David Astor

David Astor

A Life in Print

JEREMY LEWIS

JONATHAN CAPE
LONDON

1 3 5 7 9 10 8 6 4 2

Jonathan Cape, an imprint of Vintage Publishing,
20 Vauxhall Bridge Road,
London SW1V 2SA

Jonathan Cape is part of the Penguin Random House group of
companies whose addresses can be found at
global.penguinrandomhouse.com

Penguin
Random House
UK

First published by Jonathan Cape in 2016

www.vintage-books.co.uk

A CIP catalogue record for this book is available from the British Library

ISBN 9780224090902

Typeset in India by Thomson Digital Pvt Ltd, Noida, Delhi

Printed and bound in Great Britain by Clays Ltd, St Ives PLC

Penguin Random House is committed to a sustainable future for our
business, our readers and our planet. This book is made from Forest
Stewardship Council® certified paper.

MIX
Paper from
responsible sources
FSC
www.fsc.org   FSC® C018179

To my dear and much-loved wife Petra, who kept us afloat during difficult times; James Pembroke of the *Oldie*, best of friends and support *sans pareil*; and the marvellous surgeons and nurses of St George's, Tooting, without whom this book might never have been completed.

CONTENTS

List of Illustrations

Preface

This is the fifth biography I have written, but whereas I never met any of my previous subjects, I did meet David Astor, if only for an hour or two. In the early 1990s I was commissioned to write a biography of Cyril Connolly, the legendary man of letters. Not only had David Astor briefly (and unhappily) employed Connolly on the *Observer* during the Second World War, but he had been greatly influenced as an editor by *Horizon*, the monthly magazine which Connolly founded in 1939 and edited until its demise in 1950. He said he would be happy to talk to me about him, so one morning I took the Bakerloo Line to St John's Wood and, notebook in hand, walked down to Astor's large white stucco house near Lord's cricket ground to ask him about his embattled dealings with Connolly. I liked what little I saw of him very much indeed – he was helpful, amusing, informative and refreshingly modest – and it may be that our brief meeting planted a small biographical seed.

But other factors also contributed. As a young man in the 1960s and early 1970s I greatly admired the *Observer*, and not just for its contents, excellent as they often were: the typography and the layout were much more spacious than their equivalents in the cramped and grubby-looking *Sunday Times*, giving the *Observer* the same visual elegance I associated with books published by Penguin, Jonathan Cape and Faber. And, years later, my wife and I used to spend a few days every summer as the guests of Astor's nephew, also called David, and his wife Clare in Rest Harrow, Nancy Astor's magical sixteen-bedroom 'seaside cottage' in Sandwich Bay. With its dazzling white-painted floors, blue and white furniture and plethora of gables and balconies, it reminded me far more of a house in the Hamptons (or so I imagined) than a conventional English seaside house, reflecting the family's American origins and transatlantic sympathies.

Rest Harrow stimulated my interest in the Astors in general, while Richard Cockett's *David Astor and the Observer* – written with Astor's full co-operation and published in his lifetime – revived my interest in one member in particular; but I was finally prompted into asking Astor's widow, Bridget, whether I could write her husband's life after I had completed a biography of Allen Lane, the founder of Penguin Books. It struck me that two great influences on the middle-class young who had grown up in the quarter-century after the end of the war were David Astor's *Observer* and Lane's Penguin Books; and that their two lives might well complement each other. Neither man was a party political animal, but both promoted the notion of a post-war New Jerusalem, and the social-democratic values later ridiculed by Mrs Thatcher's supporters as 'Butskellism'. And they both came to look back, with nostalgia and regret, to a golden age from the end of the war to about 1960 which, once lost, could never be recovered. Lane harked back to a time when Penguin Books was regarded as one of the benign monopolies of English life, like the BBC or the National Health Service, when good books for the general reader were, almost by definition, paperbacked by Penguin, with no worries about vulgar picture jackets or low-grade competition from upstart rivals; Astor to a period when the *Observer* dominated the Sunday-paper market and, like Connolly on *Horizon*, he could publish the writers he admired without having to worry too much about the opposition, let alone about colour magazines, women's pages, consumerism and popular culture.

I approached Bridget Astor in 2005, but she wrote back to say that her son-in-law, Sean Naidoo, was writing just such a book. I was commissioned instead to write a biography of the Greene family, and very fascinating it proved to be. Not long after I'd finished it I met the writer Giles MacDonogh at a party. He had been in touch with David Astor while writing a life of Astor's hero, Adam von Trott; he told me that Sean Naidoo had decided not to continue with his book, so I wrote again to Bridget Astor, and – to my delight – she agreed that I could go ahead.

I have hugely enjoyed finding out about David Astor's life and work, and have come to like and admire him more than ever – which was a relief, since it must be a miserable business for a biographer to fall out of love with his hero. He differs from my previous subjects in that whereas one is usually exposed to a wide range of reactions to the person one is writing about, from loathing and contempt to love and admiration, opinions about David Astor occupy a much narrower band on the spectrum. Isaiah Berlin was alone in being extremely unflattering, in his letters at least, Christopher Sykes, for reasons which will become apparent, came to feel an understandable resentment, and Astor's dealings with the formidable Erin Pizzey ended in tears; but elsewhere he is invariably described as modest, self-effacing, generous, complicated, single-minded, obsessive and – essential to a man in his position – possessed of a steel hand in a velvet glove.

When I started out on this book, Diana Athill, who had dealt with Astor as an editor at André Deutsch, told me that she thought it would be difficult, if not impossible, to write an interesting or lively book about so 'saintly' a man: I hope I have proved her wrong. Astor was a brilliant editor and a good man; and because the *Observer*, invariably, looms so large in his life, my book does its best to evoke and describe a world – Fleet Street and those who worked in it – that has changed utterly since he finally severed his connection in 1981 with what had once been the family newspaper, and sometimes seems to teeter on the verge of extinction. Diana also edited the only previous biography of Astor, Richard Cockett's *David Astor and the Observer*, which was published in 1991: it is an excellent book, to which I am much indebted, but it does not deal with Astor's life outside the *Observer*.

Although I have written reviews, obituaries and occasional articles for innumerable newspapers, and have spent my working life in the related trades of book publishing, magazine editing and literary agency, I have never, to my great regret, worked on a newspaper: I hope old Fleet Street hands – a dwindling and beleaguered band – will excuse my intrusion into their domain. And since I have never been introduced to any of my subjects until now, I have made it a rule to describe them by their surnames ('Connolly' rather than 'Cyril', 'Lane' rather than 'Allen'). I broke my own rule with my book about the Greene family, simply because there were so many of them, and referred to them by their Christian names; and because I met David Astor, however briefly, and because my book is heavily populated with other members of the family, I have taken the liberty once again, and referred to him as 'David'. I hope his shade will understand.

I

Americans at Large

Elegant and well built, with bright blue eyes, a thatch of fair hair and a lopsided grin that somehow combined amusement with a rictus spasm of embarrassment, David Astor was, on the face of it, the quintessential upper-class English gentleman. Brought up in a vast country house overlooking the Thames, educated at Eton and Balliol, he had, almost in super-abundance, a very English combination of modesty, diffidence and self-deprecation with a steely determination that managed to be neither abrasive nor unpleasant; and a generosity based on a sense, imbued in him by his father, that much was expected of those to whom much had been given. And yet, in terms of his origins at least, there was nothing very English about David Astor. Both his parents were American, and the Astor fortune, which had made them, for a time, one of the richest families in the world, had been founded by the hard-featured son of a German butcher, who had left his ancestral home in the Rhineland to seek his fortune in the New World.

John Jacob Astor was born in 1763 in the small town of Walldorf, later to give its name (minus an 'l') to a long line of Astor descendants. His great-great-great-grandson, sent to live with a family in Heidelberg before going up to Oxford, paid a visit to Walldorf in the summer of 1931: it was, young David reported, a seedy, dusty little town, dominated by a tobacco factory; German Astors were still in evidence, and the achievements of its most famous son were commemorated in street names and reverential plaques. John Jacob left Walldorf in 1780, and made his way, via London, to New York. Tough, enterprising, honest and a bit of a miser, he soon made his fortune in the fur trade, garnering pelts in upper New York State and Canada, and doing business as far afield as China. With the proceeds he bought up great swathes of Manhattan, then a bosky island but soon to become the greatest and the richest city in the United States; and the Astor fortunes were made. Once described

as 'a predatory, stony-hearted, parsimonious monster of greed', he died
in 1848, one of the richest men in America.

His children and grandchildren are of no great interest to readers of
this book. John Jacob's son, William Backhouse Astor, worked hard to
maximise the revenue from the Manhattan properties, but thereafter
the Astors were more than happy to sit back and enjoy the proceeds of
vast inherited wealth; as a historian of the family once put it, 'the Astors
toiled not, neither did they spin, but an earthly father, free enterprise,
and compound interest had endowed them with the glories of Solomon'.
They diversified into hotels, some flying under an 'Astor' flag, some
under a 'Waldorf' flag, the Waldorf Astoria under a combination of the
two after the rival hotel-builders, William Waldorf and John Jacob IV,
who detested each other, agreed for once to collaborate. As the population of New York soared, with immigrants pouring in from Ireland, Italy
and Russia, where tsarist pogroms drove Jews from their shtetls to seek
refuge in the New World, the Astors' income, some of it derived from
the rack rents paid on slum dwellings on the Lower East Side, soared
in proportion. Together with the Vanderbilts and the Morgans and the
Rockefellers, they came to embody that elegant, aspiring world of late-
Victorian and Edwardian New York high society immortalised by Edith
Wharton – inhabiting huge Italianate mansions on 5th Avenue, keenly
cultivating the English aristocracy, and moving en masse between the
city and Newport, Rhode Island. Caroline Astor realised every socialite's
dream by becoming the doyenne of the ultra-exclusive '400', so enabling
her to set the tone of New York society, and decide who did or did not
belong; John Jacob Astor IV, a great-grandson of the founding father
and unkindly referred to as 'Jack Ass', achieved an endearing if transient
fame by going down with the *Titanic*, stepping aside to allow women
and children into the lifeboats and changing into evening dress in order
to meet his fate like a gentleman.

Our story begins with the *Titanic* Astor's cousin, William Waldorf
Astor. A solitary, rather melancholy figure who concealed romantic yearn-
ings behind a brusque and stern facade, he nourished political ambitions
in the Republican interest; but when the voters of lower Manhattan finally
spurned his attempts to join the House of Representatives, he flounced
off in a rage, declaring that 'America is not a fit place for a gentleman
to live. America is good enough for any man who has to make a liveli-
hood, though why travelled people of independent means should remain
there more than a week is not ready to be comprehended.' In 1882 he
settled in Rome with his wife Mary Dahlgren, a celebrated Philadelphia

beauty whose warmth offset his chilly demeanour; they had two sons, Waldorf and John Jacob V, and a daughter, Pauline. He combined his duties as the American minister in Rome with painting, drawing and sculpting, and published *Valentino: An Historical Romance of the Sixteenth Century*, the first of three gloomy, highly charged historical novels. He also amassed a collection of sarcophagi, amphorae and other antiquities: they included – much to the annoyance of the Romans – a brick and stone balustrade, complete with urns, from the Borghese gardens in Rome, which he later reassembled along the terrace at Cliveden, the house on the Thames in which his grandson David grew up.

But Italy was only a temporary posting: as with so many of the American plutocrats, England and the English aristocracy represented a beau ideal, and in 1890 William Waldorf settled in his chosen country. Three years later he bought Cliveden, a huge, rather ponderous Italianate mansion rebuilt in 1849 by Charles Barry, of Houses of Parliament fame: perched high above a heavily wooded bend in the Thames near Maidenhead, it had most recently belonged to the Duke of Westminster, who sold it for $1.25 million, much to Queen Victoria's regret ('It is grievous to think of it falling into those hands'). Its new owner soon filled its gloomy entrance hall with sarcophagi, tapestries and urns, and installed an ornate, sweet-smelling sandalwood staircase of the kind one might find in a French Renaissance chateau. To the irritation of his neighbours, who nicknamed him 'Walled-off Astor', he sealed off Cliveden's 700 acres of garden with a high wall topped with shards of broken glass; the house itself was so large that a miniature railway carried meals from the kitchens to the dining room. In 1903 William Waldorf also acquired Hever Castle in Kent, which boasted a drawbridge, a portcullis and a great many suits of armour, and had once belonged to Anne Boleyn; his London home was in Carlton House Terrace, and for office work he built a quasi-Tudor mansion on the Embankment, next to the back entrance to the Temple, replete with another elaborate wooden staircase and stained-glass windows depicting idealised scenes of Rhineland life.

Although – according to H. G. Wells – William Waldorf extracted rents from his Manhattan properties 'as effectively as a ferret draws blood from a rabbit', he made it known that he wished 'no longer to be connected with' the land of his birth. His disdain was reciprocated: when, in 1899, he became a British citizen, 'William the Traitor' was burned in effigy on Broadway. His attempts to prove that the Astors were descended from Count Pedro d'Astorga of Castile, a Crusader killed at the siege of Jerusalem, came to nothing, but a coat of arms – a silver goshawk perched on a gold gloved hand – proved easier to come by. In the meantime he worked hard to ingratiate himself with Edwardian high society, donating large sums of money to the Conservative Party, to charities, and to Oxford and Cambridge colleges. His wife's death in 1894 had made him seem still more severe and remote, and he was not always the soul of tact: he painted his carriage brown, a colour reserved for the royal family, referred to Edward VII's mistress, Mrs Keppel, as a 'royal strumpet', suggested that the king himself was impotent, and made unflattering remarks about the monarch's Jewish and South African acquaintances. Since owning newspapers and magazines is widely regarded as a useful means of acquiring influence, he bought the *Pall Mall Gazette*, a Liberal paper, in 1892. He soon sacked the editor, Harry Cust, for refusing to publish his contributions, and the following year he launched the *Pall Mall Magazine*, which went on to publish many of the leading writers of the day as well as pieces by its proprietor. And in 1911, urged on by his son Waldorf, he paid Lord Northcliffe £5,000 for the *Observer*, the editor of which, J. L. Garvin – a garrulous, gaunt-featured Liverpool Irishman – had been in the job for the last three years.

William Waldorf's children were brought up in a motherless house-hold by an increasingly reclusive father. John Jacob would, in due course, inherit Hever Castle, lose a leg in the First World War, and, in 1922, acquire *The Times*: but the 'Hever Astors' and the 'Cliveden Astors' were never that close, and the Hever branch has little part to play in this story. John Jacob's older brother, Waldorf, was born in America in 1879. At Eton he made his mark as a sportsman, edited the Eton College *Chronicle*, and became a member of Pop, the school's most exclusive society; his sporting success continued at New College, Oxford – he obtained blues in polo and fencing, rowed for his college, and enjoyed hunting, steeple-chasing and riding in point-to-points – but although he retained a lifelong interest in the turf, and became a highly successful racehorse owner, his sporting life drew to a close when it was discovered that he had a weak heart. He became a member of the Bullingdon Club, and left with a fourth in history. A gentle, generous, liberal-minded, public-spirited man, Waldorf combined self-effacement with an uncanny ability to impose his will on others in the quietest and most unobtrusive way. He was, the writer John Grigg recalled, 'remarkably kind', with 'a smile that no one who knew it could ever forget': he was also 'an excessively serious young man, with a puritan conscience and a mania for method' who 'lacked altogether the easy-going casualness and the sometimes (though not very often) deceptive amateurishness of the English upper class'.

According to his son Michael he was 'by nature a man of classical rather than romantic mould, a respecter of institutions rather than a rebel . . . Lacking from his solitary parent a living expression of humanity in his home, conscious of being largely American and respecting the need not to offend English institutions, he turned towards simple virtues as his guide to life. His life became partly a self-denying ordinance, constricted at many points.' Both Grigg and Michael Astor made much of Waldorf's American origins. 'Like his brother John', Grigg wrote, 'he emerged a model (and therefore unnatural) English gentleman, but more truly a good American,' while Michael Astor suggested that 'being American by birth, he did not fit into the English aristocratic pattern. Being puritan by nature, he did not wish to.'

'Modest, selfless, wise, prompting quietly in the wings rather than acting on the stage', in the words of his friend Tom Jones, Waldorf was to devote his life to public service, and his private life would sometimes seem inseparable from his role as a politician and newspaper proprietor. Dark, good-looking and extremely rich, he was no doubt attractive to women, and a hint of melancholy may have further softened their hearts. His fondness for the future Queen Marie of Rumania came to nothing, but on board a transatlantic liner he met his future wife, and his life was irrevocably changed.

★

Nancy Langhorne was also an American, but from a very different, and far more flamboyant, tradition. Whereas the reserved, melancholic and reclusive Astors had become quintessential Yankees, the Langhornes were Southerners, and proud of it. They claimed to be descended from a Welsh gentleman-adventurer who had settled in Virginia in the seventeenth century; like many Virginians of the hard-living, landowning, fox-hunting variety, they saw themselves as transatlantic outliers of the English aristocracy – Nancy 'really believed that to be born in Virginia was *more* British than to have been born in the UK' – though John Grigg reckoned that Nancy's father, 'Chillie' Langhorne, more closely resembled 'Squire Western than any contemporary English gentleman or aristocrat'. Witty, overbearing, hard-drinking and convivial, he was a stocky little man, more often than not sporting a bowler hat and – when not chewing and spitting tobacco – brandishing a cigar in one hand. He was a keen poker player, an inventive storyteller and an unorthodox gourmet: according to his granddaughter Nancy Lancaster – who may have inherited his gifts as a storyteller – his favourite dishes included oyster crabs in sherry, pickled watermelon rinds, pig's face, turnip salad and squirrels' brains. His working life was, and remained, a vertiginous affair. He had been, at various times, a door-to-door salesman and a tobacco auctioneer, but although the Civil War left him penniless – he later claimed that 'I had nothing but a wife, two children, a ragged seat to my pants and a barrel of whiskey' – he went on to make a fortune as a middleman in the railway contracting business. He had married Nancy Witcher Keene, known as 'Nanaire', when she was only sixteen; her gentleness offset his rumbustious ways, and they went on to have eight children, five of them girls. Nancy, the third daughter, was born in 1879.

To house his brood, and live the life of a Virginia country gentleman during the hot summer months, Chillie bought a square, red-brick Georgian house with a fanlight over the door, white shutters on the windows and a long verandah. Set in lush, rolling country near Charlottesville, surrounded by apple orchards and looking across to the Blue Ridge Mountains, Mirador came to represent, for Nancy, a kind of paradise lost, a dream home to which she longed to return or, failing that, to replicate: 'nothing could be quite as lovely as that', she recalled in old age. Two of her three brothers became heavy drinkers, so contributing to Nancy's lifelong abhorrence of alcohol and devotion to the cause of temperance; the eldest girl married a local man, and spent her life in Virginia; but it was the second daughter, Irene, who made the Langhornes famous far beyond the bounds of their home state, and even in New York itself. Tall, elegant and extremely beautiful, she came out as a Southern belle in 1890, the year in which Chillie went bust yet again. Two years later she was picked out by Caroline Astor to lead the Patriarch's Ball, the great event of the New York social season, and was the first Southern girl to do so. She met and married Charles Dana Gibson, an upper-class Bostonian whose silhouettes of beautiful social-ites were fashionable items: the ultimate 'Gibson Girl', her profile was known and admired by magazine readers throughout the United States.

Whereas Irene was tall and willowy, while Nancy's favourite sibling, Phyllis, was quiet and sweet-natured, Nancy was small, noisy and over-powering, and was compared at various times to a gnat, a grasshopper and a Chinese cracker. Blonde-haired and blue-eyed, with firm features and a fine Wellingtonian nose, she made up for her small stature by the force of her personality. 'She was not particularly striking-looking, being short and usually quietly dressed,' David wrote of her, 'but her personality was electric, attractive and compelling.' Sharp-witted, funny, fearless and a shameless show-off, she invariably dominated the proceedings: some loved her, some loathed her, and many felt a mixture of the two. Nancy Lancaster suggested that her 'strong outspokenness and teasing sense of humour came from Grandfather', and that the fearlessness he instilled in her as a horsewoman was carried through into later life. 'Aunt Nannie was the only one of my aunts who, when I was young, would make me feel small,' she added. 'The others were all charming and warm, which Nannie could be too, but she was merciless with her tongue, sparing no one.'

'The two most important things about my mother was first that she was the funniest and most compelling entertainer. No one could touch her in our family,' David Astor recalled. 'She was also socially fearless – something a lot of people claim to be but few really are.' The Langhornes had a histrionic streak, which manifested itself most famously in the actress Joyce Grenfell (Nora Langhorne's daughter and David's cousin), and Nancy indulged it more than most: she entertained children and grandees alike by putting on voices and pulling faces, slipping in a set of outsized false teeth for extra effect. 'Many people have accused her of being a show-off. But a real show-off requires an audience. Nancy was just as funny, just as witty, just as ready to stage an hilarious performance for a ragamuffin she met in the streets as for a roomful of distinguished bigwigs,' an American friend remembered. But her outspokenness and tactlessness were not always appreciated. The banker Bob Brand, who married into the Langhorne family and became a close friend and a source of sage advice, admired her 'startling combination of great beauty, extreme frankness and friendliness, brilliant wit, tremendous energy and dashing initiative', but was well aware of her disconcerting ability to 'find one's weak spot and sometimes to rub it hard', adding that 'her reflective power was not as strong as her instinct' and that 'reason was not her strongest point'. 'If there was a nerve in a tooth she'd find it,' Nancy Lancaster recalled. 'She started by punching you in the stomach and then she'd wheedle you and you'd end up staying the night. I said to her "Why don't you think before you speak?" She said, "How do I know what to think until I've said it?"' Others were less complimentary: Chips Channon, a fellow American and an energetic social climber, thought her 'dynamic, unbalanced and foolish, and only warm-hearted so long as she can patronise one'.

In 1897, Nancy met and married Robert Shaw, a well-heeled Bostonian. The marriage was a disaster: she was never in love with him; he drank

like a fish – so reinforcing her loathing for alcohol – and she resented
his sexual demands. Sex remained, for Nancy, something to be endured
rather than enjoyed, but this didn't prevent the Shaws from having
a son, Bobbie, while Nancy went on to have five more children by her
second husband. After their divorce, Nancy came to England to enjoy
some hunting in Leicestershire. 'I suppose you've come over here to
get one of our husbands,' Mrs Gordon Cunard sourly observed. 'If you
knew the trouble I've had gettin' rid of mine, you'd know I don't want
yours,' Nancy shot back (she would retain a slight Virginian twang, and
made a point of clipping her 'g's). 'I came in 1904 not to catch a husband
but to catch a fox,' she later remarked.

The kind and serious-minded Waldorf Astor must have come as a
welcome relief after the bibulous Robert Shaw. His courtship was swift
and to the point, and they were married in 1906. There was never any
question of looking for somewhere to live, or wondering how to pay the
bills: William Waldorf not only gave them Cliveden as a wedding present,
but he passed over to his two sons all his Manhattan properties, with the
Waldorf Astoria Hotel tacked on as Waldorf's birthday present. 'Think
of the joy of knowing you are absolutely independent! It is comforting –
I should have married an ogre for that!' Nancy confided to Phyllis. No
one could have been less ogre-like than Waldorf, but although – as
Victor Cunard put it – 'the exuberance of her vitality and the lightning
play of her wit tended to obscure the gentle and reserved presence of
the master of the house', he was not to be underestimated. Waldorf,
in Michael Astor's opinion, 'could not rid himself of his father's rigid,
restrictive, punctilious habits. He remained remote, difficult to approach,
fettered by his sense of obligation and duty, pleased to allow his remarkable wife to occupy the centre of the stage' – but 'when it came to an
issue, in the final analysis it was my father's will that prevailed, not hers'.
'I have the feeling that the whole time my mother was hankering after
the unobtainable because the obtainable all too quickly became a little
dull,' Michael Astor continued, adding that 'her view of people remained,
in one sense, like a child's. Some people were good and some were bad
and the distinction had always to be drawn', and that there were two
sides to her character: 'the zealot, the missionary, impelled by love, who
longed to help those she met; and the bigot, the woman of overbearing
self-will, determined at all costs to get her own way'.

Waldorf had encouraged his father to buy the *Observer*, and he was
to own and run it for the next forty years or more: but Nancy urged
him to take up politics as well, and Arthur Balfour and Lord Curzon

persuaded him to stand as an MP in the Conservative interest. In 1910 he duly entered the House of Commons as MP for the Sutton Division of Plymouth, but by temperament and conviction he was closer to the Liberal Party. Agriculture, health, imperial affairs and – not surprisingly – relations with the United States were his particular areas of interest and expertise; he favoured votes for women; he was a member of F. E. Smith's Unionist Social Reform Committee; and he infuriated many of his colleagues by voting in favour of Lloyd George's Health and Unemployment Insurance Bill, some clauses of which had been drafted at Cliveden: it paved the way for the Beveridge Report and the post-1945 welfare-state reforms, all of which were to be supported and spelt out in the pages of the *Observer*.

Poor health prevented Waldorf from joining up when war broke out in 1914; eager to do his bit, he accepted a humdrum job supervising military waste, and Cliveden became a hospital for wounded Canadian soldiers. In 1916 a coalition government under Lloyd George replaced Asquith's Liberals, and Waldorf not only became the new prime minister's private parliamentary secretary, but was made a member of Lloyd George's 'Garden Suburb', working in the grounds of 10 Downing Street. But that same year proved disastrous to Waldorf's career as an MP. William Waldorf was made Baron Astor of Hever, a reward for his donations to the Conservative Party and his support in the *Observer* and the *Pall Mall Magazine* – which meant that, as the eldest son, Waldorf would be elevated to the House of Lords after his father's death, and would have to resign his seat in the House of Commons. 'We are so knocked out by Mr Astor's taking a peerage that you would not know us,' Nancy declared. 'Waldorf was too hurt, disgusted and annoyed to even attempt hiding it . . . Never in my life have I heard of a straight man doing so shabby a trick. To be Mr Astor of New York means a great deal. To suddenly call yourself Lord Astor is quite absurd. It makes me ridiculous.' 'I am sorry that Waldorf takes my promotion so bitterly hard . . . I am delighted to have rounded off these last years of my life with a distinction,' William Waldorf retaliated. The two men did not speak for the last three years of William Waldorf's life. William Waldorf altered his will, leaving money that would have gone to Waldorf to his four 'Cliveden' grandsons – so giving them, in due course, an even greater degree of financial independence when young than would otherwise have been the case. In 1919 William Waldorf died in the lavatory of his house in Brighton; Waldorf became Viscount Astor, and life would never be the same again.

2

Country House Life

Waldorf and Nancy Astor had five children, all of them – or so Nancy claimed – 'conceived without pleasure and born without pain': Bill, who would eventually succeed his father as Viscount Astor; Phyllis, nicknamed Wissie or Wis; David, who was born on 5 March 1912 in 4 St James's Square, his parents' London house; Michael, already encountered in Chapter 1 in quotes from his memoir, *Tribal Feeling*; and John Jacob, known as Jakie. Along with their half-brother Bobbie Shaw, they were brought up in Cliveden, with occasional forays to the Hebridean island of Jura, then largely owned by the family, and to Rest Harrow, the sixteen-bedroomed 'seaside cottage' in Sandwich on the Kent coast where Nancy, always keen on exercise, could swim in the cold North Sea and enjoy a round of golf. Built in 1910, and designed by Paul Phipps, one of Nancy's nephews, Rest Harrow was more reminiscent of its American equivalent than a conventional English country house and Nancy's first act as the chatelaine of Cliveden was to lighten its prevailing gloom, replacing William Waldorf's tapestries and heavy leather furniture with chintzes and bowls of flowers. Books were in plentiful supply, including every title published in the Everyman Library, but they were more often read by guests and visitors than by their owners: although writers were welcome guests at Cliveden, Waldorf and Nancy preferred discussion and debate to the reading of books, and David would prove to be similarly inclined. Nor did they have any great interest in music, painting or the arts.

David was a fair-haired, good-looking little boy with bright blue eyes: his cousin, Nancy Lancaster, saw him first when he was three, and he reminded her of 'a perfect nectarine – I never saw such a lovely child'. Growing up at Cliveden was, he remembered, like 'living in a hotel which was also partly a museum'. According to Rose Harrison, who went to work as a maid at Cliveden in 1928, the 'indoor staff' included Mr Lee the butler, Waldorf Astor's valet, Arthur Bushell, an under-butler, footmen, two odd-job men, a hall boy and a carpenter. The kitchens were manned by a chef, three kitchen maids and a scullery maid; the housekeeper was in charge of two still-room maids, four housemaids, two dailies, four laundry staff and ladies' maids for Nancy and Wissie; also on the payroll were gardeners, chauffeurs, farmworkers, a telephonist and a nightwatchman. During the week many of the inside servants decamped to St James's Square; at weekends, when grand dinners were held at Cliveden, the butlers and footmen wore livery. Rose Harrison thought Waldorf 'the epitome of the English gentleman', courteous, liberal-minded and with a 'wonderful understanding of human frailty in others', while the children were 'friendly but not familiar'; but she found Nancy impossible to please. 'She is not a lady as you would understand a lady, Miss Harrison,' Mr Lee once told her, and on occasions she 'shouted and rampaged like a fishwife, though without using bad language'. Rose Harrison learned to stand up to her demanding mistress, and became extremely fond of her; and, as always, Nancy's ebullience was tempered by wit and comicality. On one occasion Mr Lee told her he could stand it no longer, and was handing in his notice. 'In that case, Lee, tell me where you're going – I'll come with you,' Nancy replied.

'This house is like a huge liner and that little woman is the rudder,' Bobbie Shaw once remarked, and in terms of noise, energy and sociability Nancy seemed to dominate the proceedings, not least where her children were concerned. John Grigg's father, Sir Edward Grigg, was an old friend of Waldorf, and the young Grigg retained vivid memories of Nancy, whose biography he eventually wrote. 'Two qualities most desirable in a parent she did not possess – calm and the readiness to praise,' he wrote of her, adding that 'she conveyed a sense of perpetual restlessness. Her eyes were those of a colt, not yet broken in, "tameless and swift and proud". They flashed humour, joy, exhilaration, love; or annoyance, impatience, aggression. They did not convey peace.' But where her children were concerned, 'the harmful effects of her possessiveness were aggravated by a good deal of neglect. Nancy was too busy to see very much of them, but when she did see them she tended to be overpowering.' For small children at least, she must have been both magical and alarming. Years later, her great-nephew James Fox recalled 'her sudden wheeling attacks', and how she 'enjoyed reducing single children to tears as much as driving them, en masse, to a frenzy of excitement. Her tactic, with grown-ups too, was to strike at their exposed nerve, the one that only she could see with her uncanny instinct, and then to sting again before the victim had time to react.' 'As children

we were impressed by her, even fascinated, but not really frightened,'
David recalled towards the end of his life. 'She often seemed more like
a grown-up child herself, wayward, unexpected, rule-breaking. And her
strongest card with almost all of us at almost any time in her life was
that she could make us laugh, usually at ourselves or at her . . . If ever
in my later life I did anything that took courage, I usually was reminded
of my mother, who was frightened of nobody.' But, in the last resort,
Waldorf ruled the roost. 'We all respected him and, as I grew older, and
got to know him on more equal terms, respect became devotion,' David
continued. 'If my mother said no to our requests, you waited till next
day and tried again, but we would never dare argue with my father. He
never punished us. He just had authority. Although my mother could
run rings around him as a personality, she could not move him when
his mind was made up.'

Nancy's dealings with her children were intense but intermittent, and
became more so after Waldorf had to resign his seat in the House of
Commons. She is best remembered as the first woman MP, replacing
Waldorf in his Plymouth constituency; wearing her trademark black
tricorn hat, black coat and skirt and a white open-necked shirt, she was
introduced to the House by Balfour and Lloyd George, both friends of
the family and regular visitors to Cliveden. She came to specialise in
domestic issues, sharing her husband's liberal leanings and an instinctive sympathy for the underdog which David inherited: he recalled how,
for example, she fell into conversation with a stoker while crossing
the Atlantic, and was so appalled by what he told her about working
conditions below decks that she took the matter up with the captain
and the shipping company. But although she campaigned for nursery
schools, votes for women over twenty-one, widows' pensions, juvenile
courts, equal pay and opportunities in the Civil Service, better treatment
in prison for women and juvenile offenders, cheap milk for children,
state health care, town planning, raising the school leaving age and the
abolition of the death penalty, her only legislative achievement was to
raise the pub drinking age via the Intoxicating Liquor Bill. Resented at
first by the old guard in the Commons, she soon made her mark as an
entertaining, witty if rather lightweight member of the House, well
known for heckling and interrupting longer-winded members in mid-
flow, and for her barbed exchanges with Winston Churchill. (The most
repeated of these was supposed to have taken place at Cliveden but is
almost certainly apocryphal, alas. 'Winston, if I was married to you I'd
put poison in your coffee,' she is said to have told him – to which he

replied, 'Nancy, if I was married to you I'd drink it.') Cold-shouldered
by some of the men, her closest friends in the Commons were Labour
women MPs like Ellen Wilkinson and Eleanor Rathbone, who had
followed in her wake. Waldorf, for his part, took quiet pride in her public
activities, and gave her all the support she needed: he remained active
in public life, founding and funding the Royal Institute of International
Affairs at Chatham House with Lionel Curtis and Arnold Toynbee,
looking after the *Observer* in conjunction with the overbearing J. L.
Garvin, running his beloved stud farm, and taking an active interest in
the League of Nations and in agriculture – about which he wrote two
books, including a pre-war Penguin Special.

'Cliveden to us was a world of its own. It was a maze into which
we could disappear and hide,' Michael Astor wrote in a letter recalling
his childhood. Routine was combined with 'a great deal of freedom':
they went riding at ten in the morning, followed by a pre-lunch session
with a governess and an afternoon ride in a pony cart. 'Oh Phyl, they
are wonderful children, David so robust, Wis so winsome and Bill all a
companion should be but Bobbie has my heart,' Nancy once told her
sister Phyllis, but David later suggested that her three eldest children –
Bobbie, Bill and Wissie – had been 'shockingly treated' by her. Bill may
well have suffered from emotional neglect, but Bobbie's position in the
family was more complicated and more ambivalent. Nancy loved him
most of all, but he remained something of an outsider, a court jester who
was allowed to tell her exactly what he thought of her, and disguised a
sense of exclusion with wit and self-mockery. Joyce Grenfell claimed that
he bullied the other children, and that 'his conversation is so tinged with
bitterness and his cynicism is so poisonous that it pervades and fouls the
atmosphere'. And whereas his half-brothers would, in due course, follow
their father to Eton, Bobbie was sent to Shrewsbury.

Much to his relief, no doubt, Bobbie was not expected to attend
the Cliveden equivalent of family prayers. Neither Nancy nor Waldorf
enjoyed good health, but instead of looking to Harley Street for salvation, Nancy became a Christian Scientist, and persuaded Waldorf to
follow her example. For ten minutes every morning she read her children
extracts from the Bible and Mary Baker Eddy's *Science and Health*, and
every evening she gathered her brood around her – Bobbie excepted – for
further readings. According to Michael Astor, their early indoctrination
into Christian Science not only differentiated them from their friends,
but left them 'under the impression from a tender age that we knew
the difference between right and wrong'. Not only did they believe that

their mother was 'a cross between the Virgin Mary and Mrs Eddy', but 'we did not enjoy the gradual process that many children experience of realising at an early age that one's parents are like other people, partly good partly bad, more or less affectionate and usually fallible. We had to find out all this later – rather abruptly.' All Nancy's children were to react against and eventually reject Christian Science, and their resentment was fuelled when Wissie suffered permanent damage to her spine in a hunting accident: her horse rolled on top of her, and her parents were reluctant to seek professional medical advice. David would be the first of the Astor children to reject the faith of his parents, leaving a void which was filled, years later, by an almost religious faith in the redemptive powers of psychoanalysis.

But it would be misleading to paint too stern a picture of life at Cliveden. Michael Astor remembered how 'we used to laugh a good deal, and laugh at people', and how, as children, they winced when Nancy ridiculed Waldorf's horsey friends or mocked Miss Kindersley, his loyal but buck-toothed secretary and personal assistant, and how he would sometimes calm her down by squeezing the back of her neck and murmuring 'Easy, steady', like a groom with a recalcitrant mare. According to Rose Harrison, Nancy was easy-going and jolly with the children for much of the time, although she was often away from home; but she was reluctant to give praise where praise was due, and had a disconcerting habit of teasing and drawing attention to an easily embarrassed child. Comfort and support were to hand in the reassuring form of Nanny Gibbons, who came to work for the family when Bill was born. Her domain was the day nursery, a large, comfortable, well-lit room; she slept in the night nursery with the younger children until they were old enough to have their own rooms, took them for the ride in a pony cart every afternoon, and eventually became, in Rose Harrison's opinion, 'a power in the house second only to Mrs Astor'. Nor was entertainment in short supply. Life was more constricted during the war years, when much of the house and grounds became a Canadian military hospital: although David was six when the war ended in 1918, he remembered 'a visitor speaking of modern war as something new and of untold evil possibilities and my parents listening with a gravity that I had never seen before'. He also 'quite enjoyed the melodrama of visiting our local military hospital with my mother, sometimes seeing a trainload of wounded arrive or attending a hospital funeral where the coffin was carried on a gun carriage', and only began to worry about the war when Bobbie – of whom he was to become extremely fond, albeit in a rather protective way – was called up; but normality returned after peace had been declared.

Party games and charades loomed large, particularly at Christmas and at the annual estate dance, when Arthur Bushell, Waldorf's valet, regularly dressed up as Nellie Wallace, the music-hall star, and exchanged waggish repartee with Nancy, also in fancy dress. 'My brother Jakie once noted that our family looked like theatre people,' Michael Astor noted. 'In a group they had the same friendly garrulous quality, the air of being tightly knit to each other by some intangible cord, yet at the same time self-conscious, solitary and separated.' Joyce Grenfell had reservations about Cliveden life – 'The whole unreality of the atmosphere flowed over me to suffocation point,' she confided to her diary, adding some years later that 'Cliveden was never my cup of tea, was it? The more I see of people brought up in the easy way, the more I lean towards socialism' – but she found the Langhorne histrionics hard to resist. 'Aunt N wore false teeth and her hair in a frizz on top and was any rich old woman in the Ritz,' she noted of some Christmas festivities, and the overall effect was 'quite uncanny and terribly funny'. On other occasions 'Aunt N made that awful face of the woman who has had a stroke. I thought we'd be sick we laughed so,' and played the part of Mrs Rittenhouse, Groucho Marx's comic foil, with padded bosom and bottom, while Bill, Jakie and a friend impersonated the Marx Brothers. As soon as the children were old enough, they were expected to ride and to hunt: unlike Jakie, who went on to become a great figure in that world, David never shared his father's enthusiasm for the turf, and although he became a proficient horseman he much preferred beagling to hunting. He lived in 'a cold room on top of the house', according to his brother Jakie, and 'he had a spaniel called Bruce, who was disobedient, and sometimes gave his room a doggy smell.' He tended to be late for meals, church and other family events, and Waldorf 'would repeatedly say "Don't dawdle, David." David dawdled.' 'He could be fierce,' his youngest brother continued, but he 'was loved by the "household", whose elders could be relied on to "cover up" for him in disputes, mostly about lateness'.

Tuft hunters in search of big game would have found Cliveden an earthly paradise, but for the children the household names who appeared at weekends were 'part of the inevitable herd of grown-ups who came and went and had to be treated with a modicum of good manners'. In Bernard Shaw's opinion, Cliveden was 'like no other country house in the world', where 'you meet anybody worth meeting, rich or poor'. 'Lady Astor allotted rooms, supervised menus with the French chef, arranged games, dominated the house within and the grounds without, played tennis with Lord Balfour or Sam Hoare, swung a golf club over the shaven lawns, retired to her boudoir filled with photographs of her family and friends, scribbled illegible letters, read the portions of the Bible and Mrs Eddy's *Science and Health* allocated for study by the Christian Science Church', recalled another regular visitor, Tom Jones. At dinner she presided at the head of the table, where 'she had a free hand with no Speaker to call her to order . . . Her sallies were often wildly extravagant, but they sometimes hit their target, revealing flashes of original insight into human character. However scorching she might be, her nature was fundamentally generous, and I never resented her attacks.' Shaw was a regular visitor, writing in his room for much of the day before descending – as convention demanded – in his dinner jacket when Mr Lee banged the gong, and entertaining the company with a ceaseless flow of conversation: 'he dominated the scene with his wit and his brogue and out-talked every competitor, including that other torrential Irishman, James Louis Garvin,' Tom Jones recalled. Sean O'Casey, Mary Pickford, H. G. Wells and – until he fell out with his hostess – Hilaire Belloc were frequent visitors, while Charlie Chaplin, Mahatma Gandhi and Ivan Maisky, the sociable Soviet ambassador, all made the short trip down from London. Most of the weekend guests tended to be politicians, from all three parties. Balfour and Lloyd George were particular favourites; Churchill came in the 1920s, but was increasingly disapproved of as a hard-drinking warmonger; Baldwin, Chamberlain and Eden were welcome visitors.

Closest of all the regular visitors were the members of a political discussion group known as the Round Table. Its members were Oxford graduates – some were also fellows of All Souls – and all of them, as young men, had worked with Lord Milner in South Africa after the Boer War, working on the political reconstruction of the country, earning themselves the nickname of 'Milner's Kindergarten', and elaborating their views in the *Round Table* magazine. Their members included Philip Kerr, later Lord Lothian; Geoffrey Dawson (*né* Robinson), the long-standing editor of *The Times*, best remembered (and vilified) as the arch appeaser at the time of the Munich crisis; Lionel Curtis, a fellow of All Souls much given to airy visions of world government; and, the most level-headed of them all, Robert Brand, an associate of Maynard Keynes and an international banker. With the exception of Bob Brand, they were to be associated with the policies of appeasement in the 1930s, and with the notorious – if imaginary – machinations of the so-called 'Cliveden Set';

and between them they shared a view of the world, some elements of which David Astor absorbed and retained. They were keen imperialists, but their imperialism took a defensive, constitutional form in schemes for an imperial federation of the 'old' white dominions, leading to a Commonwealth of equal and self-governing nations; they shied away from Continental alliances and entanglements; and, attuned to declining British power and the growing strength of Germany, they believed in the importance of the English-speaking nations clinging together, and in the centrality of Anglo-American relations – a point of view that came naturally to the Astors, and manifested itself, years later, in David Astor's advocacy, in the leader pages of the *Observer*, of an 'Atlanticist' foreign policy. As Michael Astor put it in his memoirs, 'I was born into an Anglo-American household', and 'this two-way pull, of the old and the new, coloured my thoughts'.

Two members of the Round Table, Philip Kerr and Bob Brand, were to become close to the young David Astor, as friends and mentors. Philip Kerr, who became the eleventh Marquis of Lothian in 1930, was brought up as a devout Roman Catholic – so devout that, for a time, he considered entering the priesthood. He graduated from New College, Oxford, before going out to South Africa; he went on to edit the *Round Table*, sharing to the full its federalist ideas, and worked with Waldorf in Lloyd George's 'garden suburb'. Following the Revolution of 1917, he came to regard Bolshevism with particular dread and abhorrence on the grounds that 'it would mean the end of Christianity, the end of tolerance and the enslavement of mankind,' Michael Astor recalled, adding that 'my parents also shared this view'. Lothian had abandoned Catholicism for Christian Science, so forging a further tie to the Astors, and to Nancy in particular: it was rumoured that they were in love, but on a strictly platonic basis. Their closeness was sometimes resented by Nancy's children, not least when he sided with her on the sometimes vexed issue of Christian Science. Good-looking and clever but indecisive and oddly gullible, Lothian was involved in drafting some of the German reparations clauses at Versailles in 1919; it was often claimed, in later years, that a sense of guilt towards Germany may have explained his readiness to regard Hitler as a reasonable statesman with whom one could do business. Bob Brand, who had worked with Keynes at Versailles, had no such illusions. Like Waldorf, he had a weak heart, which kept him out of the war. Charming, quietly spoken and extremely clever, and a fellow of All Souls, he was devoted to Nancy's sister Phyllis, whose second husband he became, and he spent much of his career as a merchant banker at Lazard's.

David's third Cliveden mentor, Tom Jones, came from a very different world. 'TJ', as he was always known, was, in his own words, 'a mere provincial in speech and dress, sporting a superannuated bowler hat': he was quick-witted, voluble (only Shaw out-talked him at Cliveden) and so small that he once described himself as a 'microbe'. Michael Astor remembered him as 'a small man with straight white hair, a prominent nose, a firm and determined mouth and a voice that was rather more prominent than was first indicated by his quiet and pallid appearance'. He was 'persuasive and devious' and 'his posture, both political and social, was humble and belied a certain inner arrogance'. Brought up in a Welsh-speaking valley in South Wales, he left school at fourteen, but went on to graduate with a first-class degree from Glasgow University. As a young man in Glasgow he had joined the Independent Labour Party (the ILP), and he was to remain a lifelong member of the Labour Party; but, thanks to the support of his fellow Welshman, Lloyd George, he worked in the Cabinet secretariat with a series of Tory and Liberal prime ministers. He was on particularly close terms with Lloyd George and Baldwin, earning a reputation as a political 'fixer' and go-between – not unlike David's close friend Lord Goodman some fifty years later. 'A brilliant manipu-lator of events rather than a participant', in Michael Astor's words, he was to play a large role in David's life, both before the war and, later, at the *Observer*. Nor were his interests purely political. Although he had little money of his own – at home with his wife and children, he never employed a servant, and was proud of doing the washing-up – he was an ardent philanthropist, albeit with other people's money: as secretary of the Pilgrim Trust he disbursed money on behalf of the American oil millionaire Edward Harkness to causes close to his heart – many of them reflecting his enthusiasm for Welsh life and culture – and, in later years, he would do the same for the young David Astor.

'This is the room with the view you love, a still summer day, a little more haze lying on the river, the trees as if cast in metal so warm and still. The most peaceful view in England,' Freya Stark wrote to a friend from Cliveden, but not all the well-known visitors were as enthusiastic. Harold Nicolson – later to become, with Philip Toynbee, one of the *Observer*'s leading book reviewers during what David would come to regard as the golden age of his editorship – confided to his diary that he found the great house 'cold and draughty', and complained of 'great sofas in vast cathedrals: little groups of people wishing they were alone: a lack of organisation and occupation: a desultory drivel', and of how 'after dinner, to enliven the party, Lady Astor dons a Victorian hat and a pair of false teeth. It does not enliven the party.' 'Oh my sweet, how glad I am that we are not so rich,' he wrote to his wife, Vita Sackville-West, already en poste as the *Observer's* first gardening correspondent. 'I simply do not want a house like this where nothing is really yours, but belongs to servants or gardeners. There is a ghastly unreality about it all . . . like living on the stage of the Scala theatre in Milan.'

The Astor children grew up surrounded by well-known names, but – according to David – their mother 'brought us up, not to admire celebrities, but people of worth, and to admire celebrities for their worth only'. Nor did she encourage them to be social snobs, even if they grew up having little real knowledge of how the great bulk of the population led their lives: she was happy to consort with the Cecils and other grand families, but one of the regular guests at Cliveden was a journalist from a Plymouth newspaper owned by Waldorf whom she had taken a shine to. As a newspaper editor, David would never be overawed by politicians and public figures, but neither did he treat them as an alien species, let alone a lower form of life. He treated them as equals and as human beings, to be assessed – most famously in his meticulously researched *Observer* Profiles – fairly and on their merits; and when, in the early 1960s, he visited President Kennedy in the White House, he met him as an equal, whom he remembered meeting as a young man when JFK visited Cliveden with his father, Joseph Kennedy, the pre-war American ambassador in London, well known if not notorious for his isolationist opinions. And growing up in a house that was always crammed with visitors led him, as an adult, to assume that such hospitality was the norm, and to open his home to all comers, many of whom were poorer and less influential than the guests at Cliveden.

★

All this lay in the future; in the meantime, the eight-year-old David was bracing himself to be sent away to school. He followed his brother Bill to West Downs, a prep school near Winchester. Nancy had first visited the school with the queen of Rumania in tow, and was encouraged to find that the headmaster, Mr Tindall, already had some Christian Scientists as pupils – and had no objection to her giving seminars on the subject in the school garden on later visits. Nancy had been very close to David, but she seldom came to see him at West Downs. 'Her visits to the school were only embarrassing in that she tended to speak to everybody there, whether I knew them or not,' he recalled: should one of her rare visits coincide with a school parade in the gym, she provided further mortification by taking over from the master in charge, and barking out orders. Like many small boys before and since, David felt abandoned and exiled: on one occasion Mr Lee the butler was deputed to take him back to school, and before they went in he marched him up and down and told him how he never wanted to go back to the trenches during the First World War.

'He is a very good-natured and altogether a very attractive little person,' Mr Tindall reported; although he thought him too self-centred for his own good or that of the school, by the end of his second year 'his selfishness, though still apparent, is much less apparent than it was.' David was wretchedly homesick at first. 'Will you be cuming to see me . . . Please rit and tell me wat is hapernig at home,' he wrote in a tear-stained letter to Nanny Gibbons. Two years later his spelling had improved a little. 'Please! Please! Wright soon and please will you ask Mummy if you can come down here and see me as you have never been able to come,' he begged her. Nancy's handwriting was notoriously illegible, and young David was as baffled by it as anyone else, including her biographers: 'I can rid your letters when you tip them,' he told her. Gradually he began to enjoy life more, reporting home that 'not half as many boys tease me'. Soon after his arrival in the school a boy named John Amery – 'short-legged, biggish-headed, dapper and with a pretentious voice' – tried to adopt him, claiming that their families were friends. Already a shrewd judge of character, David thought him a 'natural imposter', and he remembered how Amery persecuted 'a rather scrawny-looking little boy with specs and a high forehead' and an obviously Jewish name ('the scene stays with me, slightly like the early anti-Semitic confrontations of the Third Reich'); although Amery had a Jewish grandmother, was the son of Leo Amery, a leading Conservative politician and a close associate of Churchill, and the brother of the future Conservative minister Julian Amery, he spent the war years in Germany working as a Nazi propagandist, and was hanged as a traitor in 1945. David, for his part, was more politically aware than most, even at a very young age: 'A lot of the masters have asked me how the election is getting on, and I don't know what to say,' he told Nancy when she was campaigning for re-election in Plymouth in November 1922.

'He seems to be a queer mixture of extreme softness and extreme hardness,' Mr Tindall declared towards the end of David's time at West Downs. 'He is an extraordinarily attractive little creature; it is glorious to see him bubbling with amusement; he is a wonderful conversationalist for his age; and he would be doubly attractive if he could get rid of the feeling that he is the Pivot of the Universe.' In later life David would be famed for his diffidence, his modesty and his generosity of spirit, but accusations of selfishness and self-centredness would be made against him at Eton as well as West Downs. In the meantime, 'David's innate kindness and humour made the process of indoctrination easier than it would otherwise have been,' Michael Astor wrote of his own first days at West Downs. The child would prove to be the father to the man.

3

Eton and Elsewhere

Although, in retrospect, David came to love Eton – 'not sending my own children there was a real sacrifice', he later admitted – he made little or no mark on the school beyond winning the hurdles in his last year: indeed, his finest achievement may have been to invite P. G. Wodehouse to Eton, though it is unclear whether the great man visited the school in general, or David's house, or a group of boys within the house. 'Well, P. G. Wodehouse came down and was perfectly charming. He is sending me the proofs of his new book and is going to write a story with Eton as the site,' David informed Nancy: sad to say, Wodehouse never wrote an Eton story, nor is there any mention of his visit in the Eton College *Chronicle*.

David did badly in his Common Entrance exams, and 'passed in very low' to Eton. He followed Bill into Mr Conybeare's house. Poor Bill, buttoned-up and reserved at the best of times, had not had an easy time: it is said that he was held upside down out of a window in the hope that Astor gold would pour from his pockets, and that he was victimised by his classics tutor, C. J. Rowlatt, 'rather a nasty bounder at the best of times'. David was never bullied or persecuted, but he was very average academically, and took exception to the way in which Mr Rowlatt, who was in charge of the Eton Officers' Training Corps, sometimes over-loaded him with work and punishments: 'What annoys me is the way when he loses his temper with me (a daily affair) he always ends up by saying something about all the family talking much too much. I call it awful cheek but I daren't tell him so.' Mr Rowlatt's rebukes may have had some justification, since 'I am the worst soldier in the section and have to make a tremendous mental and physical effort to keep up with all the complicated movements.'

Mr Conybeare's end-of-term letters to Waldorf invariably combined affection with a degree of frustration. David was, he wrote in February 1926, 'an excellent boy, with energy, some originality, any amount of loyalty, and a sense of public duty', and 'his simplicity of outlook and his directness make him a capital boy to have dealings with'; on the other hand, 'he has a tendency to be casual and to assume as a right what he should ask for as a privilege'. He was, Conybeare reported at the end of another term, 'a very loveable and friendly boy' who was 'always ready to talk with sometimes embarrassing frankness', but he was a slow worker who suffered from an 'absence of thoroughness' and an unwelcome 'vein of obstinacy'. Mr Rowlatt, doubling up as David's form master, was less forgiving. He found the fourteen-year-old David 'altogether too self-satisfied', and he was infuriated by David's tendency to stroll into the Pupil Room a quarter of an hour late: there was no doubting his intelligence, but 'he obviously expects everything to come quite easily to him, and until he learns to put himself out a bit more about his work, I shall not be inclined to give him a good mark'.

Away from the classroom, David enjoyed playing squash on free afternoons, and going for runs through the surrounding countryside; he took part in house debates about whether lawyers should defend those they know to be guilty and – at a more parochial level – whether the school stores should be given a monopoly ('Mr Astor then got up and seemed to have a lot to say on the subject but he soon died away'). He told Nancy that he was too busy to read books, well disposed as he was to *The Pickwick Papers* and works by Surtees, Buchan, Kipling and A. P. Herbert. 'It takes me two weeks to read one book,' but 'if I can't find time to read books here, I never will,' he wrote, before asking her to send him a book 'after the style of Jorrocks and Sponge'. David would never be a great reader of books but, like many of the best publishers, he had an instinctive 'nose' for interesting books and writers; and despite his admiration for Orwell and Koestler, he had little real understanding of how authors, rather than journalists, went about their business.

Naturally shy and rather awkward, David found it hard to make friends at first, nor did he 'take to the life easily or naturally'. At one point, shortly before his fifteenth birthday, he seems to have got in with a dubious set of boys, and Mr Conybeare was not best pleased. According to reports, David had not only behaved in 'rather a despotic manner, dragooning other lower boys', but had been rude and inconsiderate to the maids. This seemed worryingly out of character, but although some of the senior boys in the house 'still think he wants sitting on', Mr Conybeare found him 'capital company, perhaps too opinionated but very loyal', and 'a shrewd critic of character, if not perhaps a very generous one'. David may have had a sharp eye for other people's weak points, but he greatly liked and admired Aunt Phyllis's stylish, half-American son Winkie, and was

devastated when his cousin decided to leave Eton and make his home in
the States. 'He forgets that he is really English and not American,' David
complained to Nancy, adding that 'the biggest danger to Winkie (besides
drink) is Bobbie . . . for goodness sake keep him away from Bobbie by
hook or by crook.' Winkie's departure left the sixteen-year-old David
weepy, shaken and demoralised: the first onset, perhaps, of the depressions
that were to blight his time at Oxford, and afflict him sporadically for the
rest of his life. Mr Conybeare, 'a bluff codger', was unable to cope, but
he alerted Nancy, who sent Philip Kerr to Eton on an errand of mercy.
Kerr had suffered some kind of nervous breakdown when he abandoned
Roman Catholicism in favour of Christian Science, and he provided
comfort and reassurance, taking David for long walks and urging him to
put his back into his academic work; 'he also told me that people who
have a happy upbringing often end up about as interesting as a sausage
on a plate; those who have to solve their own problems often do better.
And all that was kindly and reassuring.'

Kerr's advice paid off. David won the English Literature Prize for
his year group in 1928, and he became altogether more confident as a
result: still more so since 'I beat a tug – very satisfactory' ('tugs' were
the King's Scholars or Collegers, who lived in a house of their own
and were regarded as the brightest boys in the school). 'I am sure you
will be cheered by the general tone of these reports,' Mr Conybeare
wrote to Waldorf Astor. 'David has taken a tremendous interest in
his English work and I am very glad he has secured his literary prize.'
He had also won his house colours at football. 'He might have been
pardoned if his head had swelled. But I cannot see that it has, and this,
though partly due to his temperament, is partly, too, due to his sense
of moral values.' 'He must be careful to preserve this modesty, and use
his influence in the right direction,' Conybeare continued, adding that
'he is a capital boy to talk to. He has done well enough in the house,
though he hasn't much sympathy with bores and not a great deal of
patience with the weaker brethren in general. He must learn to listen
even more than to talk – that is, I think, his great danger: people who
don't know him might think him conceited.' Mr Conybeare's advice was
well judged: David would become a great listener, relishing the debates
that swirled around him in the *Observer* before deciding what line to take.
'His great danger', Mr Conybeare suggested, was being 'opinionated and
dogmatic – all part of the egoism which makes him think he is always
in the right', but when, in the summer of 1930, Mr Conybeare ceased
to be a housemaster, he reported in his valedictory note that although

David was still too self-centred, he was 'a boy who does more unselfish things than anyone else at Eton'.

David's 'saviour' at Eton was Robert Birley, who had joined the staff in 1926, teaching history, and went on to become the headmaster of Charterhouse before returning to Eton as its headmaster in 1949. 'I was a struggling schoolboy, somewhere in the middle of the school, when he first arrived as a master,' David wrote in a Festschrift published for his old teacher. 'The boys right away noticed that he was a bit different from most of the masters – more easy in manner, less conscious of his position. He would sit on his bicycle holding leisurely kerbside conversations while his colleagues marched purposefully about. Blatantly unathletic, he yet seemed more formidable and alive than anyone else.' Birley kept a Henry Moore statue in his study, and 'he did not find it unmanly to invite us to listen to classical music'. Fondly referred to as 'Red Robert' on account of his leftish views, he encouraged David to read Harold Laski's *Communism* and set up occupational centres for the unemployed in the neighbouring town of Slough, a place which most Etonians 'strove to overlook', encouraging his pupils – who included Guy Burgess and Randolph Churchill – to take an 'active interest' in it. His informality and his enthusiasm proved contagious: 'he gave all his talks the immediacy of tonight's evening paper and spoke to us as freely and amusingly as if at a dinner party. Perhaps it was his ability to see all other beings on a level with himself that made him so free and unpretentious and made his impact as a teacher so great.' He persuaded Nancy not to remove David from the school when Mr Rowlatt replaced Mr Conybeare as his housemaster: Nancy had taken against Rowlatt, and Birley made several visits to St James's Square to persuade her to think again. Nancy's fears proved unjustified: despite his earlier reservations about David, Rowlatt now found him an 'invaluable' member of his house, a great success as captain of games, 'full of public spirit and always willing to take trouble to make things go well' and 'a boy of high ideals and sterling character'. Robert Birley was equally enthusiastic. Although David 'has often been a nuisance and has rarely done as well as I should have liked with his work', he had wider interests than most boys of his age, was 'remarkably free from prejudices', thought things out for himself and was altogether 'a boy of remarkable sympathy' who would 'most probably turn his social gifts to good use'. And, as we have seen, he had more finely tuned political antennae than most boys of his age. While at Eton he met Chaim Weizmann, the future president of Israel, on a cross-Channel steamer with Nancy, 'and I noticed that he was beautifully dressed in a

quiet style. He had a neatly clipped beard and an air of quiet authority.'
Years later, during the war, he met him again at a meeting at which
Weizmann spoke about the extermination of the Jews: it was the first
David had heard of it, and it proved to be 'one of the most disturbing
and unreal occasions I have ever known'.

Between the wars public schools often ran charitable 'missions' in
the East End of London, and David found a visit to the Eton mission
'very useful as it gives me an opportunity of becoming acquainted with
members of the middle and lower classes (I hate the word!) in an unofficial
and convenient way even if at first it is all a little forced'. Towards the
end of his time at Eton he compared his prospects with those of a boy
of his own age starting work as a clerk. The real difference between
them, he decided, was that, thanks to his wealth and his education, 'my
possibilities are almost boundless. I have apparently every advantage
imaginable.' It was quite likely that both of them would prove to be a
'dull mediocrity', but he had a 'bigger scope for good'. 'You are lucky
enough to be rich; that gives you a profound responsibility towards those
who are not so lucky,' Waldorf told his sons; like his father, David had
little interest in material possessions or wealth as such, but in the years to
come his wealth and his generous instincts would provide ample opportunities for him to exercise his 'scope for good'. 'Nobility', he informed
his mother, consisted of 'an appreciation of the common good and the
unselfishness and ability to minister it', and its practitioner should be 'a
man of balanced character. Not an aesthete or a fanatic about anything.
An enrolled man of the world.'

His newly awakened interest in the 'middle and lower classes' coincided
with a distancing from Cliveden and the world in which he'd grown up.
'On the surface it is my home, yet if you look into it I have only the
faintest connection with it . . . I live a shallow, vapid, cotton-wool life
from which I learn little or nothing,' he declared. He resented the way
in which Bill's and Wissie's friends 'treat Cliveden like a hotel and think
themselves a grade above the ordinary mortal merely because they were
born with an absurd name and have since developed a fine moustache and
a marcel wave', and he asked Nancy whether they could not, for once,
see in the New Year by themselves rather than giving 'one of those awful
marrying society parties where all those highly polished and immaculate
young men come and treat me as though I was a servant and they had
lived there all their life'. And, like many sensitive young men brought
face to face with the modern world, he nourished fantasies of escape:
'When I see rows of smart cars, pampered women, pompous servants,

when I smell petrol, hear the roar of up-to-date life, I am filled with a mad desire to bury my youthful head in the quietness of a Wiltshire hamlet!' He loved, as he would always love, 'the country and nature' because they 'had so little to do with the petty bickerings of human relations', while birds 'take me into another world'.

That was all very well, but the habits of luxury were hard to shake off. 'I am working hard for that new polo pony you said you would give me if I did well this half,' he reported. 'By the way, is Henry Ford giving us one of his cars?' he asked on another occasion. If so, he'd opt for an 'open-seater'. According to Michael Astor, David was always 'more under the influence of Mr Jorrocks than W. G. Grace': between October and March he sometimes went out beagling three times a week with the Eton College Hunt (motto: 'Floreat Canes Etonenses'), sniffing out hares in the country round Eton and Windsor before coming home to a tea of scrambled eggs and sausages. David's poor reports from Eton prompted Waldorf to disband his pack of beagles at Cliveden. 'They were not house-trained, but it was impossible to keep them out of the house,' Michael Astor remembered. 'They gave tongue as all good beagles should, but only when they were shut up in the kennels for the night.' For David, their dispersal was 'a bit of a blow and I'm frightfully sorry about it', but Waldorf complained 'that I became like a kennel-boy if I had them'. 'I do miss my beagles awfully. I wish I'd kept them,' David told Nancy. 'Hunting gives me a great contact with nature', and he spent a fair amount of time brooding on 'hunting, horses and hounds'. When not beagling, running or playing squash he played the occasional game of golf, but it was as a hurdler that he made his mark, running for the school against Stowe and Lancing as well as winning the senior hurdles: Frank Pakenham, a friend of Bill who later became a great friend of David, remembered watching him hurdling with 'the same diffident smile on his face which he sustained throughout the years in the midst of great journalistic and social achievements', while the Eton College *Chronicle* noted that 'Astor from the start looked far the best hurdler.'

'On paper, of course, my Eton career has been dim in the extreme,' David told Nancy towards the end of his time at the school. 'I'm an oddish mixture. To the ordinary Etonian I'm very obscure and retiring. Beaks consider me most precocious and even provocative and I certainly cut ice in the house but I don't get across outside it. I haven't got the faculty for ready friendship on first acquaintance like you have.' But his house matron assured Nancy that 'David has personality and the other boys follow him tremendously.' 'My great regret is that during the whole of my school career I have never been in a position of authority,' he confessed: he had 'always been a critic and never a performer', and had 'learned a goodish deal by watching other people fail'. He was keen to stay on for another term, since 'I am just beginning to get a grip on my study of history'; he enjoyed singing and drawing, wanted to 'make my mark in the athletic world', in boxing as well as hurdling, and he 'had quite fun inculcating the "team spirit" into our house football side'. But a school career that had started out so unpromisingly was drawing to its close. Years later, as a founding member of the British–Irish Association, a body set up to work for peace and reconciliation in Northern Ireland, he emerged from a meeting with civil servants in the Cabinet Office, and amazed his colleagues – Marigold Johnson, Lord Longford and Anthony Kenny – by putting four fingers in his mouth to summon a taxi in Whitehall. 'I didn't learn much from Eton, but I did learn that,' he told them. As always, he was being far too modest.

Robert Birley recommended him to try for Balliol, his own old college, rather than New College, favoured by David's father and brothers, and in the spring of 1930 he went up to Oxford to be interviewed and sit the entrance exam. 'Lindsay the master of Balliol seemed rather a grim and gloomy man but no doubt he's frightfully nice when you know him,' David reported home, but 'Sligger' Urquhart, the fondly remembered dean of Balliol, seemed a 'dear old boy'. Kenneth Bell, a history tutor, told Birley that although David seemed weak on facts and details, his exam papers displayed 'much vigour and intelligence', and he assured Waldorf that 'we all liked him, and he got on extremely well and seemed to be enjoying himself'. Latin was a weak point, but 'otherwise his work was full of promise – intelligent and individual and full of life.' Oxford was to prove less congenial than Eton; but in the meantime he had set his heart on learning German, and visiting the country from which John Jacob had set forth all those years before.

Not for the last time, Tom Jones bustled forward to arrange matters on David's behalf. His son Tristan, who eventually became the business manager of the *Observer*, had spent some time in the university town of Heidelberg, and his daughter Eirene – later to become, as Eirene White, a well-regarded Labour backbencher – had stayed with a Professor Popper and his family, and warmly recommended them. In the spring of 1931 TJ and his wife accompanied David to Heidelberg, and found him a

female tutor, a Dr Gross. David took to the life at once. Frau Popper did
all the cooking, cleaning and shopping, and would have been amazed to
learn 'how we live at Cliveden with a large serf population who spend their
lives keeping up a palace for us to live in. I tell you I'm really ashamed –
we're blooming parasites!' Professor Popper was a kind and civilised man,
and his wife's food was a good deal better than that served up at Cliveden,
which always left David feeling that he had overeaten. He bought himself
a bicycle: Heidelberg lacked a golf course, but it boasted a castle and a
market and a 'Hitler propaganda shop – what more could one desire?'

'I like these 'ere Germans,' David told Waldorf. They could be
pompous and officious and humourless and uncouth, but they were
'real go-getters' and 'sound at heart', radiating an 'unselfish feeling of
fellowship', and – like many Englishmen between the wars – he favourably compared German stolidity with French frivolity. But 'politics mean
something here. People don't regard them with a tolerant smile as in
England.' Hard-working Germans were 'not given a will of their own
(unlike the Englishman, whose main concern is that his personal rights
of freedom should not be infringed)', but liked to feel 'one cog in a great
machine'. 'The place reeks of nationalism' and 'they do not believe in
an international mentality,' he told his father, adding that 'everything is
explained as a result of their being defeated in the war'. And although
'my own forecast is that the Germans will try and boss the world again
but by organised industrialisation instead of the bullet', many of the
town's students admired Hitler and the Nazis, and 'as far as I can see no
one seems to think that there is any chance of avoiding another war in
Europe.' Round Heidelberg at least, the Nazis were seen as 'the life and
soul of Deutschland, the hope of the country, its pride and revival', and if
Britain and France failed to address the contentious issue of reparations,
'the Nazis are certain to come in'.

David couldn't resist looking out of his window when the local Nazis
marched past; he came to know their songs 'almost by heart', and found
himself humming along. He was kept awake at night by the singing
of Nazis and Communists, each trying to out-bellow the other. A Nazi
Reichsparteitag was held in Heidelberg while he was there. Cheering
crowds greeted the marchers and women hurled flowers: he noted how
'most people salute the Nazi flag as if it were the national emblem', and
how children seemed particularly enthusiastic (Jewish children, on the
other hand, 'were very badly teased'). A rally was held in a field outside
the town, and widows from the last war were presented with medals.
'You were made to feel that everyone had forgotten these women,' David

remembered years later. 'It was rather moving.' As for the Brownshirts in their home-made uniforms, 'Who were these people? I looked at their faces. Were they a type? Would they show the sort of peculiarities one thought one saw in Goering, Goebbels or Hitler himself? It hit me quite strongly that these were ordinary people. It seemed more alarming that they were ordinary, rather than eccentric. It seemed that Hitler's ideas could capture the man in the street.' That evening the Nazis illuminated the castle walls with a blazing swastika, and shouts of '*Deutschland Erwache!*' rang out all night.

One day he bicycled to Walldorf, the Astors' ancestral village. 'It's on light, sandy soil among fir plantations and strips of very poor land. The loose earth blows up the streets, and the whole place is very dull and dirty. No one goes there if he can help it,' he told Mrs Jones. It was, he told Waldorf, 'a stagnant, stinking backwater of the industrial revolution, too sad and sordid-looking', with poor shops and dirty children standing around. There was a memorial to John Jacob Astor 'on a patch of grass by the church', and 'I know why he left it!' Quite a few Astors, he discovered, worked in the local tobacco factory. 'All this I found mildly reassuring: at least it was better than being connected only with New York hotels and a string of Astoria cinemas,' he wrote in a brief unpublished memoir, adding that 'I think I was probably the first member of our family to be embarrassed by our wealth.'

Although he never mastered the language, David thoroughly enjoyed the three months he spent in Heidelberg, and wished he could have stayed longer. He told Nancy that she would 'die of laughter' if she saw Nazis en masse, since they were 'the stupidest, most uninspiring lot of men imaginable', with 'stupid dull faces, suddenly opened with an air of cocksure importance'. Hitler would not be made chancellor for another eighteen months, but despite his ridicule of the Heidelberg Nazis, David was uneasily aware that should he come to power 'it would be difficult to allay the passions he has aroused'. On a return visit to Germany in the early days of Nazi rule, he told Nancy that he had expected a 'whacking great majority for Hitler': although 'I regard the present development with disapproval, one has to see its *raison d'être*', and 'anti-Semitism is apparently never heard these days . . . attention is fixed on new roads, new laws, the frugal private life of Hitler, the beneficial results of the rule of his fine, upstanding, public-spirited, sane followers. The ordinary SA man is pictured rather like the people in advertisements for Shredded Wheat – clean-living, healthy, likeable, serious, responsible, kind, trustworthy and normal.' He revisited Germany several times over the next few years: he came to hate what he saw, and to regard Hitler with a colder, clearer eye than other members of his family or their close associates.

David's exposure to totalitarian ideologies included Communism as well as Nazism. After leaving Heidelberg, he went to Berlin to join his parents and Bernard Shaw on their notorious trip to the Soviet Union, which left Shaw in particular with the reputation of being, like his friends Sidney and Beatrice Webb, one of those whom Lenin had famously described as 'useful idiots', duped into rhapsodic support for the regime after exposure to beaming peasants and well-nourished factory workers. Philip Kerr and Charles Tennant were also in the party, and they were joined in Berlin by an American, Maurice Hindus, and by Maxim Litvinov, Stalin's People's Commissar for Foreign Affairs and roving ambassador. Before leaving London the party had been advised to stock up with 'food sufficient for four days'. Russian bread was 'unpalatable', they were told, and they took with them coffee, cheese, powdered milk, lavatory paper ('cannot be purchased there'), sugar, jam, towels, soap, a corkscrew and a tin opener. Shaw shocked their hosts by hurling his supply of tinned food out of the train window, claiming that this somehow proved that hunger did not exist in the Soviet Union. They were met at the frontier by the American Anna Louise Strong, a professional apologist for Communism in Russia and, later, in China: Nancy fell into conversation with some strapping young peasant women clutching spades, and – according to the *Moscow News* – told them 'to be sure and keep their men in their place' and to 'keep the men down'.

In Moscow their train was met by 'great throngs', eager to welcome GBS in particular. It was oppressively hot, and the men discarded ties and overcoats in favour of open-necked shirts. They visited a prison, a factory and a soldiers' camp in a pine wood, where they were subjected to a blast of patriotic songs; they were taken to the races, Waldorf noting with an expert eye that 'the horses were not third class, they were fifth class'; the propaganda was unrelenting, and David bought a large collection of Soviet posters. He was not included in the visit to Stalin in the Kremlin, during the course of which Nancy asked their host how long he intended ruling by tsarist methods, only to be reminded of Oliver Cromwell; Stalin in turn asked about the possibility of Churchill coming to power, and whether he would try to repeat the 'Archangel invasion' of 1919.

David returned to Moscow a year later. He stayed at the National Hotel, which had an en suite bathroom and a view of the Kremlin. The people looked smarter than the previous year, 'well up to Margate standards'. 'I don't think Russia is paradise, but there's something to be said for the place' – and that despite visiting a collective farm run by 'Anglo-Saxon Communists,' which was like 'going into a lunatic asylum'. 'I have learned a little patience, and how bad my nerves are,' he told Nancy, but he had learned above all 'the need to work' – and, unlike many other rich men, he would never be work-shy. 'I think I have become a little less sorry for myself,' he confided to his diary. 'I don't consider my reactions quite so momentous, and my private life and intellectual attainments are absolutely absurd', and 'I refuse to accept the dictum of the intellectual snobs that the ordinary man is not interesting.' Travel had broadened his horizons, and his sympathies. In the interwar years many rich people, and many members of the British political establishment, were more worried by and fearful of Bolshevism than of fascism. Waldorf and Nancy regarded both with equal disdain, yet their support for social reforms at home was prompted not just by generosity and liberal views, but also by a very real fear that, unless such reforms were introduced, Communism could prevail. David's visits to Germany and Russia as a young man left him with an unillusioned hatred of totalitarianism of the right and the left – a view that would be reinforced, in due course, by his friend and mentor George Orwell.

Back home, David found himself confronted with a domestic difficulty in the form of Bobbie Shaw. Waspish, resentful, thin-skinned, heavy drinking and homosexual at a time when to practise homosexuality was a criminal offence, Bobbie was a permanent source of worry. After a brief spell of farming in Southern Rhodesia, he had rejoined his old regiment, the Royal Horse Guards. A keen steeplechaser, he had an appalling accident out riding; his head had to be operated on, as a result of which he was even less able to take his drink. In 1929 he lost his commission for being drunk on duty, leaving him remorseful, demoralised and more bitter than ever; and two years later he was arrested for soliciting, for trying to pick up guardsmen in a pub near Belgrave Square, and was sentenced to four months in prison. It was an appalling blow, and for Nancy in particular, but no mention was made of it in any of the papers. An unspoken code of *omertà* prevailed: as David put it, the press lords 'didn't bomb each other's headquarters', and even Beaverbrook, who was later to wage a long and vicious campaign against the Astors, toed the line. David visited Bobbie in Wormwood Scrubs, and proved, according to Nancy, a 'tower of strength'. From now on he would take a protective interest in the chequered career of his wayward half-brother; and the experience of visiting Bobbie in prison contributed, years later, to his interest in prison reform and the welfare of prisoners.

Fond as he became of Bobbie, David urged his mother both to take a strong line, and to keep her distance. She must leave Bobbie alone: that was 'the only way ever to get him to grow up mentally and to take an attitude which shows responsibility for himself', and if she failed to do so he would remain 'an irresponsible person and a danger to himself'. She must not let Bobbie pull her down: her duty to the rest of the family 'demands that you should not sacrifice yourself to this one over-grown sheep'. Nancy was the most overbearing of mothers, capricious in her choice of favourites and unable to let go; before long David would be doing battle with her, but on his own behalf this time.

4

Oxford Blues

David was normally temperate in speech and thought, eager to see both sides of any question, but Oxford brought out the extremist in him. 'I hate the beastly place, and think its atmosphere vile,' he once declared. As for the dons, and a good many of his fellow undergraduates, 'they are out of touch with the beauty of the universe, and I loathe almost everything about them. Arrogance, puppyness, small-mindedness in a dozen forms, artificiality but, first and last, pomposity.' Matters were made worse by recurrent bouts of depression, exacerbated by his agonised and embattled relationship with Nancy, whose intrusive and overbearing personality he increasingly resented. But it was while he was at Oxford that he made the strongest and most potent friendship of his life, which shaped and defined his whole career.

As in the early days at Eton, he found it hard at first to make friends. He was not good at making real friends, as opposed to 'conversational friendships': because he had 'an original and attractive manner', he got on with people at first acquaintance, but 'the gloss wears off,' leading (or so he claimed) to feelings of 'disappointment and disgust'. 'I am not making friends very fast here, despite many efforts', he reported on another occasion. Balliol had its fair share of Etonians, including his future friends Jo Grimond and Peter Calvocoressi, but although David still lived the life of a well-heeled undergraduate – 'it seems a little too much to have two horses and a groom and then only go out on an occasional day', he told Waldorf, who had asked him whether he needed a second horse to ride on Port Meadow – he seemed eager to disassociate himself from that world. When Nancy learned that he had made friends with the son of a Welsh miner, she summoned Felix Frankfurter – then a visiting professor in the Oxford law faculty, later to become a member of America's Supreme Court – in the hope that he might discourage the friendship. 'I did my best to explain to her your own independence and solidity of judgement and that instead of regretting your close friendship with the lad in question she ought to be glad that she had a son who had such generous impulses,' Frankfurter reminded David many years later.

David had decided to read PPE (or Modern Greats as it was also known), a relatively new and 'classless' subject; the leftwards-leaning master of Balliol, A. D. Lindsay, was a member of the Labour Party and active in the Workers Educational Association, and the college had long had a reputation for admitting working-class students as well as the occasional Indian undergraduate. David told Charles Collins – a middle-class young man who became a good friend at Balliol – that he was 'temperamentally and to a certain extent intellectually a radical but by birth a bourgeois': he would like to be 'an active and indignant revolutionist', was 'keen on socialist ideas', and had 'been thinking and talking socialism, going to Russia, getting to know Communists here and there'. (But, he added, he was also close to Bob Brand, 'who can ridicule nicely and discredit the socialists'.) Tom Jones's son, Tristan, who had won a Brackenbury Scholarship to Balliol from Stowe, and was also reading PPE, was an active member of the Communist Party; as an executive of the October Club, he was charged with an offence against the police during a Communist Party protest against the Reichstag Fire trials in 1933. Beaverbrook's *Daily Express* ran a story claiming that David had joined both the Labour Club and the Communist-run October Club, but 'although my closest friends at Oxford were members of these clubs, I from then onwards took good care not to make myself conspicuous, particularly as my interest was never practical enough for me to be prepared to make personal sacrifices such as undergoing public ridicule.' (Years later, recalling Beaverbrook's long-standing animus against the Astors, David wrote that 'his reporters used to try to exploit me, to my mother's embarrassment, when I was an allegedly left-wing student. It gave me my first taste of the rough methods that the gutter press are willing and able to use.') And, like many generous-spirited young men before and since, he lashed out, in a fairly conventional way, at what he considered to be manifestations of privilege. 'I can't stop in a cinema where they play "God Save the King" these days,' he told his parents. 'It means everything I dislike – privilege, grabbingness, conservatism, patriotism, deception, false education, a long-established and dangerous mental habit.'

He found it hard to concentrate on his work, or indeed to take it seri-ously: all too often he failed to complete the essays he'd been asked to write, while 'the futility of exams is proved by the unsatisfactory mental stature of those who excel at them.' Although he told Nancy that he was 'getting much fonder of Oxford as I get past its rather unattractive exterior of stuck-up undergraduates, self-conscious dons and gloomy main streets', such bouts of enjoyment were all too ephemeral. He was, he wrote in April 1932, 'perfectly miserable at being back', and 'the change from woods, fields and beauty to dank walls, dusty streets and overused quads is an unpleasant one. So is the loss of agreeable, natural, workaday people for these arrogant puppies and wrong-headed greybeards.' He took long walks around the town, convulsed by 'absolute disgust, despair, hopelessness'. He sought escape via the 'dope' of long walks and bicycle rides, and singing and whistling to himself, and tried to alleviate his misery by looking into working people's eyes, which seemed to reflect 'a different world from this fretted, futile, stuck-up Oxford-land'. 'I can't face work and discipline and regular social behaviour, and I can't face my impotence and feebleness,' he confessed in his diary. 'I don't do anything except pull myself to bits by divided desires', and 'I haven't known peace for weeks and months.' He even contemplated suicide, which, 'of course, is terribly attractive and often has seemed the logical conclusion to a train of thoughts and actions – falling in front of a bus from my window or from a bridge into the Thames.' One day he bicycled out of Oxford and spent an afternoon lying on his back in Binsey churchyard, half dozing and listening to the birds, which – together with the wind blowing in the trees – were 'an unending delight, sweeter by far than any Balliol conversation'. 'I like to look at farm labourers and hear them talk and see their caked boots and leggings and cloth caps and watch their easy unbewildered gait,' he continued, and 'I like work and its results – peace of mind, health, self-respect, a place among men, usefulness, a living life.' After brooding on all this, 'I hauled out the bike, picked up my gown which was in the ditch, and bicycled home.'

Christian Science provided consolation of a kind – or so he assured Nancy. He read his Bible every night, and found a CS practitioner: there were twelve other Christian Scientists in the university, and although he found their meetings 'stifled, forced and artificial', they provided 'anchorage'. Writing to Nancy, he referred to CS 'stuff about unhappiness coming from some sin' and the 'need to clear yourself of the sin and hence the unhappiness', before concluding that 'the one great comfort CS gives us is that one knows that eventually things are bound to come right'. 'I do trust in CS and it ought to make us happy and our paths straight. I'm sure it's the right thing . . . It's something in a world of nothings,' he told her on another occasion. Nancy, for her part, had decided that David was not only the most political of her children, but the most religious as well. 'Suddenly I woke up and discovered that she thought I should be a "practitioner", a professional healer, a terrifying sort of celibate creature who would go around preaching the word,' David recalled, and his abandonment of Christian Science was both emotional and intellectual: 'I knew that I had to break [with Nancy]: if I didn't, I was lost.' Practical issues also had their effect: the Astor boys had been outraged by their mother's reaction to Wissie's hunting accident, and when Bill, as an undergraduate at New College, fell seriously ill, the warden, H. A. L. Fisher, suggested that Nancy had prevented him from getting proper medical attention. 'He thinks Christian Science has failed him', was Nancy's reaction when David began to voice his doubts. 'Needless to say, it never occurs to him that he has failed Christian Science.'

Weaning himself away from the faith in which he had been brought up was to prove a lengthy business, and Christian Science 'left a mark' on David and his siblings in that 'we had peculiar attitudes to doctors, either going too much to doctors or thinking that using medicines was a sign of weakness.' In the meantime friends like Charles Collins provided much-needed emotional support. Years later, Collins recalled that David used to write between twenty or thirty letters a day, and that he would sometimes receive two or three a day via the college's messenger service. 'I feel frightened of being alone and very "upset" altogether. I find this thing called "the future" hard to face,' David told him in one such missive; in another he confessed to feeling a 'permanent undercurrent of fear – fear of losing control of myself, of ridicule, of contempt, of impotence in the face of new circumstances'. Writing to thank Collins for being so understanding, David told him that his interest in birds and animals and the countryside had atrophied as a result of his depression; they no longer gave him any pleasure, but he felt instead a 'strong biographical interest in people', and liked questioning them about their lives and views. His interest in nature would return in due course; his interest in people, and his shrewdness as a judge of character, would persist and play an important role in in his work as a newspaper editor.

When Collins asked him why he was so lacking in self-confidence, and was so solitary, after growing up in Cliveden surrounded by well-known names, David replied that it had been 'an absurd and enervating atmosphere to be bred in'. He was the most self-deprecating of men, but 'I feel a little silly in wanting so much praise and at being so conceitedly ambitious secretly.' He had grown up among people who 'all feel themselves to be more distinguished than the average', but 'I wish to God I'd been brought up in an intelligent, sane (but not too stiff and British)

middle-class family with a close connection with some kind of work –
productive, necessary, sobering, enlightening and respectable work. (The
parasitic element running our family life is most unpleasing.)' And 'having
been ignored and not respected at home and at school all these years,
praise to me is like drink to the teetotaler – it upsets me and makes me
want to run away. I feel it's unnatural, based on a misapprehension and
bound to be followed by "scorn and contumely".'

David was grateful to Collins for listening to him and calming him
down, and told him that 'peace is a thing I know damn little of', and
that he was 'seldom at rest, or "at peace" with myself'. Writing after
David's death, Collins remembered how uneasy he was about his family's
wealth, and how 'one of his pleasures was to stand on a hill or in a wood
and throw away pennies: a symbolism of the simplest', and how 'he
said he would have preferred to be a comfortably off middle-class intellectual living in a cosy flat.' Collins was not convinced that David had
a breakdown at Oxford – it was 'truer to say that he avoided academic
disciplines and that the subjects prescribed for his degree lost his interest
and attention. He was no slouch: on the contrary, he was socially and
in his own idiosyncratic way intellectually very active' – but at some
point he recommended David to a psychiatrist called R. D. Gillespie,
who was also a member of the British Psychoanalytical Society and, as
such, a Freudian psychoanalyst. Towards the end of his time at Oxford,
Collins remembered, David 'transferred, permanently and very privately,
a substantial part of his fortune for the formation and maintenance of a
trust that would benefit various charitable causes'. He told Collins that
he had already made his will: he had left money to 'various people who
have been kind to me', including the McNairs (who looked after him
in Glasgow towards the end of his time at Oxford) and the Poppers in
Heidelberg, but none to his family, and he had instructed his trustees
to apply 'residuary monies' to charitable causes, including 'the improvement of the condition of the wage-earning class so as to bring about
greater economic and social equality', 'the lessening of fear and therefore
hostility among the nations, and the promotion of movements calculated
to increase the sphere of international law, the development of European
political unity and ultimately the reign of a supra-national law', and the
'encouragement of the arts'. Psychoanalysis, foreign affairs and discreet
philanthropy would all loom large in his life: the York Trust, initially
administered on his behalf by Tom Jones, was the first of the bodies
through which he would channel money into causes which appealed to
his generosity and his liberal instincts. Later in the 1930s he expressed

his gratitude to Gillespie by providing money, through the York Trust, for a psychiatric unit at Guy's Hospital in London, which was eventually established in 1944.

David later diagnosed his bouts of depression at Oxford as 'a kind of self-contempt' resulting from his unhappy relationship with Nancy, in that he was torn between love and loyalty, and needed to get away. Although David was to be the most critical and independent-minded of all her children, in his teens he had become her particular favourite, together with Bobbie: so much so that she once told him, 'I wish you'd been born an ugly girl, then you couldn't leave me.' She was one of those mothers who is very entertaining to small children – showing off, making them laugh – but becomes a source of embarrassment, mortification and resentment once they move into adolescence. She was controlling and possessive, domineering rather than conventionally loving and affectionate; seemingly incapable of praise, she could never refrain from commenting on her children's appearance and achievements – or non-achievements – at a time when they were at their most self-conscious and lacking in confidence. 'It was at the onset of adolescence that Nancy's children began to be battered by the whirlwind of her domination,' wrote James Fox, who was exposed to a milder version in his great-aunt's old age, while Victor Cunard observed that 'if Nancy Astor's understanding of childhood was nearly perfect, her approach to the problems of adolescence was less happy. She felt it her bounden duty to chastise . . . those weaknesses and uncertainties that beset young men and women as they begin to grow up.' Nor would she leave them in peace to lick their wounds. 'My mother would always bring things to the point of a row,' David recalled. 'She would criticise people to the point where they'd protest. You couldn't avoid being drawn into combat, but she did it as a form of affection. It's very difficult to talk about my mother truthfully without making her sound hateful, which she really wasn't.'

'My mother's voice, coming downstairs now, would move me more than any other sound. It was as if the light was going on and everything was coming to life,' David told James Fox years later, adding that 'in spite of everything, the thought of my Ma still brings more joy and comfort and courage for me than the thought of almost anyone else'. But as a twenty-year-old undergraduate, he found her very hard to take. 'I have never felt like playing the "son". I haven't such a strong family feeling as you think, and I resent interference', he wrote from Balliol in the spring of 1932, and her relationship with him was 'much, much, much too personal. Acutely, almost violently personal.' 'You have a strong personality, a strong maternal sense, a passionate, unreasoning nature and strong affections,' he went on. 'I resent interference, dislike irrational love, loathe false praise, love freedom, disagree with my family in many views and am unable to conceal my feelings for long', and 'every time I catch a glimpse of your mother-love it makes me shudder, blush or froth at the mouth.' He would welcome some encouragement, 'but when you say that I have great abilities, rare chances, vast possibilities, I feel a nasty sugary taste in my mouth and want to make off into the woods and deliberately do what you don't want me to do.' He concluded by issuing 'my ultimatum: you've got to alter your views on family or I'm off!'

'I am afraid that I am what I appear and not what you thought I was or would like me to be', he wrote her in another of the innumerable and interminable letters he fired off on Balliol notepaper, almost all of them agonised, angry and upset. 'We mustn't allow a bitterness to come in and spoil the remainder of our temporal days. If there is one thing on earth you hate doing it is compromising. However, it happens to be an essential of existence. So try to compromise and not feel annoyed or bitter. If I attack occasionally you must remember that you are God's own attacker and can't expect always to have one-sided contests. You are so convinced of your rightness that you regard your attacks as assertions of truth. Well, I regard mine like that too.' 'I know it never entered your mind to dominate me: you do it instinctively and unconsciously,' he told her on another occasion. 'If you will take me as I am, if you will not eternally regard me as your child, if you will allow to my thoughts the same importance as to yours, then we should be able to get on all right. I am grown-up, I am different to you, I have got a life, and I want to lead it.' Many of his letters are undated, but it may be that by now he had taken Charles Collins's advice and was seeing Dr Gillespie. 'We are near to getting on well and it is only this eternal parent and child complex which spoils it,' David suggested, adding that any parent–child relationship 'is of course a sex relation'.

She must, he insisted, learn to 'play second fiddle', and not just for his own sake. He urged her to lay off Michael and Jakie, both of whom were still at Eton, but to no avail. Leaving home was 'taken as an act of defiance' given the 'strong sense of possessiveness which ran through the Langhorne family', Michael Astor recalled, and 'at times she demanded my attention and my affection to the point of insistence'. Nancy, for her part, seemed baffled by it all. 'The boys one moment think I never stop trying to meddle in their lives and won't let them alone and the next I have neglected them for public life,' she complained. 'They can't both be right – so I am really unmoved by their criticism and know that they will be sorry that adolescence took them that way.' 'Your and Papa's visit was pretty strained, wasn't it?' David wrote after his parents had paid him a visit in his digs in Ship Street, near the Oxford market. They had disagreed on every subject to 'such obvious disapproval and resentment at me from you that the atmosphere couldn't be expected to be very pleasant'. No doubt Nancy made 'scathing' remarks about David's friends. 'I've got no friends of my own,' he once told her, and 'I've never had a girl – amongst other reasons because I'm afraid of you': years later, he told James Fox that 'my mother made it impossible to bring home girlfriends', and that 'she tried to persuade me that falling in love was a "snare and an illusion"'.

'My father, who did not share this desire to keep his children at home, remained aloof', Michael Astor recalled: he may have been 'stern, benevolent, judicial in his view', but 'he reigned like Jehovah, a figure to fear, respect and increasingly resent', who regarded disagreement as a form of insubordination and seemed 'unable to recognise the individual characteristics of his sons, or offer a word of encouragement'. David's opinion of his father was a good deal more benign. 'Papa leaves me entirely to myself, and does not pretend to own or to supervise me. Yet I always know he is there if I want him,' he told Nancy; and when, in due course, David screwed up his courage, rehearsed his lines, and told his father that he could no longer get on with Nancy, Waldorf listened in silence and 'at the end he said he was sorry to hear it. He just looked a little pale but never contradicted me. From then on we had a secret pact. It was the beginning of an unspoken bond between us that lasted all his life.'

Philip Kerr was once again on hand to offer support and advice. He understood how 'your revered "mommer" can get on your and other people's nerves', but he urged David not to 'get an obsession' about her, since 'these obsessions, if they once get hold of you, make you hard and vindictive, and gradually unbalance you till you begin to qualify for an asylum. You've got to learn to keep your mentality free and calm and serene. It's not as though you have to be boxed up with your "mommer" for the rest of your life.' David came to be rightly admired for being fair-minded and even-handed, but from time to time he would be ridden by obsessions: future bees in his bonnet would include the dismal state of British propaganda in the early months of the war, the iniquities of General de Gaulle in wartime London, the inadequacies of Christopher

Sykes as a biographer, and – some might suggest – the all-redeeming, all-explaining powers of psychoanalysis itself.

★

In the meantime, David's particular obsession was to get away from Oxford, work with his hands, and get some idea of how ordinary people led their lives. He talked to Tom Jones about working in a garage or training to be a plumber. 'My "story" is going to take a little careful fabrication . . . I'm for saying my father owns a farm near Cookham (he does) and wants me to learn about cars or plumbing as a possible career or for use in farm life.' Neither fantasy came to fruition, and he turned to TJ for help. 'For God's sake, Tom, I'm going off my head,' he told him. 'I want to work with my hands. What do you suggest?'

TJ had taught for a time at Glasgow University, where he had got to know a factory-owner called Sam Mavor, whose works were in the constituency of Jimmy Maxton, a far-left Independent Labour Party MP and a friend of Nancy. TJ was also a friend of A. D. Lindsay, the master of Balliol, who was also a Glasgow University graduate, and suggested to him that David should take six months off from his studies to gain some useful 'industrial experience' with Mavor & Coulson, a Glasgow engineering firm which specialised in making coal-cutters and other mining equipment. Once Lindsay had agreed, TJ recommended David in the warmest terms to Mr Mavor. 'He wants to learn at first hand something of the life of the working people of this country,' and 'David's desire is to take his place as an ordinary working man doing whatever he is told,' TJ told him, adding that David was 'first-class material, very intelligent, of excellent character and sure to play a big part in the national life by and by'.

Mavor happily agreed, and David moved from Ship Street to lodgings in Rutherglen, for which he paid thirty-five shillings a week to Gordon McNair, an under-foreman at the works, and his mother, who worried that David might turn out to be a 'yah yah boy'. 'I live in a middle-class household (without a maid or car but still middle class, I think),' David told Nancy. 'Nobody seems to have heard of you and Papa up here, so I'm safe.' It took him a quarter of an hour to travel to the factory in Bridgeton by tram; he spent 'long dull days in a dully lit room' as an apprentice engineer and only had Sundays off, but enjoyed it all the same. Despite chipping his finger with a hammer on his first day, 'I was determined to be the best fitter and the best turner – very unlike my performance at school and university,' and was pleasantly surprised when his dour apprentice master told him that he was 'about average'.

'You will be a trifle disgusted and incredulous to know that I regard them as in most ways my superiors,' David told his mother apropos the McNairs, and he found Gordon McNair 'more interesting than most of the young Balliol gentlemen'. The food in his lodgings was excellent, he had a comfortable double bed, and altogether he was leading 'the most easy, comfortable and normal of lives – so different from the deadness of Oxford or the separatedness of Cliveden and St James's Square life'. He felt he belonged in the factory, and had begun to recognise people in the street; and because he found himself mixing with all types, workers, managers and reps – 'far from feeling that I am far from civilisation, I feel that I am right in the middle of it'. He went to the pantomime, and kept an eye out for any signs of Protestant–Catholic animosity. He found the Scots rather smug, but 'there is knowledge, chiefly scientific, and experience to be got here which is far more accurate and significant to the life of this animal, man, than most of the gup talked by the greybeards and warty-faced youths of Oxford University.'

Glasgow might be vastly preferable to Oxford, but David's bouts of depression were never far away. 'I am filled with my usual deep sense of despair,' he told Nancy. He was, he realised, introspective to the point of 'being filled with a dreary longing for death', and referred to 'the desperate feelings that have tormented me to the point of suicide'. His mother's endless fault-finding was unbearable at times: 'you can't hit a person long weighted down with unhappiness and expect a nice balanced reaction', and 'I can't take your attacks with a light-hearted smile because I haven't ever had a light heart'. Nor was he frightened of death 'as I have a private attraction towards it. I really haven't enjoyed life enough to care if I have any more of it or not.'

Although Nancy wisely kept away, Waldorf called in at the factory, and 'we took a bus out of Glasgow, then climbed a hill and ate our sandwiches basking in a spring sun'. (No doubt Waldorf was en route to Tarbert Lodge, his converted farmhouse on Jura. He owned much of the island, and Nancy used to swim in its icy waters; like many people between the wars, she had strong views on milk, and a cow from Cliveden came with them on family holidays, travelling in a specially made carriage which was attached to the train that took them to the embarkation point.) David spent his twenty-first birthday on one of Lord Lothian's estates near Edinburgh, one result of which was that he came into his share of the money left by William Waldorf Astor to his grandsons, bypassing

Waldorf after Waldrof had objected to his father accepting a peerage: known in the family as 'Grandfather's Revenge', it was to make David financially independent for the rest of his life.

David was sad to leave Glasgow and the factory, telling Nancy that he 'would *willingly* do another year or two here and infinitely prefer it to Oxford'. 'Glasgow was an attempt to regain my touch with life,' he told Charles Collins: factory life combined with visits to R. D. Gillespie's consulting room and Collins's support had helped to 'get this wretched ditched bullock onto his feet again'. He no longer felt suicidal, and would, he promised, try to be less reliant on Collins when he returned to Oxford. Tom Jones, busy as ever, arranged for David to go down a mine in the Rhondda Valley, loading and unloading trucks and visiting a working men's club. 'I like the little ant-like men who run mines and work in them – they compare very favourably with the woolly-headed uplifters of the human race,' David reported home. TJ wrote to say how glad he was that 'the engineering regime prescribed by your Consultant Tutor had worked so well', and begged him to encourage Tristan to take some exercise, since 'the Jones family don't know how to play; the Astors do'. David would never come to terms with Oxford, but it was back in Balliol that he met and became friends with a man who, with his father, would prove to be more influential than anyone else in his life.

5

Adam von Trott

David first met Adam von Trott by the porter's lodge in Balliol, and they soon struck up what was to be an intermittent, short-lived but, from David's point of view at least, extremely potent friendship. Trott was to prove a divisive and controversial figure, both in Oxford and the world at large: he was only in his mid-thirties when he was brutally executed for his part in the 20 July 1944 plot against Hitler, and David would spend the rest of his life arguing on behalf of his friend and seeking to embellish a reputation which, rightly or wrongly, had been tarnished by doubt and suspicion.

Three years older than David, Adam von Trott zu Solz was born in 1909; he was descended from a long line of Prussian lawyers and public servants, and on his mother's side he was the great-great-grandson of John Jay, one of the Founding Fathers of the United States. He had spent some time at Mansfield College, Oxford, while studying law at Göttingen University, and was keen to return to Oxford to take a full degree. A. L. Rowse – who was bowled over by the tall, good-looking young German, finding him 'charming and sensitive, intelligent, radiant with his beauty and inevitable happiness' – suggested that he should apply for a Rhodes Scholarship, for which German students had only recently been allowed to reapply. E. F. Schumacher, who was to become a good friend and a close colleague of David, had been the first post-war German Rhodes Scholar, and Trott succeeded him, winning a place at Balliol.

Trott had an immediate impact, on students and dons alike. He was older than most undergraduates, and mixed as an equal with the younger dons. 'A tall, extremely handsome young man, he was probably the most successful Rhodes Scholar in achieving popularity among dons and undergraduates,' Richard Crossman recalled. According to Diana Hubback, a half-Jewish undergraduate who fell in love with him, 'Adam's whole physical appearance was of great beauty. He was over six foot four in height, with a thin and lithe body.' He had a domed forehead, a receding hairline, heavy eyelids covering large grey-green eyes, and full lips with a duelling scar on the lower lip. He was an excellent dancer, 'his habitual expression was one of great candour and serenity', and he had the 'most beautifully modulated and expressive way of speech'. Rowse, who was almost certainly in love with him, recalled his 'immensely lofty forehead, deep violet eyes, nobility and sadness in the expression, even when young, infinitely sensitive and understanding'. 'We became friends almost at once,' Isaiah Berlin wrote of him. 'He had exceptional charm, great distinction of mind and manner, was extremely handsome, had both wit and humour, and was at all times a delightful companion. I was completely captivated. He had a far wider vision of history and culture than most of my Oxford friends: his conversation was interspersed with references to Schiller, Hegel, Kleist, Goethe – not names often mentioned in those days by students of the school of PPE . . . he seemed to me gay, carefree and invariably exhilarating.' David, for his part, 'found him open boyish, brotherly, playful and affectionate as a friend'.

For all his popularity, and his love of Oxford, Trott was, and remained, a very German figure, both in his priorities and his cast of mind. Charles Collins reckoned that 'he was deeply German, and no foreign influence, not even an English influence, ever overlaid this fundamental characteristic', while Geoffrey Wilson, another Oxford friend, told Trott's biographer that 'he was a person of intensely German mind, and the kind of ideas he had could only have come from a German': he was 'a very internationally minded man who was at the same time intensely "German-centred"', while cherishing a 'dream of a united Europe, modelled on the Holy Roman Empire'. 'Much as he enjoyed his time in England, he was never unmindful of the real business of his life, which was the future of Germany,' Charles Collins remembered. He felt it his duty in life to play an active role in Germany's affairs, as a result of which 'life in Oxford, which was on the whole carefree, seemed somewhat unreal to him, and depressed him, though never so as to mar the pleasure which his acquaintances took in his company'.

Nor was his cast of mind at all English. According to Diana Hubback, he spoke English extremely well but – as his letters to her testify – he wrote it in 'a heavy and obscure manner'. They met first at a dinner in All Souls, to which 'Adam contributed in his tortuous Hegelian style with words that ascended and sailed away like great balloons', and during their walks round Oxford he would try to explain Hegel to her. Hegel's ideas about the dialectic of history and the irresistible forces of thesis, antithesis and synthesis were anathema to even his best-disposed Oxford friends, including the younger academics. Maurice Bowra, who would do more than anyone to cast doubts on Trott's political credentials, claimed that he was 'a fluent Hegelian, and in his metaphysical approach to reality the outlines of issues became blurred, and it was not easy to say where his position lay'; Rowse, who had urged Trott to abandon politics when Hitler came to power, 'loathed Hegelianism', seeing it as an 'intellectual disease' which was 'deeply German, profoundly characteristic of their way of thinking': to Rowse's regret, Trott 'gave himself up to Hegelianism', leading to a break in their 'intense and unhappy friendship'. Isaiah Berlin, who liked Trott in person but retained lifelong doubts about him, shared his fellow Oxonians' views on Hegel (the sage's writing 'seems absolute gibberish to me', he once told a friend); Richard Crossman, who claimed in public to be a friend and admirer of Trott, later wrote a damning report in which he claimed that Trott not only 'had a great way with women and was able to discard his worshippers whenever convenient' but

> always claimed to be a Hegelian socialist which meant in fact that he had vague socialist ideals but came from too good a family to link with the working class in anything but in theory. He took his philosophy very seriously: of the quality of that philosophy one can best judge when one remembers that he did not find the Master of Balliol a confused thinker. Indeed I think that the close friendship of the Master of Balliol and Adam is due to the fact that, in the realms of philosophy, each is as high-minded as he is woolly.

David shared none of these doubts and reservations. His visits to Germany had given him an interest in the country, and he eagerly sought out Germans in Oxford, including Trott and Schumacher. Shortly after learning of Trott's death, he told Marion Doenhoff, another German friend, that Trott had been 'my alter ego and better ego, the ideal of myself whom I felt very inferior to, but loved all the more'. 'To me he was a teacher, and an elder brother as well as a well-loved friend. He was the greatest member of my generation in any country that I have ever met,' he told Trott's widow, Clarita. 'I was very attracted by the side of his nature that was both boyish and warm-hearted, by his extraordinary historical perception, and by his obvious goodness.' 'My admiration of Adam was never uncritical,' he wrote in an unsent letter to Isaiah Berlin, 'but it is true that I always envied him his intrepidity.' Charles Collins thought equally well of him, recalling 'a sense of power in his manner' as well as his 'quick sympathy and understanding, his good humour, his great kindness, his intelligence and his complete integrity of purpose.' He was never pompous or conceited, and 'there was something unspoilable and almost naive about him'. And the historian John Wheeler-Bennett attributed his popularity in Oxford to 'a charm and a sense of humour unusual in a German'.

Trott was, Collins suggested, 'a socialist (by conviction) and a liberal (by upbringing, conviction and temperament', and although he was, as a patriotic German, keen to stand up for Germany's legitimate rights – and to rectify what were seen by many, in Britain as well as in Germany, as the unjust terms imposed upon her by the Treaty of Versailles – he regarded the views and the activities of the Nazis with aristocratic disdain. He told Diana Hubback that although Germany was 'in a bad way politically', Hitler had 'repeatedly proved that he is a fool': he was reluctant to return to Oxford, since 'it now seems to me like a boy world where I have to contract my movements in an artificial and undesirable way'. Trott was in the Balliol Junior Common Room when, in January 1933, he read that Hitler had become the chancellor of Germany – and, according to Collins, 'he knew at once that a terrible disaster had befallen his country; that the prospects for his own future had undergone a funda-mental change', and that 'many of his friends and acquaintances were at once in personal danger'. Almost immediately he decided that he had to oppose the regime from within, rather than go into exile, and that 'although it would certainly handicap his own career, he would not join the Nazi Party unless it should ever become his clear duty to do so in furtherance of anti-Nazi activity'. 'My country is very sick,' he told Isaiah Berlin at a party given for him by the philosopher R. G. Collingwood, and 'I received the impression that he saw a vast transformation going on in Europe, a kind of fateful historic mutation, to which the ordinary categories did not apply, terrifying, sinister, but unlikely to be intelligible to academics like myself, so it may have seemed to him, in the exces-sively self-centred, cosy Oxford world.'

David recalled that Trott's first reaction to Hitler's accession to power was 'gloom, tempered by challenge', and in an unsigned article entitled 'How Nazis Think' – published in the first issue of the New Oxford Outlook, edited by Crossman and containing contributions from Bowra, Rowse, Goronwy Rees and Stephen Spender – Trott ridiculed the activities of the Nazi delegation to an International Students' Conference, during the course of which they had praised the racist diatribes of Gobineau and Houston Chamberlain, attacked Einstein in particular and the Jews in general, and claimed that the ancient Greeks were a pure German race. David and other friends urged Trott not to return to Germany, and to fight Nazism from without rather than within, but he was adamant. Before finally leaving Oxford, he went with David, Jo Grimond and Otto Schnetzler, a half-Jewish Heidelberg friend of David, on a tour of the great industrial cities of the Midlands and the North, and then on – minus Grimond – to the Astors' house in Jura. While walking on the island, David told Trott that he'd be a fool to go back to Germany, and that the Nazis would counter his arguments with brute force rather than reason – and to make his point, he tripped Trott up and pinned him down on the peat-sodden ground.

'What personally I fear most in the world is that the development of things here – painful enough in itself – will estrange my few friends in your country to an extent harmful to relations which are still very dear to me. I know this will not be the case with you – but there are very few that I can likewise be sure of,' Trott wrote to Diana Hubback. He was – rightly – worried that his friends in Oxford would regard with suspicion anyone who voluntarily returned to Germany rather than go into exile. David always believed that Trott was 'deeply and thoroughly anti-Nazi', that his international outlook and his devotion to both European and German culture made him 'the very embodiment of what Hitler had tried to crush and what all who fought against Hitler ought to have been inspired by', and that he 'yearned to retain some sense of common humanity between nations and hoped that Germans could be seen as part of the normal world, not as a uniquely criminal people'; but he later recalled that when they first met, Trott was 'very much involved with a circle which included Isaiah Berlin and other high intellectuals', and how he had warned his friend that 'these friends wouldn't be reliable (by this time Hitler had arrived in power and Adam's position had been strictly transformed from Prince Charming to suspect-under-examination)'. Berlin, for his part, thought Trott 'confused and therefore potentially dangerous', and he became still more doubtful when, in February 1934, Trott – by then working as a lawyer back in Germany – wrote to the *Manchester Guardian* repudiating claims of anti-Semitism in the courts of Hesse, his native province.'

Diana Hubback never had any doubts about their friend. 'He was absolutely clear from the beginning that the Nazis represented all that was evil, perverting and damaging to Germany and to Europe. He could never make any real compromise with them,' she wrote in an unpublished memoir of Trott. 'There were a few, a very few, who always believed in this fundamental integrity of his however suspicious his external actions were at times, and amidst the horrors of mistrust he had to pass, it was the absolute trust of those very few from whom he drew great strength.' She and David were among the 'very few', and it was their shared friendship with Trott that brought them together. Back in Germany, Trott urged Diana to get in touch with David (he had earlier alerted her to 'his special way of smiling with his head on one side'). 'David is a strange character – he may change a great deal still and I am not so very certain as to how much we will keep in common,' he warned her. 'But as it is I am definitely fond of him and hope that you will make friends. Don't let his shyness make you shy . . . Don't admit to him that I am a typical product of my family – it is his thesis that it is everybody's curse to be that.' Diana dutifully paid a visit to David's room in Ship Street: it was very small, but 'he says its disadvantages help him to work'. 'I'm afraid I talked too much – almost garrulous – but he seemed so easy and understanding to talk to,' she reported back. 'I liked him very much. Why does he smile so much? Is it a kind of nervousness?' She was particularly taken by his enthusiasm for Eton 'and his liking even ugly things because they mean something to other people'.

By now David's academic ties to Oxford were fairly tenuous. Roger Mynors, a Classics don at Balliol, gave him a wigging for doing so little work; David made such heavy weather of trying to read an essay to his history tutor, Humphrey Sumner, that Sumner charitably put a halt to the proceedings, and told him that there was no point in his taking his finals ('a great relief'). But his social life was a good deal brisker than it had been. Sam Beer, later to become a distinguished Harvard academic, recalled pub dinners with David, Charles Collins and Tristan Jones: 'a fairly regular episode in these larks was a wrestling match between David and Tristan. Both were very strong and quite good wrestlers, as they showed while rolling round on the ground, grunting and laughing.' When not wrestling with Tristan Jones, he fell 'half in love' with his 'Jewish girl', Diana Hubback. Late one afternoon in the autumn of 1933, after returning from a trip to Bournemouth to visit a convalescent 'Sligger' Urquhart, he drove Diana to the village of Sutton Courtenay, on the river south of Oxford, to visit a house that would come to play a crucial role in his life as an idyllic bolthole from the demands of everyday life. Set in lush meadowland on the banks of the Thames, the Manor House in Sutton Courtenay was, and still is, one of those magical English houses that seems to have slowly evolved over the centuries, like some ancient organism: a gabled-ended Tudor house, it included a Norman hall and was hemmed in by equally ancient barns, stables and paddocks. Its owner, Norah Lindsay, was a well-known garden designer who had done work for Nancy at Cliveden and at Rest Harrow ('the most enchanting large-size cottage'), for Lord Lothian at Blickling, his exquisite red-brick Elizabethan mansion in Norfolk, and at Ditchley Park, soon to belong to Nancy's niece Nancy Lancaster. Norah Lindsay was also an avid socialite: visitors over the years had included Churchill, Chips Channon and Lady Diana Cooper, who described it as 'the place above all others for romance and gathering rosebuds and making hay and jumping over the moon', and noted how 'flowers literally overflowed everything and drifted off in to a wilderness'. David was a frequent visitor during his Oxford days. On one occasion, his hostess recalled, 'David Astor and a pal from Oxford drifted in to bathe.' A group including Evelyn Waugh, Chips Channon and Mary Lygon was already installed, and David 'looked awfully upset at the unexpected crowd, all lying on cushions in the long grass outside by the swing'.

Much to David's relief, no doubt, only Mrs Lindsay and her daughter were at home when he visited with Diana. The Manor House, Diana told Trott, had a 'garden going down to or rather bordering the river', broken up by clipped hedges and statuary, and it was 'unbelievably peaceful and beautiful': years later, in her memoirs, Diana Hopkinson (as she had become) described it as 'the most romantic house and garden I have ever seen'. Their hostess had 'reddish hair, rather bepowdered', and 'talks incessantly, but amusingly and sometimes wisely'. After strolling round the garden they went into the dark-panelled room and sat in an inglenook by the fire while Mrs Lindsay talked 'very sentimentally and beautifully about birds and flowers and life and the modern world' while her daughter quietly knitted in a corner. Their hostess played Debussy on the piano, read them poems by Vita Sackville-West, and told them 'an excellent joke about mushrooms and stomach pumps'. 'One couldn't help feeling romantic in that house and garden,' Diana recalled: 'I listened to the music and watched the fire and, occasionally, David's golden head, and felt very happy.' On the drive back they discussed Mrs Lindsay and the Manor House: they wondered whether 'it was justified by any standards of social conscience', and decided that 'one couldn't apply such standards'. David parked his car by Folly Bridge, and they walked along the canal. He told her about his life in Glasgow: she found him 'very easy to talk to', and 'I like him more and more – and feel more peaceful and contented in his presence than I have been with anyone since I left you. I like his interest in details and his vitality.'

Diana had left Oxford without taking her degree and was working in London, but she tried to see her Oxford friends at weekends: apart from David, they included Isaiah Berlin, Goronwy Rees, Richard Crossman, Shiela Grant Duff and Douglas Jay, all of them known to Trott. Trott remained the love of her life, but in his absence David's 'very pink cheeks and very golden hair' had their attractions. She reported a 'lovely dream' about him – 'I can't remember any details but I was happy with him – and he had on a grey suit and a very white shirt' – quite apart from which 'he is so funny'. She announced that she would be going to see him for a day rather than a weekend – 'it will puzzle David a little – but I don't intend to enlighten him by saying I really can't afford a weekend' – and she helped him to decorate his rooms. He had repainted them in 'a beautiful pale dove grey', and she chose him 'some bold and brilliant modern designs for his curtains', and David wrote to thank her ('he really is over-polite – but charming'). They walked along the canal by Worcester, which he described as his 'especial domain'. 'He is so simple and direct – and yet imaginative and so very interested in the things one tells him,' she told Trott. 'I have only just begun to know him – but I think we are happy together. He is full of naif and charming compliments – notices clothes etc.' 'I become fonder of him – but I wonder if I don't expect too much of him – a type of friendship he would not want to give me and perhaps of which he is incapable,' she wrote in the spring of 1934. 'This is no reflection on his attitude or ideas so far – but I do expect a very great deal in appreciative perception and enthusiasms and love of poetry which he may not entirely possess . . . he has qualities which make him charming and a fine person even without those qualities.'

One evening David collected Diana from outside All Souls and took her to dinner at The Spread Eagle in Thame. He was driving 'the most beautiful new car', an American Essex Terraplane, streamlined, long, low and black, with green leather seats. After dinner they drove up into the Chilterns, where 'he took my hand and later we somehow kissed each other. Actually I think I was responsible – but he certainly showed the first signs of affection.' She felt his attitude was 'rather pitying . . . I like him and told him so – and he said he hoped I didn't like him too much.' 'If you knew my feeling for you, you would know that incident with David was so very trifling,' she assured her German admirer. 'I know you won't mind about the incident with David. He gave me a

lecture on cultivating calmness and restraint – I took it very meekly.'
'I am sure David did not kiss merely to comfort you, but I am equally
sure that he fears that certain external things about him might attract
you too much,' Trott replied. 'I am not acutely jealous, nor really frightfully surprised, as I have found some hints of the possibility in previous
letters of yours. But it makes me feel a little lost in my relation to you
as well as to him.' Since Trott had recently confessed to Diana that he
had been unfaithful to her, he was hardly in a position to lay down the
law, or take a high tone.

Romantic entanglements apart, Diana found herself acting as an intermediary between her lover in Germany and her admirer in England.
David was proving a poor correspondent, and Trott became upset when
his letters went unanswered. 'Don't worry about David,' Diana assured
Trott. 'He does behave curiously – I am sure there could have been no
estrangement between you.' But David had already 'broken the spell'
and written to his friend in Germany: 'he seems to think I'm like a strict
governess ordering him to write – and that it is his duty to inform me
when he has written!'

'I don't think David does any work – he has a lot of social engagements and wastes time, but seems happy,' but – as Diana was beginning
to discover – friendships between the very rich and ordinary mortals are
not always easy to sustain, however liberal-minded and well disposed the
very rich may be. In April 1934 Diana reported that David had flown to
Stockholm during the vacation: 'he seemed of a very different world
to either of us. He is so gay, so completely unworried (as far as one can
tell), and so happy and busy with innumerable social engagements. He
seems most contented with a graceful and varied leisure. I suppose it is
partly the simple result of the possession of wealth, and also of a very
easy natural temperament.' Because their ways of life were so different
'we would probably never be great friends', and future relations were
likely to be 'casual' rather than intimate. But 'he looked so well and
happy that it gave me pleasure to look at him – as one likes seeing very
healthy children or beautiful horses'.

A couple of months later Diana bumped into David in an art gallery
in London. 'He looked very beautiful – he had just come in from the
street where it had been raining. His cheeks were sprinkled with rain
and glowing red, his lips a little parted like a healthy child's, his eyes very
bright and his hair glowing against the dark walls of the gallery,' she told
Trott. But he didn't seem pleased to see her, so much so that his 'startled
cold expression chilled me'. 'I have no illusions any more – he doesn't in

the least want me as a friend – nor does it give him any pleasure to see me,' she admitted – and it was 'probably my own clumsy fault'. Later that year 'I heard from Shaya [Isaiah Berlin] that David Astor had come down from Oxford – but that may be only a rumour – I have heard nothing from him.' Like David, Diana would remain a loyal friend to Trott, and to his memory; her friendship with David would revive in later years, but a particular phase in their lives had ended, and they needed to make their ways in the world.

6

In Limbo

Despite the fast cars and the brisk social life, David's revulsion against his family and his background continued unabated: so much so that although he dutifully turned up on formal occasions, he kept well away from Cliveden for most of the 1930s. After leaving Oxford in 1934, he spent the next five years in a kind of limbo, demoralised, unsure of what he wanted to do with his life, flitting from one job to another: to such an extent that even Waldorf, who saw him as a kindred spirit, began to despair. Some years later, shortly after he had begun to edit the *Observer*, David referred to his 'selfish withdrawal into a purely private life' which 'began in my early twenties, when I was solitary and a sort of refugee from my family'. 'David, guided by some inner light, for a while revolted against the politics, the prescriptions and the social edifice which made up the backcloth of our lives at home,' his brother Michael recalled:

> For a time he turned abruptly against his own class in society, the class in which I numbered and valued my friends. Despite my feelings of affection and many points of recognition, I resented his experiments at living which seemed to disregard the fragile structure of our society, the subtle class differentials, the barriers through which we passed and re-passed by touch and by feeling, whose contact could become distorted if subjected to a heavy or analytical treatment. His measures appeared too literal rather than too extreme. I lost touch with his humour, which was of a particularly subtle and artistic sort.

'I have been brought up with no connections, no background, no home, no village life, no accepted and acceptable social setting,' David complained to Charles Collins, who was by now working in the East End. 'Our life is an impossible, absurd, plutocratic one to people of any taste. My father is either a saint or an unimaginative martinet. My mother is either a fascinating and clever woman or a silly egotist.' Nancy, needless to say, was much to blame for his disaffection. 'I can hardly believe she is my mother. If my father was less influenced by her I would like him better,' he told Collins: not only did she disapprove of pubs – 'Why that woman Lady Astor wants to close them, I can't think' – but he never met suitable middle-class girls because 'my mother's attitude to girls and flirting was so sarcastic that it made me shy and I covered up my shyness by pretending I "wasn't interested"'. He felt out of place at a 'hellish stupid "upper-class" party' held at Cliveden – 'I sit about and creep about and sulk and annoy almost everyone' – but Cliveden's annual sports day was no better: it ended with pillow-fighting and a dance, and 'it's not much fun being called "Sir" by your partner'. 'Grandfather's Revenge' had given him financial independence, and he soon had a house of his own in Chester Place, off Regent's Park; and – seeing him no doubt as a kindred spirit – he saw more of Bobbie Shaw than of other members of the family. But he still came home for Christmas, playing his part in the charades and amateur theatricals and manifesting what his cousin Joyce Grenfell described as 'the Langhorne imitative powers': one year he and Jakie did 'their famous ventriloquist act', as well as acting the parts of English soldiers on the North-West Frontier.

Unlike other members of his family, he shared Tom Jones's Labour-leaning sympathies: 'at that time I was leaning that way too – I was the one in the family who showed most interest in social and, indeed, in socialist ideas,' he recalled years later. But even then he looked askance at Marxism: 'I was thrilled by the simplicity of it, and the tidying up of contemporary age-old problems, but I was also horrified by the inevitability of revolution, the destructive side of the thing.' TJ was always at hand to help and give advice – not least when David wrote to him from Rest Harrow to say that he was thinking of changing his name, possibly to 'Shaw', and making a new, family-free life in America or Australia. 'If I had Randolph Churchill's brass-necked ability to thrive on publicity and criticism I might use my present one advantageously', but as it was the Astor name seemed an oppressive liability. Uncertain, like so many young people recently down from university, of what he wanted to do with his life, he thought he might 'settle in America for a year or two, getting some business experience in perhaps newspapers to please Papa and to leave open the possibility of the *Observer* to a later date' or, alternatively, 'concentrate on the entertainment business and get ground-floor experience of movies and theatres'. Waldorf had persuaded his own father to buy the *Observer* in 1911, and had already earmarked David as his heir apparent as far as the family paper was concerned, but his faith was to be sorely tested over the next few years. 'Our talks about the future of the Observer have made me feel that one of my boys ought to be fitting himself to help – at one time I thought that I should get David to undertake this – he has definite talents but unfortunately he is going through a difficult period in his development and his tastes and whole future are very much undefined,' he told Garvin in October 1934, after David had finally abandoned Oxford. 'My father made the calamitous mistake of leaving money to each of the boys on their coming of age,' he added, and 'the bequest has not been beneficial or helpful to any of them'.

'He is as kind as his mother but even more restless,' TJ noted, and David's relations with Nancy remained as agonised as ever. He resented the way in which she tried to dictate his and Bobbie's friends; he referred to a 'nightmare' discussion, during the course of which 'there were enough nasty things said last Tuesday to kill a brainless prize fighter', and signed off with 'love of a much battered and atrophied but still extant kind'; four years of 'rows and recriminations' were 'enough to make him feel thoroughly fed up with everything, to regard his home as the last place he wants to be in' and to 'kill off most of the affection and regard he had for his home'. 'You keep saying you can't go on, each time you see me it hurts, telephone conversations hurt etc. It's the same for me,' he told her, adding that 'I hate writing a letter like this.' 'You suffer from disappointment and I from despondence. But if only your disappointment and my down-heartedness could give way to something a little less poisonous – say, for example, consideration,' he wrote from Rest Harrow, signing off as 'that humourless, hateful, egotistical, selfish, introspective, self-opinionated lump of dough David'. A temporary improvement in the relations was greeted with relief, 'otherwise I would have felt more of a shipwreck than I do now'. But embattled as they were, he always appreciated her wit and her fearlessness. 'My parents were alone among prominent Conservatives to invite the "naked fakir" to their house', he recalled, and on one occasion he and Nancy found Mr Gandhi sitting cross-legged in a room in 4 St James's Square. 'So you're the wild man of God,' Nancy told him. 'I know all about you. Everybody thinks you're a saint. But I know what you really are. You're just like me. You're just an old politician.' Far from taking offence, Mr Gandhi was greatly amused.

★

David's first job had nothing to do with newspapers or the theatre. 'Uncle Banker Brand' had 'invited me to work in his bloody firm for a year or two', David told Charles Collins, though 'I find it difficult to get my ambition beyond leaning on a friendly pub counter and looking drowsily at the patches of spilt beer and empty froth.' 'It feels queer being a clerk. Very like Glasgow and slightly like school,' he reported on life at Lazard's, the merchant bank where Bob Brand worked. 'I got to know a bit about the life of City workers, but almost nothing about the money business,' he recalled in an uncompleted memoir, and he admitted to Nancy that although he was quite enjoying banking life, he found it all 'most mysterious: one buys and sells money – buys dollars with francs and pesetas with marks and lire with kroner. Why?' According to Bob Brand, David's boss reported well of him despite his doing very 'routine work' – 'he said he was doing excellently, did his fair share of the work even when the staff worked late, was much interested in the work, and was very well liked' – but for the rest of his life David would be baffled by money, trying hard (but in vain) to show interest in the business pages of the *Observer*, and amazing his staff by his ignorance of mortgages and everyday expenditure.

When not puzzling over marks and lire, David wanted to write, but – like many before and since – he had no idea what he wanted to write about. 'I greatly admired one of the few authors that I read, Turgenev, and dreamt of having literary talent myself,' he admitted years later; in due course he learned to write extremely well, but it proved a slow and laborious business, not lightly undertaken, and his genius would manifest itself in editing rather than writing. Tom Jones was once again ready with useful contacts and advice, and mentioned him to Edward Garnett, one of the linchpins of London literary life, a member of the Bloomsbury world and an influential reader at the publishers Jonathan Cape. He asked Garnett to act as a 'consulting physician to advise in the case of a young man who has Great Possessions but also has some literary promise. He wants to be a writer. The problem is, can we prevent his riches from choking his gifts? I have told him in my simple way that the way to be a writer is to write.' This was sound advice, and to implement it 'the family doctor' had urged his patient to leave London and work for a provincial paper like the *Manchester Guardian* or the *Yorkshire Post*, which 'would get him into the habit of continuous work which he has not yet achieved'. Garnett duly pronounced the 'young millionaire's case' to be 'very grave': he doubted whether David would stick life on a provincial paper, but since David had spoken about the lamentable state of British theatre over lunch, Garnett wondered whether he should somehow become involved in plans for an acting school at Dartington Hall?

In due course David would try his luck in the theatrical world, but Waldorf had different expectations. He was as keen as ever that David should eventually join the *Observer*, but felt he should gain experience on other papers before joining the family newspaper; and he was so worried by David's reluctance to commit himself to a career that he decided to involve Bill with the paper in case his heir apparent proved a broken reed. Bill had some suggestions which he wanted to discuss with Garvin, though he felt 'a bit shy about big new ideas'. 'I at one time had hoped that David might devote himself to journalism. This may come about though at the moment it seems doubtful. So I brought Bill into the *Observer*,' Waldorf informed his editor. Bill had won Fulham East in the 1935 general election, and was later made Sir Samuel Hoare's parliamentary private secretary, but by the summer of 1936 he was combining his career as a Conservative MP with lending a hand on the *Observer*, and Waldorf was consulting him on whether Joyce Grenfell had enough experience to succeed, as the paper's radio critic, the formidable Hilda Matheson, who had been Nancy's political secretary before making her name as the innovative and leftwards-leaning head of the BBC's Talks Department. But, in Waldorf's eyes at least, Bill's involvement was a stop-gap measure, taken *faute de mieux*. 'Now that Bill Astor is in the House, embarked on a political career, Lord Astor is more anxious than ever that David should look kindly towards succeeding Garvin some day at the *Observer*, and he wants me to do anything I can to influence his son in that direction,' TJ noted in his diary.

The following year David sampled the journalistic waters for himself, albeit in a rather half-hearted way. While he was still at Lazard's, Tom Jones mentioned him to Sir Robert Bruce, the editor of the *Glasgow Herald*: although 'his father has hopes that the young man may some day take an interest in the *Observer*', TJ had advised him to get some experience outside London – and there was no need to pay him a salary. David himself made an approach to the *Manchester Guardian*, but its editor, W. P. Crozier, was unimpressed when he learned that he would only be there as a 'visitor' – 'I am afraid we could not take into the office someone who was only intending to get experience with us and then go on to another paper.' Towards the end of his time as editor of the *Observer*, David waged a vociferous campaign against an attempt by the National Union of Journalists to prevent young journalists from working on national newspapers unless they had previous experience on a provincial paper – the traditional path to Fleet Street which he himself had been persuaded to follow, albeit in Leeds rather than Glasgow. 'I am slightly less of a square peg in a round hole here than I was in Lazard's, though I can't say that journalism absolutely fascinates me,' he reported in June 1937, after a month on the *Yorkshire Post*. Its editor, Arthur Mann, was a remote but generous-minded character who had edited the paper since 1919. He had earlier worked on papers in Cardiff, Birmingham and Manchester, and as editor of the *Evening Standard* he had dreamt up the 'Londoner's Diary' column: he would, in due course, become a trustee of the *Observer*, providing sound advice until 1956, when he resigned over its opposition to Suez.

Life on the *Yorkshire Post* proved a 'quiet round of mild work and mild diversions'. Arthur Mann 'spoke very highly' of David's ability to Waldorf, saying that he had 'real journalistic flair' and wrote well, but his interests were 'too diversified'. He put various ideas up to the paper, none of which were thought suitable, but in the end he 'cornered them by suggesting a series on fox hunting'. This turned out to be a 'nice little job': he wrote a series of Surteesian articles about local Masters of Foxhounds, which enabled him to hunt, enjoy the countryside and see his initials ('FDLA'), if not his name, in print. 'Charlie Littleworth, the senior huntsman in the county, is a spare, bolt-upright figure with a daring eye and an awakening voice,' David declared in one such article. When not observing the local huntsmen, David enjoyed Leeds and, in particular, watching the comedian Max Wall perform his routine: years later John Heilpern, then a young journalist on the *Observer*, was astonished when his revered and diffident editor, in order to prove a point, suddenly broke into an impeccable imitation of Max Wall on stage.

But he was still restless and unsure of what he wanted to do in life, and would remain so until the summer of 1939. 'I am not so mad on journalism as all that, and feel disinclined to spend my life at something which doesn't interest me very much,' he told Nancy. 'I would much rather be the manager of a small music hall, or even a publican. Then if I can write, well and good . . .' If he had to become a journalist, he would rather follow his father's example and take it up in middle age – whereas to do so 'at twenty-five, when one has hardly lived at all, one would have to be really keen on journalism itself'. William Waldorf and Waldorf had run the *Observer* 'because of the influence it gives them – not because their main interest in life was the technicalities of a journalist's trade. I have been here long enough to have an idea what a full journalistic training would involve, and although the idea is not

distasteful I feel that for me it is a waste of life.' He told the manager
of the Queen's Hotel in Leeds, where he stayed while working on the
Yorkshire Post, that he wished he'd gone into the hotel business 'instead
of permanently sitting at the bottom of ladders – at Oxford, Lazard's
and the *Yorkshire Post*'. He wanted to travel, like Peter Fleming: 'I often
feel inclined to hop a liner and disappear to Australia or South America.
I should have done that about seven years ago instead of always trying
to oblige someone or other, always toeing lines and being an awfully
nice and promising young man,' he confessed to Nancy – who, for all
their differences, remained his chief confidante. 'I'm just a five per cent
person who'll always be thought to have possibilities and never will be
more than that.'

'Do let me know what you thought of David – he was rather nervous
about going to take your time but I think he has very considerable possibilities,' Waldorf wrote to Garvin after the great man had agreed to see
David on one of his trips to London. A few days later he was in touch
again to ask whether David could come down to Gregories, the house
near Beaconsfield from which Garvin edited the *Observer* and filed his
sonorous editorials. 'He feels that the *Yorkshire Post* is so conservative
(in every sense of the word) that he is not getting enough experience,'
Waldorf explained. 'David wants to write – is not sure yet whether
he wants (or has the ability for) book writing or journalism. He loves
studying humanity, and has an amazing faculty for getting to know people,
getting them to talk – he is a good judge of character and observant. As
a reporter in Yorkshire he has got to know all sorts of queer people –
members of travelling circuses, gypsies – and I suspect he wants to write
about them. He is particularly interested in theatricals and art and full of
ideas.' David had been 'very much to the left in politics' at Oxford, 'but I
fancy was disillusioned and for the moment has dropped politics'. David's
interest in politics was, in fact, as lively as ever, and his views on what
was happening in Germany in particular were a good deal more realistic
than those of his elders, and of TJ and Lord Lothian in particular. David
'went through a queer phase at Oxford – was very socialistic (thank God
he was not ultra-Tory)', Waldorf concluded, but 'now he is much more
stable'. He had lacked confidence in the past, but 'Arthur Mann told me
that he has good journalistic flair and that his writing was good', and
before coming to work at the *Observer* he should gain experience, possibly
on the business side of *The Times*, or with *L'Express* in Paris.

Waldorf was delighted that Garvin seemed to like David – 'the past
two or three years have been difficult – I knew that David had real gifts

and qualities but he seemed somehow unable to find his feet – the state of the world seemed to have upset him (small blame to him)' – but the feelings were not reciprocated. 'One of these days I'll murder Garvin – out of date, pompous, dangerous, wrong-headed, hypocritical, out of proportion in every way,' David wrote of him while still at Oxford, ridiculing him as an 'old Irish toad' and a 'bulgy-eyed old maniac pouring out reactionary views with such fluency and appearance of common sense and plausibility'. ('The boy has the mother's gift of vituperation,' TJ remarked after Waldorf had shown him a letter from Balliol 'full of pungent criticism' of Garvin's articles, but in later life David would combine strong opinions with an insistence on fairness and an abhorrence of character assassination.) David never warmed to or admired Garvin, but many of those who worked with him were more kindly disposed. The Birkenhead-born son of a washerwoman and an Irish labourer, an autodidact who had read Gibbon at the age of twelve and later combined editing a national newspaper with scholarly work for the *Encyclopaedia Britannica* and writing a three-volume, never-completed biography of Joseph Chamberlain, Garvin had tripled the circulation of the *Observer* within three years of Northcliffe's appointing him editor in 1908, when the circulation had fallen to under 5,000 copies a week. By combining reliable news coverage with coverage of books and the arts, he not only saved the *Observer* from ruin, but created the modern Sunday newspaper. By the early 1930s he had built up the circulation to 200,000 copies a week, though in 1933 it was overtaken by its long-standing rival, the *Sunday Times*, which had greater resources and attracted star writers like James Agate and Desmond MacCarthy. A shambling figure in baggy trousers, with large ears, luminous eyes and specs halfway down an unusually long nose, Garvin came into the office in Tudor Street only one day a week, but his personality was pervasive and overpowering: 'for a man of just on seventy he is a miracle of suppleness in mind and body', his former deputy Robert Barrington-Ward wrote of him in 1937.

Ivor Brown, a Scottish Balliol graduate, joined the paper in the early 1920s: an old-fashioned man of letters who combined journalism with belles-lettres, he was best known as the paper's drama critic, but he also reported on cricket and reviewed novels and biographies, as well as writing the occasional leader-page article. Garvin, he recalled, was always referred to as 'the Chief', and 'so powerful was his presence that one had to be a Garvinite. He was physically large and mentally multitudinous. His enthusiasms were varied and infectious. It is unusual to combine a rapturous devotion to Wordsworth with a relish of a large brandy and a "king-size" cigar.' Garvin was, Brown continued, 'an encyclopaedic egoist' and 'incapable of saying anything commonplace. His word went because it was clear, vigorous and spoken with a justified authority.' Much of the work was left to his deputy editor, R. F. Harmer, who was for ever on the phone to Beaconsfield, but on Wednesdays, when Garvin came into the office, 'there he would sit with his prominent, luminous eyes glowing amid a wreath of cigar smoke'.

'He was generous in praise and his exuberance instead of drowning the seed-bed of his paper was a fertiliser. A man with such an appetite for life was bound to raise the eagerness and the gusto of others,' Brown recalled. 'He abounded in energy, in relish and in laughter . . . he touched nothing that he did not enlarge or quicken.' But the film critic C. A. Lejeune, who joined the *Observer* from the *Manchester Guardian* in 1928, admitted that she 'never felt wholly at ease with Garvin, although I'm certain he intended to be kind'. Clad in his 'customary suit of solemn black, the inevitable cigar clamped cater-cornered in his mouth, his tall figure restless and jerky as he prowled behind the editorial desk', he dominated the proceedings at the weekly office lunch in the Tudor Street library, reached by 'a small bronchial lift'. 'It was Garvin's habit to discourse over the soup and cold chicken in resounding phrases, on subjects such as Dickens, Meredith and Goethe. *"Mehr Licht!"* his voice would boom across the library,' she recalled. 'He brooked no interruption, although he appreciated a modest ripple of applause.' Waldorf invariably sat opposite Garvin: he would talk about horses, dogs, model farms and the best means of growing asparagus, and 'nobody could have been more considerate to a raw, provincial journalist, who came from a world so utterly unlike his own.' Ivor Brown had equally fond memories of Waldorf. 'Intended by nature to be a quiet country gentleman', Waldorf was 'all kindliness and goodwill, chivalrous and courteous' and 'blessed with a quiet chuckling humour that mitigated the pressure of his social conscience', though 'in his modesty and eagerness to see all points of view he admitted many advisers and had a ready, perhaps too ready, ear for the latest spokesman of this or that'.

The lunchers included Ivor Brown, looking like 'a kind but sad St Bernard dog'; Garvin's daughter Viola, the literary editor, 'a tall, cool elegant creature with black hair, creamy skin and astonishing violet eyes, a soft Irish voice and a low, delightful laugh'; and 'a tall, new girl, as nervous as myself, and a good many years younger', who turned out to be Joyce Grenfell, finally approved as the new radio critic. C. A. Lejeune found Bill Astor very easy to get on with, particularly if they were seated at several removes from Garvin: Bill seemed far happier talking about films than about Goethe, and seemed to exude a 'sort of defensive gregariousness'. Every now and then David would dutifully appear from Yorkshire: he was, Lejeune recalled, 'a golden-eagle version of his dark, handsome father'. He seemed 'very young and gay' with eyes 'the true blue of periwinkles', and he was – as he remained – 'a ready smiler; partly from natural kindness of heart, and largely, I believe, to cover a natural diffidence'.

But David was still far from being a committed journalist. While working on the *Yorkshire Post* he confessed to Nancy, 'in strict confidence', that 'I don't want to give up my entire life to training for the *Observer*. I wouldn't even take the *Observer* as a gift now. But at forty I am sure that I would be more than delighted to have it – so if a year or two of training now is enough to encourage Papa to keep the *Observer* open for me in ten years' time, well and good.' He was chary about talking to Waldorf about it 'as I don't want to hurt his feelings by appearing to consider the *Observer* as something one can casually take or leave ten years hence', but he would like to spend the intervening years trying 'to succeed at literature and in theatrical production – both of which subjects interest me much more than newspaper work'. He resigned his job in Leeds, and went to live in a cottage at Sandsend, near Whitby on the North Yorkshire coast. His fascination with theatre folk was as potent as ever, prompting him to take Waldorf to the circus in Leeds – 'he got to know all the ringmasters, lion-tamers, clowns etc. – their life histories, whose father was killed by an elephant etc.' – and after the show had ended he took his father behind the scenes and introduced him to the cast. Years later he confessed that during the Munich crisis of September 1938 he was 'doing nothing more world-shaking than running a concert party in the municipal theatre'.

While running his theatrical troupe he was trying, without much success, to write a book based on his interviews with Yorkshire Masters of Foxhounds. 'He is finding it a longer and tougher job than anticipated,' Waldorf told Garvin, and David himself feared that the end result would be 'as dull as a railway timetable'. The book was never completed, and before long its author would be permanently diverted by events in the wider world.

7

The Cliveden Set

'Appeasement' became a dirty word after the Munich Agreement of September 1938, and has remained one ever since; and if Neville Chamberlain was the British statesman most closely associated with the appeasement of Hitler, the so-called 'Cliveden Set', and Nancy in particular, shared the opprobrium. 'It is an extraordinary thing that my mother never understood the "Cliveden Set" view of her', David told James Fox. 'She never understood it because she was sure it was completely untrue. But the damage it did her was huge. And it affected the whole family's reputation.' He went on to compare it with the Profumo Affair of 1963, also set in Cliveden and involving a member of the Astor family, adding that 'both stories were untrue but I think they'll be there for ever'.

In retrospect we are all Churchillians, determined to stand up to Hitler and meet force with force, but in fact Churchill and his supporters – Robert Vansittart, Duff Cooper, Robert Boothby and other renegade Tories – were regarded for most of the 1930s as irresponsible warmongers, only gaining a degree of respectability after Hitler's invasion of Czechoslovakia in March 1939. Until then most Britons, of all political persuasions, shared the views ascribed to the Cliveden Set, from the pacifists of the Peace Pledge Union through the Labour Party to the great mass of the Tory Party. It was widely agreed that the slaughter of the First World War must never be repeated, and that war must be avoided at all costs; that future co-operation between nations should be manifested and reinforced by the League of Nations; and that Germany had been humiliated by the Treaty of Versailles in terms of the reparations she was expected to pay and the territory she had lost to Poland and the newly created state of Czechoslovakia. Other ingredients included a deep suspicion of the French, widely regarded as unreliable Latins who would try to inveigle Britain into making unsuitable Continental alliances; an optimistic belief that, brutal and vulgar as he might be, Hitler would inevitably be tamed by the realities of office, becoming a politician with whom one could do business and work out a modus vivendi; a widespread assumption that the politics of Mitteleuropa were none of our business; and a sense, among the upper classes at least, that Communism presented an even greater threat to the British way of life than fascism.

David remembered from his childhood 'a haunting, even alarming talk about war'. Nancy asked Arthur Balfour, a close friend and former prime minister, to hold forth on the subject. 'Tall, white-haired, gentle, a bit remote, he talked for a while in such a serious way it was as if he was speaking of a death.' Balfour predicted that the world would never be peaceful again, and 'I remember the hush he created and I think I felt frightened.' (Nancy later took David to visit Balfour as he lay dying: there was a pile of records at the end of the bed, and his niece played Mozart and Beethoven over and over again.) On another occasion 'a visitor was speaking of modern war and of untold possibilities and my parents were listening with a gravity I had never seen before': during the 1930s – and still more so after the bombing of Guernica in the Spanish Civil War – Baldwin's belief that 'the bomber will always get through' assumed the same alarming proportions in the popular and the political imagination as the atom bomb in the 1950s.

Both Waldorf and Nancy were keen internationalists, and David vividly recalled accompanying Nancy in the late 1920s to the League of Nations headquarters in Geneva, 'when it seemed to be the embryonic capital of a new world community'. Some, like Shaw and the Webbs, had put their faith in Soviet Russia instead, but as news of the great famine of 1932 and Stalin's purges filtered through, it became harder to sustain. Lord Lothian, in particular, feared and hated Bolshevism. He had been partly responsible for drafting the notorious Article 231 of the Treaty of Versailles – the war guilt clause that had saddled Germany with reparations – and the feelings of remorse this induced led him to take an over-optimistic view of Anglo-German relations, and to sympathise with German minorities in Czechoslovakia and Poland. 'In twenty years I've never known Philip [Kerr, i.e. Lothian] to be wrong on foreign politics,' Nancy once declared, though foreign affairs were never her strong point: anxious to create a new European order based on the revision of Versailles, Lothian visited Hitler in 1935 – he reported that Hitler was determined never to go to war again – and again in 1937, when the two men agreed on the need for their two countries to come to an understanding and hold out the hand of friendship, and Lothian recommended that Hitler be given a free hand in Eastern Europe, an offer he soon took up.

Despite what was later said about them, neither the Astors nor the *Observer* admired or approved of the Nazis, even if they preferred coexistence to war. 'The general impression here is that the country is in the hands of lunatics and gangsters all armed with six-shooters,' Waldorf reported two months after Hitler became chancellor, and he told Garvin that 'I detest the Nazi persecution of Jews, their attempt to crush liberty of thinking, their cruelty etc.' He met Hitler to plead on behalf of Germany's Christian Scientists: Hitler asked him why relations between their two countries were so bad, and suffered an alarming 'spasm' when Waldorf told him that friendship was impossible so long as Hitler continued to persecute the Jews. 'I came out of Germany pro the German people but very anti the Nazis,' Waldorf declared once back on terra firma.

Whereas Waldorf was generally liked and admired, Nancy excited mixed reactions – Chips Channon remembered her 'rushing about like a decapitated hen, making naive remarks' in the House of Commons – and much was made of her friendship with Ribbentrop, the German ambassador in London and Hitler's future foreign minister. 'To my regret, my parents made some attempt to get onto terms with Ribbentrop,' David recalled years later. In 1937 Nancy gave a lunch for Ribbentrop in St James's Square, and although he felt 'uneasy' about attending, David went along. At some point Nancy told Ribbentrop that no one in England could take Hitler seriously 'as long as he wears that little Charlie Chaplin moustache'. Ribbentrop, David recalled, was 'completely flummoxed'; conversation flagged and Ribbentrop left early, his burgeoning Anglophobia reinforced by yet another insult from the English upper classes. A year earlier Ribbentrop had visited Rest Harrow with Tom Jones – 'a great busybody and contacts man', according to A. L. Rowse – who persuaded the then prime minister, Baldwin, to take 'TJ's daily dose of soothing syrup' rather than listen to the advice of Robert Vansittart, the implacably anti-Nazi permanent secretary at the Foreign Office whom Waldorf regarded as a 'disastrous' influence on Churchill in particular. TJ had thought up an implausible scheme whereby Baldwin – who had never flown, and hated the sea – should meet Hitler off the coast of Kent, and was keen to discuss his idea with Ribbentrop in a suitable setting: the other guests at Rest Harrow were Lothian and Sir Thomas Inskip, described by Rowse as 'an old lawyer whose chief interest was that the Prayer Book should not be revised', and the conversation was restricted to the role of the Church in Nazi Germany.

Garvin spoke fluent German and, unlike most of his fellow editors, regularly read the German newspapers, and he was horrified by the barbarity of Nazism. An article denouncing 'repulsive cruelty towards the Jews' led to Goebbels banning the *Observer* in the autumn of 1933; earlier that year, Garvin had predicted that 'unless Hitlerism can be brought to its senses in time, it will lead with absolute certainty to European war'. Garvin was not always on the side of the angels – he supported Franco, advocated an alliance with Mussolini as a counterweight to Hitler, upheld Hitler's right to rearm and, as a long-standing opponent of Versailles, justified territorial revisions at the expense of Poland and Czechoslovakia – but he remained convinced that 'this new barbarism at the centre of Europe must end by putting Western civilisation in peril', and was 'staggered here in this country by the utter want of comprehension' of what was happening to a country whose culture he so admired. And as early as 1936 he called for the inclusion in the Cabinet of Churchill, whom he liked and admired, so risking the wrath of his proprietor.

The notion of the Cliveden Set was promoted by Claud Cockburn, an inventive, irreverent former *Times* journalist and a member of the Communist Party who had been at Berkhamsted School with Graham Greene and shared his mischievous streak. Cockburn was a great believer in what he called 'preventive journalism': effective journalists should influence as well as record events, exploiting rumours and gossip to achieve particular ends. In 1933 he had started a cyclostyled news-cum-scandal sheet called the *Week*, and he combined editing this with writing for the *Daily Worker* under the pseudonym of 'Frank Pitcairn'. Like the editors of *Private Eye* in later years, Cockburn was adept in persuading other journalists to let him have stories which their editors refused or were too timid to carry, and although the *Week* was run on a shoestring it soon became essential reading in political and diplomatic circles, exercising an influence out of all proportion to its scruffy appearance and modest circulation: his diplomatic informants included Robert Vansittart and Rex Leeper, the like-minded head of the Foreign Office's News Department, both of whom would be demoted and effectively neutered by Chamberlain, who ran a ruthless campaign against opponents of his views in the Civil Service and the press.

In June 1936 Cockburn ran a piece called 'The Best People's Front' in which he claimed that the Astors in general, and Geoffrey Dawson and *The Times* in particular, were 'important supports of German influence', but it was in November 1937 that he began his assault on the Cliveden Set as such (the term was first used by *Reynolds News*, but Cockburn claimed they had misappropriated it; another claimant was the journalist Vladimir Poliakoff, who introduced Cockburn to Vansittart). The *Evening Standard* had reported that Lord Halifax had combined a private visit to the International Hunting Exhibition in Berlin with a meeting with Nazi leaders at which Hitler said that he was prepared to drop his demands for the restoration of Germany's pre-war colonies in exchange for being given a free hand in Central Europe. According to the *Week* the scheme had been hatched over the previous weekend at Cliveden, even though, as it turned out, Halifax had not been present – whereas Eden, who took a more Churchillian line, had been among the guests. Cockburn stepped up the attack in December with talk of 'the friends of the Third Reich' and 'Schloss Cliveden'; and in January he wrote that the Cliveden Set had engineered the replacement of Eden as Foreign Secretary, and Vansittart's elevation to the grandiloquent but powerless post of chief diplomatic adviser. Cockburn's war of attrition resumed with the Munich crisis: he claimed that the decision to dismember Czechoslovakia had been taken at Cliveden, and that Geoffrey Dawson's notorious *Times* leader, in which he advocated the secession of the Sudetenland to Hitler, was planned by the '*Cagoulards*' of Cliveden in conjunction with Ribbentrop – the Cagoulards, or 'Hooded Ones', were an 'extreme right-wing faction in France'.

So influential was the *Week* that the Cliveden Set soon entered the political bloodstream. The *News Chronicle*, *Tribune* and the *Daily Worker* joined the hunt. References were made to 'Schloss Cliveden'; Low's celebrated cartoon in the *Evening Standard* featured Nancy, Lothian and Geoffrey Dawson as the 'Shiver Sisters'; the Communist Party of Great Britain published a pamphlet entitled 'Sidelights on the Cliveden Set: Hitler's Friends in Britain', which accused the Astors of having made their fortune from 'selling liquor to Negroes' and 'wielding the power of international fascism'. During the Munich crisis Harold Nicolson noted in his diary that he and Eden had agreed on 'how terrible has been the influence of the Cliveden Set': he thought Nancy 'a kindly but inordinately foolish woman' and regretted the influence of 'these silly selfish hostesses' who gave foreigners 'the impression that policy is decided in their own drawing rooms'. Even Claud Cockburn referred, years later, to the 'monster I had let loose': Cliveden had become a myth, 'the symbol of a tendency, of a set of ideas', although the picture he'd painted was 'essentially a true one'.

William Douglas-Home, the playwright brother of the future prime minister Alec, was one of the few who stood up for the Cliveden Astors. 'There was no such thing as the Cliveden Set,' he wrote years later. 'Instead, there was a very homely, very outspoken, very kind married

couple who entertained friends, acquaintances, politicians, diplomats and
foreigners, on a large and generous scale.' This was a shade disingenuous:
like most of the population, the Astors and the *Observer* favoured coexistence with Hitler rather than war, and shared Chamberlain's notorious
indifference to the 'faraway' countries of Central Europe, but Cliveden
weekenders included anti-appeasers like Eden and Bob Brand as well as
TJ and Lothian, and the idea that the politics of appeasement were devised
and dictated by Nancy and her friends was a by-product of muck-raking
journalism, the search for a scapegoat, and a sense that the upper classes
were to blame for the country's enfeebled reaction to world events. As
American arrivistes – 'ex-furriers from lower Broadway', as Cockburn
put it – the Astors were more vulnerable than most: the smear stuck,
and although David shared none of the views popularly associated with
the Cliveden Set, for the rest of his life he resented what was said about
his parents, and took any opportunity to try to set the record straight.

Nancy, needless to say, took most of the flak, which included hate
mail addressed to 'Mrs Judas' and an unsigned postcard which read
'Resign! Pro-Germans are not wanted in a British Parliament.' She
denounced Cockburn's claims as so much 'mischievous rubbish' and a
'false and stupid story published in a Communist rag', and insisted that she
opposed 'all forms of dictatorship, whether Fascist, Nazi or Communist':
when John Strachey tried to introduce her to Cockburn, she made as
if to spit at him – a gesture Cockburn rather admired. 'I distrusted
Ribbentrop from the start,' she told a friend two months after Munich,
'and I dislike the Nazi dictatorship intensely, and do not believe it is truly
representative of the Germans as a whole. What I have always wanted,
and still want, is understanding between the people of this country and
the German people.' Kristallnacht had taken place that same month,
and 'the treatment of the Jews and the recent outburst of savagery appals
me'. Outspoken, tactless and impulsive, Nancy was incapable of hiding
her prejudices, and inconsistent in their application. She was known to
be prejudiced against Jews and Roman Catholics, and her alleged dislike
of Jews could be held against her. David's Oxford acquaintance Felix
Frankfurter, himself a Viennese-born Jew and now back in the States, was
immensely grateful to her for helping to secure his uncle's release after
the Nazi takeover of Austria in March 1938, but in a letter to her shortly
afterwards he referred to the 'disquietude which the attitude of yourself
and your friends towards the Nazi regime has filled so many of us here'.
But Hitler's invasion of what remained of Czechoslovakia in March 1939
fatally discredited the policy of appeasement, though Chamberlain still

hankered after it: as Garvin put it in an *Observer* editorial, 'the last rag of human decency was discarded'. Waldorf joined his editor in pressing for the inclusion of Churchill in the Cabinet; and Nancy later discovered that, despite the *Week*, her name was included in the Nazis' Black Book of those who were to be arrested after the invasion of England.

During all this time David was in Yorkshire, far removed from the political hurly-burly and trying to write his book about hunting: yet looking back on those days, Michael Astor reckoned that 'the only member of the Cliveden Set whose opinion was never sought, who was right about Germany as well as Russia, was my brother David'. David had no illusions about Hitler or the regime, and Lothian's mission to Hitler in 1937 had led to a temporary falling-out with his mentor. 'Thank God people are beginning to have their ignorance about Adolf shaken up a bit,' David wrote from Leeds in September 1938. 'The English attitude to Adolf is so naive and ignorant – and now scared as well', he told Nancy, adding that 'as you and Papa and your bunch consider that we have almost no reason to suppose we know about these things, I'll close down . . . I'll be the one to be killed, and that will be my share in the matter.' As the negotiations in Munich proceeded, 'I can't help smiling at our bird-watching, trout-fishing, good kind Mr Chamberlain in his woollen underwear dealing with this womanishly deceptive, hysterical, homicidal coward Adolf.' Sitting on the pier at Whitby and reading a letter from Lothian to *The Times* about Hitler, David concluded that 'the ideas people hold about him are just impossible nonsense'. 'I think we are going to pay heavily for giving Hitler his head, but I'm darned if Hitler was correctly handled and that any safety has been attained by such negotiations,' he told Nancy; he listened in to German broadcasts as their troops crossed the border into the Sudetenland in October 1938, and 'you'd think they were about to start a war and not that they had signed an agreement to try in future to deal through consultations'. On one particular point he was adamant when writing to Nancy: 'I always told you it was a psychological error to treat Hitler as though he is Germany – it's discouraging to the people in Germany who might rise up.' David would use this distinction between the Nazi leadership and the German people to justify his own attempts to keep in touch with the German opposition in the months leading up to the outbreak of war, and in the early months of the war itself.

'It astonishes me that people still talk of Hitler as an idealist and an honest man', David told Tom Jones in March 1939. 'They won't understand him till he stabs them firmly in the back.' He later wrote of how, to his regret, 'my parents made some attempt to get onto terms with Ribbentrop', but he went on to say that 'my own blindness was almost as great as that of my parents. I could only think of opposing Hitler by diplomatic boycott and attempted internal subversion. I was not able to see that nothing less than military action was needed and that this must include military co-operation with the other dictatorship in Russia.' Looking back, he had come to accept that 'the point that is hardest for the gentle-minded to accept is that it is dangerous to peace to try to abolish force altogether' – a note of realpolitik that would become a recurrent theme of his *Observer* editorials.

★

'The daily press no longer gives any true idea of the feeling of the country,' Garvin told Waldorf in the late summer of 1938. 'There is at last wide anxiety – a slow, eating anxiety, though silent and feeling helpless. There is not one particle of sympathy any more with Germany. Not an atom.' Arthur Mann, David's editor at the *Yorkshire Post*, made himself extremely unpopular with his Conservative proprietors, the Beckett family, by his opposition to the Munich Agreement, but Beaverbrook, Rothermere, *The Times* and Garvin himself had all favoured appeasement in varying degrees. Like Eden at the time of Suez, Chamberlain was a ruthless manipulator of the press, putting pressure on editors and proprietors through his henchman, Sir Joseph Ball, and exiling Rex Leeper to the embassy in Bucharest after disbanding his dissident Foreign Office News Department. In the year between Munich and the outbreak of war, the newspapers' pro-appeasement line began to crack, still more so when the two Berry brothers, Lords Kemsley and Camrose, went their separate ways in 1937: Kemsley's *Sunday Times* continued to give Chamberlain uncritical support, but Camrose's *Daily Telegraph* took a more critical line, hiring Churchill as a regular columnist.

But great damage had been done to the sales and the reputation of the mainstream press – not least by the *Week*, which had enjoyed exposing the subservience of the established papers to government pressure. A slump in advertising was partly attributed to anxiety about the international situation: Waldorf prepared to dig into his pockets to help the *Observer*, in part by compensating the paper for the revenue it lost by refusing to run advertisements for alcoholic drinks. Disillusionment with the press led to a proliferation of newsletters along the lines of the *Week*, written more often than not by journalists unable to get their

views into the mainstream papers: they included the *Blue Arrow*, edited by
A. E. Voigt, formerly the *Manchester Guardian*'s Central European correspondent; the *Whitehall Letter*, the brainchild of Victor Gordon-Lennox,
the *Daily Telegraph*'s defence correspondent; and, most famously, Stephen
King-Hall's eponymous *Newsletter*, which boasted 53,000 subscribers by
the outbreak of war. Unlike the *Daily Mail*, the circulation of which
had slumped, the *Daily Mirror* had consistently opposed appeasement:
its circulation soared, and continued to soar throughout the war years.
But the greatest success story of all was Stefan Lorant's anti-fascist, anti-
appeasement *Picture Post*, the circulation of which rose from 30,000 to
1,350,000 within three months of its appearance in 1938. Owned by Edward
Hulton and edited from 1940 by Tom Hopkinson, *Picture Post* combined
progressive politics with fine writing, clear design and brilliant use of
photographs: a combination that appealed to, and influenced, the young
David Astor. When, a few years later, he began to make his mark on the
Observer, he would look for inspiration, ideas and the writers he wanted
to publish to the newsletters, to *Picture Post* and – more surprisingly – to
Cyril Connolly's *Horizon*, the first issue of which appeared in December
1939. In the meantime he was about to involve himself in a doomed
venture that had nothing to do with newspapers but was to prove the
turning point in his life, and one that transformed him from a soul in
limbo, uncertain of what he wanted to do in life, into a single-minded,
sometimes ruthless young man who combined charm and diffidence
with a determination to get what he wanted.

8

Gravitas

While David was trying to decide what to do with his life, Adam von Trott was working as a lawyer in Berlin and trying to reconcile his passion for his native land with his detestation of Nazism. His love of Germany made him acutely sensitive to outside criticism, not least from his Oxford friends: in the words of Shiela Grant Duff, a former Oxford friend, he 'regarded criticism of one's country as one regards criticism of one's family. One can criticise them oneself, but does not like others to do so.' Trott had despaired of a popular rising against Hitler, and to try to clear his mind and see Germany from outside, he decided in 1937 to spend some time in China, helped along by a grant from the Rhodes Trust and a gift from the Labour politician Stafford Cripps, whose son John had been an Oxford friend. He went via America, and visited England before he left. On a trip to Oxford he told Isaiah Berlin that he was worried by rumours that 'some English friends considered me as moving more and more to the Nazis'; Berlin had been outraged by Trott's letter to the *Manchester Guardian* three years earlier, but he nevertheless gave him an introduction to Felix Frankfurter in Washington. Trott also called at St James's Square, and met Nancy for the first time: she handed him a letter to take to Charlie Chaplin in California, bought him some riding boots and a trench coat, and declared she was 'sorry my little Trott is leaving'.

Trott was keen to keep open the option of returning to Germany and possibly joining the Auswartige Amt or Foreign Office at some future date, so he made a point of introducing himself to German embassies and consulates in America and China: this made sense in that, whatever his views of the regime, he needed to be seen as a loyal German, but his visits were noted by British and American secret service agents, and held against him. From now on he found himself in an impossible position. He had no desire to go into exile and fight Nazism at arm's length: to be an open member of the opposition, such as it was, would be suicidal and self-defeating; he had to live a double life and feign a loyalty to a regime he detested, yet by doing so he risked losing the trust of friends in England, some of whom already regarded him as a German nationalist who had imbued too much Hegel for his own good. In Shiela Grant Duff's opinion, Trott became too defensive about Germany while he was in China, as a result of which 'he excused, indeed was blinded to, the aims and methods of German foreign policy'.

Determined to resist Nazism from within, Trott returned to Germany in the autumn of 1938, shortly after the Munich crisis. A friend in the Foreign Office told him of a plot to overthrow Hitler involving Ernst von Weizsäcker (the Berlin equivalent of the permanent undersecretary at the Foreign Office), Ludwig Beck (the army chief of staff), and two Foreign Office officials, Erich and Theodor Kordt, whereby the German army would rise up in the event of Hitler invading Czechoslovakia. Theodor Kordt, a counsellor at the German Embassy in London, had been smuggled into 10 Downing Street by a back door for talks with Halifax and Alexander Cadogan, Vansittart's successor as permanent undersecretary to the Foreign Office, but although this alerted Halifax to the existence of the opposition, the plotters were overtaken by events: in October 1938 the Sudetenland, with its German majority, was annexed by Germany under the terms of the Munich Agreement, a move that made Hitler more popular than ever at home. Although the opposition's plans had been frustrated by events, Trott was so heartened by its existence that he persuaded his lawyer friend Peter Bielenberg and his English wife, Christabel, a niece of Lord Northcliffe, to drop their plans to emigrate to Ireland; and Peter Bielenberg, who shared Trott's abhorrence of Nazism and was keen to work with the opposition, gave up his job with his family firm in Hamburg to work for the Ministry of Economic Affairs in Berlin.

Trott was put in touch with the opposition, and in the nine months leading up to the outbreak of war he was actively involved in attempts to persuade the British government to pay attention to its views. This inevitably involved a degree of duplicity, in that he had to pretend to be a loyal supporter of the regime; he could not risk allowing even his closest friends in England to know what he was up to, with the partial exception of David, and he had to play the role of an appeaser, seeming to advocate further concessions to Hitler in the hope of buying time for the opposition to mount a successful coup against him. It was a dangerous and difficult balancing act, and one in which David would play an important if intermediary role. David had the political contacts he needed through his parents: as he later admitted, he was Trott's 'messenger', and he was 'perfectly aware that he was making use of me and my parents: he did not disguise the fact'. David regarded his Oxford friend as both an 'internationalist' and a German patriot, a social democrat who was horrified by the 'nationalism which Hitler was exciting in Germany and the counter-nationalism that this was exciting abroad' and 'felt it was his personal responsibility to do his utmost to thwart the regime'; and 'his consistent idea was to combat the belief that Hitler spoke for all Germans.' Isaiah Berlin met him at a dinner in All Souls late in 1938; Trott told him that war was inevitable unless Britain and Germany stood up to Hitler: 'Germany must be surrounded and stopped. This must be done very soon. German expansion must not occur.'

Trott came to England again in February 1939 on the first of four abortive missions on behalf of the opposition. At this stage he could only give David vague hints about what the opposition hoped to achieve, but he implied that 'he came to London representing substantial people, which can only have meant Weizsäcker', and that he was informally 'on attachment to the German Foreign Office'. He visited Oxford again, but 'to feel at home again at Oxford would now be difficult, although I was glad to meet with unchanged friendliness, especially by the older generation. People of my own generation, however, have become a little estranged, and I don't much like the atmosphere of their thoughts and activities any more.' Although many of his oldest English friends were still living and working in Oxford, Trott's awareness of Oxford's appetite for gossip made him more careful than ever not to give his game away, and to reveal only what it was safe to reveal; he was regarded with some suspicion already, and the German invasion of Czechoslovakia in March not only hardened British resolve but made further talk of appeasement unacceptable across the political spectrum.

Trott returned to England in early June. David had arranged for him to have dinner at Cliveden at the same time as Lothian and Halifax. William Douglas-Home, another guest and a friend of Michael and Jakie Astor, overheard Halifax talking to 'a young German called Trott', and 'listening to him, I understood how it was that so many Germans, loathing and despising Hitler as they did, yet felt that, in his insistence on the rights of Germany, he was voicing the wishes of his people'. Halifax was impressed by Trott, but 'when he had finished speaking, the minister stubbed out his cigar in an ashtray and said, "Yes, it's a fascinating problem." And it seemed to me, sitting at the other end of the table, that in the hopelessness of that answer and that gesture, he stubbed out Germany, and Europe too, for many years ahead.' (It may have been at that same dinner that Trott warned Halifax 'of whispers among officials in Berlin that "the Nazis were up to something with the Russians", but he did not know what. It turned out to be the Hitler–Stalin Pact.') 'It is quite obvious that the latent sentiment against the Nazi leaders is much stronger in Germany than some had realised,' Waldorf informed Garvin after David had taken him into his confidence, and he arranged for Trott to meet the prime minister. Alec Douglas-Home, Chamberlain's parliamentary private secretary, spoke briefly to Trott and remembered him as 'an engaging young man' who 'made no particular impact'; Chamberlain struck his visitor as a 'very old and tired man who was at the end of a very long and uncongenial road', talking to whom was 'like talking to someone already dead'. Trott also met Tom Jones, who reported that – according to Trott – Hitler 'has already decided to act this summer', and could only be stopped by cooler heads 'impressing the leader of the risks he is running'.

Back in Berlin, Trott wrote an entirely bogus report on the situation in England which, he hoped, would find its way via the German Foreign Office to Hitler's desk. Posing as a devout supporter of the regime, he larded his account with 'deliberate flattery' of Hitler, while Peter Bielenberg helped with the turgid 'Hitlerian prose', both laughing disrespectfully as they made their ritual obeisances to the Führer. Their report was typed by a half-Jewish girl called Rita Ludecke, and Trott asked David to look after her when she managed to escape to England just before the war broke out. 'He discussed these tactics with me in detail as he was staying with me in London during part of his visit,' David later wrote. 'The purpose of the visit was partly to enable Trott to report back to Berlin that influential British quarters were determined on war if Hitler made a further annexation (in contradiction to the opinion being given by Ribbentrop), but that gains, glory and useful friendships with "Germanophiles" would be Hitler's if he avoided war.' 'The incipient change in Anglo-German relations is directly due to my intervention', Trott told his mother, adding that he hoped to discuss his report with Ribbentrop, and perhaps even with Hitler himself. There is no evidence that either man ever read Trott's report, which was filed away in the Foreign Office archives; it was discovered by the Allies in 1945 and read as a genuine article, so blackening Trott's reputation still further among those who had always had doubts about him.

Not content with the destruction of Czechoslovakia, Hitler was now contemplating 'further annexations', this time at the expense of Poland, and Danzig and the Polish Corridor in particular; and it was to urge

Britain to show resolve should Hitler attack Poland that Graf Gerhard von Schwerin of the German army's general staff came on another secret mission to London in June. Once again, David was the chosen intermediary. Colonel Schwerin was a friend of Colonel Hans Oster of the Abwehr, the German secret service, who had close ties with the opposition; he also knew a young German journalist called Marion Doenhoff, who after the war would edit *Die Zeit*, and become one of David's closest friends. Schwerin was officially in London to sound out British public opinion, and David was recommended to him by Wilhelm Roloff, a Bremen businessman and a friend of Erwin Schueller, a young Austrian émigré working at Lazard's bank. Trott urged David to see Schwerin, but urged him not to mention his own activities, so David invited Schwerin – a 'genial, blunt individual' with a shaven head – to lunch at his mews house off Regent's Park. His visitor explained that Hitler planned to 'overrun the wheat-growing, coal-mining and oil districts of Eastern Europe' later that summer, and that his armies would 'if necessary defeat the Russian army and advance into the Ukraine'. Since Hitler did not believe that Britain would go to war over Poland, it was essential to impress him with a display of force. Setting up a War Cabinet and a coalition government might just 'stay their hand': Royal Navy warships should exercise in the Baltic, RAF units should be deployed to France, Churchill – the only man of whom Hitler was frightened – should be included in the Cabinet, and Waldorf's Eton contemporary Sir Nevile Henderson, the arch appeaser, should be replaced as ambassador in Berlin.

David introduced Schwerin to Admiral Godfrey, the head of Naval Intelligence, and Air Marshal Tedder; Bill Astor's friend Robert Laycock – best remembered as Evelyn Waugh's long-suffering commanding officer in Yugoslavia – passed him on to a brigadier in German intelligence, who dismissed Schwerin's approaches as 'bloody cheek'. Sir Orme Sargent, the assistant undersecretary at the Foreign Office and a fierce opponent of the Munich Agreement, accused the hapless Schwerin of 'gross treasonable disloyalty' and suspected some Machiavellian trick. Schwerin returned to Germany empty-handed, and was shortly afterwards dismissed from the general staff. David, for his part, was beginning to find his way round a world far removed from Yorkshire huntsmen and Whitby theatricals. 'That I, who was Mr Nobody Whatsoever, and no more than a layabout, should have been asked by a colonel of the German High Command in June 1939 to help him make contact with our government seems, in retrospect, amazing,' he told Trott's biographer many years later.

Schwerin's visit coincided with Trott's third and most disastrous visit to England. Weizsäcker and his fellow conspirators had come up with another scheme for mounting an eventual coup against Hitler, and Trott was told to try it out on his British contacts. Hitler should be persuaded by the British and the French to restore a degree of independence to the Czech provinces of Bohemia and Moravia in exchange for being given a free hand in Danzig and the Polish Corridor: this would flatter his sense of being the 'arbiter of Europe', and give the opposition and the army time to prepare a coup against him. Nothing could have been better guaranteed to alienate Trott's former friends in London and in Oxford: Trott failed to realise how far attitudes in Britain had hardened since the German invasion of Czechoslovakia in March, or how allergic people had become to anything that smacked of appeasement.

Trott went first to stay in Kent with his old Oxford friend Shiela Grant Duff. A passionate supporter of Czechoslovakia, she had reported from Prague for the *Observer* in the mid-1930s, but had resigned in protest against Garvin's anti-Czech prejudices: her Penguin Special, *Europe and the Czechs*, had been published at the time of Munich. Although they had been very close at Oxford, she found Trott's views increasingly uncongenial. 'I suspect that we are enemies. I do not know what you really care for and admire, but I suspect it is not what I care for', she told Trott after Munich: he had come to share Lothian's mistaken belief that Hitler would readily renounce war if given 'real equality', and had pinned his hopes on further appeasement. 'In so far as I became aware of what Adam was trying to do in 1939, I was absolutely opposed to it,' she told David years later. Breaking off friendly relations with Trott had been an 'angry, anguished' business, and he 'never explained his own aims to me beyond the necessity of securing peace (and, it seemed to me, peace at any price)'. She suggested that he should talk to Churchill, who lived nearby, but Trott showed no interest in meeting the old 'warmonger'. She also introduced him to Herbert Ripka, a Czech politician living in exile in England. Trott must have given them some indication of what the opposition had in mind, since Ripka dismissed such ideas on the grounds that Goering must have been their inspiration. Shiela Grant Duff later wondered why since Trott 'could take neither Ripka nor myself into his confidence, by what right did he demand a blank cheque of confidence in himself?'

Trott moved on to stay in St James's Square. He met Churchill's son-in-law, Duncan Sandys, and his wife Diana, but once again declined an invitation to meet Churchill; E. F. Schumacher worried that Trott

had been living in a fantasy world since his time in China, and urged
him to follow his example and go into exile. Former friends in Oxford
were increasingly suspicious of him. At a dinner in All Souls he told
his fellow diners that Hitler's coming to power represented a Hegelian
turning point, and that to go to war with Germany would be to 'rush
against the process of history'. Isaiah Berlin had come to regard him as
'an ambitious, fascinating, self-romanticising, personally delightful and
politically ambivalent figure with a passion for very high-level intrigue';
he did not see Trott on his last visit to Oxford since 'he may have felt
doubtful about my discretion, or thought, perhaps rightly, that I could
be of little political use to him'. A. L. Rowse decided to break off their
friendship since 'I was not sure that he was not reporting back to Berlin
what our opinions and attitudes were.' Trott told David that 'the general
attitude towards me was one of unusual embarrassment' – but worse
was to come when he called on Maurice Bowra, the recently appointed
warden of Wadham College.

'I was very glad to see him, since I had always thought that he was very
firmly against Hitler', Bowra recalled in his memoirs. Trott had not been
able to tell his other Oxford friends about his work for the opposition,
but he decided to make a partial exception for Bowra, and told him that
although he was formally working for the German government, his true
allegiance lay elsewhere. 'At this point I felt uneasy,' Bowra continued. 'I
could not believe that the Gestapo would allow so obvious an adversary
to go about the world expressing his views in this free manner, and I
became suspicious. My suspicions became worse when he went on to
argue that we should let Hitler keep all his conquests, and so remain at
peace with Germany. I then decided that von Trott was really on the
side of the Nazis and asked him to leave the house.' Bowra was not
well disposed towards Germans in general as a result of his experiences
in the First World War, and he had long been a passionate opponent of
appeasement, so he may not have been Trott's best choice as a confidant. Bowra knew that Trott was planning to visit America later that
year, and he wrote to Felix Frankfurter, by now very close to President
Roosevelt, to warn him against him. Bowra's letter was intercepted by
British intelligence, and never reached its destination; but Bowra opened
a second line of attack through Churchill's friend Professor Frederick
Lindemann, later Lord Cherwell, and Churchill conveyed his views to
Felix Frankfurter when he met him in Washington in July. In a later letter
to Frankfurter, Bowra said that he thought Trott was 'playing a double
game' and trying to weaken the opposition: his behaviour 'soon became

known to Trott's rich friends, who regarded me as having behaved in a criminal way. I cannot see what else I could have done.'

Looking back on his dealings with Trott at that time, David reckoned that 'the worst thing he asked me to do was to visit Berlin in the summer of 1939 to pretend to be an important British political contact (when I was really a concert-party and pantomime operator) and to meet the tame, elderly Nazi whose patronage was, he said, absolutely essential to his political camouflage'. The tame Nazi was an affable but slow-witted character named Walter Hewel, who had taken part in the Munich putsch of 1923 and had been incarcerated with Hitler in the Landsberg fortress (and would be a frequent visitor to the Bunker during Hitler's last days); after his release he had worked as a clerk for an English firm in the Dutch East Indies, as a result of which he was regarded as an authority on foreign affairs by his fellow Nazis, and was now acting as Ribbentrop's liaison officer with Hitler. Described by David as Trott's 'duped Nazi friend whom he saw so much of in public so as to keep the Nazis satisfied that he was a sound man', Hewel was genuinely alarmed at the prospect of Germany going to war with Britain, and as a Foreign Office official he had authorised Trott's trips to England. It was now David's turn to dissimulate. While in Berlin, he told himself, he had to 'swallow' his true opinion of Neville Chamberlain and present him as a 'strong-willed, stubborn and brave man with a determined country behind him': he should make his hosts understand that 'Anglo-German co-operation cannot become effective as long as Germany is organised on a war basis and utilising only power politics methods', and that although 'Nazism is in some sense a socialistic system . . . no brotherhood can be felt as long as concentration camps, Jewish persecution and power politics are part of the system.' Despite the fact that Waldorf felt 'considerably alarmed for my safety', David left for Berlin in mid-July.

Trott had, in the meantime, given Hewel an enthusiastic if misleading account of his Oxford friend. David 'gives the impression more of a blond product of the Black Forest – that's where his ancestors stem from – than a grandson from New York or Virginia', he told him. 'He has a more genuine understanding of Germany than any of the older generation of the "Cliveden Set", hence they tend to listen to him.' Warming to his theme, he claimed that David wanted to become a 'specialist in German affairs', and had 'recently mentioned that he would very much like to become a German citizen if eventually a German–English under-standing came into being'. 'Should the situation arise,' he concluded, 'you could provide Astor with useful contacts while, on the other hand,

Astor could provide worthwhile contacts for you. Heil Hitler!' Trott had
arranged for the two men to meet at a cocktail party, during the course
of which David was expected to enthuse about Anglo-German friendship
and wax lyrical about Trott's ability to influence the powers that be in
Britain. Expecting to meet a political grandee rather than a young man
in his mid-twenties, Hewel arrived at the party looking extremely smart
and wearing a rose in his buttonhole. No doubt David went through the
motions as well as could be expected, but he was hugely embarrassed
by the whole business, and amazed by the ease with which Trott led
a double life, and by what he later described as the 'fantastic, almost
Philby-like nature of Adam's duping of the Nazis'.

While in Berlin David went to Dahlem to see the Bielenbergs, who
would later become close friends. Christabel Bielenberg recalled him as
a 'tall, fair-haired and boyish-looking' young man, whose 'shy almost
diffident manner belied not only a shrewd knowledge of the political
scene but an instinctive understanding of the situation in which we found
ourselves', and how his visit 'had done us all good, lifting for a while
the sense of helplessness and isolation'. On his last day, Trott drove him
out of Berlin and showed him, at the end of a road, the concentration
camp of Sachsenhausen; they drove hastily away when a guard began to
show undue interest, and – much to his relief – David left for England
the following day.

'He paints a frightening picture of growing war spirit and efficiency,'
Waldorf informed Garvin after David's return home. Anxious to alert
the government to developments in Germany, David wrote a long memo
about his visit for Lord Halifax, the Foreign Secretary. He gave a detailed
account of his meeting with Walter Hewel before giving his own opinions. He compared the regime to 'a well-armed gangster besieged in
a house who cannot hold out much longer': Hitler, he suggested, felt
'harassed, irritated and tired; self-confident, courageous and defiant'.
'A desperado, mistrustful and highly dangerous', Hitler was too easily
swayed by Ribbentrop and Himmler: efforts were being made to align
the army with Goering, and David urged the Foreign Office to make
approaches to Goering, possibly through the American airman Charles
Lindbergh, an occasional visitor to Cliveden who was on good terms with
the commander-in-chief of the Luftwaffe, a fellow aviator. It was essential
to avoid any whiff of the 'Versailles spirit': if moderates in Germany
and statesmen in Britain could persuade Nazis to look outwards, 'then
Nazism and with it power politics may die a natural death'; the current
state of emergency in Germany would evaporate and 'concentration

camps, the Gestapo, political uniforms etc. would begin to seem out of date'. On the other hand, 'the destruction of Nazism by force must lead to a European calamity'. Halifax may or may not have read David's memo, but Orme Sargent minuted it as 'rather woolly'.

Later that month Trott came to England for the last time: he stayed with David in Chester Place, and saw only Stafford Cripps and the Astors; he told David that 'if we have a war then everyone will become a nationalist fanatic, everyone will become cruel, and you and I will kill our fellow men, and perhaps each other'. Back home in Imshausen, his family home, he wrote to say how much he wished that David was there, 'but I doubt whether you would consider it in view of your play and family concerns'. As the political situation worsened, Trott sent Peter Bielenberg to London in the vain hope that, through David, he might be able to meet Halifax and urge him, even at the eleventh hour, to get in touch with the opposition: David wrote another note to Halifax suggesting that Britain should send an old-fashioned military man like Lord Gort or General Ironside to confront Hitler, but received no reply, and 'Peter was very disgusted that I spent the summer running a theatrical company.'

'Whatever happens to you and me, we'll remain friends anyway, I know', Trott told David a fortnight before the outbreak of war. In October Trott left Germany to attend a conference of the Institute of Pacific Relations – its director had been impressed by his reports from China – and to try to persuade the American government to give non-Nazi Germans an assurance that America would ensure that equitable terms were offered to Germany should Hitler be overthrown. His contacts in America included Heinrich Brüning, the former chancellor of Germany, now in exile, and Lothian, the new British ambassador. Washington was swarming with spies, and pseudonyms were de rigueur – David later told Lothian's biographer that 'the amateurishness of Trott's and my ideas of how to be secretive are all too obviously evident, but we had to get past the censors'. Lothian (referred to as 'Anderson') wrote to David to say that 'our mutual friend' had arrived safely, and that 'what he argues is just the same as last summer: but the core of the problem is to convince the moderate elements that there is a real future for their country, not under their present leader'. 'That you are in America is the best news I have had since the war started,' David told Trott, adding that 'my attitude to this war is briefly the following: I hope that neither side wins decisively, but that after a short period of fighting as possible a new British regime faces a new German regime, both disillusioned of the chauvinistic feelings of their respective countries'. Once again, David urged Trott not to return to Germany, both for his own sake and because 'your usefulness is ten times as great outside of Germany as a planner for the future than inside Germany as a revolutionary', and he told Lothian that he hoped 'you have exerted your influence on Adam to refrain from going back to Germany until after the war'. But Trott was adamant that he must return to Germany to seek a Europe-wide solution to its problems, and he was all too aware of how he was regarded by many of his old friends. 'During the summer I seem to have developed the ill-deserved reputation of an "appeaser" in certain quarters in England,' he wrote. 'They have, apparently, proceeded to warn some Americans against me. I am obviously defenceless against such and other accusations; they originate, I feel, in certain "clever" quarters in Oxford you and I know.'

While in Washington Trott 'derived considerable comfort and support' from John Wheeler-Bennett, an authority on the German army then attached to the British Embassy in Washington. Years later, during his long campaign to rehabilitate Trott's reputation, David came to see Wheeler-Bennett as one of Trott's enemies and denigrators, on the grounds that he had not only omitted any reference to him in his memoirs of the period, but had sided with Robert Vansittart, who, after the outbreak of war, had moved on from warning about the menace of Hitler to outright condemnation of all Germans, ridiculing any distinctions between 'good' and 'bad' Germans and, by implication, any deals with the so-called opposition. In the early months of the war, however, Wheeler-Bennett sympathised with Trott, urging British and French leaders to make it plain that they were fighting Hitler and the Nazi regime rather than the German people as a whole, and referring in a letter to Vansittart to the 'present struggle for the liberation of the German people'; Trott told David that Wheeler-Bennett understood the situation better than anyone else, and 'should be very carefully listened to'. As the war progressed Wheeler-Bennett gave his support to the prevailing belief in 'unconditional surrender', which in effect precluded any dealings with German opposition movements, such as they were; but whereas some in Oxford in 1939 thought Trott to be 'a very subtle agent of the enemy', for Wheeler-Bennett, writing to the Foreign Office in 1943, 'there was nothing of the intriguer about Adam von Trott, but there was, on the other hand, considerable ambition and a certain confused political mysticism which had absorbed something of the stuff of which Nazis are made, and something of a vague Hegelianism which had induced in him a false sense of realism and a belief in power politics and his own part in them.'

'If you feel your channel is absolutely watertight I wish you would get in touch with me as soon as possible after my return in March,' Trott told David in December 1939, three months before he returned to Germany. The two friends never met again, but Trott's example would inspire David for the rest of his life, and their dealings in the months leading up to the outbreak of war proved to be the turning point in David's life.

★

David's new-found maturity was reflected in his attitude towards the *Observer*, hitherto regarded as a wearisome obligation to be endlessly postponed. 'It is extraordinary how David has managed to establish contacts and acquire information – I find a nice attractive boy has suddenly developed into a man, and into a man of considerable parts!' Waldorf told Garvin. He was keen that David and Bill should attend directors' meetings since 'the future of the *Observer* ten–twenty years hence really affects him and Bill more than it does me and it would be good to get him to face these alternatives', and suggested that David should take his place at a lunch arranged by his editor since 'I am most anxious to bring him into all these longer-term talks. He is as you say full of enthusiasm – lacks experience, but is a good judge of character.' 'He has been a slow developer – Lindsay the master of Balliol always said he would be – but he is getting keen on the *Observer*,' Waldorf told Garvin in another letter. 'I wonder whether it would be wise to put him on our board and make him feel his responsibility about these big questions of future policy.'

But David's sudden interest in the family paper was not restricted to attending board meetings and brooding on 'future policy'. Drawing on his Yorkshire experiences, he submitted a piece on circus life: he told Garvin that he was flattered by its being given 'such an exalted position on the page' over his own initials, but hoped the editor would not think him 'churlish' if he criticised the subediting. And he put forward an idea for converting Vita Sackville-West's articles on gardening into 'a feature which the *Sunday Times* would find difficulty in competing with – something of high literary (and technical) merit which might also attract some advertising'.

Before long Garvin would find himself fighting off a deluge of ideas from the young heir apparent; momentary relief was at hand when Waldorf told him that David was 'getting some experience on the business side of *The Times*' – the proprietor of which was his uncle John Jacob. 'I dread London and the bowels of *The Times*, but I expect I will take to it as I managed to take to Lazard's and the *Yorkshire Post*', David told Nancy, adding how much he preferred the company of Whitby fishermen and the waves and gales of the North Sea coast. But duty called. 'I am proposing to give David a block of shares in the *Observer* and put him on the board of directors,' Waldorf informed Garvin: he was considering giving Bill some shares, but fewer, and without a place on the board. David's life in limbo was coming to an end, and his future was taking shape.

9

Frustration

Adam von Trott's beliefs and ideals were to inspire David for the rest of his life, and, with war imminent, he determined to do all he could to put them into effect, making full use of his new-found single-mindedness and self-confidence. Like Trott, he saw the impending conflict as a European civil war, to be waged against Hitler and the Nazis and everything they stood for, and not against the German people as a whole. He became obsessed by the importance of propaganda, directed not just at the Axis powers, but at neutral countries, including the United States, and on the home front, at the British people themselves. Propaganda should be positive as well as negative: it should spell out, in detail, what Britain was fighting for as well as what she was fighting against, holding out hope not only to the tiny and fragmented opposition but to all non-Nazi Germans, and to the inhabitants of occupied Europe. Spelling out Britain's war aims should not be restricted to military matters or the post-war settlement of Europe; David passionately believed in the notion of total war, fought in the realm of ideas as well as on the battlefield, propaganda for which was combined with notions of a better Britain in which economic freedom went hand in hand with a more just and equal society. Or, as his future colleague Sebastian Haffner put it, in total war 'military operations play only a subordinate role', and it was essential to 'seek victory on other battlefields than the military one'.

Churchill, who would replace Chamberlain as prime minister in May 1940, was impatient with propaganda, though he enjoyed the mendacious and inventive 'black' variety practised by Sefton Delmer (who had been the *Daily Express's* Berlin correspondent in the early years of the Nazi regime) and deeply disapproved of by David and by Hugh Carleton Greene, the eventual head of the BBC's German Service, both of whom believed that propaganda had to be truthful to succeed; nor did he have any time for talk of post-war reconstruction, preferring to concentrate his energies on the conduct of the war itself.

But David was far from alone in holding such views, in which – in the domestic arena – the dream of a 'New Jerusalem' was combined with a rejection of Baldwinite Britain as selfish, class-ridden, complacent and short-sighted; as David put it, 'our established institutions – the political parties, Parliament, local government, the Civil Service, big business, the City, the trade unions, the churches, the press and the radio are discredited in the public mind', and regarded with 'cynicism and distrust'. Other manifestations of this spirit included J. B. Priestley's 'Postscripts' broadcasts, deeply disapproved of by Churchill, Allen Lane's Penguin Specials, Edward Hulton's *Picture Post*, the best-selling *Guilty Men*, part-authored by Michael Foot, *The Times*'s leftwards lurch under the influence of Stanley Morison and E. H. Carr, pressure groups like Political and Economic Planning (PEP), and the Beveridge Report, much of which was anticipated in articles its author wrote for the *Observer*. Between them they contributed to a transformation of the national mood which resulted in the Labour Party being returned to power in 1945, the creation of the welfare state, and the 'Butskellite' consensus which prevailed in British politics from the end of the war until the election of Mrs Thatcher in 1979.

Propaganda to Germany involved a mass of different agencies and organisations, all equipped with baffling acronyms and all at odds with one another. Chamberlain had taken a keen interest in propaganda, and after Munich he asked Sir Campbell Stuart to set up a new department to deal with propaganda to Germany in particular: based in Electra House in Moorgate, it formed a department of the Foreign Office's Political Intelligence Department. The BBC began broadcasting in German, French and Italian: early in 1939 broadcasts to Germany were extended to half an hour a day, and consisted of straightforward news items and *Sonderberichte*, talks based on the news of the day. The Joint Broadcasting Council, or JBC, secretly broadcast talks, plays and concerts from neutral countries in the hope that German listeners would assume they were broadcast from within Germany itself – a dodge later employed by the ingenious Sefton Delmer. Funded in part by the Secret Intelligence Service (SIS) or MI6, the JBC was run by Hilda Matheson, who had been sacked as the BBC's first Talks Department director for employing too many controversial or left-wing speakers, and joined MI6 as a propagandist in 1939. The lover of the poet Lady Dorothy Wellesley, she dreamt up the hugely successful 'Britain in Pictures' series of books – itself a useful contribution to British propaganda – shortly before her death in 1940. Harold Nicolson was a director of the JBC, Guy Burgess a programme director, and Stephen King-Hall and Geoffrey Crowther of *The Economist* among its regular broadcasters.

After the outbreak of war Electra House was temporarily put in charge of all broadcasting to enemy countries, including that of the BBC. Life was further complicated by the Ministry of Information, which controlled Electra House. A vast bureaucracy based on the University of London's Senate House, the ministry had a dual role: it was, in theory, responsible for providing news and presenting the official British position on issues of the day, while at the same time – again, more in theory than in practice – acting as a censor, keeping an eye out for undesirable or subversive items in newspapers, broadcasts, magazines and books; it operated a system of voluntary censorship, with editors submitting material which might breach the provisions of the Defence of the Realm Act. The government used Defence Regulation 2(d) to close down the *Week* and the *Daily Worker*, but the ministry was generally regarded as ineffectual and cumbersome, particularly in the early years of the war, easily outwitted by government ministries and the armed services, all of which insisted on presenting their own versions of events: David thought it a 'stillborn department buried in red tape', manned by 'bureaucrats and professors'. Duff Cooper was regarded as an outstandingly ineffectual Minister of Information – according to David, 'one can't imagine him stimulating one schoolboy, let alone a worldwide movement' – but matters improved in July 1941 when Churchill replaced him with his crony Brendan Bracken, a figure regarded with deep suspicion by the older Astors.

David set himself up as a one-man propaganda unit even before the outbreak of war, employing Willi Guttman, a German-Jewish lawyer who had lived in Italy before the war, to monitor German broadcasts: in due course Guttman would become a key figure at the *Observer*, a bottomless fund of knowledge as the in-house librarian, and one of a group of émigré Germans and Central Europeans whom David welcomed onto the paper. A week after the outbreak of war David told TJ that whereas German broadcasts were 'cogent in argument, quick onto weak points in our own stuff, more plausible in style and more convincingly "on the mark" – our stuff is no doubt more veracious, but it doesn't give that impression'. After ridiculing Electra House for dropping 6 million pamphlets over Germany, riddled with spelling mistakes and printed in an obsolete Gothic type, he stressed the importance of employing Germans on German-language broadcasts: they should be anti-Nazi German patriots with a love of German culture and 'a faith that what is fundamentally German is stronger and more lasting than the costume in which the Nazis have dressed it', and 'any trace of peevish reproach, moral superiority or other variations of "anti-" feelings are inappropriate'.

Sir Campbell Stuart, in David's opinion, was irremediably 'second-rate', and had made no effort to get in touch with Hilda Matheson, or make use of German émigrés: he told Stafford Cripps that 'our propaganda in German is the most important part of our foreign policy today', and 'should not be left to the secret service and to a small-minded self-seeker like Campbell Stuart'. As for the BBC, it was 'boring, unpopular and class-conscious': it made no effort to adapt to total war, and was 'totally outclassed by the Germans'. Writing to Sir James Grigg at the War Office – an old family friend, and a future trustee of the *Observer* – David claimed that there was 'a lack of a policy, or even of a consistent style, in our "enemy propaganda". They also show a lack of understanding of the German mind, a lack of thoroughness, of general intelligence.' He thought Hilda Matheson 'the best person in our propaganda effort', and Waldorf told Harold Nicolson that David would be sending him 'suggestions for dealing with Lord Haw-Haw'.

David was also involved in various think tanks and pressure groups devoted to the future shape of Europe and to post-war reconstruction: these were often funded by the York Trust and loosely connected to Chatham House and the Royal Institute of International Affairs, of both of which Waldorf had been a founding father. Contributors to a series of 'World Order' papers, among them Lionel Curtis, Gilbert Murray and William Beveridge, sought to counteract Nazi claims that should Germany lose the war it would be dismembered in an even more vindictive version of the Treaty of Versailles, and promoted instead the notion of a federal Europe that would include a denazified Germany and Austria. Members of the European Study Group included David, Waldorf, Gilbert Murray, Lionel Curtis, Sir Arthur Salter of All Souls, Erwin Schueller and Rix Loewenthal, an émigré member of the left-wing 'Neu Beginnen' group; they all belonged to the 'London Group', along with Bob Brand, Richard Crossman, Max Nicholson (the founder of PEP), William Beveridge, Arnold Toynbee and Warden Adams of All Souls. Both groups emphasised the need for 'war aims' and 'peace aims', and the importance of neutral countries knowing what Britain was fighting for. These were the halcyon days of the phoney war, six months before Germany overwhelmed Norway, Denmark and the Low Countries: David and his high-minded colleagues opposed the 'crushing' of Germany, and advocated eventual Anglo-German co-operation. Emphasis was laid on the importance of differentiating between the Nazis and Germans in general: as David told a BBC official three months before the outbreak of war, 'an anti-Nazi attitude is at present less effectual than a pro-German attitude. As long as they feel that the English are anti-German, they, the ordinary Germans, will be pro-Nazi.'

'David is said to be doing secret service work', his cousin Joyce Grenfell reported in September 1939. He had, in fact, been turned down by MI6, but his eagerness to keep in touch with Trott and the German opposition brought him, for the first time, into contact with the secret service. 'I am going to Holland ostensibly as a special correspondent of *The Times* to see various people', he told TJ in October 1939, and 'Geoffrey Dawson has given me the necessary credentials.' Although it had been infiltrated by an Abwehr agent, MI6 had a strong presence in The Hague, including Nicholas Elliott, later to play a crucial role in the Philby saga, and Lionel Loewe, a barrister who hoped to put David in touch with the German opposition. On his return to London, David sent Lord Halifax, the Foreign Secretary, reports from *The Times*'s reporter in Rotterdam as well as a passionate plea on behalf of anti-Nazi Germans – but by then the cause of the opposition had been dealt a fatal blow by what became known as the Venlo Incident. Following an abortive assassination attempt on Hitler, SIS and the JBC were led to believe that the Wehrmacht was poised to overthrow the Führer, and MI6's head of station in The Hague, Richard Stevens, and his colleague Major Payne Best – both of whom David had met in Holland, and thought little of – were persuaded to meet disaffected members of the Wehrmacht in Venlo, on the German–Dutch border. It was all a German trick, dreamed up by Walter Schellenberg of the SS's Sicherheitsdienst. The two men were bundled over the border and spent the rest of the war behind bars: MI6's reputation – in Holland at least – was in tatters, and all future attempts to get in touch with the opposition were regarded with deep suspicion. Six months later, following the invasion of France and the Low Countries, no distinctions were made between Nazis in particular and Germans in general: Vansittart's increasingly strident anti-German views prevailed, still more so after America joined the war and the policy of unconditional surrender had been proclaimed in 1943. David continued to hope that it would be possible to make contact with the opposition, and with Trott in particular, and shorten the war thereby, but the odds were stacked against him.

True to his belief in total war, David wanted to fight with weapons as well as words – and that despite the fact that, as a member of the Eton Officers' Training Corps, he had been 'the worst soldier in the section'.

At Brendan Bracken's suggestion, he joined the Royal Marines in the spring of 1940. He was to find it an intensely frustrating business, far removed from active service and too remote from London to make his voice heard in the corridors of power. He was sent to work on coastal defences in Deal, a mile or two south of Rest Harrow, Nancy's 'seaside cottage'. The house was deserted, and the lawn overgrown. 'It is amazing being here,' he told her. 'All my memories are of holidays, and here I am in the "front line".' A buttoned-up brigadier gave the Marines a speech of welcome: regimental airs were played, and oysters, stout and sherry were served to the guests. 'I feel like a frightened child. And I'm ashamed of just how out of control I feel', David confided to his diary. 'Oh God, don't let me drift for ever.' In April 1940 he applied for a commission, and two months later he was made a temporary second lieutenant.

While in Deal, David was introduced to a Marine named Smith, who had been captured by the Germans before Dunkirk, and had escaped back to England via Marseilles and Spain. Smith had been greatly impressed by the ruthless, highly disciplined efficiency of the German army, by their readiness to kill women and prisoners of war: they practised 'a gangster style of fighting', in which 'each soldier appeared to fight as a gangster belonging to a loosely organised but highly practised unit'. David sent an account of Marine Smith's adventures to Anthony Eden; and although he was the gentlest and least warlike of men, over the months David badgered the powers-that-be with his ideas about the importance of guerrilla warfare, sabotage, fifth columnists, secret agents and poisoning water supplies – the kind of irregular combat that was being practised by the newly formed Special Operations Executive, much to the disgust of more conventionally minded military men. '*Personally* I am anti-militarist to the highest degree,' David told Tom Harrisson, the co-founder of Mass Observation. 'I resigned with éclat from my school OTC and have hated every moment of my year and a bit in khaki. But it seems clear that the facts of war can only be coped with in a military way.' It was essential to 'become interested in the enemy – to be envious of his skill, to hate his brutality, to fear capture, to know his strengths and his weaknesses intimately'. On a less martial note, David continued to press for the release from internment of sympathetic enemy aliens – among them his future guru and occasional *Observer* contributor E. F. Schumacher.

With Deal's coastal defences in better order, David was moved to Hayling Island on the south coast, near Southsea. He hated both the work and the company he kept. His job was to run the camp and supervise sentries, cooks and orderlies. 'It's clerical work – hard, unremitting pen-pushing and fussing about, and I get quite worn out,' he told Nancy: he spent his days in a 'seaside bungalow' making lists about victualling, railways warrants and the housekeeping of the officers' mess, and preparing chits for the colonel to sign. Officers who had been promoted from the ranks 'are always intelligent, they've not always been bosses so are human, and like me they feel slightly out of place in an officers' mess', but the majority proved to be 'a lot of moustached fools whose silly letters I have to forward, render in other words etc.' These 'whiskered, hard-skulled dummies' spent the evenings 'swilling beer' and 'guffawing through their moustaches at nothing at all': their 'heavy horseplay' reminded him of West Downs or the worst kind of golf club, and – in a rare outburst of snobbery – he told Nancy that 'a simpleton straight from a lesser public school would be the ideal person for my job'. His attitude towards his mother was as ambivalent as ever. Embattled as they often were, she was the person he turned to most – 'I hope, dear Ma, your terrific heart and courage are absolutely unaffected by what seems the blackest hour in Europe's history', he wrote after the fall of France. 'I need your help. I always have needed it, and always will. That's the tragedy from my side of all our years of disagreement and also the reason for our disagreement', he told her. He tended to be weak and fearful – 'it's this weakness which has made me never succeed' – and, on a visit to Southsea before leaving for Washington, Lothian had told him that he had been 'maimed by my early life and was like a broken-winged bird'. With that off his chest, 'I must go back to my rows of dumb contented little middle-class officers and their whiskered and conceited seniors and try to find something in some of them I can love.'

For nearly two years David bombarded those in authority with his ideas about propaganda, at the same time begging them to release him from his 'khaki confinement' and enable him to make a more positive contribution to the war effort. Brendan Bracken put in a word for him with Walter Monckton at the Ministry of Information, but to no avail. 'I know your minister has always felt uneasy about my mother's tongue,' David told Monckton. 'This is understandable, but I hope he does not mistake me for an Allen to her Flanagan – my political thinking is not only separate but materially different from hers.' By now he was 'determined to fight on the political rather than the military front,' he told TJ. 'I feel as if a death sentence has been passed on me', he complained after Monckton had failed to pass his ideas on to Duff Cooper. 'Will my luck never change? Aren't I of any value? This setback is the worst thing that has ever happened to me. I am faced with being an exiled petty functionary of the Marines. You can't imagine how I long to be used in propaganda and how I dread infinite internment in this appallingly dull, limited and lonely Marine life.' Relief of a kind was provided by his fellow officer H. G. 'Blondie' Hasler, best remembered as the leader of the 'Cockleshell heroes' raid on German shipping in the Garonne and, years later, as the instigator of the single-handed transatlantic yacht race, sponsored by the *Observer*, and for his diligent pursuit of the Loch Ness Monster (also funded, more improbably, by the *Observer*).

'I hope I shall get a chance to hit at my old enemy, the Nazi octopus, in the way I can hit hardest – propaganda,' David told his mother in November 1940, but 'how can we hope to do propaganda if we treat it as an occupation for middle-aged ladies and professors?' He felt 'beaten and baffled by the mountains of red tape'. 'It's not only boredom and feeling out of place here that I suffer from but the certainty that I could be useful in a sphere of this war that is vital and is being neglected' was a constant refrain: TJ reported that David was enduring 'a mental hurricane again', and hoped a doctor might prescribe 'bromide in some form or other'. Among those David deluged with ideas were the Ministry of Information, Naval Intelligence, the BBC, Stafford Cripps, Bob Brand and J. L. Garvin, who was subjected to the thoughts of 'a backwoodsman subaltern who stares in horror at the Hitler menace and redoubled horror at our methods of resisting him'. Britain was still run by 'elderly men to whom the methods and whole conception of total war are alien'. Churchill might be a great war leader, but 'our cause is so much more than the Union Jack and the White Cliffs of Dover, which is all that Winston really represents', and David was frustrated by the 'Baldwinish inactivity behind the determined facade of Winston's government. We are not making all possible anti-invasion preparations and we are not doing anything to stir up a revolt on the Continent': the Allies were fighting 'an international civil war which must be conducted by the methods of total war, i.e. propaganda and fifth-column organisation', whereas Churchill was 'attempting to fight this war as though it were one of Marlborough's i.e. by soldiers only'. A 'direct defiance of Hitler's philosophy and a restatement of liberal values' should not preclude learning from the enemy, since Hitler was 'the greatest master of modern warfare, propaganda, fifth-column activity and war economy'.

David reminded Nancy that he'd been right about Hitler 'since 1931, when I saw what sort of man he was from what he did in Germany itself'; that he'd argued with Chamberlain at Cliveden while 'being smiled on reprovingly' by the other guests; that he was the only person who failed to find Ribbentrop 'charming' when he came to lunch in St James's Square; and that he had reproached Lothian for visiting the Führer. 'Well, the oracle is now telling you that we must organise this country on a military–socialist basis (rather like Nazism) but with higher ideals than anyone has dared to proclaim – such as a Federation for Europe, a more egalitarian economy, rapid advance towards equality of responsibility in the empire.' Britain should declare itself in favour of 'an embryonic federal government of Europe', 'do something spectacular in India', mount a 'massive propaganda assault on Europe as well as to Arabs, Indians, South America, Ireland', and introduce a system of government 'as efficient and as socialistic as that of the fascists' but combined with personal liberty and 'anti-nationalism'. 'Please give up discussing these ideas with defunct old back numbers like Geoffrey Dawson,' he urged her, while noting that *The Times* under Barrington-Ward, Dawson's successor, not only favoured debate about post-war reconstruction and a planned economy, but, thanks in part to E. H. Carr, was well disposed to Britain's new ally, the Soviet Union, after the German invasion of June 1941.

'I feel we should have been implementing your ideas upon guerrilla tactics-cum-propaganda long ago,' a civil servant from the Admiralty told David, adding that he had passed David's paper on the subject to the First Sea Lord. In a memo entitled 'Broadcasts to German Naval Personnel and Relatives', submitted to Naval Intelligence, David suggested that 'news and accounts of British naval affairs should avoid boastfulness, arrogance and sales talk. But skilful news, a portrait of ourselves "warts and all" could gradually be painted.' He emphasised the need for 'honesty, consistency and soundness': commentators should shun 'anything resembling a Nazi propagandist's manner i.e. contemptuous, sarcastic and overconfident', and present news of German ships and sailors 'not only with apparent veracity but with apparent sympathy'. David's views, Ian Fleming wrote in reply, were 'not far removed from our own', and Admiral Godfrey, the forward-looking head of Naval Intelligence, had suggested that David should give the occasional 'Inside England' talk, capitalising on German curiosity about what was going on in Britain. 'You bring up the political question which, of course, is right outside our brief at the moment, and all we can do is to encourage PWE [the Political Warfare Executive] to produce something sensible themselves,' Fleming concluded. Once again David had caught the mood of the moment. In June 1941 he claimed that the term 'political warfare' had first appeared, at his suggestion, in one of Stephen King-Hall's *Newsletters* – 'it had long been troubling me how to get round the hideous word propaganda' – and in a letter to Stafford Cripps he remarked on the 'impossibility of getting our authorities to take the first and simplest steps towards waging political warfare'. Directed by Robert Bruce Lockhart, the Political Warfare Executive was set up some six months later to convey government views and policies to programme-makers and propagandists: things were going David's way at last.

Nor was David alone in stressing the domestic aspects of 'war aims'. Churchill may have had little or no interest in the home front or post-war reconstruction, but with the Labour Party forming part of the coalition government, more attention was being paid to planning, urban redevelopment and greater social equality. In January 1941 Keynes was asked by the government to draw up a declaration of war aims which included social security for all and full employment; Beveridge was working along similar lines, with E. F. Schumacher advising from the wings; sympathetic support was provided by the best-selling *Daily Mirror* under Cecil King and Harry Bartholomew, by Gerald Barry's *News Chronicle*, and by Barbara Ward of *The Economist* and Julian Huxley on the BBC's Brains Trust; and the Army Bureau of Current Affairs (ABCA) was set up by William Emrys Williams, Allen Lane's right-hand man at Penguin Books, to tell the armed forces why they were fighting the war, and for what kind of Britain. Other kindred spirits included journalists like Michael Foot, Stephen King-Hall, Alastair Forbes and Francis Williams; Tom Hopkinson, who in January 1941 published the influential 'Plan for Britain' in *Picture Post*, with contributions from Thomas Balogh, A. D. Lindsay, J. B. Priestley and Julian Huxley; Tom Harrisson of Mass Observation; and Tom Wintringham, a veteran of the Spanish Civil War whose 'Home Guard Training School' in Osterley Park was funded by Edward Hulton, and who shared David's unexpected views on guerrilla warfare, bridge-blowing, sabotage and subversion. All agreed on the inadequacies of the old order and the need for a new vision of Britain to inspire the war effort; many of them would write for the *Observer* once David was in a position to make his presence felt.

'I have been seriously thinking over your suggestion that I should stand for Parliament during the war and have discussed it with my father,' David wrote to Anthony Eden: he was 'tremendously flattered' by the Foreign Secretary's interest in his career, but apart from the fact that his own 'politics are non-party', he felt that interest in old-fashioned party politics had dwindled. Rather than try to influence the existing political parties, which had 'become meaningless and outdated and lacking in reality' and belonged to the 'pre-Hitler epoch', David favoured creating a new party – or, at the very least, replacing Churchill with someone whose ideas were more in tune with those of the younger generation. Lloyd George, much favoured by his parents, was too old and too compromised by his connections with those advocating a peace deal with Hitler; but David now pinned his hopes on Stafford Cripps, who had returned to London in June 1941 after a spell as the British ambassador in Moscow, and seemed 'the most promising person in London today'. 'Please mention me if you see him so that he sees us as a great surging of youth, not as individual yappers,' David asked Tom Harrisson, who was due to meet the great man. 'These young people – David Astor and others – turn to you and me to guide them,' Isobel Cripps informed Walter Monckton, and 'all their hopes centre on Stafford', and David reported that he was 'very discreetly trying to form some little unit of right-headed younger men round Lady Cripps'. But Cripps's star was on the wane: he eventually resigned from the Cabinet, but not before announcing the publication in December 1942 of the Beveridge Report.

When not drumming his heels on Hayling Island, David attended occasional meetings of the leftwards-leaning 1941 Committee, the members of which were served 'a magnificent cold buffet' in Edward Hulton's house in Hill Street, Mayfair. According to the journalist Francis Williams, who attended the committee's meetings, Hulton was 'an intellectual manqué with a lot of money who was passionately keen on social revolution so long as it did not hit him'; David more charitably described him an 'an intrepid idealist' who had 'consistently backed and publicised progressive and intelligent ideas'. The committee's members included H. G. Wells, Kingsley Martin, Victor Gollancz, Tom Jones, Michael Foot, Tom Wintringham, Douglas Jay, Ritchie Calder, A. D. Lindsay, Stanley Unwin, Vernon Bartlett, Julian Huxley, Gerald Barry, C. E. M. Joad, and A. D. Peters, the literary agent, but the proceedings were dominated by J. B. Priestley. 'I was pleasantly surprised in Priestley,' David told his mother. 'He was more sensible and modest and unprejudiced than I had expected', and 'one feels he is sound at heart'. But Francis Williams thought 'Jolly Jack' had 'little skill as a political thinker and even less as a practical politician', and before long David felt much the same way about the committee in general, and Priestley in particular. It was, he told Stafford Cripps, 'vitiated by the presidency of Priestley, who is egotistical, fractious and politically ignorant', and it contained 'many fossils and well-wishers'. He complained to Hulton about 'the dominance of its antique class-war obsession, its adherence to the unsuccessful neo-Marxist doctrines of the past', and to TJ about the influence of 'cranks and doctrinaire intellectual backwoodsmen' like Thomas Balogh, Richard Acland and Konni Zilliacus, the Communist MP.

David soon lost interest and drifted away, and the committee itself was subsumed into Richard Acland's Common Wealth Party, an ineffectual manifestation of 'new party' aspirations. Ephemeral as it was, the 1941 Committee embodied the 'New Jerusalem' spirit, influencing not just the Labour and Liberal parties, but the Tory Reform Committee as well; and despite the cranks and fossils, it reflected David's own evolving ideas. Nothing came of his plan to hive off a splinter group of kindred spirits, consisting of Michael Foot, Ali Forbes, Tom Hopkinson, TJ and Ronald Fredenburgh, but he continued to promote pressure groups-cum-dining clubs such as Freedom House, the members of which were Hulton, Gerald Barry, John Beavan, Geoffrey Crowther and Barbara Ward.

Frustrated though he was by life in the Marines, many of David's ideas about the conduct of the war and post-war reconstruction were entering the political bloodstream. Before long he would not only be giving them space in the pages of the *Observer*, but radical changes in the paper itself would allow him to exercise a crucial influence on its future.

10

Regime Change

David's interest in propaganda, the conduct of the war and post-war reconstruction was not restricted to badgering the Ministry of Information and attending meetings of leftwards-leaning pressure groups. His new-found sense of purpose and his liberal views had led Waldorf to reinstate him as his heir apparent at the *Observer*, much to Nancy's annoyance: she blamed TJ for 'taking David leftwards and from her', while according to TJ 'she can't believe that he has a mind, and a remarkable one, of his own'. David himself was itching to be involved, but he could only do so on a very part-time basis and, while still based in Hayling Island, very much at arm's length. In 1942 he went to work for Louis Mountbatten at Combined Operations, but although he was now living and working in London, he could only devote a limited amount of time in the evenings and at weekends to the family paper. He did so to great effect, but it was not an easy business.

Now in his mid-seventies, Garvin was as formidable and as domineering as ever, and although Waldorf knew that the time had come for a change, he was reluctant to do battle with his veteran editor, and invariably tiptoed round him rather than risk an outright confrontation. David was more forthright, and less in awe of the great man: he thought it absurd that 'this national newspaper that my father owns' should be 'run by this rather elderly gentleman who really hasn't any contemporary ideas in the world'. Before the outbreak of war he had complained to Waldorf that it was 'not possible to edit a paper over the phone', and that it was not feasible for Garvin (or anyone else) to combine the roles of editor and business manager. He had suggested that Garvin should remain *en poste* as chief leader writer, that a new editor should be appointed to work closely with R. F. Harmer, the news editor, and that John Berridge, the business manager, should be given a free hand; and after speaking to Garvin 'it seemed perfectly clear that he is finding the struggle too much for him. I've no doubt that he will never admit he's beaten, but I would not be surprised if he would be secretly relieved if some of the responsibility was taken from his shoulders.'

But that was not how Garvin saw it. After war broke out he had agreed to spend Saturdays in London rather than Beaconsfield, but before long he had a much smaller paper to edit and manage. In 1940 the *Observer* consisted of sixteen pages, six of which were devoted to books and the arts, with Arthur Bryant, Frank Swinnerton, L. A. G. Strong, A. G. MacDonnell and Ivor Brown, the drama critic, as star performers: but the invasion of Norway in April 1940 had cut off British newspapers from their traditional source of newsprint, and before long paper rationing had trimmed the *Observer* to a mere eight pages, one of which was given over to books and the arts. In March 1942 the quota was cut by a further ten per cent, and it was agreed that, once a month, the Sunday papers should be reduced to six pages each. Newsprint quotas reflected pre-war sales, but although paper was in such short supply, sales of both books and newspapers flourished during the war, with the *Observer*'s circulation climbing to around 360,000.

Despite the shortage of space in the paper, Waldorf was keen that David should be involved, sooner rather than later; he had worked with Berridge on the business side before joining the Marines, and Waldorf suggested to Garvin that he should now gain some editorial experience, and perhaps even try his hand at the occasional article. 'I know we are crowded for space but David voices the views of quite a group of thinking young men,' he told his editor, to whom he was sending a piece by David about the use of propaganda, fifth columnists and sabotage in the war against Hitler. Written in his Hayling Island bungalow at night after a long day's form-filling, 'The Political Nature of War' proved far too long, and made the fatal beginner's error of trying to cover too much ground in too short a space: Waldorf 'spent a sleepless Saturday night recasting it', and after both he and Harmer had set to work with the editorial blue pencil, it was eventually published in June 1941 in two instalments – 'Psychological Warfare', followed a week later by 'Political War: A Comparison', both attributed to 'a Political Correspondent'. However unsatisfactory the first draft may have been, it made its mark in high places. 'There is a lot of sound sense in what you write,' Anthony Eden told David, and he hoped they would have an opportunity to discuss it further.

Earlier that year David had made his first editorial incursion into Garvin's sacred domain. He suggested, via Waldorf, that every Sunday the paper should carry a 900-word unsigned 'Forum' article, in which

young writers should ventilate their views on the aims and conduct of
the war; both writers and subjects would be chosen by a panel consisting
of David and TJ, who had become more involved in the running of
the paper after Waldorf had suffered a mild stroke, plus two of David's
young friends, neither of whom were on the staff of the *Observer*: Ronald
Fredenburgh, who had earlier worked on the *King-Hall Newsletter*, and
the Anglo-American Alastair Forbes, a fellow Marine and a friend of the
Churchills who, many years later, achieved momentary fame as a well-
connected, name-dropping book reviewer for the *TLS* and the *Spectator*.
David told TJ that such a series would not only be of national interest,
but give the *Observer* an edge over its long-standing rival, the *Sunday
Times*, while Waldorf assured a reluctant Garvin that *The Times* had
'raised its prestige very much' by publishing similar pieces. After a good
deal of wangling and arm-twisting, albeit of the most circuitous kind –
Waldorf was 'almost powerless vis-à-vis Garve', David complained to TJ.
'I feel he overindulges Garve's alleged sensibilities' – Garvin agreed that
a weekly Forum should appear under his leader on the editorial page.
The first Forum was published in June 1941.

'You can imagine how delighted I am at the opportunity of organising
regular contributions for the centre page of the *Observer*,' David wrote to
Garvin from Hayling Island. 'I know how sacred this page is to you and
fully understand how apprehensive you may be.' He had no 'vainglorious'
desire to see his own name in print, but he was 'acutely interested in
drawing attention to conceptions which can help in this hellish situation
we have arrived at'; he promised to 'exercise the utmost restraint and
prudence in avoiding unnecessary annoyance', and although he would
take the editor's advice, 'I cannot promise not to say some unorthodox
things or to invite writers who will only say what has already been
said . . . the situation is so grave and our accepted ideas have brought
so little success that I feel it a duty to speak what I conceive to be the
truth.' He confided to Fredenburgh that one of the aims of Forum was
to 'attack the unimaginative, easy-going Baldwinism which still pervades
our whole Civil Service, many army and naval officers, our local authorities and many ministries', and he told Miss Kindersley, a future director
of the *Observer*, that his young writers 'should deal in the name of youth
with political warfare and general ideas bearing on the future'. He sent
Garvin a list of contributors, including Michael Foot, Richard Crossman,
Francis Williams, Stephen King-Hall and Sebastian Haffner, together with
Tom Harrisson on public opinion and the home front, E. F. Schumacher
on the reconstruction of post-war Europe, and Tom Wintringham on

guerrilla warfare. David's 'The Task of Propaganda' was the second
Forum to be published; some Forums were anonymous, some carried
their authors' initials.

'Garve' was not best pleased by Forum and all it implied. Forum
writers, he confided to his notebook, were 'carpers, crabbers, grousers,
disappointed prigs, pedants, muddlers, moon-struck dreamers about war
aims: the people who don't lift a finger to fight the war but are really
skulkers in uniform', and a piece by Ali Forbes was so much 'trash'.
He shared Churchill's view that discussion of post-war plans should
be delayed until the war had been won, and that propaganda was of
little importance compared with military action: he saw the Forums as
designed to discredit Churchill – none of the Astors shared his admiration for the great man – and scribbled 'anti-Churchill' across David's list
of names. But he put a brave – or diplomatic – face on it, at least when
talking to his proprietor. 'I have a feeling that he is growing every day and
that he has the makings of a remarkable man,' he told Waldorf apropos
David, and as for Forum, 'I wouldn't now displace it for the world.' David,
for his part, was pleased, while having no illusions about Garve's feigned
enthusiasm. 'I am terribly proud of the Forum to date (and think Papa
is too),' he told Miss Kindersley. 'Even the old ogre of Beaconsfield has
been saying some reasonably nice things about this feature.'

Forums may have represented the first step in 'the gradual changeover
from the *ancien régime* to the new', but there was still a long way to go.
In the meantime, Garvin – gritting his teeth, no doubt – told Waldorf
that he would be delighted to meet David's young friends, and that he
would try to understand their points of view: and 'if I fail, it will be the
first time I have ever failed in such a business with the young'. 'Garve
is a wicked old saboteur, isn't he?' David asked TJ, no doubt suspecting
the old boy's every motive as he arranged a lunch at the Ivy for selected
Forum writers. Nor was Garvin the only hostile presence to be placated
or outwitted. Although Nancy had dismissed David's friends as so many
'yes men', he felt that, like Bill, Michael and Jakie, he should be able to
treat Cliveden as his home and invite his friends there, 'whether you
like them or not', since 'being able to do this helps me to compete with
Garve journalistically and produce a succession of articles'. Although
much of Cliveden had been closed down 'for the duration', David told his
mother that he had asked Tom Harrisson, Ali Forbes, Francis Williams,
Michael Foot, Ronald Fredenburgh, Stephen King-Hall, Edward Hulton
and the sculptor Siegfried Charoux for the weekend: quite how it went
is not recorded.

'Garve, you'll be surprised to hear, is behaving well. I almost believe I will be able to tame the old dinosaur,' David told his mother in August 1941, adding that 'Papa has definitely been very firm with Garve.' Before long Waldorf's firmness would be put to the test in a last, convulsive struggle, and David would watch on from the sidelines as his father strove to winkle Garvin out of the editorial chair. Leaving aside the fact that, so long as he remained in uniform, David was a part-timer at the *Observer*, exercising influence rather than power, Waldorf and TJ were agreed that he was still too young and untried to be put into a position of responsibility on the paper; as Waldorf put it, 'David has not had sufficient experience to justify our giving him complete control when matters are so critical. We obviously want his point of view to count, and I have great faith in his outlook and judgement, but in some respects he lacks maturity and experience.'

David would have to wait his turn, but his contribution to the slow erosion of Garvin's position revealed a tougher, more ruthless side to his character than had previously been apparent – qualities that would become even more explicit after Garvin's eventual departure. Although David was not above flattery when called for – 'I always find talks with you stimulate and delight me,' he told the old boy – he complained to TJ that the editor was 'standing in the way of all progress' at the *Observer*, that the paper was 'moribund' and that it was 'impossible to achieve serious contact with him on the simplest degree of co-operation'. But Garvin was falling out of favour even without David's helping hand. His admiration for Churchill was to prove the breaking point in his relations with Waldorf. Years earlier, Garvin had irritated the Astors by pressing for Churchill's inclusion in Baldwin's Cabinet; both Waldorf and Nancy regarded him as an irresponsible warmonger, disapproved of his bibulous ways, and would have far preferred Lloyd George to have replaced Chamberlain in May 1940. There were two Churchillian failings about which Waldorf felt ever more strongly as the war progressed: his complete lack of interest in both post-war reconstruction and propaganda, his idea of which was 'a phone call to Roosevelt or Hopkins'; and his insistence that he should combine in his own person the roles of prime minister and Minister of Defence. In May 1941 Nancy's constituency of Plymouth was heavily bombed, and although Churchill visited the city shortly afterwards, and was visibly moved by what he saw, he seemed to show no interest in the home front, including the evacuation of children. 'His mind is merely interested in moving ships and soldiers and aeroplanes,' Waldorf complained: it was not feasible for him to combine his prime-ministerial duties with an obsessive interest in the minutiae of military action. In a letter to *The Times*, Waldorf demanded that Churchill should no longer combine the two jobs, and with one military disaster succeeding another, he suggested to Garvin that 'it is not friendship to continue making Winston believe that everything is beautiful in the garden'.

Garvin was unimpressed by Waldorf's anti-Churchill rhetoric, and refused to join *The Times* and the *Daily Mirror* in condemning the prime minister's conduct of the war. In this he was egged on by Churchill's crony Brendan Bracken, by now the Minister of Information, who urged him to resist Waldorf, bearing in mind that 'it would take a lot more than the decadent descendants of Wall Street toughs to fray your nerves'. But by early 1942 the war was going from bad to worse – *Repulse* and the *Prince of Wales* had been sunk by the Japanese, who had overrun Burma and Malaya, and were heading for Singapore – and Churchill's conduct of the war was coming under heavier siege. Although Beveridge wrote a piece in *The Times* insisting that he resign as Minister of Defence, only Beaverbrook's *Express* newspapers and the *Daily Telegraph* still supported him – and Garvin in the *Observer*. Waldorf was increasingly angry and frustrated, but he continued to tiptoe round the problem, fearing and dreading the moment when he would have to take action against a formidable colleague with whom he had worked for more than thirty years.

Waldorf's kindly, liberal nature was reflected in a desire to avoid conflict whenever possible, and to minimise any conflict by providing institutionalised means for its resolution via rules and constitutions designed, as often as not, to disguise or make more palatable the hard realities of power and ownership. Three years after Garvin's departure from the scene, by which time any doubts or scruples about David's eventual succession to the editorship had long vanished, he elaborated a complicated system of trusts and trustees and directors which tried, by an unpersuasive sleight of hand, to prove that although in terms of both realpolitik and ownership of shares, David was both the editor and the proprietor of the *Observer*, the trustees owned the paper while the editor had to answer to the directors vis-à-vis its day-to-day running: TJ, who was much involved in setting it up, once described it as a 'crook-proof trust' which – in theory at least – ensured that the paper could never 'fall into the hands of a Beaverbrook or a Bottomley'. No one was taken in, but it made both David and his father feel better, and provided some kind of velvet glove for the iron fist. The Observer Trust had, in fact, been set up at the outbreak of war, and provided some clues and hints about how the paper would change and develop in the post-Garvin years, and about the beliefs David shared with his father. The *Observer* should be a non-party newspaper, representing the interests of society at large rather than a particular class, interest or party; it should broadly espouse 'Christian ethics'; it should be open to new and controversial ideas; it should favour equality of opportunity while at the same time standing up for enterprise and initiative; it would disapprove of 'any new Anglo-Saxon imperialism or chauvinism' while supporting Anglo-American co-operation; and any disputes between trustees and the editor could, in the very last resort, be referred to the arbitration of the warden of All Souls, the master of Trinity College, Cambridge, and the master of the Inner Temple.

Garvin's own tumultuous relations with his employer had, since 1918, been settled by a series of contracts, the most recent of which, in 1938, had given him as editor and manager a salary of £3,500 per annum, plus a share of the profits; any disagreements between editor and proprietor should be referred to a three-man tribunal, the members of which were Sir Edward Grigg, Arthur Mann, previously of the *Yorkshire Post*, and Geoffrey Dawson, the former editor of *The Times*. David, for his part, was impatient with the formality and long-windedness associated with the tribunal but, he assured Garvin, Waldorf insisted on its use 'because he finds the strain of personal negotiation with somebody he knows as intimately as he knows you unendurable'. Garvin owed a great deal to Waldorf, he continued: 'What other proprietor would have had the wisdom, modesty, restraint, personal disinterestedness that has enabled you to carry out your great task?'

Desperate to do the right thing while getting his own way, Waldorf now spent long hours meeting or writing to the tribunal about Garvin's iniquities. David was persistent in his support, and his determination to be shot of the 'old megalomaniac'. 'My father must have the strain of the Garvin idiocy taken off him,' he told TJ, bearing in mind Waldorf's mild stroke, and David wished that TJ could be persuaded to negotiate with Garvin instead of the tribunal, somehow breaking his 'mesmeric spell' and paving the way for a handover of power. 'Until my father decides to be strong with Garvin, nothing can be done', he told 'my dear Wizard', adding that 'his only purpose is to keep on with his Wagnerian outpourings'. Earlier in the year he had complained of how Garvin had 'bombarded overwhelmingly' during a long lunch at the Savoy, but 'I somehow think he won't be as difficult as he threatens to be – he's a blusterer who deflates rather quickly', and 'though he has now taken to speaking highly of me to Papa, I cannot see any value in him'. For his

own part, 'I confess I am very ambitious for the *Observer*. I want it to be
the best paper that there is, and in this I have quite a lot of confidence.'
Waldorf transferred £10,000 into David's account, and assured him that
he would be giving him some more shares in the paper in due course;
but after talking to TJ about who should be the next editor, 'we both
agreed that *after* the war you would do it well but we equally agreed that
during the war it would be most unwise to do this in your own interest'.

Garvin had no intention of resigning, and felt he was being shabbily
treated. He had, he claimed, created the *Observer* – 'Northcliffe himself
could do nothing with it, so he called me in.' He was 'the creator and
organiser of the whole show', and thanks to him 'the paper has been
raised from the nothingness I found to what it is today'. He refused to
accept a subordinate role while 'I have, as now, full, unimpaired faculty',
and 'my true, well-known voice will continue to be heard in Britain and
America while this struggle lasts'. A letter from Waldorf was 'an insult,
almost unique in the traditions of honest journalism in this country'. Did
Waldorf want the *Observer* to become 'an obsequious annexe to Cliveden
and a political appanage of big money?' He had 'a sixth sense which no
one else can have' as far as the *Observer* was concerned: his proprietor
was violating his 'life-connection' with the paper – 'is this justice and
decency after thirty-four years?' – and exploiting 'another man's creative
life-work in journalism'; he was being asked to 'forfeit my accustomed
free voice in this country and cease to call my soul my own'.

Waldorf's nerve held in the face of this barrage, and a steelier tone
entered his correspondence. 'I shall not reply to your letter – it was not
written by the Garve with whom I have been accustomed to work,' he
replied to a particularly fierce retaliation. But he was worried about how
Garvin's departure might affect the *Observer*'s circulation – Garvin had
claimed, rightly, that despite its reduced size, the paper was in better
financial shape than ever before – and pondered ways in which he could
stay on, albeit in a non-editorial role; and Garvin's contract with the
paper, signed in 1918, had stipulated that when he retired as editor he
could continue to work for the paper as a contributor and book reviewer.
The tribunal was becoming increasingly impatient with what Dawson
described as Garvin's 'vainglorious oratory', and suggested that he should
retain the title of editor until the end of the war, but in fact restrict
himself to writing his signed weekly article; the day-to-day running of
the paper should be passed to an associate editor. Garvin would have
none of it, but Waldorf refused to scrap the tribunal: matters 'must
be decided by an impartial jury and not by personal discussion', he

wrote, adding that 'I am not prepared to endanger our personal regard at a time when we are both advancing in years.' In a memo written in November 1941 Waldorf stated that Garvin confused 'vigour in writing' with the editor's job: for some years he had had little contact with the paper's staff and contributors, or with politicians and civil servants. 'If Mr Garvin were to continue now as editor with any power or authority and continue so till his death, the paper must inevitably suffer,' he told his solicitors, since 'he is constitutionally unable to share authority or delegate responsibility'.

'I feel very strongly about the rights of editors. They should not be shoved around like pieces of old furniture,' Brendan Bracken told Arthur Mann, but Garvin was about to be ignominiously bundled out of his editorial chair; and his support for Churchill provided the *casus belli*. In a submission to the tribunal, Garvin had said, apropos the prime minister, that 'we should thank God on our knees for his genius in this war', and that the *Observer* should 'give the same level of support to Mr Churchill's government in this war as it gave Lloyd George's government in the last war'. Matters came to a head after the fall of Singapore in February 1942. Stephen King-Hall wrote a Forum entitled 'What's Wrong' about the undesirability of Churchill continuing as both prime minister and Minister of Defence. Garvin not only flatly contradicted this in his editorial, printed on the same page, but regretted the resignation from the Cabinet of Lord Beaverbrook, of whom the Astors deeply disapproved, and hoped that he would return in due course. 'As addressed to him, of all people, this was an impossible position,' he declared, heaping derision on those who had called for Churchill to step down as Minister of Defence. 'As well might it have been suggested to Chatham that he should remain in some kind of office but cease to be Minister for War.'

'Article today runs directly counter to my known policy and makes future co-operation impossible', a furious Waldorf cabled Sir Edward Grigg, the chairman of the tribunal, and his two colleagues, Geoffrey Dawson and Arthur Mann. Grigg wrote to Garvin to say that Waldorf had 'gone up in smoke', and that there was no point in discussing the imminent renewal of his contract. Garvin's daughter Katharine learned the news from a poster at Victoria Station ('J. L. Garvin leaves the *Observer*'). 'I am going to appear again soon. I have had shoals of offers,' he told her. 'The paper he had made was a loss which cannot be underestimated,' she recalled. 'He loved it. He had always stood for the tradition in which the editor, the man responsible, is more than the proprietor.' Waldorf bought Garvin's shares in the *Observer*, and it was agreed that he would be paid £2,000 a year for the rest of his life; Beaverbrook, who always enjoyed irritating the Astors, offered him a column on the *Sunday Express*, and Garvin later contributed pieces to the *Daily Telegraph*. An era had, quite suddenly, come to an end, and Garvin's voice was heard no more over the phone from Beaconsfield or in the pages of the paper. Bill Astor wrote to say what 'happy memories' he had of working with Garvin and his daughter Viola before the war, and spoke of his 'warmest personal affection' for them both. Five years later, shortly before his death in 1947, Garvin met Waldorf by chance in a London restaurant, and the two men shook hands. The ogre had vanished at last, and David had a free hand.

Filling the Void

'Whereas under JLG the paper was almost an absolute monarchy, I wished it henceforth to be a constitutional republic,' Waldorf told Ivor Brown some months after the old tyrant's sudden departure; but converting wishes into reality proved a chaotic and problematic business. In the months running up to his sacking, various names had been discussed and discarded for the role of 'assistant', 'temporary' or 'acting' editor, among them Geoffrey Dawson, Michael Foot, Francis Williams, Arthur Mann (too conservative, in David's opinion), E. H. Carr, W. E. Williams (favoured by David) and the writer Roger Fulford. Waldorf tried to persuade a long-forgotten civil servant called Sir Wilfred Eady to take up the reins, but – mercifully – nothing came of that. To plug another gap, TJ suggested that the Oxford historian G. M. Young, best remembered for his studies of Victorian England, should inherit the chore of writing Garvin's editorials.

Contributing what he could in lunch hours and at the weekends, David insisted that the paper must have 'character, cutting edge and distinc- tion – the only thing that could sink us would be timorous, formless dullness': essential ingredients were brilliant contributors, and a strong point of view, such as that provided by the Sovietologist E. H. Carr at *The Times*, now edited by Robert Barrington-Ward. The paper should emulate *The Times*'s example in 'tackling awkward subjects and doing the advance thinking for the politicians', albeit in a less ponderous way. He agreed with Carr on the need 'to use the unique opportunities of war to prepare the country, organisationally and spiritually, for a new type of political life and a new conception of citizenship'. 'My father agrees with my views very closely,' he told Arthur Mann, 'but I think the whole JLG rumpus had made him somewhat more cautious and apprehensive of steering the paper than he would otherwise have been.'

Waldorf was sympathetic, but his feelings were prompted as much by anxiety as by idealism, and he invariably sounded a more cautious note.

Though worried in case Beveridge's recent articles were too academic for his readers – and 'I do not want the public to think that the *Observer* is simply Beveridge's mouthpiece' – he agreed that post-war reconstruction had to be on the agenda if only because 'the real danger when the war is over is from Communism, and in order to avoid this we have got to have a progressive policy.' But he reminded David that 'seventy per cent of our readers are middle-aged', held out as long as he could against following his rivals in putting news rather than classified advertisements on the front page, and frowned on signed articles on the grounds that 'the more they are signed, the more we have to compete with other papers for the name of the writer' (the *Sunday Times* had already tried, without success, to lure away C. A. Lejeune by offering her far more than she earned on the *Observer*). And he urged David to curb both his impatience and his bellicosity towards particular bêtes noires: 'I feel it is more important for the paper to examine sympathetically and constructively proposals for reconstruction than for it to jump in quick and hit the Beaver or de Gaulle ahead of other newspapers.' As it turned out, David as editor instinctively inclined to the ruminative essay as opposed to competitive front-page scoops, while character assassination was something he avoided, particularly in the paper's weekly Profiles; but these were early days, and the young David was a man in a hurry.

Geoffrey Crowther, the editor of *The Economist*, held the fort after Garvin's departure, but then left for a job at the Ministry of Production; he brought with him the Catholic writer Barbara Ward, whom David both liked and admired. Crowther was succeeded by Wilson Harris, who combined editing both the *Observer* and the *Spectator*. 'Since the *Observer* made no serious demands except at the weekends, I accepted readily,' Harris recalled, but Waldorf thought him 'disappointing' and too much an 'old-fashioned liberal' in that 'unless we are bold in our post-war constructive policy we may be swept away by Communism when demobilisation comes' – and showed him the door after learning that 'the office team are not a happy family under him'.

After a good deal of dithering and discussion, Ivor Brown was appointed the acting editor – an unsatisfactory job description from his point of view, since he always knew that he was there on a temporary and provisional basis, keeping the seat warm until the war was over and David could come into his inheritance. Rather surprisingly, given the barrage of criticism to which he would later subject the hapless Brown, David seems to have actively promoted his cause. 'I could not agree to David's suggestion that we make Ivor Brown our editor – you can't suddenly promote from the dramatic critic to the political leadership of the *Observer*!' Waldorf observed, but before long Brown was in the editorial chair. As an old-fashioned man of letters, he was far happier writing about cricket and Shakespeare than about politics and the war, let alone post-war reconstruction – 'one of my tasks', he told Arthur Mann, 'is to prevent the *Observer* from becoming a parish magazine of social reform'. Waldorf found him 'awfully nice and co-operative', but ignored his understandable wish to have the word 'acting' dropped from his title. 'IB has done very well up to a point, but his limitations have become very obvious,' he told Tom Jones. 'He neither understands politics, domestic or international, nor is he making any real effort to do so. He just isn't interested . . .'

David may have suggested Brown for the post, but he was increasingly critical of him; and when not busying himself on behalf of Combined Ops he discomfited him by sniping from the wings. Not only was Brown incapable of dealing with the new writers David brought to the paper – Cyril Connolly, George Orwell and Sebastian Haffner among them – but he repeatedly failed to cover key moments in the war at a time when the tide was, very slowly, beginning to turn in favour of the Allies. Montgomery's victory at El Alamein was ignored in favour of a 'facetious' editorial by Brown, leading David to suggest that his leaders should be restricted to domestic and cultural matters. And an article on the Eighth Army was 'too light-hearted' and 'written from the mental background of the club men I satirise' rather than the 'long-sighted imaginativeness we so much need'. Brown, David once complained to TJ, would 'make the paper flat and mediocre and unenterprising if left to himself', and he liked nothing better than to publish 'leaders on the hardships of railway travel and queueing in wartime'.

Matters went from bad to worse, and the *Observer* was the only Sunday newspaper not to cover the Allied landings in French North Africa in November 1942. 'The news is so important that our failure is doubly noticeable,' Waldorf memoed his acting editor. 'David says that as soon as the news was released at 2.30 a.m. he rang up the *Observer* but found that practically everyone had gone home' – including Harmer, the news editor. David thought Harmer 'neither a competent news-getter nor has he any political understanding', and although he was 'delightful' in person, 'sentimentalism in this matter will injure the paper and do a disservice to our readers'. Harmer left to edit the *Wilts and Gloucestershire Standard*; he later told David that 'it's rather like having been the captain of a liner and then you have to take to a rowing boat'.

He was replaced by John Beavan, from the *Evening Standard*'s 'Londoner's Diary'. Following the *Sunday Times*'s lead two years earlier, Beavan substituted news for classified ads on the front page in November 1942. The headlines included a box entitled 'The New *Observer*: A Paper and a Policy', which emphasised that it was 'not a party paper'. At home, it declared, 'much remains to be done in creating a society which will get rid of injustice without losing freedom . . . For the young opportunity must be equal; for the old and infirm, security must be assured; for all others, a proper standard of working and living must be assured' – but this must 'never be allowed to dull the initiative of the individual, to depress the spirit of adventure or the creative flame'. This was indeed the voice of the new *Observer*. Beavan eventually moved on to edit the *Manchester Evening News*, and his role as news editor was taken by the long-serving Fred Tomlinson.

'May I sing my usual dirge of criticism?' David once asked, before going on to compare Brown's editorial unfavourably with one by E. H. Carr in *The Times*: by now the beleaguered Brown was fed up with unfavourable comparisons with the donnish Carr, who – he claimed – lacked first-hand experience of industry, unlike Brown's brother-in-law in Wolverhampton. David complained that recent Profiles had been too adulatory – his proposed subjects included Evelyn Waugh, 'because he is an effete *littér-ateur* who has taken to the toughest kind of soldiering', Orwell and Beaverbrook, 'because he is one of the weirdest and most nauseous, yet least understood, of contemporary phenomena' – and suggested that editorial conferences attended by the likes of Beveridge and Haffner must be run with 'clarity, tact, confidence and soundness of judgement': 'nothing is so annoying to first-rate people as not to know where they stand; to be fumbled and messed around; to be subjected to an amateurish and vague chairman', and 'IB's contribution to editorial discussions is to whittle down and slow down the ideas and plans of his writers.' He told TJ that all the younger writers looked to him rather than to Brown, who reacted to David's suggestions with 'a sulky face, a mutter about no space, and an attitude suggesting that I am a mad perfectionist . . . I seethe with impatience at having to laboriously inject the politics and liveliness into the paper via his apathetic and somewhat amateurish and indolent mind.' All in all, Brown was an 'old-fashioned liberal' with 'antiquated opinions': Beveridge, by now a regular contributor, should write the leaders on domestic matters, while Brown should be restricted to 'occasional leaders on cultural matters or short pieces in a lighter vein, such as the fourth leader in *The Times*'.

Brown was in essence a man of letters, but this was no bar to his falling foul of one of David's best-known and more temperamental protégés. David had met Cyril Connolly early in the war, but although they were both products of Eton and Balliol, they could hardly have been more different. Short, stout and pug-faced, Connolly was a self-lacerating epicurean who agonised over his self-proclaimed indolence, an aesthete who had no interest in politics but was an influential member of the literary world, mixing, sometimes uneasily, with Waugh, Isherwood, Auden, Spender, Betjeman, John Lehmann, Harold Acton and other bright young writers. As the editor of the monthly magazine *Horizon*, which he had founded with Stephen Spender shortly before the outbreak of war, he had published a stylish mixture of poems, short stories, essays and book reviews. Their relations would never be easy, but Connolly introduced David to other writers, including George Orwell and Arthur Koestler. *Horizon* itself provided a model for David when, in due course, he succeeded to the editorship of the *Observer*: his liking for the well-wrought essay, on the leader page or elsewhere in the paper, reflected his desire to emulate what Connolly had achieved on *Horizon*, as did his lifelong enthusiasm for employing writers as well as – or sometimes in preference to – professional journalists.

In the meantime, David suggested that Connolly should be employed for £800 a year as the *Observer*'s arts editor – a job that would include that of literary editor. 'You are the person most talented and most prepared for this particular job of any person I know,' he told Connolly; he was also 'one of the best writers of English prose going around' (which was true enough), and would 'add considerably to the pure brain power of the editorial team'. The *Observer*'s stable of book reviewers – Frank Swinnerton, L. A. G. Strong, Edmund Blunden, Arthur Bryant – were just the sort of middlebrow writers Connolly had ridiculed some ten years earlier in his column in the *New Statesman*, and he soon gave them their marching orders, replacing them with a more fashionable team which included Stephen Spender, A. L. Rowse, Orwell, Maurice Richardson, Peter Quennell and Nancy Mitford. He also introduced a 'Books of the Day' feature. David was delighted by the changes – 'I have chosen YOU to be the literary editor of the *Observer*,' he assured his super-sensitive new colleague – but neither Waldorf nor Ivor Brown shared his enthusiasm. Waldorf's objections were, in part, religious: despite his and Nancy's allegiance to Christian Science, the editor of the paper was expected to be a member of the Church of England – no Catholics would be considered – and Connolly was rocking the boat. Waldorf objected to his employing that 'militant atheist' Rowse as a reviewer: 'I do want Connolly to realise that I am convinced that England owes her position to this being a Protestant country with a definitely Christian background,' he told David, and 'I refuse to believe that he cannot find good writers and critics with the correct ethical point of view.'

'You'll have to bear with limitations on the *Observer*,' David warned Connolly. 'I know it's annoying and tiresome and probably seems very silly to you, but it proves that putting any new wine at all into an old bottle has to be gone at slowly.' Waldorf complained that most of Connolly's protégés were 'completely unknown to me, and I do like to feel that I have at least heard of the man who is writing the review!' and asked TJ to suggest G. M. Young and Sir Wilfred Eady as alternatives; Brown subversively claimed that *Horizon* itself was 'beginning to look "period" already'. And David himself was unimpressed by Connolly's friend Peter Quennell, finding his writing 'so consciously fastidious it is becoming clownish'. Nor did Quennell seem to realise that there was a war on – but 'you're all the same, you superfine literary haberdashers'. 'If we are literary haberdashers, you are the customers we all dread,' Connolly replied – bearing in mind, no doubt, Osbert Sitwell's advice not to 'stand any nonsense from the Astors'. Nor was Connolly pleased when he was told that Ivor Brown would not only be taking over as arts editor, but would be invading his patch as literary editor. David was anxious to offset Brown's lack of interest in politics by appointing a more polit- ically minded news editor, so allowing IB to bend his mind to the arts pages, and demoting Connolly to the role of literary adviser and chief book reviewer. 'I don't feel Connolly would think this to be an injury as he gave up nothing to come to us and I know that he felt he was being more than well paid for what he has been doing,' David assured his father.

He could not have been more wrong. He met Connolly to explain the situation in White's, the high Tory club in St James's Street to which Connolly had recently been elected. A furious row broke out and Connolly stormed out, leaving David stranded in a club of which he was not a member. In the 'monologue of misrepresentations and insults to which you treated me in your club', Connolly had accused David of being 'anti-intellectual, anti-art, a clumsy wielder of accidental power'. 'My mistake with you was personal, not professional,' David told the outraged literary adviser. 'I treated you as an intimate before I had found out whether we could be intimate. I then found – and you found – that we couldn't.' He went on to refer to Quennell 'gnashing his teeth in harsh sayings about me'. 'My little olive branch has been stuck in my

eye,' David wrote to Connolly in another letter. 'I am surprised to find
that I still feel more affection than enmity for you, despite the very ugly
picture that you have in your mind and have frequently expressed.'

For the time being at least Connolly accepted his reduced status, and
Brown took over the arts and books pages, helped along by J. C. Trewin, a
gentle, literary Cornishman, a relic of the *ancien régime* who was unsuited
to the rough and tumble of the newsroom and was said to have fainted
when John Beavan, the news editor, barked out an order. David's overriding anxiety to improve the paper's news and political coverage had
prevailed over his desire to update the books pages in particular, but he
was uneasy about the new arrangement. He worried that Brown might
drop Orwell and Tom Harrisson as reviewers, and that 'his somewhat
middle-aged tastes in literature and entertainment would not agree with
all readers, particularly not with the younger readers whom we hope
to cultivate'. He told TJ that he thought the books pages much weaker
since Connolly's demotion, with Brown relying too much on in-house
reviewers like Trewin – 'as in his politics, so in his reviewing. IB will not
search and search adventurously. He sticks in the mud.' Connolly, for his
part, was 'feeling slightly sulky, as he cannot make himself believe that
his nominal position as literary adviser has any meaning'.

'You have just flown. So sorry,' David told Connolly early in 1943, after
Connolly had decided that enough was enough. 'I quite appreciate why
you have flown. I hope you equally appreciate why you have provoked me.
You can attribute it to "philistinism" if you like. But you must not attribute
it to ill will unless you want to dismiss me as a friend, which dismissal
I would resist.' Far removed from the *Observer*, Connolly continued to
grumble about how badly treated he had been. He portrayed David as a
dictatorial bogeyman in an unpublished piece entitled 'Spring Assignment';
Evelyn Waugh gleefully reported that Connolly had been sacked, and
'expects to be directed down the mines soon'. 'I regret the switch from
relative intimacy to absolute silence, and feel it is belittling to both parties,'
David told Connolly, who continued to grumble and disparage his former
champion. 'You have frequently tried to convince me that I am cynical,
unscrupulous, power-seeking, uncouth and barbarous; that I am an enemy
of "intellectuals" and a disparager of art,' he wrote six months after
Connolly had flounced out of the office. 'I agree that we are bad for each
other. I mean all that I have said and am deeply hurt by your egocentric
and gross malice towards me.' But David's admiration for Connolly as
a writer and editor persisted, as did a vestigial affection, and their paths
would cross in the years to come.

He was also deeply indebted to Connolly for introducing him to one of his two great heroes and mentors. He had asked Connolly whom he could recommend to write about politics, as a commentator rather than a political editor or correspondent; Connolly had suggested George Orwell, and had urged David to read the essay 'The Lion and the Unicorn: Socialism and the English Genius', which Fredric Warburg of Secker & Warburg had published in Searchlight Books, a series of short topical books edited by Orwell and Tosco Fyvel. David met Orwell for the first time in the Langham Hotel, near Broadcasting House, and 'felt I had known him all my life: he was so straightforward'. He admired his decency, his lack of dogmatism and, after the war, his dislike of Communism in general, and Stalinism in particular. 'I didn't think of him as a journalist,' he told an interviewer nearly sixty years later. 'The best thing he did for journalism were book reviews. He was a political writer, a literary critic, but not a journalist.' Be that as it may, he felt that Orwell's plain, unambiguous prose provided a model for journalists, and famously insisted that all those joining the paper should be given a copy of Orwell's essay on 'Politics and the English Language'.

Orwell contributed two Forum pieces to the *Observer*, but David was keen to enlist him as a reviewer as well – beginning with Edmund Wilson's *The Wound and the Bow*. 'I admit he needs a little handling, but he has a lot to give,' he warned IB in November 1942. But before long Orwell had come up against the old guard. IB rejected his third review, so infuriating Orwell that he returned the next book Brown sent him. 'I don't write for papers which do not allow at least a minimum of honesty,' he complained to David. 'I had no idea that silly owl Brown had anything to do with the literary pages.' TJ, on the other hand, congratulated Brown for spiking Orwell's review of C. S. Lewis's *Beyond Personality*, since it would 'give pain to a large number of our readers who are religious in spirit'. But Orwell could manage perfectly well without the *Observer*'s books pages: he was a regular contributor to *Horizon*, and in November 1943 he was made the literary editor of *Tribune*.

Orwell was a particularly fine example of David's lifelong enthusiasm for employing writers as a leavening to the journalistic dough: back in the world of professional journalists, Beavan and others complained about 'a lack of drive and consistency in editorial policy, which is reflected in the variable quality of the leading articles and notes, and in the way the paper takes up a cause one week and fails to follow it up subsequently'. To counteract Brown's lack of interest in politics, Donald Tyerman was invited to join the paper. Modest, self-effacing, hard-working and generous to aspiring writers, Tyerman walked with a limp as a result of childhood polio. Warmly recommended to David by Barbara Ward, he was Geoffrey Crowther's deputy on *The Economist*, and combined working on the weekly magazine with his duties at the *Observer*. He soon made his mark; Ivor Brown, for once, was all in favour of the new man, and hoped that he might be made editor in due course. 'He can deal with our aliens more effectively than I can,' he told TJ, referring to the voluble, opinionated and alarmingly intellectual German and Central European émigrés whom David had brought to the paper. David had mixed feelings about the new arrival. Tyerman was, he wrote from Combined Ops, 'the most valuable man we have', but although he was 'definitely worthy of the editorship, the only catch is that that cancels out my post-war vocation. I feel slightly flummoxed by this dilemma.' Editing the *Observer* was 'one of the few things I might be suited for. On the other hand the prospect of Tyerman leaving the paper before I am free to take over fills me with dismay and apprehension.'

Despite some congenial company at Combined Ops, David longed to be in Tudor Street, and was all too well aware of being a part-timer on the paper, working at several removes from the day-to-day action. Once again, David turned to TJ for advice and consolation. He sensed that Tyerman felt uneasy in his presence, and had 'definitely excluded me from the councils of Tudor Street since he arrived. I have found this a little hurtful, particularly as it means that anything I say or write now gets treated as unskilled proprietorial interference.' David frankly admitted that he wanted to be a 'full-blown editor' in due course, with – ideally – Tyerman as the political editor and Brown looking after the cultural pages, and 'it's a bit much to expect me to settle down as a sleeping partner and give him the full editorship'. Tyerman was well up to editing a national newspaper, and he 'should be told that if he's going to resent my presence in the office it would be better if he looked elsewhere'. 'I'm hoping your wizardry can find a means of resolving the problem,' he told his old mentor, since 'being cut off from the councils of the *Observer* further increases my sense of futility'.

But TJ was not a soft touch. Much of Tyerman's – and Ivor Brown's – resentment against the heir apparent had been caused by the 'unmeasured criticism you hurled at them': David's intemperate remarks 'had probably made T apprehensive of what you would be if clothed with powers of life and death', and TJ pinned his hopes on 'IB's friendly co-operation in inducing DT to remain with the paper and to accept you on top'. Tyerman had 'brought strength and precision to the leading articles;

you have rich fertility in ideas and persons which need to be checked
and sifted; IB is a bit of a Stanley Baldwin, shrewd and safe. I have an
obstinate conviction that if you are not unduly checked and can "ripen"
in the next few years without losing ardour, you may make the *Observer*
out-distance every paper of the kind, here and in America.' Brown, for
his part, found Tyerman 'a great comforter'; and when, in September
1944, Tyerman moved on to become the deputy editor of *The Times*,
IB felt his departure as 'a personal, as well as professional, deprivation'.

Although, as David once put it, 'I trotted these people out, and Ivor
gallantly took them on', Ivor Brown never felt at ease with the clever,
voluble and argumentative émigré writers whom David brought to the
Observer, once describing them as 'a load of mischief and a cartload
of monkeys as well as a Cabinet of All the Talents'. (TJ, for his part,
worried that Beaverbrook might publish a complete list of the paper's
émigré writers, since it 'could be made to *look* devastating'.) A striking
figure with a huge domed forehead, Raimund Pretzel was, perhaps, the
finest writer of them all. Trained as a lawyer in Germany, he had come
to London in 1938, and decided to stay on. The following year he sent
Fred Warburg the synopsis for his book *Defying Hitler*, a riveting memoir
of life in Nazi Germany: Warburg paid him £2 a week to complete it,
but it was not published in either of their lifetimes. With the permission
of the Foreign Office, he edited a German-language newspaper for his
fellow émigrés, and to protect his family in Germany from reprisals he
adopted the nom de plume of Sebastian Haffner – 'Sebastian' reflecting
his passion for J. S. Bach, 'Haffner' his love for Mozart's symphony of
that name. In June 1940 Warburg published his *Germany Jekyll and Hyde*,
a masterly analysis of Hitler's hold on the German people, and soon
afterwards Haffner began to contribute pieces to the *Observer* under the
pseudonyms of 'Liberator' and 'A Student of Europe'. Like David, he
made a distinction between the German people and the Nazi leadership:
he saw Germany as a 'conquered land', like France or Holland, but he
had little faith in the resistance movements on the grounds that the Nazis
were far too powerful and overbearing.

Few journalists successfully make the transition from sprinter to long-
distance runner, but Haffner was a rare exception to the rule: his books
are compelling and vividly written, and David was quick to recognise
how good he was. 'I owe my original chance of joining the paper to the
privilege of your friendship rather than to any regular or demonstrable
qualification,' Haffner once told him, and he paid tribute to David's gifts as
a hands-on editor: 'Without you, if I had stuck to political writing at all, I

would have become a rather wild, over-imaginative and irresponsible kind
of writer. You have been, and still are, one of the greatest influences in
my life and I doubt whether without you I would ever have disentangled
myself and got rid of my German overexcitability and emotionalism.'
David, for his part, told TJ that 'any statesmanship and any political
consistency you find in the paper are due exclusively to Haffner and to
me'. Haffner also proved to be a masterly writer of Profiles, including
one of Hitler, entitled 'The Crank'. David had borrowed the idea of
profiles from the New Yorker; the first, written by Lionel Fielden, was
published in March 1942, and they remained particularly close to David's
heart throughout his time at the Observer.

Haffner was a sceptical conservative; his main rival in debates at editorial
conferences was a Trotskyite. Best remembered for his three-volume biography of Trotsky, Isaac Deutscher had made his name as a journalist in
pre-war Poland – not least, as Isaac Bashevis Singer recalls in his memoirs,
for his attacks on Stalin, whose biography he later wrote. A gentle yet determined character with a pointed goatee beard, he combined detestation
of Stalinism with a lifelong faith in Marxism and the Russian Revolution.
Tyerman had employed him on The Economist; his colleague Barbara Ward
confessed herself 'torn between love and exasperation' for him, in that 'I
respect his character and detest his theories; I love his warmth and affection, but his intellectual assurance sticks in my gizzard.' During the war
years he contributed the anonymous 'Peregrine's European Notebook' to
the Observer. He fondly believed that co-operation between the Western
Allies and the Soviet Union would continue into the post-war years, and
despite his dislike of Stalin, he was unworried about Russian expansionism.
David, on the other hand, had few illusions about the Soviet Union. He
told Brown in the summer of 1943 that the Observer must point out the
dangers of 'Moscow messing up the hopes of a free and united Europe –
or of Russian imperialism, if you like it', adding that 'we must be equally
frank in castigating American economic imperialism'. And he told TJ that
'politically I have always and will always side with Communists against
Fascists. Hence I am happy with the alignment of this war. But after this
war Russia will be a highly militarist and nationalist country, autocratically
ruled by a single party.' As far as Deutscher was concerned, he was both
a Trotskyite and, for David, 'a deeply civilised person and in his working
life he behaved like a liberal. Although he engaged in long-remembered
debates in the office, he was an excellent staff member.'

Deutscher's Marxist sympathies didn't prevent him from provoking
a blazing row with the Foreign Office and infuriating Britain's Russian

allies – for which the hapless Ivor Brown took the rap. Most British newspapers, led by the Beaverbrook papers and supported by the Soviet expert E. H. Carr at *The Times*, admired or even hero-worshipped 'Uncle Joe', and were indifferent to the plight of Poland. The *Observer* took a different tack. Deutscher combined an interest in the fate of his native country with a deep suspicion of Stalin; Poland would be the first country to be entered by the Red Army on its way to Berlin, and as early as May 1943 the *Observer* was raising doubts about Russia's post-war intentions. Later that year, talks about the future of Poland began at the highest level, with the British pressing for the restoration of Poland's pre-war frontiers, whereas the Russians wanted the frontier of the Soviet Union to be extended into what had been eastern Poland. In February 1944 a top-secret Russian delegation arrived in London. The Ministry of Information asked the press not to reveal the existence, let alone the subject, of their discussions, and issued an informal D-Notice, which had no legal standing. A member of the Russian delegation leaked information to an old Polish Trotskyite living in London, who passed it on to Deutscher, who then revealed Russia's plans for post-war Poland in his *Observer* column.

Deutscher had assured an anxious Brown that his source was reliable and his piece well researched, but the acting editor was summoned to the Foreign Office and torn to shreds by an incandescent Anthony Eden: not only had IB, as acting editor, ignored the 'confidential memo' rule whereby editors were provided with background information on the understanding that it never found its way into print, but the Russians had threatened to break off relations unless Deutscher revealed his sources. Despite support from Waldorf, who muttered about 'political censorship' and promised to support him to the hilt, Brown told TJ that he felt 'rather shattered' by his interview with the Foreign Secretary; he later claimed that he had spiked some of Deutscher's subsequent articles while 'giving him to understand that he is a troublesome fellow', and that this had 'rather broken Deutscher's nerve'. This coincided with the departure of Tyerman, who might have provided some backbone to the *Observer*; he told David that the hapless Brown had 'grovelled' to Eden, who had threatened his visitor with a jail sentence. Deutscher was understandably upset, and talked of leaving the paper, and David's dim view of Brown was reinforced. 'I despair of IB', he told TJ. 'He is weak to the point of cowardice.'

Perhaps the best known of David's émigré writers was E. F. Schumacher, the future author of *Small is Beautiful*. Like Trott, he had been a Rhodes

Scholar at Oxford, and was a brilliant economist; David remembered him on the games field, so tall and thin that he looked as if he might crack in two. Unlike Trott, he had no desire to remain in Nazi Germany: he emigrated to London in 1937 and, like Haffner, he was briefly interned as an enemy alien in 1940. Bob Brand and Nancy Astor pressed for his release, after which he worked on the land at Eydon, where Brand gave him the use of a cottage. David sent him books, and he wrote long memos on post-war planning. He moved to the Institute of Statistics in Oxford, and David and Brand sent a copy of his 'Plan for an International Clearing Union' to Maynard Keynes: the two men worked closely together, and their ideas inspired the Bretton Woods Agreement at the end of the war, and the establishment of the International Monetary Fund. David also introduced him to William Beveridge, and he worked with him on his hugely influential 'Full Employment in a Free Society'. Donald Tyerman urged David to employ him as a contributor to the *Observer* – 'the one essential piece in the new pattern is Schumacher,' he suggested.

David's other émigrés included Willi Guttman, who had earlier monitored German broadcasts on David's behalf; years later, one of David's younger colleagues remembered how 'surrounded by prima donna journalists, he was courteous, calm and a little shy, and moved about the office with the benign dignity of the much-loved law professor he might have become were it not for Hitler and Stalin'. The German journalist Rix Loewenthal had moved from the far left to become a stalwart of what would be known, after the war, as the 'non-Communist left'; Jon Kimche was a Swiss-born Jew who had fought in the Spanish Civil War and run a left-wing bookshop before being recommended to David by Orwell's friend Tosco Fyvel: he was made the military correspondent, and shared the 'Liberator' column with Haffner (Kimche told David's biographer, Richard Cockett, that 'Haffner was liberating Europe from the right, while I was liberating Europe from the left'). The use of pseudonyms persisted for some time after the end of the war. The publisher George Weidenfeld regarded the *Observer* as 'the flagship of the new European spirit' and, over dinner with David, 'talked until the early hours about post-war Europe'; but David 'jealously guarded the official anonymity of his key contributors', and the two men fell out after an editor at *Contact*, the magazine Weidenfeld and André Deutsch set up after the war, inadvertently revealed the real identities of 'Peregrine' and 'Liberator'.

For a time, both David and his father pinned their highest hopes on an acquaintance of Weidenfeld, the engaging but extremely dubious Peter Smolka, alias Peter Smollett. A Viennese Jew, Smolka was already enlisted

as an NKVD agent before he settled in London in the mid-1930s. He set
up a short-lived news agency with Kim Philby, and in 1938 Hutchinson
published his account of his travels in the Arctic. He came into David's
orbit during the war years, when he worked for the Russian Section
of the Ministry of Information and organised the hugely successful
twenty-fifth anniversary celebrations of the Red Army in the Albert
Hall in 1943. Smollett (as he was known in his English years) is best
remembered for advising Jonathan Cape not to publish Orwell's *Animal
Farm* on the grounds that it would damage Anglo-Russian relations at
a critical time, and, after his return to Vienna, for tipping off Graham
Greene about the penicillin scam, as perpetrated by Harry Lime in *The
Third Man*; but in the meantime he was highly regarded at the *Observer*,
and not only by David. Waldorf visited him twice at the Ministry of
Information in Senate House, was evidently impressed, and suggested
him as a possible deputy editor, or even as an eventual editor. He was,
he told TJ, intelligent, conceited and a bit of a flatterer, but 'he is a
progressive with probably sounder judgement than David . . . I think
he realises that the bulk of our readers are old and must not have their
features on the paper "improved" too rapidly. David is inclined to go too
fast.' David shared his father's high opinion; he remained in touch with
Smolka after the war, and in an exchange of letters Smolka told him
that he had 'declined the offer [of the editorship] with regret because
I felt that I could not go into a civilian job when my contemporaries
were fighting' – he regarded his work at the ministry as 'war service' –
and fondly recalled a lunch at the Shanghai Restaurant in Soho with
David, Orwell and Isaac Deutscher. The Shanghai gave its name to a
discussion group, founded by David and Edward Hulton, the members
of which included Smollett, Frank Pakenham, E. H. Carr, Ted Castle,
Orwell, Haffner, Deutscher, John Strachey, Jon Kimche and Frank Owen,
Michael Foot's predecessor as editor of the *Evening Standard* and one of
the three authors of *Guilty Men*.

   David's foreign-born intellectuals may have provided him with 'the
Balliol I never had', but they had little appeal for Ivor Brown. He worried
that the *Observer* was 'becoming too like a magazine of foreign affairs
and too little like a newspaper', adding that 'it is very important that
we should draw on journalists trained to express themselves quickly and
shortly rather than on writers of books and reports'. Diplomatic
and emollient as ever, TJ urged David to carry on working with Brown
after the war – 'you can be spotting and insinuating gifted youngsters as
you have hitherto, and tying them to strings which can be pulled towards

the *Observer* when pulp abounds again' – but although David's gifts as a talent-spotter would flourish in the post-war years, relations with IB could only go from bad to worse.

★

Life was complicated further in the early summer of 1942, when Bill Astor returned to England from three years' military service in the Middle East. Bill had become actively involved with the *Observer* before the war, when Waldorf momentarily lost faith in his heir apparent, and was anxious to resume his connection with the paper. 'I hope we may come to a basis on which we can work together,' he told TJ apropos future co-operation with David. But the omens were not promising. 'What scares me is the complete ascendancy David has got over Papa,' he continued. 'The arguments that he [Waldorf] advanced were not his own arguments but David's', and 'it really is frightening to see it'.

Nancy had always hoped that the two brothers would be able to work together, though David had pointed out to her that 'his friends and mine are so totally different'. Waldorf sided with David, but was reluctant to humiliate Bill, not least because – recalling David's pre-war dithering – 'David was slow in coming forward in the past and thereby helped to create the present difficulty'. And, bearing the likes of Connolly in mind, 'we do not want the *Observer* to represent only the bright young things of the left-centre'. In August 1939 he had transferred to David 11,124 shares, representing twenty-five per cent of his holdings in the paper, and ten per cent to Bill. His suggestion that Bill's holding should be increased to twenty per cent in case David was killed in the war met with fierce opposition from David, who told TJ that although he was perfectly happy for the 'liberal-conservative' opinions associated with his father, TJ and Arthur Mann to be ventilated in the *Observer*, he felt 'very uneasy' about increasing Bill's influence on the paper. He was, after all, a 'right-wing Tory with a certain amount of impatience with mild progressives and an almost violent animosity towards radical progressives. My view is that the *Observer* should be run by liberal-minded people both of the left and the right. Without that liberal-mindedness in common there would be no basis for agreement.'

In a note on 'Bill's Complaints', David claimed that when his brother worked on the paper 'he merely backed up the Garvin regime', and 'had no serious complaint about it'; and that on his return to England he had made plain his disapproval of Viola Garvin's dismissal. Bill would inherit a sizeable chunk of the New York real estate, plus all his father's property in Britain and the title of Viscount Astor, and he was already installed at Cliveden: he had been a director of the *Observer* before the war, but were he to now become an active director 'he will confuse matters by not being in basic agreement with the liberal-progressive outlook of the paper; if he is a "passive" director he will be embarrassed by the connection, and so will the paper'. Despite David's opposition, Bill's directorship was renewed, and he 'promptly got truculent with me about our employment of Connolly, Harrisson and Orwell', as well as making uncomplimentary remarks about Beveridge. Nor did David want Bill as a contributor, if only because 'the name Astor should appear in the paper as infrequently as possible. The *Observer* must be a national not a family newspaper.'

Bill felt bruised by his cool reception. 'What upsets me is the general attitude of Papa and David towards myself,' he complained to TJ. 'I wasn't even asked if I minded giving up my expectations in David.' Neither his father nor David felt they could work closely with him 'although I have not, as far as I know, expressed any major disagreement with them'. He had already, at Waldorf's request, given Cliveden to the National Trust, and he was reluctant to sever his connection with the family paper as well – still more so since 'I think it very dangerous to leave it entirely in the hands of one person, David, who is brilliant but emotional and sometimes erratic.' Bill, who would lose his seat in the Commons in the 1945 general election, was nothing like as blimpish as David seemed to think – like Jakie and Michael, he supported the *Observer* over Suez, and later over the abolition of the death penalty, and he was a generous philanthropist, not least in his support for Hungarian refugees in 1956 – but the damage had been done. 'Bill remains a slight menace – one feels there's a submarine dogging the convoy,' David told TJ in the summer of 1943; Bill would remain a director of the *Observer*, and David would occasionally remind him that – unlike the trustees – the directors were solely concerned with the business side of the paper, and had nothing to do with editorial matters. In the meantime Waldorf had transferred more shares to David, giving him 24,498 out of a total of 50,000.

Earlier that year Waldorf told Bill that David would be made editor after the war. 'David is full of constructive originality whereas Bill tends to accept existing situations,' he told TJ. David, for his part, had a clear idea of what he wanted to achieve. 'I am anxious that the *Observer* should be one of the great newspapers of the world,' he told Ivor Brown, and 'this means getting read by other journalists, by intelligent politicians and civil servants and by the Cabinet, being quoted in the foreign press and on the radio. In short, what Carr achieves in *The Times* when he is trying.' Elsewhere he suggested that 'a strong and positive foreign policy, particularly as regards Europe, is the most important doctrine for any paper to have', and that the *Observer* should champion 'a progressive, constructive policy in domestic matters', combining government intervention on such matters as wages, working hours, unemployment, health, pensions and housing with encouragement for free enterprise. All these would become, in due course, part of the *Observer*'s credo, but when David should come into his inheritance remained uncertain. Waldorf felt that he still lacked experience, that he should, ideally, spend some time in America after the war, and that he was 'too apt to feel that he has to have perfection in every detail'.

David's future colleague John Pringle met David at this time, and not only remembered him as 'an absurdly youthful and handsome figure in his uniform', but was 'deeply impressed by his grasp of politics as well as by his charming personality'. Young as he still was, David was making his mark, both at the *Observer* and in public life: Basil Liddell Hart, the famous military strategist, wrote to him to say that the *Observer* 'is the only newspaper today which gives the public a truthful idea of the real facts and factors that are discussed in informed circles, privately, among those who move in them. It is a great public service to do this.' David sometimes wondered whether 'it has been a mistake to leave the post of editor lightly tenanted so that I can occupy it after the war', but – as Pringle had noticed – he was still in uniform, and he was to play a more active part in the war itself before his future role at the *Observer* could be decided.

12

Man at Arms

'I am very anxious that the services of David Astor, who is in the Marines, should not be wasted as I regard him as a remarkably able and vigorous young man,' Stafford Cripps wrote to Louis Mountbatten in March 1942. David was still drumming his heels on Hayling Island, and was trying in vain to interest the more unconventional and freebooting elements of the armed services in his ideas about combining propaganda with smuggling arms to resistance groups in occupied Europe, and mounting raids on the Continent to undermine German morale: both Cripps and Robert Laycock thought well of them, but they were 'blue-pencilled' by the Political Warfare Executive, while the Foreign Office's Political Intelligence Department dismissed them as being 'written without an understanding of current British strategy'.

Mountbatten, then in charge of Combined Operations, hurried to oblige, and later that year he offered David a job in their headquarters in Richmond Terrace, off Whitehall. Mountbatten was keen on public relations and news management, and employed a small army of young men to spread the word about Combined Ops and present their activities in as favourable a light as possible. This was sometimes easier said than done, and never more so than when dealing with the aftermath of the disastrous Dieppe Raid of August 1942, which had been masterminded by Combined Ops: David was sent down to Portsmouth to meet survivors – these included his brother Jakie, who had been on board HMS *Calpe* – and brief the press. It was not the kind of work he enjoyed. 'I wish I was doing something more interesting and important, but it seems I'm not destined to do anything serious in this war,' he complained to TJ. But he got on well with Mountbatten, and he was grateful for his support when it was learned that MI5 were worried by his friendship with so many German émigrés. 'You're perfectly right!' was Mountbatten's reaction when David told him that he had no intention of dropping his friends and was proud to consort with anti-Nazi Germans (a reasonable reaction on Mountbatten's part, whose German-born father had switched his name from Battenberg during the previous war).

Nor was David's private life any more satisfactory. His pre-war girlfriend – of whom more later – was now living in Switzerland. He was briefly involved with a black American nightclub singer called Elisabeth Welch, a London equivalent of Josephine Baker: he was extremely fond of her, but Nancy would almost certainly have disapproved. Relations with Nancy remained as agonised as ever. He told her that he must get over minding her criticisms, that he longed to be on friendly terms with her – 'I've wanted it that way all my life' – and that 'when I was younger this "mal entente" between us was the cause of more misery to me than anything else has ever been'. His busy life, torn between Combined Ops and the *Observer*, 'serves as a means to heal or forget an unsatisfactory private life' and a 'certain horror of intimacy of all kinds'. 'I am a broken reed and can't support large strains,' he told her, and 'I compensate for my diffidence by a show of intellectual arrogance.' Nancy, for her part, not only disapproved of what he was doing at the *Observer*, but had no sympathy for his overriding political passion. 'My main interest for the last six years has been European fascism and the answer to it,' he told her in August 1944. 'I live in the atmosphere of the European opponents of fascism.' Nancy had no interest in Europe, and wasn't averse to 'talking against the Jews'.

David's colleagues at Combined Ops were more congenial than the purple majors encountered in Deal and on Hayling Island – they included Goronwy Rees, the publisher Ian Collins, Francis Williams and Arthur Marshall, whom David recommended to IB for a humorous column, without success – but he longed to play a more active role in the fight against fascism, and his attempts to become involved attracted attention at the very highest level. 'Where is the report on the position of Mr David Astor, which you promised to send, showing how an officer in the Royal Marines is able to give so much time and activity to the conduct of the *Observer* newspaper?' Churchill wrote in a memo to A. V. Alexander, the First Lord of the Admiralty, three days after the Normandy Landings had begun. Alexander, who must have had other things on his mind, referred the matter to Bob Laycock, who had replaced Mountbatten at Combined Ops in October 1943. Laycock had no time for Mountbatten's PR men, and got rid of most of them: he knew that David wanted to see some action and felt he was too young to be stuck in an office job, but although Laycock said David had 'begged me to give him a job in one of the Royal Marine Commandos', David was suffering from his recurrent

sinus problems, and Laycock had asked him to stay on while Combined
Ops was reorganised. 'Captain Astor has worked extremely hard in this
HQ and has kept longer hours than the average Whitehall staff officer,'
Laycock continued. David had been interviewed by Bill Stirling, a masterful
practitioner of irregular warfare, and although that had come to nothing,
the SAS had agreed to take him on to work with the Maquis in occupied
France since 'he is a fluent French speaker, an ardent Francophile and
is keen to operate in enemy-occupied territory'. Churchill continued to
chivvy the hapless Alexander: 'Pray send this report from General Laycock.
It seems to me that there are a great many obstacles in the way of getting
at the truth of the very simple question I asked.' It was a relief to learn
that Laycock's memo 'completely exonerates him from any reproach'.

   While at Combined Ops, David had combined his work in public relations with intelligence, working closely with the newly formed Forces
Françaises de l'Interieur (FFI) and with MI9, which looked after the interests
of British servicemen who had escaped from prisoner-of-war camps and
were making their way back to Britain. Eventually seconded to the Airborne
Group of the SAS, he was to act as a liaison man between the SAS and the
Maquis, acting under the command of General Koenig, the commander-in-
chief of the FFI. Koenig in turn reported to General Eisenhower. Koenig
told David that he felt too dependent on SOE, so 'I visited Winston's man,
General Ismay, together with my colonel, Richard Broad, to tell him how
hampered Koenig felt himself to be.' 'Pug' Ismay was Churchill's closest
military adviser, and David introduced him to Koenig, who was pressing
for the Free French to be given a larger role in the planning of D-Day:
both interventions bore fruit, for which Koenig was extremely grateful.

   'The basic hitch in my present plans is that no one is being sent to
reinforce the Maquis because that near-traitor General de Gaulle does
not want to see the Maquis reinforced by the Allies and made into a
strong and independent force,' David reported to TJ, and the iniquity
of de Gaulle had become one of David's sporadic obsessions. David
believed that although de Gaulle was supported by the Foreign Office and
funded by the Treasury, his movement had 'fascist characteristics' and was
'extremely nationalistic', with a strong 'anti-Anglo-Saxon bias'; and once
in power, de Gaulle would try to impose a right-wing dictatorship on the
French people. Not only could he sow dissension between the British
and the Americans, but his vision of France was incompatible with that
of a federated and democratic post-war Europe; 'Winston alone is alive
to the danger', but Desmond Morton, Churchill's personal assistant, did
all he could to prevent complaints about de Gaulle from reaching the

prime minister. 'It would be fatal if at the end of the war we presented the French with a ready-made nucleus of military dictatorship which was anti-British in its sympathies', David told Edward Hulton.

But in David's opinion there was a deeply sinister side to de Gaulle's London operations. He was convinced that one of de Gaulle's closest aides, Colonel Dewavrin, alias 'Passy', had been a Cagoulard, a member of the conspiratorial far-right political grouping in pre-war France, previously referred to as one of Claud Cockburn's nicknames for the Cliveden Set. As head of the Bureau Central de Renseignements, Passy was involved in intelligence work, counter-espionage and secret operations, and as such he worked closely with SOE; but he also masterminded – or so his detractors claimed – a secret torture chamber in Duke Street, Mayfair, where French opponents of de Gaulle were put through the third degree. There was also, according to the historian M. R. D. Foot, who knew Passy during the war, 'an absurd tale that a Frenchman working with F Section [of SOE] was enticed to Passy's headquarters in Duke Street and murdered in the basement'.

Willi Guttman recalled that in the *Observer* offices de Gaulle was 'considered nothing short of an ogre, a tyrant and potential dictator, an enemy of Britain, a menace to a future better world and, to say the least, a confounded nuisance'. David and Ali Forbes were close to Raymond Aron and André Labarthe of the anti-Gaullist *La France Libre*, and Denis Seurat of the Institut Français was David's main source of information. But not all David's colleagues shared his dark suspicions. John Beavan, as news editor, and Donald Tyerman, as political editor, were cautious about running anti-de Gaulle stories unless they were well substantiated, partly from fear of libel. David and Fredenburgh interviewed a French SOE officer who claimed to have been tortured by Passy; David told Tyerman that he would 'cease to be such a bore on the subject' if the others would take the rumours seriously, but 'as long as I am virtually a one-man movement, my conscience compels me not to ease up'.

Despite Foreign Office pressure – 'Can Captain Astor be restrained?' – the paper launched an attack on the general on the eve of the Torch landings in North Africa in November 1942; in an editorial, David claimed that de Gaulle's followers included men 'who do not hide their approval of certain Fascist aspects of the Vichy reorganisation of France'. A row broke out in the office some eight months later. David was keen that diplomatic recognition of de Gaulle's Committee of National Liberation should be withheld until it had become more democratic, but – to his fury – IB diluted the impact of a piece Fredenburgh had written on the subject. 'It was clearly discussed at the lunch we had with WA and TJ that the paper should take a stronger line against de Gaulle,' David told Brown. 'I regard this as sabotage on someone's part.' In the meantime, he was 'going ahead collecting material for the big exposure of Gaullism'. So stirred up was he that he wrote a 30,000-word 'White Paper' on the subject, which Waldorf then showed to Churchill – who, like Roosevelt, disliked de Gaulle and was driven wild with frustration by him. But de Gaulle's position became increasingly secure, and David's anonymous Profile of the general was a milder affair than expected.

Shortly after David had first joined the Marines, Waldorf worried because 'Dr Gillespie, the nerve specialist who has had David under his care, says he is of the high-strung type that either behaves recklessly in the trenches or gets shellshock', and now David was to be put to the test. 'I have a desire due to woundable vanity to do something military and I also have a certain curiosity to see what it's like,' he told Nancy. After D-Day there was a proliferation of 'inter-allied' missions into France; some of these were parachuted in behind or near enemy lines, while others – including David's – were landed on improvised airfields. De Gaulle disapproved of SOE's involvement with the French Resistance, but although David had been seconded to the SAS, he would be forming part of a unit under French (FFI) rather than British command.

David had met his commanding officer, Colonel Richard Broad, through Combined Ops. Broad had been at Dunkirk, but instead of being taken off in one of the little ships, he and a few others had made their way west into Normandy, where they had met Pierre d'Harcourt, an upper-class Frenchman active in the Resistance. D'Harcourt had smuggled them to Paris, where they met other members of the Resistance, and then on to Marseilles, from where they made their way back to England. D'Harcourt was eventually captured by the Gestapo and sent to Buchenwald; after the war he settled in England, published a book about his experiences in Buchenwald, and became the *Observer*'s first travel writer-cum-editor.

Mission Etoile consisted of nine men, three of whom – Captain Bennett, the mission's second-in-command ('a cheerful, ugly, keen and capable man, with a quite repellent moustache', according to one report), Captain de Schonen, a French officer, and Sergeant Brierley, the radio operator – were members of the Jedburgh Team Gregory: the Jedburghs were highly trained, French-speaking three-man groups including at least one French serviceman; they had been operating to good effect since before D-Day but were now, with the Germans in evident retreat, being subsumed into larger units like Etoile. Mission Etoile was to be landed in eastern France, near the Belfort Gap, which formed a funnel between the Alps to the south and the Vosges to the north, through which the German army was making its way home across the Rhine. Wearing uniforms, and the red berets sported by airborne troops, they were to be met by Major Richard Heslop (code name 'Xavier'), an experienced SOE agent from Maurice Buckmaster's F Section who was co-ordinating Resistance groups in the Haute-Savoie, and would later liaise with an SAS unit led by a Colonel Franks.

After wearisome delays caused by bad weather, Mission Etoile left the American airbase in Harrington, Northamptonshire, on 4 September, flying in a USAAF 'Carpetbagger' Dakota and taking with them an unarmed jeep (the armoured jeep they'd been promised failed to materialise). After refuelling in Exeter, they set out for France; Colonel Broad noted the number of convoys in the Channel, and – as it grew dark – the casual attitude of the newly liberated French vis-à-vis blackout regulations. They landed on an airstrip near Gex, where they were met by 'Xavier' and a Resistance leader code-named 'Roman'. Colonel Broad was impressed by the efficiency of the reception party, but was less taken with the supper on offer: David felt unwell and complained of a stomach ache, but although his commanding officer attributed this to Resistance sausages, it seemed that he was suffering from a mild attack of dysentery.

After spending a freezing night near Gex they set off towards Lons-les-Soulines, the temporary headquarters of the US Seventh Army, travelling in the jeep and in a prison van that had earlier belonged to the dreaded Milice. They traded in the puncture-prone prison van for two cars, a Packard and a Plymouth, and the following day they set out in a convoy for Beaumes les Dames – which, the FFI warned them, had recently been retaken by a 'strong force of Boches'. They were ambushed by retreating Germans at a crossroads, and according to Bennett, who was badly wounded in the shoulder, 'the gunner was an excellent shot and the first burst of ten or fifteen rounds hit us fair and square'. Three others were wounded, including David – who, according to Colonel Broad, 'crawled round to join me and assisted me by handing out bandages etc. He made no complaint of being wounded and I attributed his lack of activity to the fact that he was suffering from dysentery. When I had completed my task as best I could, he mentioned to me that he thought he also had been hit, and on examining his back, I was horrified to find a hole big enough to take the whole of the first field dressing.' David suffered a shoulder wound; Captain de Schonen was hit in the midriff, and David always remembered how, when he took a puff on a restorative cigarette, the smoke curled through the buttonholes of his battledress top. Some American tanks appeared soon afterwards, and took the four wounded men to an American field hospital. David's war was over, at least as far as fighting was concerned.

Two years after the war had ended, David offered a job on the *Observer* to Terry Kilmartin, a tall, fair-haired, blue-eyed, untypically laconic Irishman who later became one of David's closest professional colleagues and confidants. Although both men were famously modest and self-deprecating, and the last people to indulge in boasting or bombast, it was widely known on the paper that Kilmartin had been a colleague on Mission Etoile, that he had either saved David's life during the ambush or, at the very least, handed out bandages and cigarettes, and that David's offer of a job on the *Observer* was a gesture of gratitude as well as friendship. But although there is no reason to doubt the veracity of either man, Kilmartin's formal involvement is hard to pin down. On their return to England after the completion of Mission Etoile, three of its members – Colonel Broad, Captain Bennett and Sergeant Brierley – submitted detailed reports. Colonel Broad provides a list of the mission's members, and Kilmartin's name is not included; all three describe the ambush in some detail, but no mention is made in any of them of Kilmartin's role; on the other hand, Broad refers to Kilmartin in his account of what happened to the mission after the four wounded men had been taken away, and he is included as a member of the mission in a second report written by Captain Bennett.

Kilmartin had acquired fluent French while teaching in France before the war. In 1940 he applied to join SOE, where his sister worked, and – as an Irishman educated in England – he was vetted by Scotland Yard and MI5; he was rejected for active service on medical grounds, since he had only one kidney, but joined Colonel Buckmaster's F Section in London as a civilian member, liaising with and debriefing those who had returned from SOE missions into France. He was very well thought of, and when missions to France multiplied after D-Day, it was felt that despite his medical record and despite his being, in theory, a security risk, he should be given a commission as a matter of urgency, and sent to France with the rank of captain. His absence from the official reports suggests that, despite being given clearance by F Section, he was a last-minute addition to the mission, playing truant in his eagerness to see some action at last. 'Could we not swing him onto a plane à la Kilmartin?' a colleague asked Buckmaster apropos a former member of the Resistance who was desperate to return to France, while Noreen Riols, one of the young women employed in the SOE offices at Norgeby House in Baker Street, recalls how 'one evening Terry took the matter into his own hands and left with a "Jed" team', and how, next morning, 'Buck' was puce with rage and threatened Kilmartin with a court martial. Buckmaster soon simmered down, and the *Observer* benefitted enormously from the two men's wartime encounter, however last-minute. David came to regard Kilmartin as the 'conscience' of the paper, the ultimate litmus test. Although he sometimes referred to himself as a bog Irishman, Kilmartin seemed on the surface to be the quintessential monosyllabic, rather buttoned-up Englishman, differing from David only in his attitude to drink: whereas David might, at most, sip the occasional glass of white wine, Kilmartin had the bibulous habits of an old-fashioned Fleet Street journalist.

Later that year both David and Colonel Broad had Croix de Guerres pinned to their chests by General Koenig in the courtyard of Les Invalides. In the meantime, David, weak through loss of blood, was taken to a 'Yankee tented hospital', the 'only interesting experience' of which was finding himself next to wounded Germans, 'dull, ordinary, defeatist' soldiers, anxious to disown Hitler and all in favour of the 20 July plotters. After a spell in an American military hospital near Besançon, he was flown to 'a Mussolini hospital on the edge of Naples' run by the British. It was, he recalled, 'the most disagreeable experience of all': he particularly disliked the 'jaded sorry-for-themselves nurses and callous doctors . . . but I was happy there with stacks of Penguins once my shoulder ceased giving trouble'.

'I spent three hectic days trying to locate you. The first intimation we had that you were wounded was your telegram to Mother,' Waldorf wrote, while Nancy added that 'we can hardly wait to hear about it and you can imagine how grateful I am to THE Giver of all good things.' 'You are the only member of the family who has been engaged offensively on the ground with the enemy – you, the intellectual aspirant, the all-time human benefactor,' his brother Michael remarked, but David had no time for mock-heroics. 'Well, my war experience was short and not sweet, but it was not distressing', he told TJ. 'I acquired this wound in the most unheroic and undramatic circumstances', he insisted in a letter to Nancy, adding 'no over-dramatisation, please!' It had proved to be a 'small wound – simply a bullet in the right shoulder with no complications', and 'there should be no permanent injury'. After leaving hospital, he enjoyed a 'very happy convalescence on the island of Ischia' – 'it was like stepping into a magic garden', he told his future wife. While on Ischia he wrote an affectionate letter to Elisabeth Welch, then entertaining the troops with Tommy Trinder; they met again years later, and she agreed to sing at his seventy-fifth birthday party at the Waldorf Hotel.

It was while he was still in hospital that David learned that Adam von Trott had been executed for his involvement in the abortive 20 July plot against Hitler: after a show trial conducted by Roland Freisler, the brutal and bullying president of the People's Court, he had been condemned to death, and hanged from the neck with piano wire. 'The news about Adam, though I expected it, has knocked me out. It is so horrible that I can't consider it and try to drive the whole thing out of my mind,' David told his parents. Some years later he told Marion Doenhoff, who had been involved with the German opposition from her home in Prussia, that he had heard of Trott's death in a hospital ward with sixty other people, and how 'it felt as if hope had died, as my only idea of doing anything good was that of doing things in connection with him'.

David believed that 'Adam would have shortened the war by months and saved thousands of lives if he had succeeded. He was Philip [Kerr, i.e. Lothian] with the power of action of a Lloyd George and the physical courage of Bob Laycock.' Throughout the war Trott had made futile attempts to get in touch with his friends in England, and to persuade the Allies to work with the German opposition, such as it was; but his efforts were doomed by the hostility of the Foreign Office in general, and the Foreign Secretary in particular. Nor did all his Oxford acquaintances rise to his support. 'The FO view of him is suspicious and unfriendly,' David told TJ from Combined Ops. They regarded the German opposition as old-fashioned and unapologetic German nationalists, who favoured the retention of Hitler's pre-war conquests in Austria, the Sudetenland, Danzig and the Polish Corridor: John Wheeler-Bennett, for example, suggested to the Foreign Office that although Trott was anti-Nazi, he was also a 'strong German nationalist'. The alliance with the USSR came to be seen as all-important and all-prevailing. In September 1941 Stalin had sent the British government a memo rejecting all peace-feelers on the grounds that they could weaken the alliance; and in June 1943 unconditional surrender became official Allied policy.

Earlier in the war, Trott had been in touch with the Dutch cleric Visser 't Hooft and the World Council of Churches, and when, in May 1942, Visser came to London, he brought with him a memo addressed to Stafford Cripps, with copies for Arnold Toynbee and the Oxford political scientist Sir Alfred Zimmern. Cripps – in David's opinion 'the one great exception to a sad story of neglect, not only of Adam, but of all the other Germans representing the opposition' – showed the memo to Churchill, who scrawled 'most encouraging' in the margin; but despite Cripps's assuring Eden that 'it is a complete failure to understand either him or what he stands for that dubs him politically dishonest', the Foreign Office and the Foreign Secretary reacted very differently. Trott was regarded as 'an extraordinarily suspicious character', and it was suggested that the memo was in fact the work of the German secret service, designed to sow dissension among the Allies. It was then passed to Richard Crossman, who wrote a damning anonymous report which concluded with the words 'I did not trust him very far, and he did not trust me.' Nor did a Stockholm meeting between Trott and British Embassy officials in October 1943 meet with a warmer reception. 'This sounds like our old friend von Trott,' G. W. Harrison of the FO noted after reading a memo from Stockholm. 'Note the skill with which he propagates the Communist bogey, and mixes fact with fiction.' In another memo, Harrison suggested that Trott was 'a conscious or unconscious agent of the German secret service' while Roger Makins, later to become an ambassador and a Foreign Office grandee, claimed that Trott was 'a very good mouthpiece of a certain well-known type of German propaganda', and Con O'Neill admitted, after learning of Trott's execution, that 'I certainly distrusted him, not least when I came across him during his "mission" to London a few weeks before the war began.'

'Our FO believed until this happened that Adam was a camouflaged Nazi', David wrote to TJ shortly after learning of Trott's death. Nor were doubts about Trott restricted to the Foreign Office. Hugh Carleton Greene, who had been the *Daily Telegraph*'s Berlin correspondent before the war, and ran the BBC's German Service during the war, remembered how 'Trott was amazingly indiscreet in conversation – so much so that I began to suspect (wrongly, I know) that he was an agent provocateur luring people on to expose their anti-Nazi views.' The historian Elizabeth Wiskemann, who had met Trott several times during his wartime visits to Switzerland, saw him for the last time in Berne in April 1944. 'He looked a shadow of his former self, grey and haggard', and obsessed with how the Nazis would exploit the damage done by Allied bombing. 'He was a bewilderingly brilliant creature, infinitely German in the intellectual complexity in which he loved to indulge', she recalled, adding the critical proviso that 'he would often come out with that dear old phrase about only the Germans being able to tame – or rule, or whatever it was – the Slavs'. Nor was criticism of the German opposition restricted to suspicious Foreign Office officials. Writing two years after the end of the war, Hugh Trevor-Roper dismissed it as 'a creature as fabulous as the centaur and the hippogriff', made up of 'a few high-minded aristocrats, a few disappointed officials and dismayed parsons'.

David once wrote that the one Oxford friend of Trott who never lost faith in him was Diana Hubback, 'who knew him better than any of them and, incidentally, as a Jewess, would not be without her suspicions'. Not long after Trott's death, she told David that only she, David, and Stafford and John Cripps had ever fully trusted him – and Wilfrid Israel, the Anglo-German Jewish department-store owner from Berlin who had defied Hitler for as long as he possibly could before moving to London, where he continued to work for the Jews before being shot down in a plane returning from Portugal in 1943: Israel was, in David's opinion, 'the only person in England who fully realised Adam's commitment to attempt some action in Germany'. Diana Hopkinson recalled how Trott's 'love of his country in political terms amounted to a nationalism which was so strong that I could not sympathise with it', and how 'although so many people loved him and were interested in him and admired him, ultimately so few trusted him, particularly in these last years when his strange activities and associates puzzled people so much'. The distrust persisted, and in the years to come David would do all he could to dispel it.

★

David ended the war in Paris as a 'one-man Awards Bureau', helping MI9 to compile a record of the 45,000 or so French civilians who had helped escaping British prisoners of war and pilots over the past six years. But his life was not restricted to military matters. Nancy's niece Nancy Lancaster, the co-founder of the decorating firm Colefax & Fowler, once claimed that 'David Astor's always been in love with me' – 'he used to stare at me when he was a little boy. I remember him sitting under the table the day I married Ronnie [Tree], not able to take his eyes off me. I said to him "You're in love with me, aren't you?"' – but nothing came of this youthful infatuation, if it ever existed, and on 1 August 1945, David was married in a Protestant church near the Louvre: his brother Jakie, also in uniform, was the best man, and the following day the mayor of Paris conducted a civil ceremony. 'I am so glad that he has found someone who will make him happy,' Waldorf wrote to the bride. 'He is a young man with real gifts and a love of his fellow men and I have long hoped that he would have a home of his own.' Although David recalled his wedding day as 'wonderful', their marriage was to prove – like so many wartime marriages – a short-lived, unhappy affair, the break-up of which caused him agonies of guilt and remorse over his wife and their daughter Frances. But it was far from being a sudden, shotgun romance: although they had seen little or nothing of one another since the outbreak of the war, he had known his bride-to-be since his Oxford days.

Melanie Hauser had grown up in Switzerland. Her father, an architect, was feckless, jovial and irresponsible, and although Melanie later 'talked with amusement of his semi-delinquent behaviour as a father', she was 'deeply hostile to the neglectful and joking way he had treated her' after he eventually abandoned his wife and only child. His paternal role was taken by his friend Max Emden, a wealthy financier who felt that Melanie had been sadly neglected by her parents, and often had her to stay in the house he shared with his mistress. As a child, she learned to be self-reliant, and Emden taught her to appreciate elegance and civilised living. A 'tall and handsome' young woman, she left home when she was sixteen and came to England. She was an au pair girl in Ipswich and worked in Reading before moving to London, where she shared a basement flat in Belsize Square with a German girl, and worked in a dress shop.

Melanie's father's friends included the architect Berthold Lubetkin, who had settled in London in 1931, and is best remembered for his work at the London Zoo and for the Highpoint flats in Highgate; and David met the seventeen-year-old Melanie at a party given by a mutual friend called Mary Cook, an American who worked for Lubetkin. David drove the two girls back to Belsize Square. 'I was taken by something about Melanie's manner, her genuineness and lack of pretence,' David recalled after her death in 1996. He pressed her cheek against his when they said goodbye, and 'I felt then her inner calmness that has always remained with me.' Her humour 'gave a lightness of touch to how she lived. She had a style of her own, a quiet style, a mixture of modest elegance, self-assurance and a sensible kind of ordinariness. She didn't consider herself good-looking, although she was' – so much so that she was frequently mistaken for Ingrid Bergman.

'Musi' went on to train as a sculptor at the Central School, and 'she educated me aesthetically and in how to live'. In the early 1930s she travelled to Paris with David, and they spent a summer in Florence, taking in churches and galleries. She visited Greece and America, and spent the war years working in a factory in Switzerland. She got on well with David's parents, Nancy in particular, and visited them at Cliveden after she and David had gone their separate ways; through them she met Charlie Chaplin, who became a close friend when she returned to live in Switzerland after her divorce. A strong character, she could be 'stern and stubborn. She could also in a light-hearted way put you down', David recalled. 'In our short marriage, I remember her noticing how untidy I was in dropping clothes on the floor. She said, "You're a chicken! You just drop things anywhere!"' She loved swimming and golf, and was a keen photographer. She never enjoyed coming to England; Frances remembered how 'she used to go grey and get ill within three days of ever coming to England', and she thought English upper-class voices 'phoney'.

According to David, 'Musi was always totally reliable in everything, and our relationship did not have any element of conflict – until our tragic marriage. I don't want to explain why our marriage failed, as it is too sad a story. But I can only say it was my fault. I wasn't able to give myself.'

★

David's short-lived marriage was not the only change to his domestic or family arrangements. In the spring of 1944 Chips Channon – a fellow American, and never well disposed – noted in his diary how, in the Palace of Westminster, Nancy 'barged in, with the usual jangle of bracelets, and I happened to see Lord Astor's tired lined face light up as he smiled at her with infinite tenderness: and I realised that the mad witch was still loved by her husband'. But Waldorf's insistence that Nancy should give up her seat in the 1945 general election put that love under intolerable strain. She had become an increasingly irrelevant and marginalised figure, and Waldorf was convinced that 'she was past playing any useful role in the House of Commons. She had simply become too intemperate and inconsistent and far too quarrelsome. She was also moving steadily to the right, whereas he progressed during his life steadily leftwards.' Nor could she 'have hoped to win a further election in Plymouth without his help, as he was a well-loved figure there'. Nancy's devotion to parliamentary life had taken its toll on the domestic front, and Waldorf's ordering her to retire damaged relations between them irremediably. 'Please put the family before your parliamentary career,' David begged her, adding that 'this quarrel is a frightful strain, and I personally feel exhausted by it'. Nancy threatened to return to the States; Waldorf's health suffered; David had to assure Nancy that 'there is no conspiracy between him and me to do you down, as you sometimes seem to imagine'. From now on Waldorf and Nancy led increasingly separate lives: the world in which David had grown up was crumbling away and, with his military career now ended, he could devote himself single-mindedly to the profession in which he would make his name.

13

Foreign Editor

With his military career behind him, David was at long last able to join the *Observer* on a full-time basis. 'My anxiety is not to be a dilettante in either capacity,' he told Nancy apropos both his marriage and his new position on the paper. 'It is quite difficult to become an efficient foreign editor.' Foreign affairs were to prove his overriding interest as the *Observer*'s editor, and his new position was to provide him with invaluable experience, but his ambitions for the family newspaper were not restricted to warning about the Soviet threat or promoting the dream of a federal Europe. Once the newsprint was available, the *Observer* should aim at a circulation of 500,000, publishing the 'best stuff, aesthetically and intellectually, that appears in any paper', he insisted. 'The *main* thing is to keep the paper in the same class as *The Times* in the matter of prestige. Its political opinions must be taken seriously by the serious-minded, its facts must be accepted as gilt-edged, and its literary and artistic patronage must be even more valued.'

With Waldorf increasingly frail, David was, in effect, the paper's proprietor as well as its future editor. Under the terms of a legal settlement drawn up between the then trustees (Waldorf, David, Tom Jones and Arthur Mann), Waldorf and David transferred their shares to the trustees, who were to be of 'the Protestant religion'; their aims included good relations between the English-speaking peoples, and the promotion of the freedom of the press, the independence of writers, and 'fearless educational and constructive policies'. 'I have had such disquieting experiences of cuckoos in the nest, Donald Tyerman being the most conspicuous, that I asked my father if he would insert some clause that prevented me from being pushed out of the *Observer* by future trustees, and he agreed,' David told TJ. Waldorf was equally anxious to protect David's interests. In a 'Memo re *Observer* and Family', he expressed the hope that the trustees and directors would give David 'a main share' in controlling the paper, and that he would one day take over as editor, since 'he has journalistic flair and particular aptitude and in general I support the political objectives he has in mind'. And David was bringing to the trust all his shares in the company, 'from which he might otherwise have derived a substantial income'. TJ, for his part, thought the trust 'a fine gesture on the part of Waldorf Astor to preserve the paper's independence of Political Party or Commercial Combination'.

Ivor Brown would remain the acting editor until David took over three years later, but new arrivals were already making their marks as far as the practicalities of *Observer* life were concerned. Two of them, Ken Obank and Charles Davy, had previously worked on the *Yorkshire Post*. A bluff, no-nonsense character who had also worked on the *Daily Herald*, Obank – in the words of David's future colleague Michael Davie – 'knew what life was like on a mass-circulation Fleet Street daily, which was more than anyone else at the *Observer* did'. 'Masterful and long-suffering', according to another colleague-in-waiting, Anthony Sampson, he was to become the long-serving managing editor, responsible – like the journalistic equivalent of a traffic policeman – for making sure the journalists and contributors delivered their copy on time, trimming it to size if needs be, and converting a disparate pile of articles, essays and reviews into a well-organised Sunday newspaper. According to Davie, 'the governing principle was that the *Observer* should be written by amateurs. So the amateurs would write what they wanted, and then, on Saturdays, the professionals would turn up from other papers, and produce the paper.' The 'harsh mechanics of newspaper production' took over, and whereas 'the editor proposed, Obank, most of the time, disposed'. He 'laid out every page, selected every picture, placed every story', sitting alongside and working closely with the news editor; and without him the paper 'would never have been printed on time'. Although 'the easiest and most sociable of companions' out of hours, he had a fearsome temper, and was famed for having hurled a typewriter out of a second-storey window in Tudor Street; never the man to turn down a drink, 'he could run wild after dark and was not unknown to the Bow Street constabulary', and more than once he had to be rescued from a police station after being arrested for being drunk and disorderly. His increasingly right-wing views were 'a reaction to the opinions he heard expressed at office conferences. He found the rambling and abstract nature of these occasions a sore trial as his practical mind dwelt on the prospect of late copy and missed trains.'

David's 'closest counsellor in the office was Charles Davy, who was both old and wise'. Cyril Dunn, who joined the *Observer* in 1947, and went on to report for the paper from South Africa and India, remembered Davy as 'a phenomenally aloof, remote character' who played an imaginary trombone when bending his mind to a subject. Kind, witty and considerate, he lived in Kent but slept most nights in the office and mended the tears in his shirt with Sellotape: cosy, cramped, more like a ramshackle club or common room than a conventional newspaper office, Tudor Street was his 'natural habitat', and Davy was 'the only one of us at the *Observer* towards whom D. Astor showed an unfailing deference', even though he 'invariably laughed when he talked about him, albeit lovingly'. Dunn recalled that he was 'the only reporter on the *Observer* with professional provincial training', and that Obank and Fred Tomlinson, the news editor, were the 'two real pros' on the paper, referred to by David as 'the Staff Captain' and 'Capability' Tomlinson.

Despite David's increasing dominance as editor-to-be and part-proprietor, he still deferred to Waldorf, and had to endure IB's nominal superiority. 'I feel highly embarrassed when appearing to press my claims to early accession to the editorial chair,' David told TJ in the summer of 1945, shortly after moving to the paper, but 'you don't, like me, hear the woes of the writers who, since Donald Tyerman's departure, have laboured to trim the sails of a ship whose captain is rather dormant and indecisive. They get discouraged, and without my intervention we would have lost Deutscher, Haffner and Schumacher, and may yet do so if IB isn't watched.' He despaired after Brown told him over lunch that he would like to remain as acting editor for another two years, but the old guard urged him to exercise patience and restraint. Waldorf and TJ worried that Brown might defect to the *Sunday Times* if provoked too far: Waldorf believed that 'for many readers he fills a place comparable to Miss Lejeune', and that thanks to him 'the prestige of the paper and its tone have never been higher'; TJ reported Arthur Mann as hoping that David would not 'sweep away the props like IB and Davy', and worried about his tendency 'to get obsessions, like de Gaulle and now Russia'. TJ believed that Brown's departure would be a 'calamity not easily repaired'. But David was unimpressed. 'If it is true that I have been the main creative influence on the paper since JLG went, and if the results have not been too bad, I ask that my advice be listened to on future arrangement,' he told his old mentor. Brown had a 'discouraging and pedestrian attitude' and could be 'quite rude and surly when he likes', and 'I ask *not* to be treated as an overenthusiastic and under-experienced young man.'

By the time Cyril Dunn joined the paper in 1947, 'David Astor was in total control of what was going on and Ivor Brown was making no attempt to disguise his figurehead status.' He still presided over editorial conferences 'like a wise and irritably confused old owl surrounded by all the gyrations of the Birds of Paradise': the proceedings were dominated by David's Central Europeans, and by Sebastian Haffner in particular, with Arthur Koestler sometimes in attendance. Dunn thought Koestler's first piece for the paper was 'frightful – ponderous, prolix and boring', and Dunn soon realised that IB 'didn't much care for the German exotics D. Astor had included in his new team'. 'Do you agree that Schumacher is a bore on paper? He wraps up his opinion in a swaddle of academic dullness,' IB unwisely asked David, adding that 'to me, as an editor striving to produce something people want to read, he is a pain in the orchestra stalls'. Dunn remembered Brown as 'a deeply old-fashioned character, more like somebody I'd read about in a late-Victorian novel than somebody I'd met', but he 'respected his enormous reputation, and was as fond as anyone could be of a man who seemed (from my lowly viewpoint) remote and grumpy'. But Dunn soon realised that 'the atmosphere I found throbbing in the Tudor Street air when I arrived had obviously been created by DA, and didn't seem to excite, or even to interest, IB very much'. Although 'my sympathies then were more often with IB than with DA, what I witnessed were the birth-pangs of an *Observer* sensationally different from anything in its own past and a paper unique and wonderful in Western journalism as a whole'. He soon discovered that David's modesty and diffidence were combined with determination and a degree of ruthlessness: 'I was made to realise, in spite of my ultimate devotion to David Astor, that behind that shy charm was solid steel, capable of being applied quite cruelly in what he believed to be (almost always correctly) the paper's interests.'

'My position was exalted but frustrating,' Brown recalled in his memoirs. With paper rationing still in force – it would not be lifted until 1957 – there was little room, he felt, for editorial improvements, and 'editing became subediting, a tailor and cutter's job, and writing meant the cramping into a paragraph of what needed a column'. 'I knew that I was a stopgap,' he confessed, on top of which 'I had no experience of administrative journalism and I did not care much for its minutiae.' Remembered by Dunn as 'a sweet little man, but an *obvious* misfit in the Astorian retinue', J. C. Trewin was even less suited to life in the post-war *Observer*. 'How can we have a literary editor who's afraid to use the telephone?' David demanded. Another survivor from a gentler world was the paper's Far East expert, O. M. Green, stone deaf, and 'a pure Edwardian, courtly and loveable'. TJ was worried by David's dismissive attitude towards the old guard. 'Lots of conventional readers will prefer

IB's contributors to yours, and his literary reputation is much higher than yours,' he told David after learning of a fresh row between the two men – and 'I hope you have not dismissed Trewin without securing him an alternative post.'

'Tall, handsome, apparently (though probably not actually) relaxed to the point of indifference', Hugh Massingham, the political editor, was a survivor from the old order who did meet with David's qualified approval. The son of the editor H. W. Massingham and the brother of the rural writer H. J. Massingham, he was well informed and well connected, particularly with the Bevanite wing of the Labour Party: 'a large and picturesquely untidy specimen who swears assertively', according to Dunn, he liked to give 'the impression that his week's work for the *Observer* amounted to a couple of telephone calls on a Thursday – the only day he showed up usually'. Colin Legum, soon to become the paper's African expert, remembered Massingham as 'an attractive bear of a man, a badly stuttering hypochondriac who had to be fetched in the office car from his house in Wellington Square every morning, bringing his handwritten column for a tense hour with the editor, usually devoted to toning down the Bevanite and pro-Labour slant of his column'.

According to Cyril Dunn, new arrivals on the paper were 'given a circular on green paper setting out Orwell's advice on how to write'. Some of these new arrivals went on to become permanent fixtures, such as Robert Stephens, a specialist in the Middle East who later became the diplomatic editor; the tempestuous Nora Beloff, who started her long career at the *Observer* in 1948 as the Paris correspondent; and Edward Crankshaw, who had been attached to the British Embassy in Moscow during the war, most probably as an MI6 agent, wrote books and articles on Russia and Mitteleuropa, and was 'half flattered, half bullied' by David into providing 'what was in effect a continual running commentary on what I thought the Russians were up to at home and abroad': David gave him 'the wherewithal to travel almost at will, though I was never a member of his staff'. Others proved to be more ephemeral figures. On Dunn's first day in the office he spotted the Australian journalist Alan Moorehead, who had made his name as a war correspondent for the *Daily Express* and reported for the *Observer* from India and Germany before deciding to abandon journalism for a lucrative career as a writer, and the red-haired Irish writer Honor Tracy, whom they were thinking of sending to Japan: a reluctant Fred Tomlinson had been told to develop her news sense – 'she either has a news sense or she hasn't', he complained – and since she got on David's nerves she was soon shown the door.

As foreign editor, David employed various friends and acquaintances as short-lived foreign correspondents. Orwell was sent to France and Germany in the last weeks of the war: he met Hemingway in Paris, and was frustrated to arrive in Germany too late to get a taste of what life had been like under the Third Reich; David was disappointed by his pieces, but – more importantly in terms of the *Observer*'s reputation as a campaigning newspaper over the next thirty years – Orwell urged him to interest himself in the decolonisation of Africa to make sure 'we didn't make the same mistakes we'd made in India', and to do so 'regardless of the political mistakes the Africans might then make'. The historian Hugh Trevor-Roper and the publisher George Weidenfeld reported from Central Europe, and Clare Hollingworth from Yugoslavia and Jerusalem.

David also enlisted Christabel Bielenberg, the Anglo-Irish wife of Trott's great friend Peter Bielenberg and the niece of Lord Northcliffe, who had spent the war years in Germany with her husband and small children, and briefly returned to Germany before eventually settling in the Irish countryside. Meeting David again after the war, he had 'the same boyish good looks. The same shy, almost self-effacing manner, but, above all, when it came to problems . . . a unique sense of personal involvement and an immediate searching for some solution. I could well understand why Adam considered him to be someone special.' David appointed her an official correspondent, which meant she had to wear a uniform and help out Bob Stephens, then based in Berlin; but what really excited them both was trying to help the widows of the men executed after the 20 July plot against Hitler. She took him to Imshausen to meet Trott's widow, Clarita, and their two little daughters, and David promised to do all he could to set up a fund for the widows, possibly involving the publisher Victor Gollancz, the Bishop of Chichester, George Bell, and Isobel Cripps. 'When it came to the value of friendship and to the possibility of injustice, David was like a hound on the trail,' Christabel Bielenberg recalled: the 20 July Memorial Fund had a tiny office in the top floor of Tudor Street, where 'Diana Hopkinson could be found battling with a typewriter she had not made use of since Oxford', and David maintained his support for the widows and their families long after the end of the war.

One of the most flamboyant new arrivals was Patrick O'Donovan, a product of Ampleforth, Christ Church and the wartime Irish Guards, who had been recommended to David by the diplomat Nico Henderson and the writer Robert Kee, and arrived in Tudor Street with no journalistic experience whatsoever. 'I got him on the basis of an essay he'd written on one of the Brontë sisters,' David recalled: he thought well of it, and IB for once agreed. 'I have landed a job as a journalist here. The pay is exiguous and my position could hardly be more humble,' O'Donovan reported back to his old English master at Ampleforth. 'It is very different from being an elderly major in the Irish Guards, but no doubt I shall get used to it.' Frank Pakenham intervened when he learned that O'Donovan was being paid £6 a week, telling David that 'either you pay and employ this man properly, or you sack him'. Despite Pakenham's intervention, O'Donovan continued to spend most of his time in a 'large leather chair in the library'. One day he turned up to find that the office was entirely empty. 'Even the agricultural correspondent, in some other guise, had been sent abroad to cover a story,' recalled his future wife, Hermione Fitzherbert-Brockholes, then working as David's secretary. O'Donovan saw no reason why he too shouldn't enjoy a foreign jaunt, and he was sent to Berlin – the first move in his career as a roving correspondent, reporting from every corner of the globe from China to Poland and the Middle East and covering both the Greek Civil War and Churchill's funeral.

A red-faced, hard-drinking, convivial Irishman, and a devout Roman Catholic, O'Donovan went on to lead a charmed life on the *Observer*, spending time as an erratic Washington correspondent, where he was fondly remembered for writing a report on Bobby Kennedy's funeral before it had taken place, setting it in bright sunlight when in fact it took place at night. David considered him the finest writer on the paper; in an addendum to O'Donovan's obituary in *The Times*, David noted how 'he had a baroque taste for the extravagant gesture and occasional touches of Gaelic abandon', and how 'he never lost his amused curiosity in people and the passing scene, which was what ultimately made his personality and his writing so attractive'. Robert Kee, who met him at Oxford, remembered him as a 'slightly arrogant, amusing, generous and educative friend' whose skill at blending 'a theatrical effect with a human approach to people and events was the secret of both his personal and his journalistic style'. Like so many of the best journalists, he left little behind beyond a pile of yellowing press cuttings, and today he is a forgotten figure, but he loomed large in *Observer* life. Cyril Dunn considered him 'an upper-class glamour boy', but conceded that he was a quick learner, soon mastering the journalistic essentials of writing to length and getting copy in on time, and that he was 'a wonderful Ignorant Reporter', who could 'make a Notebook of genius out of a village sale of work or summarise a vast political crisis in some foreign land with a tremendous air of authority after being there for forty-eight hours'. He was 'grossly indulged by Astor' in that he was often allowed to work from home and spend long periods of time away from the paper, and 'one of the minor hardships of my *Observer* life is listening to people praise Patrick O'Donovan, though I think he's brilliant too'.

The pre-war *Observer* had, at most, a couple of journalists covering foreign news, and to offset the costs of O'Donovan and his like, David set up Servob, a syndicated news service which commissioned pieces from the paper's journalists and sold them on to foreign and provincial papers. Ian Fleming had recently set up the Kemsley Newspapers' Foreign and Imperial News Service, known as Mercury, providing a similar service for the otherwise rather soporific *Sunday Times*, which devoted far less attention to foreign affairs, and David was anxious not to trail in the wake of the *Observer*'s only rival among the Sunday papers. Ronald Harker was Servob's first and long-serving editor: the service had six subscribers in 1946, and nearly a hundred by the end of the next decade.

Despite David's efforts to revitalise the paper, life on the *Observer* remained an engagingly casual business. Years later Michael Frayn described Tudor Street as a 'great warren of little offices, a lot of old houses joined together', and Cyril Dunn remembered how 'in the early Tudor Street days everyone seemed to drift in and out at will: of the writers I was about the only one who kept anything resembling office hours, though others had no doubt less recognisable routines of their own'. As one of the few professional journalists working on the paper, Dunn was a fast worker who made a point of meeting his deadlines, and he noted in his diary that 'this never fails to impress my colleagues who have no experience of working against the clock on a daily'. Gritta Weil, a German refugee who joined the paper as a secretary in 1945 after working for Schumacher at the Institute of Statistics in Oxford, found herself sharing an office with Willi Guttman, Ken Obank and Fred Tomlinson: she recalled how Sebastian Haffner and Isaac Deutscher argued endlessly, Deutscher perched on a stool while Haffner strode to and fro, waving his arms about; how Charles Davy's office chair converted into a bed on which he could spend the night; and how Patrick O'Donovan came into the office on Saturday mornings in a chalk-striped suit and bowler hat, and began work by rummaging through the waste-paper baskets in search of rejected copy. As was often the case in offices in those days, when phone calls were comparatively few and far between, Miss Shelton the switchboard operator listened in to conversations, yanking out the flex if they went on too long ('I don't care if you're Lord Longford or who you are!'). The front office was manned by a 'jovial cockney' called Charles Vidler, who had previously been a butler

Nancy Astor with her children: Bobbie Shaw, Bill, Wissie, David, Michael and Jakie.

At Sandwich (left to right): Michael, Bill, Waldorf, Jakie, Wissie, Nancy, David.

(*Above left* and *above*) David as a child, and (*left*) playing tennis at Rest Harrow, Nancy Astor's 'seaside cottage' in Sandwich Bay, and on horseback on Jura (*below*).

David (front) with Bobbie, Bill, Waldorf, Nancy and Wissie.

Electioneering: Bill, David, Waldorf, Nancy and Wissie.

Philip Kerr, Lord Lothian

J. L. Garvin

Ivor Brown

Tom Jones

(*Above*) David (right) and
Adam von Trott in the garden at
Cliveden in the summer of 1939.

(*Right*) Adam von Trott at his trial
for treason, August 1944.

(*Right*) Bridget and David Astor on their wedding day, 28 February, 1952.

(*Left*) Talking to a basset hound, France, 1953.

(*Overleaf*) David at Sutton Courtenay, *c*. 1960.

at Cliveden but – or so it was said – had been sacked after being found asleep in Lord Astor's bed. The lunch-hour drinking was prodigious, and a slumped figure in a mackintosh could well turn out to be a distinguished man of letters, very much the worse for wear.

'The most brilliant of our intellectuals', in Dunn's opinion, was a young man named William Clark – and he was not only 'ostentatiously brilliant', but had 'high academic achievements to justify it'. An Oxford graduate, he had spent the war years in Washington with the British Information Services, and contributed pieces to the *New Statesman*. When, in 1946, David asked Isaiah Berlin, then attached to the British Embassy, if he could recommend a bright young man to act as the *Observer*'s Washington correspondent, Berlin told him that Clark stood 'head and shoulders' above other British correspondents then working in Washington: he 'writes with great facility and sharpness, and is a pundit on American affairs', and was 'learned, accurate, brilliant and an intellectual'. Clark regretfully turned down David's offer, but within the year he would be making his mark at the *Observer*. Ebullient, gregarious and homosexual, Clark was witty, loved gossip, and was a shameless name-dropper. 'Oh no, he's *much* too close to her' was David's reaction when, a few years later, someone suggested that Clark should write a Profile of the queen.

Back in London, Clark was keen to write a piece about the Marshall Plan, the Truman administration's master plan to offset economic collapse in Europe and counteract Soviet influence, launched in 1948. The British press had, as yet, shown little interest in the subject, but after Kingsley Martin at the *New Statesman* had told him that such an article should be written by an economist, Clark walked from Great Turnstile to Tudor Street, where he asked to see David, who had recently been elevated to the editorship. He was told that David didn't normally come into the office on Mondays, but that he would be in later that day. David had a blind spot about economics, but he quickly realised what an important story this was. As an enthusiast for a united Europe, he welcomed the Marshall Plan: he regarded Stalin's Russia with deep suspicion, and resented the anti-Americanism prevalent in post-war Britain across the political spectrum, with the left raging about rampant capitalism while the right resented American views on the empire and the all-pervasive influence of American popular culture. And he agreed to Clark's radical suggestion that the *Observer* should emulate a recent issue of the *New Yorker*, in which the entire magazine had been given over to extensive extracts from John Hersey's book on Hiroshima: eight years later, prompted by Ken Obank, he cleared the decks once again, this time for Mr Khrushchev's celebrated speech denouncing Stalin to the Soviet praesidium in 1956. (Harold Ross's *New Yorker* seems to have been a great influence on David, not only in the care devoted to Profiles, but in the readiness to employ writers as well as professional journalists.)

The *Observer* was still restricted to eight pages – as a result of the 1947 dollar crisis, it had to abandon its monthly ten-page issue – and four of those were given over to the Marshall Plan, under the title 'The Rescue of Europe'. David asked Clark to help out. According to Clark, David produced 'the hard core of the *Observer*'s Marshall Plan doctrine', ably assisted by Haffner, who 'bustled into the editor's office, carrying a bundle of typescript pages'. The end product 'had the clear flavour of the *Observer*'s editorial staff, including the strong European element, the brilliant rhetoric of Haffner, and finally the moderating but still radical rationalisms of David Astor'. David's greatest contribution, in Clark's opinion, was that 'he felt on level terms with the Americans, neither suspecting them of all evil motives, nor supposing that they were without a powerful band of pirates who wished to extend American influence and trade as far as they possibly could'. According to Clark, the paper's coverage of the Marshall Plan infuriated right-wing Tories by pointing out that Britain could no longer hold the empire together, but looked to the United States for economic and military support – a premonition, perhaps, of the fury David would unleash eight years later with his opposition to Eden's Suez misadventure.

Clark was intrigued and impressed by the editorial conferences. Outside experts were often asked to attend, including Beveridge, Barbara Ward and Oliver Franks. Christabel Bielenberg came along if she was in London, and remembered how the meetings were presided over by IB in 'a small dimly lit room around a long narrow table smothered with an assortment of books and papers'; IB barely spoke, occasionally interjecting in a gruff voice with 'What about Spain?' or 'All right. Let us turn to Africa.' At his first meeting, Clark realised that 'more than half the editorial group was German or Central European', reflecting what Dunn described as 'David's sympathy for refugees and his indestructible respect for the brilliance of the Jewish mind': David modestly reminded them that 'we Astors are only German-American refugees from a little peasant holding'. But the Central Europeans were 'not a well-knitted group', and with IB seemingly bored or indifferent, 'it was always David who intervened in the discussions to settle a point with quiet authority and, as I saw it, with correct judgement'. David was greatly influenced by whoever his mentors or guiding spirits were at the time – when Clark joined the paper these included Stafford Cripps and George Bell, the Bishop of Chichester – 'but whatever David learned from his mentors he always digested and thought through for himself, never having any real doubt about the competence of his mind – without any particular expert learning – to see his way to solutions.'

'David Astor as a presiding genius was so modest, so tentative, so little claiming to specialist knowledge of far parts of the world (he had travelled very little in those days) and yet so editorially decisive on the basis of principles that he held firmly and thoughtfully that I came to admire him (though often disagreeing) more than any of my previous bosses,' Clark recalled. David was as modest as ever about his gifts and achievements. After describing a nightmare in which membership of the Athenaeum had been thrown open to all Marine officers – 'in every room and corridor there were depressing faces with big mustachios, hearty guffaws and that uniform that every time I see it makes me feel like a guilty schoolboy expecting reproof' – David told TJ that he had 'very little confidence in myself as a writer and not full confidence in my political judgement unless it is tempered by the advice of several other people'. He trusted his judgement of character, but 'I know that I am short on factual knowledge, reading, ability to write and certain qualities, such as patience, which I hope that time and perseverance will correct.'

David's political views were those to which he would adhere for most of his life. To Nancy's annoyance, the *Observer* was not opposed to the Labour government's post-war policy of nationalisation, though David himself, influenced by his friend John Strachey, favoured a mixed economy; and he was better disposed to the Attlee administration than IB, who remained 'an old-fashioned Balliol liberal'. In the run-up to the 1945 election the *Observer* published articles by representatives of the three main political parties – an even-handed approach that was followed in later years, and mirrored by Allen Lane at Penguin Books. David believed that a non-party paper 'might get a better hearing for liberal ideas and a new look at international relations'; the post-war *Observer* 'had no platform, but attempted to apply rationality and a humanistic morality to the real world'. Anxious to combine fairness with enterprise, he thought that 'a mixed capitalist and socialist economy is not just a tolerable compromise, but the most efficient and humane of economic systems'. As such, he was to become an influential exponent of 'Butskellism', opposed to extremes of left and right and sympathising with the views of moderate Tory and Labour politicians alike.

As far as foreign affairs were concerned, he continued his wartime support for a federal Europe, ideally under British leadership and including

Germany, as Trott would have wished. To advance the cause he funded Joseph Retinger, a political visionary who had been parachuted into wartime Poland in his fifties, saw a united Europe as a counterweight to the Soviet Union, and founded the influential Europe Movement. Writing to Beveridge in the summer of 1945, David emphasised the need to resist the USSR and 'her sabotage of effective international co-operation', and to work closely with the democracies of Europe. 'The great fallacy of the democratic Left all over the world is to imagine that Stalin is on the Left,' he continued. 'If Left or Progressive means "tending to liberty and internationalism" and Right or Reactionary means "tending to autocracy or nationalism", then Stalin does not belong to the Left at all. If, on the other hand, Left merely means "the increase of state control", then Hitler and Mussolini were on the Left.' And in a letter to his future colleague John Pringle, David wrote that 'I don't believe that "the Left" in this country, whether informed Fleet Street intellectuals or less informed Labour Party members, will ever find the self-confidence and courage to face the situation that is developing, in which it is Russia that presents the totalitarian threat and that plays the imperialist game. They will just bleat "Down with the Tories", fight minor domestic issues, and funk the larger international ones.'

Churchill had regarded Stalin with deep suspicion since 1943, but looking back on the post-war period, David wrote that 'the lack of understanding of what Russia's post-war policy would be under Stalin showed the same tendency to think in terms of nations and races rather than ideologies'. Anti-German rather than anti-fascist during the war, the government had been slow to realise that 'a defeated Germany would become our natural partner in holding off Russian Communist pressure. I don't like to appear boastful in saying that I did rather better than HMG in forecasting this.'

Nancy was increasingly hostile to David's, and the *Observer*'s, independent line. 'David needs your help more than any of the others and secretly wants it – so why not try to help him instead of running him down?' Waldorf implored her. She worried that David would make the *Observer* a 'socialist' paper: according to Waldorf, 'she must begin the day with a hymn of hate against the socialists', while their son Jakie listed his mother's bêtes noires as 'socialism, Roman Catholicism, psychiatry, the Jews, the Latins and the *Observer*'. Jakie would soon disgrace himself, in his mother's eyes, by marrying a Roman Catholic, and Nancy's war of attrition against the *Observer* would run for the rest of her life.

★

David's marriage, in the meantime, was unravelling. 'I know what this family disappointment must mean to you,' Waldorf told him. 'I feel sure you will grow in strength and that you can still look forward to a real home and family life.' Writing to Marion Doenhoff from the Haute-Savoie, David admitted that the imminent arrival of Melanie and their daughter 'sets me in a state of much tension': whereas Frances was 'the light of my life', Melanie 'takes an attitude towards me that suggests that *everything* about me is all wrong'. Part of the problem was 'whether she really "waited" for me sufficiently loyally during the war', and whether her attention hadn't strayed elsewhere. Nor did his grief over Trott help matters. 'My wife used to say "You live with the dead", but that was not the chief cause of her dissatisfaction,' he told Marion Doenhoff after his marriage had finally broken up. 'I, like you, have serious difficulties in "giving" myself unreservedly to the opposite sex, chiefly because of the unsatisfactory childhood relationship with my mother and its effect on my basic attitude towards all women.'

Marion Doenhoff was to remain a lifelong friend, co-operating with him on support for the widows of the July 1944 plot and, years later, for African National Congress leaders in South Africa; but she was not the only woman in his life. Writing to Annie Lacoste in the summer of 1946, David referred to their having been in Paris the previous week. 'You are simply my Paradise,' he told her. 'It would have been Paradise to spend a lifetime with you', and 'I did not believe it was possible for me to be really happy or really at home with another person.' The following year she emigrated to Argentina with her new husband, and she wrote to David before boarding ship at Le Havre. He had made her very happy, she told him, and 'I shall never regret it. Besides, you are the fair hero of all the legends.'

14

Coming into his Inheritance

'In the character of this paper, ethics matter more than politics. The particular ethics could be roughly defined as trying to do the opposite of what Hitler would have done,' David once wrote in a 'Memo on the Soul of the Paper'. He went on to say that the *Observer*'s 'personality was established in and just after the last war by people drawn together more by being "anti-fascist" than by anything else', and because he was 'haunted by what Hitler showed to exist in all us ordinary people', he was 'specially interested in antidotes to the kind of thinking he stimulated in people and they so readily adopted'. These 'contra-Hitler attitudes' should be spelt out in his own words, since they inspired and permeated David's long editorship of the *Observer*: they included

> treating opponents respectfully; opposing those who work up hatreds, but doing so non-violently; trying to understand people and to explain them to each other; valuing differences; not exaggerating your own case; avoiding overdramatisation or enjoyment of the sensational; practising moral courage, particularly daring to stand up to ridicule, and showing respect for that in others; discouraging herd thinking, particularly among those 'on our side'; religiously, pedantically respecting truth; honouring reason and its extension to the study of the overwhelmingly irrational in all of us; challenging taboos and legends, particularly those our sort of reader usually accepts; avoiding the cheap and spurious, and resisting the idea that it doesn't matter much what we say as it will soon be forgotten; cultivating moderation with 'extreme' endurance; discouraging fighting for its own sake, but daring to pursue an unpopular cause solitarily; being wary of destructiveness, even when represented as an entertaining, cleansing or rejuvenating operation; deliberately cultivating doubt and scepticism, but not cynicism; practising self-criticism – as liberals, as internationalists, as journalists – as well as dishing it out to everyone else.

'I live for my work', David once declared, and although people expected him to be an authoritative figure, 'I'm personally a great believer in doubt and hesitation': he considered doubt to be 'a positive virtue, a quality to be cultivated', and editorial decisions 'should be based on a great deal of doubt, a great deal of hesitation, to be worth reading'. But although David was sometimes portrayed as the quintessential well-meaning but woolly-minded liberal, dithering over alternatives, unable to make up his mind until the very last minute, and over-addicted to interminable editorial conferences – 'the editor's indecision is final' is usually attributed to Katharine Whitehorn and, like David's alleged ignorance of mortgages, became a cherished item of *Observer* folklore – he had, from his earliest days on the paper, a very clear idea of what the *Observer* should stand for, how it should be run, and what he believed in; and, as we have seen, his charm, his generosity and his diffidence were combined with a degree of ruthlessness and determination without which he could never have survived as the editor of a national newspaper, let alone earned an international reputation as one of the outstanding editors of the last century.

David was only in his mid-thirties when he finally took over as editor in August 1948, and his sense of coming into his inheritance at last was combined with the need for reassurance. 'Your fatherly advice will be needed now more than ever, when I am trying to discover what an editor ought to do,' he told Arthur Mann a week after assuming office. 'You are so much more knowledgeable and much more brilliant than I am,' he informed William Clark some six months later. 'You also know what misgivings I have about my own position.' 'You probably regard me as a successful person and maybe others do too, whereas with the perspective of all my 37 years, in which the last year of overseeing seems the merest episode, I see myself v opposite,' he wrote to Clark from Chamonix, where he was on a skiing holiday: he could only 'disconnect myself 100% from the paper' when away from London, but since he was reading *Scoop* at the time, he had hardly divorced himself from newspapers altogether.

Disconnecting himself from the *Observer* would become a near impossibility as he became ever more involved, but later that year he found himself wondering whether he should not stand down in the interests of the paper. William Haley had started out as a copy-taker on *The Times* and gone on to edit the *Manchester Evening News* before joining the BBC, of which he was made the director general in 1944. He had given advice about setting up the Observer Trust, and Waldorf saw him as a possible successor as chairman of the trust. David was keen to make use of his newspaper experience at the *Observer* – so much so that, for a brief moment, he contemplated stepping aside in favour of the older man. In the end, though, ambition prevailed. He had decided against giving up the editorship, he told Arthur Mann, 'as I am young and it is the work which pleases me more than any other. My other cause for reluctance is that, having a conspicuous name, I cannot easily get work elsewhere' – if cast adrift, he might fall victim to 'the idea that I am simply a "rich man's baby", the boss's son, who therefore cannot be a person of real ability'. Haley went on to become the revered editor of *The Times*, and would write David letters of advice and encouragement over the years to come.

If Haley was never a real threat, the hapless Ivor Brown was now a broken reed. 'I will do my very best to ease IB's position and make it as honourable as possible,' David had assured Arthur Mann early in 1948, though 'I perfectly realise that after 1 August IB will be generally regarded in Fleet Street as a martyr to nepotism. I also realise that the whole situation can be made disagreeable by his sulkiness, and probably will be.' Five years were to pass before Brown finally quit the scene, but in the meantime IB's eagerness to look after the arts and books pages brought its own problems. 'It is on the literary pages that the *Observer* is weakest,' David told Mann, and he was determined to do something about it: the books pages loomed large in the minds of Sunday-paper readers, and although the *Observer* could boast Harold Nicolson as its lead reviewer, the *Sunday Times* would, before long, be fielding Cyril Connolly and Raymond Mortimer in opposition. 'I would be unwilling to take on the editorship unless I am allowed to reorganise the editorial control of the books pages,' David declared, adding that 'I am of course quite willing to have the "showdown" with IB myself if that is what you decide that I should do.'

'IB likes easy safe people like Robert Lynd, or near nonentities like Trewin,' David complained: 'weak in initiative and enterprise, strong in criticism', he made no effort to get good people onto the arts pages. He had 'snubbed' Alan Pryce-Jones as a book reviewer, and grudgingly accepted William Emrys Williams as the new radio critic, but his most severe criticisms were still reserved for George Orwell. Not only had IB ignored Orwell's suggestion that he should approach E. M. Forster as a contributor, but 'he didn't want to take Orwell back on the page and I had practically to force him. Finally he wrote Orwell an invitation which was so discouraging that Orwell asked me whether he ought not to decline it.' Nor was IB averse to treating Orwell like a tyro book reviewer who needed to be told how such things should be done. He complained that Orwell's review of a new book by Kenneth Williamson did little more than summarise its contents: could Orwell 'give a bit more colour' to his review, since 'readers and publishers like to see signs of encouragement for good work'? 'I'm sorry, but it was an *awful* book,' Orwell told David. 'I am not prepared to give praise on literary grounds to books of this kind. One sinks one's standards to below zero by pretending that they exist in a literary sense at all.'

'What I need is not two indifferent literary editors but one good one,' David decided. 'This means displacing Trewin and converting IB into "Associate" instead of Lit Ed Senior, and finding a new man.' IB regarded this as a 'deep personal humiliation' and strongly objected to Trewin's dismissal: he would accept his new title provided it 'had real meaning and responsibilities', and he hoped he could still be associated with the cultural pages and deal in some capacity with reviewers, which 'is especially necessary with such small papers as we have today in which long-winded or inexperienced intellectuals are worse than useless'. He also pointed out that the circulation had risen by 150,000 during his nominal editorship: this was a slight exaggeration – it had risen from 241,000 in 1942 to 359,000 in 1947 – and, with the print unions beginning to flex their muscles, the easy profits of the war years would soon be behind them.

Alan Pryce-Jones had joined the *Times Literary Supplement* after his 'snubbing' by IB, and David tried to persuade him to join the *Observer* as literary editor rather than succeed Stanley Morison as editor of the *TLS*. Pryce-Jones declined, but recommended instead his friend Jim Rose, a product of Rugby and Balliol who had worked at Bletchley Park during the war. At his interview, Rose told David that he'd really like to work on the foreign desk, and claimed that he was not qualified to be a literary editor since he knew no writers or publishers, and was not particularly well read. 'Fine. That's just what we need,' David told him: he wanted the books pages to be free of literary cliques and aimed at the general reader, and Rose seemed ideally suited for the job. 'A highly sophisticated character' with a 'man of the world style', according to Cyril Dunn, Rose held the post from 1948 to 1951, when he left to join the International Press Institute in Geneva. Years later, after the death of Allen Lane, he proved an ineffectual and soon-forgotten boss of Penguin Books – a post occupied soon after by David's old friend from Eton and Balliol, Peter Calvocoressi, with equally disastrous results.

After Rose's departure, David asked Patrick O'Donovan whom he should appoint as the next literary editor. 'You've got one in the office,' O'Donovan replied. A year or two earlier O'Donovan, visiting the Middle East for the *Observer*, had bumped into Terence Kilmartin, then working as a radio journalist in Jerusalem under the name Kevin Hyland – 'Kevin' was his second name, 'Hyland' his mother's maiden name – and had put him back in touch with David. Despite his lack of academic or literary qualifications, Kilmartin went on to become the finest and most discriminating literary editor of his day, remaining *en poste* until 1986, and dealing firmly but politely with reviewers as distinguished and diverse as A. J. P. Taylor, Philip Toynbee, Graham Greene, Isaiah Berlin, Edwin Muir, Christopher Sykes, W. H. Auden, Malcolm Muggeridge and Angus Wilson. A reserved, rather formidable figure, he inspired huge admiration in the literary world, still more so since he seemed immune to the wiles of publishers, publicity managers and literary agents. Cyril Dunn wrongly attributed his withdrawn manner to 'pure public school reticence' – he had attended a small Catholic school in Sussex – and found him 'a most odd mixture of competence and strong character with detached dreaminess', adding that 'I admired him enormously, but was never at ease with him.'

Appointing Kilmartin was an example of David's unrivalled ability as a talent-spotter, of his reliance on hunch and instinct, on a nose for literary flair rather than the dutiful perusal of a curriculum vitae citing a spell on the provincial paper followed by service on a national daily. 'I had no interest in conventional journalism, and don't to this day,' he told his colleague John Silverlight, looking back on his time as an editor. He liked to discover 'people of real power as writers and turn them into journalists', to take a risk with stylish young writers and 'give them a very free hand and encourage the news editor and the managing editor to treat them deferentially because a good writer is more important than the man who's editing him'. 'The governing principle was that it should be written by amateurs', Michael Davie remembered.

Davie was to have a long and varied career at the *Observer*, and for many years was widely regarded as David's heir apparent, but his appointment to the paper was far from ordinary. After serving in the navy during the war, he was in his final year at Oxford when Martin Wight, who had taught him history at Haileybury and was working part-time as the *Observer*'s diplomatic correspondent, told David that he could no longer combine journalism with an academic career, and that he was handing in his notice. David asked him to suggest a replacement; Wight mentioned Davie's name as a promising young man, and showed him a letter from Davie describing his summer holiday in Sandwich. David took Davie to lunch at Boodle's, and after the preliminary pleasantries 'David leaned forward, head on one side, and asked me, to my utter bewilderment,

whether I would consider becoming the *Observer's* diplomatic correspondent.' When Davie explained that he was still at Oxford, 'I was told
that that didn't matter in the least as I could be an undergraduate in the
early part of the week and diplomatic correspondent on Thursday, Friday
and Saturday.' Davie turned down the offer, but he reapplied after leaving
Oxford, and after a stint on the *Manchester Evening News* he was made
the *Observer's* religious correspondent. This involved talking to Waldorf
at Cliveden and playing golf with Nancy, 'who complained about the
number of Communists recruited for the paper by her son'. The whole
episode, Davie recalled, 'demonstrated a crucial tenet of David's creed',
namely that 'journalism is too important to be left to journalists. The
last thing it should be is a guild or profession whose members believe
in an exclusive right to write for newspapers because of their special
skills and wisdom.'

Best remembered by *Observer* readers as its long-serving lead book
reviewer, Philip Toynbee was just the sort of literary man to tickle
David's fancy. Wild, heavy-drinking, a product of Rugby and Christ
Church, Toynbee had been a Communist while at Oxford, worked in
intelligence during the war, written several novels and contributed to
Horizon. Stephen Spender remembered him as 'an eccentric, almost
Dostoevskian character who tried to live and write out of some demonic
force of which he was conscious in himself as being his personal truth',
and admired his 'serious, religious, self-mocking attitude to life'; for
George Weidenfeld, who employed him as the editor of *Contact*, Toynbee
was 'a rebel against authority of all kinds, a brilliant conversationalist
and social magnet. Tall, stooping, with a large domed forehead and a
booming voice, lively in argument and a lover of paradox, hard-drinking
and impulsive womanising, he was passionately convivial and clannish' –
though for all his left-wing sympathies, 'never in my long friendship with
Philip and his companions do I remember having met a member of the
working class'. Patrick Leigh Fermor noted how

His clothes were unbelievably raffish and baggy, looking as if they
had been slept in (they often had): frayed tweed jacket with holes
or old leather patches at the elbow, a check flannel shirt, a stringy
and moulting tie and footwear as unwieldy as ammunition boots.
He looked a bit grey and lantern-jawed on bad mornings, brow
often furrowed, complexion cratered here and there; and yet it was
a strong and distinguished face, with decisive features and a high
and thoughtful brow. It was often divided by a slit-like grin made

very comic and dissolute by an isolated fang on one side, rather
like Disney's Pluto, its neighbours absent through some mishap.

Ferdinand Mount remembers him, from his childhood, as 'a wild and
warm character who seems to my sister and me lovably childish, more
childish than we are'.

Toynbee had been recommended by George Orwell, who thought him
'gifted and politically OK', though 'I believe he drinks a lot.' His father,
the sage and historian Arnold Toynbee, was a pillar of Chatham House
and the Royal Institute of International Affairs, causes close to Waldorf's
heart, and according to David 'he got in touch with me to say that Philip
was going through a bad time after his break-up with Anne [Toynbee's
first wife] and was there anything I could do? There was only one thing
I could do, and that was to offer Philip a job on the *Observer*. He never
knew that this was the result of his father's proposal. I approached him
as though the idea had come from me.'

Toynbee had earlier smashed up the bathroom of the American ambassador's secretary in Cairo on a drunken spree with Donald Maclean,
soon to be notorious for defecting to Moscow with Guy Burgess. Wild
as he was, David sent him first to Israel as a reporter. 'He had enormous
curiosity about the infant Jewish state,' David recalled. 'His stories were
excellent, and he picked up the knack of news writing straight away.'
David was nervous about sending him out, since 'his credentials as a journalist were nil', and 'to break through the distinction that then obtained
between literary writing and news reporting was highly experimental',
but 'the experiment was, in this case, a real success'. (David later warmly
recommended him to William Haley for freelance work at the BBC – 'he
has political brains and is, now that Orwell has died, probably the best
of our younger non-Communist progressive writer-thinkers.')

Shortly afterwards, Arnold Toynbee wrote to say how pleased he was
that Philip was now firmly attached to the *Observer*. 'He came back the
other day looking a different man from the state he was in when he left,'
he told David. 'Discovering that he could do an important job that people
valued has, I'm sure, done a very great deal to him, and I am very conscious
of the personal kindness and goodwill you have shown him.' David, for his
part, relished Toynbee's 'great capacity for friendship', adding that 'there
was no one in the office whom he ignored, and there was no visitor to
our *Observer* lunches, no matter how eminent or awe-inspiring, whom he
did not treat as a brother when the rest of us might be treating the great
man either with awe or disdain.' Terry Kilmartin was equally impressed.

'I was in a sort of way his boss – that's how he liked to put it anyway, with a tug at his forelock – though in fact I was merely the chap who sent him books to review and corrected his spelling and punctuation,' he recalled, modestly comparing their relationship to that of 'a schoolmaster with an outstandingly brilliant pupil or an uncreative don with a wayward genius of a student'. Toynbee's great qualities were 'absolute independence of judgement uncluttered by snobbery or jobbery or fashion, combined with immense curiosity and excitement about areas of knowledge he wasn't entirely familiar with . . . He never failed to deliver on time, and had none of the touchiness, the temperamental prima-donnishness which in my experience are the hallmarks of the second-rate.' He seemed untidy and disorganised, and was often the worse for wear after a session in one of the *Observer*'s local pubs, but 'I have seen him, under pressure, sit down at a typewriter and produce a sizeable article in beautifully polished prose in the time it took him to type it.'

Though highly valued as a contributor to the paper, Toynbee was, like so many of his contemporaries at the *Observer*, poorly rewarded in material terms. David may have, in Lord Longford's words, 'sustained him through good times and bad (and there were not a few of the latter) with a tenderness peculiarly his own', but Toynbee's close friend Jessica Mitford confessed herself 'shocked at the meagreness of the loaf. His wages at the *Observer* were a fraction of what top-flight American reviewers are paid by publications of like reputation and prestige.' To compare the *Observer* with American papers was unrealistic, but Toynbee was not alone in feeling hard done by. The *Observer*'s wage structure was chaotic until the National Union of Journalists made itself felt towards the end of David's time as editor, and over the years many of Toynbee's most distinguished and long-serving contemporaries – including Michael Davie – would discover, to their mortification, that young journalists who had recently joined the staff were being paid far more than they were. This was not meanness on David's part, but an embarrassed reluctance to deal with money matters, combined with a rich man's innocence or ignorance of how most people scraped a living: 'Do you mean to say that most of my staff are living in debt?' he famously remarked after the meaning of a mortgage had been explained to him; he never took a salary himself, and more than once he let slip his assumption that his colleagues had private incomes.

David reluctantly agreed that the paper should turn its attention to the economy and to business matters – though it was not until 1958 that Andrew Shonfield from the *Financial Times* was appointed the paper's first economics correspondent – but he delegated office finances, including

salaries and wages, to his business manager, Tristan Jones, who joined
the paper in 1952. TJ's son – also known as 'TJ', in the office at least –
had joined the Life Guards at the outbreak of war, but had refused a
commission, and had spent three years in Germany after the war, working
for the Control Commission. An eccentric penny-pincher, he was best
remembered in the office for turning out the lights while people were
still at work: once installed as the 'moneybags', he kept a tight control
over everyday expenditure, and issued an unenforceable edict forbidding
members of staff to reveal or compare their earnings.

David may have averted his gaze from the sordid matter of salaries,
but he was, and would remain, the most generous of men in other ways:
not least towards his hero and exemplar, George Orwell, the 'writer I
admired, and envied, more than any other', and 'the outstanding person
of my day'. After Gollancz, Faber and Cape had turned down *Animal
Farm*, Orwell asked David if he would lend him £200 to enable him to
publish it himself: David was happy to do so, but urged the dispirited
Orwell to persist with other publishers. In the event Fred Warburg happily
agreed to publish: quite why Orwell hadn't gone to him in the first place
remains unclear, since Warburg had taken him on after Gollancz's rejection
of *Homage to Catalonia*. (Although David respected Gollancz, he shared
Orwell's suspicion of Kingsley Martin, the long-serving editor of the *New
Statesman*, and another 'fellow traveller': one of Orwell's legacies, David
recalled, was 'a *New Statesman* mini-vendetta. He and I didn't admire their
role in the 1930s, when Stalin's regime was being much less than truthfully
represented.') When Orwell started work on *Nineteen Eighty-Four*, David
got in touch with Margaret Fletcher, the owner of Barnhill, a remote and
windswept farmhouse in the far north of Jura, where Orwell could work
undisturbed. Orwell moved into Barnhill in 1947; David gave him the use
of a pony and trap, and (as requested) sent him a pair of size twelve boots.

Neither David nor Fred Tomlinson was, as yet, aware of how ill Orwell
was, and there was talk in the office of sending him to East Africa to write
about the Ground Nuts Scheme, and then on to South Africa to cover
the 1948 election. Towards the end of 1947 Orwell left Jura, and was
admitted to Hairmyres Hospital in Glasgow, suffering from tuberculosis.
His typewriter was taken away, and he asked Julian Symons to send him
a newfangled Biro so he could write some reviews for the *Observer* since
'I might as well make a bit of money while I'm on my back.' David had
been sending food parcels, butter and eggs to the hospital from the Jura
estate when Orwell's doctor, Bruce Dick, asked him whether he might
be able to use his family connections to obtain some streptomycin, a new

wonder drug which was available in the States but had not yet been tested or made available in Britain. David went ahead after checking with Nye Bevan, the Minister of Health, to make sure there would be no problems in his importing the drug: he also insisted on paying for it, while emphasising that 'the only possibility of persuading him [Orwell] to be reasonable is that it should be a very private matter between him and me'.

'Thanks awfully for seeing about the streptomycin', a grateful Orwell wrote to David, but time and his health were running out. He returned to Barnhill to complete *Nineteen Eighty-Four*, but before long he had been moved to a sanatorium in the Cotswolds. 'I fear the dream of Jura must fade out', Bruce Dick told David. Orwell wrote his last review for the *Observer* in February 1949, and in September he was moved to a private room (paid for by David) at University College Hospital. 'I remember visiting you when you had the sinus, but I didn't know it was in this hospital', Orwell wrote in a letter thanking David for sending fruit and flowers. A month later Orwell married Sonia Brownell, Cyril Connolly's former assistant on *Horizon*: a special licence was needed for them to be married in hospital, and David had arranged this with the Archbishop of Canterbury. David and Robert Kee were the two witnesses at the short ceremony, and afterwards David gave the bride and a group of Orwell's friends lunch at the Ritz. Orwell died in January. He wanted to be buried in a country churchyard, so David arranged matters with the vicar of Sutton Courtenay, and erected a gravestone bearing the name of the man he admired so much, and had done his best to help.

★

In a memo to his successor, written shortly after he had retired as editor of the *Observer*, David recalled that in the early days of his editorship 'we had no division between the planning of news, features and leader-page articles', and that 'Guttman's law' prevailed. Since, in Willi Guttman's opinion, people now got their news over the radio, this left the field open for the 'scoop by interpretation'. David was, by temperament, closer in spirit to a magazine editor than to the news-hungry editor of a daily paper, thriving off scoops and maddened with anger and frustration if pipped to the post by a rival paper. He was more interested in commenting on the news than in breaking it, and Guttman's law provided him with ample justification for indulging his passion for the *Horizon*-like ruminative essay. 'The whole paper was supposed to be an extended conversation with the readers, inspired throughout by the same enquiring attitude, always intellectually lively but never snobbish, exclusive or insiderish,' he continued, and 'by "interpretation" we did not intend opinionated prediction but rather description, analysis and explanation. We did not favour personalised "colour" writing, except in the case of a few talented writers like O'Donovan. We certainly didn't permit "committed" reporting: indeed writers like Deutscher and Haffner used to watch each other and complain effectively if anyone's report departed from objectivity.'

Nor was David prepared to see the *Observer* being used in a missionary cause. When his parents' old friend Lionel Curtis wrote to suggest that the paper should publish his pamphlet on how a federation of democracies might eventually lead to his dream of world government, David was sympathetic but unyielding. 'The most formative influence' on his political education had been Philip Kerr, Lord Lothian, 'and in these central matters you and he held the same views', he told Curtis, now safely installed as an unworldly fellow of All Souls. He was prepared to give Curtis 'a firm undertaking that I will spend my life working towards the political ends to which you have dedicated your life, and in the service of which Philip spent his', but 'what is unwise is for a newspaper to use its editorial columns for crusading on a particular issue. If it does so, it risks losing its status as a newspaper and becoming a weekly (or daily) pamphlet . . . A newspaper cannot pursue a political doctrine as can and should a pamphleteer. What a newspaper can and should do is to cultivate a certain viewpoint in its readers (which is something different from advocating a policy).' Waldorf had made the *Observer* both 'trust-owned' and 'non-party', he told Kenneth Harris – 'a young, bright, aspiring Welshman' who eventually specialised in long interviews for the paper – and although 'it mustn't be not committed. It must be able to take attitudes', but 'what it is not allowed to do is to align itself with a party, right or wrong'.

'One must run a paper by deciding all questions on their merit,' David told Arthur Mann, and a paper must never become a club for the editor's friends or 'ageing pensioners' (presumably a dig at IB): as far as he was concerned, he was 'ready and desirous of being judged on merit', and 'being an Astor I am accustomed since childhood to a certain amount of public obloquy'. And, like all the best editors, he had no time for polls listing readers' likes and dislikes, or for managerial advice on editorial matters. 'We should not be guided by what readers think, otherwise the paper will have its policies decided by them,' he told a colleague, adding that 'I edit the paper for myself and my friends.' And although he once said that 'I think I am a natural journalist in that I prefer to be a spectator or a commentator' to an active participant, he recognised that 'journalists were inclined to be arrogant and to assume a know-all position', not least where politicians were concerned: when wielding the blue pencil, he tended to 'substitute "should" for "must"', so earning the paper a reputation for seeming wishy-washy or dithering at times.

Needless to say, David took a keener interest in leaders and leader-page articles than in the news pages, and he kept an eagle eye on the weekly Profile, the 250-word 'Comments' on the leader page, an innovation suggested by Charles Davy, and the Pendennis gossip column, master-minded in its early years by the well-connected William Clark. David insisted on the unsigned Profiles being both fair and accurate: in the early years, he told Haley, subjects were sent copy 'to ask their assistance in the removal of any factually incorrect statements or inaccurate remarks', a policy that was dropped after Sir Thomas Beecham had threatened to sue unless all his corrections were incorporated. Colleagues were asked to write the Profiles, but David – who was an immaculate copy-editor – would then go through them line by line with a blue pencil, amending and fine-tuning as he went. 'I would say the chief thing (in trying to be unlike Adolf) is never to remove another's dignity, even if you think he is a charlatan or himself a derider or even an oppressor – and to avoid doing this even if it means passing up a good joke,' he wrote in his 'Memo on the Soul of the Paper'. 'I always censor the Political Diary and Pendennis pretty rigidly from this angle of not holding people up to mockery,' he added, and 'nobody, not even foreign Commies, should be considered "fair game"'.

Looking back on his time as editor some fifteen years after he retired, David told his first biographer that he felt uneasy when his editorial approach was summarised as 'choosing staff for their writing ability and then giving them their head', and supporting the underdog. Both were true, but they provided an incomplete account. 'Subjects or attitudes that were often regarded as opposites, I saw as complementary,' he told Richard Cockett. 'Perhaps because I admired two parents who had diametrically opposite characteristics . . . the theme of my journalism was often one of reconciliation or of synthesis, or simply of relatedness.' He 'always resisted the pressure from our left-inclined office from those who felt that Left meant Virtue and Right meant Vice', and since 'the *Observer* looked at politics, religion and morality with a more surprised and more inquisitive stare than the other papers', he always tried to 'study both sides of every conflict of the day'. 'Some of the best journalism I ever produced was from discovering in a conference that there were two very good cases that could be put for and against. I would then insist on their both going into the paper,' he told John Silverlight – exemplified by his simultaneously printing Sebastian Haffner's and Isaac Deutscher's diametrically opposed views on the Greek Civil War in 1944, and running pieces by the pro-Arab Clare Hollingworth alongside the pro-Jewish Patrick O'Donovan in 1948.

'The great attraction of journalism is that you can be involved in public affairs without being caught in the political machine,' David once told a colleague, and 'to liberals with a small "l" journalism is their natural let-out and an awful lot of journalists are liberals with a small "l"'. But liberalism should, ideally, be strong-minded and decisive, and 'my aim has been to be militant in fighting for tolerance, freedom of expression, non-prejudice – all causes of moderation – here and abroad. What's wrong with moderates is that they lack militancy.' And in a paper circulated to the staff not long before his retirement, David returned to the subject. For the last thirty years, he wrote, the *Observer* had been a 'non-party paper of the political centre. It has criticised the policies of both major parties when it considers them to have been illiberal. It has also been consistently anti-Marxist for the libertarian reasons that its former contributor, George Orwell, was anti-Marxist.'

Where the paper should stand on particular issues, and what line it should take, was thrashed out at the celebrated editorial conferences, dominated as they were by David's Central Europeans. 'Haffner struck me as easily the greatest in the group, a typical high-domed Herr Doktor,' William Clark recalled: he 'laid things on the line at editorial conferences with god-like authority', often crossing swords with Isaac Deutscher ('He was Russian-friendly, I was German-friendly,' Haffner recalled); Edward Crankshaw was irritated by Rix Loewenthal's attempts to invade his territory, and by his insistence that the paper should have a 'monolithic' view on political matters. John Pringle, who joined the paper in 1958, found it hard to decide whether the battles between Haffner, Deutscher and Loewenthal were 'an intellectual feat or a gigantic bore. I could never understand how David could listen to them so patiently.' Very different from the volatile émigrés was Chester Wilmot, author of the best-selling *The Struggle for Europe*, later killed in the 1954 Comet crash: Michael Davie remembered him as a 'calm, bulky man . . . sitting quietly in an editorial conference, smoking a pipe, wearing a sports jacket'. David's own 'manner was shy and tentative; he retreated from argument, and was a thoughtful listener. Even when he had doubts on major issues he did not try to impose his view when faced with strongly different views at editorial conferences,' Colin Legum recalled. 'On issues he did not have strong opinions about, his manner was to listen to the specialists among his colleagues. If they happened to disagree among themselves, he left it to them to go away and argue it out among themselves.' Every now and then a writer, painter, musician or publisher would be invited to a lunch to provide a diversion from politics. On occasion Stravinsky was the guest of honour, and he asked if Graham Greene could also be invited, since he longed to meet him. Wires were crossed, and the novelist Henry Green was invited instead: Green's novels were famously obscure, Green himself was not forthcoming, and a baffled silence ensued.

But for all his diffidence, and his readiness to print conflicting points of view, David was ultimately in charge. 'The most striking feature of these conferences was the editor's chairmanship' William Clark recalled, adding that 'there was quite a lot of disagreement and quite a lot of hurt feelings, including my own'. On matters he felt strongly about – 'decolonisation, racism, minority rights, European unity, the danger of the proliferation of nuclear weapons' – David would decide who should write the leaders and the leader-page articles, and what line the paper should take. Writing to Robert Stephens about Palestine, David said that although he was all in favour of Stephens writing a factual survey of the problem, he was 'much troubled by the possibility of disagreement' over editorial policy: 'please do remember that whereas it is my duty to let you state the facts of the problem as you see them, it is also my duty to consider how much I should accept your policy ideas in determining the editorial line which, on this issue as on any other, has to remain my individual responsibility.'

15

The Golden Age

'He was far too worldly, too steely, too tactful to hark back with nostalgia to the cosier heyday of the late 1940s and early 1950s,' John Thompson recalled of David in the 1960s. Thompson joined the *Observer* as its news editor in 1962, and by the time he left the paper it was struggling to survive in, and adapt to, a very different world to that in which David had spent his early years as editor. For all his discretion, and his desire not to wound the feelings of a younger generation of journalists who had replaced his old guard of literary men and excitable émigrés, David would always look back on the fifteen or so post-war years as a golden age when the *Sunday Times* was a somnolent outrider of the Conservative Party and the *Sunday Telegraph* not yet a twinkle in the Camrose eye. The *Observer* reigned supreme in the Sunday-paper pantheon, admired editorially and steadily advancing on its old rival in terms of circulation; and it was, in Richard Cockett's words, 'the product of a thoughtful, serious generation which had fought through the Second World War, and had also seen – and in some cases experienced – the miseries of Depression and the failure to combat Fascism in the 1930s'.

David once told John Grigg that in his experience '*all* political journalism places one constantly in danger of committing acts of injustice', and his long-postponed but inevitable removal of Ivor Brown prompted cries of outrage from his victim's wife. IB's contract expired in 1953, and in August David told him that he could continue pro tem as associate editor on £2,500 a year: he would not be involved in any administrative work, and restrict himself to reviewing new plays and writing the occasional essay. But there was a sting in the tail. 'The only change I would ask (and I do so with reluctance, as I fear it may be a disagreeable change to you) is that you should let us have your room in the office' – and, to make matters worse, David was looking out for a new theatre critic, on whose appointment IB's salary would drop to £1,500 a year.

Ivor Brown's replacement was to prove one of David's most colourful, controversial and highly regarded appointments. Terry Kilmartin had alerted David to the languid, sinuous, heavy-smoking figure of Kenneth Tynan, who had made his mark at Oxford with his fake leopardskin trousers, velvet jacket and mink tie, and had recently been sacked by Beaverbrook as the *Evening Standard*'s theatre critic: he had been replaced by Milton Shulman, and had ended his last review by warning his readers that 'the older generation is knocking at the door'. David was impressed by Tynan's book *He That Plays the King* – this was soon followed by a study of Alec Guinness, and *Persona Grata*, with photographs by Cecil Beaton – and although Tynan was now reviewing for the *Daily Sketch*, he had decided to hand in his resignation, and wondered whether 'there might be any possibility of my acting as second- or third-string critic to Ivor Brown'. He met David in September, and it was agreed that he would write some freelance pieces – the first of which, 'A Bunch of Comics', was devoted to, among others, Frankie Howerd, W. C. Fields and Jacques Tati. Three months later, Tynan was appointed the *Observer*'s new theatre critic, starting in the summer of the following year and running for three years. 'It will, I expect, be not unlike moving from a brewery into a vineyard,' he remarked of his translation from the *Sketch*. David, for his part, thought it 'the bravest thing I ever did, and one of the most important'. Before long Tynan was making his mark, championing Brecht, Arthur Miller and, in 1956, John Osborne's *Look Back in Anger*, and (unjustly) ridiculing the well-made country-house plays of Terence Rattigan and the like. 'The theatre has paid him its greatest compliment,' Peter Brook observed. 'After every night it is asking "What has Tynan said?"'

Tynan's high profile could only enhance the *Observer*'s reputation as the most lively and literate Sunday paper, but although IB himself had put his successor's name forward ('There is, of course, Mr Tynan'), his elevation was not well received in the Brown household. Mrs Brown – professionally known as Irene Henschel, a theatrical producer – stormed into battles on her husband's behalf, and mobilised sympathetic theatre folk behind her. She claimed that IB's suggestion of Tynan had been 'ironic', and that he had been 'insulted' and shabbily treated. Nor was she alone in feeling that IB had been hard done by. 'More than one person has complained to me that he has been badly treated,' TJ reported, adding that '"cruelly" was the word used in one letter'. 'I have nothing but respect for your fierce loyalty, even though I think it is being misapplied,' David told Mrs Brown. He admitted that the decision to demote

IB was 'inescapably mine', but the barrage persisted. 'I don't think that rude letters are going to get us anywhere,' David replied, adding that 'I really don't think our correspondence should be continued.' Although the following year David asked TJ if he could have a word about IB's 'public grumbling', he also wrote to the prime minister's PPS to suggest (to no avail) that Brown should be given a knighthood on the grounds that 'the theatrical profession as well as the profession of journalism would greatly appreciate it if he were to receive an honour.'

Despite being remembered by C. A. Lejeune as 'a man of tremendous fortitude and loyalty' and 'a great journalist whose talents have never been sufficiently recognised', and David's reassuring Mrs Brown that 'I hold him in much greater honour than either of you seem to realise', IB faded from the journalistic scene, while Tynan went from strength to strength. 'I am delighted that my association with the *Observer* is to be extended,' he told David after his contract had been renewed. 'In the past three years I have often felt as if I were walking on egg-shells. It's wonderfully encouraging to discover that in spite of my fears none got broken.' Although David once told him that 'there is no one working for the paper who adds more to its character and credit than you do,' Tynan's widow Kathleen remembered how 'Astor thought it wise to keep his distance from his volatile young critic, though often, over the years, he regretted this self-imposed deprivation. On one occasion, passionately disagreeing with Ken's point of view, he wrote a pseudonymous letter of complaint to the paper.' John Pringle wrote that although the purple-clad critic seemed 'alarming and slightly offensive' at first, this concealed a 'natural shyness'. His foppish exterior concealed a much-appreciated professionalism. He brought his copy into the office bang on time on Saturdays, trimmed it 'on the stone' if needs be, and provided waggish captions: when Terry Kilmartin struggled to find a caption for his review of Ibsen's *The Wild Duck* for a Christmas issue of the paper, Tynan shouted 'Christmas Quacker' from the far side of the room. In later years, Tynan spent much of his time in the States, and Anthony Sampson recalled how, on his visits to London, 'he made everyone feel larger than life, arriving at the Feathers on Saturdays with a new batch of jokes and Hollywood gossip about Orson, Larry or Tennessee'.

A lean, good-looking product of Westminster and Christ Church and a former RNVR officer, Anthony Sampson had cut his journalistic teeth in South Africa as the editor of *Drum*, a magazine owned by his Oxford contemporary Jim Bailey, which was devoted to politics and current affairs as seen from a black perspective, and handsomely illustrated along the lines of *Life* or *Picture Post*. By 1955 Sampson was keen to return to England, and Bailey urged David to find him a job, not least because 'he has a first-class book on the stocks and, what is rare with books about Africa, written with great knowledge and integrity'. David invited Sampson to lunch: 'Sampson's visit here was a great success', he told Bailey. 'Everyone liked him enormously and was much impressed by his ability.' At the age of forty-three, Sampson recalled, David 'still looked boyish, with his questioning eyes, a thatch of hair and diffident mumble'; the two men got on, and Sampson was asked to join the *Observer* as an assistant editor, a dogsbody job which provided an invaluable overview of how the paper worked. Best remembered as the author of the best-selling *Anatomy of Britain*, Sampson was to become, like Michael Davie, one of David's bright young men, and another possible heir apparent; he was to enjoy a long, close and highly influential relationship with both David and the paper, reporting from around the world, and from South Africa in particular, bombarding David with new ideas as the *Observer* struggled to adjust to a rapidly changing world, editing the Pendennis column, and sporadically taking time off to write a new book. He joined the paper at a time when it was 'at the peak of its influence as a highbrow political and cultural organ, respected almost equally on the right and the left', he recalled in his posthumously published memoirs. 'Its sixteen pages every Sunday seemed to be the centre of all debates, discussed at dinner parties and setting agendas for politicians. It was original and unpredictable.' Sampson was 'amazed by its apparent casualness: it seemed more like a family charity or an eccentric college than a commercial newspaper'. Its editorial réclame was matched by soaring sales: Tristan Jones may have 'projected a deep negativity behind a big deadpan moustache', while David 'preferred not to know about circulation figures, but they went up and up without apparent effort'.

David himself, Sampson recalled, employed schoolboy phrases like 'hols', 'chums' and 'okey-dokey', and was so shy on grand occasions that, according to one of his more socialite cousins, he didn't 'even know how to get out of a room', and because he was thought to make life as complicated as possible, he was half expected to make his exit via the chimney rather than the door. Be that as it may, Sampson compared him to a Renaissance prince and, as befitted an erstwhile theatrical man, 'he had a touch of the impresario: the last of the great actor managers, we called him', who looked on his journalists as 'temperamental actors, to be humoured, reassured and given their cues, sometimes their lines'. David, for his part, liked to see himself as a head chef, mixing the ingredients. The *Observer* was sometimes referred to as 'Dr Astor's clinic' or a 'hospital for lame ducks', and David 'was a constant father figure, always prepared to discuss emotional problems or to intervene in a crisis'. Sampson recalled his colleagues tossing down prodigious quantities of booze. Philip Toynbee shambled into the Tudor Street office in his duffel coat, 'giggling like a soda fountain until he collapsed in a deep chair for the afternoon'; Patrick O'Donovan went on self-destructive binges; Alastair Buchan, the Eton- and Oxford-educated son of John Buchan, combined 'a military moustache and voice' with 'violent drunken escapades'. David had not been averse to a drink as a young man, and unlike his parents he was never a teetotaller, but bearing in mind the tidal waves of alcohol that flowed through the office, he restricted himself, in office hours at least, to an occasional glass of white wine or Mateus rosé.

Although his own prose was admirably clear and straightforward, writing never came easily to David; but he was, Sampson recalled, an exemplary copy- or line-editor (a view confirmed by David's successor, who admired him as a 'superb copy-editor and headline-writer', as well as a 'ruthless sniffer-out of humbug and weak or dodgy ideas'). When Sampson wrote his first Profile, of Albert Schweitzer, he spent hours agonising over the opening paragraph until David told him to omit it altogether – 'It's like a cough at the beginning of a speech. You just have to get it over with.' He was an appreciative editor, firing off telegrams to his foreign correspondents to congratulate them on a particularly good piece, and letters to those who were closer to home; he found talent-spotting 'the most thrilling part of the job', and liked to employ raffish, 'unsound' characters rather than dutiful plodders. A kindly man, David got rid of those whose faces didn't fit by ignoring them and letting them wither on the vine – a well-meant technique, but less tolerable, perhaps, than an old-fashioned sacking – and he was happy to pass the buck when dealing with awkward or obstreperous members of staff. He asked Sampson, for example, to persuade the formidable Mechthild Nawiasky, the picture editor and a former art editor of *Lilliput*, to use photographs on the front page (Nawiasky was 'renowned for the close relationship she developed with a tiger in London Zoo'). Nawiasky's great discovery was the photographer Jane Bown, a former Wren whose simple, beautifully composed black-and-white portraits were to become one of the *Observer*'s most distinctive features. 'Mechthild saw my picture of a cow's eye and said she knew immediately that I could photograph anyone,' Jane Bown recalled. She had no time for elaborate equipment, preferred natural to artificial light and carried her camera in her handbag: her first photograph for the *Observer*, a portrait of Bertrand Russell, appeared in 1949, and her subsequent portraits of public figures, Samuel Beckett and Kim Philby among them, combined a miraculous simplicity with an intuitive insight into her sitter's personality. David gave her away when she got married in 1953. Like Tom Hopkinson at *Picture Post*, David was ahead of his times in appreciating photography as an art: he thought it an 'under-appreciated' skill, and years later he helped to set up the Photographers' Gallery in Great Newport Street. For his own part, he was hopeless with technology of any kind and, like many writers and journalists of his generation, Alan Ross and Patrick Leigh Fermor among them, he never learned to type.

'Despite his unhappy adolescence, he never seemed insecure or unadult,' Sampson recalled, but David was never sure how much he would have achieved had he not been a member of the Astor family and the chosen heir apparent. Nancy remained a hazard, not least when the staff were taken to Cliveden for the annual summer outing. 'She is quite liable to say that there are too many Jews on the paper to one of our Semitic staff members,' David told Bill, and – apropos the Jamaican wife of a foreign correspondent – 'one would dread Mama being too hearty and Southern in the welcome she would give her'. 'So you work for my son David with all those niggers and Communists?' Nancy asked Sampson on one occasion, and no doubt she went out of her way to shock David's liberal-minded colleagues. David's high-living brother Michael, who had been returned as a Tory MP in the 1945 election, told Sampson that he envied David for having a proper job, and for having 'escaped on a silken ladder from this world of bored luxury', and Sampson noticed how David seemed to envy the lives of middle-class intellectuals, and how his houses seemed to get smaller and less heavily staffed as the years went by.

No doubt Nancy's worries about Jews and 'Communists' taking over the family paper were inflamed by David's other additions to the staff. Colin Legum, a South African Jew whose parents had emigrated from Lithuania, joined the paper in 1949. He had been involved in left-wing politics in South Africa, and had been banned from returning to the country after moving to Britain; he worked at the Tavistock Clinic before resuming his career as a journalist, and shared David's interest in psychoanalysis. 'An oak in the *Observer*'s forest, too big a man to mind if he did not always prove popular', he was to become a hugely influential figure in determining the *Observer*'s involvement in Africa in general, and South Africa in particular, but was also a forceful and voluble champion of

Israel. Nora Beloff, like Legum, was to prove a long-standing member of staff, reporting from Washington and Moscow before becoming the first female political correspondent on a British national newspaper. She was born into an academic North London Jewish family: her older brother, Max, was a fellow of All Souls and the Gladstone Professor of Government, while another brother, John, became the professor of psychology at Edinburgh. After leaving Oxford, Nora Beloff got a job at the newly reopened British Embassy in Paris in 1944, and reported from there for Reuters and *The Economist* before joining the *Observer*. 'I found it almost impossible to adjust myself to the easy-going confusion in the *Observer*' after the 'harshly regimented' life at Reuters: she once asked David why it was all so chaotic, to which the answer was 'Well, if we had a more conventional office we couldn't employ geniuses like Philip Toynbee.'

'Journalism was obviously the right choice,' Nora Beloff once said of herself. 'I had three of the necessary qualifications: inexhaustible stamina, insatiable curiosity and a thick skin.' But 'I owe my original chance of joining the paper to the privilege of your friendship rather than to my regular and demonstrable qualifications,' she once admitted to David: she had no shorthand, her typing was erratic in the extreme, and her pieces always had to be rewritten in the office, as often as not by a long-suffering Michael Davie. Though kind in private life, she was not the easiest of colleagues. 'Seen in a certain light and from a certain angle, I am a rude, overbearing, callous and cold-hearted Prussian,' she continued, and 'I can well understand that it grates on many people's nerves.' 'The backwash of Nora is terrible,' a colleague reported after her return to London from Washington: she had a particularly embattled relationship with Sebastian Haffner – she thought him 'the most stimulating and effective commentator we have', but 'we shall just go on arguing until one of us dies'. 'Tantrums and troubles' became a regular feature of Tudor Street life, with David proving 'long-suffering and eminently indulgent'.

An altogether more emollient new arrival was the Hungarian Lajos Lederer. In 1934 he had accompanied Waldorf and Nancy on a tour of his native country, and he had suggested that the crown of Hungary should be offered to Lord Rothermere, who had campaigned for the return to Hungary of land lost to Czechoslovakia under the Treaty of Versailles. Lederer had settled in Britain before the war, working for a Hungarian newspaper, and had been rescued from internment on the Isle of Man by Randolph Churchill. He was never on the staff – it was said that

David paid his salary out of his own pocket – and he was incapable of writing pieces of more than 250 words. But he had mysterious if useful connections: as early as 1948 he predicted Tito's split with Stalin, and he was proved right some four years later. A genial character, he loved the *Observer* and liked to progress through the office, handing out sweets and encouragement. 'Virginia, what a marvellous piece that was', he once told Virginia Makins, then working on Pendennis, though she hadn't published a word that week.

Lederer's fellow Hungarian Arthur Koestler was a more alarming proposition. David had met him during the war through Cyril Connolly, and immediately warmed to his 'no-nonsense style', finding him 'a great stimulant in wartime London', and 'full of confidence and vigour', and asked him to contribute a Forum piece in 1941. 'This small, passionate man, with his excruciating accent, his self-mockery, and his devotion to his political friends in Europe', was, for David, 'the embodiment of an uncompromised, unafraid, international idealism'. A Profile of Koestler described him as 'a nervous exhibitionist, an idealist beset by cynical disillusionment, an intellectual torn by all the passions' who 'has sometimes seemed like an incompatible mixture of man of the world and schoolboy in shorts, of brilliant talker and naive boaster, of subtle analyst and glib, disingenuous boaster'. Koestler was never more than a part-time contributor to the *Observer*, and his relationship with David was often embattled. On learning that Koestler thought that David was being 'more than usually ambivalent' towards him, David hurried to reassure him. 'My situation is that, being newly married and having this fairly exacting job, I seem to have extremely little time. But please don't mistake this for an increase in ambivalence. I am always pleased if you show any inclination to make use of my friendship.'

One all-important subject on which both men agreed was the threat now posed by the Soviet Union. 'No other writer of our time, not even his close friend George Orwell, has done more to shake the Western intelligentsia out of its fellow-travelling swoon,' Koestler's Profile declared. David had never had any illusions about Communism in general, and Stalinism in particular; and, like Koestler and Orwell, he was sympathetic to what was becoming known as the 'non-Communist left'. The Cold War had replaced wartime sentimentality about 'Uncle Joe'; by the late 1940s the non-Communist left had, in effect, sided with America, welcoming the Marshall Plan, the Truman Doctrine and the Atlanticism which, in David's case, was part of his family inheritance. In 1948 Ernest Bevin, the Labour Foreign Secretary, set up the semi-secret, neutral-sounding Information

Research Department to counteract pro-Soviet propaganda put out by the
Cominform on the grounds that 'we must put forward a rival ideology
to Communism'. The IRD is best remembered for having commissioned
Orwell's 'blacklist' of those 'who in my opinion are crypto-Communists,
fellow travellers or inclined that way, and should not be trusted as propagandists'. It was compiled not long after the Communist takeover in
Czechoslovakia and the Berlin blockade; a dispirited Orwell assured his
close friend Celia Kirwan, who worked for the IRD and was Koestler's
sister-in-law, that had such a list been made available earlier 'it would have
stopped people like Peter Smollett worming their way into important
propaganda jobs where they were probably able to do us a lot of harm'.

The full details of Orwell's blacklist were only revealed nearly fifty
years after Orwell's death: those named included J. B. Priestley, Kingsley
Martin, C. Day-Lewis, Michael Redgrave, Sean O'Casey, George Bernard
Shaw, Charlie Chaplin, E. H. Carr and Isaac Deutscher. 'I always knew
he was two-faced. There was something fishy about Orwell. I am pained
and sorry to hear of it and it confirms my worst suspicions of the man,'
declared Christopher Hill, the ex-Communist former master of Balliol,
after Orwell's list had been made public. Despite the inclusion on the list
of old friends and colleagues, David hurried to Orwell's defence. 'Orwell
wasn't betraying the left – the pro-Communists were betraying us,' he
declared. 'The British intellectual left in those days thought Communism
was fine, the proper side to be on. They didn't make a distinction between
the social democrats and the Communists. But at that time Communism
was a rampant doctrine which was very aggressive', and 'Animal Farm was
about how Marxism produces a regime indistinguishable from fascism.'
Orwell 'was not giving them a blacklist. He was just telling the IRD
whom not to employ.'

The IRD distributed copies of, or helped to sell foreign rights in,
Animal Farm, Nineteen Eighty-Four and Koestler's Darkness at Noon around
the world; and in the same year in which the IRD was set up, Hamish
Hamilton published The God That Failed, a widely publicised collection of
essays edited by Koestler and Richard Crossman, in which a distinguished
group of former Communists explained why they had lost their faith.
The CIA saw the non-Communist left as an invaluable means of coun-
teracting Communist propaganda – as did highly influential American
diplomats and journalists like George Kennan, W. Averell Harriman,
'Chip' Bohlen and the Alsop brothers, liberal-minded and Anglophile
Wasps who shared David's Atlanticist views. In 1950, just as the Korean
War broke out, the CIA-backed Congress for Cultural Freedom (CCF) was

launched to combat a Cominform 'peace offensive', with the American Mel Lasky, then editing *Der Monat*, acting as a link between European members of the non-Communist left like Koestler and Ignazio Silone and Sidney Hook's Americans for Intellectual Freedom, who included Dwight Macdonald and Mary McCarthy. Arthur Koestler dominated the proceedings at a rally held in Berlin, and although he resigned from the CCF the following year, he was more responsible than anyone else for spelling out what the CCF stood for. The CCF had its headquarters in Paris, and was run by Michael Josselson: among the organisations through which it channelled funds were the Ford Foundation and Julius Fleischmann's Farfield Foundation, and over the years David would get in touch with both bodies when trying to raise money for a good cause.

Subsidising magazines was one of the cultural and political areas in which the CCF was particularly active. In 1950 two of the most influential London literary magazines – Connolly's *Horizon*, which had published work by both Orwell and Koestler, and John Lehmann's *Penguin New Writing*, edited by Lehmann and published by Allen Lane – went out of business. David offered to buy *Horizon* off Connolly, and install as its editor Alan Ross, a young poet who had contributed occasional pieces to the *Observer* from Italy and Germany and would soon become a regular contributor to its sports pages: although Connolly had recommended Ross to David, he flew into a rage when David broached the idea, accusing Ross of scheming behind his back, and nothing came of it. Two years later Humphrey Slater asked David if he'd be interested in reviving his magazine *Polemic* to plug the gap left by *Horizon*, but again nothing came of it. But David had better luck with *Twentieth Century*, a monthly magazine which had started life in Victorian times as *The Nineteenth Century*, changed its name to *The Nineteenth Century and After* to keep up with the times, and had only updated itself in 1951.

Combining political articles with short stories, poems and criticism, *Twentieth Century* had attracted the attention of the CCF's British branch, the short-lived British Society for Cultural Freedom, members of which included Malcolm Muggeridge and Stephen Spender, as well as such long-standing members of the non-Communist left as Tosco Fyvel, Rix Loewenthal and Fredric Warburg. (David exchanged letters with Warburg, Koestler and Sonia Orwell about who should write Orwell's biography: Koestler ruled himself out, and there was general agreement that Muggeridge was best avoided.) The CCF offered to pay off the magazine's debts and subsidise its future publication on the understanding that its political pages would combat the neutralist or fellow-travelling ideas promoted by the *New Statesman* with an Atlanticist, pro-Europe policy, while the literary half would make amends for the loss of *Horizon* and *Penguin New Writing*. *Twentieth Century* limped along on its CIA crutch until 1958, when David bought it. The following year the Catholic journalist Bernard Wall replaced George Lichtheim as its editor: the editorial board included Rix Loewenthal, John Beavan, William Clark, Anthony Sampson, Guy Wint and John Weightman, who reviewed books on French subjects for the *Observer*, and contributors during the seven years in which David owned the magazine included *Observer* regulars like Maurice Richardson and Philip Toynbee as well as Colin MacInnes, Colin Wilson, Christopher Isherwood, Anthony Thwaite, Margaret Drabble, D. J. Enright, Brendan Behan, Rayner Heppenstall and Muriel Spark (who had won the *Observer*'s first short-story competition in 1951 with 'The Seraph and the Zambezi'; Diana Athill was a later winner). In 1962 it became a quarterly; Richard Findlater, by then on the arts pages of the *Observer*, replaced Wall as editor, Terry Kilmartin joined the editorial board, Edward Bawden provided illustrations for the covers, and the typographer Ruari McLean masterminded the layout. In 1965 David sold *Twentieth Century* to the journalist Dennis Hackett – who, like Bawden and McLean, had earlier been involved in giving the *Observer* a facelift.

The CCF's anxiety to counteract the iniquities of the *New Statesman* and *Tribune* had not been satisfied by the pre-Astor *Twentieth Century*. *Encounter*, initially edited by Irving Kristol and Stephen Spender, was founded in 1953, and although it looked very similar to *Twentieth Century* and combined politics with the arts, it had a far higher profile, becoming one of the best, and best-known, magazines of its day. MI6 and the IRD were involved in setting it up – MI6 initially paid Spender's salary – as were Tosco Fyvel, Muggeridge and Fred Warburg. Mel Lasky duly replaced Kristol, looking after the political 'front half' of the magazine, Secker & Warburg were the publishers, and by 1963 it was selling some 34,000 copies a month. David contributed articles on the Eichmann trial in 1961 and on Adam von Trott, and the writers and politicians published in *Encounter* – Roy Jenkins, Anthony Crosland, Andrew Shonfield – articulated the liberal-minded, social-democrat values which David shared with the post-war non-Communist left, and which he espoused in the *Observer*: Goronwy Rees, one of the magazine's regular columnists, once described it as an 'intellectual Marshall Plan'. In 1967 *Encounter* hit the headlines with the revelation that it had always been funded by the CIA, albeit through the innocuous-seeming CCF, with Stephen Spender in particular claiming – implausibly – that he had known nothing of it. 'It's just the sort of thing the CIA *should* be doing,' David told Anthony Sampson. Hugh Trevor-Roper, Roy Jenkins and Denis Healey were neither surprised nor alarmed by the news, and Isaiah Berlin later wrote that 'I did not in the slightest object to American sources supplying the money. I was (and am) pro-American and anti-Soviet, and if the source had been declared I would not have minded in the least.'

Arthur Koestler had been condemned to death during the Spanish Civil War, and had spent three months in the condemned cell in Seville prison; and his role in the campaign to abolish capital punishment brought him, once again, into close contact with the *Observer*. The hanging of the mentally retarded Derek Bentley in 1953 had united politicians and writers in opposition to capital punishment, as had the executions of Ruth Ellis and of Timothy Evans, wrongly accused of the murders committed by John Christie. Foremost in leading the campaign were Koestler and Victor Gollancz, whose firm's half-column advertisement was a regular feature of the *Observer*'s leader page from 1940 until his death in 1967. With Canon John Collins, they launched the National Campaign for the Abolition of Capital Punishment (NCACP), supporters of which included J. B. Priestley and Frank Pakenham, and a mass rally was held at the Albert Hall. Both Koestler and Gollancz were temperamental egotists, and each tried to upstage the other: 'Don't people realise that I'm *much* more famous than Arthur Koestler?' Gollancz demanded, while Koestler unfairly accused Gollancz of deliberately holding up publication of his book, *Reflections on Hanging*. A. D. Peters, Koestler's agent, arranged for the book to be serialised in five 3,000-word extracts in the *Observer*, and David agreed that Koestler could write an occasional column under the pseudonym of 'Vigil' – the last of which, 'Pattern of Murder', was sent to all MPs and included an attack on the judiciary which infuriated Lord Goddard, then famed as a 'hanging judge'.

Although the death penalty was not finally abolished until 1970, the NCACP had greatly advanced its cause, and David was happy to give credit to both men. A Profile of Gollancz declared that 'no single man has been more responsible for creating this sense of urgency than Victor Gollancz', while David told Koestler that 'your "hanging" journalism has contributed something of real value to this country and this newspaper. It is the episode that most deserves to be recorded in the history of this newspaper since I've been here. I'm very proud of being associated with what you've done.' Koestler remained an intermittent contributor, though he was hurt and puzzled by David's failure to take his campaign about the quarantining of dogs as seriously as his anti-hanging activities: he would be sorry if, 'after so many years of joint campaigning, the *Observer* and I fell out over dogs'. (David's lack of interest was not due to indifference to dogs. He had a soft spot for dogs and horses, which, according to John Thompson, he always referred to as 'gee-gees'; he suggested that the *Observer* should cover Crufts, and kept a keen eye on the activities of the paper's racing correspondents, the best known of whom was Richard Baerlein.)

Despite his prowess as a hurdler at Eton, David was never a games fanatic, but in the early 1950s the *Observer*'s sports pages were much admired for the quality of the reporting and the unexpected names who featured on the back page. Over dinner with Jim Rose and his wife, Alan Ross pointed out that although, thanks to Neville Cardus and others, newspapers had come to associate cricket with fine writing, this was not true of soccer. Rose put this to the current sports editor, Harold Gale, a former snooker champion, who rang Ross and suggested he should cover a match. For the next four years, Ross covered soccer matches for the paper, and when Michael Davie – who had played with him in the Haileybury cricket XI – became the sports editor, John Sparrow, A. J. Ayer, Clement Freud, David Sylvester and Louis Blom-Cooper were added to the roster of highbrow soccer reporters. Ross, who had played cricket and squash for Oxford, was, in Michael Astor's opinion, 'far the best writer on cricket today': he eventually replaced R. C. Robertson-Glasgow as the cricket correspondent, 'a job that took me abroad most winters' and gave him an opportunity to put cricket 'in a wider context, relating it to landscape, climate, politics and local life'. David approved of Michael Davie's improvements to the sports pages – later contributors included Chris Brasher, Norris McWhirter and Hugh McIlvanney, widely regarded as the finest all-round sports writer of the day – for practical as well as aesthetic reasons. He always claimed sport loomed large for the Sunday papers because Saturday was a bad day for news, as well as being the day on which the big matches were played: the *Observer* went to press earlier than its rivals, so the quality of its coverage had to compensate for its being slightly less up-to-the-minute.

The *Observer* of David's 'golden age' was a modest affair compared with a modern Sunday newspaper – as a result of which advertising space could be sold at a high price, at least until the arrival of commercial television in 1955. An easing of paper rationing had enabled the management to increase the number of pages, but there were no self-contained supplements or sections within the paper, and however admirable the content, the fabled book reviews and sports reports were little more than 200–300 words apiece. (According to Alan Watkins, the bibulous Maurice Richardson invented both the television review and the 'miniature novel review' in the form of postage-stamp-sized reviews of crime novels; with his rolling gait, pugilistic air, 'massive head and slightly protuberant, rather mad blue eyes, he resembled Randolph Churchill'. He was also the first journalist to review television in a Sunday paper.) What Nora Beloff referred to as David's 'system of administration by conference' held sway: Sampson recalled how 'Rix Loewenthal, with one eye rotating about the room, worried about outposts like Quemoy or Yemen as if they were his own big toe. William Clark, the diplomatic correspondent, brought titbits from embassy dinners, high tables or episcopal gatherings. Nora Beloff argued with Robert Stephens about Israelis and Arabs as if it were the River Jordan itself, while David – who had both Jewish and Arab friends – wrestled with an editorial which could be fair to both sides.' David's eyes glazed over when the discussion turned to economics, and an unworldly tone sometimes prevailed – Sampson remembered how, some years later, Philip Toynbee wondered why lorries could not be banned from the new motorways.

David loved the endless talking, and ultimately decided what line the paper should take, but at times he found it a lonely business. 'My greatest need is for help in the general direction of the editorial operation,' he told John Pringle, a veteran of the *Manchester Guardian* who was then editing the *Sydney Morning Herald*. There was 'a weakness at the centre' in the form of the assistant editor, Charles Davy, who was 'the mainstay of the office in many respects' but was reluctant to 'share the two heaviest duties – the making of policy and the administering of personnel': Davy displayed 'extraordinary humility in accepting his place as a team worker', and Pringle's 'presence would relieve me rather than deprive him'. Haffner, Loewenthal, Legum and Stephens were 'all full of ideas of what the paper's policy should be', but none of them was up to 'the directing of this high-powered team so that each gets used to the best possible advantage. We have no need for more instrumentalists, but an assistant for the conductor is needed.' Pringle would, in due course, bring a cool eye to the proceedings; in the meantime, David found it difficult 'to travel or be absent from the office without feeling that the centre of the system flags, and I am feeling a little overworked'.

★

David felt adrift after the collapse of his marriage to Melanie. 'Intimate and serious things scare me – with reason, as I've not yet shown that I can understand them and can live them through seriously,' he told Marion Doenhoff in the autumn of 1949. 'Life for me at present does not vary – it's just the *Observer*, this house, a motor car, Sutton at weekends and my child as the chief point of loyalty, with my father as the other.' (He had bought Norah Lindsay's idyllic Manor House in Sutton Courtenay in 1945. Brenda Colvin was employed to redesign the garden, one feature of which was a statue by the Astors' friend Siegfried Charoux; she later designed the garden of their house in Elm Tree Road, and planted trees at Compton Beauchamp, the estate under the White Horse on the Wiltshire Downs which David eventually donated to the National Trust.) The desire to lead a 'purely private life' dated back to his early twenties, 'when I was solitary and a sort of refugee from my family', and even now he still felt 'the inclination to withdraw from all communal activity and just live between my bed and garden and maybe an occasional feeble effort to write a novel'. He wished that *Die Zeit* would post Marion to London 'so as to give us a decent chance to get to know each other . . . I feel slightly world-weary just now and, as usual, mistrust my own emotional stamina. That does not mean that I doubt my affection for you, but that I doubt my constitutional ability to "live" any emotion through to its fullest extent.' He still felt greatly attracted to her, but 'I save myself from becoming frightened by the seriousness of our connection by remembering your ability to laugh, which, next to a sense of beauty and honesty, is the most valuable of gifts in what concerns personal relations.' After visiting her in Hamburg, he wrote to say that the relationship was 'too precious to be allowed to die', and how he felt 'a very tender wish to console you for the wound which my incompleteness has caused. You are a superb woman and a very sweet one, and even if I can't make you very happy I hope that I will be able to add a little happiness to your life.'

Three years later, in March 1952, David married Bridget Wreford, a gentle, good-looking, fair-haired woman whom he had met through the sculptor and painter John Skeaping. Skeaping specialised in representations of horses, which endeared him to the Astors, and after the war David had lent him money to buy a house; and Bridget, herself a sculptor, had been one of his pupils. 'I've just met the person I'm going to marry,' both parties declared after their initial meeting, but some months went by before David found an excuse to look Bridget up at the Royal College of Art, where she was then studying; and they would remain devoted to one another for nearly fifty years. 'Would you believe it, my father virtually forced me to have Bill as my best man,' David confided in Tom Jones. Fred Tomlinson reported that he had met David's new wife, but 'she was too subdued for us to decide how much more she was than pleasant and likeable'; forty years later, Stephen Spender went to dinner with the Astors in St John's Wood, and found himself sitting next to Bridget, 'a sculptress who does not dare to call herself a sculptress and seems extremely shy and helpless at her own dinner parties'. Though by nature diffident and retiring, seldom appearing at *Observer* functions, Bridget was no shrinking violet. The daughter of a Torquay solicitor, she not only provided David and their five children with the stable family life he had pined for as an adolescent, but, with her middle-class background and impatience with the more self-indulgent trappings of wealth, she enabled David to live a more 'normal' life than his siblings. David's houses in London and Sutton Courtenay were far removed from a semi in East Sheen or a terrace house in Fulham, but he had no innate taste for luxury – their London houses were functional rather than sumptuous – and over the years Bridget gradually dispensed with the army of servants whom he had hitherto taken for granted. Alice, their first child, was born in 1953, and over the next nine years she was followed by Richard, Lucy, Nancy and Tom.

Devoted as he was to his new family, David felt guilty about Melanie, and was desperately anxious that Frances should not feel excluded. He turned for help to William Clark, who was happy to act as a kindly intermediary. 'You know that Frances means the world to me and that it is a sort of nightmare to see her in distress and not be able to do anything to help her. And you know that I'm definitely pro and not anti-Melanie and would do anything I could to help her have a life which would give her some happiness and contentment,' David told him. 'I need her wellbeing for my own peace of mind, but I also wish it for its own sake – it is awful to feel that someone to whom one has been so closely related is unhappy.' 'It costs me acute embarrassment to ask for help for Melanie. It gives me correspondingly acute feelings of gratitude to hear that you are already doing so much', he wrote on another occasion. Melanie was 'at heart a very nice, honest and amusing person but is in the greatest danger of being temperamentally isolated by the effects of misfortune', and 'deserves much better of life than she gets'.

If a happy second marriage provided David with the company and the support he needed at home, psychoanalysis was a prop of a different kind, bringing comfort and an all-explaining system of belief such as Christian

Science had provided for his parents. Alastair Macleod, a Canadian psychiatrist, suggested that David should try a session of psychoanalysis. David was sceptical at first, but Koestler was well disposed, and he decided to give it a go. 'I resorted to analytical help when my first marriage failed, and found it useful generally,' David told Michael Davie many years later. 'I visit a "priest" daily to try to become more internally free, and therefore more internally reliable,' he told Marion Doenhoff. Every morning, for the rest of his working life, David was driven to the *Observer* from St John's Wood via Anna Freud's clinic in Maresfield Gardens in Hampstead, where he spent the prescribed fifty minutes talking to Anna Freud herself: he found it gave him peace of mind and improved his ability to work, as well as giving him a better understanding of other people. From Hampstead he would be driven on to have breakfast with Frances, until she went to live in Switzerland with her mother, before heading south to Tudor Street: it was rumoured that his chauffeur kept him informed about what the man in the street was thinking, and every now and then he would give a lift to another North Londoner, Nora Beloff, who would keep him posted about political developments. (At one stage, David had lived in Chelsea, but whereas his siblings tended to live in Chelsea or Belgravia, he opted for less-fashionable North London, heavily populated as it was by liberal-minded thinkers and writers, and Jewish intellectuals.) David's eagerness to provide colleagues in distress with psychoanalytical advice became, like his ignorance of mortgages, part of *Observer* folklore: Michael Davie was once told that 'I must have at least a smattering of Freud before I could hope to write a decent Profile'; Katharine Whitehorn, who revolutionised the women's pages and became one of the most popular columnists on the paper, was diagnosed as suffering from 'penis envy'; Robert Shields was made Fleet Street's first regular writer on psychological problems, just as Dinah Brooke and John Davy were pioneer education and science correspondents.

David may not have had much in common with his brothers, though he always retained a soft spot for Jakie, the youngest, whose jokes he greatly appreciated, but he took a kindly interest in his hapless half-brother, Bobbie Shaw. Shaw was briefly committed to a mental hospital in the winter of 1952, and David wrote to the lawyer and Tory MP Walter Monckton to thank him for his 'willingness to get embroiled in this sad story'. A month later, David apologised to Monckton for 'inflicting the troubles of my brother Bobbie on you again', but the mental home was proving a hell, and Shaw was in 'an alarming state of depression'. Perhaps as a result of Bobbie Shaw's experiences, David was to become a keen supporter of homosexual law reform. John Gordon, the *Daily Express*'s tub-thumping man of the people, claimed that the *Observer* had a 'shocking attitude to homosexuality', to which David replied that 'this subject ought to be approached in a scientific and humane spirit – not in that of a mediaeval witch-hunt'. When, in 1931, Bobbie Shaw had been imprisoned for four months for soliciting a guardsman, the *Express* had abided by what Northcliffe once referred to as 'the sacred cause of newspaper proprietors' whereby no mention was made in rival papers of scandals or misfortunes afflicting owners' families – the following year Waldorf had instructed Garvin to make no mention of the suicide of Lord Harmsworth's son – and, once again, no references were made in Beaverbrook's papers to Bobbie Shaw's travails.

But although David once told Kenneth Harris that he was a keen reader of the *Daily Express* – 'I find it like a sort of first cigarette in the morning' – no love was lost between Beaverbrook and the Astors. The Beaver had given Garvin a column in the *Express*, attacked the gift of Cliveden to the National Trust, and, through the Londoner's Diary column in the *Evening Standard*, ridiculed the Observer Trust's stipulation that no Catholics or Jews should qualify as trustees (a clause which David abhorred, and changed as soon as he could). David, in return, described the Beaver in a Profile as a 'golliwog itching with vitality' whose leaders were so much 'political baby talk', and after the old troublemaker's death he revealed that he'd always assumed that Beaverbrook would have been the British equivalent of Pierre Laval had the Germans invaded in 1940.

Beaverbrook's assault on the Observer Trust was prompted by David's defence of Violet Bonham Carter, who had been attacked by Henry Fairlie in the *Spectator* for standing up for Mrs Maclean after her husband and Guy Burgess had fled to Moscow in the summer of 1951. In a letter to the *Spectator*, David claimed that those who had denounced Lady Violet were all 'purveyors of various kinds of hate. One is the ideological hatred which McCarthy has shown produces cruelty, stupidity and inefficiency; another is personal hatred derived from class consciousness, which is morally no better than racial prejudice; a third is the happy hatred of the habitual trouble-seeker.' The *Sunday Express* accused David of being 'dewy-eyed' and suggested that he 'should give up trying to defend lost causes and realise that, in common with other people, he was utterly deceived by Mrs Maclean', while the Beaver himself, in gloating mood, wrote that David 'in his zeal for the underdog had backed a biter, for Mrs Maclean turned out to be in touch with her husband and duly nipped behind the Iron Curtain'. Nor was he alone in relishing David's discomfiture. Hugh

Cudlipp, the rumbustious editor of the *Daily Mirror*, described David as someone who 'occasionally strikes lofty attitudes towards the popular press, and believes it to be part of his public duty to be constantly pointing out their breaches of "good taste"'. David's 'magisterial chidings' infuriated the Beaverbrook papers, 'which are much more practised at dog-fighting and much less inhibited by the Queensberry Rules'.

No doubt Beaverbrook would have been maliciously amused to learn that Waldorf's attempt to appoint a Christian Scientist, Colonel Goulding, as an *Observer* trustee had led to one of the very few rifts between father and son; on the other hand, David told TJ, 'my mother is behaving shockingly – she may be frightening my father off the decision to make Dingle Foot the deputy chairman' on the grounds that he was the brother of the firebrand Michael Foot. Waldorf was, by now, a sick and frail old man, but Nancy had never forgiven him for insisting that she gave up her seat in Parliament in 1945. Nancy was 'in a fairly constant state of argument with him', and when he could take it no longer Waldorf moved away from Cliveden. He spent time with Bobbie Shaw, of whom he was very fond, before going to stay with David in Sutton Courtenay. 'My father is a sort of saint, but old and a bit sad because my mother behaves so aggressively,' David told Marion Doenhoff, adding that 'my brothers are making him move from here because I am not a Conservative, because I have "taken" the newspaper out of their camp, and partly because they are slightly jealous of me in various ways'. Waldorf reproached Jakie Astor for supporting his mother's disapproval of David's editorship – 'Why do you continue raising the question of the policy of the *Observer* and trying to make your mother believe it can be changed?' – and he told Nancy that he never '*hoped* David would make a mess of the *Observer* – what you said to me and others, even almost to strangers, was that you thought he would make a mess or conduct it badly'. Nancy, for her part, sometimes blamed TJ for the paper's leftwards drift. 'I wish I had never saved the *Observer*', she told him. 'You can see why it has caused me more misery than I would have thought possible.'

Waldorf suffered a heart attack, and as a Christian Scientist he spurned the help of David's doctor. He wanted to end his days at Cliveden: 'he did this not to die away from home and thus bring disgrace on my mother. It was a Captain Oates-like decision, and I greatly admired it. Having gone back to Cliveden, he was in fact treated a bit more gently by my mother.' 'The sternness which as a child I had found disconcerting had evaporated', Michael Astor remembered, adding that 'he enjoyed a short Indian summer in the evening of his life.' Waldorf died in October 1952.

'We had forty happy years together,' Nancy told TJ. 'These last seven years have been heart-breaking – but thank God he was like his old self the last ten days and oh how it makes me grieve of the years wasted!' At his insistence, Waldorf's name was never mentioned in the *Observer* during his lifetime – he was best known to the world at large as a successful breeder of racehorses – but David paid him a handsome tribute in its pages. 'It is in the balanced, yet thoroughgoing nature of the Trust that he created, and in the general character and aims of the *Observer* that his direct influence can be seen,' he told his readers. His father's 'guiding aim' had been to 'spread understanding and tolerance, to increase the sense of community': he had been 'the very embodiment of kindness, firmness and integrity', and 'his particular kind of authority was based on gentleness, a complete ignorance of all that was petty and base, the strength of single-mindedness, a capacity for being amused and none for feeling hatred, and a love of people that made him proof against all disappointment'. Anthony Sampson noted how David kept a photograph of Waldorf on his desk, and spoke of him often: he had been the great influence on David's life, greater even than Orwell or Trott, and David himself embodied many of the qualities he rightly admired in his father.

African Affairs

David was always more interested in foreign than domestic matters; and although nuclear disarmament, European unity, the Atlantic alliance and Arab–Israeli relations would always loom large in his thinking, South Africa became his particular passion – so much so that, for critics and admirers alike, the *Observer* came to be associated with Africa as far as its foreign coverage was concerned. 'London is the best centre for informed journalism about Africa,' the best-selling American writer John Gunther proclaimed in *Inside Africa*, published in 1955, and 'one might almost say that the "capital" of Africa is the office of the London *Observer*'. As we have seen, Orwell had urged David to turn his attention to the decolonisation of Africa once India had been granted its independence in 1947, adding the proviso that independence should be granted 'regardless of the mistakes the Africans might then make'. David was to follow a very similar line: many years later he told Donald Woods, the liberal South African newspaper editor who had fallen foul of the authorities in Pretoria, that 'although liberals have the right to claim the role of ally (as have Communists or Christians) they would be mistaken to assert that the cause is anything other than the right of the Africans to majority rule, even if that majority is not liberal'.

'I am so glad that the *Observer* is taking up Africa, so to speak,' Orwell wrote in November 1948, but elsewhere David's advocacy of the African cause excited both derision and hostility. 'So this is the man you have hired to turn our paper into a Coon Gazette?' Nancy asked after David introduced her to Colin Legum, while Beaverbrook warned the journalist Bob Edwards that if he wanted to meet David he should 'put some boot polish on your face and then he'll see you' (he also claimed that 'the *Observer* is for the blacks, and the *Spectator* is for the buggers'). At a more elevated level, David crossed swords with his old mentor Bob Brand on the subject of Africa. Africans, Brand told him, have 'the extraordinarily attractive qualities of humour, rhythm and happy-go-luckyness', but 'the natives of South and East Africa are totally incapable of running a modern state'. 'I have never said that the natives of South and East Africa are capable of running a modern state or are capable of developing their territories without great assistance,' David replied after Brand had described his leaders on the subject as 'hopelessly impractical', but it was vitally important to move away from a situation in which 'the Africans have only Communism or what is called "Black Nationalism" of the Mau-Mau type to which to look for hope'. Eight years later, Brand remained unconvinced. 'I know you know a lot about Africans but I have had much more experience of different tribes', he insisted, after reminding David of his experience with Milner's Kindergarten. 'Do you think they are likely to be good leaders of a modern democracy?' he asked after showing David photographs of Kikuyu in native dress.

Nor was Bob Brand alone in his views. Years later Sebastian Haffner told *Der Spiegel* that he and David fell out over South Africa and 'David's policy on race, which was basically anti-white and pro-black', while TJ wrote to say that people were criticising the *Observer* for being 'rather self-righteous', and 'perhaps this may refer to your Black and White Policy'. Leonard Woolf, like Orwell, had urged British politicians to 'forestall events' by decolonising in Africa, but the Labour grandee Hugh Dalton was appalled when Attlee offered him the job of Secretary of State for the Colonies ('I had a horrible vision of a pullulating, poverty–stricken, diseased nigger community'). And in a letter to his father about Basutoland, David wrote that 'one can only understand the atmosphere in which public affairs in these South African territories are transacted if one remembers the way in which the Southern whites of the USA have for long been accustomed to dealing with their negro questions. There is the same basic assumption that members of the subordinate races are children and should be treated accordingly.'

In 1948 D. F. Malan's National Party defeated General Smuts's United Party in the South African general election, and a year later the apparatus of apartheid began to be introduced. Although the election result was unreported by most of the British press, the *Observer* greeted it with an anxious leader, written by David, entitled 'The Meaning of Malan', and from now on the paper would be increasingly involved with African affairs. It was well equipped for the purpose. Colin Legum had come to England to fight apartheid from outside: he was a formidable figure, more than able to hold his own, though when David learned that Bob Brand and Arthur Mann had been complaining to him about the paper's interest in Africa, he told Legum to let him know if it happened again, as 'I won't stand for it.' Stanley Uys and Cyril Dunn both reported from South Africa, as did Patrick O'Donovan on flying visits; and when Anthony Sampson joined the paper he brought with him invaluable knowledge and contacts from his time on *Drum*. But the man who was to influence David more than any other, and was to join Trott and Orwell in his pantheon of heroes, was a tall, emaciated, shabbily dressed and single-minded Anglican priest named Michael Scott.

'You have only to spend a weekend, or half an hour, with Michael Scott to know that he is emptied of self,' Tom Driberg once wrote of him. 'He lives his cause. He can talk of little else. He has, indeed, the irritatingly lovable "absent-mindedness" of the proverbial philosopher – absent-mindedness meaning a mind so full of one dominant passion that it is detached from the trivial details of its body's comforts.' After serving as a priest in India before the war, Scott had moved to South Africa in 1943. He was appalled by the conditions endured by the non-white popu-lation, and had become actively involved in the Campaign for Right and Justice; he had also campaigned for the restitution of their lands to the Herero people of the mandated territories of South-West Africa, and against South-West Africa's absorption into South Africa. In 1950 he was refused readmission to South Africa and settled in London, making an occasional trip to New York, financed by Indian admirers, to press the Hereros' case at the United Nations. 'He was horribly pained by the racial brutality in South Africa, which for him was not only an affront to his principles, but an almost physical hurt,' Peter Calvocoressi recalled. 'He was bitterly disappointed by the strong-arm methods adopted by some leaders in new African states, whom he rebuked privately. He was not an easy man to work with or for, partly because he saw the world and its problems in extraordinarily simple terms.' 'The non-violent breaking of laws that are regarded as morally wrong is to him a positive act, deriving from respect for law, and is the opposite of lawlessness,' David wrote of him, adding that, according to Scott, 'the trouble with moderate men is that, often, they are only moderately willing to fight for their beliefs'.

Robert Stephens brought Scott to Tudor Street, and introduced him to David. 'I was very taken with him,' David recalled: he was 'immediately struck by the fact that Michael was the last one to speak', and by his 'funny combination of modesty, selflessness and intransigence' – though 'it takes you a little while to come to the intransigence'. Before long David had published a Profile of his new friend. It was read by Mary Benson, a good-looking, fair-haired South African who was working in New York for David Lean, the film director, but decided there and then that she must work for Scott instead. A close friend of Alan Paton, the author of the best-selling *Cry the Beloved Country*, she was to become an occasional contributor to the *Observer* and a tireless champion of Scott's work. She was taken on as his assistant in 1950, typing up his letters, his petitions to the UN and his autobiography, and noting how he kept his voluminous papers under the bed in his tiny room at the Quaker-run Friends' Centre. Scott was a fine-looking man – Mary Benson remembered how 'his face revealed the two sides of his nature, one austere, the other mischievous, but he radiated spiritual strength and the overpowering impression was one of beauty'– and before long she had fallen in love with him, despite his warning her that he had no room for anything 'personal' in his life. As a boy he had been molested by a schoolmaster, as a result of which he was, in David's words, 'an obvious celibate'. 'Can't you see that for Michael marriage is an impossibility?' David asked her, but the hopeless passion persisted – signifying, in David's opinion, 'a powerful neurotic drive' on her part. She followed him on one of his missions to New York, where she found him ill and living in poverty in Brooklyn. 'I felt like a very clumsy maid handling the fragilest piece of Dresden,' Mary Benson reported to David. 'His eyes are dull, desperate and unhappy – no spark ever. His mind races from one problem to another.' Shortly afterwards David happened to be passing through New York en route to Washington, and booked Scott into the Astor-owned Carlton House Hotel.

'As Scott's reputation for fearless championship of the Africans spread, his name became associated with trouble, and white South Africans regarded him as a dangerous crank, a misinformed fanatic,' Mary Benson recalled in her memoirs, but his activities were by no means restricted to South Africa. In March 1952 Scott wrote an article for the *Observer* about his visit to St Faith's Anglican Mission in Southern Rhodesia, which he saw as a rare but encouraging example of multiracial living. Offers of money and help were forthcoming, leading to the establishment of the African Development Trust (ADT), which pressed for the eventual independence of Northern and Southern Rhodesia and Nyasaland. Both Scott and Benson supported the ADT, which years later was merged with E. F. Schumacher's Intermediate Technology Group, with which David was also involved; but an altogether more influential body was the Africa Bureau, designed, in Scott's words, to be a 'well-informed and impartial intermediary between Britain and Africa, providing a channel through which Africans, and other communities in Africa, Europe and Asia, can convey their opinions to wide sections of the British public and to MPs'.

The Africa Bureau was set up in 1952: it was always run on a shoestring, but David provided the initial funding, and was still writing the occasional cheque some twenty years later. The Bureau was, in David's words, 'a vehicle for Michael', with Scott as the director and Mary Benson the secretary. As was invariably the case with the good causes he supported, David was more than happy to take a back seat once the Bureau was up and running: he was never a director, but advised from the wings, along with Colin Legum. The Bureau was non-party: its first chairman, Lord Hemingford, was a Conservative, the initial executive committee consisted of Elizabeth Pakenham and Arthur Creech Jones, a Labour MP and former Secretary of State for the Colonies, and the honorary presidents included Maurice Bowra, Isaac Foot and Mary Attlee.

Over the years the Bureau put African politicians including Hastings Banda, Tom Mboya, Jomo Kenyatta and Kwame Nkrumah in touch with British politicians, academics, journalists and businessmen. It campaigned to safeguard communities against domination by majorities as well as minorities, so prompting David's involvement in what became the Minority Rights Group, and against unfair discrimination and inequality of opportunity. It arranged public meetings, and published a roneo'ed *Information Digest* and pamphlets, among them Patrick O'Donovan's 'Africa: Which Way Now?'; it opposed the setting up of the Central African Federation and lobbied for reforms in Britain's other African colonies. Its ethos pervaded the 1951 Penguin Special *Attitudes to Africa*, a book suggested by David to which Scott, Legum, Martin Wight and W. Arthur Lewis were the contributors: when Allen Lane wrote to ask whether the *Observer* would be running a review, David told him that it would loom large on the leader page – an altogether more satisfactory state of affairs from the publisher's point of view.

David was horrified when, in 1955, Scott was caught sunbathing naked at Parson's Pleasure in Oxford, and charged with indecent exposure. He dreaded the news being taken up by the tabloids: luckily the case was never reported, and David sent Scott – who had earlier been treated for insomnia and depression – to the York Clinic. Scott, he pronounced, was 'fearless as a lion, but unable to look inside himself', so Anna Freud was put on the case. David also recommended Mary Benson to take a course of psychoanalysis to cure her of her doomed infatuation. No doubt Scott was grateful to David for his support – 'as always, you treat a neurotic and recalcitrant nuisance with the utmost understanding and calm' – but his self-absorption left little room for other people. Three years after the Parson's Pleasure incident, Faber published Scott's autobiography, *A Time to Speak*: very little was said about his friends and helpers, and David was only mentioned for suggesting *Attitudes to Africa*.

In an unpublished history of the Africa Bureau, Scott wrote that although it made a 'noteworthy contribution towards assisting progress towards independence by orderly means' in Central Africa, Kenya and Ghana, 'it was unable to convince Western nations, Britain and the USA in particular, of the dangerous fallacy of the South African position and its relying on its system as an indispensable part of the West's economy and military strategy of defence against Communism', while noting with regret the influence in Britain and America of the 'combined Israeli and South African lobby'. Scott's condemnation of British and American companies which insisted in doing business in South Africa never abated, leading to clashes with colleagues at the Bureau – Jock Campbell of Booker Brothers, for example, championed Harry Oppenheimer of the Anglo-American Corporation as being both liberal and progressive, and claimed that such businesses would eventually lead to the creation of a black middle class. But for all their occasional differences of opinion, South Africa would dominate the *Observer*'s coverage of Africa, and Scott's own involvement with the continent. In 1953 Mary Benson visited her home country, and got in touch with Nelson Mandela and Walter Sisulu of the African National Congress: Mandela was still a practising lawyer, running a firm in Johannesburg with Oliver Tambo, and both men had been active in the ANC's Youth League. 'One had only to mention Scott's name to be welcomed by a multitude of Africans,' Benson reported.

In 1956 the authorities staged a mass arrest of ANC leaders, including Mandela and Albert Luthuli, and the following year the long-running Treason Trial began. Anthony Sampson covered the trial for the *Observer*. Mary Benson was made the secretary of the Treason Trial Defence and Aid Fund, which had been set up by Canon John Collins, and wrote to David to say that 'we are very grateful for the *Observer*'s continual and excellent reporting'. Back in London, the anti-apartheid movement was riven by disagreement between its most eminent advocates. Trevor Huddleston, Michael Scott and the publicity-craving Canon Collins detested one another, and being taken out to lunch en bloc by David at the Waldorf Hotel did little to ease the tension. Collins wrote to David from Christian Action to ask if he would sponsor the Treason Trial Defence and Aid Fund; David wrote back to say that although he would be honoured in principle to be associated with Henry Moore, Victor Gollancz, Bertrand Russell, A. J. P. Taylor, Dingle Foot, Maurice Bowra, Frank Pakenham and Benjamin Britten, 'my difficulty is that, as a newspaper editor, I am responsible for the reporting and commenting on the subjects that appear in the *Observer*. If I am actually involved as a sponsor of a body active in the political field, it seems to me that this compromises my paper's objectivity.' This went down badly with the canon, and relations deteriorated still further when Robert Sobukwe's short-lived Pan Africanist Congress (PAC) split from the ANC. David and Michael Scott favoured the PAC, but Collins stuck with the ANC. Collins was finally infuriated by an *Observer* article entitled 'Canon Jumps the Gun'; a blazing row between Collins and Scott took place in Tudor Street, so ad hominem that – or so David told Trevor Huddleston – 'the way John spoke to me far exceeded in licence and extravagance anything I can remember since my adolescence'.

Late in 1959, the prime minister, Harold Macmillan, began to prepare for his now-famous 'wind of change' tour of Africa, starting in Ghana and ending in South Africa, in which he combined speech-making with promoting the interests of the family publishing firm. Albert Luthuli and Alan Paton were among the signatories to an open letter to the prime minister, published in the *Observer*, begging him not to say 'one single word which could be construed to be in favour' of apartheid, the iniquities of which had been expanded and reinforced by the new South African prime minister, Hendrik Verwoerd, the architect of 'grand apartheid'. Anthony Sampson would be covering the tour for the *Observer*, and David wrote to Macmillan in the hope that he would find time to talk to him 'off the record', adding that Sampson was 'an entirely honourable and discreet person' and 'one of the best men on my staff'.

In March 1960 the world was horrified by the Sharpeville Massacre, in which sixty-nine black protesters objecting to an extension of the notorious 'pass laws' were gunned down by the police. The following month the ANC and the PAC were made illegal under the terms of the new Unlawful Organisations Bill, so pushing the ANC closer to the banned South African Communist Party (SACP). Oliver Tambo went into exile, while Mandela went into hiding. Ruth First of the SACP took Patrick O'Donovan to meet Mandela in his secret hideout. Sometimes referred to as the 'black pimpernel', Mandela had reluctantly come round to the belief that the ANC should forsake peaceful opposition for violence, and had founded the ANC's military wing, the Spear of the Nation. Anthony Sampson, in the meantime, reported on a failed assassination attempt on Prime Minister Verwoerd.

In March 1961 the judges at the Treason Trial finally came up with a verdict of not guilty, but Mandela was still a wanted man. Later that year he was smuggled out of South Africa, and made his way to London via Tanzania, Ethiopia, West Africa and Algeria. Trevor Huddleston had earlier introduced David to Oliver Tambo; Tambo arranged for Mandela to meet David in Tudor Street, and both Scott and Mary Benson were present. 'I've come to thank you for all your paper has done for our people,' Mandela told David. David later introduced him to Hugh Gaitskell and Jo Grimond. In a letter to Grimond marked 'Private and Confidential', David revealed Mandela's name. Neither Grimond nor Gaitskell had ever heard of him, but David assured Grimond that 'while it is important to keep his visit here dark, you obviously ought to be clear about his future actions', adding that 'I personally found him distinctly impressive.'

Just as he had urged Trott not to return to Germany in 1933 but to fight Nazism from without, so David now advised Mandela not to go back to South Africa to face immediate arrest, but to campaign against apartheid from outside, basing himself in Washington DC. But Mandela was adamant. He told Colin Legum that the armed struggle must now be the priority, and spent six months in Ethiopia receiving military training before making his way home, where he was promptly arrested and charged with leaving South Africa without a passport and inciting strikes, including the 1961 'Stay at Home' strike. When David discovered that Mandela had been jailed, he hurried to make his life more bearable by sending him some reading matter. 'Many people I know have a particularly high opinion of Nelson Mandela,' he told Sir John Maud, the British ambassador in Pretoria. 'Obviously one would not want to send books that were deliberately provocative of the South African authorities. The idea would be to send him historical and scholarly works to enable him to continue his general intellectual growth.' Maud was more than happy to act as a go-between, and the first batch of books included H. A. L. Fisher's *History of Europe*, Koestler's *The Sleepwalkers*, Theodore White's *The Making of the President*, Alan Moorehead's *The White Nile*, Churchill's *My Early Life*, Sampson's *Anatomy of Britain* and Edmund Wilson's *Patriotic Gore*. After Mandela had been moved to Robben Island, David supplemented these with law books so that he could continue his legal studies at London University.

In 1963 Mandela and nine others, including Govan Mbeki, Sisulu and Ahmed Kathrada, were put on trial in Pretoria, charged with sabotage, and once again Sampson covered what became known as the Rivonia Trial for the *Observer*. All the defendants faced the death penalty under the 1962 Sabotage Act, and David wrote on Mandela's behalf to R. A. Butler, the Foreign Secretary, begging him to intercede, copying in McGeorge

Bundy, the National Security Advisor at the White House. There was an urgent need to 'save the life of the outstanding African leader in South Africa, and also one of the most moderate', he wrote: his colleagues who knew about South Africa 'believe it is desperately important, both for South Africa and the rest of the continent, that Mandela's life should be saved'. Butler thought it would be unwise to intervene while the trial was still in progress; the defendants were sentenced to life imprisonment, and Mandela was returned to the tiny cell on Robben Island where he was to spend the next eighteen years. David commissioned Bram Fischer, who had led the defence, to write an account of it for the *Observer* – the page on which it appeared was torn from copies distributed in South Africa – and Mary Benson helped Cyril Dunn with a Profile of Mandela. 'I wonder whether you realise how much you and the *Observer* must be largely responsible for saving Nelson's life?' Mary Benson wrote to David. 'In the UN and in Washington people were tremendously inspired by the various articles, including the Profile – and the fact that so great a newspaper was pointing to the stature of the man and the significance of the case hugely impressed people of influence.' These may well have included David's old history master from Eton, Robert Birley, who in 1963 resigned as the headmaster of Eton to become the professor of educa-tion at Witwatersrand University. David greatly admired his old teacher, and after Birley's death he co-edited a collection of essays in his honour: before returning to Eton, Birley had worked for the Allied Control Commission, where he had been active in Anglo-German reconciliation and in setting up the annual Anglo-German Königswinter Conference, both causes dear to David's heart; he had kept in touch with his old pupil, and during the four years he spent in South Africa he helped to make his university into a liberal-minded enclave, and he and his wife were active in trying to ameliorate or ignore the effects of 'petty' apartheid. Nancy, in the meantime, angrily opposed David's stand on apartheid, and ridiculed him for 'putting so many black people on the front page' of the *Observer*: some things, it seemed, would never change.

★

In 1953 Churchill's government, implementing an idea first suggested by Clement Attlee's administration, merged the three British colonies of Northern Rhodesia, Southern Rhodesia and Nyasaland into the Central African Federation. The *Observer* opposed federation from the start, on the grounds that it had been imposed on the hostile black majority, and would perpetuate white minority rule. In March 1959 the *Observer* looked back, regretfully, on 'six years of failure of the Central African Federation', and called for an 'honest partnership' based on 'the full and free consent of the Africans'. Shortly afterwards riots broke out in Nyasaland, in the course of which fifty-two Africans were killed, and the governor declared a state of emergency. Lord Home, the Secretary of State for Commonwealth Relations, claimed that the *Observer*'s policy was 'harmful to the best interests of Britain and the Commonwealth', but David found an ally in his old friend Sir Walter Monckton, who was sent out to the Central African Federation as the head of a Royal Commission. In the meantime, the Devlin Report, to the government's embarrassment, declared Nyasaland to be a 'police state', and found no evidence that Hastings Banda and his supporters planned violent revolution. David was on holiday when the report was published, but his deputy, John Pringle – following the earlier examples of the Marshall Plan and Khrushchev's denunciation of Stalin – printed the Devlin Report in full. The following year the Monckton Report was published: it recommended that the federation's constituent states should be allowed to 'secede' at some future date, and was warmly welcomed by the *Observer*.

South Africa became a republic in 1961, but the British retained responsibility for the three mandated territories of Basutoland, Bechuanaland and Swaziland, all of which were stranded, like islands, inside South Africa itself. In 1948 Bechuanaland hit the headlines in London when Seretse Khama, the nominal chieftain of Bechuanaland since his father's death in 1925, who was reading for the bar in London, married an English girl called Ruth Williams. This caused a scandal in London, in South Africa, and in Bechuanaland itself. Seretse's uncle, Tshekedi Khama, who was acting as regent in his nephew's absence, demanded that the marriage be annulled; Malan's government in Pretoria, which was about to introduce the Prohibition of Mixed Marriages Act, was appalled; the Labour government in London, always fearful of upsetting the South Africans, on whom they depended for supplies of uranium, worried that Pretoria might impose sanctions on Bechuanaland, or even use the scandal as an excuse to annex the territory. In 1950 the government suspended Seretse's right to inherit the chieftainship, and forbad him from returning to Bechuanaland for five years. In a leader-page article in the *Observer*, Dingle Foot wrote that if the British government broke its promise to Seretse, it would simultaneously 'appease the South African advocates of racial discrimination' and 'present world Communism with one of its greatest victories'.

Patrick O'Donovan was sent by David to see Tshekedi, and reported that the British High Commissioner in Pretoria opposed Tshekedi's wish to come to London to meet his banished nephew. 'People have very mixed opinions about him here – everything from the biggest rogue in the Bechuanaland Protectorate to the saviour of his people,' O'Donovan reported. 'Certainly he is the most intelligent and impressive African of any sort I have ever met.' Tshekedi – who had encouraged Michael Scott to campaign for the Hereros at the UN – was then banished from the protectorate, and made his way to London, hoping to persuade the government to take a more lenient line. Michael Scott introduced the 'strong but naturally courteous and good-humoured' Tshekedi to David, and took him to Sutton Courtenay for a meeting also attended by Mary Benson and Margery Perham, the Oxford don and an authority on Africa, who had been campaigning on Seretse's behalf: Mary Benson remembered how they listened to Tshekedi talking while 'sitting in front of the fire in the panelled hall, with pictures of eighteenth-century huntsmen looking down'.

The ban on Seretse returning to Bechuanaland was eventually lifted, and in 1956 he was finally made the chieftain in what was to become Botswana. David, in the meantime, had interested himself in the education of Tshekedi's two sons, nicknamed Peachy and Secky; and because Tshekedi was keen that they should go to a Catholic school, David turned for help to his old friends Christabel and Peter Bielenberg. After the war the Bielenbergs had decided to settle in Ireland, and David lent them the money to buy a farm near Tullow, in Co. Carlow. The boys' school was in Cashel, and they lived with the Bielenbergs, who acted as foster parents. 'Tshekedi's outward behaviour is one of extreme modesty, almost of servility, which is apparently the manner which all Africans of South Africa automatically adopt when dealing with Europeans,' David warned the Bielenbergs, adding that 'like all Africans these days, he is so conditioned to being suspicious of the likes of us that it is really very hard to get on open and intimate terms of conversation with him'. Guy Clutton-Brock, who had farmed the land in Rhodesia belonging to St Faith's Anglican Mission, kept David informed about the Khamas' activities in Africa, and both David and Martin Wight helped with Secky's education. Dealing with the boys and their father was not always an easy business – Christabel Bielenberg once described Tshekedi to David as a 'pain in the arse' – but somehow they struggled through. Years later, David funded Mary Benson to write a biography of Tshekedi Khama.

Michael Scott resigned as the director for the Africa Bureau in 1968, a year after learning to his horror that the CIA-funded Farfield Foundation had been supporting the Bureau to the tune of £3,000 a year. Ten years later the bureau was finally wound up, after being run by Peter Calvocoressi and then Guy Arnold. David tried, in vain, to persuade Cyril Dunn to write a biography of Scott: Dunn remembered the poorly house-trained Scott spilling gravy all over the carpet at Sutton Courtenay, and trampling it in. Despite the carpet, David continued to pay Scott an annuity until Scott's death in 1983.

David's involvement with South Africa and the ANC would revive after his retirement, but in the meantime Rhodesia provided a plat-form on which he could combine his knowledge of newspapers with advancing the cause of black Africans. In 1959 Richard Hall, a young Oxford graduate, and his friend Alexander Scott put forward plans for a new newspaper which would represent the views of the black inhabit-ants of Northern Rhodesia. Jim Bailey of *Drum* and Anthony Sampson were all in favour, and Jock Campbell of Booker Brothers put up some money towards the start-up costs. On a visit to London, Hall met David through Anthony Sampson, and David agreed to invest £70,000 of his own money in the weekly *African Mail*, based in Lusaka. Hall ran the paper single-handedly; by 1961 the circulation had reached 15,000 copies, and the following year he added 'Central' to its title after deciding to sell copies in Southern Rhodesia as well. 'I am immensely proud of my participa-tion in this splendid paper,' David told Jim Rose, while Rose, who had visited Hall in Lusaka, reported that the *Mail* was 'the only publication in N or S Rhodesia which digs for the facts when they are unpleasing to the govt and the only publication which Africans trust'. In 1961 Roy Welensky, the prime minister of the Central African Federation, sued the *Mail* for libel, and David provided Hall with the support he needed: Hall later described the *Mail* as 'the *Observer*'s echo on the spot, in that very part of Africa where the drive for independence was meeting the harshest resistance'.

In 1964 the Central African Federation fell apart, and Zambia, the former Northern Rhodesia, declared its independence. Hall, who also freelanced for the *Observer*, kept the *Mail* afloat thanks to occasional injec-tions of cash from David's private Cushion Fund. 'David's pre-eminent role is most vital,' Hall told Anthony Sampson. 'His support for the *Mail* through the toughest days became a legend out here with everyone from Kenneth Kaunda downwards'; and President Kaunda himself told Jim Rose that 'we don't know what we should do without it.' It remained a very small-scale production: although the circulation had now reached 35,000, the pages were still collated by hand.

Later that year David was to be sadly disillusioned. He needed to
raise every penny to finance the new *Observer* colour magazine, and
felt he had no option but to sell the *Mail*. He told Kaunda that despite
outside offers, including one from 'Tiny' Rowland, the future owner of
the *Observer*, he would far sooner sell it to the Zambian government. He
reckoned he had, over the years, invested at least £70,000, and possibly
as much as £100,000, in the *Mail*, and although Richard Hall disapproved
of his selling the paper in order to finance a magazine for Hampstead
trendies, he was understandably anxious that David should get his money
back (by a strange irony, a few years later he would find himself back
in London, editing the *Observer* colour magazine). Hall and Kaunda met
David in London: Kaunda told David that he was a 'true freedom fighter',
and Hall remembered 'Astor sitting there smiling, his head slightly on one
side, seeming too overwhelmed to speak'. 'Are you sure they will give us
the right amount? I don't want any more – just what I have put in,' David
asked Hall after the meeting. 'Don't worry about that,' Hall reassured
him. 'Kaunda won't let us down.' In the event, Kaunda's accountants
valued the *Mail* at £40,000. 'David Astor is bitterly wounded at the way
things have gone,' Hall told Kaunda, but to no avail. 'So that was the
tawdry way it ended,' Hall wrote many years after the event. 'Supporting
Kaunda's struggle for independence had cost David Astor almost £70,000.'
Kaunda refused to meet David on his next visit to London, but David's
commitment to black Africa remained as firm as ever.

Michael Scott was also involved in what became one of David's most
celebrated, if arcane, political crusades. The Nagas are a Mongol people,
just over a million strong, hemmed in between the far north-east corner
of Assam and the Burmese border. In 1947 A. Z. Phizo, the head of the
Naga National Council, declared Nagaland's independence from India;
he spent the next two years in prison, and on his release he set about
organising a plebiscite on independence. An overwhelming vote in favour
was recorded in 1952, but was ignored by Mr Nehru's government in
Delhi, prompting a campaign of civil disobedience. Phizo had sided with
the Japanese during the Second World War in the hope of advancing his
cause, and he now began to import weapons from China. The Indian
army retaliated with unexpected ferocity, burning villages and killing or
torturing those suspected of siding with the rebels. In 1960 Mr Phizo,
who was wanted for murder by the Indian authorities, went into exile.

David first heard about Mr Phizo and the travails of the Naga people
through Michael Scott. Alerted to Scott's endeavours on behalf of the
Hereros, Phizo had got in touch with Scott, who met him in Zurich,

brought him to London, where he settled in the south-east suburb of
Bromley, and provided the Naga National Council with a room in the
Africa Bureau office in the Vauxhall Bridge Road. David and Scott were
convinced by Phizo's claims that the Indian army had been responsible
for over 70,000 deaths in Nagaland, that over 100,000 Nagas were being
held in concentration camps, and that some 500 villages had been burned
to the ground: according to Scott, 1956 to 1958 had been the worst years,
with crops and granaries burned, Baptist churches destroyed, and village
elders hung upside down from trees. David's first port of call was his
former C-in-C Lord Mountbatten who, as the last viceroy, had overseen
Indian independence and the division of the subcontinent between
India and Pakistan. Phizo, David told Lord Louis, seemed a 'serious,
determined and impressive little man', and the horrifying stories he had
to tell were reminiscent of the French in Algeria in the late 1950s. Phizo
spoke in terms of genocide, and David begged Mountbatten to speak or
write to Nehru since 'the whole matter seems to me terribly grim and
totally regrettable' and 'may be Nehru's Waterloo'.

David also wrote to Nehru's sister, Mrs Pandit, the Indian High
Commissioner in London. She was not pleased by his intervention.
'It seems rather odd that a group of people should form themselves into
a committee and sit in judgement between the government of a country
and a man who has committed acts of violence, looting and subversion in
that country and is a fugitive from justice,' she replied. Mr Nehru himself
had been offended by the tone of David's letter to Lord Louis, and David
admitted that he was 'conscious of having displeased you over the kind of
attention the *Observer* has given the Naga situation'. The Indian government's ire was further piqued when they learned that David had somehow
smuggled Gavin Young into Nagaland without their permission – 'Actually,
I don't suppose you'll manage to get there, but I think you ought to try',
David warned his intrepid reporter. Young was the first Western journalist
to reach the remote territory since 1948: he had spent three weeks there,
and had photographed and interviewed the crew of an Indian air force
DC3 which had been shot down by the rebels. 'I can assure you that it
will be written in the most objective manner possible and we will ensure
that the Indian government's point of view is properly represented,' David
assured Mrs Pandit vis-à-vis Young's three articles on 'The Unknown War'.
'We would be poor champions of the aggrieved if we would only report
and sympathise with the grievances against some governments and not
others. I know how disagreeable it is to governments when journalists
assume this role – I have a lot of experience of this.'

In 1964 Michael Scott went out to Nagaland as a peace commissioner; he arranged a short-lived ceasefire, but was deported two years later. Conor Cruise O'Brien, the Irish journalist and politician, was refused permission to visit Nagaland on behalf of the *Observer*, as was Cyril Dunn; David, in the meantime, helped with Phizo's son's school fees. In 1968 Colin Legum reported that Mrs Gandhi had condemned an 'objectionable article' in the *Observer*, and five years later he wrote a piece on 'The War That India Hides'. The following year David was appalled by an article in the *Guardian* by Walter Schwarz, who suggested that he might also write a piece on the Nagas for the *Observer*. Schwarz, he felt, had given the Indian army a carte blanche, and had visited the country 'with none of the scepticism that I expect a reporter to take into any situation where there is an army occupying territory against an underground resistance movement'. Schwarz retaliated by claiming that David's information was out of date, that he was too reliant on exiles like Phizo, and that the desire for independence had waned.

And that was, almost, the end of the story. In November 1974 David asked Colin Smith, an adventurous and footloose young reporter, to accompany Naga rebels making their way 'over unbelievable terrain' to collect arms from the Chinese. A year later David resigned as editor, and with him went his paper's admirable if lonely campaign for the people of Nagaland. It had been a noble example of campaigning journalism, an *Observer* exclusive in the best sense of the term, but to many readers and commentators David's single-minded obsession with the sufferings of a remote and little-known people had seemed baffling and even faintly comical at times.

17

Suez

'May I take this opportunity of saying how much we have all admired your conduct of foreign policy over the last historic year?' David wrote to Anthony Eden in December 1954. Eden was then the long-serving Foreign Secretary in Churchill's government, and had accepted an invitation to one of David's editorial lunches at the Waldorf Hotel. Two years later, as prime minister, he would be savaged by his erstwhile host in what must be the most frequently quoted leader ever printed in the *Observer*. A glamorous, stylish figure who had specialised in Arabic at Oxford, Eden had been a successful and independent-minded Foreign Secretary, admired as an opponent of pre-war appeasement and hand-picked by Churchill as his heir apparent, yet he is best remembered for the debacle of Suez, which brought his career to an abrupt end and blighted for ever his political reputation. David had known Eden since Eden's pre-war visits to Cliveden and, like Eden, he is best remembered for his part in the Suez crisis, albeit as a critic rather than a proponent of government policy. Suez was to prove a high point in David's career, and, to some extent, a turning point in the fortunes of the post-war *Observer*; and his reaction to Eden's calamitous misadventure reflected his dedication to anti-colonialism and the Anglo-American alliance, tested as they both were by the British government's delusions of post-imperial grandeur.

Because he had devoted the greater part of his professional career to foreign affairs, Eden was less accustomed to the rough and tumble of dealing with the press than his more domestic colleagues; he was also more thin-skinned than most, given to fearful outbursts of rage, and from early on in his premiership he felt embattled. Despite holding and winning a general election shortly after taking over as prime minister, he soon found himself coming under attack. He was seen as a ditherer, and was deeply wounded when Donald McLachlan in the *Daily Telegraph* called for 'the smack of firm government'; in January 1956, only eight months after he had assumed office, Hugh Massingham in the *Observer* reported rumours that he would be elevated to the Lords on the grounds of ill health, while Evelyn Shuckburgh, his former principal private secretary, thought him 'totally disintegrated – petulant, irrelevant, provocative at the same time as being weak'. To make his life easier, as he hoped, Eden appointed William Clark as his press officer. Eden had few contacts in the press apart from Lord Kemsley, the owner of the *Sunday Times* and a loyal supporter of the Conservative Party, and felt he needed an insider's advice; Clark's career at the *Observer* had reached an impasse and, fond as David was of him, David felt that they had come to a temporary parting of the ways. He agreed that Clark had 'outgrown the particular post in London that happens to be the only one available and suitable for you here', and likened the status quo to 'a situation between brothers when it is mutually agreed that it is best if the younger one moves out of the family business and starts up on his own'. Gritta Weil, the office secretary-cum-dogsbody, dreaded losing an ebullient member of staff 'who will bounce around the place – playing leapfrog over high stools, turning somersaults, making a very elegant handstand – and all that on a quiet Saturday afternoon in the newsroom', but A. P. Wadsworth, the editor of the *Manchester Guardian*, regretted Clark's departure for graver reasons. 'As a journalist, I really don't know whether you are doing the right thing,' he told Clark. 'William Clark muzzled would be a sad thing', and 'I can only wish you well – in black coat and striped trousers.'

Once installed in Downing Street, Clark hurried to reassure Wadsworth, telling him that he had 'found the prime minister extremely obliging and absolutely prepared to let me try and play this as a non-party, impartial job. I think in fact it is a credit to have picked on someone who is not a regular, safe party man.' But Clark had misread his man. Like Chamberlain before the war, Eden combined paranoia with a determination to meddle with and, if needs be, muzzle the press, making full use of the lobby system of non-attributable briefings, and, later in the year, threatening to revive wartime powers of censorship. According to James Margach, the veteran *Sunday Times* political correspondent, 'in the conflict for power between Downing Street and Fleet Street Anthony Eden was the natural loser – the easiest and quickest victim on record', but despite that Clark soon found himself being sidelined by his super-sensitive master. Writing in his diary in the summer of 1956, he felt low-spirited 'as a result of a general persecution complex arising out of a whispering campaign designed to make me appear disloyal to the PM. I no longer see enough of the PM to feel that I enjoy his full confidence.' He was frustrated by the prime minister's 'heavy-handed approach', noting how 'several times when papers have attacked him he has sent for the editor or the proprietor, over my strong protests'. And Eden already sensed the *Observer* as a potential enemy. 'I hear Massingham is never out of your room,' he told Clark. 'He's my enemy, so it's not much good my seeing him, is it?' According to Clark's memoirs, Massingham was close to Eden's arch rival, Rab Butler, which may have explained the enmity. Events in Egypt only made matters worse.

Though never formally part of the British Empire, Egypt had long been regarded as a colonial outpost: Lord Cromer had, in effect, ruled the country during the late nineteenth century, and during the Second World War Cairo in particular played a crucial role in the British war effort both before and after the German army had been defeated at El Alamein. The Suez Canal itself had been created by the French diplomat Ferdinand de Lesseps, and was opened in 1869. Based in Paris, the Suez Canal Company had been granted the concession to operate the canal until 1968; Britain owned forty-four per cent of the shares in the company and was the biggest single user of the canal, which provided a priceless link to India, the Far East and the Antipodes as well as being the conduit whereby Middle Eastern oil could be shipped to Britain.

In 1953 the monarchy, widely regarded as corrupt and ineffectual, was overthrown: the portly, pleasure-loving King Farouk was sent into exile, and a republic declared. In 1954 Gamal Abdel Nasser, Eden's nemesis, became prime minister of Egypt after winning a power struggle with the country's president, General Neguib; and that same year the Anglo-Egyptian Agreement was signed, whereby British troops would leave the country within eighteen months. Although the CIA had encouraged Nasser's rise to power, the Americans soon became disillusioned with their protégé, who had not only done a massive arms deal with the Soviet Union, but – together with presidents Nehru of India and Tito of Yugoslovia – was an energetic advocate of 'neutralist' policies, committed to neither of the superpowers; nor did he endear himself to the French by supporting the National Liberation Front in Algeria, which had recently begun its fight for independence from France. In July 1956 Britain and America withdrew their offer to help to finance the hugely ambitious Aswan High Dam project on the upper Nile, as a result of which the World Bank cancelled its crucial funding. Later that month, Nasser announced that he was going to nationalise the Suez Canal, freeze the assets of the Suez Canal Company, which operated but did not own the canal, and use the proceeds of nationalisation to finance the Aswan Dam.

'If we cannot hold the Suez Canal, the jugular vein of world and empire shipping communications, what can we hold?' asked Lord Hankey, a director of the Suez Canal Company, on hearing the news, while Sir Norman Brook, the Cabinet Secretary, warned that 'if he [Nasser] succeeds, we lose our oil and, with it, our standard of life in this country, not to mention our position in the Middle East and our influence as a world power'. According to William Clark, Eden insisted that Nasser 'must not be allowed to get away with it' or to 'have his hand on our windpipe'; nor was he alone in insisting that the Egyptian president (as he had now become) should be met with force. 'We should hit Nasser hard and quickly,' King Faisal of Iraq told Eden and his Cabinet at a dinner party in Downing Street, and although British forces had been withdrawn from the Canal Zone the previous month under the terms of the Anglo-Egyptian Agreement, Eden told his chiefs of staff to prepare plans to occupy the canal. Nasser was portrayed as an Arab incarnation of Mussolini, and then of Hitler, and as a Soviet stooge; and Eden was determined to move against him to keep the canal open, ensure that essential supplies of Middle Eastern oil were not disrupted, keep the Russians out of the Middle East, and (best of all) remove Nasser from power. The reaction of the press was, on the whole, favourable to the prime minister, with the leftwards-leaning *Daily Herald* picking up the Hitler analogy ('No More Hitler!') while the equally leftish *News Chronicle* declared that the government would be justified in taking retaliatory action. The *Sunday Times* would prove unwavering its support; *The Times* less so, though Eden exploited his pre-war friendship with its foreign and deputy editor, Iverach McDonald, who had reported from Berlin before the war, with the result that the paper initially took a strong anti-Nasser line, with one leader comparing his nationalisation of the canal with Hitler marching into the Rhineland.

But over the summer dissident voices began to be heard. Patrick O'Donovan reported from Washington that Eisenhower's administration was opposed to the use of force against Egypt. Alastair Hetherington, standing in for the terminally ill A. P. Wadsworth at the *Manchester Guardian*, wrote that there was no justification for British military intervention, and that to press ahead would align much of the world against Britain; and although the Labour Party had initially sided with the government, its new leader, Hugh Gaitskell, was impressed by Hetherington's arguments, and Labour support gradually turned into outright opposition. The *Observer*, the *Daily Herald* and the *News Chronicle* followed Hetherington's lead in calling for 'negotiations first', claiming that there was no justification for war so long as the canal remained open, rejecting both the Hitler analogy and the use of force unless Nasser used it first, and calling for UN involvement; the *Observer*, which had initially called Nasser's nationalisation 'Hitlerian', now opposed 'childish retaliation' on the grounds that it would ruin Anglo-Arab relations and damage Britain's standing in what was becoming known as the 'Third World'. Eden, for his part, made adroit use of D-Notices, which had no legal standing but called on editors to refrain from commenting on 'sensitive' defence and military matters, so prompting them to exercise a degree of self-censorship which prevented the public from learning about the British military build-up; and he kept up the pressure via twice-daily lobby briefings. He also tried to prevent the BBC's overseas services from reporting the views of Gaitskell and the *Manchester Guardian*, and even asked the Lord Chancellor to prepare plans for taking over the BBC as a whole. Writing in his diary, Richard Crossman reported that Hugh Massingham was 'convinced that Eden and Macmillan really want a war' and were plotting a coup against Nasser, and 'it is the belief that this is their mood which has set off most of the left press in supporting the line which has been taken by the *Manchester Guardian*'. And Rab Butler admitted to Massingham that 'When I sit with some of my colleagues, I sometimes think that I am surrounded by madmen, talking about things I can't understand.'

The state of Israel had only been founded eight years earlier, and felt itself to be under siege from the Arab world in general, and Egypt and Jordan in particular. On 22 October Selwyn Lloyd, who had replaced Macmillan as the Foreign Secretary, met French and Israeli officials at Sèvres, near Paris, to elaborate a top-secret plan whereby the Israelis invaded Egypt via the Sinai, and the British and the French then intervened to separate the combatants and keep the canal open: so secret were these discussions that most members of the Cabinet knew nothing of them, and Eden tried, unsuccessfully, to have every copy of the 'Sèvres Protocol' destroyed. Eight days later Eden presented Nasser with an ultimatum, and when this was rejected British troops were landed at Port Said; a seaborne assault was combined with the bombing of Egyptian airfields. But Eden's timing could hardly have been worse. The Americans were in the middle of an election campaign, but indifference swiftly turned to outright disapproval. The invasion also coincided with the Russians putting down the anti-Soviet revolution in Hungary. In the House of Commons, Gaitskell denounced the invasion as 'an act of folly whose tragic consequences we shall regret for years'.

James Morris, who covered the landings for the *Manchester Guardian*, had been the first correspondent to reveal the 'collusion' hatched up between the British, the French and the Israelis at Sèvres, but so tight was the censorship and control of the press that access to the front was restricted and journalists had to make do with briefings and official 'guidance'. According to the veteran foreign correspondent James Cameron, journalists were 'denied the right to express such things as doubt, or bitterness, or shame, because of an iron-clad censorship'. The censorship was lifted the day after the fighting was called off, with only a third of the canal under British control, but until then all reports had been vetted by the Joint Press Censorship Unit, based in Cyprus: only sanitised accounts were allowed through, with no details of the actual fighting, and casualties underplayed. The hapless William Clark could only watch on from the wings. 'I don't envy your job in the next few days; this will be the hardest war to justify ever,' Mountbatten told him shortly before the attack was launched. Clark only learned of the Israeli incursion into the Sinai via the *News Chronicle*. But if journalists on the front line were shackled by authority, their editors could speak their minds. The *Daily Mail* and the *Daily Express* still supported Eden, but *The Times* and *The Economist* were increasingly critical, while the *Daily Mirror* and the *Daily Herald* were opposed. Clark had been kept in the dark, but he came to believe that William Haley at *The Times* had been briefed about collusion by Eden himself: according to David, 'Clark did not know what had been said to *The Times* but as the briefing took place before the alleged surprise attack by Israel on Egypt, he assumed it must have included an implied admission of collusion', as a result of which *The Times* switched from supporting Eden to being 'silent but hostile'. Once again the *Manchester Guardian* set the pace. By now Wadsworth had died; Hetherington, formerly the defence correspondent, had replaced him as editor, and he took the lead in attacking the government. In a leader Hetherington described the Anglo-French ultimatum as 'an act of folly, without justification in any terms but brief expediency'. Eden's policy, he declared a few days later, had been 'hideously miscalculated and utterly immoral'. Some sales were lost in the *MG*'s heartland in the north of England, but were more than made up for in London and the south – presaging, perhaps, the paper's eventual move from Manchester to London, and the dropping of 'Manchester' from its title in 1959.

David had never been convinced by those who compared Nasser with Hitler, seeing him instead as a 'weak man in a weak country asserting his minimum rights', playing his part in the anti-colonial movement in Africa as a whole; and he worried that attacking Egypt would not only alienate other Arab countries but neutral states torn between 'the Western and Communist power blocs'. Leaving aside the claims of morality and realpolitik, Britain was no longer powerful enough to impose its will in a single-handed, Palmerstonian way, and back in August the *Observer* had joined Hugh Gaitskell in suggesting that the canal should be put under the jurisdiction of the United Nations since 'no single state or combination of states can now effectively police the world. The choice in our time is between paying the price of world anarchy – disastrous for a trading nation such as ourselves – or creating effective organs of international control.' 'Surely something terrible is happening. I have the feeling the nation is being disgraced. Please excuse this urgent cry,' David wrote to Walter Monckton – but even as he wrote he was bracing himself to take a strong line. Because the *Observer* was a Sunday paper, and events were moving very fast, he had to bide his time before unleashing his attack on Eden. 'The bottom has fallen out of my world. Worse than you know even, or will ever know,' a distraught Clark told David. Clark had drafted his resignation two days before the Anglo-French invasion on the grounds that he could no longer 'defend a policy I candidly dislike', and now 'all I ask is your compassion in overwhelming disaster. I dread and anticipate reading you tomorrow.' His worst fears were soon realised.

The *Observer*'s famous editorial, baldly headed 'EDEN', claimed that the British and the French had acted 'not as policemen but as gangsters' and that 'in our view there is one essential: Sir Anthony Eden must go'. It had, in fact, been written by Dingle Foot, but David added the lethal words 'we had not realised that our government was capable of such folly and such crookedness'. Foot specialised in Commonwealth affairs; he had succeeded Waldorf as chairman of the Observer Trust, but although he had been sacked by his fellow trustees Lord Portal and Keith Murray for involving himself in editorial matters, he had remained close to David, whom he had earlier defended against Portal and Murray's disapproval of the paper's policy on Africa. An *Observer* Profile had once described Eden as 'essentially likeable', adding that 'to achieve fame and remain modest; to have authority and remain gentle; to contend for power without being coarsened and cunning – these are major virtues', but the former friendship and admiration were consigned to the past. 'Of course I understand why you wrote it,' Monckton told David: he couldn't give a 'considered reply' under the circumstances, but 'silence does not mean that I should not like a talk with you when we can arrange it'. Others were less forgiving. Julian Amery, the leader of the Tory Suez Group, denounced the *Observer* in the House of Commons for displaying 'weakness', while Isaiah Berlin warned Clarissa Eden that 'the *Observer* is surely going to preach with the peculiar mixture of sanctimoniousness and hysteria which is more nauseating even than the *New Statesman*', and 'I should like to offer the PM all my admiration and sympathy. His action seems to me very brave, very patriotic and – I should have thought – absolutely just.' Berlin later changed his mind, but the prime minister's wife went on to say how 'for the past three months I have felt as if the Suez Canal was flowing through my drawing room'.

'David Astor has written to Iain Macleod urging him to overthrow the government,' Clarissa Eden wrote in her diary a week after the withdrawal of British troops. 'He is said to be using all his money and resources to prove collusion between us and the French and Israelis, and for that reason *The Times* stopped supporting us because they suspected collusion. I suggest we tell John Astor' – the Astor in this case being John Jacob, the recently created first Baron Astor of Hever Castle, who owned *The Times* from 1922 to 1966, and was a close friend of her husband. The Conservative Party had not been united behind their leader. Sir Walter Monckton, who worried that Eden was 'on the verge of a breakdown' and later wrote that he 'did not like the idea of our allying ourselves with the French and the Jews in an attack on Egypt', had resigned as Minister of Defence shortly before Eden's ultimatum, but accepted the post of Paymaster General in order to preserve Cabinet unity; two junior ministers, Edward Boyle and Anthony Nutting, had resigned in protest; and David's youngest brother, Jakie – the Tory MP for his mother's old constituency, the Sutton Division of Plymouth – had been one of six Tory MPs to vote against the government. 'Bloody good!' David wrote to Jakie. 'Very brave indeed. I don't think I would have had the courage to do it. It must have been quite an ordeal to speak in the House against the government at such a time', and he told Colin Legum that his brother had 'made a very brave speech, of which I'm very proud'. 'The anti-Astor feeling is rising, and will continue to rise,' Michael Astor reported. 'It will reach its peak, of course, when we are proved right.' Bill had joined the attack in the House of Lords, sharing his brothers' belief that government policy was damaging Anglo-American relations and the Atlantic Alliance. 'How odd that the four of us, who cannot very often agree about anything, should, from separate points of departure, arrive at the same spot at practically the same time,' Michael continued. 'Courage to your arm and to your pen! You're absolutely right for once!'

Iain Macleod, one of the Conservative Party's rising stars and a member of the Cabinet as the Minister of Labour, had always had doubts about the whole operation on the grounds that the Cabinet had not been kept sufficiently well informed, while the Americans had been deliberately misled. David wrote to him to say that he believed 'the collusion charge is going to be proved – that we knew of a French–Israeli military understanding which we either endorsed or connived at, but certainly did not seek to prevent'. 'The damage to the Conservative Party will be very great and of long duration,' he continued. 'As I believe the collusion was arranged by two ministers and was made known only to a minimum of others, it is in fact unfair that this fate should befall your party. Certainly the backbenchers had no knowledge of it. Presumably most ministers also did not know.' David had put his finger on a sore point, but no reply was forthcoming. Sir Frederick Bishop, a senior civil servant, forwarded David's letter to Eden: Macleod had no intention of replying, but 'wanted you to see it as soon as possible, as Astor may have made similar approaches to others', Bishop told the prime minister. 'That Astor is using these tactics makes us feel quite sick, but it shows that he, and others, are pressing this view hard.' The government continued to deny the charges of collusion, Eden's health had suffered, and Butler held the fort while he recuperated at Goldeneye, Ian Fleming's house in Jamaica; he resigned in January 1957, and was succeeded by Harold Macmillan. David was not forgiven by the new prime minister, who refused to speak to him at a reception in Downing Street for the UN's Dag Hammarskjöld.

Only two members of the *Observer* staff – the cartoonist Haro Hodson, and O. M. Green, the elderly authority on the Far East – opposed the paper's line on Suez, but Arthur Mann, Lord Portal and Sir Keith Murray resigned as trustees in protest. Arthur Mann had lost his job at the *Yorkshire Post* for defending Eden's opposition to appeasement, and had remained a friend of the prime minister; according to the *Observer*, he had resigned because 'the style of our leading article was out of keeping with the kind of journalism that he himself has stood for and that the *Observer* had hitherto upheld'. David would remain forever grateful to Sir Ifor Evans, the chairman of the trustees, for supporting him throughout. Sir Ifor was an academic, specialising in English literature, and a close friend of his fellow Welshmen Tom Jones and William Emrys Williams, and David had earlier expressed doubts about his suitability as chairman: Evans was 'a nice man, intelligent, friendly and altogether civilised', but he had 'not much experience of public life', and David worried that he might feel out of his depth 'if we ran into serious difficulties'. A deluge of letters poured into Tudor Street, all of which were answered by Charles Davy: 302 were in favour of the *Observer*'s stand and 866 against, including one which began 'I read with growing nausea your vicious attack on Sir Anthony Eden.' Ten heads of Oxford colleges gave David their support – led by Alan Bullock, who would in due course be made chairman of the *Observer* trustees. Hugh Trevor-Roper, on the other hand, outraged David's brother Michael by describing the *Observer* as 'the traitors' paper', and was asked to leave house. (This was not the only occasion on which Trevor-Roper disgraced himself over dinner at Bruern Abbey, Michael Astor's house in Oxfordshire. When a fellow guest idly wondered what Guy Burgess would do if he were allowed back to England, Trevor-Roper suggested that he 'would go to work at the *Observer*'. A furious Michael Astor laid down his knife and fork. 'My father owned the *Observer*, my brother edits the *Observer*, and I will have no one speak of the *Observer* in that offensive way in my house,' he declared, and the Trevor-Ropers beat a retreat. Like his Oxford colleague Isaiah Berlin, Trevor-Roper had an uneasy relationship with the *Observer*, and eventually stopped reviewing books for the *Observer* and moved to the *Sunday Times* instead.) C. P. Snow wrote privately to David, lending his support; David's old mentor, Robert Birley, argued that had Egypt not been attacked, it would have destroyed Israel.

One of the myths about the *Observer* and Suez has it that, as a result of angry readers cancelling their subscriptions, sales began to drop away in favour of the *Sunday Times*. This was not true: the *Sunday Times* was poised to challenge and soon surpass the sales of its old rival, but the *Observer* had nudged ahead that September, with sales of 568,969 in one week, and despite some cancelled subscriptions and some angry letters, the *Observer* retained its lead, notching up sales of 633,000 by the second half of the following year. But whereas the readers who jumped ship tended to be middle-aged and well-heeled, those who switched to the *Observer* because of its stand on Suez were, as often as not, young, idealistic and relatively hard-up, and therefore of much less interest to advertisers: or, as Bill Smart, the paper's advertising director, put it, 'We had readers who had gardens but switched to readers who had window-boxes.' (A precursor of the more conservative readers who cancelled their subscriptions was the Garrick Club member who, in May that year, wrote to say that devoting an entire issue to Khrushchev's denunciation of Stalin was 'an iniquity and an impertinence' which had ruined his Sunday, and that David must have suffered 'a rush of eccentricity to the brain'.) J. Walter Thompson, the advertising agency which looked after the paper's interests, warned about an inevitable withdrawal of advertising, and Tristan Jones was duly depressed. 'Don't let Tristan get you scared,' David told Anthony Sampson, who had conveyed JWT's warning to his editor. 'The only way to get into real trouble is if we lose our self-confidence. After all, we've been right over this crisis and will be proved so. We only need not to get alarmed, and should of course avoid saying "I told you so." All will be well if we keep our heads.' Holding his nerve had not been easy – as he told Hugh Gaitskell, 'I know in my little way what the pressures have been on anyone who stood out against the semi-hysteria of the whole Suez episode.' Some large firms, including English Electric, withdrew their advertising, and ten years later English Electric still refused to reconsider their embargo; the advertising agency Masius & Fergusson advised its clients, on political grounds, not to place advertisements with the *Observer*.

Some of the firms which withdrew their advertising were Jewish-owned: as David put it, because 'the *Observer* had always taken a special interest in Israel and probably had a higher percentage of Jewish readers than most papers, it suffered a sharp rebuff. I have met many Jewish readers who have not read the paper since.' Marcus Sieff of Marks & Spencer told David that he was very upset by the *Observer*'s claiming that Nasser's behaviour was 'to a large extent the product of years of bad Western policy': according to Sieff, Nasser had not only refused to negotiate with Israel, but had 'openly planned Israel's destruction' and had used fedayeen gangs to murder Israelis in Israel itself. In his reply, David said that the *Observer* had always tried to explain both sides of the Arab–Israeli conflict while discouraging 'military adventures' – and the fact that 'the present government has utterly departed from the above maxim is our reason for our strong line against them'. Sieff was unconvinced. 'Frankly I think the reputation of your great newspaper has been lowered,' he wrote a few days later. 'We have done our best to be impartial,' David replied. 'As this office contains its pro-Israeli contingent, we have arrived at our judgement after more protracted and two-sided discussions than I imagine have happened in any other office in this city. So I am not unduly daunted by your verdict on us.' But he hated losing the support of the Jewish world, and not for purely commercial reasons. David had a lifelong love for the Jewish people, and said on more than one occasion that he wished he had been born a Jew. Years later, David reiterated that he had 'met many Jewish individuals who have never read the paper since then', but over the next twenty years he did everything he could to repair relations with the Sieffs, the Raynes

and other members of the Jewish community, with Lajos Lederer acting
as an engaging and ever-active intermediary. As the *Observer*'s resident
Hungarian, Lederer had covered the Hungarian rising: David and his
brother Bill were actively involved in sending money and medicine as
the Russians took their revenge.

Michael Scott had marshalled what he called 'the group' to support
David's line on Suez: its members included Jo Grimond, David Gilmour,
Richard Scott of the Guardian Trust, Donald Tyerman, Edward Boyle,
Stephen King-Hall, John Grigg, Peter Calvocoressi and Lady Violet Bonham
Carter – who, two months after the Suez debacle had ended, wrote
David a New Year letter of 'gratitude and *deep* admiration for the great
leadership you have given, and are giving – with such shining courage
and such matchless integrity', adding that 'it needed more courage for
the *Observer* (with its Conservative tradition) than for the *Manchester
Guardian* or *The Economist*'. 'Suez was a traumatic experience for David
Astor,' Hugh Massingham wrote some years later. 'Before he became
editor, when Ivor Brown was in the chair, he had organised the paper's
foreign news with great success. He took over and had a dazzling period
when everything went right for him. Then came Suez, with its loss of
circulation, and it sapped his confidence.' The loss of circulation became
part of Fleet Street folklore, but a far greater threat to the future of the
Observer was looming – triggered, in part, by the final disappearance of
paper rationing, an advertising boom that coincided with Macmillan's
declaration that 'You've never had it so good', and by the appearance in
Britain of a small, genial Canadian wearing heavy pebble-lensed specs
and a crumpled double-breasted suit. But David would always be more
concerned with world affairs than the economics of newspaper publishing.
'The tragedy of Suez was that Britain should have allowed itself to see
the world as it looks to France and Israel,' he told Bob Brand, and he
worried that, as a result, 'Asia would be pushed more and more into an
anti-Western attitude, to the ultimate advantage of the Communists.'
Suez had been his 'Agincourt', the fine embodiment of his moral and
political courage, and the single incident for which he is best remembered;
and although he felt in retrospect that his attack on Eden had been too
emotive, 'I think I would do it again. You couldn't keep quiet.'

18

Changing the Guard

In 1957 paper rationing finally came to an end, and two years later the Newsprint Supply Company, which had controlled the supply of newsprint to the newspaper industry, was wound up; rather than drawing on a shared pool of newsprint, managers were now free to negotiate directly with suppliers, and haggle over the price they would pay. Since the end of the war slightly more generous quotas had been made available, but now a bonanza beckoned. This sudden largesse coincided with the consumer boom of the late 1950s, early intimations of youth culture and the permissive society, and an explosion of consumer advertising, whipped up by the advent of commercial television in 1955 and reflected in the popularity of books like Vance Packard's *The Hidden Persuaders*. Newspaper proprietors and editors felt free to increase the pagination of their papers, to emulate the Americans by adding new sections devoted to the arts or sport or business, to increase the number of photographs on offer, and to venture into the less familiar terrain of women's pages, travel, gardening, furnishing and DIY, cookery and wine-tasting – all of it made possible, it was hoped, by increased sales and the support of the advertising industry. The printing unions saw, and exploited, the opportunities offered to tighten their stranglehold on the printing and production process, vulnerable as it was to industrial blackmail in the form of exorbitant wages for sometimes non-existent jobs, and the threat of a strike which could kill off the next day's issue; and bright young journalists hovered in the wings, waiting to exploit the opportunities offered by extra pages and new subject areas, and – in the case of the *Observer* – to take the place of an increasingly disaffected old guard.

It was agreed that the *Observer* should expand, ideally to forty pages, and in 1960 both the *Observer* and the *Sunday Times* followed the American lead by dividing their papers into two sections. Ken Obank's attempt to design the front page for the new Weekend Review, which included an essay on the front page, followed by books and arts reviews, travel and the women's page, was not a success, and outside help was summoned. David turned to Ruari McLean, the elegant and well-regarded typographer and designer who had worked with Allen Lane in the early days of Penguin Books before designing *Eagle*, the wholesome boys' comic much favoured in the early 1950s by middle-class parents worried that their offspring might be corrupted by American 'horror' comics. Like Allen Lane, David was the most stylish of editors, in print as well as in person, and McLean not only produced an elegant template for the new Weekend Review, but designed new mastheads for the Review Front and for the front page of the paper itself, the lettering of which was reproduced on a fascia board outside the Tudor Street offices: when the paper eventually moved into the *Times* building in New Printing House Square, it was then engraved in stainless steel above the entrance. McLean also commissioned Edward Bawden to redraw the paper's royal coat of arms, later used as 'ears' on either side of the front-page masthead.

At a less rarefied level, the twenty-seven-year-old Clive Irving joined from the *Daily Express* as features editor of the Weekend Review, and was involved in redesigning the paper as a whole; and Dennis Hackett (ex-*Mail* and *Express*) replaced Mechthild Nawiasky as the picture editor, ushering in a more 'newsy' use of photographs, and employing young photographers, including Don McCullin. Neither Irving nor Hackett stayed long at the *Observer*, but with Ruari McLean they helped to create the elegant, spacious layout and typography that characterised the *Observer* from the early 1960s. The front page, the Weekend Review and the leader-page double-spread were particularly good to look at, improving still further in 1965 when Wally Fawkes, alias 'Trog', replaced 'Abu' as the regular cartoonist. David used to say that his favourite moment in the working week was when Fawkes came into the office on Friday to discuss the subject of that week's cartoon. (Fawkes doubled up as a jazz clarinettist, playing with George Melly – who was to become a frequent contributor to the paper.)

But the improved look of the paper was not simply due to more paper being available, and David's hiring of Ruari McLean. Since Garvin's day, the *Observer* had been printed by the Argus Press in Tudor Street, but in 1958 their contract was not renewed, and the printing was moved to *The Times* – so making it possible for *The Times*'s machines to keep rolling seven days a week. (According to Tom Baistow, who reported on the press for the *New Statesman*, the Hever Astors charged David 'at a consanguine cut rate'.) The look and feel of the 'host' paper inevitably rubbed off on the once-weekly 'guest': the *Sunday Times* had long been printed on the

Daily Telegraph's presses, and both papers had a cramped, over-cluttered look, and were printed on grey-looking paper; thanks to Stanley Morison, an authority on typography and the creator of the ubiquitous Times New Roman typeface, *The Times* was elegant, generously laid out and printed on better-quality paper, and the *Observer* reaped the benefits. On Saturday mornings the key editorial staff, including David, Ken Obank and the news editor, decamped to New Printing House Square, on the other side of New Bridge Street.

Both Michael Davie and Anthony Sampson brimmed over with ideas for new areas into which the *Observer* might venture: too much so, at times, for David's liking. Writing to Davie, who was temporarily working in Australia – he had an Australian wife, and was very attached to the country – David hoped he hadn't seemed too dismissive of Davie's sugges-tion of a series of articles on British institutions in the Weekend Review. He wanted to steer clear of enlarged versions of what Sampson did so well in Pendennis – 'a quick, gossipy, witty insight into the worlds of bankers and bishops' – and had no desire to 'join the *Sunday Times*, the *Spectator* and the Beaverbrook lads in providing bright and entertaining flapdoodle'. He worried about 'introducing more vulgar material into the bumph', and diluting 'those characteristics which made the paper a suitable vehicle for George Orwell to write in and a place where other minority views that were not simply playing to public prejudice could be heard' – adding that 'I bring these conflicts on myself by staffing the office with people likely to pull in opposite directions from some of those in which I believe we ought to go.'

'What I am not sympathetic to is the general tendency towards bright-ness at the expense of intelligence, which follows fairly inevitably from the general office concern at the circulation advances made by the *Sunday Times*,' he continued two days later. He worried about the 'decay' of his beloved Profiles – 'they used to be the outcome of a much more intensive study', and should ideally draw upon 'the qualities of a failed novelist and an amateur psychologist' – and 'if my letters sound grumpy, tired and slightly defeatist, that is simply due to the fact that that is the way I am these days.' Davie agreed about the Profiles, the best of which 'had your blood on their hands', but felt they should be more ruthless about bad books by established writers – he cited the latest Graham Greene as an example – and felt that the paper should cover 'business and pop music as well as trade unions and ballet', and that 'material solely designed to lift circulation' was acceptable provided it was 'up to the paper's general standard'. As far as popular culture was concerned, Kingsley Amis was regularly writing about jazz; the paper had already run Profiles of Tommy Steele, Brigitte Bardot and the Goons, and Anthony Sampson had provided a full report on Bill Haley's hugely popular tour of Britain in 1956.

Sampson was equally fertile with ideas, and was particularly keen that the *Observer* should turn its attention to business – a sore subject at the time, since it was widely agreed that British industry and commerce were blighted by the old school tie and outdated business methods, and that Britain should follow the examples of the French and place its faith in planning and professional management: notions spelt out in innumerable blue-covered Pelicans such as Michael Shanks's *The Stagnant Society*. Sampson was all in favour of devoting the new, free-standing section to business: writing from Washington, he told David that 'we would have the immense advantage of our Sunday date, when most people's thoughts turn to Mammon'. No other general interest paper devoted space to business, 'but I don't see why the *Observer* shouldn't do some pioneering in this field'. Andrew Shonfield had proved a brilliant economics editor – William Clark remembered how at conferences he would 'shine his searchlight mind into the dark corners of political economy, so that we were able to make up our minds with understanding' – and despite being 'economically illiterate', in Nora Beloff's words, David picked the young and unknown Sam Brittan as his successor; but Sampson had something less specialised in mind, and was convinced that takeovers and tycoons, advertising and City news, could be made of interest to the lay reader. Like Davie, he was keen to run a series on British institutions, including the Foreign Office, the Treasury, the BBC and the public schools: before long he would take time off to write his best-selling *The Anatomy of Britain*, in which he would put this approach into practice at book length. In the meantime David tamped down his natural indifference to business articles by commissioning his friend Roy Jenkins to write 8,000 words, spread over three Review Fronts, on the takeover struggle between ICI and Courtaulds. 'The concept was entirely his, although the treatment was entirely mine,' Jenkins admitted. Jenkins was a natural ally, combining enthusiasm for the Common Market with Atlanticism, liberal social policies with faith in the mixed economy.

'We are finding the *Observer* at its present size a struggle to produce with our existing staff, and the prospect of its becoming larger (which is economically very desirable) is quite alarming to my editorial colleagues and me,' David told Tom Hopkinson. 'We have plenty of writers of all kinds. Our weakness is in the higher administration.' The time had come to summon the help of John Pringle, then editing the *Sydney Morning*

Herald, who had earlier admitted that 'there is no paper for which I would rather work; there is no one for whom I would rather work', and that he had no desire to be an editor again, since 'I haven't the physical and moral toughness which editors need.' Sampson met Pringle in Delhi, and reported back that he had 'just the right mixture of drive and niceness. He's bubbling with ideas, and is obviously rarin' to go.' 'I think the *Observer* is in a thorough mess,' Alastair Buchan told William Clark. 'The organisation hasn't evolved at all from the days of a ten-page paper to the needs of twenty-fours.' Fred Tomlinson had taken to the bottle, 'David's editorial judgement is much less good than it used to be', and 'everyone is waiting for Pringle, *comme on attend* Godot – and such a large load will be dumped on his shoulders that he may not be able to cope'. Morale was low, but for David 'what has been worrying me is a tendency to put speed, slickness, wit and circulation above the retention of the paper's hard-won reputation for being serious, truthful and fair', and although some people dismissed its 'careful regard for fairness as a joke or a fault, I think it the paper's chief asset', he told Pringle shortly after his new deputy editor had joined the paper in 1958 on a salary of £2,500, half what he had been getting in Australia.

Pringle quickly realised that 'for all practical purposes David Astor was both the editor and the proprietor': the trustees were 'distinguished, civilised, liberal men and women who knew little or nothing of the newspaper business' and were more than happy to leave David in control; every now and then he gave them dinner at the Savoy, after which 'they went back to their universities and City offices in a glow of brandy and mutual admiration'. But it would be wrong to assume that David exercised power in an 'arbitrary or dictatorial way. On the contrary, I found the *Observer* to be more like an experiment in participatory democracy or even a Maoist commune. Every decision was discussed, interminably, by everyone.' Once a fortnight the entire staff was invited to voice their opinions: David was not a good chairman, so 'the proceedings tended to be chaotic', but the exercise was good for the morale and encouraged staff loyalty. Editorial policy was decided by small groups meeting once or twice a day from Tuesday to Friday. 'These meetings tended to last for hours, and though the discussions were brilliant and often informative, they used to drive me nearly frantic because of the difficulty of getting a decision', Pringle recalled. He particularly remembered David 'listening attentively with a smile on his handsome, boyish face, occasionally brushing his fair hair off his forehead with a characteristic gesture, and sometimes intervening shyly but effectively'.

In a memo to Ifor Evans, David tried to clarify the interminable meetings. He claimed that there were four meetings a week. On Wednesdays, a small group of six to eight people went through the main features for the week and discussed long-term projects; on Thursday there was a meeting open to all the staff, at which Profiles and leader-page articles were discussed; on Friday there was a 'Comments' meeting, attended by four or five people, in which that week's leaders were finalised, and writers were assigned to write up the 200-word 'Comment' features; and on Saturday afternoon a final meeting was held, after the first edition had gone to press to catch the 6.30 train to Edinburgh, at which the current issue was assessed, plans were made for the following week's issue, and foreign correspondents were alerted to possible stories they might want to follow up.

One of Pringle's jobs was to bridge the gap between the voluble Central Europeans and the dependable Fleet Street lags. David was 'never happier than when surrounded by his staff, talking, talking, talking', but he could be fickle at times, moving from one guru to another, with the result that 'the first adviser, never rudely dismissed but politely set aside, would often feel hurt and rejected'. Of the Central Europeans, Deutscher was, for Pringle, 'the most lovable and the most brilliant of the lot, but was neither quiet nor sensible'; Loewenthal, a 'slightly comical figure', was 'convinced that he, and he alone, understood the world political situation'; he seldom spoke for less than ten minutes, and 'lunch would seem infinitely distant'. They were not always appreciated by their Anglo-Saxon colleagues. Alastair Buchan, the defence correspondent, 'got even angrier at the European Mafia than Edward Crankshaw', though Robert Stephens proved to be a 'quiet, gentle and kindly man who concealed his irritation rather better than most of us'. Not everyone attended the endless meetings and lunches. Patrick O'Donovan and Hugh Massingham stayed away; Ken Obank and Michael Davie were often too busy; Terry Kilmartin and Nigel Gosling were taken up with the arts pages, while Philip Toynbee, a 'tall, gaunt figure with a pale craggy face and a loud and boisterous laugh', only came into the office once a week, though as soon as he appeared 'everyone seemed to be smiling'. David 'presided over this intellectual bear-garden with extraordinary patience and good temper. He was an admirable listener, and talk of one kind or another was both his chief recreation and the main way in which he absorbed knowledge.' He couldn't bear to delegate, and 'all decisions were eventually taken by him even if only after prolonged hesitation and delay which drove the production staff to frenzy'.

During the years in which Pringle worked with him, David was obsessed by the notion that the two superpowers, America and the USSR, 'could impose peace and disarmament on the rest of the world'. But although politics was his passion, he was always open to ideas. 'You could not work with David for a week without realising that the essential feature of his character was an almost simple goodness', Pringle concluded. 'In his relations with his staff he was infinitely kind and generous', but sometimes Pringle found his 'intense moral earnestness and intellectual seriousness wearying', and turned for light relief to Patrick O'Donovan, Terry Kilmartin, Anthony Sampson or William Clark.

Much as David appreciated their contributions to editorial meetings, the old guard were slowly fading from the scene. Sebastian Haffner had dominated conferences in the early days of David's editorship, but by the time Pringle arrived he was no longer in attendance. Years later, David told Haffner's daughter that her father had been 'the ablest colleague I had', as well as a 'good friend', but as early as 1953 Haffner wondered, in a letter to David, whether the time had come for him to leave the paper, citing the German proverb that one should 'stop eating when it tastes best', and he worried that he was now 'playing the odious role of the court favourite rather than the respectable one of a responsible minister'. He felt that his views and David's were diverging, leading to, 'on your side, a feeling of loss of confidence, on my side a feeling of loss of freedom', with the result that he felt he had to 'soft-pedal and equivocate' in his articles. Now in his mid-forties, he wondered whether he should 'live out my days in the comfortable groove of the *Observer*', becoming 'an increasingly unhandy and obsolete piece of ancient office furniture standing in the way of younger people'. Nor did he see eye to eye with his fellow Central Europeans. Colin Legum recalled the battles between 'the feisty, brilliant and self-opinionated Loewenthal and the stolid Haffner': Loewenthal shared David's Atlanticism, whereas Haffner was becoming, in Pringle's words, 'a premature Gaullist', strongly opposed to American involvement in European affairs.

The following year Haffner returned to Germany as the paper's Bonn correspondent. As such, he enthusiastically advocated a united and neutral Germany. 'Haffner has gone neutralist or, to put it in less political terms, he has become anti-David,' William Clark told Patrick O'Donovan. 'His big three articles in recent issues represent roughly the opposite of *Observer* policy.' Hugh Gaitskell complained to David about an editorial on Germany, written by Haffner, which 'surely is exactly the opposite of what the paper has always said previously. It is in fact going a very long way to conceding the Communist cause.' In 1961, as the Berlin Wall went up, Haffner resigned from the *Observer*, and he spent the rest of his life in Germany, writing for German papers. He had been one of the finest writers ever to work for the *Observer*; towards the end of his life he told *Der Spiegel* that 'being able to influence David Astor was practically an affair of the heart. When I could no longer succeed at it, I lost a significant purpose in my life.'

Rix Loewenthal also felt that the time had come for a parting of the ways. After being particularly 'irritated by a large piece of Astorian prose', he wrote to David in 1957 to say that life at the *Observer* was becoming 'more and more of a strain', and that he did not want to 'hang on till our relations really deteriorate' – the bone of contention being the great gulf set between 'my inclination to think in terms of power politics and self-interest and your inclination to think in terms of co-operative international machinery': for all his suspicion of Stalinism, David increasingly spoke of co-operation between the Communist bloc and the West, but for Loewenthal this was 'both unobtainable and undesirable', and he left to teach at the Free University of Berlin.

Isaac Deutscher also had academic aspirations, bolstered by the critical success of his biographies of Stalin and Trotsky. In 1961 David offered Deutscher a retainer of £2,000 for ten to fifteen pieces a year, after learning that the *Sunday Times* had asked him to write about the Sino-Soviet split. But fond as David was of the 'sage of Wokingham', his younger colleagues were less sympathetic. Pringle told Deutscher that he was spiking one of his articles on the grounds that it contradicted 'other stories we were receiving from correspondents in Moscow and Berlin', putting the political editor, Mark Arnold-Forster, in an 'impossible position'; and David himself later admitted that Deutscher's 'basically Marxist position and that of the paper were incompatible'. The following year he decided not to renew Deutscher's annual retainer – but any feelings of guilt were assuaged by the knowledge that Deutscher had applied for a job at the new University of Sussex, and that both Asa Briggs and David's old friend Martin Wight, now a professor of history at Sussex, were so keen to have him that they were planning to create a chair in Soviet studies specially for him.

What none of them had reckoned on was the animosity felt towards Deutscher by Isaiah Berlin, to whom the chancellor of Sussex, John Fulton, turned for advice. Although they only met twice, Berlin detested Deutscher on both personal and ideological grounds. Some years before, Deutscher had reviewed Berlin's *Historical Inevitability* in the

Observer. Berlin told David that Deutscher's review was 'nastier than I had conceived possible', a travesty of his views which revealed the 'cunning, dishonest and cheap' reviewer to be 'a diffident Bolshevik and not a defender of any kind of liberal values': David offered him a right of reply, but he refused it on principle. A few years later they fell out again over Deutscher. 'As regards his general position, I certainly don't find myself close to him, but I very much doubt whether your idea of where he stands is correct. What binds me to him is that I have many times seen examples of his independence of judgement,' David insisted, before going on to cite Deutscher's readiness to criticise the Soviet Union during the war, when 'the honeymoon atmosphere was so strong in this country that it required considerable moral courage to write of Russia in unsentimental terms'. Berlin was unmoved by David's hope that closer knowledge would lead to a more favourable opinion. 'You say he is a man of courage, integrity and independence; you know him and I have only met him casually, and you speak from long experience,' he replied, but 'beneath his appearances of cool judgement and the temperate tone there is, I am sure, an icy fanaticism. He is a complete Bolshevik of Lenin's time.' Fulton's approach provided Berlin with an opportunity to do down a man for whom he felt the 'greatest contempt' both as 'a person and a writer'; the Sussex offer was withdrawn, and Deutscher continued life as a freelance writer, but no longer for the *Observer*.

Berlin not only disagreed with David over both Deutscher and Trott, but he was one of the very few to diverge, in private at least, from David as a liberal hero, combining modesty, kindness and generosity with a necessary dash of steely determination, describing him more than once as 'a neurotic, muddled, complicated, politically irresponsible, unhappy adventurer, permanently resentful of somebody or something and a typical poor little American rich boy surrounded by a court of dubious toadies which gives his newspaper its queerly disoriented look', and a type 'of whom pre-Nazi Germany was full, and who flourish most richly in New York'. (He was even more damning about Nancy, describing her as 'the most detestable woman in England: boring, rude and guilty of interference in British politics which has brought nothing but disaster'.)

Like Deutscher, Arthur Koestler had reached the end of the road as far as the *Observer* was concerned. Michael Davie was scathing about some of the pieces submitted by Koestler ('Coming from anyone else, I think we'd reject them as newspaper copy'); his agent A. D. Peters pressed for higher fees, and reminded David that other papers were keen to publish his client. 'I much regret that his long association with the *Observer* has ended,' Peters wrote eventually, after reminding David how Koestler was always being asked to rewrite his pieces. David told Koestler that he thought of him as 'just about my oldest surviving friend and mentor', and hoped that his writing for other papers would not 'affect our personal relations. I have too few friends, and would feel upset if that happened.' 'I do appreciate the friendly things you say, but if you, or your collaborators, dislike every single thing I wrote, what's the point?' Koestler replied – and although he would always be happy to review books for Terry Kilmartin, 'with whom, unlike some other members of your staff, co-operation has always been smooth', relations would never be the same again.

But it was not only the Central Europeans who were moving on. Edward Crankshaw wrote to say that his health was not too good, and that, 'Rix or no Rix, I should have had by now to withdraw a little from the rough and tumble': he remained a contributor, but no longer came up from Kent to do battle with Loewenthal at editorial conferences. William Clark was accorded heroic status when he returned to Tudor Street from his unhappy stint at Number 10 – according to Pringle, 'he was seen as a man who could act with the greatest courage when he believed that his principles were at stake' – but he became increasingly bored by journalistic life: he was keen to work with Third World countries, and after running the Overseas Development Institute he ended his career with the World Bank. Alastair Buchan had preceded Patrick O'Donovan as the paper's Washington correspondent before being made the defence and then the diplomatic correspondent. Like O'Donovan, he was a heavy drinker, but although David was prepared to indulge O'Donovan's every foible, Buchan was never a kindred spirit. Whereas David confessed to having 'a weakness for keeping office life informal and familiar', Buchan preferred a 'more clear-cut and contractual' relationship, finding 'the informalities of a home or the closely corporate life of a school to be inappropriate to office work and uncongenial to one's adulthood'. 'Any familiar working relationship with a fatherly or older brother element in it was unwise': it would be more sensible, David suggested, for them to 'avoid a close working relationship', and for Buchan to keep away from conferences. This was not a matter of their disagreeing over politics – if so, 'I would not choose Rix as my chief leader writer, his being a more opinionated and forceful mind than any other in the firm' – but more a question of his wanting to 'avoid the irrational from interfering in the office'.

In what must have been one of the most bizarre and short-lived appointments in the history of the *Observer*, David made the reserved

and scholarly Buchan the assistant manager (public relations), expected
as such to drum up advertising for the paper, while Robert Stephens
took over as diplomatic correspondent. Michael Davie regaled William
Clark with an account of how the hapless Buchan was expected to take
'Lord Chandos out to lunch at Brooks's and explain that the *Observer* is
not just a left-wing vehicle for nigger-lovers and central European Jewish
intellectuals', after which Chandos would give orders for 'thousands of
pounds' worth of advertising'. Not surprisingly, Buchan, who ended his
career as the professor of international relations at Oxford, left the paper
in 1958 to become the first director of the Institute for Strategic Studies.
That same year Bill Smart joined from the *Daily Telegraph*. 'There was no
queue of advertisers at the door of the *Observer*,' he recalled. The paper's
opposition to apartheid ruled out any South African advertising, and the
long-standing ban on advertising alcoholic drinks was still in force. Smart
pointed out to Tristan Jones that the money brought in by drinks ads
made it possible for the *Sunday Times* to produce a thirty-two-page paper,
as opposed to twenty-four at the *Observer*; the ban was finally lifted in
1958, with an ad for dry sherry. The *Observer* pioneered the printing of
Consumers' Association surveys, and was involved in setting up *Which?*
magazine; and although David dutifully toured the advertising agencies with Smart, he instinctively mistrusted the relationship between
advertisers and the coverage of consumer goods, particularly where
cars were concerned. A scathing report on the 1961 Earls Court Motor
Show, in which British cars came in for a drubbing, led to the threat of
a withdrawal of all their makers' advertising: David's penance consisted
of attending a car manufacturers' dinner at the Lancaster Gate Hotel,
during which he had to discuss hubcaps and petrol consumption rather
than transatlantic relations or the possibilities of a Lib–Lab pact.

By then, rather to his relief, he had learned to do without Hugh
Massingham, the last survivor from the Garvin era. According to
Anthony Sampson, David disagreed with Massingham's line on domestic
politics, and heavily edited his copy – still unsigned, as in the old days.
Sampson remembered Massingham emerging from the editor's office,
looking furious and muttering 'the stiletto's out'. Alan Watkins, a keen
admirer of Massingham, suggested that whereas David wanted explan-
ations of government policy rather than elegant yet informative essays,
Massingham was bored rigid by having to explain the workings of the
Ministry of Housing or the Common Market; he also felt that the new
generation of politicians was less colourful than the last, and complained
about the lack of expenses. The final straw came when the oleaginous

Kenneth Harris wrote a long Profile of Reginald Maudling without having 'the wit or the decency to consult me or show me a proof'. Maudling was 'an invaluable contact of mine', and would assume that Massingham was the piece's author: 'I do not believe that this was an ordinary or harmless slip-up: I am quite satisfied that Harris deliberately kept me in the dark.'

Five years later, in the autumn of 1963, another – if less long-serving – political editor handed in his notice in a fit of understandable fury. It was well known that Harold Macmillan was going to stand down as prime minister and party leader for health reasons, and it was widely assumed that he would be succeeded, against his own wishes, by his old rival, Rab Butler. Mark Arnold-Forster, who had recently joined the *Observer* from the *Manchester Guardian*, was tipped off at the Tory Party Conference that Macmillan had chosen the improbable figure of Alec Douglas-Home, still Lord Home and a member of the House of Lords, to be his successor. It was an exclusive coup, and Arnold-Forster phoned his story through to London in a state of high excitement. Peter Crookston, a young journalist who had recently joined the paper, remembers a clutch of senior journalists including Nora Beloff, Ivan Yates and Kenneth Harris talking about it to David in *The Times* newsroom on Saturday morning, with Nora Beloff endlessly exclaiming 'It can't be true.' In the end they decided against, and the paper ran a headline reporting that Butler would be taking over. Arnold-Forster immediately handed in his resignation, and went back to the *Manchester Guardian*. 'My agonised best wishes to you,' David wrote to him in his letter of farewell. 'I really can't say more without weeping.'

New Faces

David still pined for the days when he had been inspired by Connolly's *Horizon*: he told Mark Arnold-Forster that he was still keen to use 'novelists and other writers without journalistic training as occasional reporters. The idea was to introduce a new and more personal style of reporting which aimed at conveying atmosphere rather than fact.' Most of the new writers were, in fact, professional journalists, but the odd exception still slipped through; and the new travel editor was a fine example of the 'amateur' journalist, a literary man who was parachuted in without any previous experience on a newspaper. In 1964 Eric Newby succeeded Pierre d'Harcourt, with far more space at his disposal. A dashing adventurer with bright blue eyes and a broken nose, Newby was one of the best and most entertaining travel writers of the day, and luring him to the *Observer* was quite a coup. As a young man he had sailed from Australia to England in a four-master, as recounted in *The Last Grain Race*; he had had a good war, and later described his exploits as a prisoner of war on the run in *Love and War in the Apennines*; he had worked in the rag trade, in the publicity department of Secker & Warburg, and was the author of the much-admired *A Short Walk in the Hindu Kush*. 'David Astor offered me one of the most coveted posts in Fleet Street, and for the next nine years I led its readers a merry dance,' Newby recalled – too merry, as it turned out, from the *Observer*'s point of view.

In 1958 the paper decided to appoint a 'woman's editor' to work alongside Alison Settle, a 'dear, aunty, old-fashioned' figure who had been *en poste* since shortly before the war, and 'who is staying with us to write and advise on fashion for a further period', and 'to keep an eye on all the other existing "home" subjects (cooking, consumer research, etc) as well as to organise or write additional articles on general topics of interest to women readers'. The successful applicant, Patience Gray, was a well-known cookery writer, and had recently co-authored, with Primrose Boyd, the groundbreaking *Plats du Jour, or Foreign Food*, published by Penguin and illustrated by the young David Gentleman, whom she later employed at the *Observer*. Although she stayed in the job for over three years, she retained an uneasy feeling that 'a woman was not exactly *persona grata* in Tudor Street'. David offered her the job 'in a kind if unenthusiastic way' after informing her that the 'ideal' candidate – whom she later assumed to be Anne Scott-James – was then unavailable; her immediate boss, Nigel Gosling, seemed unsure of how she could be best employed on her sporadic visits to her 'little cell' in the office; Alison Settle took her out to lunch, and made her feel irremediably amateur: '"It's all right for you," she said with a touch of acidity, "you have looks. I have had to make my way without them."' Making her escape down a narrow staircase at the end of her first day, she came face to face with Philip Toynbee, 'inhospitably ejected from some Soho haunt hours after closing time' – and 'I wasn't always able to evade his bearlike embrace.'

Although food and drink were Patience Gray's areas of expertise, Cyril Ray was already installed as the wine correspondent, while the pseudonymous 'Syllabub' wrote about food; but 'it was the European scene I wanted to bring home to English people' in her page, which was entitled 'A Woman's Perspective'. 'I cherished the feeling, acute after the war, that Europe was our real inheritance. England was very isolated still', and 'I came to realise just how indifferent was the *Observer* to the innovative genius flourishing in foreign parts.' Writing about modern architecture or design, about Swedish glass or Scandinavian furniture, risked crossing wires with well-entrenched colleagues, and reinforced her sense that the paper manifested 'a singular indifference on the visual side'; and her efforts to interest Nigel Gosling in the genius of Marcel Marceau came to naught. In due course she received 'a kind note from David Astor' bringing her time at the *Observer* to a close.

The appointment of a new women's page editor was to prove a more harmonious affair, as well as providing the paper with one of its most popular and longest-lasting columnists. The man responsible was a 'laid-back, rumpled figure, slow of speech and patient in dealing with David Astor's Freudian hang-ups over the role of women and motherhood'. George Seddon joined from the *Manchester Guardian* in 1959, and before long he had traded in his tweed jacket and baggy flannels for a white suit and a pink shirt, and belatedly come out as a homosexual despite having a wife and two children. Patience Gray, who assumed that Seddon had masterminded her dismissal, later claimed that under his aegis 'the paper, heading for Consumerland, began to descend the treacherous slope – to sing the deceptive but seductive joys of acquisition'; but he was to prove an exemplary features editor, remembered with gratitude and affection by those who worked with him.

David told Seddon that he wanted to 'humanise' the paper, and asked him to mastermind the expansion of the women's pages. Seddon decided to follow the example of his old colleague Mary Stott at the *Manchester Guardian*, for whom women's pages 'should cover anything and everything that wasn't work'. He approached Katharine Whitehorn, the Cambridge graduate who had worked on *Picture Post* and *Woman's Own*, and was now one of Brian Inglis's star columnists on the *Spectator*. David had decided that he wanted two women's editors, 'one doing the frocks and one the gravitas (a very *Observer* word, that) because they thought that anybody who could do the fashion couldn't possibly have enough gravitas to do the rest', Whitehorn recalled. She told Seddon that she wouldn't do the gravitas, since she didn't want to leave the *Spectator*, but she'd be happy to do the fashion part-time, replacing Anne Scott-James, who had left for the *Daily Mail*. As such she campaigned against cardigans and twinsets, much to the consternation of the advertising department, who worried that advertisers like Marshall & Snelgrove would withdraw their patronage.

But Seddon was reluctant to leave his protégée looking after fashion, and encouraged her to 'do the gravitas bit'; and in 1963 Katharine Whitehorn abandoned the rag trade to start writing what was to become one of the most admired and talked-about columns in the business. 'I was one of the first to bridge the divide between women's writing and what I suppose the blokes would have called serious writing,' she recalled, 'at the moment when writing for women ceased to be a matter of exhorting them to be perfect – at the stove, round the cradle, head down in the broom cupboard if necessary – and started telling it how it really was: a confusion of purposes, a mess, against which we all struggle.' But life was complicated by David's ambivalent views about working women. John Bowlby's influential tome *Child Care and the Growth of Love* had been published in 1953, and suggested that children lost out if mothers went to work, and suffered from 'deprivation anxiety': according to Seddon, David 'didn't believe that any working woman journalist was fit to write about women, on the Catch-22 grounds that only a wife and mother could write about women faithfully. On the other hand, he also believed that if a woman journalist happened to be a wife and mother, then she should be at home looking after her family and not working in a newspaper office.' Patience Gray and other applicants for the job of 'woman's editor' back in 1958 had been asked to write a sample article on 'Can a Career

Woman be a Good Mother?' Gray, for her part, was a single parent with
two young children, and when Claire Tomalin, then working at Cape,
applied for a job at the *Observer*, David sent a message to say that she
should be at home with her children. Every now and then, on a Friday
evening, just as Katharine Whitehorn was struggling to give her children
a bath or get them into bed, David would ring to query some point in
her copy. It was maddening at times, but 'David could tolerate readable
eccentricity in both the prose and the lives of his writers.' (David's well-
meaning interest in the welfare of mothers and babies was reflected in
the serialisation, in 1968, of Dr Spock's *Baby and Child Care*. Spock was
then the leading guru on the subject, and every subsequent book he
wrote would be serialised in the *Observer*.) Whitehorn's husband, Gavin
Lyall, worked on the *Sunday Times*, and between them they worked out
that 'the *Sunday Times* told you what views were or were not acceptable to the paper, but they didn't care, and didn't ask, what your private
views were', whereas the *Observer* reckoned 'you could write what you
liked and they'd support your integrity – but they only hired people of
the same mind in the first place'.

One of the most unusual minds employed on the *Observer* was that of
John Gale. Perhaps the most brilliant writer ever to work full time for the
paper, he is best remembered – though not as well as he should be – for
Clean Young Englishman: poignant, funny and disconcertingly honest, it is
one of the great English autobiographies. 'I am what they call a manic-
depressive', runs its opening line, and his fits of depression verged on
lunacy at times. Attached to the Guards Armoured Division at the end
of the war, he noticed – inimitably – how the SS guards loading the
bodies of concentration-camp victims onto trucks had 'stitched creases' in
their trousers; he then served in Palestine with the Transjordan Frontier
Force, where he fought a duel with champagne bottles. He worked on a
local paper in the Midlands and on the *Sunday Express* before joining the
Observer – his first article for which was entitled 'In Defence of Suede
Shoes', controversial items of footwear at the time.

'He was floppy-haired and fair, handsome in a big-boned, easy, smiling
fashion, slightly teasing in manner, with a faint undercurrent of competi-
tiveness,' Alan Ross wrote in his introduction to a reissue of *Clean Young
Englishman*. 'When I first met him he looked, with his bright-eyed, joking,
obtrusively physical presence, about as far removed from a candidate for
breakdown as you could possibly imagine.' 'Clothes were talismanic
for him,' John Heilpern remembered, and the most widely reproduced
photograph of Gale shows him standing, notebook at the ready, in a

wasp-waisted tweed jacket, tubular trousers and suede shoes ('baggy trousers deaden the imagination', Gale believed). 'He had an electric presence, springy, slightly manic, gesturing with big strong hands, laughing and hoping for the best,' Heilpern wrote of him, while Ross noted 'a certain unease about him, a tension, which I put down to restlessness. He was the sort of person who needs a lot of exercising, like certain breeds of dog.'

Gale contributed occasional pieces to the sports pages, but North Africa, and what he experienced there, was to shape and blight the rest of his life. He was in Morocco for the paper in 1955 – David reported that he was doing better there than expected, still more so since 'he has an exaggerated modesty that compels him to assert his utter incompetence before taking on any job' – and in Egypt at the time of Suez. Back in London, 'I took to waving my arms and shouting about Suez. I shouted at a clergyman. I shouted at people in a greengrocer's in Hampstead. I had been ashamed of England.' In the summer of 1957 David asked him to go to Algeria, where a vicious war had broken out between the French and the FLN, fighting for independence. 'Write nothing while you're there,' David told him. 'Then come home and take the lid off.'

What Gale witnessed in Algeria, directly or at one remove – the brutalities, the massacre of civilians, the torture of captured FLN fighters by French paras, some of them former members of the SS – tipped him over the edge. He came home via Paris, where he was convinced that he was being followed by paras, and that his drinks were being spiked: his feet felt fuzzy and he swung his arms too high when walking – both worrying symptoms as far as he was concerned. On his return to London he took a taxi from Heathrow to David's house in St John's Wood, where a dinner party was taking place. 'Funny things happened in Paris,' he told Bridget. 'Do I seem a bit odd?' David drove him to see a doctor, 'a thin, dark man' with a practice 'deep into what was either Kilburn or West Hampstead'. His behaviour became steadily more erratic; on one occasion he seized a pneumatic drill from an Irishman who was working in Tudor Street, and began to drill holes in the pavement.

Alan Ross – himself no stranger to paralysing bouts of depression – was summoned by David, and asked to stand in for Gale in North Africa. David told him that Gale 'had apparently gone off his head'. Gale himself was 'in no state to talk to me. Instead I had to make do with rereading John's dispatches, which were of a fraught and violent nature.' 'From the misery of that time, his acute distress at the butchery and torture, John never properly recovered,' Ross suggested, and a trip to America made matters worse: 'he became quite unhinged' as a result, and on his return he spent four months in a clinic, where he was subjected to electroconvulsive treatment.

Gale's days as a foreign correspondent were numbered, and for the next ten years he became the *Observer*'s star interviewer, recording his encounters with Louis Armstrong, Groucho Marx, Chaplin, Marlene Dietrich, Tommy Steele and the Chief Scout: 'skilful at drawing even the least co-operative people out and letting them do the talking, John's innate voyeurism and genuine curiosity enabled him to create fascinating portraits by the most economical and unobtrusive methods'. Encouraged by David, he became a master of perfectly shaped 'colour' pieces about dog shows or village fetes or seemingly unimportant members of the public, whom he drew out by asking them whether they liked sherry or telling them about his dandruff problems. Every piece was written in a prose that was, in John Heilpern's words, 'as sharp and clean as a bleached bone on a beach'. He worked in Hong Kong after leaving the *Observer*, and committed suicide at the age of forty-eight, leaving behind his wife and family, and an uncompleted novel. Tristan Jones made a hash of his pension arrangements, and David made up the difference.

Gale had many admirers in the journalistic world – among them Michael Frayn, who moved from the *Manchester Guardian* to the *Observer* in 1962. 'The great draw for me was John Gale,' Frayn recalled. 'I was captivated by the apparent innocence of his observation, the apparent naivety of his style. He had an eye for the inconsequential detail and an ear for the oblique remark. He absented himself from his reports, but left somehow lurking behind this absence the faint ghost of a detached, wryly amused onlooker.' Frayn had applied to the *Observer* while still at Cambridge, and now he had been asked to write a regular humorous column in place of the current incumbent, Paul Jennings. This had involved a lunch at the Waldorf Hotel in Aldwych, where – according to Frayn – 'David Astor used to bring people to lunch to sack them, because it was owned by the family and he got special rates' (in fact it had been owned since 1958 by Charles Forte). David told Jennings that 'in future they wanted him to do a lot more – travel writing and women's pieces and fill-in bits for the business pages, but of course still continue his very funny column. Paul immediately got the message and resigned promptly. You were never fired from the *Observer*,' Frayn concluded – 'they just made your life so uncomfortable that you had to go.'

One of the paper's most popular columnists, Michael Frayn famously evoked Tudor Street life in *Towards the End of the Morning* – which must be, after *Scoop*, the funniest novel ever written about life in a newspaper office. The central character, John Dyson, was based on John Silverlight, a much liked and long-standing member of staff; the editor has David-like qualities of self-effacement, insinuating himself into the office unnoticed by the staff, but the 'short, rather fat man in a shapeless raincoat and a shapeless trilby hat' is more evocative of William Shawn, the mole-like editor of the *New Yorker*, nor would David have taken a bus to lunch at the Athenaeum. 'He was always very kind to me, but really my contacts with him were minimal,' Frayn recalled years later. 'All I can remember now is that he was said to feel that I was *unsound* on psychoanalysis, which John [Silverlight] thought cast a shadow over my prospects on the paper . . . John also said that David felt I saw him as a symbolic father whom I had symbolically to kill.'

David may have been disappointed by Frayn's lack of interest in psychoanalysis, but he greatly admired his columns. 'It is fantastic how you keep up the standard of your originality and surrealist good sense week by week,' he wrote in one of his handwritten notes of appreciation. Just occasionally they failed to see eye to eye. Although Frayn claimed that Alastair Hetherington had been happy for him to mock the *Guardian*'s advertising, David vetoed his suggestion that the *Observer*'s ads should be subjected to similar treatment, on the grounds that this could have a damaging effect given the strength of the competition and the paper's own increasingly precarious position. Nor was he prepared to allow the repetition of a piece which had ridiculed some of the more downmarket pieces published in the paper, upsetting their authors in the process – 'which is not to say that I will publish no criticism of this paper in the paper – on the contrary, we have always published an exceptional amount of highly critical letters from readers and gained thereby a reputation for self-flagellation among journalists. I don't mind that, but I don't want to pretend that it's a pleasure – it would, anyhow, turn it into a vice if one enjoyed self-flagellation.' Frayn contributed his column for six years, after which he wrote the occasional Review Front travel piece, before eventually abandoning journalism for life as a playwright and novelist.

Like Eric Newby, Gavin Young is best remembered as a travel writer. A product of Rugby and Oxford, he had worked in Iraq before finding a job with Radio Maroc. Ian Fleming, whom he met in a bar in Rabat, suggested he try his hand at journalism and approach the *Sunday Times*, but Young had so admired the *Observer*'s stand on Suez that he applied to them instead. After being interviewed by David, 'a floppy-haired, shy-voiced man popping multicoloured sweets into his mouth from a tin on his desk', he was appointed the paper's 'stringer' in Tunis during the war in Algeria, for which he was paid a small retainer plus so much per word printed. He received encouragement from John Gale, 'an intensely warm and manically humorous man', and from Patrick O'Donovan, 'a tall stately galleon of a man' with a 'fine W. C. Fields nose'; Michael Davie, the news editor at the time, 'possessed an unmatchable ability to instil confidence into a neurotic correspondent shivering at the end of a telegraphic cable', and his congratulatory telegrams 'acted on me like a handful of pop pills'. Young reported from around the world, but was best known on the *Observer* for his reports from Nagaland.

Mark Frankland was another footloose reporter, spending two stints in Moscow and spells in Saigon and Washington. He had taken the highly regarded Russian course while doing his National Service and had spent a year with MI6, where he learned to fire guns, pick locks and use invisible ink. *The Times* had refused to send his contemporary Jeremy Wolfenden to Moscow on the grounds that, as a homosexual, he was particularly vulnerable to blackmail, but Frankland's homosexuality presented no problems at the *Observer*. Edward Crankshaw briefed him about Moscow life, and Michael Davie, sporting scarlet braces, assured him that 'there'll be times when you think we've forgotten you. But we won't have' – good advice, since 'the *Observer*'s apparent forgetfulness and difficulty of communication were advantages for any correspondent who liked to be his own master'. Frankland hugely enjoyed his occasional visits to Tudor Street. 'Some of the staff were as knowledgeable as dons, but they were a good deal more worldly-wise, and without a hint of donnish drabness,' he recalled. 'There were eccentrics and there were brilliant drunks, but what everyone seemed to share was a sense of being involved in something uncommonly worthwhile.' Frankland made an invaluable contribution to the *Observer*'s foreign coverage – as did Dennis Bloodworth, the long-serving Far East correspondent based in Singapore, who joined the paper in 1949 'on the basis of a single test piece' he wrote for David.

Neal Ascherson compared his colleagues at the *Observer* to a 'brilliant dysfunctional family' run by a man whose 'enduring qualities were kindness and courage'. A super-intelligent young Scot, educated at Eton and Cambridge, Ascherson reported from Germany and Eastern Europe, later putting his knowledge to great effect in his book *The Black Sea*. He recalled how although the old guard talked obsessively about the head of the family, 'David fed them, and his feeding hand was sometimes sharply bitten. It was a frightfully emotional paper.' Early on in his time at the

Observer, Ascherson was asked to write a Profile of Kingsley Martin. None of his colleagues would take it on, knowing David's views on its subject, and Ascherson's attempt failed to make the grade. Martin, David told him, was a 'profoundly evil' man, who had failed to understand that Hitler and Stalin were 'almost equally satanic' – suggesting that David's long-held dislike for the long-serving editor of the *New Statesman* may have prevailed over his insistence on fairness in the paper's Profiles.

John Silverlight joined the paper in 1960 as an assistant editor: as befitted the anti-hero of *Towards the End of the Morning*, he was one of the most popular members of staff, responsible for the claim that 'We are all Astoroids now'. One day he returned from lunch to find on his desk an envelope addressed to 'John Silverlight Esquire'. Inside was a note from the editor. 'I know I'm often lamentably late for conferences myself', it read. 'But if I try to improve, will you too?' Trying to keep tabs on who succeeded whom as news editor or assistant editor or political editor or letters editor would call for an elaborate family tree, but when in 1962 Paul Ferris left to write full-time – he is best remembered for his biography of his fellow Welshman Dylan Thomas – he was replaced by John Thompson. Rather to his surprise, since he assumed that the editor would be run off his feet getting the first edition of the paper ready for press, Thompson was interviewed for the job on a Saturday afternoon: David assured him that 'by this stage I'm way back from the front line. I can hear the howitzers in the distance – just.' David had, Thompson recalled, 'an almost childlike willingness to be amazed by the new and the good', and 'unusually for a working editor, he was unfussed about coming first with an idea or a feature: for him the crucial thing was to try and "get things right"'. Two years later Thompson was promoted to assistant editor: the job was no different, but 'I think it's time we gave you another pip on your shoulder.'

Other new arrivals were Clifford Makins, the sports editor, Godfrey Hodgson, and John Lucas, a Cambridge graduate. Despite some fierce competition, Makins may well have been the heaviest of all the *Observer*'s heavy drinkers; in 1972 he succeeded Chris Brasher as the sports editor after working as a stage manager and as the editor of the *Eagle*. Hugh McIlvanney, who started writing for the *Observer* in 1962, recalled that although Makins 'looked like one of the homeless', he introduced him to champagne. On one occasion, when the guest at an editorial lunch dropped out at the last minute, David announced that 'We will do without the drink. It will be good for us.' 'It might be good for you, David, but seriously harmful to me,' Makins announced, and headed off to El Vino – from where, it was said, he commissioned his sporting articles. Towards the end of his time at the *Observer* he stupefied his colleagues by marrying Nora Beloff. 'It's the best news since the Fall of Rome,' David exclaimed when he heard the news, before adding 'But was that a good thing?'.

Godfrey Hodgson was the Washington correspondent in the early 1960s. He moved on to the *Sunday Times*, and provided astute insights into the closing months of David's editorship and the eventual sale of the paper: his 'clearest physical memory of David is of a peculiar sawing gesture of his hand, accompanied by a hesitant smile'. John Lucas was recommended to George Seddon by Michael Frayn ('Michael Frayn says you're all right. So you're in'). One of his jobs was reducing Eric Newby's copy to publishable length; he also recalls how Nigel Gosling – an Eton contemporary to whom David offered a job after meeting him at a bus stop – provided the *Observer* with a coup after Rudolf Nureyev defected to the West in 1961. Gosling reviewed art exhibitions under his own name, and ballet as 'Alexander Bland', and when Nureyev first arrived in London, he camped out in the Goslings' basement. Gosling, Tynan and Peter Heyworth, the *Observer*'s highly regarded music critic, formed part of Terry Kilmartin's domain – as did Penelope Gilliatt, 'a small, vital, vigorous red-haired girl who always seemed charged with energy and enthusiasm' who replaced the veteran C. A. Lejeune as the film critic, working in tandem with Tynan.

The *Observer* had adjusted to the end of paper rationing and the advertising boom by expanding into new subject areas, and taking on younger journalists and contributors; but the competition was more intense than ever, and rising to its challenge would involve editorial changes that David found even less congenial than those he had endured so far, as well as placing intolerable strains on the finances of a newspaper which, unlike the other daily and Sunday papers, was a free-standing, self-financing entity, lacking the support of more lucrative if less elevated siblings. Conservative spirits such as Terry Kilmartin were averse to joining in the race for circulation, and compromising standards as a result, but the advertising department pointed out that a 'Top People's' newspaper with modest sales could only survive by attracting advertising which would appeal to the rich readers who had jumped ship after Suez, and been replaced by impoverished undergraduates and intellectuals. David's heart was with Kilmartin, but his head reluctantly prevailed.

Competing on Two Fronts

A stocky, myopic Canadian who peered at the world through thick pebble glasses, Roy Thomson had made a fortune as a newspaper proprietor in his native country, and in 1953 he decided to expand his horizons by buying the *Scotsman* newspaper, based in Edinburgh. He was a friendly, straightforward and unpretentious man, and – from an editor's point of view – the perfect proprietor in that he kept an expert eye on the accounts, took a keen interest in attracting advertising, and classified ads in particular, and made a point of not interfering with editorial matters. David took to him at once: he hurried to offer the new arrival advice and useful contacts, and recommended Alastair Buchan (then in Washington), John Pringle (still in Sydney) and Ivor Brown, Scots to a man, as possible editors of the *Scotsman*. But whereas David had opposed the arrival of commercial television in 1955, and had turned down an offer for the *Observer* to join one of the original syndicates – 'That's one more case where the *Observer* has been totally wrong,' he admitted to Anthony Sampson. 'Not only has commercial TV been a success, but the commercials are the best part' – Thomson had invested in the Scottish franchise, famously describing it as a 'licence to print money'.

In 1959 Thomson bought the *Sunday Times* and a range of other papers from Lord Kemsley for £5 million, and David's affable new friend became, overnight, a rival proprietor. David once said of Kemsley that he 'orders his politics from Central Office as if it were a commodity like newsprint', and he ridiculed the way in which the paper's reverential editorials about the royal family were printed in italics. The paper's most recent editors had been slow-moving, if not soporific: in 1950 W. W. Hadley, by then in his eighties, had finally retired, and his successor, H. V. Hodson, was a fellow of All Souls and a former civil servant with no experience of journalism apart from editing the *Round Table* magazine; his conditions of employment included a clause, inserted at his wife's insistence, that he should not have to work on Saturday evenings. But salvation was to hand in the shape of Lt Col. C. D. Hamilton, DSO, a tall, lean figure with a military moustache who had had a good war – so good that Monty had tried to persuade him to join his staff after hostilities ended – and whose previous journalistic experience consisted of spells on local newspapers in Middlesbrough and Newcastle. Denis Hamilton was made the editorial director of Kemsley Newspapers in 1950, and he was to prove one of the most influential newspapermen of the twentieth century. Most journalists are, almost by definition, tacticians, short-term thinkers who react instantly to events, and quickly move on to the next; Hamilton, the old soldier, was a strategic thinker, prepared to invest money and time in long-term projects which might not pay off for months or even years.

Although the *Sunday Times* had always outsold its old rival – according to Leonard Russell, its long-serving arts and literary editor, 'the *Observer* under its unconventional young editor, David Astor, might be breezing along close to the *Sunday Times*, but it had become a point of honour to keep ahead' – by the mid-1950s the gap was beginning to close. Lord Kemsley, Russell reported, 'would feel personally disgraced if his paper had to take second place to the inspired amateurs of Tudor Street', but disgrace stared him in the face when, shortly before Suez, the *Observer* finally drew ahead. Although, as we have seen, the *Observer* acquired a different kind of readership after Suez, rather than losing circulation, Hamilton attributed the revival of the *Sunday Times* to Suez, and to his invention of what he called 'the Big Read'. Both the Sunday papers had to compete with television for advertising and public attention, but the 'Big Read' was also, as he put it, his 'secret weapon' which 'blasted the *Observer* out of the water'; and it involved the serialisation, at great length and over several weeks, of best-selling books, as often as not the memoirs of Second World War generals, beginning with those of Field Marshal Alanbrooke, for which an enormous advance was paid to Collins, its publisher. Ever the long-term strategist, Hamilton would do more than simply buy the rights in books that had been already written: very often they were bought well in advance of book publication, and sometimes the *Sunday Times* would jointly commission a book from scratch with its publisher. As early as 1954, well before Suez, Hamilton and Billy Collins co-commissioned Monty's memoirs: published four years later, by which time the *Sunday Times* had become the first paper to publish a free-standing supplement, it became the most celebrated manifestation of the 'Big Read', running over fourteen weeks and adding 100,000 to the weekly sales. Leonard Russell – whose wife, Dilys Powell, had been the paper's film critic for almost as long as C. A. Lejeune at the *Observer* – proved to be a nimble in-house editor, and the introduction of a new free-standing supplement provided the necessary elbow room in which to print the extracts he had chosen. Collins and Hamilton later co-operated on Alan Moorehead's account of the Russian Revolution; and over the next few years Hamilton negotiated with publishers and agents to acquire the rights in books by Somerset Maugham, Chaplin and Lady Diana Cooper, as well as John Betjeman's *Summoned by Bells*. Investing in these books and their authors was an expensive business, tying up capital for months or even years – not an expense the *Observer* could easily afford. By the time Kemsley sold the *Sunday Times* its circulation was over 850,000, and Roy Thomson was poised to take it up to forty-eight pages.

David usually spent his holidays, such as they were, in Sutton Courtenay, from where he could pop up to London easily enough if a crisis occurred; but in the summer of 1959, with John Pringle as deputy editor at hand to relieve David of some of his responsibilities, David felt relaxed and confident enough to take his family on holiday on Jura. Like his mother before him, he swam in its icy seas: he introduced his children to the local people, many of whom had worked as ghillies for the Astors, and he settled one family, Mrs Mackenzie and her four children, in a cottage in the grounds of the abbey at Sutton Courtenay, a mediaeval house opposite the Manor House which he owned; he later built a low wooden holiday house down the hill from Tarbert Lodge, the white-painted farmhouse where he had spent so many holidays as a young man. In his absence, the news broke about the sale of the *Sunday Times*, and Pringle asked Michael Davie to write a Profile of its new owner. As Pringle later recalled, Profiles represented for David 'the final judgement of the paper: they were moral as well as political judgements': he 'always insisted on absolute fairness' and would 'strike out a witty remark if he did not think it absolutely justified'. David read the Thomson Profile on holiday, and wrote Pringle a long letter 'telling me that he thought the Profile grossly unfair to Roy Thomson and a disgrace to the paper. He had, he said, lost all confidence in my judgement.' In David's opinion, the piece had been too jokey, presenting Thomson as a crude businessman and 'the Henry Ford of newspapers': it should have extended welcome to the new arrival and emphasised his good qualities, still more so since 'we so obviously have an interest in the matter that it would be difficult to write about this man without risking some loss of whatever reputation we have for fair-mindedness'. He had been more than happy to give Pringle a free hand, but had begged him to show him any Profiles he commissioned; it was no good claiming that other people

in the office thought well of this particular Profile, since 'the editing of
a paper is not a matter of following majority opinion'. He was so angry
that he had written to Roy Thomson to apologise.

Pringle was equally upset: he felt that David's letter was 'tantamount
to a notice of dismissal', and that it had 'destroyed the very basis of
our relationship'. Over the eighteen months they'd worked together,
David had treated him 'with ever-increasing kindness and confidence',
and encouraged him to take on more responsibilities: 'is it really cred-
ible that all this can have been changed overnight by one article?' David
had introduced into their relationship an 'element of capriciousness and
unfairness which has shocked me', and he was 'simply not prepared to
submit all articles and decisions to you, or sit in Tudor Street wondering
whether you will approve of this or that – I'm too old, too proud and,
perhaps, too headstrong for that'. 'The loss of you would be the loss of
the most distinguished journalist on this paper,' David told Pringle once
he had simmered down, but the trust had been broken, and Pringle left
the *Observer* in 1963. In retrospect, he thought David's reaction dispropor-
tionate, and wondered whether 'he could not bear to leave the *Observer*
to me and was bound, by some inner compulsion, to find something to
which he could object'. Although he had been hurt at the time, 'perhaps it
was my fault that I could not care so much, that I did not take journalism
so seriously. When I thought of all the daft things that are printed, even
in the *Observer*, I wondered whether it was so important.'

Roy Thomson, for his part, was not remotely offended. 'I have a
very high regard for you and it makes me happy to feel that I enjoy
your friendship and respect,' he replied. He was very excited about
the *Sunday Times*: they would now be competitors, 'but I am sure that
some measure of co-operation will be possible and, certainly, it will not
disturb our friendship'. 'I enjoy our competition very much and I'm sure
it is good for both of us,' he wrote a few months later. David invited
'my old pal Thomson' to dinner at the Savoy to meet senior members
of the *Observer* staff, recommended his osteopath to him, and urged
his brother Bill to invite him to Cliveden ('I think you would find him
very good fun'). Although Thomson disconcerted his host over lunch
in Tudor Street by announcing that he planned to 'bury the *Observer*',
their relationship combined mutual liking with mutual incomprehen-
sion. Asked by Thomson how much money the *Observer* was making,
David told him that 'I don't deal with that side of the paper, you will
have to ask the general manager.' Thomson moved on to the *Observer*'s
circulation, to which David replied, 'I'm not sure, but it isn't as big as

the *Sunday Times*.' David then asked Thomson what his policy was on Berlin. 'I don't know,' the tycoon is said to have replied, 'but I am sure I could buy one.' They may have inhabited very different worlds, but they exchanged birthday cards ever year.

Writing to the businessman Ronald Grierson, David claimed that people owned newspapers to make money or to exert influence, and that whereas Beaverbrook and Cecil King of the *Daily Mirror* thought they exerted influence 'because they can frighten people by mentioning them in their gossip columns', the *Economist* was in reality far more influential – and 'what I have said is precisely what Thomson does not understand, and constitutes the real advantage we have over him. I predict that he will beat us commercially, without noticing that we will have won in the competition for which paper is most heeded – which suits us fine, as we have no shareholders, being owned by a trust which is a legal charity (a shocking idea in itself to someone like our worthy friend Roy).'

Brave words – but misguided, in that the revived *Sunday Times* was to combine commercial acumen with editorial excellence, thereby winning influence of the kind David valued. The 'Big Read' was not the only way in which the *Sunday Times* was making its mark. Urged on by Ian Fleming, Roy Thomson replaced H. V. Hodson as editor with Denis Hamilton in 1961. That same year the contract whereby the *Sunday Times* was printed on the *Daily Telegraph*'s presses in Fleet Street was terminated – the Berry family had their own plans for using their machines seven days a week – and the printing was moved to purpose-built premises in Gray's Inn Road, with machines capable of printing a seventy-two- or eighty-page paper. Thomson himself was happy to concentrate on his other interests – Yellow Pages, North Sea oil, package tours – all of which provided the solid financial backing that the *Observer* soon found itself sadly lacking; and, as the *Evening Standard*'s editor, Charles Wintour, put it, the *Sunday Times* 'flourished under his policy of benign neglect'. The paper moved from being staunchly Conservative to becoming what its political editor, William Rees-Mogg, described as 'the great independent paper of the centre' – a shift that would be accentuated when the young Harold Evans replaced Hamilton as editor in 1967, encroaching on the centre-left territory hitherto monopolised by the *Observer*. 'I had this strong feeling that there was an immense amount of sale lying round in the middle classes waiting to be tapped,' Hamilton recalled. 'I felt they did not want to read a rehash of the week's news, and in those days little seemed to happen on a Saturday.' A shrewd talent-spotter, he attracted young journalists to the paper, including Nicholas Tomalin, Alan Brien and Ron Hall; inspired in part by Roy Jenkins's articles in the *Observer* about the ICI–Courtaulds takeover battle, and drawing on Irving's experience on the rather similar 'Daylight' column in the *Observer*, dreamed up by Anthony Sampson in 1963, Ron Hall and Clive Irving started the groundbreaking Insight column, with its successful spin-off books. *Observer* writers were targeted: 'the only one we wanted and didn't get was Michael Frayn', Hamilton claimed in a moment of understandable hyperbole. 'He wanted to come but by this time we were drawing so far away from the *Observer* that he felt it was his duty to help it.'

Hamilton's most radical departure was the creation of Britain's first Sunday colour magazine. 'My God! This is going to be a disaster!' Thomson exclaimed when first told about it. Cecil King told his hosts at an *Observer* lunch that it was doomed to failure, and that it was widely expected to last three months at the most, but Hamilton was convinced that it would add another 200,000 to sales. Mark Boxer was made its first editor, ably assisted by Francis Wyndham, and the magazine was launched in January 1962, with one of Ian Fleming's James Bond stories as its main feature. Initially it lost £20,000 a week, but before long it had added 150,000 to sales, and was proving a huge success with advertisers. The decision to employ Lord Snowdon as an in-house photographer prompted outrage from the *Mail* and the *Express* as well as the *Observer*, all of whom saw his employment as a ploy to attract advertisers. But Dee Wells, writing in the *Daily Herald*, would have none of it. 'Let Lord Beaverbrook howl, let David Astor be cross,' she declared. 'But both of them would have been delighted to hire Tony if they could have got him.' In 1964 Godfrey Smith replaced Boxer as editor of the colour magazine. 'We go for all the middle-class preoccupations – the car, houses, the cinema, antiques, health,' he declared. By the following year the *Sunday Times*'s circulation had passed 1.3 million, leaving the *Observer* far behind. Journalism was indeed changing, and in ways David found increasingly unsympathetic.

At the increasingly beleaguered *Observer*, costs were rising, advertisers were looking elsewhere, and a large staff still had to be paid. David, Tristan Jones and the trustees became preoccupied with keeping the paper afloat; and for the rest of his time as editor David would find himself devoting more time than he would have liked to the managerial and financial side of things, and under pressure to popularise the paper and even take it downmarket. As Pringle noted, the *Observer*'s plight was not helped 'by the extraordinary nature of the Observer Trust which did not allow the paper to earn profits and thus made it almost impossible to borrow money. The *Observer* had no capital except its goodwill; it owned neither its building nor its printing press.' Nor were the omens good when it came to competing headlong with the *Sunday Times*. 'After much conferring, it has been decided that the *Observer* ought to compete with the *Sunday Times* in trying to obtain the rights to publish extracts from the memoirs of important personages', David told a former trustee, and he wrote to Lord David Cecil to ask if he would let him have the rights to his forthcoming biography of Max Beerbohm. But the *Sunday Times* was impregnable, and David had neither the will nor the funds to do battle. The *Observer* found it increasingly hard to compete for serial rights, and the only time David outbid his great rival, paying £100,000 for Svetlana Stalin's *Letters to a Friend*, proved to be a disaster. Many of David's colleagues shared his reluctance to compete, and his fear that imitating the *Sunday Times* could dilute the quality and the character of the *Observer*. 'We are madly trying to beat the *ST* at the dreadful game of big-name serials,' complained a gloomy Alastair Buchan, who was still trying to combine the sale of advertisements with acquiring serial rights. David told Terry Kilmartin and Nigel Gosling how appalled he was to see that the *Sunday Times* had beaten them to it with a profile of F. R. Leavis, the controversial Cambridge don, but winning that particular battle would not have made an iota of difference in terms of sales or advertising revenue. Before long the *Observer* would reluctantly set in motion plans for its own colour magazine, but in the meantime it found itself coming under siege from another old denizen of Fleet Street.

Michael Berry of the *Daily Telegraph* had been outraged when his uncle, Lord Kemsley, sold the *Sunday Times* to Roy Thomson: when Kemsley's and Berry's father, Lord Camrose, divided up the family papers in 1937, it had been agreed that neither would sell without giving the other the first offer. It had also been agreed that so long as Kemsley owned the *Sunday Times*, Berry would tamp down his long-held ambition to start a rival Sunday paper, but now he felt free to press ahead. The *Sunday Times* was no longer printed on the *Telegraph*'s machines, which could now be used on Saturdays to print the new *Sunday Telegraph*. The first new Sunday paper in forty years, edited by the well-regarded Donald McLachlan, it was sold on the slogan 'Filling the Gap', but although it could exploit its parent paper's unrivalled news-gathering operation, its initial printing of 1.4 million copies proved a disaster. The type was grey and dense, there was no picture on the front page, and it looked and read like a Sunday version of the daily. Two months after its launch in February 1961 it was selling a mere 625,000 copies. But matters slowly improved. Peregrine Worsthorne proved to be a popular columnist; Nigel Lawson started a business section; Hugh Massingham left the *Observer* to become the political correspondent; Rebecca West and Nigel Dennis became the lead reviewers on Anthony Curtis's excellent books pages, and the *Sunday Telegraph*, with its greater resources, was better able to compete on the serial front than the *Observer*, scoring highly with its serialisation of the Chips Channon diaries. In 1964 Berry launched his own colour magazine; published on Fridays, it was brilliantly edited by John Anstey, and attracted advertisers as well as first-rate writers.

After a lunch with Lady Pamela Berry, Richard Crossman reported a rumour that Randolph Churchill might be replacing Mark Arnold-Forster as the *Observer*'s chief political correspondent, indicative (in Crossman's opinion) of 'chronic instability and fear' on David's part. 'The battle between the *Observer* and the *Sunday Telegraph* for the conscience of the nation is something worth watching,' Crossman concluded. The journalist Ernestine Carter suggested that the *Sunday Times* and the *Sunday Telegraph* were 'both playing the piano, while the *Observer* was playing the violin', and suggested that the violinist should make the most of its quality writers and its superior looks. David claimed that because his two rivals had more space and more money at their disposal, it became all the more important for the *Observer* to be concise and accurate – all too often 'we get the big things right and little details wrong' – and 'if we all give the very best that's in us, we shall fight the coming battle with courage, with fun and with honour. The unforgivable thing will be to die in our sleep.'

David had told his staff, apropos the *Sunday Times* colour magazine, that 'it's not the sort of thing the *Observer* would go in for', while Ken Obank insisted that 'it cannot be right, and must in the end be disastrous, to allow ourselves to be pushed by commercial rivalry along any path that is not of our own choosing'. The colour magazine was 'a North American pre-television gimmick for which there is no public demand here'; Thomson was only interested in making money, and – for his part – Obank was keen to 'reverse the trend towards "feature-isation"'. But with the *Observer* losing both sales and money, and the *Sunday Express* tempting some of its advertisers away, David came to the reluctant conclusion that unless the *Observer* became a weekly magazine rather than a newspaper, losing both sales and influence in the process, he would have to emulate his two main rivals. It was decided that Michael Davie should be brought back from Washington to edit the new colour magazine, and that Hilary Rubinstein should be his deputy.

Rubinstein had joined the *Observer* after working for his uncle, Victor Gollancz, where he had made his reputation by signing up Kingsley Amis's *Lucky Jim*, and was well known to publishers and literary agents. 'His manner was excitable and he fizzed with energy and he had the glossy face of a *bon vivant*, but he was not a nuts and bolts journalist,' his colleague Jeremy Hunt recalled. Unlike most publishers, 'Uncle Victor' had been a highly influential public figure, not least through his pre-war Left Book Club, but his nephew had never worked for a newspaper, and soon discovered that whereas publishing 'was a lake, full of interesting fish, but slow-moving and without tides', newspapers 'by contrast inhabited a restless ocean'. He soon returned to the book world as a director of A. P. Watt, the literary agents: Michael Davie was left to steer the magazine towards publication, helped along by the American Paul Mandel, a veteran of *Life* magazine, who advised Davie on layout and the unfamiliar demands of magazine production, and persuaded his colleagues to share his own fascination with Swinging London and the Beatles – rather to the dismay of Bill Smart and the advertising department. The art editor was Romek Marber, late of Penguin Books, described by Hunt as 'a charming but obstinate Continental with a thick accent who imposed a bleak and alien typographical style on our pages and had a preference for moody pictures which did not lend themselves to good reproduction on cheap paper'. Running to sixty-four pages, half in colour and half in black and white, the first issue appeared in September 1964, and was 'appallingly printed' on cheap paper by Purnell's – who, since the *Observer* lacked the necessary funds, jointly owned the colour magazine on a fifty–fifty basis.

Denis Hamilton's 'Big Read' had got off to an explosive start with Alanbrooke's memoirs, and David's colour magazine also looked back to the war for its opening fusillade. Writing to his old C-in-C at Combined Ops as 'Dear Chief', David asked Lord Mountbatten if he would be interviewed by Kenneth Harris, and Lord Louis agreed to go ahead 'in view of our serving together during the war and the fact that I admire what you are doing in the field of journalism'. Mountbatten was pleased with the interview itself, which was to be spread over three successive issues, but he was (or claimed to be) horrified by the accompanying advertising, with its slogan of 'Mountbatten Speaks', and by seeing his face plastered all over the Tube and other public places. 'You do not realise the appalling repercussions the advertising campaign has had on my friends and relations,' he told David, adding that 'they are all upset that I should have joined the ranks of garrulous generals and feel that I have largely destroyed my image in doing so'. David replied that although he was upset by Mountbatten's reaction, 'with the actual fate of this paper depending on the successful launch of this magazine, it has not been easy to restrain our agents from doing the best advertising campaign they could'. Mountbatten was not mollified – 'if you were not so deeply immersed in the struggle for Fleet Street you would have seen for yourself what this publicity was doing for my image' – but, image-conscious and publicity-hungry as ever, he went on to thank David for the extra copies of the magazine provided for his family.

Less controversial fare was provided in succeeding issues by concentrating on remoter periods of history, on the Industrial Revolution or the Tudors. After TJ complained that younger readers were being neglected, a 'Young Observer' section was introduced. In a 'secret memo', David – surprisingly – suggested that the magazine should differentiate itself from the *Sunday Times* by appealing to younger readers via 'more use of pictures of pretty girls', a Willie Rushton type of comic strip, and articles about setting up house. Raymond Hawkey replaced Marber as the design director, and his friend Len Deighton provided a cartoon-strip cookery column entitled 'Ou Est le Garlic?' Elizabeth David decided against writing a cookery column but recommended instead her friend Jane Grigson, who remained in the job until her death in 1990. Michael Davie was replaced by Anthony Sampson, who – 'frustrated by the lack of entrepreneurial drive from Tristan Jones' – eventually retired to concentrate on writing books, and was replaced in turn by John Thompson. The magazine never had the glamour or the weight of its *Sunday Times* equivalent – or, indeed, of John Anstey's *Telegraph* magazine, which was shuttled on to Saturdays before finally coming to rest as a Sunday publication.

Two months after the first issue had appeared, Karl Miller in the *New Statesman* dismissed the *Observer* colour magazine as a very dim affair, the unwelcome embodiment of 'the new brightness which is part of a swing through the quality papers towards a heightened awareness of fashion, presentation, leisure and consumer goods'. Christopher Booker in the *Spectator* saw it as symptomatic of Britain's moral decay in the 1960s, with Sampson branded as the villain of the piece. 'The amiable and agreeable Sampson has become one of the most influential figures in British journalism,' he declared. 'Through a succession of columns in the *Observer* – Pendennis, Mammon and Daylight – and through his book he has fathered a whole new style of writing about people and public figures that has been subtly pervasive not just through the *Observer* but throughout newspaper and magazine "feature-writing".' Booker described this as the 'new sycophancy', the net effect of which was to glamourise and sanitise his subjects by the use of flattering epithets – 'a development of the *Time* technique of capsule descriptions' combined with the 'jargon of the advertising world'. Loyal as he was to his ablest lieutenants, David may well have sympathised with the puritan strictures of Messrs Miller and Booker.

★

But life at the *Observer* was not devoted to fighting the competition, to the exclusion of all else; and 1963 was to prove a particularly busy and embattled year for David. It began with the flight to Moscow of the paper's most notorious correspondent. Kim Philby had worked as a journalist in the late 1930s, reporting for *The Times* from Franco's side during the Spanish Civil War, and later from France during the phoney war. In 1951, after the flight to Moscow of Guy Burgess and Donald Maclean, he returned to London from Washington, where he had been working for MI6. Suspected of being the 'Third Man' and responsible for tipping off his friends, he was put through the mill by Dick White and William Skardon of MI5, both of whom were convinced of his guilt. MI6 did not share MI5's suspicions, but it was agreed that he should resign from the service.

Philby found himself adrift and out of a job, but set about exercising his famous charm. André Deutsch, who found him 'witty, charming and intelligent', offered him a contract and a £600 advance to write a book: nothing came of it, and the advance was repaid, but Malcolm Muggeridge, a wartime colleague from MI6, suggested that he should approach the *Observer*, 'that Salvation Army for the ideological drunks and bums of our time'. Writing to 'My dear Astor' in February 1952, Philby explained that he had recently resigned from the Foreign Office after eleven years' service, and was keen to get back into journalism, 'my regular profession from 1935 to 1940'. 'He seems an extremely reliable chap and he has created a good impression on David, Philip Toynbee and myself. Deakin, *The Times*'s foreign editor, speaks very highly of him,' Fred Tomlinson wrote to Robert Stephens in Cairo. Philby hoped to be in Cairo in the near future, and although 'he does not know whether he will be able to give the *Observer* any time', he was a 'first-rate journalist' and it would be well worth Stephens talking to him. Nothing came of the Cairo trip, but the following year Philby was 'given accreditation in Madrid' and sent three reports from Spain to Servob, the *Observer*'s foreign-news syndication service. Philby then told Tomlinson that he had been 'offered a commercial opening of a nature so attractive that I cannot refuse it', and returned his press card.

Two years later, Philby was formally cleared of the accusation that he was the Third Man by Harold Macmillan in the House of Commons, after which he held his notorious press conference in his mother's flat in Drayton Gardens at which he dismissed as nonsense the notion that he could ever have been a Soviet spy. MI6 took him back, ostensibly on the grounds that he was a good man who had been hard done by, and posted him to Beirut: Philby's father was a well-known Arabist, and according to George Young of MI6, 'Philby was given Arab affairs because his family was connected with the Arab world.' A cover was needed, and Nicholas Elliott of MI6 was sent to see David and Donald Tyerman, by now the editor of *The Economist*, to ask if they could use Philby as a Middle Eastern stringer. (Ten years earlier, as it happened, both papers had employed another of the Cambridge spies, John Cairncross, as their Rome correspondent.) Philby told his biographer, Phillip Knightley, that 'Elliott assured me that he had cleared my cover with David Astor, but Astor has since denied that he knew anything about it.' Philby was hardly a reliable source, but Elliott's colleague George Young later wrote that 'I would have thought that Astor knew.' David also denied that he had ever heard of Nicholas Elliott, and had never met him before: this seems unlikely, since he may well have met him when he went to The Hague in October 1939, shortly before the Venlo Incident; Elliott had recently been posted to The Hague by MI6, and David discussed with MI6 representatives the possibility of getting in touch with the German opposition.

Both the *Observer* and *The Economist* were prepared to employ Philby, paying him £500 a year (£300 of which was the *Observer*'s share), which went up by stages to £1,000 by 1958. Philby arrived in Beirut shortly before Suez, and quickly set to work covering the Middle East in general apart from Israel and Egypt. According to Patrick Seale, a long-serving *Observer* journalist who specialised in the Middle East and was there at the same time, Philby 'was judicious in analysing the news, rather than being the first with it'. Writing to Fred Tomlinson in 1957, Stephens reported that he'd had 'a good talk, in fact several, with Philby' in Beirut: it was felt that he wrote better pieces for *The Economist*, but 'part of the trouble was a mixture of diffidence and not being quite sure what we wanted', in that Philby assumed they didn't want heavyweight articles and 'has seen himself as a rather marginal stringer and hasn't liked to push himself'. A year later Philby found himself dealing with Michael Davie, who had replaced Tomlinson as the news editor. Davie remembered Philby as 'a very quiet presence, usually in a tweed suit when he came to London, and with a disarming stammer': Davie told him that they were pleased with his work, but he had removed some of Philby's personal comments from his reports – 'I can well imagine that it is hard to keep your irritation with some aspects of Western policy out of your stories, but it must be done.' He also noted Philby's 'staggering expenses'. Philby provided a leader-page article on Nasser's achievements; he wrote his father's obituary for the paper in 1960, and covered the much-publicised discovery of the Dead Sea Scrolls. He hid behind the pseudonym of 'Charles Garner' for trivial or lightweight pieces, as when Ronald Harker, who ran Servob, asked him to write about Arab slave girls.

Hugh Trevor-Roper, who had been a wartime colleague of Philby in MI6, met him again in Iraq in the spring of 1957, and although he was 'satisfied that he had been a Russian spy for over twenty years', and 'inwardly shrank from him as a traitor', he 'found his company as attractive as ever, his conversation as disengaged, and yet as enjoyable'. By now Trevor-Roper's friend Dick White had left MI5 to take charge of MI6. He continued to believe that Philby was a Soviet agent, and was determined to winkle him out. It was never clear whether his predecessors at MI6 had, quite genuinely, sent Philby to Beirut to act as a British agent, or whether they did so in the belief that he would inadvertently let something slip, so enabling them to close in on him. White was very much in the second camp, and in 1960 a reluctant Elliott was sent to Beirut as MI6's station commander with instructions to provide Philby with disinformation to pass on to the Russians. Two years later even Philby's closest friends in MI6, including Elliott, were finally convinced: partly by the revelations of the KGB defector Anatoli Golitsyn, and partly by Flora Solomon, whom Philby had tried to enlist as a Soviet agent before the war. 'How is it that the *Observer* uses a man like Kim Philby?' she asked Victor Rothschild at a reception in Jerusalem, apropos what George Weidenfeld, who was present at the time, described as 'particularly hostile stories about Israel'. 'Don't they know he's a Communist?'

In November 1962 Philby asked David for a spell of home leave. 'I enlisted him – to my cost,' David admitted to Phillip Knightley. 'But after that he kept away from me. So it's more likely he would have written to the foreign editor. But he could have written to me. I just don't remember it.' MI6, in the meantime, had prepared their case against Philby, and in early January the disillusioned Elliott was sent back to Beirut to confront him and offer him immunity from prosecution in exchange for a full confession. Philby's last despatch to the *Observer* was very different to its predecessors: he had bought a young fox in a bazaar and taken it back to his flat five floors up, from the balcony of which it had fallen to its death. Robert Stephens thought it unsuited to the *Observer* and passed it on to *Country Life*, which ran the piece and sent Philby, via the *Observer*, a cheque for £12. It was never cashed: Philby had boarded his Russian freighter at the end of January, and was in Moscow when the cheque reached Beirut. Clare Hollingworth, the intrepid foreign correspondent who had occasionally filed stories for the *Observer* and *The Economist*, was the first to suggest that Philby had fled to the Soviet Union, but her story was spiked by the *Manchester Guardian*. 'Be your age,' Alastair Hetherington told her when she objected, pointing out that to have run the story might have incurred 'millions of pounds' worth' of libel fees. 'Journalist Missing in the Middle East' ran an *Observer* headline two months after Philby fled: the paper admitted that it had no idea of the whereabouts of its Beirut stringer, but had asked the Egyptian authorities to keep an eye out for him. In June *Newsweek* finally broke the story that Philby had been the Third Man, and in July Ted Heath told the House of Commons that Philby had worked for the Soviet Union.

In a Review Front article published later that month, Roy Perrott, an *Observer* staffer, shed some light on Philby's employment by the paper. 'A member of the Foreign Office staff known to the paper, who made it clear that his approach was official, asked the editor of the *Observer* if he had a place for Philby,' he wrote. 'He said the Foreign Office felt it was unfair that, in spite of the full clearance of Philby's name in 1955, he was finding it impossible to practise his profession of journalism. A cast-iron promise was given that he had no further connection with British intelligence, and that he would not be involved in government work of any kind while in *Observer* employment.' Working for the KGB was a very different matter. 'We knew Philby as a colleague during six years, and we were completely deceived by him,' David later admitted. The *Daily Express* had 'bayed for his official exposure', and 'to employ him after all that was, to put it mildly, a quixotic act' – but 'in taking on Philby, the *Observer* believed it was helping a stranded individual, not the government'. Years later David told the *Sunday Times* that his dealings with the Foreign Office had seemed entirely above board, but that when Philby 'finally turned up in Moscow they rushed over and apologised and said "Very sorry we didn't warn you."' In the meantime, Robert Stephens reread Philby's reports for the paper, looking for clues, but 'found it impossible to see anything in his writing beyond diligent and honest reporting on the Middle Eastern scene. His writing was clear, better than competent, and where he sought to interpret political trends seemed to have a remarkable degree of accuracy in the light of subsequent political events.'

Early in 1968 Eleanor Philby, Philby's American third wife, returned to the West, unable to stand Moscow life any longer. David asked Patrick Seale to bring her to the office. They barely exchanged a word, but she showed David a scrap of paper on which was written 'Japan is a disease of the skin; Communism is a disease of the heart' – a cryptic quotation taken from a forthcoming biography of Richard Sorge, the Soviet spy who had been based in Japan during the early years of the war, and had provided his Russian masters with invaluable information about Axis plans. David, Seale recalled, was greatly moved, hugged his visitor to him, and no more was said. Seale then helped her to write, in six weeks, *The Spy I Loved*, which was serialised in the *Observer* later that year, coinciding with the *Sunday Times*'s serialisation of *Philby: The Spy Who Betrayed a Generation*, written by their Insight team of Phillip Knightley, Bruce Page and David Leitch, and published, appropriately enough, by André Deutsch.

Philby was not the only spy to hit the headlines in the early 1960s: others included the Portland spy ring, George Blake, and John Vassall, the Admiralty clerk blackmailed into spying for the Soviets. But one story above all – the Profumo Affair – gripped the nation's attention over the summer of 1963, and it too contained an element of espionage, albeit bogus – and was widely thought to have contributed to Macmillan's resignation later in the year. It also provided a dreadful example of the popular press at its worst, and the kind of journalism – sensationalist, vindictive, gossipy, inaccurate – that David had always deplored. Newspaper sales had peaked in the early 1950s, and although they were still enviably high by modern standards, the Queen's coronation in 1953 and the advent of commercial television two years later had diverted both readers and advertisers from print to the 'gogglebox'. The furore over the Profumo case was led and orchestrated by Cecil King and Hugh Cudlipp of the Labour-supporting Mirror Group, who scented in it a godsent opportunity to boost sales with some salacious scandal, savage what they saw as a decadent, overprivileged and self-sustaining Establishment, and possibly bring down Macmillan's government. Beaverbrook readily joined the hunt in order to pursue his vendetta against the Astors. He had refrained, just, from exposing Bobbie Shaw in his papers, but the involvement of Nancy's and Waldorf's son, the current Viscount Astor, made this a story that was too hard to resist.

Stephen Ward was a society osteopath whose patients had included, at various times, Churchill, Eden, Gaitskell, Rab Butler, Paul Getty, Frank Sinatra, Ava Gardner, Elizabeth Taylor, Danny Kaye – and Bill Astor, to whom he had been recommended by Bobbie Shaw. Ward was, at worst, indiscreet, voluble and something of a show-off – and, for all his grand connections, osteopathy was not a greatly respected profession. Bill Astor had let a cottage on the Cliveden estate to Ward, and it was at one of Ward's parties round the Cliveden swimming pool in July 1961 that John Profumo, the Secretary of State for War in Macmillan's government, met the nineteen-year-old Christine Keeler, a friend of Ward and a 'dancer' at Murray's Club in Soho – the 'dancing' involved standing bare-breasted and immobile at the back of the stage while the dancers proper went through their motions. Also present was Yevgeny Ivanov, a Russian naval attaché and one of Christine Keeler's lovers. Profumo, a veteran womaniser, started an affair with Keeler; the story leaked out, and although Profumo initially denied the whole story, he later admitted that he had lied to the House and had to resign as a minister and as an MP. A further frisson was provided by the fact that MI5 had kept tabs on Ivanov as a possible Soviet agent, and noted his occasional meetings with Stephen Ward: Ward unwisely joked to Keeler about her making improbable pillow talk with Profumo regarding the possibility of West Germany being provided with nuclear warheads, and although MI5 rightly refused to take this seriously, the story leaked out and intimations of espionage were added to the toxic mixture.

Cliveden was depicted in the popular press as the epicentre of upper-class decadence and immorality, and no one suffered more than the stiff, awkward, buttoned-up Bill Astor, absurdly described by Beaverbrook as a 'callous libertine'. His house in Upper Grosvenor Street was broken into, presumably on behalf of a journalist in search of incriminating material; Spring Cottage, the Tudor-beamed cottage on the Cliveden estate which had been let to Stephen Ward, was vandalised; he was interviewed by the police, who muttered about his being charged as a brothel-keeper on the grounds that he had once written out a cheque to pay the rent owed by Keeler and her friend Mandy Rice-Davies on a flat they shared in Barons Court. And his denial of Mandy Rice-Davies's claim that they had had an affair prompted the quip from her by which the whole affair is best remembered – 'Well, he would say that, wouldn't he?'

'Ward on "Immoral Earnings" Charge', ran the Observer's front page, while a leading article on 'Sex and Politics' declared that 'Nothing can excuse Mr Profumo's conduct in deliberately lying to his government

colleagues, the House of Commons and the public, though even his
severest critics could hardly wish his career to end in so painful a way.'
Deserted by most of his fair-weather friends – Bill Astor had earlier given
him notice to quit Spring Cottage – Stephen Ward was put on trial at
the Old Bailey in July 1963, charged with living off immoral earnings,
even though neither Christine Keeler nor the more ebullient Mandy Rice-
Davies had ever worked as prostitutes. Bill, David, his brother Jakie, Bill's
lawyer and Bill's father-in-law, Sir Alun Pugh, met beforehand to discuss
whether Bill should give evidence. 'David was breathing fire and talked
about the fight for the honour of the Astor family,' Sir Alun recalled.
'He was begging Bill to go into the witness box. Bill was quiet, almost
apathetic.' In fact Bill wanted to give evidence, but was advised against
doing so; and David thought that Bill's 'awful lawyer' had given him
further dud advice by urging him to carry on as usual, doing 'asinine
things like going to Ascot', whereas 'he should have given him good
common-sense advice which would have been to show that he was upset
by all his friends being involved in the Ward case. By smiling in public
and saying nothing, it was as if he thought he could buy his way out
of anything.' Bill may have 'made the most calamitous impression', but
Ward's reputation was shredded in court by the prosecuting counsel,
Mervyn Griffith-Jones – best remembered for his role in the *Lady Chatterley*
trial three years earlier – and after the judge's summing-up Ward took
a fatal overdose. 'The fate of Stephen Ward has shaken me a lot. I wish
I was not on holiday so I could control what the *Observer* says,' David
wrote to Bill from Jura. Ward was 'the scapegoat, the person from
whom all public sympathy is withdrawn and who is imagined to have
been corrupting society. Psychologically this just represents the public's
constant fear of its own dangers from its own sexuality.' And David's
friend and adviser Arnold Goodman once described Ward as 'a British
Dreyfus', and 'the historic victim of an historic injustice'.

'I only regret that I did not say something in protest against the whole
build-up of hostility when it was happening. But one only sees these
things too late,' David confessed. He found it a nightmare, and worried
that his family and the house in which he had grown up would be for
ever associated with the Profumo Affair as well as the Cliveden Set.
John Pringle 'never admired David Astor more than during that dreadful
period': he kept his head, refused to believe stories unsupported by the
evidence, dismissed allegations of a security leak and 'was absolutely
right in his detestation of the vindictive cruelty of the Ward trial. Thanks
to him, the *Observer* behaved with generosity and restraint.' Bill's wife

Bronwen wrote to say how 'very touched' she had been by a letter from David. 'Not many people can write such wonderfully kind and comforting words,' she told him, adding that she hoped 'we will not let the family down any further by our conduct during the next few weeks'. David also wrote to Profumo, extending sympathy and support. 'Bill is one of the people connected with your troubles whom you have found it difficult to entirely forgive,' he wrote: he urged Profumo to visit Bill, then in the Middlesex Hospital, since, according to Bronwen, Profumo was 'the one person he wants to see. She thinks it would make an enormous difference to his peace of mind if you and he could have some kind of reconciliation.' When Bill died of a heart attack in 1966 at the age of fifty-eight, David added a note to his obituary in *The Times*. 'My elder brother's upbringing was more stilted than those of the rest of us,' he wrote. 'A lack of warmth in his earliest years seemed to produce an awkwardness in his human relations, which he strove all his life to overcome.' And he added how, after the Profumo Affair, Bill and Bronwen had 'withstood misrepresentation, vilification and the ostracism of some former friends with lonely courage'. Bill had died a broken man; C. P. Snow wrote an obituary of him for the *Observer*, but after Bronwen had read it she asked David to 'throw it in the fire'.

David once reminded his brother Michael, who had suggested that he might write some articles about America, that he made it 'a point of principle not to put my own or my relatives' names into the paper', but the publication by John Murray of Michael's family memoir, *Tribal Feeling*, put his ruling to the test. It provided a 'welcome diversion' from the horrors of the Profumo Affair, and although Michael alerted David to the fact the *Sunday Times* had bought the serial rights 'as I felt that as the book had been written by me it would automatically be disallowed', he knew that Stephen Spender, who rented a cottage at Bruern from him, was keen to review it for the *Observer*. In the end David broke his self-imposed rule, just as he had when Waldorf died, and Bob Brand was asked to write the review, rather than Spender, declaring it to be 'an admirably written book' which was both 'very interesting and a work of art'. 'No one is ever able to get the Astor family straight,' declared the *Observer* at the height of the Profumo crisis, but Michael Astor made better sense of it than most.

Bill's second wife, Bronwen's predecessor, had been a niece of Dorothy Macmillan, and David felt that Macmillan deeply resented the Astors' involvement in the Profumo Affair. 'I don't think he ever forgave Bill or me,' David recalled. 'He had to ask me to Downing Street and made out that he hardly knew me. But he had almost lived in our home in my mother's day.' (There was another element to the story: Macmillan had earlier confided in Nancy about the deep unhappiness caused him by his wife's long-standing affair with Bob Boothby, and this confession of weakness had, for some reason, set him against the Astors in general.) David, for his part, was equally unforgiving where Beaverbrook was concerned. The year after the Profumo Affair Roy Thomson invited David to a grand dinner to celebrate the Beaver's eighty-fifth birthday. 'This puts me in a difficulty,' David replied. He made no mention of Beaverbrook's coverage of the Profumo Affair, but a series of 'malicious' and 'specially commissioned' articles about Nancy in the *Sunday Express* and an unpleasant obituary of Waldorf in the *Evening Standard* made it 'rather hard for me to pretend that I am full of admiration and goodwill. I cannot pretend to like his behaviour and do not mind if you tell him why I am absent': it would have been 'humbug' to accept.

A bad year ended with the assassination of President Kennedy on 22 November. JFK and David had much in common, including a stylish, lean-limbed elegance and the self-confidence of men accustomed to wealth and the best education their respective countries could provide. But Kennedy was five years younger than David, and his family were arrivistes on the American scene when compared with the Astors; and one has the sense that, on the few times they met, they did so as equals: David recalled a 'high old time' in Washington with JFK, Bobby Kennedy, Robert McNamara and McGeorge Bundy, during the course of which 'they confirmed (what I had not dared to hope would be the case) that the idea of how to avoid war which the *Observer* has long advocated (a biopoly of nuclear power in the hands of the Americans and Russians with some agreement between them and their allies to prevent it being acquired by anyone else) was not at all uncongenial to the current thinking in Washington'. John Thompson was the news editor at the time of the assassination, and was keen to send more reporters to Dallas to cover its aftermath; David, on the other hand, was far more interested in what was going on in Washington, in the political implications of Kennedy's death. Peter Crookston remembers editorial grandees gathering outside David's office, just as they had gathered a month earlier to discuss Mark Arnold-Forster's report about Macmillan's successor: only this time the matter was never in doubt.

The Perils of Biography

David's relations with his mother remained uneasy – provocative as ever, she supported the whites of Southern Rhodesia, comparing them to the paternalistic Virginians of her childhood – but as she moved into old age an ancient fondness revived on both sides. The house in St James's Square was sold, and although Nancy bought a much smaller house in Hill Street in Mayfair, she spent much of her time at Rest Harrow or with her daughter Wissie, the Countess of Ancaster, at Grimsthorpe in Lincolnshire. David visited her at Grimsthorpe: she thought she was back in Virginia, and for all their past difficulties 'I was a very welcome visitor. She was happy, light and charming, and in a holiday mood. She treated me as an equal. It was a complete transformation, and it was delightful.' But happy as she was on that occasion, she became increasingly anxious towards the end of her life, ringing David every day to say that she was worried and unhappy, and felt a failure because her children weren't looking after her in her old age: 'she said it without self-pity, and it was tragic'. She died in May 1964 at the age of eighty-four: the front page of the *Observer* carried a report by Kenneth Harris, and Clement Attlee and Mary Stocks wrote appreciations of her life.

She left behind her favourite child, and the saddest and loneliest member of her family. In the early 1950s Bobbie Shaw had been arrested for committing a sexual offence with a mentally retarded man; once again no mention was made of this in the press, but he was given the choice of prison or psychiatric treatment. Ten years later, Bobbie was being treated for depression with ECT: all his old irreverence and gaiety had gone, he had money problems – although he had 'substantial trust funds in America', his reluctance to pay his own medical bills reflected 'a childish attitude towards money which is quite unreasonable but cannot be overcome' – and David reported that he was 'threatening to return to the bottle if he is not treated more fairly'. Bobbie felt 'deeply touchy about being her eldest child and yet having no status in the family and in what concerns Mama'; he was being treated by David's psychiatrist friend Alastair Macleod in the York Clinic, but seemed 'increasingly morose and suicidal'.

Bobbie committed suicide in 1970. David remembered how 'he had the nerve and the decency to ring up and thank everybody', and how 'he was quite himself and very touching. He just said "I'm terribly grateful and I'm just ringing to say goodbye."' 'You wouldn't be so unkind, would you, as to make me stay on?' he replied when David tried to dissuade him. 'Bobbie was a very big item in my landscape ever since I can remember,' David told a friend: he was not surprised by his suicide, but was far more affected by it than expected. Bobbie used to tell people that 'David's all I've got', and that he was the 'linchpin' of the family; David, for his part, had appreciated the way in which Bobbie 'was always able to upset the official apple cart on any occasion in a way that I found a great relief'.

Nancy was an obvious subject for a biography, and as early as 1955 Harold Nicolson had written to David to say that 'although I disagreed with your mother on almost every cause she held dear, I think her one of the most striking people that I have ever known', and suggest the names of possible biographers. After Nancy's death, the family began in earnest to hunt for a suitable biographer, and although her two literary executors were Jakie Astor and Sir Edward Ford, an amiable and emollient royal courtier who had married into the Langhorne family, David took effective charge of the proceedings. A list of possible biographers provided by Terry Kilmartin included Elizabeth Longford and Nancy Mitford as well as Robert Blake, Philip Magnus and Robert Rhodes James. David initially favoured a young writer, preferably female, who appreciated 'Mama's originality and audacity', but he eventually urged the claims of another of Kilmartin's suggestions, Christopher Sykes. A florid, hard-drinking, convivial Roman Catholic who had travelled in Persia with Robert Byron before the war, a friend of Cyril Connolly and Evelyn Waugh, and the well-regarded author of *Four Studies in Loyalty* and a biography of Orde Wingate, Sykes was not the obvious choice for Nancy, given her abhorrence of drink and Roman Catholics, but David was insistent. 'I think very highly indeed of Christopher Sykes as a writer and quite believe he might be very good at dealing with Mama,' he told Jakie. 'He is about the fairest-minded man in the world and I would have no doubt at all about his generosity.' Not only that, but he was 'sympathetic to the family and quite intrigued by the political role our parents played'. Sykes and David may not have been kindred spirits, but they had the war in common: like David, Sykes had been dropped by the SAS into eastern

France, near the Belfort Gap, to liaise with the Maquis in the autumn of 1944, and like David he had been awarded the Croix de Guerre. After the war David had employed him as a regular contributor to the *Observer*, writing book reviews, articles and the occasional Profile.

Nor was Nancy's the only life Sykes had undertaken to write on David's recommendation. The year before Nancy's death he had embarked upon an even more sensitive mission: to write a biography of Adam von Trott. David's devotion to his old friend was as strong as ever, but Trott remained a controversial figure – not least in Oxford, where both Isaiah Berlin and Maurice Bowra retained their doubts about him. Writing to Felix Frankfurter in early 1951, Berlin referred to 'a really vicious and horrible attack' on Bowra in the *Observer*, the gist of which was that Bowra 'has always been at his weakest in judging the more serious problems of real life, such as those of an anti-Nazi German determined to resist Hitler'. It was, Berlin told another friend, 'the most offensive and vicious attack I have ever seen delivered on a human being by a British newspaper', and he 'wondered why David Astor hated him so much'. Despite his role in the 1944 plot, Trott was a 'nationalist and an ambitious, handsome, complicated man who played with fire and took large risks, and lost, but was no democrat'. Bowra had never liked or trusted him; as a result of his pre-war intercepted letter to Felix Frankfurter, 'the orders of the FO were not to touch him', and 'David Astor therefore attributes his subsequent death to Maurice Bowra and regards him as a murderer.' The article about Bowra was no more than a 'most violent revenge'.

Trott's bogus report to the German Foreign Office about British attitudes towards Germany in the summer of 1939 had come to light in 1956, reviving suspicions that he might have been a Nazi agent rather than a member of the opposition posing as a loyal civil servant. David repudiated such suspicions in a long article entitled 'Von Trott's Mission' for the *Manchester Guardian*, referring to Trott's 'deliberate flattery of Hitler' in his report and mentioning how Trott was regarded by some of his former friends in Oxford. 'All David Astor's accusations are delivered ominously at unmentioned persons (among whom I vaguely, but very vaguely, count myself),' Berlin told Shiela Grant Duff. Three years later, David found himself fighting to put the record straight when J. R. M. Butler – a fellow of Trinity College, Cambridge – sent him the typescript of his forthcoming biography of Lord Lothian. 'I am in despair about Butler's references to Trott in his life of Philip,' David told Bob Brand; Trott's seemingly duplicitous behaviour in the summer of 1939 'makes him almost unintelligible to the ordinary conventional

Englishman, such as Professor Butler'. Nor was Trott's cause helped by
the publication in 1961 of A. L. Rowse's contentious and widely reviewed
All Souls and Appeasement, in which he wrote that Trott had 'entered
deeply, ambivalently, into relations with the Nazis' and that 'it was this
Hegelianism in action that caught him in its toils in the end'.

In 1960 David broached the subject of a biography with Trott's
widow Clarita, whom he was helping with the education of her children. Constantine FitzGibbon and Peter Fleming were discussed as
possible authors, but in June 1962 David approached Christopher Sykes
instead. Seven years earlier he had discussed a possible book about the
September 1944 plot with Peter Calvocoressi, then a director of
the publisher Chatto & Windus, and they had decided between them
that Sykes would be the perfect author for such a book, and now he set
about introducing Sykes to Clarita and the all-important Bielenbergs. 'I
cannot tell you how delighted I am that you have voted for doing the
book on Adam,' he told Sykes. 'We've been looking for the right man
literally for years. We are all agreed that you could do it best – it would
have been a disaster if you had declined. I *won't* breathe down your
neck', and Peter Fleming assured the Bielenbergs that 'Christopher is the
ideal choice: his biography of Wingate was absolutely brilliant, and his
command of German will be a great asset. You couldn't have taken a
sounder decision.' All the relevant papers and letters would be at Sykes's
disposal: he would have 'complete freedom to write it your way', and
'we would all be willing to help in any way you may think fit, but you
need not fear that we would try to supervise your work'. 'I know Sykes
personally and can affirm he deserves his reputation for great independence of mind,' David assured Freya von Moltke, whose husband, Helmuth
von Moltke, had been executed by the Nazis in January 1945: Moltke had
known David and A. L. Rowse in Oxford – a disillusioned Rowse later
declared him to be 'a finer type than Adam' – and, with Trott, had been a
leading member of the Kreisau Circle opposition group. 'It is this quality
above all which specially qualifies him to tell this complicated story with
impartiality and fairness to all involved,' David concluded. Like the Nancy
Astor biography, the book would be published by Collins, and to cap
his commitment David agreed with A. D. Peters, Sykes's literary agent,
that he would contribute from his own pocket £600 to cover a trip to
America, to be repaid from future earnings.

But the honeymoon proved all too short. By the summer of 1964, a year
after Sykes had accepted the commission, Peter Bielenberg reported that
both Clarita and her friend Margret Boveri were 'vehemently opposed'

(*Above left*) William Clark

(*Above*) Charles Davy

(*Left*) Colin Legum

(*Right*) E. F. Schumacher

William Guttman

Sebastian Haffner

Philip Toynbee

Patrick O'Donovan

(*Right*) Nora Beloff

(*Below*) Gavin Young

(*Above*) John Gale

(*Left*) Jane Bown

(*Left*) Rev. Michael
Scott

(*Above*) Clifford Makins

(*Above right*) Terence Kilmartin

(*Right*) Tristan Jones

(*Above*) Michael Davie

(*Left*) Ken Tynan

(*Below left*) Edward Crankshaw

(*Below right*) Anthony Sampson

(*Above*) Ken Obank and Donald Trelford

(*Left*) Lord Goodman

(*Below*) Michael Davie and David Astor

(*Right*) Travelling at speed with Alice.

(*Left*) Preparing to bowl.

(*Right*) At the races with Bridget.

(*Left*) At Elm Tree Road: (back) David, Bridget (front) Alice, Lucy, Nancy, Tom and Richard. The Henry Moore statue was often used as a climbing frame by the children.

to his continuing with the book; seventeen months later David reported
'a slight anxiety' about the Trott biography. 'I think we're in trouble,'
David told Sykes in July 1966: Sykes seemed to be out of sympathy with
the pre-war German opposition, a subject on which Peter Bielenberg
felt him to be 'way adrift'. David wrote Sykes long letters about his
own involvement with Trott, but to no avail. 'You do not accept that
Adam and his friends were indeed primarily motivated by anti-Nazi
sentiment: on the contrary, you imply that they were motivated by a
cloudy mixture including much German nationalism,' he told Sykes.
The 'cloudy mixture' included the Hegelianism which Berlin, Bowra
and A. L. Rowse had viewed with such suspicion in pre-war Oxford, and
David suggested to Shiela Grant Duff that 'the clumsy, muddle-headed
Hegelian that appears in Sykes's book is their invention'.

Sykes agreed that Christabel Bielenberg should read the typescript:
a necessary but fatal move as far as relations between Sykes and David
was concerned. Peter Bielenberg wrote to Sykes to say that he and
Christabel wanted to disassociate themselves from a book which 'conveys
an impression or picture which we find unacceptable'. 'I'm happy to
become the "baddy" in Sykes's mind who is responsible for all his troubles
if that makes it easier for him to make concessions to you and Clarita,'
David told Christabel Bielenberg, but it was too late for harmony to
be restored. An increasingly embattled Sykes felt that what he called
'the Trott Committee', consisting of David, Margret Boveri and the
Bielenbergs, were ganging up against him: the Committee tried to suggest
that Trott had no close friends apart from its members, yet both Shiela
Grant Duff and Diana Hopkinson thought well of the book. 'These
people are all in love with Trott and won't look at any facts that leave him
as anything but perfect. Which he wasn't,' Sykes noted after a dinner in
David's house attended by the Bielenbergs. 'I respect your great love for
Adam and the way he inspired devotion in his friends, but a biographer
must regard truth – the *evidenced* truth – as the soul of his craft,' he
told David. David seemed to have no real idea of 'what being a writer
entails': he was 'a strange case of complex mental elaboration, not so
much *open* to misunderstanding as an *invitation* to misunderstanding',
but although 'David has not behaved pleasantly to me of late, yet I like
him, mainly for the obvious reason that he is likeable.'

Collins were delighted with the finished book, and keen to press ahead
with publication. Sykes's editor, Richard Ollard, himself a historian,
thought it a 'magnificent and moving book, and if David Astor wants to
play the Queen of the Night to your Sarastro, his squeakings only make

your basso more profondo'. 'I do think David Astor is really asking a great deal too much, as you are already much more than generous to Trott's verbose and overheated romanticism,' Ollard assured his author after reading one of David's 'effusions'. 'It's all so well meant, but one can only stand amazed at his daring to accuse you – or anyone else – of intellectual confusion.' In the meantime, Sykes continued to do battle with the Committee, the members of which forgot that 'to get the pliable and obedient author they wanted meant sinking low in the literary scale, to book-makers and hacks'. 'You and the Committee wanted more agreement than the evidence would yield,' he told David. 'You were all asking for "unconditional surrender". Not a practical policy. Not the way to get a book worth reading.' Nor were relations improved by Clarita and Christabel sending David copies of Sykes's letters to them, or letting him know that Sykes had referred to Nancy as a 'wicked woman'. Sykes complained to David about this, describing it as 'outrageous mischief-making', and in a letter to Clarita, no doubt passed on to the Committee, he said of David that 'if he could only conjoin his undoubtedly fine qualities with a more rational outlook, and if he could lose his addiction to intrigue – then what a splendid man he would be!' 'I was reacting against David Astor's ludicrous hero worship, which was expressed by his usual intrigue and natural dishonesty,' Sykes told Ali Forbes.

David found himself coming under fire from another quarter when Shiela Grant Duff wrote a furious letter in which she said that 'the real disaster of Adam's life was that he put his trust in you and Cliveden and Chamberlain in 1939'. Both Sykes and David had written pieces in *Encounter* setting out their differing views on Trott: Christabel Bielenberg's memoir, *The Past is Myself*, had been published at the same time as Sykes's biography, and Shiela Grant Duff claimed that it had 'poisonous passages in it like your article. It's time somebody challenged your right to speak on Adam's behalf.' 'I quite agree with you that Adam suffered enormously, indeed fatally, from his association with Lothian and his contact with my parents', David replied, adding that Trott 'was trying to make use of them,' and that he himself 'had no influence on Adam. If he had listened to me he would have emigrated, but he was never in the least bit impressed by my arguments.'

Reviews of Sykes's book were very favourable. Alan Bullock told David that he thought it a 'very fair memorial to your friend', the effect of which 'was to make me understand, with more sympathy than before, the dilemma in which Adam von Trott found himself'. David took Richard Crossman to lunch, and 'after ascertaining his general attitude towards

Adam and that he understood the limitations of Sykes's approach', asked him to write what he hoped would be a 'useful review': Crossman dutifully wrote a long review in praise of Trott – without, needless to say, mentioning how he had stabbed his old friend in the back when, in the middle of the war, the Foreign Office had asked him for his views on Trott's abortive attempts to put the British government in touch with the German opposition. Trott was, he declared, the only hero he had known as a friend, and although he 'could not take Adam's Hegelian philosophising as seriously as he did' at Oxford, 'I was one of the very few who never for a moment doubted his integrity.' Sykes's book was 'scrupulously fair', but 'it will pain many of those to whom Christopher Sykes is indebted' and was the work of 'a biographer out of love with his subject'. Despite the good reviews, the Committee continued to grumble in the background. 'The full story of the intrigue against your book would make fascinating if hardly elevating reading,' Ollard told his author. As for 'stopping David Astor bitching up your book, it is loathsome and even contemptible, but what can one usefully do?' He had come to regard David as 'effectively insane on this subject', but were Collins to have a 'blood row' with him, 'all kinds of persons and interests totally uninvolved in the matter would suffer as a result'.

Trott's Oxford friends remained ambiguous to the last, and none more so than Isaiah Berlin. 'I have been radically shaken in my view,' he had told David in 1965 after David had taken Clarita to see him in Oxford. What David had told him 'lifts the mist – not even a cloud – that seemed to hang over him. I am very glad of this: I was very fond of Adam and am relieved and happy to have an unsullied memory; and you are the only – literally the only – person who has ever explained Adam's behaviour to me, to make this view of him plausible . . . I am pleased and grateful to you.' But he told Sykes that despite the *Manchester Guardian* row – 'I did forgive him, though I thought that David Astor in particular had been very tiresome and had made particularly bad blood' – he had been well disposed to Trott until the summer of 1939, when 'although his anti-Nazi views were not in doubt, his talk was *too* ambiguous'. As for David, 'Grasp of reality is not the Astors' strongest suit. In this case he seems to have been blinded by love and worship.' And, like his friend Hugh Trevor-Roper, he was unimpressed by David's article in *Encounter*, thinking it a poor riposte to Sykes's piece. It 'seemed to me pathetic and embarrassing; his intentions may be good, his motives pure, but the interpretation of events was foolish, the psychology fanciful, the history faulty – in short, it's all no go – it was not like that at all, and no wholly sane person could have supposed that it was. Still, I suppose that he is besotted with love and admiration for old Adam, and there is nothing to be done.'

'I didn't know that you ever counted Bowra as a friend – only as a malicious acquaintance,' Diana Hubback had written to Trott back in the early 1930s, and despite Bowra's public *mea culpa* in his *Memoirs* – he wrote of how, when he learned of Trott's execution, 'I saw how mistaken I had been, and my rejection of him remains one of my bitterest regrets' – Bowra, like Berlin, retained his doubts. 'That's one Nazi who was hanged,' he once told Hugh Trevor-Roper: he described Trott as 'an upper-class Hun' who had 'duped' his Oxford friends, and he told an American academic that Sykes's biography was 'about a German Rhodes Scholar who was eventually hanged, but not before he had done a great deal of harm. I played a part in it – which I still think was OK, but was not approved by the Astors.' According to Shiela Grant Duff, Bowra 'does not regret anything he did, and I should not think needs to'. David once told Christabel Bielenberg that he had a 'bad conscience' about not approaching Bowra on Trott's behalf after their encounter in Wadham, but 'I considered it hopeless': Bowra and Felix Frankfurter 'are the people who, by malicious gossip, rendered Adam's efforts impossible and that is really shameful. I would feel happier had I braved them.' He confessed to Sykes that he should have done more to help his friend, and 'probably this feeling of inadequate effort on my part makes me more bitter than I ought to be about people like Bowra, who were actively acting against Adam'. Many years later, David went so far as to admit to Michael Davie, who was contemplating a biography of Bowra, that the warden had made 'a wholly reasonable mistake'.

Having failed to sabotage the Trott biography, David now turned his attention to the biography of his mother. Jakie Astor insisted that there was 'no question' of Sykes being replaced despite David's warning that 'my experience of him is rather seriously alarming', but David would not be dissuaded. Sykes's mental health was being undermined by 'age and alcohol', and since 'Mama was in many ways a much more objectionable character than Trott, I fear that Christopher in his present state will make a monkey of her'. He assured his sister Wissie that 'I have had my little say and am perfectly willing to say no more. I will certainly not stir up any relatives to have doubts about him or do anything else to embarrass Jakie's and Edward's plans', but 'I have my doubts about his capacity to sympathise or understand some aspects of Mama and Papa which they thought important but he probably won't – I mean their puritanical, high-minded and reforming zeal, which I suspect he will regard as fairish nonsense.' Michael Astor intervened to say that he thought well of the Trott biography, and that Sykes came across as 'an intelligent, professional and rather penetrating biographer. But no one can write a biography that will coincide with the views of everyone.' David offered to compensate Sykes in exchange for his abandoning the biography, but Sykes would have none of it. 'I appreciate your generosity, but the proposal comes much too late,' he told him. 'If you are a writer you write. One cannot stick around being paid and helped *not* to write books every time doubts are raised as to one's worthiness.'

David found himself fighting an increasingly lonely battle. As befits a professional courtier, Sir Edward Ford wrote him diplomatic and conciliatory letters of the 'on the one hand' and 'on the other hand' variety, but his brothers did not mince their words. After pointing out that David kept promising that his latest barrage would be his 'last word' on the subject, only to return to the attack a few days later, Michael suggested that his assault on Sykes was a 'purely destructive act' which stemmed from their feud over Trott, and had nothing to do with a life of their mother. David's attitude to Sykes was 'little short of preposterous', and he should let a 'very competent author get on with his work'. 'You had an emotional "thing" about Trott, which later became an emotional "thing" about Christopher Sykes,' he continued. 'In my hearing you suggested that Christopher was senile, maybe alcoholic', while claiming that the Trott book was so dull that it would get no reviews. Jakie was more restrained, but reminded David that 'no one member of the family is in a privileged position which justifies trying to undermine the arrangements that Mama's appointed literary executors reached after considerable family consultation'.

Although David seems to have told Sykes that he liked and admired the Trott biography, Sykes wished that 'you would act with more simplicity and directness', adding that 'you are a terribly difficult man to have dealings with'. Michael begged David to stop circulating letters about Sykes, but to no avail. 'It is easy enough to bombard an author and to criticise him. It's a damn sight harder to produce a book. I think your approach to the author would be a little different if you had actually gone through the experience,' he insisted. Michael knew from his own experience that 'the author has to write his own book. You, presumably, have to edit your own newspaper'. (Michael's forceful opinions may have reflected a growing hostility on his part: when he lay dying, in 1980, David tried to visit him at Bruern, but Michael refused to see him. Twenty years later, when Jakie was on his deathbed, David sat beside him for hours, holding his hand.)

David continued to denounce Sykes as an 'intellectual crook', undermined by 'age and drink', while assuring his brothers that 'that, I assure you, is the last word I will volunteer on the subject' and that if they disagreed 'I shall try to keep as quiet as a mouse and say no more.' In the end he agreed to co-operate with Sykes, but not without regretting that his opponents had 'taken so little notice of my evidence or so little regard for my feelings', and reminding Edward Ford that Nancy had originally wanted him to be her literary executor: he had stood aside in favour of Jakie and a third party rather than upset Bill – which 'suggests that my mother had some regard for my judgement; that my father had some is suggested by the confidence he showed in me over the *Observer*'. Sykes's biography was finally published in 1972. Richard Ollard told Sykes that the *Sunday Times* had bought the serial rights since 'I am told that he [David] has some phobia about nepotism.'

'I am greatly impressed by the book,' David told the embattled Sykes. 'My fears that you would not be able to sympathise with my mother's more unorthodox views were certainly exaggerated.' Eight years later, John Grigg's much shorter biography of Nancy was published, and David said he much preferred it to Sykes's version. For all the critical praise they received, Sykes's biographies of Trott and Nancy are ponderous, heavy-laden affairs, but it's hard not to sympathise with him given the battering he received from David, who, fair-minded as he usually was, sometimes gave way to an overriding obsession which made him seem both unreasonable and unjust. Sykes continued to write occasional book reviews for the *Observer*, and in the last months of David's editorship he agreed to the serialisation of Sykes's biography of Evelyn Waugh.

Despite his admiration for Orwell, Connolly and Koestler, and his readiness to print prepublication extracts from books as diverse as Dylan Thomas's *Under Milk Wood* and Waugh's *The Ordeal of Gilbert Pinfold* – and his enthusiasm for publishing writers who were not professional journalists – David never seemed entirely at home in the literary world; his gift for dealing with journalists was both intuitive and practical, but he had never been a great reader of books, and his dealings with Sykes suggest that he had little understanding of how writers went about their business. Nor was Sykes the only writer with whom he fell out: Alan Ross told his friend

Michael Astor that he no longer enjoyed writing for the paper, and that he resented not being paid when 'totally incapacitated' by a nervous break-down, partly induced by the strain of taking over the *London Magazine* from John Lehmann in 1961. And Eric Newby's departure as travel editor proved an unhappy, bad-tempered business. Although Newby later wrote that 'no one gave a damn what one did with one's spare time, and in all the years I worked for the paper no one ever told me that I was doing badly, just as no one told me I was doing well', this was not strictly true. Newby was a brilliant writer, but a hopeless editor and administrator; he was hardly ever in the office; his own pieces were far too long and had to be savagely cut by George Seddon or John Lucas; he had no interest in commissioning pieces by other writers, and 'no ability to cut or edit copy'. The advertising department wanted pieces tailored for the booming holiday market, complete with prices, details of hotels and the like, rather than travel articles as Newby understood them: David warned him that the 'Time Off' pages needed to be planned in advance in order to attract advertising, quite apart from which 'we feel we are wasting the talents of one of the country's best travel writers by asking you to put your experi-ences into 800-word pieces addressed to holidaymakers'. But flattery got him nowhere, and before long David was writing again to say that his footloose editor had been doing 'too much travelling and too little editing', and that his prolonged absences, which included a round-the-world trip, had 'added greatly to the workload and nervous strain of other members of staff and disrupted the running of the department unnecessarily and unprofitably'. After an angry confrontation, Newby resigned after what he described as 'nine years' faithful and devoted service', and Edward Mace took over the travel pages.

A writer for whom David felt both affection and admiration was the Irish playwright Brendan Behan. David was alerted to Behan's heavy drinking, and the disastrous effect it was having on his health, by an article about him in the *Observer* by the American journalist Clancy Sigal. David told Behan that although 'it seems fairly clear that your days are numbered' if he didn't give up drinking, 'disturbances or imperfect development of personality are matters that to my certain knowledge can be dealt with by psychoanalysis', and 'I would feel much honoured if you would allow me to be of help.' He visited Behan in the Middlesex Hospital, taking with him his medical correspondent, Dr Abraham Marcus, who repeated his warning about the lethal consequences of his drinking: Behan subjected his visitors to a torrent of abuse, and within a short time of their visit he was dead. David saw Behan's most famous play, *The Hostage*, four times, and serialised *Brendan Behan's Island* in three parts in the Weekend Review: he admired him 'because of his tremendous humanity, his detachment. He seemed to me like George Orwell, incapable of prejudice against any class because it was a class', and he hated the idea of 'this marvellous man destroying himself'.

After David's old sparring partner Cyril Connolly had expressed interest in moving from the *Sunday Times* in the summer of 1960, David offered him the post of principal book reviewer and 'cultural reporter': Philip Toynbee was said to be all in favour of 'getting you out of the roller-shafts and giving you the full freedom to do what you want', and David's offer included a trip to Africa ('provided the expenses could be kept within reasonable bounds'), a 'Connolly notebook column', and the serialisation of Connolly's autobiography (never written) – and 'we would treat you like a prince'. Nothing came of it, but their correspondence reminded David 'of what fun you are – only my stepbrother Bobbie and Ali Forbes are as amusing, and I seldom see them either', and 'what an ass I was in those days'. But although he wrote to Anthony Burgess to suspend him as a fiction reviewer after learning that he had reviewed his own novel in the *Yorkshire Post*, and suggested to Graham Greene that he should write a piece on 'fashionable hypocrisies' – Greene liked the idea, but was too busy to put it into practice – David was more than happy to leave Terry Kilmartin to deal with the literary contributors. Kilmartin had quickly established a reputation as the most distinguished literary editor in London, and his regular book reviewers now included Greene, D. J. Enright, Angus Wilson, Anthony Burgess, John Gross, Malcolm Muggeridge, Bernard Levin, Paul Bailey and Kingsley Amis (whose controversial 'More Means Worse' reaction to the new universities recommended by the Robbins Report was published in the main body of the paper in February 1961).

Kilmartin 'looked like an army officer – handsome, upright and slightly reined in – the perfect English gentleman', according to Al Alvarez, the paper's long-serving and influential poetry editor. 'In fact he was Irish and iconoclastic, very much his own man and a shrewd judge of literature and prose style' – and he was happy to give his contributors a free hand once he trusted them. Reviewers and critics 'accept – and are grateful for – criticism from Terry which they would accept from nobody else', Edward Crankshaw reminded David, adding that Kilmartin 'keeps Tynan from going right off the rails – a superhuman task' and 'winds A. J. P. Taylor round his finger' – which no doubt came as a relief to David, who found the pugnacious Oxford historian a heavy cross to bear. Taylor, who began reviewing for the *Observer* in 1953, had a curious passion for the Astors' old enemy, Lord Beaverbrook, and was a regular and highly valued contributor to the *Sunday Express*. 'I was influenced by the idea that AJP would gain us circulation, but I really think he is rather a terrible little man,' David told Kilmartin, and after Taylor had ridiculed the *Observer* in the *Evening Standard* while at the same time asking to be given more work on its pages, David informed him that 'it would be asking a lot to expect the paper used in this way to get a similar enjoyment from the relationship'. Taylor's 'drive to naughtiness' made him 'the hardest to justify of our contributors'.

The young Australian Clive James, who had been lured away from the *Listener* to replace Maurice Richardson as the television critic, recalled how 'Astor gave Kilmartin a free hand to run the arts pages as a kind of university campus', but Kilmartin's self-contained empire came under siege when David invited Richard Findlater, an authority on theatrical low-life and the perils of authorship, to become the cultural features editor – a job he initially combined with editing *Twentieth Century*. David told Kilmartin that, as part of the hunt for new readers, 'necessity has led me to ask you to accept Richard's journalistic leadership in trying to get Part II more popular. I also wanted you to get an assistant who would be less Oxbridge and more Redbrick than you – and more alert to newsy books.' Kilmartin would have none of it. His assistant, Miriam Gross, was a product of Oxford, and went on to become the classiest literary editor of her generation, very much in the mould of her mentor; and he spurned David's suggestion that reviews should be followed by a short biographical note about the reviewer, regarding it as a waste of valuable reviewing space. Clive James remembered how, as an editor, Kilmartin 'proved a much tougher nut to crack' than the amiable Findlater, and how 'he stared at me over the top rim of his half glasses as his blue pencil softly struck'.

Dealing with agents and publishers never greatly appealed to David – Peter Calvocoressi at Chatto and Mark Bonham Carter at Collins were his only close friends in the publishing world: George Weidenfeld was the one publisher whose name regularly surfaced in his desk diaries, but although Terry Kilmartin had healed the breach between them, he remained a professional acquaintance rather than a friend – so he was more than happy to leave Findlater and, in due course, his deputy editor, Donald Trelford, to haggle over terms for serial rights with 'whizz-kid' agents and publishers like Pat Kavanagh at A. D. Peters and Tom Maschler at Jonathan Cape. Nor were his ventures into the booming world of serial rights happy experiences. He decided against

William Manchester's *The Making of the President*, which then added more to the *Sunday Times*'s circulation than any of its 'Big Reads' since Monty's memoirs; much to the relief of Nigel Hawkes, the newly appointed science editor, who thought David too credulous at times, he was only prevented from buying the rights in a new book by Uri Geller by Tristan Jones, who refused to pay up the £50,000 being asked for the rights (Geller, who addressed David as 'Dave', demonstrated his powers in the Ritz to David, Hawkes, Simon Master of Pan Books and David Burnett of Heinemann, performing a near-miraculous trick involving the synchronisation of their watches). In a rather half-hearted attempt to emulate the success of the *Sunday Times*'s Insight books, he encouraged Patrick Seale, who combined journalistic and entrepreneurial gifts, to set up Observer Books and Features to exploit and sell the publishing rights in books written by *Observer* journalists. This was easier said than done, since most of the writers who wrote books already had agents and publishers. David asked his new friend Arnold Goodman to talk to the prime minister about the possibility of an *Observer* book about the cracking of codes by the British during the Second World War – a subject that was slowly emerging from the cocoon of secrecy. British and American publishers, he assured Goodman, 'are already sniffing around the subject and there is a distinct possibility that a determined effort, say on the scale of the *Sunday Times* Philby enquiry, would result in the publication of a substantial book'. Nothing came of it; Patrick Seale then started a service whereby artists' prints could be sold through the paper to its readers before setting up on his own as a literary agent.

'I made many appointments but none that had such consequences as yours. The paper was excellent in its most important department entirely through you. And nobody taught you how to do it. You're a wonder,' David told Kilmartin when he finally stood down as literary editor, eleven years after David himself had retired as editor. '"Look at all those bloody books," he would groan as he surveyed his cluttered office,' Gavin Young recalled after Kilmartin's death in 1991, while Lorna Sage, a relative newcomer, wrote of how 'no flattery would move him, in fact it had the opposite effect. Even Ken Tynan wouldn't cross Terry.' He had been the outstanding literary editor of his day, and no member of the staff had been closer to David.

Drifting Apart

In the summer of 1969 the ultra-fashionable *Queen* magazine ran a profile of David. He was, his readers learned, referred to in the office as 'the Boss': a 'person of enormous, insidious charm', he hummed loudly but tunelessly when striding the corridors of New Printing House Square, 'hardly ever raises his voice or bawls anybody out', and was 'given to running large brown hands nervously through untidy brown hair, thus producing an engaging harassed look'. 'Although the paper has been, in theory, owned and administered by a trust, he has always had absolute power over the whole organisation – a crude fact that he seems to want to disguise, as if it is a slight embarrassment to him,' the profile-writer continued, adding that 'his way with power is diffuse, self-deprecating, self-conscious: but the power is there, and everyone in the *Observer* knows it'. And a couple of years earlier Sir William Haley, the former editor of *The Times*, had told David that 'the *Observer* of today is your creation to a degree and in a way that no other paper is any other man's. The achievement is all the more remarkable because you did not imprint your character on a nondescript sheet, but on a journal which your predecessors had made famous by its being highly personalised.'

To the outside world at least, life at the *Observer*, and David's place in it, seemed reassuringly stable and familiar, but the reality was much more worrying. Harry Evans, the young and energetic editor of the *Sunday Times*, was reported as saying that he no longer regarded the *Observer* as serious competition, and that its place had been taken by the *Sunday Telegraph*. David found himself increasingly unsympathetic to the social and political changes of the 1960s, and was regarded as out of touch by his younger colleagues and by commentators on the press; his lifelong Atlanticism, and his sympathy for the Americans over Vietnam, were seen as evidence of a move to the right, at variance with notions of what the *Observer* had always stood for. Money problems loomed larger than ever, causing David to dip into his own pockets, and solicit other members of the family for financial support; and he found himself doing battle not just with the print unions, but with a revitalised National Union of Journalists and with a Labour government which fully supported its demands.

Help was to hand in the rotund, avuncular form of the solicitor Arnold Goodman, who was appointed chairman of the Observer Trust in 1967 and was to become David's right-hand man during his last years as the *Observer*'s editor. A close confidant and adviser to Harold Wilson, Goodman was the best-known fixer and intermediary of his day, flitting – or rather lumbering – between the worlds of politics, the media, culture and high society, and holding court in his flat in Portland Place: he was, at various times, involved with the British Council, the National Theatre, the Royal Opera House and the Royal Shakespeare Company; he chaired the Arts Council from the Astors' old house in St James's Square, as well as the British Council, the Housing Corporation and, more relevantly from David's point of view, the Newspaper Proprietors Association (NPA), the largely ineffectual and disunited body which represented the interests of the owners of the press; and after his formal retirement from the law firm Goodman Derrick, he became the master of University College, Oxford, from where he continued to intercede and negotiate.

Sir Ifor Evans had urged David to meet Goodman to discuss the possibility of the *Observer* acquiring shares in ITV licences, and Tristan Jones had been greatly impressed by him. Goodman was fascinated by newspaper proprietors, and thought David 'as big-hearted and liberal a man as can be found on this earth': he admired his 'talented, if not wholly businesslike' running of the *Observer*, and had 'always been in broad sympathy with his aspirations and notions'. David, for his part, soon 'developed an admiration for my qualities, wildly undeserved and totally excessive', and in 1970 David and Max Aitken of the *Express* nominated Goodman to be chairman of the NPA. Ifor Evans had earlier convinced David that Goodman should replace him as chairman of the trustees. The managerial team also included Roger Harrison, who joined the paper in 1966 via Oxford, the Harvard Business School and *The Times*, and John Littlejohns, the *Observer*'s finance director and a former partner in the accountancy firm of Sayers Butterworth; and on most Fridays Goodman joined David, Harrison and Littlejohns for a working lunch.

Although he concentrated on the managerial side of the paper, Goodman would sometimes intervene on editorial matters. He persuaded David not to name the Fifth Man, and threatened to resign if the paper published a disobliging story about George Brown, the bibulous Foreign Secretary. Every now and then the 'friends of Arnold' would fall out, and even his powers of reconciliation were thwarted: he tried in vain to get an out-of-court settlement when Sidney Bernstein of Granada TV sued the *Observer*, and was awarded £35,000 in damages by the High Court. And he threatened to resign in 1967 after reading an as-yet-unpublished piece by Anthony Howard about Harlech TV's franchise deal. After conferring with Goodman, David emerged from his office scratching his nose ('always a bad sign', according to Howard); Howard was subjected to a 'very unpleasant' interview with Goodman; David, unusually indecisive, asked Howard what he should do, and 'I fear I sent him away, as it were, with a flea in his ear, and the article duly appeared.'

Goodman came into his own when discussing possible mergers with other newspapers. In 1965 the *Observer* offices were moved from 'our crazy patchwork of Victorian offices in Tudor Street to the hygienic modernity of the New Printing House Square'; and before he joined the paper, Littlejohns negotiated the contract for the use of *The Times*'s presses, and the rent for the front building at NPHS. 'Much look forward to showing you this part of your own building and to offering you some of your own lunch', David told his cousin Gavin, chairman of *The Times*, adding that 'we greatly enjoy having access to your excellent kitchen and those charming old butlers'. But despite the butlers, times were hard for the newspaper business: a prices and wages freeze was combined with a reduction in advertising and increased printing costs. There was talk of the *Observer* and the *Guardian* forming a joint company to buy New Printing House Square, of a *Times–Guardian* merger, of a consortium of *The Times*, the *Guardian* and the *Observer* publishing a merged daily paper as well as the *Observer*, of the *Guardian* taking over the *Observer*, which would then, like its parent paper, be subsidised by the *Manchester Evening News* . . . Nothing came of these circuitous negotiations. According to Alastair Hetherington, 'David was looking for a means to inject new money into the *Observer* and to let the *Guardian* keep something of itself alive. He was willing to sacrifice something of his own editorial and managerial control', but the Scott Trust decided to keep the *Guardian* independent despite huge losses: by 1967 the paper had not only recovered, but had poached the *Observer*'s first-rate manager, Peter Gibbings; and Tristan Jones's acrimonious relations with Gibbings made future co-operation with the *Guardian* impossible. Jones was a keen collector of antiques, owned a pet fox, wore a Roman helmet, and kept his coffin in his garage, filled with chocolates, and he was increasingly out of his depth in the newspaper world. In Michael Davie's opinion, 'the only management principle he observed was never to hand out money for anything', and 'he was psychologically incapable of thinking about the future, possibly believing, on Marxist principles, that it was predetermined', while Goodman recalled that 'he was not particularly liked or trusted by the rank and file, since he neither liked nor trusted the rank and file'.

In September 1966 Roy Thomson bought *The Times*, and increased the charge levied for printing the *Observer* on *The Times*'s machines. Goodman insisted that Thomson should give the *Observer* five years' notice if he decided to leave NPHS, and six years later, with *The Times* still losing money, Thomson decided it should join the *Sunday Times* in Gray's Inn Road. New Printing House Square would be sold to pay for the move, and under the terms of their lease the *Observer* had the option to buy the property. Goodman's friend Max Rayne had informally valued the buildings at £7 million, though by the early 1970s 'its notional value was reckoned to be more like £18 million'; Goodman asked Hamilton how much they would cost; Hamilton produced the estate agent's evaluation, which was far lower than Goodman had expected, and Goodman instantly made an offer of £5 million. 'I am sure the Astors can always find a penny or two,' he told Hamilton. According to Marmaduke Hussey, Hamilton's plan to sell NPHS to the *Observer* 'may have looked good on paper' but proved to be 'idiotic', in that an immensely valuable piece of City property was disposed of at a 'bargain price'. But Goodman's shrewd acquisition – he once described it as 'the business coup of my career' – was offset by new and crippling costs. *The Times* finally moved to Gray's Inn Road in 1973, leaving the *Observer*, in Tom Baistow's words, 'with a technical force of 600 highly paid men to produce one paper a week': David's paper had become 'that most uneconomic of Fleet Street propositions, a Sunday paper without a partner to minimise unit costs'. The print unions had negotiated terms whereby they were paid six days' wages for one day's work; wages now represented 'a crippling thirty-six per cent of turnover', and whereas sales of the *Sunday Times* and the *Sunday Telegraph* were steadily increasing, those of the *Observer* were static by comparison. David contemplated keeping the paper's editorial offices in London but printing in the provinces, but the unions got wind of this, and nothing came of it.

'You must tell me when the lights turn to amber,' David asked John Littlejohns, but they were already showing red. Under the terms of the Observer Trust, the paper could neither borrow money nor earn profits; there was not enough money in the trust itself to pay for ever-increasing paper and manning costs, plus the cost of the printing works and the NPHS building, so David had to draw upon his own resources and family trusts. In September 1967, after revealing that he had already put in £750,000 of his own money, and was planning to invest a further £500,000, he turned to other members of the family for possible support, while emphasising that only his contribution would be at risk. Jakie Astor, by now a director of the *Observer*, was reluctant to contribute to the 'proposed *Observer* consortium'. David's 'cash investment' had given the paper a reserve to draw on for the next three to five years, but whereas the planned consortium would have a capital value of £2 million, Roy Thomson and the *Telegraph*'s Berry family had infinitely greater resources at their disposal, and 'I am not convinced that a solitary independent paper can survive financially unless it has control of large cash reserves which it can spend in times of need.' Waldorf had left the paper to David, 'with the trustees as some mock set-up to appear as if the paper really was independent of Astor money. This has proved unworkable, despite your heroic efforts as editor', and 'I feel we must not involve the money of the next generation in any uneconomic enterprise which made political sense to our father, who acted regardless of money.'

David also approached his sister Wissie, the Countess of Ancaster. Owning a newspaper, he told her, was a 'way in which private individuals can interfere in public affairs', but was 'only a suitable investment for people with enough capital resources to provide for their "living allowance" by other means'. The trust was being 'drastically altered' to give control to new investors and new money – 'yours, mine, and anybody else's' – and all shares in a new company, Observer Holdings Ltd, would be held by the amended trust. The plan was to make the new company 'thoroughly businesslike and commercially seaworthy' and, by diversifying into areas like book publishing and Patrick Seale's literary agency, 'build up a group of companies engaged in publishing that will last for years and years'. A loan from Wissie of £700,000 would be guaranteed by David himself; Wissie's daughter, Jane Willoughby, could, if she so wished, become more involved in the *Observer*'s affairs, and it was agreed that 'Jacob [Rothschild] will indeed be the Merchant Banker on the Board, if he so wishes.' Efforts at diversification included setting up the consortium which established Capital Radio, the brainchild of a dentist from Woking: Tristan Jones persuaded his colleagues that a music station would be much more profitable than a news station, and his hunch paid off. The buildings and the shareholdings in Capital Radio and London Weekend Television were put into a family trust-owned holding company, and the income (but not the capital) could be used to support the *Observer*.

After he had retired as editor, David wrote a rueful note to the effect that a paper's 'political and intellectual standing' was inevitably reduced if it became too dependent on editorial devices designed to increase circulation and advertising, while the editor himself was in danger of becoming 'a shopkeeper, subservient to the whims of his customers and advertisers'. 'I ought to know, as I kept the *Observer* afloat for a decade or more by just such devices', he added. 'I don't regret this, as I had no other means available. But the decline in the paper's standing was unmistakeable.' Nor did he have any time for managerial devices such as readers' questionnaires or opinion polls since 'the idea of question-naires to readers is based on the (to my mind false) analogy with normal commercial operations, where the task of the purveyor is to provide precisely what his market is demanding. This is not the situation in any serious publication.'

'I spend a great deal of time racking my brains for devices to sell extra copies,' he told William Haley, and the strain was beginning to show. Enforced economies including the axing of the annual Christmas dinner-dance at the Café Royal, and in early 1967 David told the trustees that 'in view of the present economic difficulties, the *Observer* felt it necessary to impose cuts in almost all the departments including the editorial'. With more journalists employed but with fewer resources, greater emphasis was put on news-gathering at the expense of David's beloved conferences, with the result that he became a more remote figure in the office. Richard Hall, who had returned from Africa in 1969, noted that 'although David kept his fair-haired boyish looks, he was really tired': he had edited the paper 'for far too long – and he knew it'. Neal Ascherson felt that David had run out of steam by the late 1960s, and that 'most of its [the *Observer*'s] aims had been achieved: decolonisation, East–West détente, Roy Jenkins's reforms of morals legislation'. Anthony Howard, who had returned to London after a spell as the Washington correspondent, thought that David had stayed on too long, that some of his new columnists weren't up to scratch, and that serialising Svetlana's memoirs had been indicative of a loosening grip at the helm.

Bill Grundy in the *Spectator* hardly evoked the festive spirit when noting David's twenty-first anniversary as editor: the *Observer* had become 'trendy to the point of being tiresome', while its fascination with clothes and design 'borders on the ridiculous, for all the world like an elderly hippy' (albeit a hippy with a taste for creature comforts, as suggested by the promo line 'Shirley Conran Goes Shopping for Central Heating', as well as for a long leader-page interview with John Lennon and Yoko Ono, conducted by Tariq Ali and Robin Blackburn). Tom Baistow in the *New Statesman* suggested that the paper had 'become more woolly liberal than compassionate liberal, still relatively radical on the Third World but increasingly right-wing on the domestic front, with a middle-aged yearning for the tidy order of a centrist Utopia that must have cost it many young potential readers'. Baistow thought the *Observer* devoted too much energy to imitating the *Sunday Times*, leading to an apparent lack of confidence; another commentator noted that 'what was good about the *Observer* was David Astor: its amateurishness, its generosity, its high-mindedness, and a brilliant staff': on the other hand, it was prone to a 'certain primness' and 'an extreme reluctance to undertake investigative journalism just when that became an urgent item in an increasingly secretive society', and it seemed unable to 'bring in talented people in their twenties and thirties to blend in with those in their fifties and sixties'.

David once referred to professional journalists as 'plumbers', and many of the younger generation of *Observer* employees had more in common with their colleagues in Fleet Street than with London literary life or Oxbridge common rooms. Eric Clark started life on a local paper before working for a news agency and the *Daily Mail*; when David rang him at the *Guardian* to offer him a job he assumed it was a practical joke by one of his colleagues, and put the phone down. Clark was followed by Peter Deeley, a foot-in-the-door journalist of the old school, and by Robert Chesshyre, who had joined the *Sheffield Telegraph* from Oxford and worked his way up from there. Colin Smith was a grammar-school boy who started life on his local paper and moved on to the *Birmingham Post* before joining the *Observer* as a home-news reporter. Since there was no executive lavatory in the offices, Smith would put ideas to David if ever they found themselves standing side by side in the urinals. David took a particular shine to Colin Smith, and encouraged him to think in terms of becoming a foreign correspondent ('Don't you think the Kurds look interesting?'). Smith's lavatorial technique was also employed by Peter Wilby, an ambitious Sussex University graduate who later became the paper's long-serving education correspondent. Nigel Hawkes, who had read metallurgy at Oxford, worked for John Maddox on *Nature* before replacing Gerald Leach as the science correspondent: he noticed a division on the papers between the 'thinkers' – grandees of the older generation including Legum, Kilmartin, Robert Stephens and David himself – and the 'doers' like Obank and William Millinship, the news

editor, who were much more like conventional newspapermen. For
Richard Hall, life on the *Observer* 'quickly began to remind me of my
distant undergraduate days on the *Isis*'; he unkindly recalled how 'one of
his closest associates said in exasperation after another futile conference
about the financial crisis, Astor would have made an excellent master
in the better sort of preparatory school', and David himself, in low
moments, sometimes wondered whether he could have made it had he
not been his father's son.

Every now and then David would cross swords with his more sleuth-
like younger colleagues. Consisting of Eric Clark, Peter Wilby and Robert
Chesshyre, Inquiry had been set up as a modest rival to the *Sunday
Times*'s Insight team, and when Eric Clark learned that Hugh Carleton
Greene, soon to become a trustee of the *Observer*, was planning to resign
as the director general of the BBC, the story was printed without David
having read it. 'You have upset a lot of important people,' Kenneth Harris
ominously informed Clark soon after the piece had appeared. Clark was
summoned before David, who brandished a letter from Greene denying
that he had any intention of resigning. Clark suggested that the letter
should be printed in the next week's issue, but David said that Greene
did not want it quoted in any way; six months later, almost to the day
suggested in the offending article, Greene resigned as director general.
(Despite being the subject of several Profiles, and an occasional reviewer,
Graham Greene, Hugh Carleton's older brother, found less favour with
David. 'I should not like that. Greene is mischievous. He is anti-American.
He is a fellow traveller,' was David's reaction when Richard Hall told
him that Greene would be delivering a piece on Salvador Allende to the
colour magazine: Hall slipped it in while David was on holiday, and no
more was said on the matter.)

Robert Chesshyre thought David too kind-hearted to be a news-driven
editor of the hard-nosed variety. With Peter Deeley, he once followed
up the activities of a fraudster, but their story was spiked when the
fraudster's son contacted David and told him that his father had a weak
heart and might suffer a heart attack were it published. A long piece
about Keith Joseph by Polly Toynbee, Philip Toynbee's daughter, went
the same way on the grounds that Joseph was in poor health, and the
piece would expose him to ridicule: Peter Crookston, who had returned
to the paper as features editor in 1973, did his best on Toynbee's behalf,
but David was adamant. And David thought the *Sunday Times*'s lengthy
revelations about Lord Lucan 'an unjustified piece of sensationalism.
After all, there was no point of public policy involved. And the fact that

the idle rich are socially indefensible does not mean that they are fair game for use as entertainment.'

Sue Arnold remembers David saying that 'You can sit in your high chairs and bang your spoons as loudly as you like, but it is *not* going in' apropos a contentious item in Pendennis, but he stoutly stood by her when the occasion demanded. Peter Heyworth, the *Observer*'s long-serving and highly regarded music critic, had suggested a possible story about the conductor Sir Adrian Boult for the Pendennis column: he gave Sue Arnold Boult's private phone number, but warned her that the great man was fiercely guarded by his wife and his secretary. She rang Boult, who was charm personified, and said he would be delighted to meet her at the Festival Hall, but when she got there she found Boult's secretary on the prowl. Somehow she managed to get past the secretary, and speak to the famous conductor – who spluttered with indignation, denied ever having spoken to her, and ordered her to leave at once. Edward Mace, who was now running Pendennis, decided to make a story out of it under the heading 'Conduct Unbecoming'. The following day David received a furious letter from Boult demanding to know 'Since when did the *Observer* employ illiterate little wops who can barely speak English?' (Boult muddled his abusive epithets: Sue Arnold is half-Burmese, not Italian, and is a graduate of Trinity College, Dublin.) David wrote to Boult, pointing out that he should be the one to apologise. Looking back at the editors he worked for during a long career in journalism, John Clare chose David as 'the one I most admired, for his moral integrity, his gentle wisdom and, although it could be mocked, his otherworldliness, a rare and precious quality in journalism'. While still in his early thirties, Clare joined the *Observer* as its labour correspondent towards the end of David's editorship, and he recalls how David stood up for him after he had written disobliging pieces about Len Murray and Jack Jones, two of the most powerful trade union barons of the early 1970s: Jones – later revealed to have been in the pay of the KGB – was subsequently invited to lunch at the paper, and made a point of refusing to speak to Clare, let alone shake his hand.

David may not always have sympathised with the views of the younger generation, but despite the occasional spiking, he encouraged them to follow their hunches and their enthusiasms, and did his best to look after them when times were hard. When Andrew Wilson fell ill in what was still Rhodesia, David flew out a surgeon to look after him; he paid for him to take a course in war studies at London University after he had been made defence correspondent, and backed him to the full in his long if futile campaign against the building of Concorde. David came

to abominate the IRA, but when Mary Holland, who had joined the
paper as a fashion correspondent, alerted him to the civil rights marches
and anti-Catholic discrimination in Northern Ireland, way ahead of any
of the other London papers, he told her to 'Go away and write it – it's
our problem to find the space.' And although he disapproved of the
1968 student riots, he gave Peter Wilby room to ventilate their views.
(At about this time the paper ran a story about an IRA informer. After
the first edition had gone to press, Ken Obank and Robert Chesshyre
popped out to the *Observer* pub, and on their way back they noticed a
police car drawn up in front of the office. Inflamed by drink, Obank
gave the car a sharp kick; he was immediately whisked off to a police
cell, but was released in time to work on the third edition. 'Good God,
and Ken a grandfather' was David's reaction when he heard the news.)

   But looking back on David's career, a perceptive commentator
suggested that after 1968 the *Observer* 'lost its tolerance for new ideas.
It denounced student demonstrations, sexual liberation, political radi-
calism and trade union militancy in tones which became increasingly
shrill and almost absurd'. Mark Frankland felt that, for David, 'the Cold
War remained the central issue of the age', and that 'the attitudes associated with it had become obstacles to change': David may have been
'seductively modest', but 'he towered like an oak tree above everyone else
on the paper, and his view of the world was shaped by Hitler's rise to
power and the later realisation that Stalin's Soviet Union was an equally
powerful threat to the democratic countries of the West'. For Richard
Hall, 'the *Observer* was never a socialist paper, whatever the opinions
held about it in Conservative Central Office', and 'no British journal
was more detested in the Kremlin'. Writing in the *New Statesman* the
year before David's resignation, Corinna Adam claimed that whereas
the *Sunday Times* under Harry Evans was moving to the left, the *Observer*
was heading in the opposite direction. 'Even its most loyal subscribers
seem to be distressed by its current obsession with Red extremists,' she
wrote: Nora Beloff was 'a firm believer in Reds-under-the-bed. That
attitude prevails in Mr David Astor's leader columns as well.' No doubt
she was confirmed in her views when, without consulting his colleagues,
David bought the rights in Brian Crozier's 'Sources of Conflict in British
Industry': first published by the right-wing Institute for the Study of
Conflict, it examined the influence of the Communist Party on British
trade unions, and David ran it over two pages.

   David's closest political allies had always been on the right wing of the
Labour Party, so Ted Heath was a surprising new friend. Heath's letters

to David were affectionate, warm-hearted and far more literate than most, and much appreciated by the recipient. 'I tremendously admire the way you have withstood the many disparaging attacks on you over the last few years – but, even more, the way you have obviously thrived and grown on them,' David told the newly elected prime minister, who had sent him flowers in hospital. Four years later David wrote to Heath about the miners' strike: his paper had supported Heath 'with a consistency that has annoyed some of our readers', and he wished him 'good luck in the strenuous and brave cause you are pursuing'. In a leader entitled 'The Arrival of the Militants', Ivan Yates claimed that a 'free society' was threatened by a combination of 'fashionable Marxists' and miners' leaders. This infuriated some of his writers, and a letter was sent to David signed by Neal Ascherson, Peter Wilby, Polly Toynbee, Philip Toynbee, Peter Crookston, Nigel Hawkes and Jeremy Bugler, the paper's first environmental correspondent: they resented the implication that the miners were the 'dupes of a few fanatics', and saw the leader as a 'hardly concealed invitation to the readers to vote Conservative'. David denied that the views of news reporters and leader writers were diverging, pointing out that 'the only papers that are politically consistent throughout are the ideologically straight-jacketed ones – the Nazis invented a word for this, *Gleichschaltung*'. In the meantime he continued to provide Heath with epistolary support. 'How greatly I have admired your fearlessness and your high morality,' he told him, adding that, as far as the premiership was concerned, 'your qualities have given the job a shining character that it had somehow lost'. Later that year, after Heath had been defeated in the general election, David invited the new Tory leader, Margaret Thatcher, to a lunch attended by Ivan Yates, Laurence Marks, Nora Beloff, Bill Millinship and Katharine Whitehorn. 'You were less perfect and, there-fore, less daunting than your telly image', he told her after the event.

According to Rudolf Klein, who had joined the paper in the 1960s, 'Astor's interests were no longer the sure guide they had been. There was more interest in domestic issues, but it was extraordinarily difficult to enlist Astor's enthusiasm for such matters as public spending or devaluation.' David always seemed 'anxious to demonstrate his tolerance of divergent opinions. Yet there was an element of humbug about it all. On issues that mattered to him, only one opinion mattered: Astor's. Dissidents were sooner or later edged out.' David was the kindest of men, but he 'liked dependence, if not deference', and the staff were poorly paid because he 'wanted people to work for him because they loved or admired him, not because he rewarded them well'.

Nor did David endear himself to his younger colleagues by his ambivalent attitude towards the Vietnam War. In 1963 the *Observer* had printed extracts from *The Wall Has Two Sides*, a rhapsodic account of life in Mao's China by Graham Greene's cousin Felix Greene. Greene continued to contribute occasional pieces after he had lost faith in Communist China and transferred his allegiance to Ho Chi Minh, but despite that David had urged Lyndon B. Johnson to carry the war into North Vietnam in 1964. Nor did David's liking and admiration for President Nixon and Henry Kissinger go down well with many of his journalists. In 1958 Isaiah Berlin, who thought Nixon 'a most shifty, vulgar, dishonest and repellent human being', attended a party given by David to meet Stravinsky at which their host 'spoke with furious indignation about the monstrous campaign against him [Nixon] being conducted by the American left, which had fortunately not deceived the English, who had realised what a sterling true good man he was'. Fifteen years later Peter Crookston suggested that Mary McCarthy, rather than the *Observer*'s Washington correspondent, should be commissioned to write about Watergate, and David agreed after Terry Kilmartin and Gavin Young had given it their blessing: the story ran over several weeks, providing much-needed publicity for the paper, but after Nixon's resignation David rejected Crookston's suggestion that McCarthy should cover it since 'I don't want Mary McCarthy dancing on Nixon's grave.'

David had been in touch with Kissinger since the late 1950s. In June 1974 Anthony Lewis of the *New York Times* wrote to David, disputing an *Observer* leader about Kissinger's role in the Vietnam War and claiming that the Secretary of State had, in fact, prolonged an unjustifiable war. 'Everyone knows it was a disaster,' David replied. 'But I can think of several things in American history that are a great deal more disgraceful (killing of Indians for land greed, exploitation of slaves) than this war. I believe that it was waged for motives that were infinitely more disinterested and impeccable, even unselfish, than was the case in most wars. I realise that it is not fashionable to speak of the American past in Vietnam in other than terms of execration. But I don't believe that this is how history will see that episode.' 'I have thought of you very often in the last few months, particularly in that monstrous period when some newspapers were behaving so extremely badly towards you,' he told Kissinger. 'You are irredeemably lined with Beelzebub–Nixon', he wrote in a later letter. 'You make the ideal scapegoat for fantasies about Nixon, fears for Israel and guilt for the most tragic war of modern times. I cannot tell you how strongly I feel about the grotesque injustice of all this.'

The old guard had slowly faded from the scene, but Nora Beloff was still firmly in place as the political correspondent – much to the frustration of ambitious young political writers like Anthony Howard, who longed to supplant her, and those of her colleagues who had to rewrite or type up her copy before it could be passed to the printers. Though kind and considerate in private life, Beloff was not an easy colleague, but David always humoured her. According to Alan Watkins, who joined the paper in 1976, Beloff was 'famous for grasping the wrong end of any stick that might be in sight': she reproduced what her colleagues told her in her pieces, but 'while she did not always get things entirely wrong, she did not usually get them entirely right'. Harold Wilson, paranoid at the best of times, was driven to fresh heights of persecution mania. She was the first political correspondent to write about the influence of Marcia Williams and the prime minister's 'kitchen Cabinet'; Wilson, in turn, claimed that this 'dangerous woman' tipped off Ted Heath about what his ministers had revealed at briefings, and that he had her shadowed to discover her sources.

In the spring of 1968 Wilson boiled over after reading a piece entitled 'Wilson Glad to Be Rid of Brown'. According to James Margach, Beloff's equivalent on the *Sunday Times*, 'over Miss Beloff Wilson grew more than angry, he became a man possessed'. Arnold Goodman warned David that the prime minister was incandescent, and David was summoned to Downing Street. He was conducted into Wilson's room by a private entrance rather than via the anteroom occupied by Marcia Williams, 'done so as to indicate how painful Nora's reports (which were perfectly straightforward political commentary) were supposed to have been to the future Lady Falkender'. Wilson addressed him about the iniquities of Beloff in a 'fast monologue' and produced a fat file of objectionable cuttings, which he thrust in David's direction ('Read this, for example. And this one'). 'That woman hates me, she hates me,' Wilson insisted: her column was full of 'gossip she picks up from my enemies', and 'she can't write about serious politics'. He went on to say that 'our people keep an eye on her', and concluded with 'a nasty innuendo that she was prepared to sleep with [a] minister in exchange for titbits from the Cabinet table'.

Back in the office, David wrote a calming letter to the prime minister. 'I remain unconvinced by what you said of my colleague, Miss Beloff,' he told him. Of course she made mistakes, but she was 'essentially an honest and decent person'. He was 'profoundly shaken by the terms in which you spoke of her' and he begged Wilson 'not gratuitously to injure a reputation in this fashion'. He saw no point in trawling through old cuttings: 'What you are really saying is that you don't like what she is writing, think it unfair, and so on. Well, I come from a family which has been much more unfairly treated than you have, and I don't really think you need feel so aggrieved.' (The following year David wrote to Roy Jenkins, Wilson's Chancellor of the Exchequer, about the vexed issue of 'the relations between politicians and journalists'. Unlike most of his colleagues, he favoured 'a certain amount of distance' between the two parties to allow for 'what I put under the heading "private life". But I think this is because I come from a family of politicians and am not quite a thoroughbred journalist.')

Three years later Nora Beloff was in trouble again. Anthony Bambridge, the *Observer*'s business editor, and Paul Foot of *Private Eye* were investigating the involvement of Reginald Maudling, a former Tory minister, in the shady affairs of Jerome Hoffman's Real Estate Fund of America. David deeply disapproved of the ad hominem attacks made in *Private Eye* on individuals, however justified they might be; Beloff admired Maudling, and in her column she accused *Private Eye* of smearing him, and writing 'pure fabrication' about him. In their next issue, Paul Foot reproduced, under the title 'The Balsoff Memorandum', an *Observer* internal memo in which Beloff had described to David and other colleagues the details of a long conversation about Maudling she had recently had with William Whitelaw, the Conservative MP and Leader of the House of Commons. Peter Carter-Ruck of Oswald Hickson, Collier & Co., the most feared libel lawyer of the day, urged Beloff to take two separate actions for damages against *Private Eye*: breach of copyright, to facilitate which he sent her an assignment of copyright form, to be signed by David, in which copyright in the memo was to be transferred to her from the *Observer*; and libel, prompted by a self-evidently absurd article by Auberon Waugh in which he claimed that Beloff was 'frequently to be found in bed with Mr Harold Wilson and senior members of the previous administration, although it is thought that nothing improper occurred'. Like so many *Observer* journalists, Beloff was never averse to a drink – Alan Watkins recalled her asking for 'a large whisky, please. I find that a small one just dirties the bottom of the glass' – but this was going too far.

The copyright case lasted for four days in March 1972. David gave evidence for the plaintiff, but Anthony Bambridge and Anthony Howard spoke up for the defence, as did Richard Ingrams, who remembers how David clutched his stomach while giving evidence, as if in agony. Mr Justice Ungoed-Thomas eventually decided against the plaintiff: he considered that reproducing the memo was a case of 'fair dealing' on a subject of public interest, and despite Carter-Ruck's claim that it represented 'a most serious and irresponsible infringement of copyright', he declared that the copyright remained with the *Observer*, that David never had the right to assign it to Ms Beloff, and that the document Carter-Ruck had sent her was invalid. A week later Beloff's libel case was heard: she was awarded £3,000 in damages, and *Private Eye* was ordered to pay the costs; the 'Balsoff Fund' was inaugurated in the next issue of the magazine, and David was unkindly referred to as 'the millionaire drip Astor' (Michael Astor suggested that David had become an obsession of 'that strange man Richard Ingrams'). It was not David's finest hour. He had never been well acquainted with the legal aspects of journalism, and although he had employed Louis Blom-Cooper as Fleet Street's first legal correspondent, it was not until fairly late in his editorship that he brought in Anthony Lincoln QC to vet the pages before the paper went to press (followed in due course by Michael Beloff QC, Nora Beloff's nephew and a future president of Trinity College, Oxford).

David was tired and increasingly out of touch, and brooding on who should succeed him led him to make one of the most bizarre appointments of his career. A career diplomat with no experience of journalism, Ronald Higgins was briefly married to Mary Holland, later to become the *Observer*'s writer on Irish affairs. Higgins was based for a time in Jakarta, but Mary Holland loathed it, and returned to England. David wrote to Higgins in Jakarta to say that 'my hope is that I may in due course be able to recommend to the trustees to appoint you to be the editor'; sworn to silence, Higgins resigned from the Foreign Office in 1969 and returned to London to take up a vague and undefined role as David's 'special adviser' while he learned about the editorial and the managerial sides of running a newspaper. His new colleagues were mystified and resentful; although he managed to cling on until shortly before David's own departure – he was the first to go in an editorial culling, on the 'last in, first out' basis – he was reduced to organising Observer Management Seminars, in which eminent thinkers and writers addressed assembled businessmen, and Observer Offers, whereby readers were offered furniture, garden tools and classical music records on advantageous terms. Shortly before Higgins's departure, David encouraged him to write a long piece entitled 'Is Mankind Committing Suicide?' It prompted his first book, and led to a new career as an environmental writer.

Michael Davie, the deputy editor, was generally regarded as David's obvious heir apparent, but at about the same time as Ronald Higgins joined the paper he disgraced himself in David's eyes by leaving his wife, Robin, for Anne Chisholm, an Oxford graduate who had earlier worked on *Time*, the *Telegraph* magazine and, briefly, *Private Eye* and was now employed on Pendennis. David and Bridget were very fond of Robin, and rallied to her side; Anne Chisholm was asked to resign, albeit in the kindest way; Nora Beloff, who had relied on Davie to rewrite her copy and felt proprietorial about him, downed the whiskies and denounced him as a 'murderer'; Michael Davie infuriated David by vanishing for weeks on end. He returned to the paper as news editor, started a new 'Notebook' column on the back page of the paper, covering politics, the arts, sport and public affairs; nominated Journalist of the Year in 1976, he was appointed associate editor of the Melbourne *Age* the following year, becoming its editor in 1979. After his return to Britain he edited *The Diaries of Evelyn Waugh*, which were serialised in both the *Observer* and the *Sunday Times*. Davie may have been 'the ablest journalist I ever had', but he was no longer the heir apparent, and he eventually became a freelance author, writing, with Anne Chisholm, a much-admired biography of the Astors' old adversary, Lord Beaverbrook.

Davie's eventual successor as deputy editor and heir apparent was a young and ambitious journalist called Donald Trelford. While at Cambridge, where he took a double first in English and edited *Varsity*, he asked Chris Brasher, then the *Observer*'s sports editor, if he could cover a rugger match for the paper (and, on another occasion, the first Oxford vs Cambridge tiddlywinks match). After learning the trade on the *Sheffield Telegraph* he edited the *Nyasaland Times*, which he combined with occasional freelance work for the *Observer* and *The Times*; Richard Hall met him in Addis Ababa, and found him 'good company, quick and knowledgeable, with a humour that was rather conspiratorial, making you feel that you were sharing in his cache of light-hearted secrets'. He returned to England in 1966, joining the *Observer* as assistant news editor – just in time to persuade Ken Obank, who had no interest whatsoever in sport, to run a piece on the World Cup final, with Hugh McIlvanney dictating his piece to the printers 'on stone'.

Not long after Trelford had accepted the job, John Silverlight told him that his colleagues could not decide whether he was a 'plumber' or a 'journalist': was he there 'to help David sell newspapers or to help him save the world?' 'A bit of both', Trelford replied, and he came to see himself as a bridge between technicians like Ken Obank and the more writerly type of journalist. Although the old guard thought him too young, it was widely felt that, after Davie's debacle, Trelford would most probably be the next editor: 'It's your shoes,' John Gale told him, after noting that Trelford was sporting a pair of suedes. Trelford was the de facto editor for several weeks when David was laid low with a viral disease and a long bout of depression. 'I am enormously helped by having at last got a really good deputy in the form of Donald Trelford,' David told Mary Benson. 'He runs the paper much better than I do when I'm away.'

23

End Game

Always vulnerable to the introduction of new technology and 'direct input' by journalists seated behind a computer, the printing unions were finally toppled from power by Rupert Murdoch's decision to move his newspapers en bloc to Wapping in 1986, and today they seem as remote and as implausible as the dinosaur: but for forty years from the end of the war they were overpaid, overindulged and more than ready to hold press barons and their managers to ransom by the threat of withdrawing their labour. Back in 1947 the *Observer*'s general manager had complained to Waldorf and Arthur Mann about 'the number of needless men that trade union rules compelled newspaper owners to employ in the machine, stereo and packing departments', and since then matters had steadily worsened. Newspaper proprietors were understandably obsessed with sales and circulation; and because they dreaded, above all else, production of the next day's paper being delayed or cancelled by the printers downing tools or going on strike, they were far more vulnerable than most industries, and would far sooner give in to the unions' demands than suffer disruption, accompanied by the loss of sales and advertising revenue. Highly profitable newspapers like the *Mail* and Beaverbrook's *Express* could afford to buy off the printers, but other papers were much more exposed. Or, as a printer told Roy Thomson shortly after he bought the *Sunday Times*, 'You may own it, but I run it.' During the 1960s a raft of papers went out of business, including the *News Chronicle*, the *Daily Herald*, the *Daily Sketch* and the *Daily Graphic*, thanks in part to the printing unions.

During the 1960s smaller unions were merged with or swallowed up by larger rivals, the most influential of which were the NGA, NATSOPA and SOGAT – names which sent shivers down the spine of newspaper managers, but are completely forgotten today. Print unions were usually closed shops, entry to which was restricted to particular families, but their members' allegiance was to the 'chapels' within a particular paper rather than to the unions, who had little power to discipline individual chapels and the fathers of the chapels. Union members were, in effect, paid and employed by the chapels, and what were known as 'old Spanish practices' prevailed. 'Ghost' payments were made for notional work on 'ghost' machines; workers were paid extra for 'blows', or rest time; there was a long list of extra charges or 'special payments' due for changing a typeface, inserting corrections, altering the pagination or dealing with late-running stories. Wages were paid to imaginary workers who clocked in under fictitious names ('Gordon Richards of Tattenham Corner' and 'M. Mouse of Sunset Boulevard' were frequent claimants); at one stage the *Daily Telegraph* machine room theoretically employed 306 men, but only 252 regularly turned up for work, and the wages of the 'ghosts' were divided between the genuine employees. Sabotage was employed if necessary: familiar wheezes included tearing the paper by sticking chewing gum to the side of the roll, or squirting the reel with oil. Further confusion was caused by demarcation disputes between particular unions, as often as not involving the NGA, a craft union, and NATSOPA, a non-craft union, whose members were less well paid; newspaper strikes proliferated in the 1960s, and the closure of papers put more men on the jobs market, and swelled the number of 'casuals' working – or pretending to work – in Fleet Street. Preparing evidence for the 1961 Royal Commission on the Press, John Pringle reminded David that when the *Observer* was divided into two parts, although it 'involved no extra work for anyone, we had to pay the whole machine room staff more money, including the men who sweep the floor'. So powerful was the hold of the unions that Tristan Jones, as general manager of the paper, was not allowed into the printing works.

In May 1971 David commissioned a report in the Business section on conditions in the newspaper industry. The wording of the piece was amended after SOGAT officials threatened to stop production, and the following week an anonymous letter from a print worker agreeing with the article prompted another possible shutdown unless the letter was withdrawn or its author's name revealed; production was only resumed after the letter had been dropped. Six months earlier, Richard Briginshaw, the general secretary of NATSOPA, had threatened to close down the paper after it had published a report on union activities. Two years after his resignation as editor, David wrote a piece entitled 'How the British Press Censors Itself' for *Index on Censorship* in which he cast doubts on managerial claims that they would never allow printers to censor copy in their newspapers: they made 'this bold claim easier to maintain by not asking printers to handle copy they might want to censor', since 'a newspaper might easily commit suicide by challenging the censorship of the print unions' – and 'some of the present practices are so outrageous that exposure to the light would at last reveal them as public scandals'. Production of the *Guardian* and *The Times* was held up after they had reported on David's article, and when William Rees-Mogg, the editor of *The Times*, revealed that he hoped to reprint it, unofficial action by the paper's machine minders' chapel led to the loss of a complete edition. As Rees-Mogg put it, 'the chapel has, in effect, made Mr Astor's point about union censorship for him'. In a letter to *The Times*, David congratulated them on reporting on his article – 'I never dared go that far myself, as an editor.' The following year Fleet Street lost 105 million copies to industrial action: 1,378,000 from the *Observer*, and over 5 million from the *Sunday Times*.

The Times's departure to Gray's Inn Road had left the *Observer* with plant and printers used only one day a week, plus a Saturday-night influx of casuals paid at exorbitant overtime rates. Negotiations with the unions were handled by Clive Bradley, who had first been approached by the *Observer* in 1969, when the paper was given notice by *The Times*. A barrister who had worked for the BBC, the Labour Party and as the group labour adviser to IPC Newspapers, and was about to be made deputy general manager of the *Daily* and *Sunday Mirror*, Bradley had declined this initial approach since he felt that the *Observer* could only be viable if it shared plant with, ideally, the *Guardian*. In 1973 Bradley was approached again, successfully this time, and by now the *Observer*'s future was in serious doubt. The following year negotiations with the print unions about the *Observer* taking over responsibility for its printing from *The Times*, with the necessary transfer of printing staff, were completed within time and within the budget, while also achieving manning reductions of ten per cent. Littlejohns and Harrison had earlier entered into negotiations with the *Financial Times* and the *Yorkshire Post* about printing the *Observer* on their machines – the technology of page transmission was new but proven, and the *Observer* would no longer have to pay or employ its own printing staff – but the scheme was opposed by Tristan Jones and the printing unions, whose consent had been a condition of going ahead. It was, Harrison told Richard Cockett, 'several years ahead of Wapping, but the *Observer* had none of the resources to do it'.

The failure to share printing costs or find other work for the *Observer*'s presses, and the excessive costs of production, led, in 1975, to a further round of negotiations with the unions. Widespread rumours that the

Observer stood to make a substantial profit from the acquisition of New Printing House Square prompted Bradley to suggest that the unions should be given full access to the paper's accounts. This was accepted by the management; it was also agreed that six weeks should be allowed for negotiations with the unions, and that if no agreement had been reached by the end of that time, formal notice would be given to the staff of the closure of the *Observer*. Management called for a thirty-three per cent reduction in printers' manpower: after weeks of hard negotiation, cuts of twenty-five per cent to regular and casual printing jobs were agreed, with the loss of eighty-eight full-time and 160 part-time jobs. Tristan Jones had no appetite for battling with the unions, and negotiations with the unions were conducted by Clive Bradley, with occasional interventions by Arnold Goodman and ACAS, the conciliation service. 'The real hero of our struggle is Arnold Goodman,' David told Robert Birley. 'Although he is only a trustee with a token remuneration, he devoted most of a week – throughout the worst of the heatwave – to sitting through lengthy meetings, sometimes going on into the evenings', and 'he apparently never blinked throughout the whole performance and only said one cross word, that to one of our team'. Despite being the recipient of the 'cross word', for which Goodman rang next day to apologise, Clive Bradley, who had borne the brunt of both sets of negotiations, was denied such fulsome acknowledgements: not surprisingly, perhaps, he looked back on his time at the *Observer* as a 'hell on earth' and 'the hardest years of my life by a long way'. He regretted his failure to heed Dennis Hackett's warning that 'the *Observer*'s management is made of cotton wool', and although David's 'liberal instincts were largely the same as mine', he thought him 'an aloof, shy patrician, out of touch with the world', and 'met him only about six times in my two years there'.

But the printers were not the only ones to face redundancies as the paper struggled to survive. They were better paid than most journalists, and in a stronger position to twist the arms of proprietors and management, but – unlike the gentlemanly Institute of Journalists – the increasingly militant and left-wing National Union of Journalists was affiliated to the TUC, and was determined to flex its muscles. They pressed for a 'post-entry' closed shop, for the 'blacking' of copy submitted by writers who were not members of the union, and for restrictions on the use of columnists not in the NUJ; and they had already come to an agreement with the Newspaper Proprietors Association that Fleet Street was not a suitable place to train journalists, and graduates must serve a two-year apprenticeship in the provinces before working for a national newspaper. Such ideas were anathema to David, given his belief that anyone should be free to write for the press, and his long-standing preference for writerly amateurs over well-qualified 'plumbers', but life had changed a great deal since the post-war years, when journalists frequently joined national newspapers straight from serving in the armed forces; many of the *Observer*'s younger journalists had started out on provincial papers, gaining invaluable experience as a result – as indeed had some of the older hands, including Michael Davie.

Both sides of the argument were ventilated in the paper's pages: Michael Beloff was given three pages on 'The Closed Shop and Press Freedom', and the full text of a pamphlet entitled 'The Threat to Press Freedom' by David, Alastair Hetherington and Denis Hamilton was reprinted; Michael Foot and Kenneth Morgan of the NUJ were allowed to give an opposing view. But David and his fellow editors faced a formidable opponent in the shape of his old friend and erstwhile Forum contributor Michael Foot, who, despite being a former journalist and editor of both *Tribune* and the *Evening Standard*, was firmly on the side of the NUJ. Harold Wilson attributed his victory in the 1974 general election to the support of the unions, and was determined to reward them by repealing Heath's 1971 Industrial Relations Act and replacing it with a Trade Union and Labour Relations Bill, masterminded by Michael Foot as Minister of Employment.

Charles Wintour, now editing Foot's old evening paper, wrote that 'it would be insane for journalists who profess a belief in freedom of expression to curtail it by refusing to handle the copy of gifted people from outside the profession', while David suggested that 'journalism is not simply an industrial process in which the manpower can be met by a form of technical apprenticeship, but a creative or semi-artistic occupation' which 'depends for its quality on a free supply of talents from all walks of life'. The NUJ's campaign threatened to 'lower the ability and talent in quality journalism', and 'the idea of qualifying tests to engage in politics or writing is nonsense in a free society and journalism belongs to both politics and literature'. 'I can't help sending you a personal note as I feel a bad misunderstanding is growing up between yourself and whatever we, the protesting editors and broadcasting people, represent,' he told Foot, adding that newspapers were 'far too politically important to be treated as merely industries'. But his plea that 'you ought to be our patron in this effort' fell on deaf ears. Meetings of editors were held in Denis Hamilton's office, with David and Freddy Fisher of the *Financial Times* as the hardliners, while Alastair Hetherington of the *Guardian* and Charles Wintour were more ready to compromise: according to

David, 'we had no idea where we were going. It was easy for Foot to drive a wedge between us.' Foot told his Cabinet colleagues that the editors were 'blithering idiots' and 'a poor bunch who had not done their homework', and dismissed Arnold Goodman, the chairman of the NPA, as a 'babe in arms'. (He was equally dismissive of a letter to the *Times Literary Supplement* signed by, among others, Isaiah Berlin and Hugh Trevor-Roper.) Nora Beloff, who later wrote a book about the dispute, was fully on David's side: she resigned from the NUJ and joined the rival Institute of Journalists; colleagues warned her that she faced losing her job if a closed shop was imposed on the *Observer*, but David said 'he would rather close the paper than accept a veto on who should be its political correspondent'. She remembered how David 'gives a misleading impression of vagueness and diffidence. But if he takes up a cause, as he did the principle of editorial freedom, he is inclined to be single-minded to the point of obsession.' He continued his campaign after he had resigned as editor, but in 1976 Foot's bill received the royal assent.

Robert Chesshyre was the father of the *Observer*'s NUJ chapel in 1975. Although most of his colleagues were leftwards-leaning, he was well aware that many of them also shared David's views on the unionisation of journalists, and sided with him over, for example, the NUJ's attempts to weed out some of the paper's best sports writers, including Clem Thomas, the great Welsh rugger player. The chapel saw itself as a staff association, attached to the NUJ but keeping its distance from it: one of Chesshyre's happiest moments was when a rather embarrassed Ken Obank, hitherto firmly opposed to the NUJ, revealed that he would like to join. The paper lost £750,000 that year, and journalists were expected, like the printers, to accept their share of redundancies. Voluntary redundancies were accepted by twenty-five per cent of the staff: one hundred per cent of the staff were now members of the NUJ, and since Tristan Jones virtually refused to have dealings with the NUJ, Robert Chesshyre and Jeremy Bugler negotiated on their behalf with Clive Bradley. According to a critical commentator 'it was the nucleus of older writers, many of them – to put it charitably – stiff in the intellectual joints, and all of them cronies of David Astor, who stayed'. The management knew perfectly well that many of those who 'left' with pay-offs would be back the following week as freelances: among the younger journalists who happily accepted redundancy were Peter Wilby, Jeremy Bugler and Christine Doyle, the medical correspondent, all of whom immediately resumed work on the paper. After it was all over, David stopped Chesshyre in the corridor and told him that Chesshyre had 'saved' the *Observer*, but negotiations with the printers and the journalists had been filmed, in part, by the BBC for a ninety-minute documentary entitled *Crisis at the Observer*; according to Roger Harrison, its effect was 'catastrophic' in that advertisers assumed the paper was going out of business, and withdrew their patronage.

Printers and journalists were not the only ones to be losing their jobs. David had decided that the time had come to leave the job he loved, and had held for so long. On 24 August 1975 he wrote 'A Letter to the Reader', his last contribution to the *Observer* as its editor, in which he wrote that independent newspapers could only hope to survive by 'drastically' reducing their costs and introducing a 'technological revolution'. He then rang Bob Chesshyre, who was in Blackpool for the Labour Party Conference, and told him that, as father of the chapel, he should be the first to know of his imminent resignation: he would be announcing the news to the staff that evening, and asked Chesshyre to return to London immediately. According to Katharine Whitehorn, David 'made the announcement in such a low-key, petering-out sort of way that it left no room for anyone to say "How frightful" or "How we'll miss you"'. Afterwards she followed him into his office and found him 'sitting bleakly behind his desk by himself; we had five minutes of melancholy retrospection which I treasure'. Tributes flowed in from his older colleagues. 'You were far and away the best editor I've ever had any dealings with,' Philip Toynbee told him, looking back to 'the years of our innocence' before Suez; Patrick O'Donovan thanked him for 'those many years of kindness and tolerance', and for enabling him to 'live the sort of life I would choose to live again'. 'I guess you must be feeling pretty glum,' Cyril Dunn wrote from a penurious retirement in Bridlington, 'so let me say that, if you do nothing else, the *Observer* of the 1950s and 1960s was more than enough to guarantee you a place in the National Portrait Gallery.' Henry Kissinger wrote from the White House to say how 'distressed' he was – 'you know how highly I have always valued your thoughts, and I find the idea of your lapsing into silence unsettling' – while Roy Jenkins acclaimed his editorship as 'one of the most outstanding feats of journalism in this generation'. Less lamented, perhaps, was Tristan Jones's departure that same week.

It was decided that the trustees should consult the staff, each member of which would, in theory, be given a vote to elect David's successor. The NUJ chapel suggested that it should have a say in the matter; as father of the chapel, Chesshyre was its spokesman, and he asked Michael Davie to join him in interviewing possible candidates, liaising with the trustees, and sounding out other members of staff in the hope that he or she would be democratically elected. The six candidates for the post included Anthony Sampson, Donald Trelford, David Watt, Joe Rogaly and Geoffrey Cannon. Chesshyre and Davie made several visits to Goodman's flat, where they invariably found him padding about in a dressing gown. He told them that democracy usually led to the lowest common denominator, and revealed that 'some sort of runner' called 'Brassher' also wanted to stand. (Goodman was mistaken in thinking that Chris Brasher, the well-known runner and the former sports editor of the *Observer*, saw himself as a possible editor: he had rung Goodman to suggest who David's successor should be.) It soon became apparent that Anthony Sampson and Donald Trelford were the front-runners. Sampson was the favourite of many of the journalists, including Michael Davie, but his connection with the paper had loosened over the years, and he had devoted most of his time to writing books. He told David that he hoped to 'bring some new ideas and energy to the paper, and that I might be able to extend its circulation while maintaining its standards'; he planned to introduce the new technology, and replace Nora Beloff and Colin Legum with young journalists like Simon Jenkins and Simon Winchester. Although Trelford was often dismissed as a technician, adept at the nuts and bolts of the trade but short on ideas and ideals, he appealed to those who wanted continuity and a 'safe' pair of hands, and according to the soundings carried out by Chesshyre and Davie he 'won' by a fairly wide margin.

Although David assured Sampson that he would 'not allow any office politicking to affect my personal feeling', the outcome had been decided well in advance. The trustees were of no use whatsoever: two of them had recently resigned, Lady Albemarle was too busy, and Hugh Carleton Greene, the only one with any experience of journalism, was in Greece – leaving Sir Mark Turner, a businessman, and the ubiquitous Arnold Goodman to run the show. Although Trelford could not have been appointed had the majority of the journalists made their opposition apparent, Richard Hall reckoned that David was 'quite single-minded about wanting Donald to take over'; Goodman hinted to Chesshyre that the election was unnecessary since the result had been fixed in advance ('It's a man named Treffle'). According to Michael Astor, David regarded the *Observer* as a sinking ship: he favoured Trelford because he was already on board, and advised David Watt to stay on dry land. Fond as he was of Sampson, David was also swayed by the knowledge that Terry Kilmartin was rooting for Trelford. 'I suppose it was always inevitable that they should play for safety, or what they took to be safety,' Sampson told Davie. The choice of David, the trustees and the journalists

coincided, giving the lie to Goodman's dismissive views of office democracy. Not for the last time, Trelford had been underestimated: he was to
remain at the helm for the next eighteen years, fighting off unwelcome
advances from potential predators, and holding his own against difficult and demanding proprietors. David, in the meantime, urged him to
revive editorial conferences: 'although addicted to discussion conferences
myself, I have gradually given them up' since colleagues found them
'irksome' and time-wasting, and as a result 'the policy of the paper has
become noticeably undistinguished and imprecise'.

Terry Kilmartin organised a dinner at the Gay Hussar, and in his letter
of thanks David gave vent to further regrets. 'I've always been aware of
the gulf between what I feel and what may be good for the paper. If I
were to have gone on editing the paper, giving full rein to whatever were
my strongest feelings, as I tended to in our early days, and the paper
had consequently appealed to fewer and fewer readers, and had by now
died, you would have given me no dinner,' he told Kilmartin afterwards.
He had 'sabotaged my own inclinations' by not publishing more on 'the
coming fuel and ecology crisis', 'war prevention techniques', 'the major
misdeeds of uninteresting countries like India and Indonesia', the malign
influence of the NUJ and blackmail by the printing unions – but 'if the
paper has lacked fiery causes in recent years, it might have fared even
worse if I had allowed my convictions more play'. Left to his own devices,
David would have laid into 'a host of recent fashionable causes and
attitudes that were either overrated or plain wrong', including women's
lib ('the libbers are misery makers'), the Provisional IRA ('a provincial
fascism that no one else is able to love') and 'those fatuous LSE students'.

Some years later, Peregrine Worsthorne – not, on the face of it, a
kindred spirit – wrote of David's time at the *Observer* that 'his paper
was wrong on most of the major issues – absurdly unrealistic about the
prospects for democracy in black Africa, about the blessings of permis-
siveness, about Suez and so on. But it was wrong with such intelligence,
and such an abundance of seriousness and knowledge, that even those
who disagreed preferred its freshly minted arguments on the wrong side
to a routine repetition of truisms on their own.' It was a tribute that
David must have appreciated: in the meantime, in a letter of thanks to
Linda Blandford, a young and relatively new arrival, David wrote that
'I have enjoyed my dealings with you every bit as much as you have.
You have always been so kind and considerate to me. Many people think
that if one is in authority one doesn't require such treatment. But you
know better, and I am enormously grateful for this.'

24
Last Rites

'My overwhelming recollection of the period from autumn 1975 to autumn 1976 is of trustees' meetings at which we heard long reports from Freshfields, the solicitors, about the complex and frustrating problems of putting more Astor family money into the newspaper,' David later recalled, and he remembered Jakie Astor saying, at one such meeting, that 'If this was a racing stud, I know what I'd be doing now: I'd be drawing up a list of likely buyers on the back of an envelope and finding out who's interested.' Life had become increasingly hard for the *Observer* in the 1970s: rising paper costs, inflation and reduced advertising had taken their toll; Harry Evans's *Sunday Times* was flourishing with the thalidomide story and the Crossman diaries, and the liberal-minded readers who had once been the *Observer*'s staple were deserting ship for a paper that was livelier and now occupied the non-party political middle ground traditionally reserved for its old rival; in 1974 the *Observer*'s circulation dropped below 700,000, with the result that the classified ads no longer poured in. The predators were prowling, and the Astor Family Trust was no longer convinced that investing in the family paper was in the interests of its beneficiaries. The time had come to find a new proprietor with deep pockets and – ideally – a commitment to the values of the *Observer*.

Those expressing a short-lived interest included Sir James Goldsmith, who – according to Alan Watkins – shocked even the most hard-drinking *Observer* journalists by inviting a select group to dinner and positioning an extremely expensive bottle of red wine in front of each place, alongside the wine glass; the heiress Olga Deterding, who wanted to make the paper 'more whimsical'; and Sally Aw Sian, the Tiger Balm heiress, whom David's nephew David, Michael Astor's son, interviewed in Hong Kong, travelling under the confusing pseudonym of 'David Attenborough': she was prepared to buy the *Observer* provided the building was included in the sale – which was not the case. David himself rang Eric Clark, by

then working for the Haymarket Press, and asked him to ring the magazine publisher Si Newhouse in New York, to no effect; 'Tiny' Rowland
of Lonrho expressed interest, but Roger Harrison was despatched to
Cheapside to tell him that he was not thought to be a suitable buyer.
After talks with Goodman, Harold Wilson had suggested an approach to
IPC, the owners of the *Daily Mirror*, or even a government subsidy
to enable the *Observer* to tackle overmanning and introduce the new
technology; but IPC showed no interest, and an approach to the TUC
by his successor, James Callaghan, was similarly rebuffed.

The first serious contender was Rupert Murdoch, the Australian owner
of the *News of the World*. Roy Thomson died in August 1976, and in due
course it became evident that his son Kenneth did not share his father's
interest in British newspapers. Murdoch would eventually acquire *The
Times* and the *Sunday Times*, and was keeping a keen eye on the situation,
but in the meantime his MD, Bert Hardy, encouraged him to consider
the *Observer*.

David famously remarked of a possible Murdoch takeover that it was
'better to have an efficient Visigoth than nothing at all'. The two men
got on well as board members of London Weekend Television – the
Observer had bought ten per cent of the voting stock in 1967 as part
of their diversification plans, and according to Roger Harrison 'the
company was a disaster' until Murdoch became involved – and David
invited his nephew David and his wife to dinner to meet the Murdochs;
but he disapproved of the serialisation of Christine Keeler's memoirs
in the *News of the World*, and muddied the waters by (or so it was
rumoured) telling Arnold Goodman, the first to learn of Murdoch's
interest, that he hoped he would not 'sell my paper to that pornographer': David's remark found its way into the pages of *Newsweek*,
Murdoch took umbrage, and David wrote to the magazine denying
that he had ever said such a thing.

A meeting was held in Goodman's flat to discuss a possible offer from
Murdoch. Goodman was doubtful about Murdoch's suitability, but it
was agreed that Harrison should ring him in the States to sound him
out. 'That's a surprise. He *is* interested,' Harrison reported, and the
wheels were set in motion. Donald Trelford flew to New York to see
Murdoch, and soon realised that his own job was at risk: Murdoch had
a low opinion of the *Observer*'s editorial approach, and planned to make
Bruce Rothwell, a former editor of the *Sunday Australian*, the editor-in-
chief with Anthony Shrimsley of the *Sun* as his deputy. Back in London,
Trelford met Rothwell for lunch, and his worst fears were confirmed.

Observer journalists were appalled at the prospect of being taken over by the man *Private Eye* termed the 'Dirty Digger'. Trelford reported Murdoch's views on the paper's coverage of Africa and Asia ('The Third World doesn't sell newspapers') to a staff meeting at which Clive James remarked that 'giving the *Observer* to Rupert Murdoch is like giving your beautiful daughter to a gorilla', and that Murdoch 'was one of the main reasons why people like me have come 12,000 miles to work in Britain'. According to Alan Watkins, a new arrival on the paper, David looked 'uneasy, even shifty, as if wanted to get home to St John's Wood as soon as he decently could', while Goodman waffled vaguely about a man on a white horse galloping to the rescue. Two weeks later the *Daily Mail* broke the story of Murdoch's negotiations with Trelford; Murdoch accused Trelford of leaking the story, and withdrew his offer. One commentator suggested that 'all the *Observer* had to offer Murdoch was the respect of his peers in the newspaper business, plus additional printing capacity for his successful papers', and wondered whether Roger Harrison's approach to Murdoch hadn't been a ploy to excite rival bids. Murdoch told Harry Evans that 'We'd have given you a run for your money with the *Observer*', adding that 'all that Third World garbage would have gone . . . So would Trelford' – but he later admitted that 'the biggest mistake I made was in underestimating Donald Trelford'.

Trelford told David that any new owner must feel free to change the editor: he was 'ready to go quietly, with the minimum of fuss', but if he stayed he couldn't be confident of increasing the paper's circulation or market share – 'it may simply not be possible with the kind of paper I want to produce against a *Sunday Telegraph* that is 3p cheaper and a *Sunday Times* that is twice as fat'. His fears were confirmed by the circulation manager – sales were dropping whereas those of the two rivals were steadily increasing – and by the advertising director, who reported that speculation about the paper's future had led to a decline in forward bookings. Despite these gloomy tidings, Vere Harmsworth told Goodman that Associated Newspapers were contemplating an offer whereby the *Observer* would remain 'an independent newspaper left of centre', with Trelford at the helm unless 'his talents proved inadequate to the task'. On the sidelines, Woodrow Wyatt talked to David about a possible Saudi-based offer, and Patrick Seale murmured about Libyan government interest. (Worried that none of the suitors would 'keep the *Observer* remotely resembling its present character', David rather favoured Woodrow Wyatt on the grounds that he was 'an *Observer* man politically, culturally and internationally, including having an even-handed, reconciliatory attitude to the Middle East'.)

Despite his angry withdrawal, Murdoch had kept in touch with
Goodman, and had flown to London to resume discussions when Kenneth
Harris was invited to dinner at Rules by an American called Douglass
Cater – very much a last-minute invitation, since several others, including
Harry Evans, had already declined the offer. Cater was a colleague of
Robert O. Anderson, the boss of Arco, the seventh largest oil company
in the States, which was keen to increase its stake in North Sea oil now
that licences were about to be renewed: both men were involved with
the Aspen Institute, a high-minded cultural-cum-political body based in
Colorado. 'Perhaps Bob Anderson would be interested,' Cater remarked
when Harris told him of the *Observer*'s problems; he insisted that they
go round to Goodman's flat in Portland Place at once to ring Jo Slater,
the head of the Aspen Institute, and tell him to get in touch with
Anderson. Cater then spoke to Anderson, who asked that representatives of the *Observer* should fly out to California instantly. David and
Roger Harrison set out next morning by economy class in time to have
breakfast with Anderson in Los Angeles. Anderson told them that he had
never contemplated buying a newspaper, but 'when the chance came to
buy the world-famous *Observer*, standing for the kind of values we were
already working for through the Aspen Institute, we said "Why not?"'
Their 'values' would eventually prove incompatible, but in the meantime
David observed that 'I think he's a man with whom we could do business – he's got a hole in the sole of his shoe.'

'Anderson seemed too good to be true, with his pixie smile under his
ten-gallon hat', Anthony Sampson wrote years later. 'He saw himself as
a world patron and statesman, advising world leaders and presiding over
the Aspen Institute, which reconciled big business with culture.' Arco
paid £1 for ninety per cent of the shares in the *Observer*, with a promise
to invest £5 million in the paper: Observer Holdings Ltd retained ten
per cent for the Astor Family Trust; neither New Printing House Square
nor the shares in London Weekend Television and Capital Radio were
included in the sale, and the NPHS offices were leased back to Anderson
at a competitive rate. The sale went through on 18 November 1975, and
the takeover was announced in the Domino Room of the Café Royal:
not surprisingly, perhaps, Arnold Goodman – unkindly described as a
'corpulent, cross-looking solicitor', sitting in the middle of the long
table – refused to disclose the sale price. Although the *Times* diarist
thought David 'seemed not to share in the general elation, and looked
a little sour throughout', David wrote to the paper to say that however
tired he may have looked, he had 'seldom felt happier', and described the

paper's new proprietor as 'a man who can compare with any newspaper publisher in the world in his command of wealth and, I believe, in his genuine disinterestedness'.

'How do you thank someone who has saved what you regard as your life's work?' he asked Anderson. 'I don't think I have ever experienced such a thrill as the three packed days beginning with our journey to LA and climaxing in the news that you were indeed ready to come in and do so on the most generous terms.' He welcomed the appointment as chairman of the new company of Lord Barnetson of Reuters and United Newspapers ('the most intelligent and successful of all our newspaper publishers'), with Douglass Cater as the vice chairman. A dinner was arranged in the hall of Lincoln's Inn to welcome Anderson: among the 150 guests were Yehudi Menuhin, Peter Hall, Max Aitken, Jo Grimond, Alan Bullock, Lord Hailsham, Woodrow Wyatt, Vere Harmsworth and Lord Hartwell. As for Kenneth Harris, 'it was a long time since anyone had taken him seriously at the *Observer*, but now he was the hero of the hour', in his own mind at least – and delusions of grandeur soon set in.

'It seemed to me a godsend when these wealthy and high-minded Americans arrived to save us from the prospect of having to pass the paper to Rupert Murdoch,' David told William Haley, but he wrote to Murdoch to thank him for 'the speed of your original willingness to move into the *Observer* situation and for the patience you showed during the long hours when we were trying to make up our minds'. He was 'confident that you would do a creditable job with the paper and told the editorial staff that this was my view', and 'Arnold and I have always held you in high regard and have not been surprised that you have treated us so decently through our hour of trial and confusion.' Murdoch was not mollified by sweet words. After referring to David's description of him as a 'pornographer', Murdoch claimed that 'the only dividend I have received from your plea for help has been to be vilified throughout the world. This is no exaggeration and is certainly not a comfortable experience, especially without a word of public thanks (or apology) from your side.' Arnold Goodman hurried to mend fences by giving a dinner in Murdoch's honour at University College, Oxford, to which Harold Wilson, Anderson, Trelford, Roger Harrison, Douglass Cater and David were invited.

In 1981, Murdoch finally bought the *Sunday Times* and *The Times* from Kenneth Thomson. In the late 1970s Gordon Brunton of the Thomson Organisation had decided to go for the 'big bang' and introduce the computer-based new technology and with it (he hoped) uninterrupted

production. The unions would have none of it: both papers were closed
for a year, with the journalists on full pay, and when publication resumed
in November 1979 Thomson had lost over £40 million as a result; the
circulation of the *Sunday Times* had slumped to 150,000, with the *Observer*
picking up extra sales in the short term, and almost doubling its circulation in its rival's absence. Five years later Murdoch had forcibly introduced
the new technology, revolutionising the newspaper business in a stroke
(David never felt Murdoch got the credit he deserved for this).

As Arco soon discovered, the *Observer* was still bedevilled by the old
problems of overmanning, and was as vulnerable as ever to the threat
of strike action: so much so that the management threatened to close
down the paper altogether in 1980. Millions of dollars were pumped into
the paper to increase the number of pages and attract more advertising,
but to no great effect. Despite having advanced the claims of Trelford
over Anthony Sampson in the sham elections to appoint a new editor,
David told Haley that the editorship remained a problem since Trelford
'was generally regarded as being a very good Number 2 but not quite
satisfactory as Number 1': he confessed to the new proprietor that the
Observer lacked 'editorial brilliance', and worried whether 'the editorial
staff of the paper itself is going to prove capable enough'. 'Since you and
I do not have full confidence in the present set-up', he looked to Cater 'to
advise our proprietorial colleagues on the master factor of who should
edit': among those he suggested were Bernard Levin, Hugo Young, David
Watt and Michael Scammell, the editor of *Index*. Cater then launched a
savage attack on a recent issue of the paper. Trelford was appalled by the
'choleric tone' of his note, since 'your comments seem to me to verge
on contempt for the style of journalism that appears in the *Observer* and
the people who produce it'. 'If Arco wants more editorial brilliance than
Donald provides, Michael Davie, now editing a paper in Australia, but
formerly the *Observer*'s ablest editor, would probably be the best bet,'
David suggested. As it turned out, Trelford was much more resilient,
independent-minded and fleet of foot than his critics liked to think, and a
great survivor: Alan Watkins once described him as 'the Rocky Marciano
of newspaper politics', while Richard Hall noted that he had grown into
the job and 'seemed audaciously confident, his mind as sharp as a whippet'.

David, as ever, combined diffidence with strong opinions. 'I am very
much aware of the delicacy of my own position in *Observer* matters, as
representing the old and failed regime', he modestly informed Thornton
Bradshaw, another Arco executive. 'It is not for me to be offering anyone
advice.' And he added, apropos discussions over the paper's future, that

'I have absolutely no wish to play an active part in these possibilities, and am ready to retire at any time.' But after Roy Jenkins, his first choice, had declined the offer, David had no compunction about recommending Conor Cruise O'Brien as the *Observer*'s editor-in-chief – providing, it was hoped, the intellectual fireworks, while Trelford the technician was left with the day-to-day running of the paper. David insisted that although O'Brien's appointment was his idea, 'I keep quiet about that', and he urged O'Brien to give the credit for his appointment to Messrs Anderson, Cater and Bradshaw. (O'Brien, on the other hand, remembered how, at a meeting with the new owners, David 'positively fizzled with joy' when he accepted the job.)

A hard-drinking, disconcertingly clever Dubliner, O'Brien had been, at various times, a writer, an academic, a United Nations official and a politician; he had contributed occasional pieces to the *Observer* since 1964, reporting from Ireland, South Africa and the USA, and had abandoned Irish politics in 1977. According to Richard Hall, 'the Cruiser was rarely seen on the editorial floor, and his main occupation was to dictate a column of dazzling casuistry once a week over the phone from Dublin'; John Cole, an Ulsterman who had joined the paper from the *Guardian*, where he had been pipped at the post by Peter Preston to succeed Alastair Hetherington, described working with O'Brien as 'a perpetual switchback ride', and 'his concept of the editorial function was nearer to Socratic dialogue than to conventional Fleet Street practice'. O'Brien agreed to take the job 'on the assumption that, as editor-in-chief, I would be responsible for full and final control of editorial policy', but, 'as I later realised, the stipulation was quite unrealistic. No one is ever in full control of anything that someone else owns.'

Although most of the staff, including Trelford, seemed happy enough to have him on board, there was one glaring exception. Having saved the *Observer* from Murdoch, Kenneth Harris felt he should reap his reward. In 1977, the year in which O'Brien was made editor-in-chief, he produced two long documents about the paper's future, harking back to the great days between 1948 and 1956. He was also, in Richard Hall's words, 'an assiduous courtier', taking time off to visit Robert Anderson in New Mexico, where he 'gave a lot of pleasure with his plummy British ways'. His hostility to Conor Cruise O'Brien was 'formidable, deep-laid and dangerous': according to O'Brien, 'it was only when David began to lose control that Harris, through the American connections that he had cultivated, became a significant, even a pivotal figure' on the paper, and a 'poisonous presence in my professional life'.

Harris's ambitions, combined with the *Observer*'s precarious finances
and inevitable political differences between the Republican Anderson and
the editorial staff, and O'Brien in particular, led to a gradual deterior-
ation of relations. Partly as a result of printing extra copies when the
Sunday Times was laid off in 1978–9, the machine minders demanded that
manning be restored to former levels, and after a protracted unofficial
strike in the summer of 1980 Arco threatened to close down the paper
altogether. Although the Astors' last ten per cent share had now been
bought out, David continued to urge its owners to make it once again a
moral and intellectual force like *Die Zeit* or *Le Monde* rather than trying
to compete with the *Sunday Times* as 'a "department store" type of
newspaper, aiming to be all things to all men, which is what is happening
at present'. 'The main point to try to get across to Anderson is that he
didn't take on the *Observer* to make money, but to save a respected newspaper,' he complained to Goodman. Trelford and O'Brien were moving
the paper in the right direction, but any changes 'should be dictated
by a knowledge of the British scene, not by the whims of an absentee
proprietor'. And, like all the best editors, he remained convinced that
'you can't give a paper character by market research'.

O'Brien, for his part, was feeling increasingly embattled. He objected
to Cater's 'rather heavy-handed interference on the editorial side'; he
found Mary Holland too sympathetic to Sinn Fein, and often disagreed
with Colin Legum and Robert Stephens about the Middle East. He was
uneasily aware that 'Anderson's ruthless business methods had earned
him a rather unsavoury reputation both in America and internationally';
he worried that Roger Harrison and his deputy Brian Nicholson felt he
'represented the continuance of David's high-minded but stubbornly
unprofitable policy', and that he embodied 'the fatal Astor albatross'.
And Harris's attitude towards him had transmuted from 'faintly
menacing' to 'openly bullying'. When Harris told him that a piece he
had written about military coups in Africa was 'not in accordance with
the national mood', 'I laughed in his face and we never spoke to one
another again.'

David assured Thornton Bradshaw that O'Brien was 'one of the most
distinguished and constructive commentators in the English-speaking
world and I cannot think of anyone who would confer more distinction on your publication', but the Arco men were not convinced; and
when, taking his cue from John Cole, O'Brien openly lent the paper's
support to Labour's Jim Callaghan in the 1979 general election, relations
went from bad to worse. O'Brien knew that Anderson would not be

pleased, but 'I was determined to do my Astorian duty for the short remainder of my time as editor-in-chief.' Terry Kilmartin was among those who lamented O'Brien's eventual departure: he was 'the most powerful, original and interesting columnist in the business', he told Donald Trelford; his removal was 'worse than a crime' and his leaving 'makes me despair of our future as a civilised newspaper'.

By a strange irony, Kenneth Harris prompted Anderson's decision to sell the *Observer*. As early as 1978 Barnetson told David that Anderson was keen to put Harris on the board: he had editorial ambitions, and hoped to unseat O'Brien as editor-in-chief. David urged Goodman to tell Anderson that 'Harris has a reputation only as a contact man and public relations promoter', and that Anderson would become a 'laughing stock' if he promoted him.

Douglass Cater had by now returned to America to head the Aspen Institute, and Thornton Bradshaw had left Arco to run RCA; and in February 1981 Anderson informed Goodman that Anderson himself was to be the new chairman, with Harris as his deputy. A stormy board meeting ensued, at which David, Goodman, Trelford and O'Brien insisted to a furious Anderson that Harris must not be promoted: as Goodman put it to Trelford, 'Have you heard that Caligula wants to make his horse deputy chairman?' By now David was convinced that Anderson would sell the paper, but on a flying visit to New York Goodman was assured by the new chairman that he had no intention of selling up, or elevating Harris: Vere Harmsworth had been expressing interest, but 'you do not need to worry. I do not intend to sell the paper to Associated', and – Goodman later confessed – 'as a simple soul I arrived at the conclusion that this was an assertion that he was not going to sell it to anybody'. (Richard Hall was convinced that the six years Goodman had now spent as master of University College, Oxford, has transformed him 'from a legal eagle into an academic dove'.) On 25 February Anderson rang Goodman in Oxford. 'I have some knowledge that might interest you,' he said. 'I have sold the *Observer* to Tiny Rowland. He'll call you within the hour.' George Outram & Co., the newspaper subsidiary of Tiny Rowland's Lonrho empire, had paid £6 million for two thirds of the shares. Goodman immediately rang David at home in Cavendish Avenue. No one at the *Observer* had been given advance warning, though Richard Hall had written to Rowland to say that although he might not be 'in the least interested in braving Fleet Street's troubles', he would 'naturally be willing to help' if Rowland wanted to 'know more about the internal scene'. 'I really was almost speechless,' the ever-articulate

Goodman later revealed. The last phase in David's long relationship with his beloved paper had begun.

★

Donald Trelford once said of David and Tiny Rowland that 'both are tall, fair men of German extraction with a charm and seeming diffidence that hide a strong will to have things done their way'. Be that as it may, David was not pleased by the buccaneering Rowland's irruption into *Observer* life. 'I was led up the garden,' he recalled, and 'Rowland is not the right man.' The news was broken to the staff in suitably dramatic form: Trelford 'bounded into the newsroom, stood on a table and announced "We've been sold."' A few minutes later, Rowland rang Richard Hall, one of his few supporters – 'Tiny never did me a bad turn when I was editor of the *Times of Zambia*,' Hall insisted – to ask 'What are they saying? Are people pleased? You can tell them I want to make it the best paper, with the best writers. Tell them we shall take on the *Sunday Times*.' A 'visibly nervous' Rowland was then let into NPHS by a back door to address the staff from behind a canteen table. Colin Legum led the voluble opposition. He had met Rowland in what had been Southern Rhodesia, and although he approved of his love for Africa and his scorn for the white settlers, he distrusted him and 'couldn't maintain my integrity as an independent journalist if my proprietor was Tiny Rowland'. Trelford, caught in the crossfire, assured his colleagues that they could 'rely on me to keep Tiny Rowland out of tiny Trelford's editorial conferences'.

Rowland had assured both Goodman and David that he wanted them to remain on the board, but both handed in their resignations – Goodman insisted that 'not all the instruments of torture in the Tower of London would keep me on the board' – and David's house became the nucleus of the unofficial opposition to the takeover. Lord Shawcross, newly appointed to the board, assured David that, far from planning to move the paper to the right, leaving the *Guardian* as the only outlet for the liberal left, Rowland was 'almost apolitical' and had no desire to use the paper as a 'propaganda vehicle', but David was unconvinced. In a letter to *The Times*, he wrote that if the government agreed to the takeover, 'it is hard to see how the paper can avoid being dead or unrecognisable within three years'.

Rowland already owned two Scottish papers, including the *Glasgow Herald* – George Bolton, the eighty-year-old deputy chairman of Lonrho, even suggested that the *Observer* might be moved to Glasgow – and

because John Biffen, the Secretary of State, had been criticised for
nodding through Murdoch's acquisition of *The Times* and the *Sunday
Times*, the takeover was referred to the Monopolies Commission. David,
Goodman and Conor Cruise O'Brien gave impassioned evidence against
the takeover. O'Brien 'went into some detail about Rowland's shady
African interests and how these were likely to influence his use of the
Observer'; Colin Legum weighed in with a fourteen-page memo; Richard
Hall, a lone voice, lent Rowland his support in a written submission.
David emphasised the non-party nature of the *Observer* in his day –
'in all the years that I was editor I never voted because I didn't want
to cloud my feelings' – and ridiculed Rowland's proposed editorial
safeguards, including independent directors, on the grounds that such
'assurances from a suspect leadership are worse than valueless, since
they convey a specious assurance to the public'. And he tried to find an
alternative buyer in the form of a consortium consisting of the Aga Khan
and the Melbourne *Age*, now edited by Michael Davie, which 'would
have the expertise and the liberal outlook that Lonrho lacks, and just
as many resources'.

Rab Butler, Roy Jenkins and David Steel wrote to *The Times* to protest
at the sale, and they were supported in another letter signed by, among
others, Henry Moore, Peggy Ashcroft, Iris Murdoch, David Hockney,
Philip Larkin, Tom Stoppard, V. S. Pritchett, Michael Tippett, Asa Briggs,
Angus Wilson, Hugh Casson, Laurens van der Post and Brian Rix. But
Lonrho's opponents laboured in vain. Arco acquired a twenty per cent
share of Outram and $4.5 million in cash, and Anderson remained
chairman for three years before handing over to the new owner. Rowland
owned the *Observer* until 1993, when it was sold to the *Guardian*; and
despite the doubts expressed about him by David and others, and a
blazing row with his proprietor in 1984 after he had published a long
article about the murderous activities of Mugabe's Fifth Column in
Matabeleland, prompting a threat to sell the *Observer* to Robert Maxwell,
the nimble-footed Donald Trelford remained at the helm for the next
twelve years. David's long connection with the family newspaper had
finally come to an end.

Home Affairs

'My inclination is not to retire into more public life but rather to the golf club and the grandchildren department,' David told his old friend Ali Forbes soon after his resignation as editor, while Roy Thomson was convinced that 'if David Astor gives up the *Observer* it will kill him. That paper is his life. It keeps him going.' Neither forecast proved correct. David would be involved in public life for the rest of his days, more often than not as an *éminence grise* working behind the scenes for innumerable good causes. As he headed towards old age he remained as keen as ever on taking exercise: his golfing partners included Laurence Gandar, the former editor of the *Rand Daily Mail*, and Des Wilson, the founder of Shelter and a latter-day *Observer* columnist; he walked as much as possible – he had retained his passion for birds and the natural world – and he still swam in the icy waters off Jura. The grandchildren lay in the future; as far as his own children were concerned, he was kind and easy-going, if sometimes abstracted. He did everything he could to make Frances feel a member of the family, and kept in touch with Melanie, who spent her last days with Frances in Ireland; rather than have them board away from home, he sent his children to day schools in London, albeit of the fee-paying rather than the state variety; and as they grew older, he gave each of them a sum of money to invest in a charity of their own choosing. He enjoyed having more time in which to go to the theatre – Pinter was a particular favourite – and although he tamped down his old theatrical proclivities, and refrained from imitating other people's voices or gestures for fear of seeming to mock or give offence, he still wore his jacket draped over his shoulder like any good actor would. According to John Pringle, David's theatrical tastes reflected the fact that 'the contemporary always seemed more exciting to him than the past'. When Pringle told him that he was going to see *The Marriage of Figaro* at Covent Garden, David said he could not understand 'what you can see in an opera where everyone is dressed in eighteenth-century clothes and wigs'. One of David's more critical colleagues suggested that he 'smiles a great deal, but lacks humour', but his taste in books, films and television programmes hardly suggests a man who inhabited a joke-free zone: he enjoyed reading James Thurber, and retained his youthful enthusiasm for P. G. Wodehouse; he admired *Dad's Army* and Woody Allen as well as Max Wall; Kenneth Williams came to dinner – both David and Bridget were fans of his – and Arthur Marshall was always a welcome visitor. He enjoyed modern art, but when Lucian Freud asked if he could paint him – David's children were keen to commission a portrait – he declined on the grounds that, despite a family connection, he was reluctant to spend too much time in the painter's company, and opted for Michael Andrews instead. Michael Andrews suggested that his wife June should join them at their sessions in his studio in Chelsea, talking to David and putting him at his ease. David, now in his early eighties, hugely enjoyed their conversations, trading gossip about mutual friends with such enthusiasm that Michael Andrews sometimes stopped in mid-brush stroke in his eagerness to learn more. And June Andrews recalls how David, that most self-effacing of men, loved being, for once, a legitimate focus of attention.

Despite heavy investments in the *Observer*, money was not in short supply, thanks in part to Arnold Goodman's having shrewdly refused to include David's forty per cent share in the New Printing House Square building when the paper was sold to Arco. Bridget had always felt ill at ease with the trappings of grandeur, and although they still lived in a succession of large white stucco houses in St John's Wood, they led a more middle-class life: the staff was reduced to a driver, a housekeeper and a Czechoslovakian cook, and Bridget often did the cooking herself. But for all the talk of golf and grandchildren, David was as busy as ever. Pat Burge became one of his two private secretaries in 1972, and worked from Cavendish Avenue after David retired. 'Never assume my wife and I talk to each other,' David told her. One of her jobs was to type out 'the Bible', a list of the following week's engagements giving details of time, place and what to wear, copies of which were left on the hall table (for Bridget) and in David's office and dressing room. They continued to spend their weekends at Sutton Courtenay, as often as not in the company of African bishops, battered wives and their offspring, and other groups or individuals whom David had taken under his wing: he had grown up in a large house always filled with guests and visitors, and Cliveden habits of hospitality persisted – so much so that his children wished at times that they could have more of the house, and their father, to themselves. Nor were their London houses reserved exclusively for family use. Their former

home in St John's Wood, 12 Elm Tree Road, had been knocked through into
the house next door, and the Mistrys, a family of Ugandan Asians, lived in
what had been the servants' quarters; and when, years later, David took up
the cause of Myra Hindley, Tricia Forrester, a former prison warden who
had had an affair with Hindley and felt threatened by the hostile publicity
surrounding the case, came to live at Cavendish Avenue. 'I have never known
anyone who cared so much about being kind, from rescuing a donkey from
a bad master to helping battered women to financing anti-apartheid efforts'
David's old Oxford friend Sam Beer once recalled.

  David continued to agonise over his past, and his relationship with
Nancy in particular. When the South African journalist and editor Donald
Woods suggested a series of interviews, David suggested that its theme
should not be 'How did a rich boy come to be so idealistic?' but 'How
did a cripple come to have some success?' 'The crippling in my case was
partly because of my partly unsuccessful relationship to my mother in
childhood. This produced educational failure, a breach in family relations, some years of non-achievement and lengthy psychoanalysis. It also
produced an affinity with other people's disadvantages,' he told Woods.
He needed to seek out heroes as a result, and 'where the cripple element
comes in is that I was able to appreciate odd people with bad disadvantages of their own', including Michael Scott, Orwell, Myra Hindley, Anna
Freud and, 'one of the oddest', Richard Nixon.

  Not surprisingly, friends, colleagues and publishers pressed him to write his
memoirs in the years following his retirement. André Deutsch, then nearing
retirement himself, told him that publishing his autobiography would be the
'crowning achievement' of his career; Michael Davie pondered the idea of
a book about David's time at the Observer, but warned David that 'Tristan
might not come out of it too well'; John Silverlight spent long hours with
David and a tape recorder. But nothing came of these possible collaborations,
nor did David himself seem willing to embark on a memoir. Eventually, in
1989, Deutsch commissioned Richard Cockett, a young London University
history lecturer, to write David Astor and the Observer, published in 1991. David
gave Cockett his full co-operation, so much so that Diana Athill, the book's
in-house editor, worried that the end product might turn out to be 'just too
much of a panegyric', and urged David to allow the occasional criticism voiced
by former colleagues since 'they add credibility and a touch of amusement,
which is not unwelcome in such a serious book'. Cockett was impressed by
his subject's 'capacity for honesty', recalling how, as 'an analysand of Anna
Freud', David would open an interview by 'saying that he had been unable
to sleep properly because he had held back something the previous day'.

Although David had no formal religious beliefs, he loved visiting cathedrals, finding 'the sensation of looking and walking round them so delicious that I have to restrain myself'; he relished 'religious ritual of the most theatrical kind', and developed a 'passion for the symbolism of Orthodox Judaism'. He once said that although he couldn't believe in God, he did believe in Sigmund Freud, and he remained loyal to the end. In 1956 the *Observer* had run a series of articles marking the centenary of Freud's birth. He was 'a man who made a discovery as important as that of Columbus' and 'not only did Freud approach his studies with the classic humility of the genuine seeker after truth: he always maintained the highest respect for his patients, and indeed for all mankind, which is of course the foundation of true morality . . . The assumption on which his whole process of treatment is founded – that the more people acquire freedom from illusions and greater control over themselves: or, conversely, that bad behaviour is generally the product of enslavement to buried fears – is an immensely optimistic one.'

Anna Freud, Sigmund Freud's daughter, lived and worked in her father's house in Maresfield Gardens, Hampstead, until her death in 1982. She had made her reputation by working with children, founding the Hampstead War Nursery in 1941 and the Hampstead Child Therapy Course in 1947, and opening the Hampstead Clinic in 1952. Like any other all-explaining system of thought, psychoanalysis was prone to schisms and heresies, and Maresfield Gardens was no exception: Anna Freud's colleague Melanie Klein split away and established a rival practice and philosophy, known as the Kleinian school of psychoanalysis. Anna Freud herself had, according to her long-standing colleague Clifford Yorke, an 'extraordinary ability to connect the right ends, to bring into relief the core of a problem and its essential characteristics, in a manner of which few people are capable'. David had great faith in her and in Clifford Yorke and, as we have seen, he spent a daily 'analytic hour' on the couch at Maresfield Gardens before being driven on to work. Freud sent David to Clifford Yorke – then the medical director of her clinic – for psychiatric help during a depressive crisis, and Yorke in turn referred him to Dr Bernheim, who prescribed lithium, which was still relatively unknown. David remained on this treatment for the rest of his life. After Anna Freud's retirement, Yorke took over her roles as director of the Hampstead Clinic and as David's psychoanalyst, but the frequency of his sessions was reduced to once weekly. In due course David joined the board of the clinic, then renamed the Anna Freud Centre, other members of which included, at various times, Claus Moser, Louis Blom-Cooper and Lois Sieff.

Shortly before his death, David donated £500,000 to the centre, forty per cent of which was earmarked to support Mark Solms's neuropsychoanalysis project, which was then based at the Anna Freud Centre: he had funded the project for the three previous years, believing that a link with neuroscience was the most promising future development for psychoanalysis. Over his lifetime, David gave more to support psychoanalytic efforts to improve mental health than to any other philanthropic cause; he also supported the Richmond Fellowship, founded in 1959 by the Dutch former theology student Elly Jansen, who had opened her home in Richmond to people suffering from mental health problems.

David had been actively involved in psychoanalytical matters since his days as an editor. 'Psychoanalysis, even of an elementary kind, has scarcely begun to be studied in our universities; it will, it seems, be some time before Oxford does more than point out certain illogicalities in Freud's writings; decades before what he proved is part of the curriculum,' he wrote in the centenary celebrations; doctors were 'conservative and cautious', and British writers were nothing like as well informed as Americans like Lionel Trilling and Edmund Wilson. David's claims prompted a swift reply from B. A. Farrell, the Wilde Reader in Mental Philosophy at Oxford. Far from being overcritical of Freud, Oxford philosophers were 'apt to view him and psychoanalysis with excessive respect', and the teaching of psychology at the university 'covers a much wider field than that with which Freud was primarily concerned'. Eleven years later, David wrote that 'the most important advance' psychiatry could make 'would be to include psychoanalytic studies (Freud and all that) in its training', and that 'the psychoanalytic knowledge of the functioning of the unconscious mind not only has something to offer medicine but all other human studies i.e. sociology, anthropology, politics etc', as well as child-rearing, education, the penal system and industrial relations. He told Lionel Trilling that he was thinking of funding a 'visiting lectureship' in 'applied psychoanalysis' at Oxford. Trilling was all in favour, but warned David that although his own university, Columbia, had agreed to include psychoanalysis in the degree course, it was being offered by the English department, 'of all places'. Trilling urged David to get in touch with Alan Tyson, a fellow of All Souls and a musicologist who was also a doctor of medicine and practised as a psychoanalyst. Tyson spoke to Stuart Hampshire; they agreed that such a post should be under the auspices of the Oxford medical faculty, which had recently set up a chair in psychiatry, and Hampshire reported that the new professor of psychiatry, M. G. Gelder, was well disposed. Not so, it seemed: Gelder told David that psychoanalysis was too narrow a subject for a university post, and although David sought to reassure him that, in defiance of

Tyson's strictures, he would be happy to allow rival schools and heresies to voice their views, Gelder refused to budge.

But all was not lost. Tyson now spoke to Noel Annan, who had recently moved from being provost of King's, Cambridge, to the provostship of University College London. Annan was all in favour, as were the philosopher Richard Wollheim and Frank Kermode, the professor of English. David offered to endow a chair, with a new professor being appointed every year, and put up £175,000 for the purpose; Annan told David that its occupants should be able to 'expound the history, cultural significance and new developments in the subject', and suggested that it should be attached to Wollheim's philosophy department. W. H. Gillespie, the president of the British Psychoanalytical Society, a Freudian body, was all in favour, and Anna Freud was happy for the new post to be called the Freud Memorial Visiting Professor in Psychoanalysis. David declared that he had longed to see psychoanalysis taught as a university subject 'ever since I was a student myself', and Stuart Hampshire told him that it 'was a most wonderful thing to have done', and wished that Oxford had availed itself of the opportunity. In October 1974 the opening lecture was given by the chair's first occupant, J. D. Sutherland.

But before long war had broken out on the campus, and not just between the 'B-Group' – supporters of Anna Freud – and the Kleinians, headed by Wollheim. Annan, who was caught in the crossfire, had optimistically hoped that the newly appointed committee would be 'brave enough' to appoint incumbents who were not necessarily in the 'mainstream' of psychoanalysis, but David – despite his earlier reassurances to Professor Gelder – now insisted on a more exclusive approach: although 'obviously I am not in favour of religious orthodoxy in religious matters', he felt very strongly that psychoanalysis should be expounded by believers rather than doubters or schismatics. Wollheim, supported by Annan, favoured the idea of the occasional lecturer being a layman; the British Psychoanalytical Society objected to this, and insisted on sticking to the original brief; David found himself stranded between the two when he agreed that Trilling – a Freudian, but a layman – could be a suitable candidate (nothing came of it). An increasingly embattled Annan told David that these feuds were 'making life awfully difficult for those who are trying to make a success of the chair', while David agreed that 'if the divisions of psychoanalysts weren't a bit comic, they would be very sad. I dislike them as heartily as you do.' 'Please do not press me too hard!' Annan begged his benefactor three years later. 'It is agreed that the Freud Professor must be clinically qualified, and we have dropped all idea of an amateur holding the chair,' though he thought laymen should be allowed to give the occasional Freud lecture. A year later Annan wrote that he understood David's wish that the professorship should be used to 'further the state of clinical psychoanalysis (and the wider impact of that subject on the Western world)', but 'I am a little anxious about the continual sensitivity which you display on this issue. The college cannot agree, and never has agreed, to appoint to the chair only those belonging to one particular group of psychoanalysts.'

The battle rumbled on, with David complaining that Richard Wollheim persisted in his attempts to 'bounce' the committee into making 'objectionable' decisions. Noel Annan retired later that same year, no doubt with a sigh of relief. Nor can it have been a very satisfactory business from David's point of view. He later claimed that he had two aims in setting up the chair: that 'Freud's work and ideas should be expounded in an English university by persons trained in the discipline he founded, i.e. psychoanalysis'; and that 'his work should not be treated only in terms of its clinical use. Freud invented "lay" as well as medical analysis because he thought his findings had an application outside medicine.' Oxford had rejected his offer 'chiefly because there was unwillingness to accept that a grounding in psychoanalysis was necessary to teach this subject. I was not only asking that practising psychoanalysts should hold the chair, but that those who held it should be acceptable to the psychoanalytical profession as being able to represent their body of knowledge' – with Lionel Trilling as a prime example. It was all very confusing, and a can of worms – but, as the psychoanalyst Moses Laufer put it, the chair made 'psychoanalytical thinking available to young people' at an early stage in their 'academic and professional lives'.

The Freud chair at UCL was not the only university post to benefit from David's generosity and his passion for psychoanalysis. He was increasingly interested by 'the psychology of irrational political acts, such as Hitler's policy towards the Jews', and was convinced that 'it should become possible to learn more about the irrational element which must exist in mass thinking, just as it exists in individual thinking'. During the Eichmann trial in Jerusalem in 1961, David wrote a leader-page article entitled 'The Meaning of Eichmann' in which he argued that we all had the potential to act like an Eichmann, and that the terrifying thing about him was his apparent normality – a line very similar to that taken by Hannah Arendt in her reports on the trial for the New Yorker, in which she claimed that 'the trouble with Eichmann was precisely that so many were like him, and that the many were neither perverted nor sadistic, that they were, and still are, terribly and terrifyingly normal'. Constantine FitzGibbon congratulated him on this 'long, well-argued and intensely interesting article', adding that 'the study of social psychosis is young and its findings still highly disputable – findings ignored by historians and philosophers'. FitzGibbon referred to the 'dehumanising' and 'demonising' of alien groups or individuals, to which David replied that 'it is always unwise to regard any person or persons as demons – and I certainly include the Nazis in this. On the other hand, to regard people as "fellow human beings" is not to regard them as safe and harmless. Both the older religious view of men as all possessing "original sin" and contemporary psychological knowledge seem to me to confirm this approach.'

The following year David addressed a Warsaw Ghetto Memorial Meeting in St Pancras Town Hall; his speech was reprinted in *Encounter*, where it attracted the attention of Norman Cohn, then teaching at Durham University, who wrote to say that his own groundbreaking study, *The Pursuit of the Millennium*, was itself 'a major excursion into the almost unexplored territory of what you call "political psychopathology"'. David was keen to set up a study centre to examine the political psychopathology of Nazism, and an approach was made to Asa Briggs and Martin Wight at the University of Sussex, both of whom warmed to the idea. It was agreed that they should set up a centre, funded by David, to study the irrational in politics, including not just Nazism but millenarian fantasies such as those described by Norman Cohn, racial prejudice, the persecution of the Jews, mass hysteria, collective fantasies, the European witch-hunts of the sixteenth and seventeenth centuries, and – a subject about which David felt ever more strongly – the universal tendency to dehumanise and demonise both groups and individuals. Norman Cohn seemed the obvious man to head what became known as the Columbus Centre for Research in Collective Psychopathology; he resigned his post at Durham, and David agreed to pay him an equivalent salary at Sussex, to be paid until he retired, and lent him the money to buy a house in London.

'Your initiative has opened up a prospect which I had come to regard as closed for ever. If this scheme, or even a major part of it, can be successfully carried through, it will be for me the fulfilment of a dream which has haunted me practically all my adult life. To the world at large it will offer a chance, however slight, to make all the horror and misery of this century yield at least some scrap of wisdom, some accession to our poor stock of sanity,' Cohn told David, adding that 'if I were able to devote myself wholly to such research, I should regard that as the greatest imaginable privilege and the proper fulfilment of my working life'. Writing from All Souls, Max Beloff, who had made the initial approach to Sussex, struck a cautionary note. 'Do you not prejudge a

little too soon the view that the key to these phenomena lies in individual and more particularly Freudian psychology?' he wondered, before
going on to say that, while agreeing that 'the area you wish to study is
desperately important to us all', as a historian and political scientist he
favoured an interdisciplinary approach to the subject, and 'if what you
are interested in is further work in individual psychology, then I am sure
that I have nothing further to contribute'. 'What I want studied is the
Third Reich and cognate examples of catastrophic politics, so that we can
learn lessons for the avoidance of similar political catastrophes,' David
replied. Many academics were reluctant to study the unconscious mind
'because it contains the alarming or animal-like aspects of our nature'
but 'unless we take a conscious and deliberate decision to investigate
the deeper psychological aspects, we will remain in the shallow waters
of sociological studies or of psychological-political studies carried out
in British academic circumstances where psychoanalysis itself is not yet
accepted. I wish I had the deep knowledge of psychology you attribute
to me', he concluded, but 'all I have is a hunch it may be helpful'.

David's *Observer* colleague Andrew Shonfield shared Beloff's reservations, and David hastened to reassure him. He was keen to pursue 'a
psychological study of the incidence of madness in politics', but was
all too well aware of the great gulf set between those who 'believe in
the existence of the unconscious mind and in the value of studying it,
although by its very nature such studies must, always and for ever, be
imprecise and unverifiable', and those who do not.

> My thesis is (a) that madness, irrationality and imperfect mental
> health are as constant and inescapable a part of human nature as
> imperfect physical health (b) that whereas this fact is *beginning* to
> be realised in terms of the individual and social group, it is not yet
> realised that nations and governments also are constantly subject
> to irrationality (c) that it is in this political field that irrationality
> is at its most dangerous by far (d) that in the Third Reich we have
> been presented with an extreme example of this phenomenon from
> which we can obtain priceless knowledge.

The Third Reich was insufficiently studied – in the 1960s at least – because
'it alarms people to consider what ordinary people like themselves have
done', and fear of the unconscious mind was reflected in universities,
treatment of children, and 'the resistance of people like my colleagues
at the *Observer* to publishing anything more direct on this subject than

Dr Spock'. And intellectuals, David suggested, were particularly reluctant to accept influence of the irrational on their minds. 'What I am suggesting is the most difficult study that could be attempted in any field', namely tracking down 'the irrational source of large-scale violence'.

In a joint memo, David and Cohn declared that the Columbus Centre would deal with 'the politics of obsession' and 'demonological thinking' in politics, starting with the Nazis, and Cohn stressed the need to examine how 'social disintegration – the breakdown of traditional norms of whatever kind – tends to weaken the ego-structure of individuals and so encourage outbreaks of gratuitous violence'. Sceptical academics continued to doubt the value of trying to apply psychoanalytical diagnoses to groups or even nations, as opposed to individuals. David dismissed Solly Zuckerman's opposition to the 'Project' as indicative of the universities' distrust of Freud and his ideas – 'one of the exciting aspects of the Sussex project is that it will be the first clear breaching of this shameful taboo in British academic life' – but although Norman Cohn was eternally grateful for David's support, he too had his reservations. The Columbus Centre encouraged the writing and publication of some marvellous books, including Cohn's *Europe's Inner Demons* and *Warrant for Genocide*, but years later Cohn cast doubts on what he saw as David's oversimplistic view that Nazism could be explained by psychoanalysis ('He went so far as to describe Nazi Germany as a study in collective psychopathology. That's absurd. It's a country of 60 million people. They were not all Hitler-worshippers'). The psychoanalytical interpretation of history, which had flourished after the war, had fallen from intellectual grace, and attempts to widen the Columbus Centre's activities in such a way as to deal with contemporary problems presented fresh problems. 'I am not at all sure whether we could undertake a special study of race relations such as we were toying with a year or two ago,' David wrote in 1973, adding that 'I must say, too, that I have a slight feeling of exhaustion myself and am not really inclined to go through the struggle of getting a further study launched.' Although he may have hoped that the Columbus Centre would become a permanent fixture, rather like Chatham House, it closed in 1980: Cohn had reached retirement age, and one of its major sponsors, the Wolfson Foundation, had withdrawn its support.

David's loathing for the demonising of groups or individuals was combined with a belief in redemption and forgiveness: both were to inspire derision and even hatred when, in later life, he took up the cause of Myra Hindley. His passion for prison reform and the welfare of prisoners may well have reflected his concern for the welfare of Bobbie Shaw – as did his interest in reforming the law on homosexuality, which remained a criminal offence until 1967. In 1954 the country was gripped by the trial of Lord Montagu of Beaulieu, the journalist Peter Wildeblood and the landowner Michael Pitt-Rivers for committing 'consensual homosexual practices', and after their release from prison Frank Pakenham gave a dinner for Lord Montagu and Wildeblood, attended by David, Victor Gollancz and Sonia Orwell, who later married Michael Pitt-Rivers. The Howard League for Penal Reform and the British Social Biology Council approached David on reforming the law; David got in touch with, among others, Hardy Amies, Oliver Messel and John Gielgud, whose reply indicated what a social and professional minefield they were entering ('I am naturally in sympathy with your project, but for personal reasons I could not lend my name officially in support of your scheme'). Whereas Anna Freud regarded some forms of homosexuality as a condition which could be cured by psychoanalysis, David saw it in social rather than medical terms; and, along with J. B. Priestley, Canon Collins, Gollancz, Julian Huxley, Bertrand Russell, Maurice Bowra and Stephen Spender, he lent his support to the Wolfenden Report of 1957, which led to the legalisation of homosexual relations.

David's interest in prison reform and the welfare of prisoners was shared by Arthur Koestler, whose experience of imprisonment had not only included his three months in the condemned cell in Seville, but the Le Vernet prison camp in France and a spell in Pentonville after his arrival in England in 1940. 'Vat is our next crusade?' David recalled Koestler asking after the Abolition Campaign (David liked to imitate Koestler's Hungarian accent, not least when he referred to their mutual friend George 'Orvell'): quarantining dogs had not proved a shared enthusiasm, but in 1961 Koestler suggested that annual prizes – later known as the Koestler Awards – should be offered to prisoners for literary and artistic works, and he approached David for support and possible funding. David was, in the words of the writer and campaigner C. H. Rolph (Bill Hewitt), 'a man in whom he had, as I think everyone had, boundless trust and confidence. If you got the sympathetic ear of David Astor in any such scheme, an early outcome was usually a lunch party in a private room at the Waldorf Hotel.' This was no exception, and David's guests at the Waldorf included Koestler and his future wife, Cynthia Jefferies, A. D. Peters, C. H. Rolph and Hugh Klare from the Howard League for Penal Reform. The Home Office's Prison Commission lent its support; David became a trustee of the Koestler Awards, along with A. D. Peters and C. H. Rolph, and wrote to Koestler to say how pleased he was to be involved since 'the idea is such a good one and because it will mean, I hope, that we will see each other occasionally'. In November 1963 the first prizes were awarded: £500 in prize money was distributed to thirty-six prisoners in eighteen institutions, and J. B. Priestley, V. S. Pritchett and A. D. Peters awarded the £25 literary prize to a first novel. Some unwelcome publicity occurred when the winning novel, published by Hutchinson, was revealed as an act of plagiarism and had to be withdrawn, but the awards flourished, and continue to flourish, with future judges including Sir Kenneth Clark for arts and crafts, and Sir Arthur Bliss for musical composition. David eventually resigned as a trustee in 1994.

In 1966 David, Louis Blom-Cooper and Terence Morris saw Roy Jenkins, the new Home Secretary, and persuaded him to include a parole board – itself an innovation – in the 1967 Criminal Justice Act. David also started the Prison Reform Trust, which sponsored the short-lived experiment of Prison Weeks, whereby governors were persuaded to open their prisons to the press and to local people. The Prison Reform Trust duplicated and soon overshadowed the work of the Howard League, thanks in part to the activities of David's new friend Peter Timms, a former governor of Maidstone jail who had become a Methodist minister, and would be involved in David's efforts to help Myra Hindley. When, in 1982, David succeeded Hugh Casson as chairman of the Koestler Awards, he introduced Timms to his fellow trustees. 'We don't want a bloody screw,' Koestler growled. 'Did you expect me to come in jackboots?' Timms wondered when they eventually met. Timms felt that the awards should be extended to prison staff as well as to the prisoners. Rab Butler's widow liked the idea, as did her son, Sir Richard Butler, and the Butler Trust was set up in 1985, with Veronica Linklater as its first administrator. The Butler Awards were launched in 1985 as 'sister' awards to Koestler; David put up £10,000, and Princess Anne provided royal patronage. Other developments supported by David and Peter Timms included the short-lived Prison Charity Shops, chaired by Richard Attenborough, and the Replay Trust, concerned with the rehabilitation of women prisoners. Founded in 1991 by David's son Richard and his daughter-in-law Sarah, the Prisons Video Trust, on the other hand, still flourishes. Prisoners and prison staff were able to exchange mutually beneficial ideas and information via six-weekly videos, which also provided training. David became a trustee and helped to fund the trust; Jon Snow, Derek Lewis, Jim Meyer and Sally Sampson were among those who provided support, and the trustees included Roger Graef, Terry Waite and the lawyer Ben Birnberg. A Southwark-based solicitor specialising in civil liberties and miscarriages of justice, Birnberg was instrumental in setting up the charities initiated by David, and had been recommended by the minority-rights campaigner Mary Dines. 'You won't know who I am,' David insisted when he first turned up at Birnberg's office in Borough High Street one day in 1981.

Ian Brady and Myra Hindley were tried and imprisoned for the horrific Moors Murders in 1966, but although Maurice Richardson wrote a long piece about their trial for the *Observer*, David did not become involved with Myra Hindley until the early 1980s. Lord Longford, who believed that no one was beyond redemption, and that Hindley was at worst an 'infatuated accomplice' of Brady, had long championed her cause on the grounds that she was one of the few 'lifers' not to be given a 'tariff date' for possible release. Believing that she was truly penitent and a reformed character, he had persuaded her to return to the Roman Catholic Church, encouraged her to take an Open University course, and convinced the authorities that it would be safe to move her from Durham jail to the more relaxed Cookham Wood. But Longford's addiction to publicity and his high public profile rankled with Hindley, who begged him to desist and to stop visiting her. David regarded his old friend as 'one of nature's innocents': Longford 'was absolutely right to defend her as a human being when no one else would, but accidentally he did her harm by exciting the press, encouraging them to treat him as a "loony lord" and therefore making her position worse'. David got in touch with Hindley, who complained about the way she was demonised by the popular press, making it impossible for her to be considered for parole. He told her that the public associated her with 'what they are frightened of in themselves', and urged her to make public 'some statement of your real feelings in areas of compassion, remorse etc' since 'by changing their view of you to a more human one, they would be ridding themselves of fantasies and coming to terms with their own fears'.

David visited Hindley for the first time in September 1983, accompanied by Peter Timms. On his return he told the journalist Maureen Cleave that 'one feels she's come through some incredible experiences and is the nobler for it'. Writing to Hindley four years later, he praised her endurance as 'a spiritual achievement', and when he learned that she was writing her autobiography, he told her that he had written about it to André Deutsch, 'the publisher I know best and trust most'. Diana Athill was put onto the case and, very reluctantly, went to see Hindley: much to her relief, the book proved unpublishable. By now David and Peter Timms had replaced Lord Longford as Hindley's champions and links with the outside world: Longford, for his part, 'has been pretty good about keeping silent since Peter and I came into the business and made our coming in depend on him keeping quiet'. 'You must realise that I would never have visited Myra and encouraged Peter to take on the role he has played in her affairs, if I had not had your full approval,' he reassured Longford, who felt bruised at being sidelined. 'You are mistaken if you imagine I don't greatly value and respect what you have done for Myra.' He arranged for her to be sent the *New York Review of Books*, assured her that 'you have the love and loyalty of all our little team', and told her that she had 'already made an astounding achievement which I think is seriously comparable to that of Nelson Mandela'. Bizarre and even outrageous as the Mandela analogy seems at first, it reflected David's belief that they were both political prisoners, albeit in very different ways, and that both were survivors who had been strengthened and, in Hindley's case, redeemed by what they had endured. Hindley was also provided with a solicitor: Ben Birnberg was already acting for Ian Brady, so Peter Timms introduced her to Andrew McCooey, who acted on her behalf for ten years – initially on a pro bono basis, though David soon took on Myra Hindley's legal costs.

David believed very strongly that politicians should not involve themselves in legal arguments; but the villains of the piece, in his opinion, were the tabloid newspapers, whose demonisation of her had perverted the course of justice by making it impossible for successive Home Secretaries to offer her parole, let alone the promise of eventual release. In a letter to *The Times* he referred to 'a unique campaign of hatred carried on by the popular tabloid newspapers over a quarter of a century' and in the *Guardian* he compared her demonisation to the witch-hunts of the seventeenth century, adding that 'any trial by newspaper is a form of mob rule'. In 'A Witch-Hunt that Demeans Us All', published in the *Observer* ten years after his first meeting with Hindley, he derided the notion of Hindley as being 'innately evil as is no other human being': he claimed that 'the public have become accustomed to a person being publicly ill-treated for their entertainment', and that 'it's about time this sordid circus was disowned by the rest of us'.

The tabloids quickly fought back. 'MONEYBAGS BEHIND MYRA', screamed a headline in the *Daily Star*, which went on to reveal how an 'elderly toff' was paying Hindley's legal fees. After learning that David had written to the Home Secretary, the *Daily Star* warned its readers that 'FIEND MYRA TO GO FREE' thanks to the efforts of 'Old Etonian David Astor, 77'. Nor were David's critics restricted to the tabloids. 'Mr Astor this week added a new dimension to this war of attrition between the lobby for Hindley's release and public opinion. He described her as a "political prisoner"', a *Times* leader declared in December 1994. Joe Chapman, who had counselled Hindley in prison, later told David that 'some day, perhaps, Myra will find the courage to declare what her involvement was in the crimes and to stop the futile attempt to shift the blame . . . The sooner you can face the truth about her situation the sooner you will move on. There are over 4,000 lifers currently in the system, all with needs as important as Myra's. It is offensive that she should command so much undeserved attention.' Nor was David immune to the worst efforts of the green-ink brigade, venomous examples of whose anonymous, ill-written abuse are contained in his papers. Quite how guilty Hindley was, and how penitent, remains a matter of debate, and despite David's best efforts she was to die in prison; but it was her demonisation above all else that persuaded David to take up her cause, to rage against the 'effects on our society of treating someone as demonic – just as the Jews were grotesquely treated in Germany'.

David and Bridget remained on good terms with Myra Hindley, but his relations with the formidable Erin Pizzey were much more embattled. Erin Pizzey set up Chiswick Refuge Aid in 1971, providing accommodation for battered wives and their children in a house in Chiswick High Road. Polly Toynbee described the 'shambling Victorian house' in the *Guardian*: visiting the 'squalid, dirty, broken-down, patched-up building seething with women and children' – eighty-five of them that day alone – provided 'an abrupt reminder of some unpleasant truths'. Jack Ashley, the Labour MP, had raised the question of battered wives in the Commons in 1973, but David was alerted to Pizzey's activities by his nephew David, Michael Astor's son – 'I am much interested in this subject of battered wives, and will gladly team up with my namesake', he declared – and in 1976 Pizzey received a visit at the refuge from a man with 'fair silvery hair and a damaged smile': he offered to act on her behalf in her battle with Hounslow Council, who claimed that the refuge was overcrowded and had received complaints from the neighbours. David introduced her to Arnold Goodman, whom she instantly disliked, and suggested setting up an advisory committee, on the understanding that they would not interfere with the running of the refuge. Erin Pizzey told him he could only become involved 'if you will come and work here', so he dutifully visited the refuge once a week: he was struck by the smell of carbolic soap, and compared the inmates to 'an intelligent extended family'. 'I sensed that David felt cut off from the world I inhabited, and part of the attraction of the refuge was that he could share the warmth of its atmosphere,' Pizzey wrote in the most recent of her three autobiographies. 'Often when I looked up in a morning meeting I could see him sitting quietly in a corner. The mothers soon got used to his presence, and he seemed to me like an emotionally frozen man, holding out his hands to the flame of our laughter.'

David did valuable work on behalf of the refuge, helping to raise its profile in the world at large. He talked to Hounslow Council – Pizzey was 'surprised to find that David was so succinct and assertive in public, because he usually spoke so quietly. He had a tendency to put his head down and mumble, but on this occasion he was defiant and forthright' – and persuaded the GLC to provide a grant of £60,000, and he enlisted the support of Jack Ashley, Lord Rayne and Colin and Margaret Legum as well as of celebrities like Sally Anne Howes, Joanna Lumley and Pete Townshend: but although Pizzey thought of him as a 'dear friend and saviour', she found her forays into his world uncongenial. She remained unreconciled to Lord Goodman, who recalled that 'she had the force of persuasion of a steamroller', Roy Jenkins reminded her of 'a puddle of car oil', and she was not happy when, over lunch at the Gay Hussar, Lord Longford tried to enlist her support for Myra Hindley. Erin Pizzey was the kind of forceful woman who appealed to David, and she was very happy to enlist his support, but relations between them gradually deteriorated. 'David became increasingly controlling', she wrote. 'Some nights he drove down to my house to push letters through my front door accusing me of ingratitude and bewildering me with references to my "inner child".' David had arranged for some of the mothers and children to spend time at Sutton Courtenay, but Mrs Coupland, the housekeeper, made it plain that they would not be welcome: she referred to a Namibian bishop whose family had 'trashed the house', and Pizzey said she 'knew it was a warning'.

In a neat reversal of roles, Pizzey was not averse to subjecting David to amateur psychoanalysis, since she believed that they had both endured uneasy parental relationships. She felt vulnerable 'because I needed so desperately to keep the refuge open', but 'the relationship was bound to turn sour because David, in spite of years of therapy, had never really come to terms with his difficult relationship with his mother'. She began to dread his persistent phone calls, so much so that she installed an answerphone so that 'I need not fear his early morning commands any longer. I did feel guilty when I heard the anger and confusion in his voice when he first had to speak to the machine and not me.' The GLC had offered another £250,000, so 'I no longer needed to jump at David's command.' 'I was upset that our relationship was now so fraught with bad feelings on both sides,' but 'appeasing David was too high a price for protecting the future of the refuge'. In 1979 David wrote to her to say that he felt he should step down as chairman since 'I think I have unhappily joined the ranks of those who seem to you to be a Bad Father. Given your history and way of thinking, this is probably a bad development.' He asked her not to think too unkindly of him, and reminded her that he had contributed around £100,000 to the costs of the refuge.

★

Woodrow Wyatt, an assiduous gossip, reported the Duke of Devonshire as saying that 'David Astor, whom I regarded as the archetypal wet, is now an ardent supporter and has been for some time of Mrs Thatcher, whom he regards as perfect. What a revolution she has performed'; but although David had outraged some of his younger colleagues with his seemingly right-wing views during his last years at the *Observer*, and shared some of Mrs Thatcher's views on the trade unions, his loyalties still lay, as they always had, with the Liberals and the Jenkinsite wing of the Labour Party: Tony Benn thought him 'a sentimental old liberal' who was 'generally speaking not incisive or effective. But he is a fundamentally decent guy.' 'I may be starry-eyed about it, but it has seemed to me that the very fact that you have had no single leader has added powerfully to the impact you have made,' he told David Owen, who, along with Roy Jenkins, Shirley Williams and Bill Rodgers, had splintered away from the Labour Party to found the Social Democratic Party in 1981. 'I will be voting for you if you have a candidate in this area, and will also be making a modest contribution' – a reference to his nephew David, who was standing for the SDP in his grandmother's former constituency in Plymouth.

David's great friend E. F. Schumacher died in 1977. At his memorial service in Westminster Cathedral, David compared him to St Benedict, and he was determined to continue and support his work. In the early 1970s the Club of Rome and others had alerted the public to the dangers of overpopulation, global warming, pollution and the ruination of the environment – with such success that, after he retired from the *Observer*, David made more than one trip to New Zealand, and seriously contemplated moving his whole family there. Towards the end of Schumacher's life, the two men had often discussed organic farming techniques and the work of Schumacher's Intermediate Technology Group. A few years after Schumacher's death David donated £250,000 to the group, then run by Dennis Stevenson; and with his son-in-law, Lawrence Woodward, he

set up the Elm Farm Research Centre near Newbury to develop techniques of organic farming which were sustainable and less dependent on
oil products. In 1980 the Progressive Farming Trust was set up, chaired
by the Bielenbergs' son Christopher; five years later David became the
president of the Soil Association, then chaired by Woodward, and in
1997 he made a contribution to the New Renaissance Group, set up by
Max Nicholson, an eminent ornithologist and the founder of the World
Wildlife Fund, whom David had first encountered before the war when
Nicholson helped to set up the pressure group Political and Economic
Planning. After reading an article by David Fleming in *Prospect* magazine,
David encouraged him to write *The Lean Economy*; Fleming died before
it could be published, but he put into wider circulation the notion
of tradable carbon emissions. David's final involvement in matters
ecological, undertaken when he was eighty-nine, was to help to fund
the Oil Depletion Analysis Centre, a charity set up by Richard and Sarah
Astor in association with the petroleum geologist Dr Colin Campbell.

Mediaeval archaeology seems far removed from unpasteurised milk
and the work of homeopathic vets, but David was active here as well.
Back in 1963 the *Observer* had run a series of articles about the excava-
tion of Masada – a hill fort in the Judaean desert where, in AD 70, the
Jews had made their last stand against the Romans – and had called
for volunteers to help in the excavations; three years later the paper
sponsored the hugely successful Masada exhibition at the Royal Festival
Hall, with an accompanying book by Ronald Harker, the *Observer* journalist who had covered the excavations. Masada may well have whetted
David's appetite for archaeology, for when he read about excavations in
Winchester being undertaken by Martin Biddle, an academic archaeolo-
gist, he visited the site with Bridget, and went on to offer Biddle a job
as the *Observer*'s archaeological correspondent, a post formerly occupied
by Jacquetta Hawkes. The Astors became great friends of the archae-
ologist and his wife, and in 1989 David gave £250,000 to Biddle's Oxford
college, Hertford, to establish a personalised Astor Research Fellowship
in Mediaeval Archaeology – which later prompted the university to set
up a chair of mediaeval archaeology.

David's retirement was proving busier than expected, and although, in
theory, he disapproved of the honours system, he was delighted when,
in 1993, he was made a Companion of Honour, like his mother before
him, and greatly enjoyed going to Buckingham Palace to receive his
award. But foreign affairs had always been his overriding interest, and
they provide the final chapter to his life.

Happy Endings

Despite his fascination with foreign affairs, David was never a great traveller, restricting himself to the occasional trip to Washington and New York, and preferring to work from home or the office, as often as not as an *éminence grise* supporting what he felt to be good causes. In the early summer of 1961, at Louis Blom-Cooper's suggestion, an Old Etonian Roman Catholic lawyer named Peter Benenson had approached David with an article entitled 'The Forgotten Prisoners', which drew attention to the plight of eight 'forgotten prisoners' from around the world. Benenson, Blom-Cooper and the Quaker Eric Baker had formed a group called 'Appeal for Amnesty', which collected information about 'prisoners of conscience', and campaigned for them to be given a fair trial, and for the release of those imprisoned for their opinions. David ran the article in the *Observer*; it caused a furore, and was republished in *Die Welt* and the *New York Times*, and it led to the establishment of Amnesty International by Benenson and Neville Vincent, a left-wing barrister. Amnesty soon became – as its name suggested – an international movement; Nelson Mandela was adopted by them in 1962, and Neville Vincent went on to manage the Prisoner of Conscience Fund.

As with the Koestler Awards and other good causes, David was scrupulous about keeping Amnesty at arm's length, and not allowing the *Observer* to become a mouthpiece for particular campaign groups. 'To a large extent, I regard Amnesty as a godchild of yours,' Sean MacBride – a former IRA man and Irish foreign minister – once told him, but in a letter to Benenson David insisted that 'I feel bound to stick to my journalistic role and not personally engage in these campaigning efforts as it is impossible to praise a political campaign that one is oneself involved in conducting!' MacBride was one of those involved in the early years of Amnesty, as was David's old friend Peter Calvocoressi. It was, in those days, a fairly feud-ridden organisation: Benenson was prone to paranoia, and suspected one of his colleagues, Robert Swann, who had formerly worked for MI6, of being a government mole; there were rumours of government funding, and of the CIA financing the International Commission of Jurists. Benenson withdrew from Amnesty in 1967, and life became less troubled.

The following year *The Times* and *Le Monde* published an open letter from the dissident Pavel Litvinov protesting against the trial and imprisonment in Moscow of the writers Yuri Galanskov and Alex Ginzburg. Stephen Spender sent a telegram of support, to which Litvinov replied with a letter suggesting that Spender should set up an organisation to publicise the fate of writers suffering censorship and persecution. David, a neighbour of Spender in St John's Wood, joined Spender, Stuart Hampshire and Edward Crankshaw in setting up a charitable trust, Writers and Scholars International, and they agreed to publish a magazine entitled *Index on Censorship*. Four years earlier the Congress for Cultural Freedom had funded a short-lived magazine called *Censorship*, edited by Murray Mindlin and including on its advisory board Richard Hoggart, Ignazio Silone and Daniel Bell; it provided a model for *Index*, which received an initial grant from the Ford Foundation, and David made an annual donation of £5,000. The first issue of *Index* was published in 1972, and five years later it published David's controversial views on the printing unions' stranglehold on Fleet Street. Its council in 1986 included David, Harry Evans, Spender, Blom-Cooper, Stuart Hampshire, Philip Roth, Dan Jacobson, Ronald Dworkin, Jim Rose, Tom Stoppard and Robert McCrum. David resigned from the council in 1990, by which time its editor was Michael Scammell, later to be the biographer of Arthur Koestler.

Amnesty and *Index* were the best-known internationally minded organisations to receive David's support, but they were not alone. The Minority Rights Group stemmed from David's and Michael Scott's support for the Nagas, and reflected, in part, their belief that – in David's words – 'the United Nations, being an organisation of governments, is a particularly inhospitable forum for the rights of minorities'. Once again, it began life with a lunch at the Waldorf Hotel, attended by David, Michael Scott, Guy Wint and Conor Cruise O'Brien in 1962; David told Keith Kyle that it was set up 'to act as a friend, adviser and introducer of minorities, without becoming their propagandist'. As always, David was happy to take a back seat once he had set a scheme in motion and provided the necessary funding, and once again he was keen to keep the *Observer* at a distance: as he told Jim Callaghan, 'I feel a certain need to advance this thesis discreetly. One does not want it to appear as merely the pet notion of one newspaper.' The Congress for Cultural Freedom provided some of its funding, as did the Ford Foundation: its directors included Laurence Gandar and Ben Whittaker. David eventually resigned as trustee, disapproving of what he saw as its increasingly strident tone.

The interests of minorities and political refugees were also looked after by Rights and Justice and World Wide Research, both of which had been set up by Michael Scott but were now run single-handed by his friend Mary Dines from a chaotic office in Islington, and funded by David, who had been introduced to her by Scott: Sarah Astor, David's daughter-in-law, remembers David sitting quietly in the background, perched on a rickety chair and sipping tea out of a cracked mug, while Mary Dines smoked one cigarette after another, and Kurdish, Eritrean and Ethiopian refugees queued on the stairs outside. David's secretary, Pat Burge, suggested to Richard and Sarah Astor that they should get in touch with Mary Dines, and they helped to organise her work with asylum-seekers into a charity, Asylum Aid, which was funded by David and built up by its first co-ordinator, Alasdair Mackenzie. Many of Mary Dines's clients were from the Horn of Africa, which led her into supporting Eritrean efforts to win their independence from Ethiopia. The Eritrean cause appealed to David, with his long-standing involvement in African liberation movements: he invited Isaias Afwerki, the leader of the Eritrean People's Liberation Front, to Sutton Courtenay, where he introduced him to leading Africanists, including Basil Davidson, and arranged for him to visit Chatham House. Mary Dines also put David in touch with an Ethiopian asylum-seeker, Kebede Berhanu, who became David's driver and the family's odd-job man, first in St John's Wood and later at the Manor House in Sutton Courtenay.

David's involvement in practical politics focussed on the Middle East, Ireland and South Africa. He was involved in setting up the World Security Trust (WST) in 1963, the advisory council of which included Lord Harlech, William Deakin, Hugh Foot, Philip Mason, Robert Stephens and his former colleague Alastair Buchan, now running the Institute for Strategic Studies. Brooding on how 'some kind of world order' could be established, David noted that the WST had 'found much more acceptance of the need for such a study among the practical politicians (both here and in the USA) than among the academics – who tend to feel you cannot study something until it has already happened'. And he increasingly came to believe that 'what Philip [Lothian] and my parents were trying to do in the 1920s and 1930s in the field of international politics makes sense today. Indeed my own efforts inside the paper and outside it are motivated by that belief.'

According to Richard Cockett, who had it from David himself, David's interest in Israel 'dated back to a family visit to Palestine during the 1920s when he and his mother had been threatened in a field by Arabs wielding their farm implements who had mistaken them for Zionist land prospectors', and the Middle East had always loomed large in editorial meetings in which Colin Legum, Robert Stephens, Nora Beloff and others gave vent to their forcefully held and often opposing views. The *Observer* had supported the creation of Israel in 1948, and again during the Six Day War of 1967, which had inspired some of Patrick O'Donovan's most inspired reporting, but Israel's subsequent occupation of the West Bank had prompted a leader entitled 'The Two Rights', which put the case for the Palestinians and was critical of Israel. David sympathised with both sides: his stand on Suez was still remembered in the Arab world, but his subsequent efforts to repair relations with the Jewish community in Britain, ably assisted by Lajos Lederer, had led to friendships with, among others, Max Rayne, Harold Lever, Jacob Rothschild and Lois Sieff. 'I have long taken an interest in Israel and its problems,' he told Jonathan Power. 'My personal relations are almost entirely with the Israelis, but I also have a political sympathy for the Palestinians.' Israel's victory in the Six Day War was, he wrote in a leader-page article, evidence of the 'superior efficiency of democracy', while 'the Jews have, individually and collectively, made a greater contribution to human progress than any other comparable category of people'.

After he retired from the *Observer* he was asked to write a book for the World Security Trust about the Middle East, and Robert Stephens suggested that help could be provided by Valerie Yorke, then in her late twenties and working in the Foreign Office's Research Department. They met for lunch in the ladies' annexe at the Athenaeum, and agreed that, before setting pen to paper, they should go on their travels, interviewing political leaders, senior officials, diplomats, newspaper editors and opinion-makers. In 1976 they visited New York, Washington and Paris, at a time when David was deeply involved in the sale of the *Observer*, and the following year they travelled to Moscow, where they met Yevgeny Primakov, the future Soviet prime minister, before spending five weeks in the Middle East. In Cairo they met Gavin Young, and a PLO representative who gave them an introduction to Abu Iyad, a leading figure in the PLO based in the Lebanon; Lebanon was racked by civil war, but there and elsewhere David found time to look at churches, mosques and museums. From there they took a ramshackle taxi on a hundred-mile journey, in freezing conditions, through the Bekaa Valley and over the Lebanon mountains to Damascus; they went on to Amman, the West Bank and East Jerusalem, and Israel. Among those they interviewed were Shimon Peres and King Hussein of Jordan, whose 'normally impassive face gave way to animated delight as he caught the logic' of David's plan. 'The chemistry worked particularly well between David and the PLO', but an infuriated official at the Israeli foreign ministry threw them out of his office for suggesting that Israel might 'have to rely on outside guarantees'.

Peace in the Middle East was completed in six weeks after their return to Britain: David provided an eight-page introduction, and the rest was written by Valerie Yorke. Before starting work, Patrick Seale, the authors' literary agent, showed a synopsis to André Deutsch. Deutsch longed to publish David, but 'Oh, how disappointed we were when we read the outline, which is, I am afraid to say, rather flat and lacks any vibration or excitement.' Following Deutsch's suggestion that David should approach Transworld Publishers, it was published in 1978 by Corgi Books, who eventually printed 10,000 copies: although the commitment, time and energy David gave to the project was never in doubt, the modesty of his written contribution to the book suggests that, like so many of his former colleagues, he was a sprinter rather than a long-distance runner when it came to putting pen to paper. Preceded by a long article written by him for *The Times*, and carrying a foreword by Lord Harlech, the book argued that because of the arms race and the Cold War, only the two superpowers could guarantee stability and new frontiers once Israel had withdrawn from Gaza and the West Bank, the territories invaded and occupied after the Six Day War in 1967: a Control Commission should supervise the establishment of an independent Palestinian state in the occupied territories, and a demilitarised zone should run astride Israel's borders, with the superpowers present in a non-combatant role. Ambitious and even audacious, *Peace in the Middle East* captured the imagination of political and diplomatic circles in Europe, North America, the Soviet Union and the Middle East. Shimon Peres wrote to say that it was 'an essential document, likely to assist us in the crucial debates we are now having'; Keith Kyle hailed it as 'a vitally relevant text' in the *Listener*; Colin Legum described it in the *Observer* as 'the first comprehensive plan for creating a security system for the Middle East', and – optimistically, as it now seems – suggested that 'the great majority on both sides are now ready to live together as peaceful neighbours, provided only that they can be sure that the concessions required from each side will not leave either of them vulnerable to future attacks'. The *Middle East International*'s reviewer struck a more cautious note, claiming that 'the great strength of the Astor–Yorke proposals is also their great weakness: they postulate a rational world'.

But it by no means marked the end of his involvement in the conflict between Israel and the Palestinians. A planned seminar in Ditchley Park, sponsored by the World Security Trust, came to nothing, but in 1978, together with Lord Harlech, David Owen, Garret FitzGerald and Harold Lever, David helped to set up the Council for Palestinian Social and Economic Development, designed to channel economic aid to Gaza and the West Bank. In 1980 he donated £10,000 to the Trust for International Development and Education, which was supported by several eminent British Jews, including Lever, Arnold Goodman and Max Rayne; its Palestinian director, George Assousa, later paid tribute to David's 'enormous contribution to the Palestinian people, against all odds'. In 1984 David visited the Palestinian Israeli Saleh Baransi, a former schoolmaster who had long campaigned for peaceful coexistence between Palestinians and Israelis, and had been imprisoned for ten years. Two years later Baransi was again under house arrest in Israel, and David took up his cause in letters to *The Times* and Shimon Peres; he told Anthony Kenny, the master of Balliol, that he was convinced that Baransi was 'gilt-edged', though 'I cannot help doubting whether Isaiah [Berlin], who has never been a great fighter, would be willing to offend his Israeli friends by taking Baransi seriously.' And in 1994 David and Jacob Rothschild each contributed £10,000 to Medical Aid for Palestinians, a charity which provided money for Palestinian doctors and nurses working in Israeli hospitals.

The problems of Northern Ireland were almost as intractable as those of Israel and the Palestinians, and although Ulster Unionists may bridle at the province being included in foreign parts, David once again found himself trying to reconcile the irreconcilable. As early as 1946 Frank Pakenham had urged David to publish articles about the division of Ireland, and had warned him of the dire consequences of continued discrimination against the Catholic population of Northern Ireland. 'I would not have backed Mary Holland so confidently if Frank hadn't implanted in my mind so many years before the idea that a terrible injustice was being done,' David recalled after Mary Holland – despite being told by fellow journalists that Ulster politics were of no interest to the British reading public – raised the subject at a Wednesday-morning editorial meeting, and he went on to publish her account of the October 1968 Civil Rights march in Derry under the heading of 'John Bull's White Ghettoes'. In 1972 Brian Inglis, Robert Kee and others founded the British–Irish Association (BIA), a gathering of politicians, academics, journalists and others from Britain and both sides of the Irish border who met to discuss ways of improving Anglo-Irish relations and relations between Unionists and Republicans in the North; only members of Sinn Fein, and those advocating violence, were excluded. David later became involved, and in 1984 he declared that 'of my activities in retirement, much the most useful is my chairmanship of the British–Irish Association'.

Anthony Kenny first met David to discuss a series of lectures on the German Resistance, held in Balliol in 1982 to commemorate the fiftieth anniversary of Trott's arrival in the college. 'People who want to avoid taking on jobs do well to give David a wide berth,' he once observed: David was 'most dangerous when most diffident', and people found themselves being 'profoundly influenced' by this 'most gentle and unthreatening of men'. Kenny had become an active member of the BIA, arguing for the establishment of a 'New Ireland Forum' to promote acceptance of a 'unitary state' of Ireland in which London and Dublin would be jointly responsible for Northern Ireland, and the identities of both Unionists and nationalists would somehow be respected and guaranteed. David was a keen supporter of Kenny's ideas, and with Marigold Johnson, the secretary of the BIA, he visited Charles Haughey, the Irish prime minister, in Dublin, and went with Kenny to the Cabinet Office in London to talk to Robert Armstrong, Mrs Thatcher's Cabinet Secretary. Early in 1985 Lord Kilbrandon published the New Ireland Forum Report, based on Kenny's proposals. Mrs Thatcher's instinctive reaction was hostile – a view shared by most Unionists, who regarded the New Forum ideas as the first stage in the ultimate annexation of the North by the Republic – but that November she and Garret FitzGerald, who had succeeded Haughey as the Irish prime minister, signed the Anglo-Irish Agreement at Hillsborough which, for the first time, allowed the Dublin government a formal role in the administration of Northern Ireland. David resigned from the BIA in 1990: Marigold Johnson has fond memories of him dossing down, improbably, in a B&B in Belfast, and his summoning a taxi in Whitehall by putting two fingers in his mouth and unleashing that piercing whistle he had learned at Eton.

★

Ever since George Orwell urged David to bend his mind to the decolonisation of Africa, the continent had dominated David's thoughts, and the pages of the *Observer*, much to his mother's distress. By the 1970s most of Africa had achieved independence, but white minority rule, and the injustices that went with it, was as firmly in place as ever in South Africa; and the most promising African leader, Nelson Mandela, was still serving his interminable sentence on Robben Island. In 1970 the British ambassador in Pretoria told David that Mandela's cell was 'bursting at the seams' with books, and that the prison would no longer accept the law books and journals which David had arranged to be sent to Mandela. Mary Benson reported that Mandela's living conditions had worsened, that he spent much of his time in solitary confinement in his tiny cell when not breaking stones in the quarry, that his diet was now restricted to mealie-meal, fat and salt, and that he was no longer allowed to study for a London University law degree. (Later in that decade Mandela was allowed to read the newspapers, and the London University ban was revoked.)

In June 1976 the world at large was shocked by the massacre of over 600 students and schoolchildren in Soweto, and fifteen months later Steve Biko of the Black Consciousness Movement died after being beaten and tortured in police custody. Grass-roots opposition to the regime increased in both numbers and confidence. Mandela once said, apropos David's support, that he would 'do everything in my power to justify the confidence he has in me', but not all his ANC colleagues were as appreciative. In 1978 David contributed over £5,000 to the travel costs of a group of ANC leaders, led by Joe Matlon, so that they could attend a conference in the Ivanhoe Hotel in Bloomsbury organised by the chain-smoking Mary Dines. David had been worried by Communist 'usurpation of leadership' of the ANC and 'inappropriate class-war dogma', and was convinced that Matlon and his colleagues were 'serious and experienced' politicians, but his visitors took full advantage of his trust and his habitual generosity. Pat Burge in David's private office queried air tickets from Lusaka to London which had been paid for but never used, only to discover that David had not only paid the travel expenses of previously unmentioned delegates, but for flights all over Africa. 'As a sovereign liberation organisation we view your investigation of our legitimate business with Express Air Travels as a gross interference in our internal affairs and therefore highly undesirable,' she was told. 'We therefore request you kindly to desist therefrom.' Soon afterwards Matlon was expelled from the ANC.

In 1978 Donald Woods, a friend of Steve Biko and a former editor of the *Daily Dispatch*, moved to London after falling foul of the apartheid laws,

and was soon befriended by David. Woods was very taken with his new
friend: he liked the way he uttered 'the most emphatic opinions in tones
of excruciating diffidence, accompanied by semi-coughs, mini-grunts and
self-deprecatory sounds in the throat', and noted how 'sometimes when
David is listening he slumps sideways with his head bowed, his eyes shut
and a look of acute dyspepsia'. David feared that the ANC would turn
to the Soviet bloc for support and assistance if help was not forthcoming
from the West, and he discussed with Woods the possibility of reviving
the anti-apartheid movement through the newly formed SDP, 'which is
free of Communist connections, whereas the Labour Party is all tied up
with the present London supporters of the ANC'. 'It is important that
such an enterprise should be working, plainly and visibly, as the *servant*
of the black African cause, rather than as the spokesman of liberalism
(or, for that matter, of Communism or Christianity),' David told Woods
in words that echoed Orwell's over thirty years before. Woods was keen
to involve the centre and the right of British politics in the anti-apartheid
cause, and to provide ANC leaders with better access to Western politicians. The Lincoln Trust was set up to facilitate this; David was one of
the trustees, and the committee included Robert Birley, Jock Campbell,
Denis Healey, Trevor Huddleston, Roy Jenkins, David Owen, David
Steel, Shirley Williams and, from the USA, Edward Kennedy and Robert
McNamara.

In 1982 Mandela was moved from Robben Island to Pollsmoor
maximum security prison on the mainland, where he shared a cell
with five others, including Walter Sisulu and Ahmed Kathrada from
the ANC. In a submission to the UN Working Group on Human
Rights, based on her discussions with Winnie Mandela, Mary Benson
reported that although there was 'no torture, no brutality', 'the treatment is extremely subtle in its cruelty. And in all the twenty-one years
of Nelson Mandela's imprisonment, I have never before detected such
a note of desperation in her description of a visit.' But after visiting
Mandela in Pollsmoor, Helen Suzman, the South African politician and
anti-apartheid campaigner, told David that he was in good spirits and
good health: medical and dental care were available, he was able to
study and read the papers, and had the use of a shower with hot water.
'I do not believe that the authorities at Pollsmoor are "trying to break
Mandela's spirit" – an aim that is unlikely to succeed with that indomi-
table man', she wrote, adding that she would be grateful if David would
show her letter to Mary Benson. David also showed it to Denis Healey,
David Steel and the Duke of Devonshire. 'Her findings are almost

totally at variance with the report that Winnie Mandela had sent us,' he told them. Helen Suzman suggested that Winnie Mandela must have visited her husband when he was depressed, or that conditions must have improved since her last visit: either way, she was 'unable to give a really unemotional visit, and it is a pity that Mary went ahead without confirmation'. Two years later, in 1985, Nicholas Bethell told David that he had found Mandela in good health: he was still sharing a cell with five others, but he had the use of a radio, the South African papers, *Time* and the *Guardian Weekly* were delivered to his cell, and he grew fruit and vegetables in a small garden; but he still supported the armed struggle, which deprived him of Amnesty's support 'and provides the authorities with the ideal pretext for not putting his name forward to State President Botha for clemency'. In the meantime, David supported members of Mandela's family: in 1983 he arranged for Winnie to be paid £500 per annum; Mandela had proved to be a neglectful father and grandfather – hardly surprising, given the years he had spent behind bars – and David helped with a grandson's education, and paid for a daughter to do a secretarial course.

David's 'obsession about Communist infiltration' and his liberal lean-ings led to a falling out with Trevor Huddleston, who raged against 'the proven uselessness of the liberal approaches which I have come to hate so much'; David, for his part, had come to regard Huddleston as something of a prima donna, and resented the way he rode roughshod over Michael Scott. In an angry exchange of letters, David denied that he was trying to 'divide' the leadership of the ANC, claiming that it needed the support of both East and West, and that – to quote from an earlier letter to Huddleston – he had 'always accepted the use of force as a necessary ingredient in bringing about a change to a one-man-one-vote regime in South Africa'. 'I am pretty certain I defended this in print well before you did in public statements,' he insisted. 'Our disagreement is about whether it is in the best interests of the Africans to have fallen so much into the hands of white South African Communists.' From exile in Zambia, Oliver Tambo, who had become acting president of the ANC after Luthuli's death in 1967, issued a call to make the South African townships 'ungovernable' and, rather reluctantly, accepted arms from the Soviet Union for the use of guerrillas making sporadic forays into his home country. Still doing battle with Huddleston – who had infuriated him by suggesting that Donald Woods was a South African agent – David defended the involvement of the United States by referring to a recent trip that Tambo had made to Washington on the grounds that 'I doubt whether you and I have yet introduced him to such influential people here as his American friends have done there.'

Scott himself had always believed that the Africa Bureau had too readily accepted the idea that South Africa was an integral part of the Western economy; he remained sceptical about the notion that ordinary South Africans benefitted from Western investment in the country, and was convinced that a sinister Israeli–South African lobby had far too much influence in London and Washington. But like Trevor Huddleston – whom David now dismissed as a 'spent force' – Scott now seemed a voice from the past. Ever more frequent battles in the townships were beginning to worry American and British companies and investors, and although the South African government still claimed that Mandela was a Communist and a terrorist, business leaders began to realise that the ANC represented the future of South Africa, and that they needed to have dealings with its leaders. David, Anthony Sampson and Mary Benson led a campaign to introduce Tambo and his colleague Thabo Mbeki to British businessmen, bankers and politicians. Although Mrs Thatcher, like Ronald Reagan, seemed strident in support of the status quo, and firmly opposed to sanctions, Tambo wrote to David in May 1985 to say that he had 'given some thought to ways in which the British government might be influenced towards taking a more positive policy', and asked David for help 'in this crucial time'. David called a meeting with Donald Woods, Anthony Sampson and Mary Benson, at which they agreed on the need to emulate the more forward-thinking Americans. Oliver Tambo had met President Reagan, Edward Kennedy and Katharine Graham, the owner of the *Washington Post*, in Washington: black South African leaders – including Desmond Tutu, who had won the Nobel Peace Prize in 1984 – should meet British politicians, and counter the misguided Foreign Office belief that Chief Buthelezi was their country's most important black politician. In July 1985 President Botha declared a state of emergency; Chase Manhattan's decision not to roll over loans to South Africa not only led to a run on the rand, but was indicative of changing attitudes among Western financiers and businessmen.

In October that year Tambo and Mbeki came to London. Gavin Relly, the new chairman of Anglo-American, one of the largest and most influential businesses operating in South Africa, had earlier flown to meet Tambo in Geneva, and David wrote to Denis Healey, Shirley Williams, James Prior and Jo Grimond to alert them to Tambo's arrival in London. Mrs Thatcher instructed members of her government not to meet him: she described the ANC as a terrorist organisation, and set her face against the notion of sanctions, but in due course she would not only allow Geoffrey Howe, the Foreign Secretary, to meet Tambo, but privately urged President Botha to release Mandela, realising him to be the ANC's most effective and charismatic leader. Tambo addressed the House of Commons Foreign Affairs Committee and Chatham House, and lunched at *The Economist*. Anthony Sampson had spoken to Robert McNamara about the 'importance of the businessman's role as go-betweens' between British politicians and ANC leaders: Anne Yates – a South African academic who had been introduced to David by Robert Birley, and was co-writing Michael Scott's biography – told David that 'Anthony's meeting of businessmen for this evening has a list that reads like the *Financial Times* list of biggest fish – not the most liberal, but the most powerful.' The following year Sampson held a lunch for Tambo and Mbeki in his house in Holland Park, attended by senior figures from Consolidated Gold Fields, Rio Tinto, Courtaulds, Barclays Bank and BP. But most influential of all was the change of tack by Consolidated Gold Fields, widely regarded as the most reactionary of companies and a keen supporter of the National Party. Anxious to ensure the company's future against the possible collapse of the existing order, its chairman, Rudolf Agnew, authorised his English political adviser, Michael Young, to bring together ANC leaders and Afrikaners in a series of top-secret meetings, held in an English country house. David had earlier lent Oliver Tambo his house in Sutton Courtenay, and he now arranged a lunch for Tambo, Mbeki and Jacob Zuma at the Connaught Rooms, attended by, among others, Michael Young, George Soros, Evelyn de Rothschild and Anthony Sampson. The ANC leaders, he told Tambo, had made a 'tremendous impression': all those present wanted 'closer talks with the ANC', and 'the traditional pro-Pretoria business lobby is now being undermined, though it still includes some very nasty people'.

In October 1986 David and Bridget spent a month in South Africa – his first visit to the country in which he and the *Observer* had been so long and so intimately involved. Although a state of emergency had been declared, they 'criss-crossed the country seeing famous anti-apartheid leaders' on a state-of-emergency tour planned and guided by Shaun Johnson, a young academic, writer and activist whom David had taken under his wing when he was studying in England on a Rhodes Scholarship, and who now worked on the *Weekly Mail*. While he was in Johannesburg David promised to raise money on behalf of the *Weekly Mail*, which was edited by Anton Harber and Irwin Manoim and was highly regarded by Laurence Gandar, who had edited the *Rand Daily Mail* from 1957 to 1969: Gandar had transformed the South African press by covering black politics and conditions, but he had been sacked after losing many of his white readers and had moved to London, where he had become the first director of the Minority Rights Group. Back in London, David successfully solicited support from, among others, Jock Campbell and Peter Palumbo, raising £30,000 in the process; and when Shaun Johnson brought Harber to London, David introduced him to Mary Benson, Neal Ascherson, Colin Legum, Dan Jacobson and Christopher Hope. The previous year David had offered £15,000 to enable Shaun Johnson to investigate the mood of young people in the country. Anne Yates, now living in Oxford, had suggested to Anthony Kenny that a trust should be set up to provide practical training for exiled members of the ANC. David and Anthony Sampson warmed to the idea, as did Oliver Tambo. David, Shell and the Rockefeller Brothers Fund in New York put up the money for the Southern Africa Advanced Education Project; young black people from South Africa were placed with businesses, in newspapers and in local government in England, and encouraged to attend courses at the London Business School and elsewhere. By the time the trust was wound up in 1991, some 700 young people had received training and experience of the kind so desperately needed in a rapidly changing South Africa. (The David Astor Journalism Awards Trust, which trains promising young journalists from east Africa, was set up in 2006, five years after David's death, by his son Richard and Jim Meyer.)

The following year David turned to another old friend, and a bête noire of some of his former colleagues on the *Observer*. Not all Americans, it seemed, were as enlightened as Robert McNamara, David Rockefeller and Wayne Fredericks of the Ford Motor Company, all of whom had earlier attended a meeting in London of the 'Rockefeller Group', together with Tambo, Mbeki and David's old friend Marion Doenhoff. David wrote to Henry Kissinger to ask 'whether you might be able to use your great influence to persuade Americans to take a more realistic view of the ANC . . . Might you be able to grasp that nettle, as you grasped the nettle of Chinese Communists ten years ago?' David, Anthony Sampson and Ronald Dworkin, the professor of jurisprudence at Oxford, set up meetings between white South African judges and ANC lawyers, including a dinner at Sutton Courtenay; two years later, David reported another 'confidential meeting', attended by four South African judges 'in spite of great pressure from their Minister of Justice to stay away'.

In December 1986 David wrote an article in the *Independent* entitled 'Why the West Must Act on South Africa Now', in which he claimed that the South African government was resorting to arbitrary police power and the cultivation of fear, 'the method of government perfected by Stalin and adapted by Hitler', and that although 'a few freedoms remain, chiefly for the whites', the black majority was still 'denied all means of expression'. But South African politics were changing inexorably, under internal and external pressure. In 1989 F. W. de Klerk replaced P. W. Botha. The new president was more flexible and more realistic than his predecessor, and Sampson told David, after talking to Thabo Mbeki, that de Klerk was coming under pressure to start talks with the ANC 'even before it renounces violence'. The following year Nelson Mandela was finally released, and nothing was the same thereafter. Anthony Sampson accompanied Anton Harber and Shaun Johnson to Soweto to conduct one of the first interviews with Mandela as a free man, and Mandela told him that the first books he had read in prison – both sent by David all those years before – were Sampson's *Anatomy of Britain* and Edmund Wilson's *Patriotic Gore*. Shortly after his release, Mandela flew to Sweden, where he was reunited with Oliver Tambo; he rang David to ask if he could join him there, but it proved impossible. David continued to be involved in South African affairs – in 1991 he arranged for £15,000 to be paid to Donald Woods at the Institute for the Advancement of Journalism in Johannesburg, which Woods had set up on his return to South Africa two years earlier – but Mandela's release, and all it brought with it, was the culmination of a long involvement, first set in motion over forty years earlier by his mentor, George Orwell.

David was in his late eighties by the turn of the millennium, but apart from occasional vagueness and the inevitable physical slowing-down, he remained as alert and as interested in the world as ever, dividing his time between London and Sutton Courtenay, with occasional family holidays in Trenain, a square white house in Trebetherick, on the north Cornish coast. But his sinuses continued to give him trouble, and following the bad bout of depression which had kept him off work in 1969 he was prescribed Prozac as well as lithium. But in March 2001, shortly after his eighty-ninth birthday, he was taken to St Mary's, Paddington, with severe abdominal pains. His doctor thought he might be suffering from appendicitis, but when they operated on him they discovered, and removed, a tumour in his colon. Although he still swung a golf club, enjoyed weekends in Sutton Courtenay, and agreed to be interviewed about his life on video by Jim Meyer, David never recovered from the combination of a general anaesthetic and a major operation. He became increasingly frail and confused, and a carer was brought in to look after him in the house in St Anne's Terrace into which he and Bridget had moved in the 1990s.

David Astor died in the Royal Free Hospital in Hampstead on 7 December 2001. His ashes were scattered in a stream that runs through the grounds of the Manor House into the Thames, and in due course a headstone was erected in the graveyard at Sutton Courtenay church, close to that of his great friend and mentor, George Orwell. A well-attended memorial service was held in St Bride's, the journalists' church, only yards from the old *Observer* offices in Tudor Street. He had been a truly good man, a great editor, and he had influenced our lives, and the lives of people around the world, in innumerable different ways, almost always to the good. He deserves to be better remembered.

Acknowledgements

Writing and researching this book has been an undiluted pleasure, and I'm extremely grateful to David Astor's widow, Bridget, for giving me permission to write it, and for all her help and advice. Her eldest son, Richard Astor, has proved a marvellous friend and patron – generous, hospitable, helpful, excellent company and an eagle-eyed subeditor – and I shall always be in his debt. Of their other children, I'm very grateful to Alice, Lucy and Tom; to David's daughter Frances; to Sarah Astor, Micky Astor, Viscount Astor, Jane Willoughby, James Astor, Polly Astor and Emily Astor who helped with the picture research; to Sean Naidoo, the most generous of lunchers; and to my old friend David Astor, my subject's nephew, who not only entertained my wife and me over many summers at Rest Harrow, Nancy Astor's 'seaside cottage' on Sandwich Bay, but has talked to me at length about the book, and provided an invaluable reading of the first draft, so saving me from quite a few howlers and wrong dates.

Piers Brendon, the Cambridge historian and a writer I hugely admire for his wit and elegance, volunteered to read the book in its first draft. Having a historian of such distinction read one's work in painstaking detail is a great and salutary privilege; for over three weeks in the autumn of 2014 he emailed me his thoughts and suggestions on a chapter-by-chapter basis, and the book was vastly improved as a result.

Once a week Robert Chesshyre and I go for a long early-morning walk in Richmond Park. Bob worked for many years at the *Observer* under both David Astor and Donald Trelford: our conversations proved invaluable, from my point of view, and he too provided a detailed reading of the first draft.

Other *Observer* members of staff to whom I'm extremely grateful include Sue Arnold, Neal Ascherson, Michael Beloff, Marcelle Bernstein, Linda Blandford, the late Jane Bown, Jeremy Bugler, Pat Burge, Carol Cattley, John Clare, Eric Clark, Anne Chisholm, Peter Crookston, Peter Deeley, Christine Doyle, Peter Dunn, the late Mark Frankland, Michael Frayn, the late Philip

French, Miriam Gross, Roger Harrison, Nigel Hawke, Ronald Higgins, Godfrey Hodgson, Jeremy Hunt, Bill Keegan, John Lucas, Virginia Makins, the late Hermione O'Donovan, Oliver Pritchett, the late Hilary Rubinstein, the late Patrick Seale, Colin Smith, John Thompson, Polly Toynbee, Donald Trelford, Katharine Whitehorn, Peter Wilby and Des Wilson.

I would also like to thank the following for their help and advice: June Andrews, Mel Andrews, Diana Athill, Roderick Bailey, Ariane Bankes, Michael Barber, Paula Barkay, Dennis Barker, Jose Bellido, Martin Biddle, Ben Birnberg, Louis Blom-Cooper, Amy Boone, Stephen Bourne, Clive Bradley, Candida Brazil, Felicity Bryan, Ben Buchan, David Buchan, Michael Burleigh, David Burnett, Ethan Casey, Ian Chapman, Nicky Cherrott, Maureen Cleave, Richard Cockett, John Cornwell, Nicky and Anne Cottam, Bruce Coward, Derek Cross, Tam Dalyell, Richard Davenport-Hines, Robin Davie, Valentine Davies, Laurian d'Harcourt, Gabriel Denvir, Luke Dodd, Gervase Duffield, Max Egremont, Adam Federman, Laura Feigel, Elspeth Forbes-Robertson, Adrian Fort, Jill Gale, Patrick Garrett, Trish Gibson, Graham C. Greene, James Greene, Richard Greene, Laurence Grissell, the late Professor M. R. D. Foot, Peter Goodwin, Henry Hardy, Steve Hare, Ernest Hecht, Henry Hemming, Nick Hodson, Anthony Holden, James Hughes-Onslow, Richard Ingrams, Judy Innes, Oliver James, Marigold Johnson, Shaun Johnson, Ben Jones, Danae Karydaki, Sir Anthony Kenny, Christopher Kilmartin, Olivia Kilmartin, Phillip Knightley, Carol Leadenham, Paul Levy, Professor I. M. D. Little, Bob Low, Andrew Lownie, Andrew McCooey, Robert McCrum, Giles MacDonogh, Callum Mackenzie, Patrick Marnham, Alex May, Patricia Meehan, Jim Meyer, Angela Neustatter, the late Francis Nichols, Antonia Owen, Graham Page, Maggie Parham, Pearson Phillips, Daniel Pick, Erin Pizzey, Patricia Potts, Stanley Price, David Pryce-Jones, Diana Rawstron, Noreen Riols, Julian Roop, Jean Rose, Malise Ruthven, Michael Scammell, Andrew Schuller, Lois Sieff, Sue Simmons, Christopher Sinclair-Stevenson, James Skinner, Adrian Smith, Carol Smith, Godfrey Smith, Mark Solms, Lord Stevenson, Anthony Stoll, John Stubbs, Andrew Thompson, Pierre Tille, Dr Bridgette Timmermann, Peter Timms, Philip Tinline, Claire Tomalin, Hugo Vickers, Michael Ward, Anthony Warne, Lord Weidenfeld, Lawrence Woodward, Lord Woolf, Blair Worden, Peregrine Worsthorne, the late Ilsa Yardley and Valerie Yorke.

Dan Franklin has been the most patient of publishers – I spent much of 2013 in and out of hospital, and had to put the book aside for almost a year – and his enthusiasm for the finished product, when it eventually arrived, was particularly gratifying, and a major boost to the morale. He has been my publisher at Cape since 1997, when my biography of Cyril Connolly came out; this is the fourth book we have worked on together. My agent, Gillon Aitken, has been with me even longer; he has had his own travails over the last couple of years, but has been unstinting in his advice and support. David Milner is the most diligent and keen-eyed editor I have encountered in nearly fifty years in the publishing business; he has saved me from innumerable howlers, and I am hugely indebted to him. I am also greatly indebted to Alison Rae for her impeccable proofreading and would like to thank Clare Bullock for her editorial assistance and Christopher Gibbs for his masterly index.

David Astor's papers are held by his family solicitors, Boodle Hatfield. Working in their Bond Street offices proved immensely enjoyable, still more so since, in the early days at least, tea and biscuits were brought round by a tea lady pushing a trolley – something I hadn't seen in an office since the early 1960s. I am very grateful indeed to Geoffrey Todd at Boodle Hatfield, and his colleagues Paula Corbett, Karen Johnson, Kim Christie and Joe Ritchie-Bennett for making me so welcome and for looking after me so well. The *Observer*'s archives are housed in the ultra-modern *Guardian* building, and working with Mariam Yamin, Susan Gentles and Hannah Jenkinson was a very pleasant business. It was good to find myself working once again with Verity Andrews and Brian Ryder and Nancy Jean Fulford at Reading University Library, which houses Nancy and Waldorf Astor's papers; with Pat Fox and Andi Gustavson at the Harry Ransom Humanities Research Center at the University of Texas in Austin, where J. L. Garvin's papers are kept; with Helen Langley, Colin Harris and Russell Edwards at the Bodleian Library in Oxford; and with Nicholas Scheetz of Georgetown University Library, the guardian of Christopher Sykes's papers. I particularly enjoyed my visit to the National Library of Wales in Aberystwyth, where J. Graham Jones made Tom Jones's papers available to me. I'm also grateful to Penny Hatfield at the Eton College Archives; Rona Morrison and Patricia Boyd at Edinburgh University Library, who sent me copies of letters from Arthur Koestler; Hannah Lowery at Bristol University Library; Anna Sander at the archives of Balliol College, Oxford, where many of Adam von Trott's papers are housed; Alison Greenlee at Tulsa University Library; the assistant archivist at the Hoover Institution Archives; Sabrina Rowlatt at the Imperial War Museum; Joanne Halford at the Institute of Psychoanalysis; and Charles Arkwright, who very kindly showed me round 2 Temple Place, the extraordinary mock-baronial mansion which David Astor's grandfather, William Waldorf Astor, built on the Embankment, just by the back entrance to the Middle Temple.

Picture Credits

Photographs nos. 1, 2, 3, 4, 5, 6, 7, 8, 9, 12, 13, 14, 15, 16, 17, 41, 42, 43 and 44 are from Astor family collections. No. 11 is © National Portrait Gallery, London. No. 49 is © Photo by Central Press/Getty Images. No. 34 is by courtesy of Anne Chisholm. No. 39 is © Photo by Fred Mott/Evening Standard/Getty Images. No. 40 is © David Rubinger/The LIFE Images Collection/Getty Images. Nos. 18, 19, 20, 21, 22, 23, 24, 26, 27, 28, 30, 31, 32, 35, 36, 37 and 38 are reproduced by permission of Guardian News and Media Ltd. 'David Astor' by Trog © Willy Fawkes.

The author and publishers have made every effort to trace and contact copyright holders. The publishers will be pleased to correct any mistakes or omissions in future editions.

Bibliography

Addison, Paul, *The Road to 1945: British Politics and the Second World War* (Jonathan Cape, 1975)

Alvarez, Al, *Where Did It All Go Right?* (Richard Cohen, 1999)

Andrew, Christopher and Mitrokhin, Vasili, *The Mitrokhin Archive: The KGB in Europe and the West* (Allen Lane, 1999)

Arendt, Hannah, *Eichmann in Jerusalem: A Report on the Banality of Evil* (Viking, 1965)

Ascherson, Neal, Introduction to Haffner, Sebastian, *Germany: Jekyll and Hyde* (Secker & Warburg, 1940)

Astor, David, 'Why the Revolt against Hitler was Ignored', *Encounter*, June 1969

Astor, David, 'How the British Press Censors Itself', *Index on Censorship* Vol. 6, No. 1, January–February 1977

Astor, David, 'Adam von Trott: A Personal View' in Bull, Hedley (ed.), *The Challenge of the Third Reich: The Adam von Trott Memorial Lectures* (Clarendon Press, 1996)

Astor, David and Benson, Mary (eds.), *Robert Birley 1903–1982* (privately printed, n.d.)

Astor, David and Yorke, Valerie, *Peace in the Middle East* (Corgi, 1978)

Astor, Michael, *Tribal Feeling* (John Murray, 1963)

Astor, Nancy, *A Lightning Sketch* (Wilton 65, 2003)

Athill, Diana, *Stet: A Memoir* (Granta, 2000)

Ayerst, David, *Garvin of the Observer* (Croom Helm, 1985)

Barnett, Correlli, *The Audit of War: The Illusion and Reality of Britain as a Great Nation* (Macmillan, 1986)

Barton, Frank, *The Press of Africa: Persecution and Perseverance* (Macmillan, 1979)

Becker, Robert, *Nancy Lancaster: Her Life, Her World, Her Art* (Knopf, 1996)

Bellido, José, 'The Failure of a Copyright Action: Confidences in the Papers of Nora Beloff', *Media and Arts Review* 249 (2013)

Beloff, Nora, *Freedom Under Foot: The Battle over the Closed Shop in British Journalism* (Temple Smith, 1976)

Benn, Tony, *Out of the Wilderness: Diaries 1963–7* (Hutchinson, 1987)

Benson, Mary, *Tshekedi Khama* (Faber, 1960)

Benson, Mary, *A Far Cry* (Viking, 1989)

Berlin, Isaiah, *Flourishing: Letters 1928–1946* (ed. Henry Hardy) (Chatto & Windus, 2004)

Berlin, Isaiah, *Enlightening: Letters 1946–1960* (eds. Henry Hardy and Jennifer Holmes) (Chatto & Windus, 2009)

Berlin, Isaiah, *Building: Letters 1960–1975* (eds. Henry Hardy and Mark Pottle) (Chatto & Windus, 2013)

Bielenberg, Christabel, *The Past Is Myself* (Chatto & Windus, 1968)

Bielenberg, Christabel, *The Road Ahead* (Bantam, 1992)

Billen, Andrew, *Jane Bown Observer* (Herbert Press, 1996)

Bourne, Stephen, *Elisabeth Welch: Soft Lights and Sweet Music* (Scarecrow Press, 2005)

Bower, Tom, *Tiny Rowland: A Rebel Tycoon* (Heinemann, 1993)

Bown, Jane, *Women of Consequence* (Introduction by Suzanne Lowry) (Chatto & Windus, 1986)

Bowra, Maurice, *Memories 1898–1939* (Weidenfeld & Nicolson, 1967)

Bradley, Clive, *The Observer, 1973–1975* (privately printed, n.d.)

Brendon, Piers, *The Life and Death of the Press Barons* (Secker & Warburg, 1982)

Brivati, Brian, *Lord Goodman* (Richard Cohen, 1999)

Brown, Ivor, *The Way of My World* (Collins, 1954)

Brown, Ivor, *Old and Young* (The Bodley Head, 1971)

Bryant, Chris, *Stafford Cripps: The First Modern Chancellor* (Hodder & Stoughton, 1997)

Bull, Hedley (ed.), *The Challenge of the Third Reich* (Clarendon Press, 1986)

Burk, Kathleen, *Troublemaker: The Life and History of A. J. P. Taylor* (Yale University Press, 2000)

Calvocoressi, Peter, *Threading My Way* (Duckworth, 1994)

Campbell, John, *Roy Jenkins: A Well-Rounded Life* (Jonathan Cape, 2014)

Card, Tim, *Eton Renewed: A History from 1860 to the Present Day* (John Murray, 1994)

Carney, Michael, *Stoker: The Life of Hilda Matheson OBE* (privately printed, 1999)

Caute, David, *Isaac & Isaiah: The Covert Punishment of a Cold War Heretic* (Yale University Press, 2013)

Chisholm, Anne and Davie, Michael, *Beaverbrook: A Life* (Hutchinson, 1996)

Clark, William, *From Three Worlds: Memoirs* (Sidgwick & Jackson, 1986)

Clarke, Peter, *The Cripps Version: The Life of Sir Stafford Cripps 1889–1952* (Allen Lane, 2002)

Cockburn, Claud, *I, Claud . . .* (Penguin, 1967)

Cockburn, Patricia, *The Years of the Week* (Macdonald, 1968)

Cockett, Richard, *Twilight of Truth: Chamberlain, Appeasement and the Manipulation of the Press* (Weidenfeld & Nicolson, 1989)

Cockett, Richard, *David Astor and the Observer* (André Deutsch, 1991)

Cockett, Richard, 'The Government, the Press and Politics in Britain, 1937 to 1945', PhD thesis, London University, 1988, BH

Cole, John, *As It Seemed to Me: Political Memoirs* (Weidenfeld & Nicolson, 1995)

Coleman, Peter, *The Liberal Conspiracy: The Congress for Cultural Freedom and the Struggle for the Mind of Post-war Europe* (The Free Press, 1989)

Collis, Louise (ed.), *Maurice Collis Dairies: 1949–1969* (Faber, 1971)

Connolly, Cyril, 'The Spring Assignment', unpublished MS, 1943

Cowles, Virginia, *The Astors: The Story of a Transatlantic Family* (Weidenfeld & Nicolson, 1979)

Crankshaw, Edward, *Putting Up with the Russians: 1947–84* (Macmillan, 1984)

Crick, Bernard, *George Orwell: A Life* (Secker & Warburg, 1980)

Cudlipp, Hugh, *At Your Peril* (Weidenfeld & Nicolson, 1962)

Curtis, Anthony, *Lit. Ed.: On Reviewing and Reviewers* (Carcanet, 1998)

Curtis, Sarah (ed.), *The Journals of Woodrow Wyatt: Volume 1* (Macmillan, 1998)

Davenport-Hines, Richard (ed.), *Letters From Oxford: Hugh Trevor-Roper to Bernard Berenson* (weidenfeld & Nicolson, 2006)

Davenport-Hines, Richard, *An English Affair: Sex, Class and Power in the Age of Profumo* (HarperCollins, 2013)

Davie, Michael, *Anglo-Australian Attitudes* (Secker & Warburg, 2000)

Davison, Peter (ed.), *Orwell: A Life in Letters* (Harvill Secker, 2010)

Davison, Peter (ed.), *George Orwell: Diaries* (Harvill Secker, 2010)

Dorril, Stephen, *MI6: Fifty Years of Special Operations* (Fourth Estate, 2000)

Douglas-Home, William, *Half-Term Report: An Autobiography* (Longmans, 1954)

Dudley Edwards, Ruth, *The Pursuit of Reason: The Economist 1843–1993* (Hamish Hamilton, 1993)

Dudley Edwards, Ruth, *Victor Gollancz: A Biography* (Gollancz, 1987)

Dunn, Cyril (ed.), *Shouts and Murmurs: A Selection from the Observer 1962–3* (Hodder & Stoughton, 1963)

Eden, Clarissa (ed. Kate Haste), *A Memoir: From Churchill to Eden* (Weidenfeld & Nicolson, 2007)

Edwards, Robert, *Goodbye to Fleet Street* (Jonathan Cape, 1988)

Elkins, Caroline, *Britain's Gulag: The Brutal End of Empire in Kenya* (Jonathan Cape, 2005)

Ellis, E. L., *T. J.: A Life of Dr Thomas Jones, CH* (University of Wales Press, 1992)

Evans, Harry, *Good Times, Bad Times* (Weidenfeld & Nicolson, 1983)

Evans, Harry, *My Paper Chase: The Stories of Vanished Times* (Little, Brown, 2009)

Faught, C. Brad, *Into Africa: The Imperial Legacy of Margery Perham* (I. B. Tauris, 2012)

Foot, M. R. D., *SOE in France: An Account of the Work of the British Special Operations Executive in France, 1940–1944* (Cassell, 2004)

Ford, Roger, *Steel from the Sky: Behind Enemy Lines in German-Occupied France* (Cassell, 2004)

Fort, Adrian, *Nancy: The Story of Lady Astor* (Jonathan Cape, 2012)

Fox, James, *The Langhorne Sisters* (Granta, 1998)

Frankland, Mark, *Child of My Time* (Chatto & Windus, 1999)

Frayn, Michael, *Towards the End of the Morning* (Collins, 1967)

Frayn, Michael, *Travels with a Typewriter* (Faber, 2009)

Gale, John, *Clean Young Englishman* (Hodder & Stoughton, 1965)

Gannon, Franklin Reid, *The British Press and Germany 1936–1939* (Clarendon Press, 1971)

Garvin, Katharine, *J. L. Garvin: A Memoir* (Heinemann, 1948)

Gibb, Mildred and Beckwith, Frank, *The Yorkshire Post: Two Centuries* (Yorkshire Conservative Newspaper Co. Ltd, 1954)

Gibson, Trish, *Brenda Colvin: A Career in Landscape* (Frances Lincoln, 2011)

Glancey, Jonathan, *Nagaland: A Journey to India's Forgotten Frontier* (Faber, 2011)

Glees, Anthony, *The Secrets of the Service: British Intelligence and Communist Subversion* (Jonathan Cape, 1987)

Goodman, Arnold, *Tell Them I'm On My Way* (Chapman, 1993)

Grant Duff, Shiela, *The Parting of Ways: A Personal Account of the Thirties* (Peter Owen, 1982)

Gray, Patience, *Work Adventures Childhood Dreams* (Edizioni Leucasia, 1999)

Gray, Tony (ed.), *Fleet Street Remembered* (Heinemann, 1990)

Green, S. J. D. and Horden, Peregrine, *All Souls and the Wider World: Statesmen, Scholars and Adventurers c.1850–1950* (Oxford University Press, 2011)

Greenslade, Roy, *Press Gang: How Newspapers Make Profits from Propaganda* (Macmillan, 2003)

Grenfell, Joyce, *Darling Ma: Letters to Her Mother 1932–1944* (Hodder & Stoughton, 1988)

Griffiths, Dennis, *A History of the NPA 1906–2006* (Newspaper Publishers Association, 2006)

Grigg, John, *Nancy Astor: Portrait of a Pioneer* (Sidgwick & Jackson, 1980)

Gross, Miriam, *An Almost English Life: Literary, and not so Literary, Recollections* (Short Books, 2012)

Gunther, John, *Inside Africa* (Hamish Hamilton, 1955)

Heawood, Jonathan (ed.), *Orwell: The Observer Years* (Atlantic, 2003)

Haffner, Sebastian, *Offensive Against Germany* (Secker & Warburg, 1941)

Haffner, Sebastian, *Defying Hitler: A Memoir* (Weidenfeld & Nicolson, 2001)

Hall, Richard, *My Life with Tiny: A Biography of Tiny Rowland* (Faber, 1987)

Hamilton, Denis, *Editor-in-Chief: Fleet Street Memories* (Hamish Hamilton, 1989)

Harris, Harold (ed.), *Astride the Two Cultures: Arthur Koestler at Seventy* (Hutchinson, 1975)

Harris, Kenneth, *The Wildcatter: A Portrait of Robert O. Anderson* (Weidenfeld & Nicolson, 1987)

Harris, Wilson, *Life So Far* (Jonathan Cape, 1954)

Harrison, Rosina, *Rose: My Life in Service* (Cassell, 1975)

Harrison, Rosina, *Gentlemen's Gentlemen: My Friends in Service* (Arlington Books, 1976)

Hart-Davis, Duff, *The House the Berrys Built* (Hodder & Stoughton, 1990)

Harvey, Robert, *The Fall of Apartheid: The Inside Story from Smuts to Mbeki* (Palgrave, 2001)

Haslam, Jonathan, *The Vices of Integrity: E. H. Carr 1892–1982* (Verso, 1999)

Hayward, Allyson, *Norah Lindsay: The Life and Art of a Garden Designer* (Frances Lincoln, 2007)

Hearnden, Arthur, *Red Robert: A Life of Robert Birley* (Hamish Hamilton, 1984)

Heilpern, John, Introduction to Gale, John, *Camera Man* (Hodder & Stoughton, 1979)

Hetherington, Alastair, *Guardian Years* (Chatto & Windus, 1981)

Hichens, Mark, *West Downs: A Portrait of an English Prep School* (Pentland Press, 1992)

Hobson, Harold, Knightley, Phillip and Russell, Leonard, *The Pearl of Days: An Intimate Memoir of the Sunday Times 1822–1972* (Hamish Hamilton, 1972)

Hoggart, Richard (ed.), *Your Sunday Paper* (University of London Press, 1967)

Hollingworth, Clare, *Front Line* (Jonathan Cape, 1990)

Hopkinson, Diana, *The Incense-Tree: An Autobiography* (Routledge, 1968)

Hopkinson, Tom, *Of This Our Time: A Journalist's Story 1905–50* (Hutchinson, 1982)

Horowitz, David (ed.), *Isaac Deutscher: The Man and His Work* (Macdonald, 1971)

Howard, Anthony (ed.), *The Crossman Diaries: Selections from the Diaries of a Cabinet Minister 1964–1970* (Jonathan Cape, 1979)

Hunt, Jeremy, *Original Sinner* (privately printed, n.d.)

Hussey, Marmaduke, *Chance Governs All: A Memoir* (Macmillan, 2001)

Ignatieff, Michael, *Isaiah Berlin: A Life* (Chatto & Windus, 1998)

Ingrams, Richard, *My Friend Footy: A Memoir of Paul Foot* (Private Eye, 2005)

Jacobs, Eric, *Stop Press: The Inside Story of the Times Dispute* (André Deutsch, 1980)

James, Clive, *North Face of Soho: Unreliable Memoirs, Vol. IV* (Picador, 2006)

Jenkins, Simon, *The Market for Glory: Fleet Street Ownership in the Twentieth Century* (Faber, 1986)

Jones, Benjamin F., *Freeing France: Eisenhower's Guerrilla War and the Liberation of France* (Oxford University Press, 2014)

Jones, Thomas, *A Diary with Letters 1931–1950* (Oxford University Press, 1954)

Kaplan, Justin, *When the Astors Owned New York: Blue Blood and Grand Hotels in a Gilded Age* (Plume, 2007)

Kenny, Anthony, *A Life in Oxford* (John Murray, 1997)

King, Cecil, *The Cecil King Diary 1965–1970* (Jonathan Cape, 1972)

Klemperer, Klemens von, *A Noble Combat: The Letters of Shiela Grant Duff and Adam von Trott zu Solz 1932–1939* (Clarendon Press, 1988)

Knightley, Phillip, *Philby: The Life and Views of the KGB Masterspy* (André Deutsch, 1988)

Knightley, Phillip and Kennedy, Caroline, *An Affair of State: The Profumo Case and the Framing of Stephen Ward* (Jonathan Cape, 1987)

Koss, Stephen, *The Rise and Fall of the Political Press in Britain. Volume Two: The Twentieth Century* (Hamish Hamilton, 1984)

Kyle, Keith, *Suez* (Weidenfeld & Nicolson, 1991)

Lamb, Richard, *The Ghosts of Peace 1935–1945* (Michael Russell, 1987)

Langbehn, Elke, *Adam von Trott: An Account for His Friends* (TS, translated from German, n.d., p.c.)

Leapman, Michael, *Barefaced Cheek: The Apotheosis of Rupert Murdoch* (Hodder & Stoughton, 1983)

Lejeune, C. A., *Thank You for Having Me* (Hutchinson, 1964)

Lewis, Jeremy, *Cyril Connolly: A Life* (Jonathan Cape, 1997)

Lighthill, James, *The Freud Memorial Professorship at University College, London* (Carnac, 1989)

Longford, Lord, *Diary of a Year* (Weidenfeld & Nicolson, 1982)

Longford, Lord, *Avowed Intent: An Autobiography* (Little, Brown, 1994)

MacDonogh, Giles, *A Good German: A Biography of Adam von Trott zu Solz* (Overlook, 1992)

McLean, Ruari, *True to Type* (Oak Knoll Press, 2000)

Margach, James, *The Abuse of Power: The War between Downing Street and the Media from Lloyd George to Callaghan* (W. H. Allen, 1978)

Marnham, Patrick, *The Private Eye Story: The First Twenty-One Years* (André Deutsch, 1982)

Marnham, Patrick, *Wild Mary: The Life of Mary Wesley* (Chatto & Windus, 2006)

May, Derwent, *Critical Times: The History of the Times Literary Supplement* (HarperCollins, 2001)

Meehan, Patricia, *The Unnecessary War: Whitehall and the Resistance to Hitler* (Sinclair-Stevenson, 1992)

Mitchell, Leslie, *Maurice Bowra* (Oxford University Press, 2009)

Mitford, Jessica, *Faces of Patrick: A Memoir of Philip Toynbee* (Heinemann, 1984)

Morgan, Janet (ed.), *The Backbench Diaries of Richard Crossman* (Hamish Hamilton and Jonathan Cape, 1981)

Morris, Benny, *The Roots of Appeasement: The British Weekly Press and Nazi Germany during the 1930s* (Frank Cass, 1991)

Mount, Ferdinand, *Cold Cream: My Early Life and Other Mistakes* (Bloomsbury, 2008)

Muggeridge, Malcolm, *Tread Softly for You Tread on My Jokes* (Collins, 1966)

Newby, Eric, *A Traveller's Life* (Collins, 1982)

Nicolson, Harold, *Diaries and Letters 1930–39* (Collins, 1966)

Nicolson, Harold, *Diaries and Letters 1939–45* (Collins, 1967)

Nicolson, Harold, *Diaries and Letters 1945–62* (Collins, 1968)

O'Brien, Conor Cruise, *Memoirs: My Life and Times* (Profile, 1998)

O'Connor, Ulick, *Brendan Behan* (Hamish Hamilton, 1970)

O'Donovan, Hermione and Kee, Robert (eds.), *Patrick O'Donovan: A Journalist's Odyssey* (Esmonde Publishing, 1985)

Peters, Uwe Henrik, *Anna Freud: A Life Dedicated to Children* (Weidenfeld & Nicolson, 1985)

Pick, Daniel, *The Pursuit of the Nazi Mind: Hitler, Hess and the Analysts* (Oxford University Press, 2012)

Pimlott, Ben (ed.), *The Second World War Diary of Hugh Dalton 1940–1945* (Jonathan Cape, 1986)

Pomian, John (ed.), *Joseph Retinger: Memoirs of an Eminence Grise* (Sussex University Press, 1972)

Pizzey, Erin, *Scream Quietly or the Neighbours Will Hear* (Penguin, 1974)

Pizzey, Erin, *Infernal Child: A Memoir* (Gollancz, 1978)

Pizzey, Erin, *This Way to the Revolution: A Memoir* (Peter Owen, 2011)

Power, Jonathan, *Like Water on Stone: The Story of Amnesty International* (Allen Lane, 2001)

Pringle, John Douglas, *Have Pen, Will Travel* (Chatto & Windus, 1973)

Rhodes James, Robert (ed.), *Chips: The Diaries of Sir Henry Channon* (Weidenfeld & Nicolson, 1967)

Riols, Noreen, *The Secret Ministry of Ag. and Fish: My Life in Churchill's School of Spies* (Macmillan, 2013)

Rolph, C. H., *Further Particulars* (Oxford University Press, 1987)

Rose, Norman, *The Cliveden Set: Portrait of an Exclusive Fraternity* (Jonathan Cape, 2000)

Rose, Peter, *How the Troubles Came to Northern Ireland* (Macmillan, 2000)

Ross, Alan, *Coastwise Lights* (Collins Harvill, 1988)

Ross, Alan, Introduction to Gale, *Clean Young Englishman* (q.v.) (Vintage edn, 1988)

Rowse, A. L., *All Souls and Appeasement* (Macmillan, 1961)

Sampson, Anthony, *The Changing Anatomy of Britain* (Hodder & Stoughton, 1982)

Sampson, Anthony, *Mandela: The Authorised Biography* (HarperCollins, 1999)

Sampson, Anthony, *The Anatomist: Autobiography* (Politico's, 2008)

Sampson, Anthony (ed.), *David Astor: Tributes by Friends and Colleagues on the Occasion of his Eightieth Birthday* (privately printed, 1992)

Saunders, Frances Stonor, *Who Paid the Piper? The CIA and the Cultural Cold War* (Granta, 1999)

Scammell, Michael, *Koestler: The Indispensable Intellectual* (Faber, 2010)

Schofield, Victoria, *Witness to History: The Life of Sir John Wheeler-Bennett* (Yale University Press, 2012)

Seale, Patrick and McConville, Maureen, *Philby: The Long Road to Moscow* (Hamish Hamilton, 1973)

Sears, Kenneth A. G., *Opposing Hitler: Adam von Trott zu Solz 1909–1944* (Sussex Academic Press, 2009)

Shaw, Tony, *Eden, Suez and the Mass Media: Propaganda and Persuasion during the Suez Crisis* (I. B. Tauris, 1996)

Shawcross, William, *Rupert Murdoch: Ringmaster of the Information Circus* (Chatto & Windus, 1992)

Shelden, Michael, *Friends of Promise: Cyril Connolly and the World of Horizon* (Hamish Hamilton, 1989)

Shelden, Michael, *Orwell: The Authorised Biography* (Heinemann, 1991)

Shepherd, Naomi, *Wilfrid Israel: German Jewry's Secret Ambassador* (Weidenfeld & Nicolson, 1984)

Skeaping, John, *Drawn from Life: An Autobiography* (Collins, 1977)

Smith, Adrian, *Mountbatten: Apprentice Warlord* (I. B. Tauris, 2010)

Stanford, Peter, *Lord Longford: A Life* (Heinemann, 1994)

Stanford, Peter, *Bronwen Astor: Her Life and Times* (HarperCollins, 2000)

Stubbs, John, 'Appearance and Reality: A Case Study of the *Observer* and J. L. Garvin' in Boyce, George, Curran, James and Wingate, Pauline (eds.), *Newspaper History from the Seventeenth Century to the Present Day* (Constable, 1978)

Sutherland, John, *Stephen Spender: The Authorised Biography* (Viking, 2004)

Sykes, Christopher, *Troubled Loyalty: A Biography of Adam von Trott* (Collins, 1968)

Sykes, Christopher, *Nancy: The Life of Lady Astor* (Collins, 1972)

Taylor, Geoffrey, *Changing Faces: A History of the Guardian 1956–88* (Fourth Estate, 1993)

Trelford, Donald (ed.), *The Observer at 200* (Quartet, 1992)

Trevor-Roper, Hugh, *The Last Days of Hitler* (Macmillan, 1947)

Trevor-Roper, Hugh, *The Secret World: Behind the Curtain of British Intelligence in World War II and the Cold War* (ed. Edward Harrison, I. B. Tauris, 2014)

Tynan, Kathleen, *The Life of Kenneth Tynan* (Weidenfeld & Nicolson, 1987)

Tynan, Kathleen (ed.), *Kenneth Tynan: Letters* (Weidenfeld & Nicolson, 1994)

Wall, Bernard, *Headlong into Change: An Autobiography and a Memoir of Ideas Since the Thirties* (Harvill, 1969)

Watkins, Alan, *Brief Lives* (Hamish Hamilton, 1982)

Watkins, Alan, *A Short Walk down Fleet Street: From Beaverbrook to Boycott* (Duckworth, 2000)

Waugh, Auberon, *Will This Do? An Autobiography* (Century, 1991)

Weidenfeld, George, *Remembering My Good Friends: An Autobiography* (HarperCollins, 1994)

West, W. J., *Truth Betrayed* (Duckworth, 1987)

Whitehorn, Katharine, *Selective Memory* (Virago, 2007)

Wilford, Hugh, *The CIA, the British Left and the Cold War: Calling the Tune?* (Frank Cass, 2003)

Williams, Francis, *Nothing So Strange: An Autobiography* (Cassell, 1970)

Wintour, Charles, *Pressures on the Press: An Editor Looks at Fleet Street* (André Deutsch, 1974)

Wintour, Charles, *The Rise and Fall of Fleet Street* (Hutchinson, 1989)

Wiskemann, Elizabeth, *The Europe I Saw* (Collins, 1968)

Wood, Barbara, *Alias Papa: A Life of Fritz Schumacher* (Jonathan Cape, 1984)

Woods, Oliver and Bishop, James, *The Story of The Times* (Michael Joseph, 1983)

Woods, Rex, *A Talent to Survive: The Wartime Exploits of Lieutenant Colonel Richard Lowther Broad* (William Kimber, 1982)

Worsthorne, Peregrine, *Tricks of Memory: An Autobiography* (Weidenfeld & Nicolson, 1993)

Yates, Anne and Chester, Lewis, *The Troublemaker: Michael Scott and His Lonely Struggle Against Injustice* (Aurum, 2006)

Young, Gavin, *Worlds Apart: Travels in War and Peace* (Hutchinson, 1987)

Young-Bruehl, Elisabeth, *Anna Freud: A Biography* (Macmillan, 1989)

Ziegler, Philip, *Mountbatten: The Official Biography* (Collins, 1985)

Notes

Where it is obvious who is writing to whom, I have given the date only (or n.d. where unknown), followed by the source from which it is quoted or the collection in which it is to be found. I have used the following abbreviations:

Aberystwyth: the papers of Tom Jones in the National Library of Wales, Aberystwyth
Balliol: the Adam von Trott papers in Balliol College, Oxford
Bodleian: the papers of Isaiah Berlin, William Clark, Lionel Curtis, Arthur Mann, Walter Monckton and Anthony Sampson in the Bodleian Library, Oxford
BH: the David Astor papers in Boodle Hatfield
Georgetown: the Christopher Sykes papers in Georgetown University, Washington DC
HRHRC: the papers of J. L. Garvin in the Harry Ransom Humanities Research Center, University of Texas at Austin
NA: National Archives
Obs. Arch.: Observer Archives
Reading: the papers of Nancy and Waldorf Astor in Reading University
n.d.: no date
p.c.: private collection

Chapter 1: Americans at Large
p. 2 'a predatory, stony-hearted . . .': Kaplan, p. 14.
p. 2 'the Astors toiled not . . .': ibid., p. 120.
p. 2 'America is not . . .': q. in ibid., p. 45.
p. 3 'It is grievous . . .': q. in Norman Rose, p. 13.
p. 3 'as effectively as a ferret . . .': q. in Kaplan, p. 118.
p. 4 'remarkably kind': Grigg, p. 41.
p. 5 'by nature a man . . .': Michael Astor, p. 44.

p. 5 'Like his brother John . . .': Grigg, p. 40.

p. 5 'being American by birth . . .': Michael Astor, p. 47.

p. 5 'Modest, selfless, wise . . .': Thomas Jones, p. xxvi.

p. 5 'really believed that . . .': DA, 'Memoir Material', n.d., BH.

p. 5 'Squire Western': Grigg, p. 16.

p. 6 'I had nothing but a wife . . .': q. in Becker, p. 17.

p. 6 'nothing could be quite as lovely . . .': q. in Fox, p. 9.

p. 6 'She was not particularly . . .': DA, 'Memoir Material', n.d., BH.

p. 7 'strong outspokenness . . .': Becker, p. 13.

p. 7 'The two most important things . . .': q. in Fox, p. 338.

p. 7 'Many people have accused . . .': q. in Sykes, *Nancy*, p. 249.

p. 7 'startling combination . . .': q. in Norman Rose, p. 88.

p. 7 'If there was a nerve . . .': q. in Fox, p. 339.

p. 7 'dynamic, unbalanced . . .': 20.2.40, Rhodes James (ed.), p. 233.

p. 8 'I suppose you've come . . .': q. in Grigg, p. 34.

p. 8 'I came in 1904 not to . . .': q. in Fort, p. 55.

p. 8 'Think of the joy . . .': q. in Grigg, p. 55.

p. 8 'the exuberance of her vitality': q. in Michael Astor, p. 41.

p. 8 'could not rid himself . . .': ibid., p. 48.

p. 9 'We are so knocked out . . .': q. in Fox, p. 271.

p. 9 'I am sorry that Waldorf . . .': q. in Kaplan, p. 172.

Chapter 2: Country House Life

p. 10 'conceived without pleasure . . .': q. in Fox, p. 384.

p. 10 'a perfect nectarine . . .': Lancaster in Sampson (ed.), p. 3.

p. 10 'living in a hotel . . .': q. in Cockett, *David Astor and the Observer*, p. 9.

p. 11 'the epitome . . .': q. in Norman Rose, p. 44.

p. 11 'She is not a lady . . .': ibid., p. 46.

p. 11 'shouted and rampaged . . .': ibid., p. 82.

p. 11 'In that case, Lee . . .': q. in Michael Astor, p. 63.

p. 11 'This house is like . . .': q. in Norman Rose, p. 123.

p. 11 'Two qualities most desirable . . .': Grigg, p. 134.

p. 11 'her sudden wheeling . . .': Fox, p. 2.

p. 12 'As children we were impressed . . .': DA, 'Memoir Material', n.d., BH.

p. 12 'Winston, if I was married . . .': q. in Sykes, *Nancy*, p. 127.

p. 13 'Cliveden to us . . .': MA to DA, 28.6.54, BH.

p. 13 'Oh Phyl . . .': q. in, Fox, p. 366.

p. 13 'shockingly treated': q. in ibid., p. 384.

p. 13 'his conversation is so tinged . . .': 8.1.38, Grenfell, p. 35.

p. 13 'under the impression': MA to DA, 28.6.54, BH.

p. 14 'we used to laugh . . .': MA to DA, 28.6.54, BH.

p. 14 'a power in the house . . .': q. in Norman Rose, p. 113.

p. 14 'a visitor speaking . . .': untitled TS, n.d., BH.

p. 15 'My brother Jakie . . .': Michael Astor, p. 75.

p. 15 'The whole unreality . . .': Grenfell, p. xviii.

p. 15 'Cliveden was never . . .': ibid.

p. 15 'Aunt N made that awful face . . .': ibid., p. 18.

p. 15 'a cold room on top . . .': Jakie Astor in Sampson (ed.), p. 4.

p. 15 'part of the inevitable herd . . .': MA to DA, 28.6.54, BH.

p. 15 'like no other country house . . .': q. in Fox, p. 337.

p. 16 'Lady Astor allotted rooms . . .': Thomas Jones, p. xxxvi.

p. 16 'she had a free hand . . .': ibid., p. xxxvii.

p. 16 'he dominated . . .': ibid., p. xxiv.

p. 17 'I was born into . . .': Michael Astor, p. 3.

p. 17 'it would mean the end . . .': ibid, p. 143.

p. 18 'a mere provincial . . .': Thomas Jones, p. xxi.

p. 18 'a small man . . .': Michael Astor, p. 81.

p. 18 'This is the room . . .': to Stuart Perowne, q. in Fox, p. 94.

p. 18 'cold and draughty . . .': Nicolson, *Diaries and Letters 1930-39*, 29.11.30, p. 60.

p. 19 'Oh my sweet . . .': ibid., 28.6.36, p. 266.

p. 19 'brought us up . . .': q. in Norman Rose, p. 39.

p. 20 'Her visits to the school . . .': DA to West Downs Society, n.d., BH.

p. 20 'He is a very good-natured . . .': winter 1922 school report.

p. 20 'his selfishness . . .': undated school report, Reading.

p. 20 'Wil you be cuming . . .': n.d., BH.

p. 20 'Please! Please! . . .': September 1922, BH.

p. 20 'I can rid your letters . . .': n.d., BH.

p. 20 'short-legged, biggish-headed . . .': DA, 'Memoir Material', n.d., BH.

p. 20 'a rather scrawny . . .': ibid.

p. 20 'A lot of the masters . . .': 12.11.22, BH.

p. 21 'He seems to be a queer . . .': Tindall to WA, n.d., BH.

p. 21 'David's innate kindness . . .': Michael Astor, p. 87.

Chapter 3: Eton and Elsewhere

p. 22 'not sending my own children . . .': DA, 'Memoir Material', n.d., BH.

p. 22 'Well, P. G. Wodehouse . . .': n.d., Reading.

p. 22 'passed in very low': DA, 'Memoir Material', n.d., BH.

p. 22 'rather a nasty bounder . . .': q. in Davenport-Hines, p. 74.

p. 22 'What annoys me . . .': DA to NA, n.d., Reading.

p. 22 'an excellent boy . . .': 8.2.26, BH.

p. 23 'a very loveable . . .': 30.7.26, BH.

p. 23 'altogether too self-satisfied': 4.4.26, BH.

p. 23 'Mr Astor then got up . . .': 1926, Eton Archives.

p. 23 'It takes me two weeks . . .': DA to NA, n.d., Reading.

p. 23 'take to the life . . .': DA, 'Memoir Material', n.d., BH.

p. 23 'rather a despotic manner . . .': 2.2.27, BH.

p. 23 'still think he wants . . .': 27.7.27, BH.

p. 24 'He forgets that he is really English . . .': n.d., Reading.

p. 24 'a bluff codger': DA, 'Memoir Material', n.d., BH.

p. 24 'he also told me that people . . .': q. in Fox, p. 390.

p. 24 'I beat a tug . . .': DA to NA, n.d, Reading.

p. 24 'I am sure you will be cheered . . .': 23.12.28, BH.

p. 24 'His great danger . . .': March 1929, BH.

p. 25 'a boy who does more . . .': July 1930, BH.

p. 25 'saviour': q. in Cockett, *David Astor and the Observer*, p. 26.

p. 25 'I was a struggling schoolboy . . .': Astor and Benson (eds.), p. 15.

p. 25 'invaluable': 27.12.30, BH.

p. 25 'has often been a nuisance . . .': Birley to Rowlatt, 26.3.31, BH.

p. 25 'and I noticed that . . .': DA, 'Memoir Material', n.d., BH.

p. 26 'very useful . . .': q. in Cockett, *David Astor and the Observer*, p. 20.

p. 26 'my possibilities are . . .': ibid., p. 21.

p. 26 'You are lucky enough . . .': q. in Norman Rose, p. 27.

p. 26 'Nobility . . .': ibid, p. 20.

p. 26 'On the surface . . .': DA to NA, n.d., Reading.

p. 26 'one of those awful . . .': DA to NA, 1929, n.d., Reading.

p. 26 'When I see rows . . .': ibid.

p. 27 'I am working hard . . .': DA to NA, n.d., Reading.

p. 27 'By the way, is Henry Ford . . .': DA to NA, n.d., Reading.

p. 27 'more under the influence . . .': Michael Astor, p. 71.

p. 27 'They were not house-trained . . .': ibid.

p. 27 'a bit of a blow . . .': DA to NA, n.d., Reading.

p. 27 'I do miss my beagles . . .': n.d., Reading.

p. 27 'the same diffident smile . . .': Longford, *Avowed Intent*, p. 194.

p. 27 'Astor from the start . . .': 26.3.31.

p. 27 'On paper, of course . . .': q. in Cockett, *David Astor and the Observer*, p. 25.

p. 27 'David has personality . . .': n.d., Reading.

p. 27 'My great regret . . .': DA to NA, n.d., Reading.

p. 28 'I didn't learn much . . .': Marigold Johnson to DA, 11.12.01, BH.

p. 28 'Lindsay the master . . .': DA to NA, n.d., Reading.

p. 28 'much vigour . . .': 20.3.30, Reading.

p. 29 'how we live at Cliveden . . .': DA to Mrs Jones, 19.6.31, Aberystwyth.

p. 29 'Hitler propaganda shop . . .': DA to NA, 19.4.31, BH.

p. 29 'I like these 'ere Germans . . .': n.d., BH.

p. 29 'politics mean something . . .': DA to WA, 6.5.31, BH.

p. 29 'most people salute . . .': DA to NA, 20.6.31, BH.

p. 29 'You were made to feel . . .': q. in Cockett, *David Astor and the Observer*, p. 38.

p. 30 'It's on light, sandy soil . . .': 19.6.31, Aberystwyth.

p. 30 'a stagnant, stinking backwater . . .': 31.7.31, BH.

p. 30 'All this I found . . .': DA, 'Memoir Material', n.d., BH.

p. 30 'die of laughter': 20.6.31, BH.

p. 30 'difficult to allay . . .': ibid.

p. 30 'whacking great . . .': n.d., BH.

p. 31 'food sufficient . . .': q. in Norman Rose, p. 133.

p. 31 'to be sure and keep . . .': *Moscow News*, 28.7.31.

p. 31 'the horses were not third class . . .': WA, diary, 26.7.31, Reading.

p. 31 'well up to Margate . . .': DA to WA and NA, n.d., BH.

p. 32 'I have learned a little patience . . .': n.d., BH.

p. 32 'I think I have become . . .': DA, diary, 15.8.32, BH.

p. 32 'didn't bomb each other's . . .': q. in Fox, p. 425.

p. 33 'tower of strength': q. in Fox, p. 433.

p. 33 'the only way ever . . .': n.d., BH.

Chapter 4: Oxford Blues

p. 34 'I hate the beastly place . . .': q. in *Daily Telegraph* obituary of DA, 8.12.01.

p. 34 'conversational friendships': DA to NA, 22.3.32, BH.

p. 34 'I am not making friends . . .': DA to NA, 11.8.32, BH.

p. 34 'it seems a little too much . . .': n.d., BH.

p. 34 'I did my best . . .': 4.5.64, BH.

p. 35 'temperamentally and to a certain extent . . .': n.d., BH.

p. 35 'although my closest friends . . .': DA, 'Dossier', n.d., BH.

p. 35 'his reporters used to . . .': DA to Christopher Sykes, 22.11.72, BH.

p. 35 'I can't stop . . .': n.d., BH.

p. 35 'the futility of exams . . .': DA, diary, 17.6.32.

p. 35 'getting much fonder of Oxford . . .': 28.5.32, BH.

p. 36 'perfectly miserable . . .': DA, diary, 23.4.32, BH.

p. 36 'absolute disgust . . .': DA, diary, 2.6.32, BH.

p. 36 'a different world . . .': ibid.

p. 36 'I can't face work . . .': ibid.

p. 36 'an unending delight . . .': ibid.

p. 36 'stifled, forced and artificial': DA to NA, n.d., BH.

p. 36 'stuff about unhappiness . . .': 2.5.32, BH.

p. 36 'I do trust . . .': 11.8.32, BH.

p. 36 'Suddenly I woke up . . .': DA, 'Memoir Material', n.d., BH.

p. 37 'He thinks Christian Science . . .': q. in Fox, p. 389.

p. 37 'left a mark': DA, 'Memoir Material', n.d., BH.

p. 37 'I feel frightened . . .': n.d., BH.

p. 37 'permanent undercurrent . . .': n.d., BH.

p. 37 'strong biographical interest . . .': n.d., BH.

p. 37 'an absurd and enervating . . .': 21.1.34., BH.

p. 38 'peace is a thing . . .': n.d., BH.

p. 38 'one of his pleasures . . .': *Balliol College Annual Record*, 2002.

p. 38 'various people who . . .': DA to Collins, 23.6.34, BH.

p. 39 'a kind of self-contempt': q. in Fox, p. 455.

p. 39 'I wish you'd been born . . .': q. in ibid., p. 388.

p. 39 'It was at the onset . . .': Fox, p. 386.

p. 39 'if Nancy Astor's . . .': q. in Michael Astor, p. 44.

p. 39 'My mother would always . . .': q. in Fox, p. 388.

p. 39 'My mother's voice . . .': q. in ibid., p. 387.

p. 39 'I have never felt . . .': 21.5.32, BH.

p. 40 'I am afraid that . . .': n.d., BH.

p. 40 'I know it never entered . . .': n.d., BH.

p. 40 'We are near to . . .': n.d., BH.

p. 40 'taken as an act of defiance . . .': Michael Astor, p. 125.

p. 40 'The boys one moment think . . .': q. in Fox, p. 455.

p. 41 'Your and Papa's visit . . .': n.d., BH.

p. 41 'I've got no friends . . .': n.d., BH.

p. 41 'my mother made it impossible . . .': q. in Fox, p. 389.

p. 41 'My father, who did not share . . .': Michael Astor, p. 126.

p. 41 'stern, benevolent . . .': ibid., p. 119.

p. 41 'Papa leaves me . . .': 7.6.32, BH.

p. 41 'at the end he said . . .': q. in Fox, p. 455.

p. 41 'your revered "mommer" . . .': 18.7.32, BH.

p. 42 'My "story" . . .': n.d., Aberystwyth.

p. 42 'For God's sake, Tom . . .': DA, 'Memoir Material', n.d., BH.

p. 42 'He wants to learn . . .': 28.7.32, BH.

p. 42 'yah yah boy': DA to NA, 2.10.32, BH.

p. 42 'I live in a middle-class . . .': n.d., BH.

p. 42 'long dull days': DA to NA, 14.11.32, BH.

p. 43 'You will be a trifle . . .': 29.11.32, BH.

p. 43 'there is knowledge . . .': 5.11.32, BH.

p. 43 'I am filled . . .': n.d., BH.

p. 43 'we took a bus . . .': WA to Garvin, 13.3.33, BH.

p. 44 'would *willingly* do . . .': DA to NA, n.d., BH.

p. 44 'Glasgow was an attempt . . .': n.d., BH.

p. 44 'I like the little ant-like men . . .': DA to NA, 11.10.32, BH.

p. 44 'the engineering regime . . .': TJ to DA, 30.3.33, Aberystwyth.

Chapter 5: Adam von Trott

p. 45 'charming and sensitive . . .': Rowse, p. 23.

p. 45 'A tall, extremely handsome . . .': Foreign Office report FO371 30912 by 'an Oxford contemporary', n.d., BH.

p. 45 'Adam's whole physical appearance . . .': unpublished memoir of Adam von Trott, n.d., Balliol.

p. 46 'his habitual expression . . .': Diana Hopkinson, p. 96.

p. 46 'immensely lofty forehead . . .': Rowse, p. 93.

p. 46 'We became friends . . .': Berlin, *Flourishing*, p. 718.

p. 46 'found him open . . .': DA to Klemens von Klemperer, 27.5.80, BH.

p. 46 'he was deeply German . . .': q. in MacDonogh, p. 38.

p. 46 'he was a person of . . .': q. in Sykes, *Troubled Loyalty*, p. 59.

p. 46 'Much as he enjoyed . . .': q. in Cockett, *David Astor and the Observer*, p. 42.

p. 46 'a heavy and obscure manner': q. in Sykes, *Troubled Loyalty*, p. 75.

p. 46 'Adam contributed . . .': Diana Hopkinson, p. 89.

p. 47 'a fluent Hegelian . . .': Bowra, p. 305.

p. 47 'loathed Hegelianism . . .': Rowse, p. 94.

p. 47 'seems absolute gibberish . . .': Berlin to Morton White, 21.4.58, *Enlightening*, p. 263.

p. 47 'had a great way with women . . .': Foreign Office report FO371 30912 by 'an Oxford contemporary', n.d., BH.

p. 47 'my alter ego . . .': n.d., BH.

p. 47 'To me he was a teacher . . .': q. in Cockett, *David Astor and the Observer*, p. 42.

p. 47 'My admiration of Adam . . .': unsent letter, n.d., BH.

p. 47 'a sense of power . . .': 'Notes on von Trott', 19.11.46, BH.

p. 48 'a charm and a sense of humour . . .': 1943 Foreign Office report FO371 344449.

p. 48 'a socialist (by conviction) . . .': 'Notes on von Trott', n.d., BH.

p. 48 'in a bad way politically . . .': 28.3.32, Balliol.

p. 48 'he knew at once . . .': 'Notes on von Trott', n.d., BH.

p. 48 'My country is very sick . . .': Berlin, *Flourishing*, p. 718.

p. 48 'gloom, tempered by challenge': Bull (ed.), p. 18.

p. 49 'What personally I fear . . .': 1.4.33, Balliol.

p. 49 'deeply and thoroughly . . .': q. in Cockett, *David Astor and the Observer*, p. 43.

p. 49 'very much involved with . . .': DA to Klemens von Klemperer, 27.5.80, BH.

p. 49 'confused and therefore . . .': Berlin to Sykes, 7.7.65, BH.

p. 49 'Adam entered deeply . . .': Rowse, p. 96.

p. 49 'He was absolutely clear . . .': unpublished memoir of Trott, n.d., Balliol.

p. 50 'his special way . . .': Diana Hopkinson, p. 111.

p. 50 'David is a strange character . . .': November 1933, Balliol.

p. 50 'he says its disadvantages . . .': 24.10.33, Balliol.

p. 50 'a great relief': q. in Cockett, *David Astor and the Observer*, p. 33.

p. 50 'a fairly regular episode . . .': Sam Beer to Bridget Astor, 11.12.01, BH.

p. 50 'half in love': DA 1932 diary, n.d., BH.

p. 51 'the most enchanting . . .': q. in Hayward, p. 150.

p. 51 'the place above all others . . .': q. in ibid., p. 42.

p. 51 'David Astor and a pal . . .': q. in ibid., p. 189.

p. 51 'garden going down . . .': 20.11.33, Balliol.

p. 51 'the most romantic house . . .': Diana Hopkinson, p. 117.

p. 51 'reddish hair . . .': Hubback to Trott, 20.11.33, Balliol.

p. 52 'very easy to talk to': ibid.

p. 52 'very pink cheeks . . .': ibid.

p. 52 'lovely dream': Hubback to Trott, 16.1.34, Balliol.

p. 52 'He is so simple . . .': Hubback to Trott, 29.1.34, Balliol.

p. 52 'I become fonder . . .': Hubback to Trott, 6.2.34, Balliol.

p. 52 'the most beautiful new car': Hubback to Trott, 26.2.34, Balliol.

p. 52 'If you knew my feeling for you . . .': 2.3.34, Balliol.

p. 53 'I am sure David . . .': 7.3.34, Balliol.

p. 53 'Don't worry about David . . .': n.d., Balliol.

p. 53 'broken the spell': 21.2.34, Balliol.

p. 53 'I don't think David does . . .': Hubback to Trott, 26.2.34, Balliol.

p. 53 'he seemed of a very different . . .': Hubback to Trott, 30.4.34, Balliol.

p. 53 'He looked very beautiful . . .': 28.6.34, Balliol.

p. 54 'I heard from Shaya . . .': Hubback to Trott, 20.12.34, Balliol.

Chapter 6: In Limbo

p. 55 'selfish withdrawal . . .': DA to Marion Doenhoff, 20.10.49, BH.

p. 55 'David, guided by . . .': Michael Astor, p. 123.

p. 55 'I have been brought up . . .': n.d., BH.

p. 56 'I can hardly believe . . .': 7.7.34, BH.

p. 56 'Why that woman . . .': 10.7.34, BH.

p. 56 'hellish stupid . . .': 26.3.34, BH.

p. 56 'it's not much fun . . .': 14.8.34, BH.

p. 56 'the Langhorne imitative . . .': Grenfell, p. 19.

p. 56 'at that time . . .': DA, 'Memoir Material', n.d., BH.

p. 56 'If I had Randolph . . .': n.d. 1934, Aberystwyth.

p. 56 'settle in America . . .': ibid.

p. 57 'Our talks about the future . . .': 5.10.34, HRHRC.

p. 57 'He is as kind . . .': Thomas Jones, 28.7.36, p. 232.

p. 57 'there were enough nasty things . . .': DA to NA, n.d., BH.

p. 57 'You keep saying . . .': 1.11.35, BH.

p. 57 'You suffer from disappointment . . .': ibid.

p. 57 'otherwise I would have felt . . .': DA to NA, n.d., BH.

p. 57 'My parents were alone . . .': untitled TS, n.d., BH.

p. 57 'So you're the wild man . . .': q. in Fox, p. 338.

p. 58 'invited me to work . . .': 1.10.34, BH.

p. 58 'It feels queer . . .': DA to Collins, 25.3.35, BH.

p. 58 'I got to know a bit . . .': DA, 'Memoir Material', n.d., BH.

p. 58 'most mysterious . . .': n.d., BH.

p. 58 'he said he was doing excellently . . .': Brand to WA, 2.3.35, BH.

p. 58 'I greatly admired . . .': DA, 'Memoir Material', n.d., BH.

p. 58 'consulting physician . . .': 21.10.36, Aberystwyth.

p. 58 'young millionaire's case . . .': Garnett to TJ, 2.11.36, Aberystwyth.

p. 59 'a bit shy about . . .': WA to Garvin, 8.3.35, HRHRC.

p. 59 'I at one time had hoped . . .': 4.3.36, HRHRC.

p. 59 'Now that Bill Astor . . .': Thomas Jones, 14.1.36, p. 161.

p. 59 'his father has hopes . . .': 27.10.36, Aberystwyth.

p. 59 'I am afraid we could not . . .': 29.3.37, BH.

p. 60 'I am slightly less . . .': DA to NA, 14.6.37, BH.

p. 60 'quiet round . . .': DA to NA, 16.6.37, BH.

p. 60 'spoke very highly': WA to Garvin, 29.11.37, HRHRC.

p. 60 'cornered them by . . .': DA to NA, n.d., BH.

p. 60 'I am not so mad . . .': 22.11.37, BH.

p. 61 'instead of permanently . . .': DA to NA, n.d., BH.

p. 61 'I often feel inclined . . .': ibid.

p. 61 'Do let me know . . .': 8.11.37, HRHRC.

p. 61 'He feels that . . .': 29.11.37, HRHRC.

p. 61 'Arthur Mann told me . . .': 6.12.37, HRHRC.

p. 61 'the past two or three years . . .': ibid.

p. 62 'One of these days . . .': DA to Charles Collins, 15.3.34, BH.

p. 62 'The boy has the mother's gift . . .': Thomas Jones, 28.4.34, p. 129.

p. 62 'for a man of just on seventy . . .': q. in Ayerst, p. 238.

p. 62 'so powerful . . .': Brown, *Old and Young*, p. 130.

p. 63 'He was generous in praise . . .': Brown, *The Way of My World*, p. 285.

p. 63 'never felt wholly at ease . . .': Lejeune, p. 134.

p. 63 'It was Garvin's habit . . .': ibid., p. 133.

p. 63 'Intended by nature . . .': Brown, *The Way of My World*, p. 288.

p. 63 'a kind but sad . . .': Lejeune, p. 132.

p. 64 'a sort of defensive . . .': ibid., p. 209.

p. 64 'in strict confidence . . .': 22.11.37, BH.

p. 64 'he got to know . . .': WA to Garvin, December 1938, HRHRC.

p. 64 'doing nothing more world-shaking . . .': DA to Christopher Sykes, 27.10.67, BH.

p. 64 'He is finding it . . .': 9.6.38, HRHRC.

p. 64 'as dull as a railway . . .': DA to NA, n.d., BH.

Chapter 7: The Cliveden Set

p. 65 'It is an extraordinary thing . . .': q. in Fox, p. 507.

p. 66 'a haunting, even alarming . . .': DA, 'Memoir Material', n.d., BH.

p. 66 'a visitor was speaking . . .': untitled TS, n.d., BH.

p. 66 'when it seemed to be . . .': ibid.

p. 66 'In twenty years . . .': q. in Norman Rose, p. 171.

p. 67 'The general impression here . . .': WA to Garvin, 28.3.33, HRHRC.

p. 67 'I detest the Nazi . . .': n.d., HRHRC.

p. 67 'I came out of Germany . . .': WA report on visit to Germany, n.d., HRHRC.

p. 67 'rushing about like . . .': Rhodes James (ed.), 24.2.36, p. 313.

p. 67 'To my regret . . .': untitled TS, n.d., BH.

p. 67 'as long as he wears . . .': q. in Cockett, *David Astor and the Observer*, p. 40.

p. 67 'completely flummoxed': ibid.

p. 67 'a great busybody . . .': Rowse, p. 35.

p. 67 'TJ's daily dose . . .': ibid., p. 39.

p. 67 'disastrous': WA report on visit to Germany, n.d., HRHRC.

p. 67 'an old lawyer . . .': Rowse, p. 35.

p. 68 'repulsive cruelty . . .': q. in Ayerst, p. 243.

p. 68 'unless Hitlerism . . .': May 1933, q. in ibid., p. 245.

p. 68 'this new barbarism . . .': Garvin to WA, September 1936, q. in Morris, p. 33.

p. 69 'extreme right-wing faction . . .': Rose, p. 179.

p. 69 'how terrible has been . . .': Nicolson, *Diaries and Letters 1930–39*, 19.9.38, p. 361.

p. 69 'a kindly but . . .': ibid., 10.4.38, p. 396.

p. 69 'the monster I had let loose': Claud Cockburn, p. 180.

p. 69 'There was no such thing . . .': Douglas-Home, p. 112.

p. 70 'ex-furriers . . .': q. in Patricia Cockburn, p. 237.

p. 70 'Resign! . . .': n.d., BH.

p. 70 'mischievous rubbish': q. in Norman Rose, p. 181.

p. 70 'I distrusted Ribbentrop . . .': NA to Isobel Keith, 15.11.38, Reading.

p. 70 'disquietude which . . .': 7.4.38, BH.

p. 70 'the last rag . . .': *Observer*, 19.3.39; q. in Morris, p. 160

p. 71 'the only member . . .': Michael Astor, p. 147.

p. 71 'Thank God people . . .': DA to NA, 19.9.38, BH.

p. 71 'The English attitude . . .': n.d., BH.

p. 71 'I can't help smiling . . .': DA to NA, 24.9.38, BH.

p. 71 'the ideas people hold about him . . .': DA to NA, 5.10.38, BH.

p. 71 'I think we are going . . .': 8.10.38, BH.

p. 71 'you'd think they were about . . .': DA to NA, 3.10.38, BH.

p. 71 'I always told you . . .': n.d., BH.

p. 71 'It astonishes me . . .': 15.3.39, Aberystwyth.

p. 71 'my parents made some attempt . . .': untitled TS, n.d., BH.

p. 71 'the point that is hardest . . .': ibid.

p. 72 'The daily press . . .': 30.8.38, q. in Cockett, 'The Government, the Press and Politics in Britain, 1937 to 1945'.

Chapter 8: Gravitas

p. 74 'regarded criticism . . .': Grant Duff, p. 58.

p. 74 'some English friends . . .': q. in Mitchell, p. 215.

p. 74 'sorry my little Trott . . .': Trott to Shiela Grant Duff, March 1937, in Klemperer, p. 218.

p. 75 'he excused . . .': Grant Duff, p. 58.

p. 75 'messenger': DA to Christopher Sykes, 27.10.67, BH.

p. 76 'nationalism which Hitler . . .': DA to Christophor Sykes, 18.12.67, BH.

p. 76 'Germany must be surrounded . . .': Berlin, *Flourishing*, p. 719.

p. 76 'he came to London . . .': untitled notes, 14.4.91, BH.

p. 76 'to feel at home again . . .': 15.2.39, BH.

p. 76 'a young German called Trott': Douglas-Home, p. 113.

p. 76 'when he had finished . . .': ibid., p. 114.

p. 77 'of whispers among . . .': DA to Christopher Sykes, q. in Sykes, *Troubled Loyalty*, p. 246.

p. 77 'It is quite obvious . . .': 20.4.39, HRHRC.

p. 77 'an engaging young man . . .': Lord Home to DA, 19.5.71, BH.

p. 77 'very old and tired man . . .': q. in Cockett, *David Astor and the Observer*, p. 52.

p. 77 'has already decided . . .': Thomes Jones, 6.6.39, p. 436.

p. 77 'deliberate flattery': DA, 'Von Trott's Mission', *Manchester Guardian*, 4.6.56.

p. 77 'Hitlerian prose': DA in Bull (ed.), p. 27.

p. 77 'He discussed these tactics . . .': DA, 'Von Trott's Mission', *Manchester Guardian*, 4.6.56.

p. 77 'The incipient change . . .': 11.6.39, q. in Langbehn, p. 130.

p. 78 'genial, blunt individual': DA in Bull (ed.), p. 25.

p. 78 'overrun the wheat-growing . . .' DA, 'confidential' note, n.d., BH.

p. 78 'bloody cheek': notes from John Silverlight's conversations with DA, n.d., BH.

p. 78 'gross treasonable disloyalty': q. in Meehan, p. 205.

p. 78 'That I, who was Mr Nobody . . .': DA to Christopher Sykes, 17.6.66, BH.

p. 79 'I suspect that we are enemies . . .': Grant Duff, p. 204.

p. 79 'In so far as I became . . .': n.d., April 1969, BH.

p. 79 'could take neither Ripka . . .': Grant Duff, p. 210.

p. 80 'rush against the process . . .': Sykes, *Troubled Loyalty*, p. 265.

p. 80 'an ambitious, fascinating . . .': q. in Ignatieff, p. 76.

p. 80 'he may have felt doubtful . . .': Berlin, *Flourishing*, p. 719.

p. 80 'I was not sure that . . .': Rowse, p. 96.

p. 80 'I was very glad to see him . . .': Bowra, p. 305.

p. 80 'playing a double game': q. in Mitchell, p. 306.

p. 80 'soon became known . . .': Bowra, p. 306.

p. 81 'the worst thing he asked me to do . . .': DA to Christopher Sykes, 27.10.67, BH.

p. 81 'duped Nazi friend . . .': DA to 'Nicholas', 12.11.45, BH.

p. 81 'strong-willed, stubborn . . .': DA, draft letter to 'Ben', n.d., BH.

p. 81 'gives the impression . . .': 14.7.39, BH.

p. 82 'fantastic, almost Philby-like . . .': DA to Christopher Sykes, 27.10.67, BH.

p. 82 'tall, fair-haired . . .': Bielenberg, *The Road Ahead*, p. 53.

p. 82 'He paints a frightening . . .': 1.6.39, HRHRC.

p. 82 'a well-armed gangster . . .': DA to Lord Halifax, 9.7.39, BH.

p. 83 'rather woolly': q. in Cockett, *David Astor and the Observer*, p. 55.

p. 83 'if we have a war then . . .': q. in Sykes, *Troubled Loyalty*, p. 272.

p. 83 'but I doubt whether . . .': 31.7.39, BH.

p. 83 'Peter was very disgusted . . .': DA to Trott, 20.10.39, BH.

p. 83 'Whatever happens to you and me . . .': 24.8.39, q. in Sykes, *Troubled Loyalty*, p. 285.

p. 83 'the amateurishness of Trott's . . .': DA to J. R. M. Butler, 16.1.59, BH.

p. 83 'our mutual friend': 7.10.39, BH.

p. 83 'That you are in America . . .': 20.10.39, BH.

p. 84 'your usefulness . . .': 10.11.39, BH.

p. 84 'you have exerted your influence . . .': 22.11.39, BH.

p. 84 'During the summer I seem . . .': 26.12.39, BH.

p. 84 'derived considerable comfort . . .': ibid.

p. 84 'present struggle . . .': q. in Schofield, p. 122.

p. 84 'should be very carefully . . .': ibid., p. 123.

p. 84 'a very subtle agent . . .': Foreign Office report FO 371 344449, 1943.

p. 85 'If you feel your channel . . .': 26.12.39, BH.

p. 85 'It is extraordinary . . .': 6.7.39, HRHRC.

p. 85 'the future of the *Observer* . . .': 6.6.39, HRHRC.

p. 85 'I am most anxious . . .': 8.6.39, HRHRC.

p. 85 'He has been a slow developer . . .': 21.6.39, HRHRC.

p. 85 'such an exalted position . . .': n.d., HRHRC.

p. 85 'a feature which . . .': DA to Garvin, 3.5.39, HRHRC.

p. 85 'getting some experience . . .': 21.6.39, HRHRC.

p. 85 'I dread London . . .': n.d., BH.

p. 86 'I am proposing to give David . . .': 31.7.39, HRHRC.

Chapter 9: Frustration

p. 87 'military operations play . . .': Haffner, *Offensive Against Germany*, p. 16.

p. 88 'our established institutions . . .': DA, notes, n.d., BH.

p. 89 'stillborn department . . .': DA, TS of 'The Need', n.d., BH.

p. 89 'one can't imagine . . .': DA to Garvin, 4.7.41, BH.

p. 89 'cogent in argument . . .': 9.9.39, Aberystwyth.

p. 89 'a faith that what is . . .': DA to TJ, 9.9.39, BH.

p. 90 'second-rate': DA to Samuel Hoare, 2.11.39, BH.

p. 90 'our propaganda in German . . .': DA to Stafford Cripps, 10.11.39, BH.

p. 90 'a lack of a policy . . .': 25.11.39, BH.

p. 90 'the best person . . .': DA to WA, 13.11.39, BH.

p. 90 'suggestions for dealing with . . .': 19.1.40, BH.

p. 91 'an anti-Nazi attitude . . .': DA to F. W. Ogilvie, 5.6.39, BH.

p. 91 'David is said to be doing . . .': Grenfell, p. 109.

p. 91 'I am going to Holland . . .': 6.10.39, BH.

p. 91 'the worst soldier . . .': DA to NA, n.d., BH.

p. 92 'It is amazing being here . . .': n.d., BH.

p. 92 'I feel like a frightened child . . .': DA, diary, 31.3.40, BH.

p. 92 'a gangster style of fighting': DA, notes on Marine Smith, n.d., BH.

p. 92 '*Personally* I am anti-militarist . . .': 14.6.41, BH.

p. 92 'become interested in the enemy . . .': DA, memo, n.d., BH.

p. 92 'It's clerical work . . .': n.d., BH.

p. 93 'whiskered, hard-skulled . . .': DA to NA, n.d., BH.

p. 93 'swilling beer': DA to NA, 25.2.41, BH.

p. 93 'a simpleton straight . . .': n.d., BH.

p. 93 'I hope, dear Ma . . .': 18.6.40, BH.

p. 93 'I need your help . . .': 28.1.41, BH.

p. 93 'maimed by my early . . .': ibid.

p. 93 'khaki confinement': DA to NA, n.d., BH.

p. 93 'I know your minister . . .': 10.8.41, BH.

p. 93 'determined to fight . . .': DA to TJ, n.d., Aberystwyth.

p. 93 'Will my luck never change . . .': DA to TJ, n.d., 1941, Aberystwyth.

p. 94 'I hope I shall get a chance . . .': DA to NA, 12.11.40, BH.

p. 94 'How can we hope . . .': DA to TJ, 3.2.41, Aberystwyth.

p. 94 'It's not only boredom . . .': DA to NA, n.d., BH.

p. 94 'a mental hurricane . . .': TJ to Dr Carl Lambert, 7.2.41, Aberystwyth.

p. 94 'a backwoodsman subaltern . . .': DA to Garvin, n.d., HRHRC.

p. 94 'elderly men to whom . . .': DA, TS of 'The Need', n.d., BH.

p. 94 'our cause is so much more . . .': DA to NA, n.d., BH.

p. 94 'Baldwinish inactivity . . .': DA to NA, n.d., BH.

p. 94 'attempting to fight this war . . .': DA to TJ, 21.5.41, Aberystwyth.

p. 94 'direct defiance of Hitler's . . .': DA, TS of 'The Need', n.d., BH.

p. 94 'since 1931 . . .': n.d., BH.

p. 95 'I feel we should have been . . .': Tony Simpson to DA, 30.6.41, BH.

p. 95 'news and accounts . . .': TS, n.d., BH.

p. 95 'not far removed from . . .': 18.11.41, BH.

p. 95 'it had long been troubling me . . .': DA to Geoffrey Dawson, 22.6.41, BH.

p. 96 'impossibility of getting . . .': 21.6.41, BH.

p. 96 'I have been seriously thinking . . .': 2.12.41, BH.

p. 96 'become meaningless . . .': DA to TJ, 26.11.40, Aberystwyth.

p. 97 'the most promising person . . .': DA to WA, 20.6.41, BH.

p. 97 'Please mention me . . .': 14.6.41, BH.

p. 97 'These young people . . .': 30.6.41, q. in Bryant, p. 267.

p. 97 'very discreetly trying . . .': DA to WA, 13.10.41, Aberystwyth.

p. 97 'a magnificent cold buffet': Williams, p. 160.

p. 97 'an intellectual manqué . . .': ibid., p. 159.

p. 97 'an intrepid idealist': DA to Stafford Cripps, 19.6.41, BH.

p. 97 'I was pleasantly surprised . . .': n.d., BH.

p. 97 'little skill as . . .': Williams, p. 159.

p. 97 'vitiated by the presidency . . .': 19.6.41, BH.

p. 97 'the dominance of its antique . . .': 21.4.41, BH.

p. 97 'cranks and doctrinaire . . .': n.d., BH.

Chapter 10: Regime Change

p. 99 'taking David leftwards . . .': q. in Ellis, p. 464.

p. 99 'she can't believe . . .': ibid.

p. 99 'this national newspaper . . .': DA in conversation with John Silverlight, n.d., BH.

p. 99 'not possible to edit . . .': n.d., BH.

p. 99 'it seemed perfectly clear . . .': ibid.

p. 100 'I know we are crowded . . .': 12.5.41, HRHRC.

p. 100 'spent a sleepless Saturday night . . .': WA to Garvin, 26.5.41, HRHRC.

p. 100 'There is a lot of sound sense . . .': 29.7.41, BH.

p. 101 'raised its prestige . . .': 21.1.41, HRHRC.

p. 101 'almost powerless . . .': n.d., February 1941, BH.

p. 101 'You can imagine . . .': 26.3.41, HRHRC.

p. 101 'attack the unimaginative . . .': 6.7.41, Aberystwyth.

p. 101 'should deal in the name . . .': 25.8.41, BH.

p. 102 'carpers, crabbers . . .': in 'Notebook 78', HRHRC.

p. 102 'I have a feeling . . .': n.d., Reading.

p. 102 'I am terribly proud . . .': n.d., BH.

p. 102 'the gradual changeover . . .': DA to TJ, 19.12.40, Aberystwyth.

p. 102 'if I fail, it will . . .': n.d., Reading.

p. 102 'Garve is a wicked . . .': n.d., Aberystwyth.

p. 102 'whether you like them . . .': n.d., July 1941, BH.

p. 103 'Garve, you'll be surprised . . .': 27.8.41, BH.

p. 103 'David has not had . . .': WA to TJ, 8.8.41, Aberystwyth.

p. 103 'I always find talks . . .': n.d., HRHRC.

p. 103 'standing in the way . . .': 16.2.41, Aberystwyth.

p. 103 'impossible to achieve . . .': 8.5.41, Aberystwyth.

p. 103 'a phone call to Roosevelt . . .': WA to Garvin, 14.5.41, HRHRC.

p. 103 'His mind is merely interested . . .': WA to Garvin, 3.5.41, HRHRC.

p. 104 'it is not friendship . . .': 31.7.41, HRHRC.

p. 104 'it would take a lot more than . . .': 4.11.41, HRHRC.

p. 104 'crook-proof . . .': q. in Ellis, p. 449.

p. 105 'any new Anglo-Saxon . . .': draft document on Observer Trust, n.d., BH.

p. 105 'because he finds the strain . . .': 28.8.41, HRHRC.

p. 105 'old megalomaniac': DA to TJ, 8.5.41, Aberystwyth.

p. 105 'My father must have . . .': 29.11.41, Aberystwyth.

p. 105 'mesmeric spell': DA to TJ, 16.3.41, Aberystwyth.

p. 105 'Until my father decides . . .': 8.5.41, Aberystwyth.

p. 105 'bombarded overwhelmingly': DA to TJ, 19.2.41, BH.

p. 105 'I somehow think . . .': DA to TJ, 30.8.41, Aberystwyth.

p. 105 'though he has now . . .': 21.7.41, Aberystwyth.

p. 106 'I confess I am very . . .': DA to NA, n.d., BH.

p. 106 'we both agreed that . . .': 10.7.41, BH.

p. 106 'Northcliffe himself . . .': Garvin to WA, 25.8.41, HRHRC.

p. 106 'the creator and organiser . . .': Garvin to DA, 25.8.41, BH.

p. 106 'an insult . . .': Garvin to WA, 14.8.41, Reading.

p. 106 'a sixth sense . . .': Garvin to WA, 1.9.41, Reading.

p. 106 'life-connection': Garvin, memo, 25.11.41, BH.

p. 106 'I shall not reply . . .': 18.8.41, HRHRC.

p. 106 'vainglorious oratory': Dawson, diary, 26.11.41, q. in Cockett, 'The Government, the Press and Politics in Britain, 1937 to 1945'.

p. 106 'must be decided . . .': WA to Garvin, 12.9.41, Reading.

p. 107 'vigour in writing': WA, memo, 23.11.41, BH.

p. 107 'If Mr Garvin were to continue . . .': WA to Lewis & Lewis, solicitors, 27.9.41, BH.

p. 107 'I feel very strongly . . .': 3.9.41, Mann papers, Bodleian.

p. 107 'we should thank God . . .': Garvin submission to tribunal, BH.

p. 107 'As addressed to him . . .': *Observer*, 22.2.42.

p. 107 'Article today runs . . .': 22.2.42, BH.

p. 107 'gone up in smoke': q. in Cockett, 'The Government, the Press and Politics in Britain, 1937 to 1945', p. 210.

p. 107 'I am going to appear . . .': q. in Garvin, p. 132.

p. 107 'The paper he had made . . .': ibid.

p. 108 'happy memories': Bill Astor to Garvin, n.d., HRHRC.

Chapter 11: Filling the Void

p. 109 'Whereas under JLG . . .': 20.10.42, Reading.

p. 109 'character, cutting edge . . .': DA to TJ, 29.3.42, Aberystwyth.

p. 109 'tackling awkward subjects . . .': DA to Arthur Mann, 19.6.42, Mann papers, Bodleian.

p. 109 'My father agrees . . .': ibid.

p. 110 'I do not want the public . . .': WA to TJ, 17.2.43, BH.

p. 110 'the real danger . . .': WA to Arthur Mann, 3.9.42, Mann papers, Bodleian.

p. 110 'seventy per cent . . .': 7.5.42, BH.

p. 110 'the more they are signed . . .': WA, memo, 4.5.42, BH.

p. 110 'I feel it is more . . .': n.d., BH.

p. 110 'Since the Observer . . .': Harris, Life So Far, p. 269.

p. 110 'disappointing': WA to TJ, 10.6.42, Aberystwyth.

p. 110 'the office team . . .': WA to Arthur Mann, n.d., BH.

p. 110 'I could not agree . . .': WA to TJ, 10.6.42, Aberystwyth.

p. 111 'one of my tasks . . .': IB to Arthur Mann, 5.10.42, Mann papers, Bodleian.

p. 111 'awfully nice . . .': WA to TJ, 12.2.43, Reading.

p. 111 'IB has done very well . . .': 10.11.42, Aberystwyth.

p. 111 'too light-hearted': DA to IB, 8.11.42, BH.

p. 111 'make the paper flat . . .': 26.5.44, Aberystwyth.

p. 111 'The news is so important . . .': WA to IB, 9.11.42, BH.

p. 111 'leaders on the hardships . . .': DA to TJ, 20.2.45, Aberystwyth.

p. 111 'neither a competent . . .': DA, memo to WA and TJ, n.d., BH.

p. 111 'it's rather like . . .': DA in conversation with John Silverlight, n.d., BH.

p. 112 'not a party paper': Observer, 1.11.42.

p. 112 'May I sing . . .': DA to IB, 29.11.42, BH.

p. 112 'because he is an effete . . .': DA to IB, 11.12.42, BH.

p. 112 'clarity, tact . . .': DA to TJ, 9.12.42, BH.

p. 112 'a sulky face . . .': 27.3.43, Aberystwyth.

p. 112 'an old-fashioned liberal . . .': DA to TJ, 9.12.42, BH.

p. 113 'You are the person . . .': n.d., BH.

p. 113 'I have chosen YOU . . .': q. in Lewis, p. 372.

p. 114 'militant atheist': 3.7.42, BH.

p. 114 'You'll have to bear . . .': 1.7.42, BH.

p. 114 'completely unknown . . .': WA to TJ, 4.11.42, Aberystwyth.

p. 114 'beginning to look "period" . . .': IB to TJ, 2.2.43, Aberystwyth.

p. 114 'so consciously fastidious . . .': q. in Lewis, p. 372.

p. 114 'If we are literary . . .': ibid.

p. 114 'stand any nonsense from . . .': q. in ibid., p. 371.

p. 114 'I don't feel Connolly . . .': DA, memo to WA and TJ, n.d., BH.

p. 114 'monologue of misrepresentations . . .': 17.8.43, BH.

p. 114 'My mistake with you . . .': n.d., BH.

p. 114 'My little olive branch . . .': n.d., BH.

p. 115 'his somewhat middle-aged . . .': DA, memo to WA and TJ, n.d., BH.

p. 115 'as in his politics . . .': DA to TJ, 27.11.42, Aberystwyth.

p. 115 'feeling slightly sulky . . .': DA to TJ, 12.1.43, Aberystwyth.

p. 115 'You have just flown . . .': 22.2.43, BH.

p. 115 'expects to be directed . . .': q. in Lewis, p. 374.

p. 115 'I regret the switch . . .': 4.3.43, BH.

p. 115 'You have frequently tried . . .': 20.8.43, BH.

p. 116 'felt I had known . . .': DA interview with Richard Keeble, 20.1.00, BH.

p. 116 'I didn't think of him . . .': ibid.

p. 116 'I admit he needs . . .': 22.11.42, BH.

p. 116 'I don't write for papers . . .': q. in Shelden, *Orwell*, p. 104.

p. 116 'give pain to . . .': 16.10.44, BH.

p. 116 'a lack of drive . . .': DA to WA, 25.7.43, BH.

p. 117 'He can deal with our aliens . . .': 15.5.44, Aberystwyth.

p. 117 'the most valuable man we have . . .': n.d., BH.

p. 117 'definitely excluded me . . .': ibid.

p. 117 'it's a bit much . . .': DA to TJ, 25.3.44, Aberystwyth.

p. 117 'I'm hoping your wizardry . . .': n.d., Aberystwyth.

p. 117 'unmeasured criticism . . .': 6.4.44, BH.

p. 117 'brought strength and precision . . .': TJ to DA, n.d., BH.

p. 118 'a great comforter': Brown, *The Way of My World*, p. 291.

p. 118 'I trotted these people . . .': DA in conversation with John Silverlight, n.d., BH.

p. 118 'a load of mischief . . .': IB to TJ, 15.5.44, Aberystwyth.

p. 118 'could be made to *look* . . .': TJ to DA, 6.4.44, BH.

p. 118 'I owe my original . . .': 5.5.53, BH.

p. 118 'Without you . . .': 25.2.51, BH.

p. 119 'any statesmanship . . .': 17.6.43, Aberystwyth.

p. 119 'torn between love . . .': q. in Dudley Edwards, *The Pursuit of Reason*, p. 754.

p. 119 'Moscow messing up . . .': 27.5.43, BH.

p. 119 'politically I have always . . .': 7.1.44, Aberystwyth.

p. 119 'a deeply civilised . . .': DA in Servob, 28.12.75, BH.

p. 120 'rather shattered': 18.4.44, Aberystwyth.

p. 120 'giving him to understand . . .': ibid.

p. 120 'grovelled': q. in DA to TJ, 26.5.44, BH.

p. 120 'I despair of IB . . .': 26.5.44, Aberystwyth.

p. 121 'the one essential piece . . .': q. in Wood, p. 158.

p. 121 'surrounded by prima donnas . . .': Frankland, p. 211.

p. 121 'Haffner was liberating . . .': q. in Cockett, *David Astor and the Observer*, p. 96.

p. 121 'the flagship of the new European . . .': Weidenfeld, p. 126.

p. 121 'jealously guarded . . .': ibid., p. 127.

p. 122 'he is a progressive . . .': 10.4.42, Aberystwyth.

p. 122 'declined the offer . . .': 2.8.77, BH.

p. 122 'the Balliol I never had': q. in Cockett, *David Astor and the Observer*, p. 136.

p. 122 'becoming too like . . .': IB to WA, 2.9.44, BH.

p. 122 'you can be spotting . . .': n.d., BH.

p. 123 'I hope we may come . . .': 12.5.42, Aberystwyth.

p. 123 'his friends and mine . . .': n.d., BH.

p. 123 'David was slow . . .': WA to TJ, 21.2.43, Aberystwyth.

p. 123 'very uneasy . . .': 9.12.42, Aberystwyth.

p. 123 'he merely backed up . . .': DA, 'Bill's Complaints', n.d., BH.

p. 124 'promptly got truculent . . .': DA to TJ, 19.2.43, Aberystwyth.

p. 124 'the name Astor . . .': DA to IB, 22.11.42, BH.

p. 124 'What upsets me . . .': 7.4.43, Aberystwyth.

p. 124 'Bill remains a slight . . .': 17.6.43, Aberystwyth.

p. 124 'David is full of . . .': 3.2.43, Aberystwyth.

p. 124 'I am anxious that . . .': 27.5.43, BH.

p. 125 'a strong and positive foreign . . .': DA to IB, 27.5.43, BH.

p. 125 'a progressive, constructive policy . . .': DA to WA, 10.8.45, BH.

p. 125 'too apt to feel . . .': WA to TJ, 4.5.44, Aberystwyth.

p. 125 'an absurdly youthful . . .': Pringle, p. 137.

p. 125 'is the only newspaper . . .': 14.11.44, BH.

p. 125 'it has been a mistake . . .': DA to TJ, 26.5.44, Aberystwyth.

Chapter 12: Man at Arms

p. 126 'I am very anxious . . .': 11.3.42, BH.

p. 126 'blue-pencilled': DA, note, July 1942, BH.

p. 126 'written without an understanding . . .': ibid.

p. 126 'I wish I was doing . . .': n.d., Aberystwyth.

p. 126 'You're perfectly right!': q. in Cockett, *David Astor and the Observer*, p. 100.

p. 127 'I've wanted it that way . . .': DA to NA, 7.11.43, BH.

p. 127 'My main interest . . .': 30.8.44, BH.

p. 127 'Where is the report . . .': Churchill, memo, 9.6.44, PREM 4/66/6B, NA.

p. 127 'begged me to give him . . .': Laycock to A. V. Alexander, 12.7.44, ibid., NA.

p. 128 'Pray send this report . . .': 10.7.44, ibid., NA.

p. 128 'completely exonerates him . . .': 17.7.44, ibid., NA.

p. 128 'I visited Winston's man . . .': DA, memo to John Stubbs, n.d., BH.

p. 128 'The basic hitch . . .': 25.6.44, Aberystwyth.

p. 128 'fascist characteristics . . .': DA to WA, n.d., BH.

p. 128 'Winston alone . . .': ibid.

p. 129 'It would be fatal . . .': 16.6.42, BH.

p. 129 'an absurd tale . . .': Foot, p. 209.

p. 129 'considered nothing short . . .': q. in unpublished essay by John Stubbs, n.d., BH.

p. 129 'cease to be such a bore . . .': 5.12.43, q. in ibid.

p. 129 'Can Captain Astor . . .': q. in ibid.

p. 129 'who do not hide . . .': *Observer*, 1.11.42.

p. 130 'It was clearly discussed . . .': 25.7.43, BH.

p. 130 'Dr Gillespie . . .': WA to Garvin, 25.1.40, HRHRC.

p. 130 'I have a desire . . .': 30.8.44, BH.

p. 130 'a cheerful, ugly . . .': SOE report, n.d., HS6/518, NA.

p. 131 'strong force of Boches': Captain Bennett's report, HS6/518, NA.

p. 131 'the gunner was . . .': ibid.

p. 131 'crawled round to join me . . .': Colonel Broad's report, HS/518, NA.

p. 132 'Could we not swing . . .': Vera Atkins to Maurice Buckmaster, 20.9.44, HS9/1089/3, NA.

p. 133 'one evening Terry . . .': Riols, p. 145.

p. 133 'Yankee tented hospital . . .': Pringle, p. 138.

p. 133 'a Mussolini hospital . . .': ibid.

p. 133 'I spent three hectic . . .': 22.9.44, BH.

p. 133 'We can hardly wait . . .': 21.9.44, BH.

p. 133 'You are the only . . .': 11.10.44, BH.

p. 133 'Well, my war experience . . .': 8.10.44, Aberystwyth.

p. 133 'I acquired this wound . . .': 16.9.44, BH.

p. 133 'very happy convalescence . . .': 16.9.44, BH.

p. 133 'it was like stepping . . .': DA to Melanie Hauser, 9.4.87, BH.

p. 134 'The news about Adam . . .': 28.9.44, BH.

p. 134 'it felt as if hope . . .': n.d., BH.

p. 134 'Adam would have . . .': DA to WA and NA, 28.9.44, BH.

p. 134 'The FO view of him . . .': n.d., Aberystwyth.

p. 134 'the one great exception . . .': DA to John Cripps, 30.5.79, BH.

p. 135 'it is a complete failure . . .': 20.6.42, Foreign Office report FO 371 30912.

p. 135 'most encouraging': q. in Sykes, *Troubled Loyalty*, p. 380.

p. 135 'an extraordinarily suspicious . . .': Foreign Office memo, 1942, BH.

p. 135 'I did not trust him . . .': Foreign Office report FO371 30912 by 'an Oxford contemporary', n.d., BH.

p. 135 'This sounds like . . .': Foreign Office memo, FO371 34462, 5.11.43, BH.

p. 135 'a conscious or unconscious . . .': Foreign Office memo, FO371 39059, 30.4.44, BH.

p. 135 'a very good mouthpiece . . .': ibid.

p. 135 'I certainly distrusted him . . .': Foreign Office memo FO371 39066, 25.9.44, BH.

p. 135 'Our FO believed . . .': 8.10.44, Aberystwyth.

p. 135 'Trott was amazingly . . .': q. in Lamb, p. 271.

p. 135 'He looked a shadow . . .': Wiskemann, p. 168.

p. 135 'a creature as fabulous . . .': Trevor-Roper, *The Last Days of Hitler*, p. 267.

p. 136 'who knew him better . . .': DA to Professor J. R. M. Butler, 21.1.59, BH.

p. 136 'the only person in England . . .': 'Draft Memorandum to Christopher Sykes', 9.1.67, BH.

p. 136 'love of his country . . .': 13.3.45, BH.

p. 136 'one-man Awards Bureau': DA to Tyerman, 3.10.45, BH.

p. 136 'David Astor's always been . . .': Becker, p. 361.

p. 136 'I am so glad . . .' WA to Melanie Hauser, 3.8.45, BH.

p. 137 'talked with amusement . . .': DA, unpublished tribute to Melanie Hauser, n.d., BH.

p. 138 'she used to go grey . . .': q. in ibid.

p. 138 'barged in . . .': Rhodes James (ed.), 23.3.44, p. 390.

p. 138 'she was past playing . . .': DA to James Astor, 30.6.97, p.c.

p. 138 'Please put the family . . .': 22.1.45, BH.

p. 138 'there is no conspiracy . . .': n.d., BH.

Chapter 13: Foreign Editor

p. 139 'My anxiety is not to be . . .': n.d., BH.

p. 139 'best stuff . . .': DA to IB, 11.3.45, BH.

p. 139 'the Protestant religion': legal settlement, 27.2.45, BH.

p. 139 'I have had such disquieting': n.d., January 1945, BH.

p. 139 'a main share . . .': 10.1.45, Aberystwyth.

p. 140 'a fine gesture . . .': Thomas Jones, 28.9.46, p. 544.

p. 140 'knew what life was like . . .': draft obituary for Obank, n.d., December 1991, Obs. Arch.

p. 140 'Masterful and long-suffering': Sampson, *The Anatomist*, p. 46.

p. 140 'the governing principle . . .': Michael Davie, the *Age*, 2.7.81.

p. 140 'laid out every page . . .': John Silverlight to Donald Trelford, 16.9.80, Obs. Arch.

p. 140 'a reaction to the opinions . . .': Michael Davie, the *Age*, 2.7.81.

p. 140 'closest counsellor . . .': DA to Richard Cockett, 7.3.91, BH.

p. 141 'a phenomenally aloof . . .': Cyril Dunn to John Stubbs, 1.9.77, p.c.

p. 141 'I feel highly embarrassed . . .': n.d., July 1945, Aberystwyth.

p. 141 'for many readers . . .': WA to TJ, 16.12.45, BH.

p. 141 'sweep away the props . . .': 20.12.45, BH.

p. 141 'If it is true that . . .': n.d., July 1945, BH.

p. 141 'David Astor was in total . . .': Dunn to John Stubbs, 1.9.77, p.c.

p. 142 'like a wise . . .': Dunn, diary, 1.1.48, p.c.

p. 142 'frightful – ponderous . . .': Dunn, diary, 16.2.48, p.c.

p. 142 'didn't much care . . .': Dunn to John Stubbs, 1.9.77, p.c.

p. 142 'Do you agree . . .': n.d., BH.

p. 142 'a deeply old-fashioned . . .': Dunn to John Stubbs, 1.9.77, p.c.

p. 142 'My position was exalted . . .': Brown, *Old and Young*, p. 132.

p. 142 'I had no experience . . .': Brown, *The Way of My World*, p. 288.

p. 142 'a sweet little man . . .': Dunn to John Stubbs, 1.9.77, p.c.

p. 142 'How can we have a . . .': ibid.

p. 142 'a pure Edwardian . . .': Dunn to John Stubbs, 29.9.77, p.c.

p. 142 'Lots of conventional readers . . .': 16.2.48, BH.

p. 143 'Tall, handsome . . .': Dunn to John Stubbs, 1.9.77, p.c.

p. 143 'an attractive bear . . .': Colin Legum, unpublished memoir of DA, n.d., p.c.

p. 143 'given a circular . . .': Dunn to John Stubbs, 1.9.77, BH.

p. 143 'half flattered . . .': Crankshaw, p.ix.

p. 143 'she either has a news . . .': Dunn, diary, 10.12.47.

p. 144 'we didn't make the same . . .': DA, Servob report, 28.12.75, Obs. Arch.

p. 144 'the same boyish good . . .': Bielenberg, *The Road Ahead*, p. 53.

p. 144 'When it came to . . .': ibid., p. 92.

p. 144 'Diana Hopkinson could be found . . .': ibid.

p. 144 'I got him on the basis . . .': DA in conversation with John Silverlight, n.d., BH.

p. 145 'I have landed a job . . .': q. in O'Donovan and Kee (eds.), p. 12.

p. 145 'either you pay . . .': ibid.

p. 145 'Even the agricultural . . .': ibid.

p. 145 'he had a baroque . . .': *The Times*, 28.1.81.

p. 145 'slightly arrogant . . .': q. in O'Donovan and Kee (eds.), p. 8.

p. 145 'an upper-class glamour boy': Dunn to John Stubbs, 1.9.77, p.c.

p. 146 'one of the minor . . .': Dunn, diary, 1.2.48, p.c.

p. 146 'great warren . . .': q. in Gray (ed.), p. 168.

p. 146 'in the early Tudor Street . . .': Dunn to John Stubbs, 27.9.77, p.c.

p. 146 'I don't care if . . .': Michael Davie, the *Age*, 2.7.81.

p. 146 'jovial cockney': Sampson, *The Anatomist*, p. 44.

p. 147 'The most brilliant . . .': Dunn to John Stubbs, 1.9.77, p.c.

p. 147 'head and shoulders': Berlin to DA, 18.2.46, Berlin papers, Bodleian.

p. 147 'Oh no, he's *much* . . .': Dunn to John Stubbs, 1.9.77, p.c.

p. 148 'the hard core . . .': Clark, p. 97.

p. 148 'a small dimly lit room . . .': Bielenberg, *The Road Ahead*, p. 58.

p. 148 'more than half . . .': Clark, p. 94.

p. 148 'David's sympathy . . .': Dunn to John Stubbs, 1.9.77, p.c.

p. 148 'we Astors are only . . .': Clark, p. 94.

p. 149 'David Astor as a presiding . . .': ibid., p. 116.

p. 149 'in every room and corridor . . .': 28.2.45, Aberystwyth.

p. 149 'an old-fashioned Balliol . . .': DA in conversation with John Silverlight, n.d., BH.

p. 149 'might get a better hearing . . .': DA, Servob report, 28.12.75, Obs. Arch.

p. 150 'her sabotage of . . .': 15.5.45, BH.

p. 150 'I don't believe that "the Left" . . .': q. in Pringle, p. 138.

p. 150 'the lack of understanding . . .': DA to Noble Frankland, 2.8.57, BH.

p. 150 'David needs your help . . .': n.d., BH.

p. 150 'she must begin the day . . .': q. in Norman Rose, p. 205.

p. 150 'socialism, Roman Catholicism . . .': ibid.

p. 151 'I know what this family . . .': 4.5.48, BH.

p. 151 'sets me in a state . . .': n.d., BH.

p. 151 'My wife used to say . . .': n.d., BH.

p. 151 'You are simply . . .': 1.6.46, BH.

p. 151 'I shall never regret it . . .': 21.5.47, BH.

Chapter 14: Coming into his Inheritance

p. 152 'In the character . . . .': n.d., BH.

p. 152 'I live for my work . . .': DA on 'Frankly Speaking', BBC Home Service, 18.7.62.

p. 153 'Your fatherly advice . . .': 7.8.48, Arthur Mann papers, Bodleian.

p. 153 'You are so much more . . .': 16.2.49, William Clark papers, Bodleian.

p. 153 'You probably regard me . . .': n.d., William Clark papers, Bodleian.

p. 154 'as I am young . . .': 3.11.49, Arthur Mann papers, Bodleian.

p. 154 'I will do my very best . . .': 9.3.48, ibid.

p. 154 'It is on the literary pages . . .': ibid.

p. 154 'I would be unwilling . . .': DA to Arthur Mann, 7.4.48, ibid.

p. 154 'IB likes easy, safe . . .': ibid.

p. 154 'he didn't want to take . . .': ibid.

p. 155 'give a bit more colour': IB to Orwell, 18.2.48, q. in Davison (ed.), *Orwell: A Life in Letters*, p. 392.

p. 155 'I'm sorry, but it was . . .': Orwell to IB, 20.2.48, ibid., p. 391.

p. 155 'What I need . . .': DA to Arthur Mann, 9.3.48, Arthur Mann papers, Bodleian.

p. 155 'deep personal humiliation': IB to trustees, 3.3.48, ibid.

p. 155 'Fine. That's just what . . .': Rose in Sampson (ed.), p. 11.

p. 155 'A highly sophisticated . . .': Dunn to John Stubbs, 1.9.77, p.c.

p. 155 'You've got one . . .': q. in Claire Tomalin, obituary of Terence Kilmartin, *Independent*, 19.8.91.

p. 156 'pure public school . . .': Dunn to John Stubbs, 1.9.77, p.c.

p. 156 'I had no interest . . .': DA in conversation with John Silverlight, n.d., BH.

p. 156 'The governing principle . . .': the *Age*, 2.7.81.

p. 156 'David leaned forward . . .': Davie in Sampson (ed.), p. 10.

p. 157 'I was told that that . . .': the *Age*, 2.7.81.

p. 157 'who complained about . . .': ibid.

p. 157 'an eccentric . . .': q. in Mitford, p. 8.

p. 157 'a rebel against authority . . .': Weidenfeld, p. 120.

p. 157 'His clothes were . . .': Patrich Leigh Fermor to Jessica Mitford, 29.10.82, p.c.

p. 158 'a wild and warm character . . .': Mount, p. 47.

p. 158 'gifted and politically OK': Orwell to DA, 9.5.49, BH.

p. 158 'he got in touch with me . . .': q. in Mitford, p. III.

p. 158 'He had enormous curiosity . . .': ibid.

p. 158 'he has political brains . . .': 24.1.51, BH.

p. 158 'He came back . . .': 5.2.51, BH.

p. 158 'great capacity for friendship': q. in Mitford, p. 169.

p. 158 'I was in a sort of way . . .': q. in ibid., p. III.

p. 159 'sustained him through . . .': Longford, *Diary of a Year*, p. 132.

p. 159 'shocked at the meagreness . . .': Mitford, p. 5.

p. 159 'Do you mean to say . . .': Robert Chesshyre to author, and elsewhere.

p. 160 'writer I admired . . .': interview for CBS with Steve Wadhams, March 1984, BH.

p. 160 'a *New Statesman* mini-vendetta . . .'

p. 160 'I might as well . . .': q. in Crick, p. 371.

p. 161 'the only possibility . . .': q. in Davison (ed.), *Orwell: A Life in Letters*, p. 391.

p. 161 'Thanks awfully . . .': 9.2.48, ibid., p. 388.

p. 161 'I fear the dream . . .': q. in Crick, p. 385.

p. 161 'I remember visiting . . .': q. in ibid., p. 399.

p. 161 'we had no division . . .': DA to Donald Trelford, 30.12.75, Obs. Arch.

p. 162 'The most formative influence . . .': 18.2.54, BH.

p. 162 'a young, bright, aspiring . . .': Clark, p. 115.

p. 162 'it mustn't be not committed . . .': Kenneth Harris interview with DA, 16.1.63, Obs. Arch.

p. 162 'One must run a paper . . .': 9.3.48, Arthur Mann papers, Bodleian.

p. 162 'We should not be guided . . .': Colin Legum, unpublished essay on DA, n.d., BH.

p. 162 'I think I am a natural . . .': Kenneth Harris, interview with DA, 16.1.63, Obs. Arch.

p. 163 'journalists were inclined . . .': Colin Legum, unpublished essay on DA, n.d., BH.

p. 163 'to ask their assistance . . .': 5.6.59, BH.

p. 163 'I would say the chief . . .': n.d., BH.

p. 163 'choosing staff for their . . .': DA to Richard Cockett, 7.3.91, BH.

p. 163 'Some of the best journalism . . .': n.d., BH.

p. 164 'The great attraction . . .': Kenneth Harris, interview with DA, 16.1.63, Obs. Arch.

p. 164 'my aim has been . . .': DA to Anthony Howard, q. in Cockett, *David Astor and the Observer*, p. 134.

p. 164 'non-party paper . . .': 15.2.74, Obs. Arch.

p. 164 'Haffner struck me . . .': Clark, p. 116.

p. 164 'He was Russian-friendly . . .': Haffner to DA, 5.5.53, BH.

p. 164 'monolithic': Crankshaw to DA, 28.1.52, BH.

p. 164 'an intellectual feat . . .': Pringle, p. 141.

p. 164 'calm, bulky man . . .': Davie, p. 190.

p. 164 'manner was shy and tentative . . .': Colin Legum, unpublished essay on DA, n.d., BH.

p. 165 'The most striking feature . . .': Clark, p. 116.

p. 165 'decolonisation, racism . . .': Colin Legum, unpublished essay on DA, n.d., BH.

p. 165 'much troubled by . . .': 2.12.55, Obs. Arch.

Chapter 15: The Golden Age

p. 166 'He was far too worldly . . .': unpublished notes on DA, p.c.

p. 166 'the product of a thoughtful . . .': Cockett, *David Astor and the Observer*, p. 133.

p. 166 '*all* political journalism . . .': 22.11.55, BH.

p. 166 'The only change I would ask . . .': 21.8.53, BH.

p. 167 'the older generation . . .': q. in Greenslade, p. 67.

p. 167 'there might be any possibility . . .': Tynan to DA, 30.7.53, Tynan (ed.), p. 198.

p. 167 'It will, I expect . . .': Tynan to DA, 19.12.53, Obs. Arch.

p. 167 'the bravest thing I ever did . . .': q. in Tynan (ed.), p. 198.

p. 167 'The theatre has paid him . . .': q. in Tynan, p. 109.

p. 167 'There is, of course, Mr Tynan': q. in ibid., p. 107.

p. 167 'More than one person . . .': 3.4.54, BH.

p. 167 'I have nothing but respect . . .': 23.11.53, BH.

p. 168 'inescapably mine': 3.12.53, BH.

p. 168 'I don't think that rude . . .': 7.12.53, BH.

p. 168 'public grumbling': 2.4.54, Aberystwyth.

p. 168 'the theatrical profession . . .': 13.6.56, BH.

p. 168 'a man of tremendous . . .': Lejeune, p. 193.

p. 168 'I hold him in . . .': n.d., BH.

p. 168 'I am delighted . . .': 18.8.57, Tynan (ed.), p. 211.

p. 168 'there is no one working . . .': 16.9.58, Obs. Arch.

p. 168 'Astor thought it wise . . .': Tynan, p. 135.

p. 168 'alarming and slightly offensive': Pringle, p. 147.

p. 168 'he made everyone feel . . .': Sampson, *The Anatomist*, p. 59.

p. 169 'he has a first-class book . . .': 14.3.55, BH.

p. 169 'Sampson's visit here . . .': 12.6.55, BH.

p. 169 'still looked boyish . . .': Sampson, *The Anatomist*, p. 43.

p. 169 'at the peak of its influence . . .': ibid., p. 44.

p. 169 'even know how to . . .': q. in ibid., p. 45.

p. 169 'he had a touch of . . .': ibid., p. 49.

p. 170 'giggling like a soda fountain . . .': ibid., p. 48.

p. 170 'superb copy-editor . . .': Donald Trelford in Sampson (ed.), p. 30.

p. 170 'It's like a cough . . .': q. in Sampson, *The Anatomist*, p. 61.

p. 170 'the most thrilling . . .': q. in ibid., p. 58.

p. 170 'renowned for the close . . .': Colin Legum, unpublished memoir of DA, n.d., p.c.

p. 170 'Mechthild saw my picture . . .': q. in Billen, p. ix.

p. 171 'under-appreciated': DA to Donald Trelford, 14.1.76, Obs. Arch.

p. 171 'Despite his unhappy . . .': Sampson, *The Anatomist*, p. 50.

p. 171 'She is quite liable . . .': 21.5.54, BH.

p. 171 'So you work for my son David . . .': q. in Sampson, *The Anatomist*, p. 50.

p. 171 'escaped on a silken ladder . . .': ibid., p. 53.

p. 171 'An oak in the *Observer*'s . . .': obituary of Colin Legum, *The Times*, 16.6.03.

p. 172 'I found it almost impossible . . .': Beloff, p. 59.

p. 172 'Well, if we had a more . . .': ibid.

p. 172 'Journalism was obviously . . .': q. in Donald Trelford, *Oxford Dictionary of National Biography* entry on Nora Beloff.

p. 172 'I owe my original . . .': 5.5.53, Obs. Arch.

p. 172 'The backwash of Nora . . .': Haffner to DA, 25.2.51, BH.

p. 172 'the most stimulating . . .': Beloff to DA, n.d., BH.

p. 172 'Tantrums and troubles': ibid.

p. 173 'Virginia, what a marvellous . . .': Virginia Makins to author.

p. 173 'no-nonsense style': q. in Scammell, p. 213.

p. 173 'This small, passionate man . . .': ibid.

p. 173 'a nervous exhibitionist . . .': *Observer*, 15.3.56.

p. 173 'more than usually ambivalent': 6.1.53, BH.

p. 174 'we must put forward . . .': q. in Saunders, p. 58.

p. 174 'who in my opinion . . .': q. in Tim Garton-Ash, *Independent on Sunday*, 14.7.96.

p. 174 'it would have stopped . . .': ibid.

p. 174 'I always knew . . .': q. in ibid.

p. 174 'Orwell wasn't betraying . . .': q. in ibid.

p. 176 'intellectual Marshall Plan': q. in Dorril, p. 481.

p. 177 'It's just the sort . . .': q. in. Sutherland, p. 454.

p. 177 'I did not in the slightest . . .': q. in Ignatieff, p. 199.

p. 177 'Don't people realise . . .': q. in Scammell, p. 446.

p. 177 'no single man . . .': *Observer*, 15.3.56.

p. 177 'your "hanging" journalism . . .': q. in Scammell, p. 447.

p. 178 'after so many years . . .': 8.4.62, BH.

p. 178 'far the best writer . . .': Michael Astor to DA, 19.10.62, BH.

p. 178 'a job that took me . . .': Ross, *Coastwise Lights*, p. 105.

p. 179 'massive head . . .': Watkins, *Brief Lives*, p. 155.

p. 179 'system of administration . . .': Beloff to DA, 5.5.53, Obs. Arch.

p. 179 'Rix Loewenthal . . .': Sampson, *The Anatomist*, p. 46.

p. 179 'My greatest need . . .': 29.3.55, BH.

p. 179 'all full of ideas . . .': DA to Pringle, 8.10.54, BH.

p. 180 'Intimate and serious . . .': 2.10.49, BH.

p. 180 'purely private life . . .': 22.7.49, BH.

p. 180 'so as to give us . . .': 30.8.49, BH.

p. 180 'too precious . . .': n.d., BH.

p. 180 'I've just met the person . . .': Lucy Astor in conversation with the author.

p. 181 'Would you believe it . . .': 26.2.52, Aberystwyth.

p. 181 'she was too subdued . . .': Tomlinson to Robert Stephens, 13.3.52, Obs. Arch.

p. 181 'a sculptress who . . .': Spender, unpublished journals, 9.1.92, p.c.

p. 181 'You know that Frances . . .': 16.10.55, Clark papers, Bodleian.

p. 181 'It costs me acute . . .': 9.8.55, ibid.

p. 182 'I resorted to . . .': 1.10.86, BH.

p. 182 'I visit a "priest" . . .': n.d., BH.

p. 182 'I must have at least . . .': Davie to DA, 29.9.86, BH.

p. 182 'willingness to get . . .': 26.11.52, Monckton papers, Bodleian.

p. 182 'inflicting the troubles . . .': 31.12.52, ibid.

p. 183 'shocking attitude . . .': *Daily Express*, 3.12.53.

p. 183 'this subject ought . . .': DA to *Daily Express*, 3.12.53.

p. 183 'I find it like . . .': Kenneth Harris interview with DA, 16.1.63, Obs. Arch.

p. 183 'golliwog itching . . .': *Observer*, 29.5.49.

p. 183 'purveyors of various . . .': *Spectator*, 18.10.55.

p. 183 'dewy-eyed': *Sunday Express*, 2.10.55.

p. 183 'in his zeal for . . .': q. in Cudlipp, p. 304.

p. 184 'occasionally strikes . . .': ibid.

p. 184 'my mother is behaving . . .': 16.4.52, Aberystwyth.

p. 184 'in a fairly constant state . . .': 30.8.49, BH.

p. 184 'My father is a sort of . . .': ibid.

p. 184 'Why do you continue . . .': q. in Fort, p. 315.

p. 184 'hoped David would make . . .': q. in Fox, p. 530.

p. 184 'I wish I had never . . .': q. in Ellis, p. 513.

p. 184 'he did this not to die . . .': DA to James Astor, 30.6.97, p.c.

p. 184 'The sternness which . . .': q. in Sykes, *Nancy*, p. 508.

p. 185 'We had forty happy years . . .': q. in ibid.

p. 185 'It is in the balanced . . .': *Observer*, 5.10.52.

Chapter 16: African Affairs

p. 186 'London is the best centre . . .': Gunther, p. 332.

p. 186 'although liberals have . . .': n.d., BH.

p. 186 'I am so glad . . .': Orwell to DA, 19.11.48, Davison (ed.), *Orwell: A Life in Letters*, p. 422.

p. 186 'So this is the man . . .': q. in Colin Legum, unpublished memoir of DA, n.d., p.c.

p. 186 'put some boot polish . . .': q. in Edwards, p. 83.

p. 186 'the *Observer* is for the blacks . . .': q. in Chisholm and Davie, p. 8.

p. 186 'the extraordinarily attractive . . .': 18.5.51, BH.

p. 187 'the natives of South . . .': 7.12.54, BH.

p. 187 'I have never said . . .': 8.12.54, BH.

p. 187 'I know you know . . .': 8.3.62, BH.

p. 187 'David's policy on race . . .': letter to *Der Spiegel*, 2011.

p. 187 'rather self-righteous': 6.5.54, BH.

p. 187 'forestall events': q. in Michael Scott, TS of 'The Africa Bureau: A Prospective History of its Life and Times', n.d., BH.

p. 187 'I had a horrible vision . . .': q. in ibid.

p. 187 'one can only understand . . .': 9.2.52, BH.

p. 188 'I won't stand for it': Colin Legum, unpublished memoir of DA, n.d., p.c.

p. 188 'You have only to spend . . .': introduction to TS of *Shadow over Africa*, n.d., BH.

p. 188 'He was horribly pained . . .': Calvocoressi, p. 56.

p. 188 'The non-violent breaking . . .': DA in *Observer*, 31.7.77.

p. 188 'I was very taken . . .': q. in Yates and Chester, p. 121.

p. 189 'his face revealed . . .': Benson, *A Far Cry*, p. 58.

p. 189 'an obvious celibate': ibid., p. 92.

p. 189 'Can't you see that . . .': ibid., p. 89.

p. 189 'a powerful neurotic drive': ibid., p. 92.

p. 189 'I felt like a very clumsy . . .': 19.11.52, BH.

p. 189 'As Scott's reputation . . .': Benson, *A Far Cry*, p. 57.

p. 189 'well-informed and impartial . . .': Scott, unpublished history of the Africa Bureau, BH.

p. 190 'a vehicle for Michael': q. in Yates and Chester, p. 127.

p. 190 'fearless as a lion . . .': ibid., p. 172.

p. 190 'as always, you treat . . .': 23.2.65, BH.

p. 191 'noteworthy contribution . . .': Scott, unpublished history of the Africa Bureau, BH.

p. 191 'One had only . . .': TS of 'My Early Days at the Africa Bureau', n.d., BH.

p. 191 'we are very grateful . . .': 16.8.57, BH.

p. 191 'my difficulty is that . . .': DA to Canon Collins, 25.11.58, BH.

p. 192 'the way John spoke . . .': 23.1.61, BH.

p. 192 'one single word . . .': *Observer*, 20.12.59.

p. 192 'off the record': 31.12.57, Sampson papers, Bodleian.

p. 193 'I've come to thank . . .': q. in Sampson, *Mandela*, p. 168.

p. 193 'while it is important . . .': 3.7.62, BH.

p. 193 'Many people I know . . .': 10.8.62, BH.

p. 194 'save the life . . .': 2.4.64, BH.

p. 194 'I wonder whether you . . .': 12.6.64, BH.

p. 194 'putting so many black . . .': q. in Norman Rose, p. 207.

p. 195 'six years of failure': *Observer*, 1.3.59.

p. 195 'harmful to the best . . .': q. in Cockett, *David Astor and the Observer*, p. 191.

p. 195 'police state': ibid.

p. 195 'secede': ibid.

p. 195 'appease the South African . . .': *Observer*, 12.3.50.

p. 196 'People have very mixed . . .': q. in Benson, *Tshekedi Khama*, p. 211.

p. 196 'sitting in front of the fire . . .': ibid., p. 216.

p. 196 'Tshekedi's outward . . .': 21.5.56, BH.

p. 196 'pain in the arse': 14.9.60, BH.

p. 197 'I am immensely proud . . .': 28.10.61, BH.

p. 197 'the only publication . . .': Rose to DA, n.d., September 1961, BH.

p. 197 'the *Observer*'s echo . . .': Hall, p. 21.

p. 197 'David's pre-eminent role . . .': ibid., p. 22.

p. 197 'We don't know what . . .': ibid.

p. 198 'true freedom fighter': Hall, p. 27.

p. 198 'Astor sitting there . . .': ibid.

p. 198 'David Astor is bitterly . . .': 1.6.65, BH.

p. 198 'So that was the tawdry . . .': Hall, p. 27.

p. 199 'serious, determined . . .': 25.6.60, BH.

p. 199 'It seems rather odd . . .': 27.6.60, BH.

p. 199 'conscious of having . . .': 15.3.61, BH.

p. 199 'Actually, I don't suppose . . .': q. in Young, p. xvii.

p. 199 'I can assure you that . . .': 5.4.61, BH.

p. 200 'objectionable article': unpublished memo on DA by Legum, n.d., p.c.

p. 200 'with none of the scepticism . . .': 8.3.74, BH.

p. 200 'over unbelievable terrain': DA to William Millinship, 21.11.74, BH.

Chapter 17: Suez

p. 201 'May I take . . .': 16.12.54, BH.

p. 201 'the smack of firm government': *Daily Telegraph*, 3.1.56.

p. 202 'totally disintegrated . . .': q. in Kyle, p. 95.

p. 202 'outgrown the particular . . .': DA to Clark, 11.2.55, Clark papers, Bodleian.

p. 202 'who will bounce around . . .': Weil to Clark, 29.10.55, Clark papers, Bodleian.

p. 202 'As a journalist . . .': 19.9.55, ibid.

p. 202 'found the prime minister . . .': q. in Shaw, p. 17.

p. 202 'in the conflict for power . . .': q. in ibid., p. 20.

p. 202 'as a result of a general . . .': 5.6.56, Clark papers, Bodleian.

p. 203 'several times when papers . . .': diary, 9.4.56, ibid.

p. 203 'I hear Massingham . . .': q. in Shaw, p. 20.

p. 204 'If we cannot hold . . .': q. in Kyle, p. 43.

p. 204 'if he succeeds . . .': q. in ibid., p. 205.

p. 204 'must not be allowed . . .': q. in ibid., p. 136.

p. 204 'We should hit Nasser . . .': q. in Hetherington, p. 2.

p. 205 'childish retaliation': *Observer*, 12.8.56.

p. 205 'convinced that Eden . . .': Crossman, diary, 5.9.56, Morgan (ed.), p. 507.

p. 205 'When I sit with . . .': q. in Sampson, *The Anatomist*, p. 54.

p. 205 'an act of folly . . .': q. in Hetherington, p. 15.

p. 206 'denied the right . . .': q. in Shaw, p. 81.

p. 206 'I don't envy . . .': 29.10.56, Clark papers, Bodleian.

p. 206 'Clark did not know . . .': DA to Richard Lamb, 16.1.87, BH.

p. 206 'an act of folly . . .': *Manchester Guardian*, 30.11.56.

p. 206 'hideously miscalculated . . .': q. in Hetherington, p. 19.

p. 206 'weak man in a weak country . . .': q. in Cockett, *David Astor and the Observer*, p. 212.

p. 207 'no single state . . .': *Observer*, 12.8.56.

p. 207 'Surely something terrible . . .': n.d., November 1956, Monckton papers, Bodleian.

p. 207 'The bottom has fallen out . . .': n.d., BH.

p. 207 'not as policemen . . .': *Observer*, 4.11.56.

p. 207 'essentially likeable': *Observer*, 22.1.50.

p. 207 'Of course I understand . . .': 5.11.56, Monckton papers, Bodleian.

p. 208 'the *Observer* is surely . . .': 1.11.56, Berlin, *Enlightening*, p. 54.

p. 208 'for the past three months . . .': Eden, p. 258.

p. 208 'David Astor has written . . .': 15.11.56, ibid., p. 256.

p. 208 'on the verge of . . .': q. in Kyle, p. 336.

p. 208 'did not like the idea . . .': q. in ibid., p. 304.

p. 208 'Bloody good!': q. in Cockett, *David Astor and the Observer*, p. 224.

p. 208 'made a very brave speech . . .': 13.11.56, Obs. Arch.

p. 208 'The anti-Astor feeling . . .': 13.11.56, BH.

p. 209 'the collusion charge . . .': 14.11.56, PREM/11/1127, NA.

p. 209 'wanted you to see it . . .': 16.11.56, BH.

p. 209 'the style of our leading . . .': q. in Cockett, *David Astor and the Observer*, p. 225.

p. 209 'a nice man . . .': DA to Lord Portal, n.d., BH.

p. 210 'I read with growing nausea . . .': *Observer*, 11.7.56.

p. 210 'the traitors' paper': q. in Sampson, *The Anatomist*, p. 55.

p. 210 'would go to work . . .': q. in Davenport-Hines (ed.), p. 163.

p. 210 'We had readers who . . .': Roger Harrison to the author.

p. 210 'an iniquity . . .': *Observer*, 10.5.56.

p. 211 'Don't let Tristan . . .': q. in Sampson, *The Anatomist*, p. 56.

p. 211 'I know in my little way . . .': 14.8.57, BH.

p. 211 'the *Observer* had always . . .': q. in Cockett, *David Astor and the Observer*, p. 233.

p. 211 'to a large extent . . .': 7.11.56, BH.

p. 211 'military adventures': 8.12.56, BH.

p. 211 'Frankly I think . . .': 12.12.56, BH.

p. 211 'We have done our best . . .': 14.12.56, BH.

p. 211 'met many Jewish individuals . . .': DA to Dr Negrine, 6.11.79, BH.

p. 212 'gratitude and *deep* admiration . . .': 2.1.57, BH.

p. 212 'Suez was a traumatic . . .': q. in Hobson, Knightley and Russell, p. 297.

p. 212 'The tragedy of Suez . . .': 2.4.57, BH.

p. 212 'I think I would do it again . . .': q. in Sampson, *The Anatomist*, p. 56.

Chapter 18: *Changing the Guard*

p. 214 'at a consanguine cut rate': *New Statesman*, 27.6.75.

p. 215 'a quick, gossipy . . .': 4.2.59, BH.

p. 215 'What I am not sympathetic to . . .': DA to Michael Davie, 6.2.59, BH.

p. 215 'had your blood . . .': 31.3.59, BH.

p. 216 'we would have the immense . . .': 22.10.59, Sampson papers, Bodleian.

p. 216 'but I don't see why . . .': 21.10.58, ibid.

p. 216 'shine his searchlight . . .': William Clark papers, Bodleian, n.d.

p. 216 'The concept was entirely . . .': q. in Campbell, p. 219.

p. 216 'We are finding the . . .' n.d., BH.

p. 217 'there is no paper . . .': Pringle to DA, 7.9.54, BH.

p. 217 'just the right mixture . . .': Sampson to DA, 19.1.58, BH.

p. 217 'I think the *Observer* . . .': 10.8.57, William Clark papers, Bodleian.

p. 217 'what has been worrying . . .': 25.7.59, BH.

p. 217 'for all practical purposes . . .': Pringle, p. 135.

p. 217 'listening attentively . . .': ibid., p. 136.

p. 218 'never happier . . .': ibid., p. 141.

p. 218 'a tall, gaunt figure . . .': ibid., p. 148

p. 218 'all decisions . . .': ibid., p. 142.

p. 219 'the ablest colleague . . .': DA to Sarah Haffner, 11.7.01, BH.

p. 219 'playing the odious role . . .': Sebastian Haffner to DA, 5.5.53, BH.

p. 219 'the feisty, brilliant . . .': Colin Legum, 'David's Style of Editing', n.d., Obs. Arch.

p. 219 'a premature Gaullist': Pringle, p. 140.

p. 219 'Haffner has gone neutralist . . .': 15.12.53, William Clark papers, Bodleian.

p. 219 'surely is exactly . . .': 25.1.55, BH.

p. 220 'irritated by a large . . .': 30.12.57, BH.

p. 220 'other stories . . .': 4.11.61, q. in Caute, p. 192.

p. 220 'basically Marxist . . .': DA letter to staff, 15.2.74, Obs. Arch.

p. 221 'nastier than I had . . .': 27.1.55, Berlin, *Enlightening*, p. 474.

p. 221 'As regards his general . . .': 7.5.58, q. in ibid., p. 624.

p. 221 'You say he is a man . . .': 14.5.58, ibid.

p. 221 'a neurotic, muddled . . .': Berlin to Rowland Burdon-Miller, 18.1.51, ibid., p. 208.

p. 221 'of whom pre-Nazi Germany . . .': Berlin to Arthur Schlesinger, 27.8.53, ibid., p. 386.

p. 221 'the most detestable woman . . .': Berlin to Rowland Burdon-Miller, 21.6.54, ibid., p. 449.

p. 221 'Coming from anyone . . .': Michael Davie to DA, 9.10.68, BH.

p. 221 'I much regret . . .': 24.9.68, BH.

p. 222 'just about my oldest . . .': 20.12.63, BH.

p. 222 'affect our personal relations . . .': 4.10.68, BH.

p. 222 'I do appreciate . . .': 22.12.63, BH.

p. 222 'with whom, unlike . . .': 9.10.68, BH.

p. 222 'Rix or no Rix . . .': 27.12.57, BH.

p. 222 'he was seen as . . .': q. in Clark, p. 217.

p. 222 'a weakness for keeping . . .': 19.11.57, BH.

p. 222 'I would not choose Rix . . .': 28.11.57, BH.

p. 223 'Lord Chandos . . .': 20.10.57, Clark papers, Bodleian.

p. 223 'There was no queue . . .': q. in Cockett, *David Astor and the Observer*, p. 241.

p. 223 'the stiletto's out': q. in Sampson, *The Anatomist*, p. 60.

p. 224 'the wit or the decency . . .': Hugh Massingham to DA, 24.2.58, BH.

p. 224 'It can't be true': Peter Crookston to the author.

p. 224 'My agonised best wishes . . .': 22.11.63, Obs. Arch.

Chapter 19: New Faces

p. 225 'novelists and other . . .': 14.4.60, BH.

p. 225 'David Astor offered . . .': Newby, p. 221.

p. 225 'dear, auntly, old-fashioned': Colin Legum, unpublished memoir of DA, n.d., p.c.

p. 225 'who is staying with us . . .': Fred Tomlinson to Patience Gray, 29.2.58, p.c.

p. 226 'a woman was not exactly . . .': Gray, p. 38.

p. 226 'it was the European scene . . .': ibid., p. 40.

p. 226 'a singular indifference . . .': ibid., p. 44.

p. 226 'a kind note . . .': ibid., p. 46.

p. 226 'laid-back, rumpled . . .': Hunt, TS of *Original Sinner*, n.d., p.c.

p. 226 'the paper, leading . . .': Gray, p. 45.

p. 227 'should cover anything . . .': Whitehorn, p. ix.

p. 227 'one doing the frocks . . .': q. in Gray (ed.), p. 196.

p. 227 'do the gravitas bit': Whitehorn, p. 120.

p. 227 'I was one of the first . . .': ibid.

p. 227 'didn't believe that . . .': q. in Gray (ed.), p. 200.

p. 227 'Can a Career Woman . . .': Fred Tomlinson to Patience Gray, 29.2.58, p.c.

p. 228 'David could tolerate . . .': Whitehorn, p. 136.

p. 228 'the *Sunday Times* told you . . .': ibid., p. 125.

p. 228 'I am what they call . . .': Gale, p. 10.

p. 228 'He was floppy-haired . . .': Ross, introduction to paperback reissue of Gale, unnumbered pages.

p. 228 'Clothes were talismanic . . .': Heilpern, p. vii.

p. 229 'baggy trousers . . .': Gale, p. 17.

p. 229 'he had an electric . . .': Heilpern, p. vii.

p. 229 'he has an exaggerated . . .': DA to Nora Beloff, 18.11.55, BH.

p. 229 'I took to waving . . .': Gale, p. 134.

p. 229 'Write nothing . . .': ibid., p. 139.

p. 229 'Funny things happened . . .': ibid., p. 169.

p. 229 'had apparently gone . . .': Ross, *Coastwise Lights*, p. 148.

p. 229 'in no state to talk . . .': Ross, introduction to Gale.

p. 230 'skilful at drawing . . .': ibid.

p. 230 'as sharp and clean . . .': Heilpern, p. vi.

p. 230 'The great draw for me . . .': Frayn, *Travels with a Typewriter*, p. 6.

p. 230 'David Astor used to bring . . .': q. in Gray (ed.), p. 168.

p. 231 'short, rather fat man . . .': Frayn, *Towards the End of the Morning*, p. 11.

p. 231 'He was always very kind . . .': Michael Frayn to Anthony Sampson, 11.12.91, Sampson papers, Bodleian.

p. 231 'It is fantastic how . . .': 12.6.65, p.c.

p. 231 'which is not to say . . .': 2.10.65, p.c.

p. 231 'a floppy-haired . . .': Young, p. xii.

p. 232 'there'll be times . . .': q. in Frankland, p. 206.

p. 232 'the *Observer*'s apparent . . .': ibid., p. 207.

p. 232 'Some of the staff . . .': ibid., p. 208.

p. 232 'on the basis of . . .': Bloodworth, 24.2.02, p.c.

p. 232 'brilliant dysfunctional family': Ascherson, 'Some Memories', unpublished TS, n.d., p.c.

p. 232 'David fed them . . .': ibid.

p. 233 'I know I'm often . . .': Silverlight in Sampson (ed.), p. 26.

p. 233 'by this stage . . .': Thompson, unpublished memoir of DA, n.d., p.c.

p. 233 'looked like one . . .': McIlvanney, taped interview, n.d., Obs. Arch.

p. 233 'We will do without . . .': Robert Chesshyre to the author.

p. 234 'It's the best news . . .': Nora Beloff in Sampson (ed.), p. 39.
p. 234 'clearest physical memory . . .': unpublished TS, n.d., p.c.
p. 234 'Michael Frayn says . . .': John Lucas to the author.
p. 234 'a small, vital, vigorous . . .': Pringle, p. 147.

Chapter 20: Competing on Two Fronts

p. 235 'That's one more . . .': q. in Sampson, *The Anatomist*, p. 57.
p. 235 'orders his politics . . .': q. in ibid., p. 56.
p. 236 'the *Observer* under its . . .': q. in Hobson, Knightley and Russell, p. 278.
p. 236 'would feel personally disgraced . . .': q. in ibid., p. 288.
p. 236 'secret weapon': Hamilton, p. 86.
p. 237 'the final judgement . . .': Pringle, p. 149.
p. 237 'telling me that . . .': ibid., p. 150.
p. 237 'the Henry Ford . . .': DA to Pringle, 25.7.59, BH.
p. 238 'tantamount to . . .': 28.7.59, BH.
p. 238 'The loss of you . . .': 1.8.59, BH.
p. 238 'he could not bear to leave . . .': Pringle, p. 150.
p. 238 'I have a very high regard . . .': 15.8.59, BH.
p. 238 'I enjoy our competition . . .': 10.6.60, BH.
p. 238 'my old pal Thomson': DA to Ronald Grierson, 13.6.60, BH.
p. 238 'I think you would find him . . .': 19.3.60, BH.
p. 238 'bury the *Observer*': q. in Cockett, *David Astor and the Observer*, p. 236.
p. 238 'I don't deal with that side . . .': q. in Cockett, *David Astor and the Observer*, p. 141.
p. 239 'because they can frighten . . .': 13.6.60, BH.
p. 239 'flourished under his . . .': Wintour, *The Rise and Fall of Fleet Street*, p. 120.
p. 239 'the great independent paper . . .': q. in Hobson, Knightley and Russell, p. 388.
p. 239 'I had this strong feeling . . .': q. in Hobson, Knightley and Russell, p. 374.
p. 240 'the only one we wanted . . .': q. in ibid., p. 407.
p. 240 'My God! . . .': q. in Wintour, *The Rise and Fall of Fleet Street*, p. 116.
p. 240 'Let Lord Beaverbrook . . .': q. in Hobson, Knightley and Russell, p. 359.
p. 240 'We go for all . . .': q. in ibid., p. 370.
p. 240 'by the extraordinary . . .': Pringle, p. 152.

p. 241 'After much conferring . . .': DA to Lord Portal, 30.5.57, BH.

p. 241 'We are madly trying . . .': q. in Cockett, *David Astor and the Observer*, p. 240.

p. 242 'chronic instability and fear': Crossman, *The Backbench Diaries*, 1.11.63, Morgan (ed.), p. 1,036.

p. 242 'both playing the piano . . .': Sampson to DA, 31.12.60, Sampson papers, Bodleian.

p. 242 'we get the big things right . . .': 'Conference Notes for Editor's "Keynote Speech"', November 1961, BH.

p. 242 'it's not the sort of thing . . .': q. in Hobson, Knightley and Russell, p. 368.

p. 242 'it cannot be right . . .': Obank to DA, n.d., October 1961, BH.

p. 243 'His manner was excitable . . .': Hunt.

p. 243 'was a lake, full . . .': Rubinstein, unpublished note on DA, n.d., p.c.

p. 243 'a charming but obstinate . . .': Hunt.

p. 243 'appallingly printed': Hunt.

p. 243 'in view of our serving together . . .': 10.6.64, BH.

p. 243 'You do not realise . . .': 1.9.64, BH.

p. 244 'with the actual fate of . . .': 4.9.64, BH.

p. 244 'if you were not so deeply . . .': 8.9.64, BH.

p. 244 'more use of pictures . . .': 26.2.64, Obs. Arch.

p. 244 'frustrated by the lack . . .': Sampson, *The Anatomist*, p. 67.

p. 244 'the new brightness . . .': *New Statesman*, 13.11.64.

p. 244 'The amiable and agreeable . . .': *Spectator*, 11.6.65.

p. 245 'witty, charming and intelligent': q. in Knightley, p. 190.

p. 245 'that Salvation Army . . .': Muggeridge, p. 188.

p. 245 'My dear Astor': 14.2.52, BH.

p. 245 'He seems an extremely . . .': 27.2.52, BH.

p. 246 'offered a commercial . . .': 23.6.52, Obs. Arch.

p. 246 'Philby was given Arab . . .': q. in Knightley, p. 199.

p. 246 'Elliott assured me . . .': q. in ibid.

p. 246 'I would have thought that . . .': q. in ibid.

p. 246 'was judicious in . . .': Seale and McConville, p. 238.

p. 246 'a good talk . . .': 14.5.57, Obs. Arch.

p. 246 'a very quiet presence . . .': Michael Davie, the *Age*, 2.7.81.

p. 247 'I can well imagine . . .': 4.9.58, Obs. Arch.

p. 247 'staggering expenses': note, October 1958, Obs. Arch.

p. 247 'satisfied that he had been . . .': 'The Philby Affair' in Trevor-Roper, *The Secret World*, p. 95.

p. 247 'How is it that . . .': q. in Knightley, p. 213.

p. 247 'particularly hostile stories . . .': Weidenfeld, p. 192.

p. 247 'I enlisted him . . .': q. in Knightley, p. 215.

p. 248 'Be your age': q. in Hollingworth, p. 192.

p. 248 'A member of the Foreign Office . . .': Observer, 7.7.63.

p. 248 'We knew Philby . . .': Observer, 8.10.67.

p. 248 'finally turned up . . .': Sunday Times, 20.3.88.

p. 248 'found it impossible . . .': n.d., Obs. Arch.

p. 249 'Japan is a disease . . .': Patrick Seale, unpublished note on Philby, n.d., p.c.

p. 250 'callous libertine': q. in Davenport-Hines, p. 272.

p. 250 'Ward on "Immoral Earnings" . . .': Observer, 9.6.63.

p. 250 'Nothing can excuse . . .': ibid.

p. 251 'David was breathing . . .': q. in Stanford, Bronwen Astor, p. 259.

p. 251 'awful lawyer': DA, q. in Knightley and Kennedy, p. 210.

p. 251 'he should have given him . . .': q. in ibid., p. 254.

p. 251 'made the most calamitous . . .': DA, q. in ibid.

p. 251 'The fate of Stephen Ward . . .': 24.6.83, BH.

p. 251 'a British Dreyfus': q. in Knightley and Kennedy, p. xiv.

p. 251 'I only regret . . .': DA to Bill Astor, n.d., BH.

p. 251 'never admired David Astor . . .': Pringle, p. 151.

p. 252 'very touched': Bronwen Astor to DA, 11.6.63, BH.

p. 252 'Bill is one of the people . . .': DA to Profumo, 20.11.65, BH.

p. 252 'My elder brother's . . .': The Times, 10.3.66.

p. 252 'throw it in the fire': q. in Collis (ed.), p. 182.

p. 252 'a point of principle . . .': DA to Michael Astor, 24.10.53, BH.

p. 252 'welcome diversion': DA to Bill Astor, 24.6.63, BH.

p. 252 'as I felt that . . .': Michael Astor to DA, 14.5.63, BH.

p. 252 'an admirably written book': Observer, 30.6.63.

p. 252 'No one is ever able . . .': Observer, 16.6.63.

p. 252 'I don't think he ever . . .': q. in Stanford, Bronwen Astor, p. 268.

p. 253 'This puts me in . . .': 1.5.64, BH.

p. 253 'they confirmed . . .': DA to Sykes, 11.7.62, BH.

Chapter 21: The Perils of Biography

p. 254 'I was a very welcome . . .': q. in Fox, p. 546.

p. 254 'substantial trust funds . . .': Bill Astor to Bobbie Shaw, 14.11.62, BH.

p. 254 'a childish attitude . . .': DA to Michael Astor, 2.9.64.

p. 254 'threatening to return . . .': DA to Bill Astor, n.d., November 1962, BH.

p. 255 'he had the nerve . . .': q. in Fox, p. 546.
p. 255 'Bobbie was a very big . . .': DA to Lady Helen Nutting, 25.7.70, BH.
p. 255 'was always able to upset . . .': DA to James Astor, 18.8.70, BH.
p. 255 'although I disagreed . . .': 9.9.55, BH.
p. 255 'I think very highly . . .': 20.11.65, BH.
p. 256 'a really vicious . . .': 10.1.51, Berlin, *Enlightening*, p. 205.
p. 256 'the most offensive . . .': Berlin to Rowland Burdon-Miller, 18.1.51, ibid., p. 207.
p. 256 'deliberate flattery . . .': *Manchester Guardian*, 4.6.56.
p. 256 'All David Astor's accusations . . .': 21.6.56, Berlin, *Enlightening*, p. 534.
p. 256 'I am in despair . . .': 6.3.59, BH.
p. 256 'makes him almost . . .': DA to Brand, 10.3.59, BH.
p. 257 'entered deeply . . .': Rowse, p. 96.
p. 257 'I cannot tell you . . .': 12.5.63, BH.
p. 257 'Christopher is the ideal . . .': q. in Christabel Bielenberg to DA, 24.5.63, BH.
p. 257 'I know Sykes . . .': 19.7.63, BH.
p. 257 'a finer type . . .': Rowse, p. 96.
p. 257 'vehemently opposed': 22.7.64, BH.
p. 258 'a slight anxiety': DA to Sykes, 28.12.65, BH.
p. 258 'I think we're in trouble': 1.7.66, BH.
p. 258 'You do not accept . . .': 12.2.68, BH.
p. 258 'the clumsy, muddle-headed . . .': 10.4.69, BH.
p. 258 'conveys an impression . . .': 19.7.68, Georgetown.
p. 258 'I'm happy to become . . .': 6.5.68, BH.
p. 258 'These people are all . . .': Sykes notes on letter to him from DA, 1.7.66, Georgetown.
p. 258 'I respect your great . . .': 4.4.68, BH.
p. 258 'what being a writer entails': Sykes to DA, 10.9.68, BH.
p. 258 'a strange case of . . .': Sykes to Clarita von Trott, 6.2.69, Georgetown.
p. 258 'magnificent and moving . . .': Ollard to Sykes, 15.11.68, BH.
p. 259 'I do think . . .': 23.2.68, Georgetown.
p. 259 'to get the pliable . . .': Sykes to Christabel Bielenberg, 7.3.69, BH.
p. 259 'You and the Committee . . .': 1.6.69, Georgetown.
p. 259 'outrageous mischief-making': 10.5.69, BH.
p. 259 'if he could only . . .': 8.4.69, BH.
p. 259 'I was reacting against . . .': 8.7.80, Georgetown.
p. 259 'the real disaster . . .': 18.2.69, BH.

p. 259 'poisonous passages . . .': Grant Duff to DA, 18.2.69, BH.

p. 259 'I quite agree with you . . .': 22.2.69, BH.

p. 259 'very fair memorial . . .': 27.1.69, BH.

p. 259 'after ascertaining . . .': DA to Clarita von Trott, 17.8.68, BH.

p. 260 'could not take . . .': *Observer*, 24.11.68.

p. 260 'The full story . . .': 4.9.69, Georgetown.

p. 260 'I have been radically . . .': 8.7.65, BH.

p. 260 'I did forgive him . . .': Berlin to Sykes, 24.5.68, Georgetown.

p. 260 'seemed to me pathetic . . .': 10.6.69, Georgetown.

p. 261 'I didn't know . . .': 20.12.34, Balliol.

p. 261 'I saw how mistaken . . .': Bowra, p. 316.

p. 261 'That's one Nazi . . .': q. in MacDonogh, p. 5.

p. 261 'an upper-class Hun': q. in Mitchell, p. 215.

p. 261 'about a German Rhodes . . .': q. in ibid., p. 217.

p. 261 'does not regret anything . . .': Grant Duff to Berlin, 2.7.62, q. in ibid.

p. 261 'bad conscience': DA to Christabel Bielenberg, 21.5.62, BH.

p. 261 'probably this feeling . . .': DA, 'Draft Memorandum to Christopher Sykes', 9.1.67, BH.

p. 261 'a wholly reasonable mistake': q. in Mitchell, p. 217.

p. 261 'no question': Jakie Astor to DA, 15.5.68, BH.

p. 261 'my experience of him . . .': DA to Jakie Astor, 3.5.68, BH.

p. 261 'age and alcohol': DA to Jakie Astor, 21.8.68, BH.

p. 261 'I have had my little say . . .': 3.10.68, BH.

p. 262 'an intelligent, professional . . .': Michael Astor to DA, 4.9.68, BH.

p. 262 'I appreciate your generosity . . .': 1.6.69, BH.

p. 262 'purely destructive act': 9.4.69, BH.

p. 262 'no one member . . .': 8.4.69, BH.

p. 262 'you would act . . .': 9.4.69, BH.

p. 262 'It is easy enough . . .': 21.4.69, BH.

p. 263 'intellectual crook': DA to Edward Ford, 4.6.69, BH.

p. 263 'age and drink': DA to Jakie Astor, 9.5.69, BH.

p. 263 'that, I assure you . . .': ibid.

p. 263 'taken so little notice . . .': DA to Edward Ford, 17.7.69, BH.

p. 263 'suggests that my mother . . .': ibid.

p. 263 'I am told that he . . .': 3.2.72, Georgetown.

p. 263 'I am greatly impressed . . .': 11.1.72, BH.

p. 264 'totally incapacitated': Michael Astor to DA, 23.10.62, BH.

p. 264 'no one gave a damn . . .': Newby, p. 221.

p. 264 'no ability to cut . . .': Richard Findlater memo, 14.9.72, Obs. Arch.

p. 264 'we feel we are wasting . . .': 9.2.73, Obs. Arch.

p. 264 'too much travelling . . .': 16.3.73, Obs. Arch.

p. 264 'nine years' faithful . . .': 20.8.73, Obs. Arch.

p. 264 'it seems fairly clear . . .': 7.4.60, BH.

p. 265 'because of his tremendous . . .': q. in O'Connor, p. 234.

p. 265 'getting you out of . . .': q. in Lewis, p. 502.

p. 265 'of what fun you are . . .': 29.4.60, BH.

p. 265 'fashionable hypocrisies': DA to Graham Greene, 21.9.63, HRHRC.

p. 265 'looked like an army . . .': Alvarez, p. 207.

p. 265 'accept – and are grateful for . . .': 8.5.63, Obs. Arch.

p. 266 'I was influenced by . . .': 29.10.57, Obs. Arch.

p. 266 'it would be asking . . .': 25.10.57, Obs. Arch.

p. 266 'drive to naughtiness': Kenneth Harris interview with DA, 16.1.63, Obs. Arch.

p. 266 'Astor gave Kilmartin . . .': James, p. 58.

p. 266 'necessity has led . . .': 11.6.66, Obs. Arch.

p. 266 'proved a much tougher nut . . .': James, p. 109.

p. 267 'are already sniffing . . .': 29.10.69, NA.

p. 267 'I made many . . .': 26.11.86, BH.

p. 267 '"Look at all those . . ."': *Observer*, 18.8.91.

p. 267 'no flattery would move . . .': ibid.

Chapter 22: *Drifting Apart*

p. 268 'person of enormous . . .': *Queen*, 20.8.69.

p. 268 'the *Observer* of today . . .': 23.3.67, BH.

p. 269 'as big-hearted . . .': Goodman, p. 379.

p. 270 'always a bad sign': q. in Brivati, p. 220.

p. 270 'I fear I sent him . . .': q. in ibid., p. 221.

p. 270 'our crazy patchwork . . .': John Pringle, q. in Cockett, *David Astor and the Observer*, p. 246.

p. 270 'Much look forward . . .': 9.10.65, BH.

p. 270 'David was looking . . .': Hetherington, p. 162.

p. 270 'the only management . . .': Michael Davie, the *Age*, 2.7.81.

p. 271 'he was not particularly . . .': Goodman, p. 379.

p. 271 'its notional value . . .': Clive Bradley, 'The *Observer* 1973–1975', n.d., p.c.

p. 271 'I am sure the Astors . . .': Goodman, p. 390.

p. 271 'may have looked good . . .': Hussey, p. 130.

p. 271 'the business coup . . .': Goodman, p. 390.

p. 271 'with a technical force . . .': Baistow, 'Anatomy of the Observer Crisis', *New Statesman*, 27.6.75.

p. 271 'You must tell me . . .': Roger Harrison to the author.

p. 272 'proposed *Observer* consortium': Jakie Astor to DA, n.d., September 1967, BH.

p. 272 'I am not convinced . . .': ibid.

p. 272 'way in which private . . .': 16.10.67, BH.

p. 272 'drastically altered': 20.8.67, BH.

p. 272 'thoroughly businesslike . . .': 1.9.67, BH.

p. 272 'Jacob will indeed . . .': 21.3.68, BH.

p. 273 'political and intellectual . . .': unsent letter from DA to Thornton Bradshaw, n.d., BH.

p. 273 'the idea of questionnaires . . .': ibid.

p. 273 'I spend a great deal . . .': 11.12.73, BH.

p. 273 'in view of the present . . .': n.d., BH.

p. 273 'although David kept . . .': Hall, p. 80.

p. 273 'most of its aims . . .': 'Some Memories', n.d., p.c.

p. 273 'trendy to the point . . .': *Spectator*, 20.9.69.

p. 274 'become more woolly . . .': Baistow, 'Anatomy of the Observer Crisis', *New Statesman*, 27.6.75.

p. 274 'what was good about . . .': author unknown, 'Efficient Visigoths and Noble Romans', TS, n.d., Sampson papers, Bodleian.

p. 274 'Don't you think . . .': Colin Smith to author.

p. 275 'quickly began to . . .': Hall, p. 78.

p. 275 'You have upset . . .': Peter Wilby to author.

p. 275 'I should not like that . . .': q. in Hall, p. 85.

p. 275 'an unjustified piece . . .': DA to Donald Trelford, 16.9.75, Obs. Arch.

p. 276 'You can sit . . .': Sue Arnold to the author.

p. 276 'Since when did . . .': ibid.

p. 276 'the one I most admired . . .': John Clare to the author, 17.10.14.

p. 277 'Go away and write it . . .': Holland in Sampson (ed.), p. 26.

p. 277 'Good God, and Ken . . .': Robert Chesshyre to author.

p. 277 'lost its tolerance . . .': author unknown, 'Efficient Visigoths and Noble Romans', TS, n.d., Sampson papers, Bodleian.

p. 277 'the Cold War remained . . .': Frankland, p. 209.

p. 277 'the *Observer* was never . . .': Hall, p. 87.

p. 277 'Even its most loyal . . .': *New Statesman*, 15.2.74.

p. 278 'I tremendously admire . . .': 27.6.70, BH.

p. 278 'with a consistency . . .': 26.1.74, BH.

p. 278 'dupes of a few . . .': 18.2.74, Obs. Arch.

p. 278 'the only papers that . . .': n.d., Obs. Arch.

p. 278 'How greatly I have . . .': 12.3.74, BH.

p. 278 'You were less perfect . . .': 27.11.74, Obs. Arch.

p. 278 'Astor's interests . . .': Rudolf Klein, review of Cockett, *David Astor and the Observer, Political Quarterly*, Vol. 63, No. 1, January–March 1992, pp. 114–15.

p. 279 'a most shifty, vulgar . . .': Berlin to Rowland Burdon-Miller, 17.12.58, *Enlightening*, p. 663.

p. 279 'I don't want Mary . . .': Peter Crookston to author.

p. 279 'Everyone knows . . .': 19.6.74, BH.

p. 279 'I have thought of you . . .': 4.9.74, BH.

p. 279 'You are irredeemably . . .': 26.4.75, BH.

p. 280 'famous for grasping . . .': Watkins, *A Short Walk Down Fleet Street*, p. 157.

p. 280 'dangerous woman': q. in Margach, p. 147.

p. 280 'over Miss Beloff . . .': ibid.

p. 280 'done so as to indicate . . .': ibid., p. 149.

p. 280 'I remain unconvinced . . .': 9.4.68, PREM 13/2301, NA.

p. 281 'What you are really saying . . .': q. in Margach, p. 148.

p. 281 'the relations between . . .': 28.5.69, Obs. Arch.

p. 281 'pure fabrication': *Observer*, 27.12.71.

p. 281 'frequently to be found . . .': *Private Eye*, 12.3.71.

p. 281 'a large whisky . . .': Watkins, *A Short Walk Down Fleet Street*, p. 156.

p. 282 'a most serious . . .': Peter Carter-Ruck to Richard Ingrams, 5.4.71.

p. 282 'the millionaire drip . . .': *Private Eye*, 3.11.72.

p. 282 'that strange man . . .': Michael Astor to DA, n.d., BH.

p. 282 'my hope is that I may . . .': 28.3.68, BH.

p. 283 'the ablest journalist . . .': DA evidence to the Monopolies Commission, 2.6.81.

p. 283 'good company . . .': Hall, p. 31.

p. 283 'to help David sell . . .': Trelford in Sampson (ed.), p. 30.

p. 284 'It's your shoes': Trelford in interview with Robert McCrum, n.d., Obs. Arch.

p. 284 'I am enormously helped . . .': 22.7.70, BH.

Chapter 23: End Game
p. 285 'the number of needless . . .': q. in Griffiths, p. 224.

p. 285 'You may own it . . .': q. in Jenkins, p. 73.

p. 286 'involved no extra work . . .': Pringle, memo to DA, 11.4.61, q. in Cockett, *David Astor and the Observer*, p. 258.

p. 286 'this bold claim easier . . .': *Index on Censorship*, Vol. 6, No. 1, January–February 1977.

p. 287 'the chapel has . . .': q. in *Evening Standard*, 13.1.77.

p. 287 'I never dared . . .': *The Times*, 19.1.77.

p. 287 'several years ahead . . .': q. in Cockett, *David Astor and the Observer*, p. 271.

p. 288 'The real hero . . .': q. in ibid., p. 273.

p. 288 'hell on earth': Bradley, 'The *Observer*, 1973–1975', n.d., p.c.

p. 289 'it would be insane . . .': Wintour, *Pressures on the Press*, p. 82.

p. 289 'journalism is not simply . . .': DA to NPA, 30.2.70, q. in ibid., p. 83.

p. 289 'I can't help sending . . .': 20.12.74, Obs. Arch.

p. 289 'you ought to be our patron . . .': q. in Beloff, p. 32.

p. 290 'we had no idea . . .': q. in ibid., p. 60.

p. 290 'blithering idiots': ibid., p. 123.

p. 290 'a poor bunch . . .': ibid., p. 62.

p. 290 'he would rather close . . .': ibid., p. 49.

p. 290 'gives a misleading . . .': ibid., p. 58.

p. 290 'it was the nucleus . . .': author unknown, 'Efficient Visigoths and Noble Romans', TS, n.d., Sampson papers, Bodleian.

p. 291 'made the announcement . . .': Whitehorn in Sampson (ed.), p. 19.

p. 291 'You were far and away . . .': 7.9.75, Obs. Arch.

p. 291 'those many years . . .': 6.10.75, Obs. Arch.

p. 291 'I guess you must . . .': 4.8.75, BH.

p. 291 'you know how highly . . .': q. in Cockett, *David Astor and the Observer*, p. 276.

p. 291 'one of the most outstanding . . .': ibid.

p. 292 'some sort of runner': Robert Chesshyre to author.

p. 292 'bring some new ideas . . .': 5.7.75, Sampson papers, Bodleian.

p. 292 'not allow any . . .': 14.10.75, Sampson papers, Bodleian.

p. 292 'quite single-minded . . .': Hall, p. 118.

p. 292 'It's a man named . . .': Robert Chesshyre to author.

p. 292 'I suppose it was always . . .': n.d., Sampson papers, Bodleian.

p. 293 'although addicted to . . .': 7.11.75, Obs. Arch.

p. 293 'I've always been aware . . .': 17.12.75, BH.

p. 293 'his paper was wrong . . .': *Sunday Telegraph*, 6.10.91.

p. 293 'I have enjoyed my dealings . . .': 14.10.75, p.c.

Chapter 24: Last Rites

p. 294 'My overwhelming . . .': DA notes on Cockett's final chapter of *David Astor and the Observer*, n.d., Obs. Arch.

p. 294 'If this was a racing . . .': ibid.

p. 294 'more whimsical': q. in Hall, p. 121.

p. 295 'better to have . . .': q. in ibid., p. 119.

p. 295 'the company was . . .': q. in Cockett, *David Astor and the Observer*, p. 250.

p. 295 'sell my paper to . . .': q. in Hall, p. 11.

p. 295 'That's a surprise . . .': q. in Leapman, p. 83.

p. 296 'The Third World . . .': q. in ibid., p. 96.

p. 296 'giving the *Observer* . . .': q. in ibid., p. 86.

p. 296 'uneasy, even shifty . . .': Watkins, *A Short Walk Down Fleet Street*, p. 164.

p. 296 'all the *Observer* had . . .': q. in author unknown, 'Efficient Visigoths and Noble Romans', TS, n.d., Sampson papers, Bodleian.

p. 296 'We'd have given you . . .': q. in Evans, *Good Times, Bad Times*, p. 212.

p. 296 'the biggest mistake . . .': Murdoch to Times Newspapers executives, q. in DA notes, n.d., Obs. Arch.

p. 296 'ready to go quietly . . .': 29.10.76, BH.

p. 296 'an independent newspaper . . .': 3.11.76, BH.

p. 296 'keep the *Observer* remotely . . .': DA to Goodman, 4.11.76, BH.

p. 297 'Perhaps Bob Anderson . . .': Kenneth Harris, p.vii.

p. 297 'when the chance came . . .': ibid., p. 148.

p. 297 'I think he's a man . . .': Roger Harrison to author.

p.297 'Anderson seemed too good . . .': Sampson, *The Changing Anatomy of Britain*, p. 393.

p. 297 'corpulent, cross-looking . . .': author unknown, 'Efficient Visigoths and Noble Romans', TS, n.d., Sampson papers, Bodleian.

p. 297 'seemed not to share . . .': *The Times*, 25.11.76.

p. 297 'seldom felt happier': DA to *The Times*, 26.11.76.

p. 298 'How do you thank . . .': 26.11.76, BH.

p. 298 'the most intelligent . . .': ibid.

p. 298 'it was a long time . . .': Hall, p. 123.

p. 298 'It seemed to me . . .': 29.3.79, BH.

p. 298 'the speed of your . . .': 3.11.76, BH.

p. 298 'the only dividend . . .': 8.12.76, BH.

p. 299 'was generally regarded . . .': 29.3.79, BH.

p. 299 'editorial brilliance': 3.12.76, BH.

p. 299 'the editorial staff . . .': DA to Anderson, 20.1.77, BH.

p. 299 'Since you and I . . .': DA to Cater, 13.5.77, BH.

p. 299 'choleric tone': Trelford to Cater, 9.9.77, BH.

p. 299 'If Arco wants more . . .': DA to Goodman, 7.1.79, BH.

p. 299 'the Rocky Marciano . . .': Watkins, *A Short Walk Down Fleet Street*, p. 177.

p. 299 'seemed audaciously confident . . .': Hall, p. 133.

p. 299 'I am very much aware . . .': 18.8.77, BH.

p. 300 'I keep quiet . . .': q. in Watkins, *A Short Walk Down Fleet Street*, p. 177.

p. 300 'positively fizzled with joy': O'Brien in Sampson (ed.), p. 38.

p. 300 'the Cruiser was rarely . . .': Hall, p. 134.

p. 300 'a perpetual switchback ride': Cole, p. 196.

p. 300 'on the assumption that . . .': O'Brien, p. 364.

p. 300 'an assiduous courtier': Hall, p. 134.

p. 300 'formidable, deep-laid . . .': O'Brien, p. 366.

p. 300 'it was only when David . . .': ibid., p. 367.

p. 301 'a "department store" . . .': DA, memo, 5.7.79, BH.

p. 301 'The main point to try . . .': 9.1.79, BH.

p. 301 'you can't give a paper . . .': DA to Lord Barnetson, 24.8.77, BH.

p. 301 'rather heavy-handed . . .': O'Brien, p. 365.

p. 301 'Anderson's ruthless . . .': ibid., p. 368.

p. 301 'not in accordance . . .': ibid., p. 370.

p. 301 'one of the most distinguished . . .': 10.11.77, BH.

p. 302 'I was determined . . .': O'Brien, p. 376.

p. 302 'the most powerful . . .': n.d., Obs. Arch.

p. 302 'Harris has a reputation . . .': DA to Arnold Goodman, 9.1.79, BH.

p. 302 'Have you heard that . . .': Trelford interview with Robert McCrum, n.d., Obs. Arch.

p. 302 'You do not need . . .': q. in Cockett, *David Astor and the Observer*, p. 286.

p. 302 'as a simple soul . . .': ibid.

p. 302 'from a legal eagle . . .': Hall, p. 141.

p. 302 'I have some knowledge . . .': q. in Bower, p. 395.

p. 302 'in the least interested . . .': Hall, p. 136.

p. 302 'I really was almost . . .': q. in ibid.

p. 303 'both are tall . . .': n.d., Obs. Arch.

p. 303 'I was led up the garden . . .': q. in Hall, p. 142.

p. 303 'bounded into the newsroom . . .': q. in ibid., p. 138.

p. 303 'Tiny never did . . .': ibid., p. 144.

p. 303 'What are they saying . . .': ibid., p. 140.

p. 303 'couldn't maintain my . . .': q. in Bower, p. 398.

p. 303 'rely on me . . .': q. in ibid., p. 399.

p. 303 'not all the instruments . . .': q. in ibid., p. 396.

p. 303 'almost apolitical': 5.3.81, BH.

p. 303 'it is hard to see how . . .': q. in Hall, p. 158.

p. 304 'went into some detail . . .': O'Brien, p. 377.

p. 304 'in all the years . . .': DA evidence to Monopolies Commission, 2.6.81, BH.

p. 304 'assurances from a suspect . . .': DA to John Biffen, 24.6.81, BH.

p. 304 'would have the expertise . . .': q. in Cockett, *David Astor and the Observer*, p. 289.

Chapter 25: Home Affairs

p. 305 'My inclination is not to . . .': 25.10.75, Obs. Arch.

p. 305 'if David Astor gives up . . .': q. in Hall, p. 81.

p. 305 'the contemporary always seemed . . .': Pringle, p. 144.

p. 306 'smiles a great deal . . .': Hall, p. 77.

p. 306 'Never assume . . .': Pat Burge to the author.

p. 306 'I have never known anyone . . .': Sam Beer, q. by Donald Trelford in speech at DA's memorial service.

p. 307 'How did a rich boy . . .': DA notes, n.d., BH.

p. 307 'crowning achievement': 25.11.85, BH.

p. 307 'Tristan might not . . .': 29.9.86, BH.

p. 307 'just too much of . . .': 26.2.91, BH.

p. 307 'capacity for honesty': Cockett in Sampson (ed.), p. 50.

p. 307 'the sensation of looking . . .': DA, 'Memoir Material', n.d., BH.

p. 308 'a man who made . . .': *Observer*, 6.6.56.

p. 308 'an extraordinary ability . . .': q. in Peters, p. 196.

p. 309 'Psychoanalysis, even of . . .': *Observer*, 6.6.56.

p. 309 'apt to view him . . .': letter to *Observer*, 20.5.56.

p. 309 'the most important advance . . .': DA to Sir William Hayter, 21.6.67, BH.

p. 309 'visiting lectureship': 8.9.67, BH.

p. 309 'of all places': 4.11.67, BH.

p. 310 'expound the history . . .': 26.11.71, BH.

p. 310 'ever since I was . . .': DA to Sir Edward Playfair, 2.7.72, BH.

p. 310 'was a most wonderful . . .': 5.7.72, BH.

p. 310 'brave enough': q. in DA to Annan, 20.12.72, BH.

p. 310 'obviously I am not . . .': DA to Annan, 20.10.72, BH.

p. 310 'making life awfully . . .': 5.11.74, BH.

p. 310 'if the divisions . . .': 13.12.74, BH.

p. 310 'Please do not press . . .': 5.7.77, BH.

p. 310 'further the state . . .': 31.8.78, BH.

p. 311 'bounce': 18.9.78, BH.

p. 311 'Freud's work and ideas . . .': DA, notes on the Freud chair, n.d., BH.

p. 311 'psychoanalytical thinking . . .': Laufer in Sampson (ed.), p. 32.

p. 311 'the psychology of . . .': DA to Alastair Buchan, 3.12.63, BH.

p. 311 'the trouble with Eichmann . . .': Arendt, p. 276.

p. 311 'long, well-argued . . .': 26.3.61, HRHRC.

p. 312 'it is always unwise . . .': 1.4.61, HRHRC.

p. 312 'a major excursion . . .': Cohn to DA, 23.7.62, BH.

p. 312 'Your initiative . . .': 14.11.62, BH.

p. 312 'Do you not prejudge . . .': 5.12.62, BH.

p. 313 'What I want studied . . .': 7.12.62, BH.

p. 313 'a psychological study . . .': 1.12.62, BH.

p. 314 'the politics of obsession': DA and Cohn, joint memo, n.d., February 1963, BH.

p. 314 'social disintegration . . .': report by Cohn, 22.9.63, BH.

p. 314 'one of the exciting . . .': DA to Leonard Wolfson, 26.11.65, BH.

p. 314 'He went so far . . .': q. in Gabriel Denvir, 'An Analysis of the Columbus Centre', BA dissertation, Birkbeck College, 1.5.14.

p. 314 'I am not at all sure . . .': DA to Tommy Wilson, 31.5.73, q. in ibid.

p. 315 'I am naturally in sympathy . . .': 11.2.56, BH.

p. 315 'Vat is our next crusade?': q. in Scammell, p. 485.

p. 315 'a man in whom . . .': Rolph, p. 151.

p. 315 'the idea is such a good . . .': 25.4.61, BH.

p. 316 'We don't want . . .': Peter Timms in conversation with the author.

p. 316 'Did you expect . . .': ibid.

p. 316 'You won't know who I am . . .': Ben Birnberg in conversation with the author.

p. 317 'infatuated accomplice': Longford to DA, 23.2.82, BH.

p. 317 'one of nature's innocents': q. in Stanford, *Lord Longford*, p. 275.

p. 317 'was absolutely right . . .': q. in ibid., p. 442.

p. 317 'what they are frightened of . . .': 14.12.82, BH.

p. 317 'one feels she's come . . .': 6.9.83, BH.

p. 317 'a spiritual achievement': 11.3.87, BH.

p. 317 'the publisher I know best . . .': 23.3.88, BH.

p. 317 'has been pretty good . . .': DA to Hindley, 25.1.90, BH.

p. 317 'You must realise . . .': 4.7.89, BH.

p. 318 'you have the love . . .': 10.9.90, BH.

p. 318 'a unique campaign . . .': *The Times*, 5.11.90.

p. 318 'any trial by newspaper . . .': *Guardian*, 2.1.90.

p. 318 'innately evil . . .': *Observer*, 25.4.93.

p. 318 'elderly toff': *Daily Star*, 28.9.89.

p. 318 'Old Etonian . . .': *Daily Star*, 16.8.90.

p. 318 'Mr Astor this week . . .': *The Times*, 10.12.94.

p. 318 'Some day, perhaps . . .': 25.2.99, BH.

p. 319 'effects on our society . . .': DA and Longford, letter to *The Times*, 14.12.94.

p. 319 'shambling Victorian house': *Guardian*, 16.10.78.

p. 319 'I am much interested . . .': DA to Philippa, Lady Astor, 22.1.75, BH.

p. 319 'fair silvery hair . . .': Pizzey, *This Way to the Revolution*, p. 161.

p. 319 'if you will come . . .': q. in *Guardian*, 11.1.78.

p. 319 'an intelligent extended . . .': ibid.

p. 319 'I sensed that David . . .': Pizzey, *This Way to the Revolution*, p. 184.

p. 320 'surprised to find . . .': ibid., p. 161.

p. 320 'dear friend and saviour': ibid., p. 193.

p. 320 'she had the force of persuasion . . .': Goodman, p. 379.

p. 320 'a puddle of car oil': Pizzey, *This Way to the Revolution*, p. 193.

p. 320 'David became increasingly . . .': ibid., p. 271.

p. 320 'trashed the house': ibid., p. 281.

p. 320 'because I needed . . .': ibid., p. 284.

p. 320 'I need not fear . . .': ibid., p. 288.

p. 320 'I think I have unhappily . . .': 10.9.79, BH.

p. 321 'David Astor, whom I . . .': Curtis (ed.), p. 581.

p. 321 'a sentimental old liberal': Benn, p. 44.

p. 321 'I may be starry-eyed . . .': 15.4.81, BH.

Chapter 26: Happy Endings

p. 323 'To a large extent . . .': 2.11.68, BH.

p. 323 'I feel bound to stick . . .': 31.8.63, BH.

p. 324 'the United Nations . . .': DA to Aubrey Jones, 2.2.65, BH.

p. 324 'to act as a friend . . .': 17.1.77, BH.

p. 324 'I feel a certain need . . .': 11.8.62, BH.

p. 325 'some kind of world order': DA to Sir Miles Clifford, 15.4.64, BH.

p. 325 'what Philip . . .': DA to Betty Langhorne, 1.3.65, BH.

p. 326 'dated back to . . .': Cockett, *David Astor and the Observer*, p. 252.

p. 326 'I have long taken . . .': 18.7.86, BH.

p. 326 'superior efficiency . . .': DA, 'Israel: The Real Challenge', *Observer*, 11.6.67.

p. 327 'normally impassive face . . .': Yorke in Sampson (ed.), p. 32.

p. 327 'Oh, how disappointed . . .': 19.4.77, BH.

p. 327 'an essential document . . .': Peres to Pat Newman of Corgi Books, 17.10.78, p.c.

p. 327 'a vitally relevant text': *Listener*, 21.12.78.

p. 327 'the first comprehensive plan . . .': *Observer*, 10.9.78.

p. 327 'the great strength . . .': Sydney Bailey, *Middle East International*, December 1978.

p. 328 'enormous contribution . . .': Assousa in Sampson (ed.), p. 41.

p. 328 'gilt-edged': 12.12.86, BH.

p. 328 'I would not have backed . . .': q. in Peter Rose, p. 94.

p. 329 'of my activities . . .': DA to Sir John Prideaux, 4.7.84, BH.

p. 329 'People who want to avoid . . .': Kenny in Sampson (ed.), p. 42.

p. 330 'bursting at the seams': Sir Arthur Snelling to DA, 9.11.70, BH.

p. 330 'do everything in my power . . .': Mandela to Sir John Maud, q. in Sampson, *Mandela*, p. 204.

p. 330 'usurpation of leadership': 22.9.78, BH.

p. 330 'As a sovereign . . .': secretary of ANC to Pat Burge, 4.6.80, BH.

p. 330 'the most emphatic opinions . . .': Woods in Sampson (ed.), p. 40.

p. 331 'which is free of . . .': 13.4.81, BH.

p. 331 'It is important that . . .': 28.7.80, BH.

p. 331 'no torture . . .': 25.5.83, BH.

p. 331 'I do not believe . . .': 4.7.83, BH.

p. 331 'Her findings are . . .': 21.7.83, BH.

p. 332 'unable to give . . .': Suzman to DA, 1.8.83, BH.

p. 332 'and provides the authorities . . .': 29.1.85, BH.

p. 332 'obsession about Communist . . .': Huddleston to DA, 29.5.85, BH.

p. 332 'always accepted . . .': DA to Huddleston, 3.11.83, BH.

p. 332 'I am pretty certain . . .': 22.8.85, BH.

p. 332 'ungovernable': 1985 broadcast, q. in *New York Times* obituary of Tambo, 25.4.93.

p. 332 'I doubt whether you . . .': 21.5.85, BH.

p. 333 'spent force': DA to Legum, 19.10.83, BH.

p. 333 'given some thought . . .': 21.5.85, BH.

p. 334 'importance of the . . .': Sampson to DA, n.d., BH.

p. 334 'Anthony's meeting . . .': 24.10.85, BH.

p. 334 'tremendous impression': 8.7.86, BH.

p. 334 'criss-crossed the country . . .': Shaun Johnson in Sampson (ed.), p. 48.

p. 335 'whether you might be able . . .': 7.1.87, BH.

p. 335 'confidential meeting': DA to Marion Doenhoff, 10.7.89, BH.

p. 336 'the method of government . . .': *Independent*, 17.12.86.

p. 336 'even before it . . .': 28.4.89, BH.

Index

League of Nations 13, 65, 66
Lean, Sir David 188
Leavis, F. R. 242
Lebanon 327–8; Philby in 247, 248–9
Lederer, Lajos 172–3, 212, 327
Lee, Edwin (Cliveden butler) 10, 11, 16, 20
Leeds 60, 64; Queen's Hotel 61
Leeper, Sir Reginald (Rex) 68, 72
Left Book Club 244
Legum, Colin: background, character and interests 171–2, 275; at *Observer* 171, 179, 186, 293, 302; reporting on Africa 171, 187–8, 193, 336; advisor to Africa Bureau 190; contribution to *Attitudes to Africa* 190; reporting on Nagaland 200; and Middle East conflict 327, 328; and Lonrho's purchase of *Observer* 304, 305; and Chiswick women's refuge 321; views on DA 164–5; views on *Observer* and its staff 143, 220
Legum, Margaret 321
Lehmann, John 113, 265; *Penguin New Writing* 175, 176
Leitch, David 250
Lejeune, C. A. 110, 141, 235, 237; on Bill Astor 63–4; on DA 64; on Garvin 63; on Ivor Brown 168
Lenin, Vladimir 31, 222
Lennon, John 275
Lesseps, Ferdinand de 203
Lever, Harold (*later* Baron Lever of Manchester) 327, 329
Levin, Bernard 266, 300
Lewis, Anthony 280
Lewis, Sir (William) Arthur 190
Lewis, C. S., *Beyond Personality* 116
Lewis, Derek 317
Lichtheim, George 176
Liddell Hart, Sir Basil 125
Life (magazine) 244
Lilliput (magazine) 170
Lincoln, Anthony 283
Lincoln Trust (anti-apartheid group) 332
Lindbergh, Charles 82
Lindemann, Frederick (*later* Viscount Cherwell) 80
Lindsay, A. D. (Sandie; *later* 1st Baron Lindsay of Birker) 28, 35, 42, 85, 96, 97
Lindsay, Norah 51, 180
Linklater, Veronica, Baroness 317
Listener (magazine) 267, 328
lithium 309, 337
Littlejohns, John 270, 271, 272, 288
Littleworth, Charles 60
Litvinov, Maxim 31
Litvinov, Pavel 325
Lloyd George, David, 1st Earl Lloyd-George of Dwyfor 9, 12, 16, 18, 97, 103, 107
Lloyd, Selwyn (*later* Baron Selwyn-Lloyd) 205
Loch Ness Monster 94
Loewe, Lionel 91
Loewenthal, Richard (Rix) 90, 121, 164, 175, 176, 179, 219, 220, 221, 223
'London Group' (wartime think-tank) 90
London Magazine 265
London School of Economics (LSE) 294
London Weekend Television: *Observer* investment in 273–4, 296, 298
Longford, Elizabeth Pakenham, Countess of 190, 256
Longford, Frank Pakenham, 7th Earl of 27, 28, 122, 145, 159, 329; and campaign for abolition of death penalty 177; and South Africa Treason Trial Defence

Fund 191; and Montagu trial 315–16; and Myra Hindley 318–19, 321
Lonrho (corporate conglomerate) 296, 303–5
Lons-les-Soulines, France 131
Lorant, Stefan 73
Los Angeles 298
Lothian, Philip Kerr, 11th Marquess of Lothian: background, character and career 17, 61; at Cliveden 16–17; friend and mentor to young DA 17, 23, 41, 71; visits Soviet Union with Astors and Bernard Shaw 31; properties and estates 43, 51; and rise of Hitler and coming of war 66, 67, 69, 70, 71, 79, 95, 326; and Trott's peace missions 76, 83, 84, 260; visits DA during military service 93; and Lionel Curtis 162; *Lord Lothian* (Butler) 257–8
Low, Sir David: cartoon of 'Cliveden Set' 69
LSE (London School of Economics) 294
Lubetkin, Berthold 137
Lucan, John Bingham, 7th Earl of 276–7
Lucas, John 234, 235, 265
Ludecke, Rita 77
Lumley, Joanna 321
Lusaka 197
Luthuli, Albert 191, 192, 333
Lyall, Gavin 229
Lygon, Lady Mary 51
Lynd, Robert 154

MacBride, Sean 324
MacCarthy, Sir Desmond 62
McCarthy, Mary 175, 280
McCarthyism 183
McCooey, Andrew 319
McCrum, Robert 325
McCullin, Don 214
Macdonald, Dwight 175
McDonald, Iverach 204
MacDonnell, A. G. 100
MacDonogh, Giles x
Mace, Edward 265, 277
McIlvanney, Hugh 178, 234, 284
MacInnes, Colin 176
Mackenzie, Alasdair 326
McLachlan, Donald 201, 242
Maclean, Donald 158, 183, 246
Maclean, Melinda 183
McLean, Ruari 176, 214
Macleod, Alastair 182, 256
Macleod, Iain 208, 209
Macmillan, Lady Dorothy 253, 254
Macmillan, Harold (*later* 1st Earl of Stockton): Foreign Secretary 205, 247; clears Philby 247; and Suez Crisis 205; succeeds Eden as prime minister 209; 'never had it so good' speech 212; 'wind of change' tour of Africa 192; and Profumo Affair 250, 253–4; resignation and announcement of successor 225, 250, 254
McNair, Gordon (and family) 38, 42–3
McNamara, Robert 254, 332, 335, 336
McWhirter, Norris 178
Maddox, Sir John 275
Magnus, Sir Philip 256
Maisky, Ivan 16
Makins, Clifford 234–5
Makins, Roger (*later* 1st Baron Sherfield) 135
Makins, Virginia 173
Malan, D. F. 187, 195
Malaya 104
Manchester, William: *The Making of the President* 268

Manchester Evening News 112, 153, 157, 271
Manchester Guardian 49, 202; DA seeks position with 58, 59; on Suez Crisis 204, 205, 206, 212; women's pages 228; and Philby affair 249; DA's article on Trott 257, 261; becomes national newspaper and changes title 206; see also *Guardian*
Mandel, Paul 244
Mandela, Nelson 191, 192–4, 319, 324, 331–33, 334, 335, 337
Mandela, Winnie 332, 333
Mann, Arthur: background and character 60; editor of *Yorkshire Post* 60; opposition to Munich Agreement 72; *Observer* trustee 60, 123, 139; and Garvin's tribunal 105, 107; as possible successor to Garvin 109; and Brown's appointment as editor 109, 111; concerns about Brown's possible departure 141; and DA's takeover as editor 153, 154; and DA's interest in Africa 187; resignation over Suez 60, 209
Manoim, Irwin 335
Mansfield College, Oxford 45
Mao Tse Tung 280
Marber, Romek 244, 245
Marceau, Marcel 227
Marcus, Abraham 265
Margach, James 202, 281
Marie, Queen of Rumania 5, 19
Marlborough, John Churchill, 1st Duke of 94
Marshall, Arthur 127, 307
Marshall & Snelgrove (department store) 228
Marshall Plan 147, 148, 173
Martin, Kingsley 97, 147, 160, 174, 234
Marx Brothers 15, 231
Marxism: DA's views on 56, 97–8, 165
Masada (ancient fortification) 323
Maschler, Tom 267
Masius & Fergusson (advertising agency) 211
Mason, Philip 326
Massingham, H. J. 143
Massingham, Hugh 143, 218, 224–5, 243; on Eden and Suez Crisis 201–2, 203, 205, 212
Massingham, H. W. 143
Master, Simon 268
Matabeleland 305
Matheson, Hilda 59, 88, 90
Matlon, Joe 331
Maud, Sir John (*later* Baron Redcliffe-Maud) 193
Maudling, Reginald 225, 282
Maugham, W. Somerset 238
Mavor, Sam 42
Mavor & Coulson (engineering company) 42–3, 44
Maxton, James 42
Maxwell, Robert 305
Mbeki, Govan 193
Mbeki, Thabo 334–5, 336, 337
Mboya, Tom 190
Melly, George 214
Menuhin, Yehudi, Baron 299
Meredith, George 63
Messel, Oliver 316
Meyer, Jim 317, 336, 338
MI5 126, 132, 246, 248, 251
MI6 (Secret Intelligence Service; SIS): and wartime propaganda 88; DA turned down by 91; wartime operations in Holland 91, 247; and *Encounter* magazine 176; Mark Frankland's